German Orientalism in the Age of Empire

Religion, Race, and Scholarship

Nineteenth-century studies of the Orient changed European ideas and cultural institutions in more ways than we usually recognize. "Orientalism" certainly contributed to European empire-building, but it also helped to destroy a narrow Christian-classical canon. This carefully researched book provides the first synthetic and contextualized study of German *Orientalistik*, a subject of special interest because German scholars were the pacesetters in oriental studies between about 1830 and 1930, despite entering the colonial race late and exiting it early. The book suggests that we must take seriously German orientalism's origins in Renaissance philology and early modern biblical exegesis and appreciate its modern development in the context of nineteenth- and early twentieth-century debates about religion and the Bible, classical schooling, and Germanic origins. In ranging across the subdisciplines of *Orientalistik*, *German Orientalism in the Age of Empire* introduces readers to a host of iconoclastic characters and forgotten debates, seeking to demonstrate both the richness of this intriguing field and its indebtedness to the cultural world in which it evolved.

Suzanne L. Marchand completed her BA in history at the University of California, Berkeley, in 1984 and her PhD at the University of Chicago in 1992. She then served as assistant and associate professor at Princeton University (1992–9), before moving to Louisiana State University, Baton Rouge, where she is now professor of European intellectual history. She is the author of *Down from Olympus: Archaeology and Philhellenism in Germany, 1750–1970* (1996) as well as numerous articles on the history of art, archaeology, anthropology, classical studies, and the humanities generally.

More Praise for *German Orientalism in the Age of Empire*

"Suzanne Marchand has written a dazzling work of scholarship, a tour de force as an intellectual history of modern Germany. The erudition and breadth of material presented demonstrates that Suzanne Marchand is one of the great scholars of her generation. Essential reading for students in numerous fields, including religion, biblical studies, history, Asian studies, ancient Near East studies, and philology, her book is also an extremely important contribution to the field of Jewish studies, brilliantly illuminating its rise, development, influence, and significance."
   – Susannah Heschel, author of *The Aryan Jesus: Christian Theologians and the Bible in Nazi Germany*

"Suzanne Marchand's enormously learned, contextually rich, and conceptually complex study of the scholarly traditions and cultural practices that defined the 'peculiarities' of German Orientalism in the modern Imperial age finally provides a comprehensive, convincing response to questions that historians of modern Germany have been asking since the publication of Edward Said's *Orientalism* more than thirty years ago. But her book does more than simply fill a gap in historical scholarship or supplement existing paradigms of analysis. Marchand's work reframes the issue by setting the processes whereby representatives of the 'West' constructed their own cultural identities by appropriating and 'othering' the 'Orient' within the longue duree of Europe's own cultural civil wars. By emphasizing the immense diversity and motivational ambivalence of German Orientalism, she has produced a story that opens the tradition to critical, reciprocal, post-Imperial appropriations."
   – John Toews, University of Washington

PUBLICATIONS OF THE GERMAN HISTORICAL INSTITUTE

Edited by Hartmut Berghoff
with the assistance of David Lazar

The German Historical Institute is a center for advanced study and research whose purpose is to provide a permanent basis for scholarly cooperation among historians from the Federal Republic of Germany and the United States. The Institute conducts, promotes, and supports research into both American and German political, social, economic, and cultural history; into transatlantic migration, especially in the nineteenth and twentieth centuries; and into the history of international relations, with special emphasis on the roles played by the United States and Germany.

Recent books in the series

German Orientalism in the Age of Empire

Religion, Race, and Scholarship

SUZANNE L. MARCHAND

Louisiana State University

GERMAN HISTORICAL INSTITUTE

Washington, D.C.

and

 CAMBRIDGE
UNIVERSITY PRESS

CAMBRIDGE UNIVERSITY PRESS
Cambridge, New York, Melbourne, Madrid, Cape Town,
Singapore, São Paulo, Delhi, Mexico City

Cambridge University Press
32 Avenue of the Americas, New York, NY 10013-2473, USA

www.cambridge.org
Information on this title: www.cambridge.org/9780521169073

German Historical Institute
1607 New Hampshire Avenue NW, Washington, DC 20009, USA

First published 2009
Reprinted 2010 (thrice)
First paperback edition 2010
Reprinted 2010, 2011 (thrice), 2013

A catalog record for this publication is available from the British Library.

Library of Congress Cataloging in Publication Data

Marchand, Suzanne L., 1961–
German orientalism in the age of empire : religion, race, and scholarship /
Suzanne Marchand.
   p.   cm.
Includes bibliographical references and index.
ISBN 978-0-521-51849-9 (hardback)
1. Orientalism – Germany – History – 19th century.   2. Middle East – Study and teaching
– Germany – History – 19th century.   3. Asia – Study and teaching – Germany – History –
19th century.   4. Orientalism – Germany – History – 20th century.   5. Middle East – Study
and teaching – Germany – History – 20th century.   6. Asia – Study and teaching – Germany
– History – 20th century.   I. Title.
DS61.9.G3M37   2009
950.072´0943–dc22   2008053038

ISBN 978-0-521-51849-9 Hardback
ISBN 978-0-521-16907-3 Paperback

For my mother who insisted we go to Istanbul;
my husband who cheerfully moved to Berlin;
my sister, who cherishes the ancients' idiosyncracies;
And in memory of my father, who marveled at the contradictions
of the modern world

Contents

Acknowledgments

It would be the height of insolence, not to mention an act of inexcusable ingratitude, to open a book that offers a contextual, critical history of the practice of scholarship without acknowledging that this book too "came from somewhere." It came chiefly from my very cluttered office in Baton Rouge, Louisiana, but it was also shaped by my visits to German archives and libraries, my years as a faculty member at Princeton University, and by my encounters, personal and electronic, with a large number of people who provided me with crucial references or made helpful criticisms. This book – very long in gestation – was also made possible by grants from various patrons, who have been extremely supportive without being at all intrusive, or even impatient. In what follows, I will try to express my appreciation to those who have been most important in helping me put together this long and complicated study, but the fact remains: a book that takes a dozen years to research and write will owe debts to many people and circumstances, debts the author will never entirely manage to acknowledge, much less repay.

Let me begin at the beginning, and thank, first of all, my wonderful Princeton colleagues amongst whom I was living and working when I first began this project. Here especially I would like to thank Hans Aarsleff, Peter Brown, Natalie Zemon Davis, Lionel Gossman, Anthony Grafton, Peter Lake, and Anson Rabinbach, as well as the members of the team with whom I wrote *Worlds Together, Worlds Apart*, Jeremy Adelman, Stephen Aron, Stephen Kotkin, Gyan Prakash, Robert Tignor, and Michael Tsin; the rich (and contentious!) discussions we had about how to conceive this world history textbook greatly influenced my thinking on many things, one of which was German orientalism. In 1997, I profited greatly from a Humboldt Stiftung fellowship, which I used to begin my archival research in Berlin and to discover just how enormous and complex the topic I had chosen to write on really was. In 2000–1, I was lucky enough to be chosen to be a Fellow at the Wissenschaftskolleg zu Berlin; this year was vital both to my further exploration of the libraries and archives and to my reshaping of the project. At the Wiko, I benefited particularly from my conversations with Philippe Burrin, Deborah Shuger, and Jacques Waardenburg, and from my interactions with the members of the "Indische Schwerpunkt," Partha Chatterjee, Navid Kermani, Velcheru Narayana Rao, David Shulman, and Sanjay Subramanyam, all of them "orientalists" of the most distinguished and insightful kind, and all of them delightful iconoclasts too, each in his own way.

I am very grateful also to the staff members of the Geheimes Staatsarchiv in Berlin, the Museum für Indische Kunst, and the Handschriftsabteilung at the

Staatsbibliothek Berlin for their assistance in locating and using archival materials;
I have also used in this book some material I gathered in researching my previous
one, then located in the Auswärtiges Amt Archiv in Bonn and the Zentrales
Staatsarchiv in Potsdam (I have indicated new locations for this material in the
bibliography). But I found that most of the subjects I was dealing with were so
under-researched that the published primary and secondary material on them had
not yet been put into synthetic form, or properly contextualized, and so there are
many individuals or topics surveyed herein for which an exploration of archival
sources is still needed; in fact, it is one of the author's hopes that this book will stir
interest in some of these long-forgotten subjects and that other scholars will now
seek out unpublished letters, diaries, and documents. In any event, I discovered
that the printed primary source material left behind by modern German orientalists was vast and, to really get to know it, I would need, first of all, a great library
and, secondly, some time to read it.

Here is where the ACLS and LSU played critical roles. The ACLS offered me a
Burkhardt Fellowship, which I took in 2003–4; LSU very generously gave me a
year off then as well as another year off in 2005–6 to read and to begin writing my
book. The second year off was supported by an Atlas Grant from the LSU Board
of Regents, a marvelous program, which, like the Burkhardt Fellowship, helps
busy associate professors get that second book finished. I owe the completion of
this volume to these granting agencies and to Paul Paskoff and Gaines Foster, my
excellent departmental chairmen, who have helped me organize leaves and supported my research in every possible way. As for the library – though LSU's isn't
world-class, the Interlibrary Loan Office made it seem like it is, and I cannot
fail to include them in my thanks. Finally, I would like to thank Cambridge
University Press for its willingness to publish this long manuscript, and the
German Historical Institute in Washington, D.C., for its generous support for
its publication. It has been an honor to work with both of these great cultural
institutions.

Of course, books are also the products of personal exchanges of ideas and
information, and I have many people to thank as well. Among those who provided
me with very helpful references I would especially thank Mustafa Aksakal,
Margaret Anderson, Ali Anooshahr, David Armitage, Tuska Benes, Nina Berman,
Thomas Broman, Peter Brown, John Connelly, Natalie Zemon Davis, Omnia El-
Shakry, Anthony Grafton, Anselm Hagedorn, Ludmila Hanisch, Stefan Hauser,
John Henderson, Susannah Heschel, Steven Korenblatt, Anthony La Vopa, Kris
Manjapra, Peter N. Miller, Klaus Mühlhahn, David Mungello, Perry Myers,
Lynn Nyhart, Elisabeth Oliver, Jürgen Osterhammel, Reza Pirbhai, Till van
Rahden, Karl Roider, Dietmar Rothermund, Martin Ruehl, David Schimmel-
pennick von der Oye, Ismar Schorsch, Jonathan Sheehan, Harvey Shoolman,
Helmut Walser Smith, Jacques Waardenburg, George Williamson and Margherita
Zanasi. I have also benefited greatly from exchanging work with Nina Berman,
Heiner Feldhoff, Nick Germana, Alexander Haridi, Wolf Liebeschütz, Douglas
McGetchin, Peter Park, Indra Sengupta, Sergei Stadnikov, and my own students,
Roshunda Belton, Eva Giloi, Heather Morrison, Martin Ruehl, and Derek Zum-
bro from whom I learned so much about their subjects, and about mine.

Some people have gone the extra mile (or given my verbosity, the extra marathon) and read and critiqued whole chapters for me, in many cases saving me from errors or unsound lines of argument. I would like to offer them a special thanks: Alex Bevilacqua, Gary Cohen, Marwa El-Shakry, Anselm Hagedorn, Bradley Herling, Peter Jelavich, Christine Kooi, Michael Laffen, Harry Liebersohn, David Lindenfeld, Tomoko Masuzawa, John Pizer, Bernard Porter, Brian Porter-Szucs, Martin Ruehl, Jonathan Sheehan, Harvey Shoolman, Andreas Sommer, Jonathan Sperber, and Lynn Zastoupil. I will be eternally grateful to David Lazar for checking the whole manuscript for footnote typos. My deepest thanks goes to five people I have endlessly hounded for references and plied for information, reactions, and ideas: Margaret Anderson, Anthony Grafton, Ludmila Hanisch, Kris Manjapra, and George Williamson. I can't imagine what this book would look like without them; I wouldn't even want to try.

Finally, a brief and wholly insufficient line of gratitude to my friends, many of whom are listed above, and to my family members – thanks for putting up with me and my German orientalists for so long. My husband, Victor Stater, deserves far more thanks for his wisdom, wit, patience, and never-failing confidence in me than a line or two in the acknowledgments – but I expect he will be embarrassed even by this. Having heard about "Mom's book" for so long, my sons, Bertie and Henry, will be as glad as I am to see it off my desk. They too have contributed to it, mostly by making my extra-textual life boundlessly joyful. They are not mentioned in the dedication this time only because they are already in possession of something more valuable than my book: my heart.

Introduction

In an essay published in 1907, the Indologist and orientalist popularizer Hermann Brunnhofer offered a revealing account of the Orient's interest to Westerners, one that bears quoting at length:

> The longing for the Orient accompanies the Occidental from the cradle to the grave. When the young farmer's wife of the Far West, deep in the most remote forest valley of the Rocky Mountains, holds her first-born child on her lap and imparts to him the elements of the Christian faith, she tells him about the shepherds of Bethlehem in the land of Judea, far, far on the other side of the Atlantic Ocean. She tells him about the star, which the wise men from the land of Chaldaea followed, and then of the rivers of the Nile and the Euphrates, of Mount Ararat on which Noah's ark came to rest after the Flood, of Mount Sinai from which Moses brought the earliest tables of the law to the people of Israel, of the great cities of Nineveh, Babylon, Tyre and Sidon, of the world conquerors Cyrus of Persia and the Pharoah in Egypt-land.
>
> . . . The Bible is the book through which the world of the West, even in times of the most melancholy isolation, remains persistently tied to the Orient. Even when one ignores its character as a sacred book of revelation, and examines it from a historical and geographical standpoint, the Bible can be seen as a world-historical book of wonders, as the book which ever again reawakens in the Aryans of the West, who have deserted their homeland, that longing for the Orient which binds peoples together. . . .

Brunnhofer then followed this immediately with a brief sketch of the origins and history of European oriental studies:

> It was also religious need which in the educated circles of the West provided the most powerful impetus for the study of the Orient. The world of the West was captivated in its inner being by the information that it received through the Bible about the peoples of the Orient. But that which sufficed to please the taste did not satisfy the curiosity, which was afterward awakened. The Bible's accounts of language, morals and religions of the Egyptians, Assyrians, Babylonians, Phoenicians, Medes and Persians were too scant not to inspire the desire, in the era of the renascence of the sciences, for richer and more trustworthy information about the lives of the peoples of the East. So arose, at first, in closest connection to the Biblical scholarship inspired by the Reformation, an oriental philology and archaeology. These [sciences] limited themselves for many centuries to the study of the language and religion of the Semitic people. But towards the end of the previous century the languages and literatures of the Sanskrit-Indians and the Zoroastrian Persians were rediscovered, and then arose, quickly and at the same time as the philological study of Semitic

languages and religions, Sanskrit and Zend philology, to which soon too Egyptology and Sinology were added.[1]

Brunnhofer was in some ways an exceptional scholar; he authored several books on Homer, Goethe, and the Hermeticist-heretic-magus Giordano Bruno, and – probably to ingratiate himself with Russian patrons – translated into German the oriental travels of the Czarevich.[2] What made him confident to speak as an orientalist, about the history of orientalism, was his specialized knowledge of Sanskrit philology and his publications on ancient "Aryan" culture and languages – but here he was saying nothing his contemporaries would have found surprising, or even particularly interesting. Indeed this whole passage was nothing more than a rather anodyne prologue for a rave review of Indologist Max Müller's enormously important series of classics in translation, *Sacred Books of the East* (50 vols., 1879–1904). The point is that Brunnhofer's career and his picture of western orientalism have virtually nothing to do with the one recent studies have conjured, and we begin this book by wondering why that might be, and in what ways we can reconcile the two points of view.

Some sort of reconciliation, or reckoning, is necessary if we are finally to answer the question, which was posed immediately upon the publication of Edward Said's *Orientalism* in 1978, but which has never been treated in detail: what lies at the heart of German orientalism? Said famously, and self-consciously, left the Germans out of his analysis, despite the well-known fact that they were the pacesetting European scholars in virtually every field of oriental studies between about 1830 and 1930. He said simply that Britain and France "were the pioneer nations in the Orient and Oriental studies," and that their positions, politically and intellectually, were taken over by the Americans after World War II. He reproached himself for seeking "to provide an understanding of academic Orientalism and pay[ing] little attention to scholars like [Heymann] Steinthal, [Max] Müller, [Carl Heinrich] Becker, [Ignaz] Goldziher, [Carl] Brockelmann, [Theodor] Nöldeke" (all of whom do have attention paid to them in this book), but insisted that

at no time in German scholarship during the first two-thirds of the nineteenth century could a close partnership have developed between Orientalists and a protracted, sustained national interest in the Orient. There was nothing in Germany to correspond to the Anglo-French presence in India, the Levant, North Africa. Moreover, the German Orient was almost exclusively a scholarly, or at least a classical, Orient: it was made the subject of lyrics, fantasies, and even novels, but it was never actual, the way Egypt and Syria were actual for Chateaubriand, Lane, Lamartine, Burton, Disraeli or Nerval.... What German Oriental

---

[1] Hermann Brunnhofer, "Die heiligen Bücher des Orients," in idem, *Oestlisches Werden: Kulturauschtausch und Handelsverkehr zwischen Orient und Okzident von der Urzeit bis zur Gegenwart* (Bern, 1907), pp. 25–7.

[2] Brunnhofer's works include *Urgeschichte der Arier in Vorder-und Centralasien* (Leipzig, 1893); *Arische Urzeit* (Bern, 1910); *Homerische Rätsel* (Leipzig, 1898); *Russlands Hand über Asien* (St. Petersburg, 1897); *Goethes Bildkraft im Lichte der ethnologischen Sprach- und Mythenvergleichung* (Leipzig, 1893); *Giordano Bruno's Weltanschauung und Verhängniss* (Leipzig, 1882); and the translation of Prince Espere Esperovich Uchomski's two-volume *Orientreise seiner kaiserlich Hoheit des Grossfürsten-Thronfolgers Nikolaus Alexandrowitsch von Russland*, trans. Hermann Brunnhofer (Leipzig, 2 vols., 1894–99).

scholarship did was to refine and elaborate techniques whose application was to texts, myths, ideas, and languages almost literally gather from the Orient by imperial Britain and France.[3]

Said's statements were immediately recognized to be misleading, for the Germans did not merely follow in the tracks of others. Nor did they lack an "actual" relationship with the East – the German-speaking polities have had a very long and important relationship with both the Holy Land and the Ottoman Empire, and the Wilhelmine Empire did have colonial interests, and even colonial territories (Qingdao and Samoa, for example) in the East.[4] It seemed clear that by excluding the Germans – as well as the Russians, Dutch, Greeks, and Italians – Said was engaging in a deliberate sort of deck-stacking: focusing exclusively on French and British literature and scholarship produced during the high imperial age, he was able to conclude that "orientalism" was a product of empire. But Said's paradigm took hold, perhaps because his grand claims did teach us to see so much that we had missed. And despite its dodges and flaws, Said's analysis has, until recently, continued to structure virtually all discussions about the relationship between the European mind and the cultures of the East, even when the Germans are added to the mix.

The last few years have seen an increasing number of attempts to redress Said's omissions and efforts to refine his model. There have been highly sophisticated critiques of the intimate relationships between European science and colonialism, and equally sophisticated challenges to the subalternist "iron cage."[5] While earlier work focused heavily on England, and secondarily on France, we have recently seen the appearance of a number of fine studies of Russian and Dutch imperialism, and many more seem to be in the works.[6] There are now a number of excellent treatments too of orientalizing "othering" as the process occurred in Japan and the Ottoman Empire.[7] In literary studies and art history in particular, scholars

---

[3] Edward W. Said, *Orientalism* (New York, 1978), pp. 17, 19.

[4] Said, *Orientalism*, p. 19; Nina Berman has shown, with emphasis on the Crusades and other religious encounters, that Said vastly overstated the case in claiming that the German Orient was never "actual." See Berman, "Thoughts on Zionism, in the Context of German Middle East Relations," in *Comparative Studies of South Asia, Africa and the Middle East* 24, no. 2 (2004): 134. Berman's forthcoming book will document myriad forms of "actual" encounter between Germans and Asians and force us to rethink the exclusion of the Germans from studies of orientalism. Professor Berman has kindly allowed me to read several chapters of her manuscript, the provisional title for which is *Beyond Orientalism: Germany and the Middle East, 900–2000*.

[5] To cite just a very few: Gyan Prakash, *Another Reason: Science and the Imagination of Modern India* (Princeton, NJ, 1999); Bernard S. Cohen, *Colonialism and Its Forms of Knowledge* (Princeton, NJ, 1996); C. A. Bayly, *Empire and Information: Intelligence Gathering and Social Communication in India, 1780–1870* (Cambridge, 2000); David Washbrook, "Orient and Occident: Colonial Discourse Theory and the Historiography of the British Empire," in *The Oxford History of the British Empire*, vol. 5, ed. Robin Winks; J. J. Clarke, *Oriental Enlightenment: The Encounter between Asian and Western Thought* (London, 1997). On Germany specifically, Russell Berman, *Enlightenment or Empire: Colonial Discourse in German Culture* (Lincoln, NE, 1998); George Steinmetz, *The Devil's Handwriting: Precoloniality and the German Colonial State in Qingdao, Samoa and Southwest Africa* (Chicago, IC, 2007).

[6] Michael Francis Laffen, *Islamic Nationhood and Colonial Indonesia* (London, 2003); on Russia, Daniel R. Brower and Edward Lazzerini, eds., *Russia's Orient: Imperial Borderlands and Peoples, 1700–1917* (Bloomington, IN, 1997); Alexander Etkind, "Orientalism Reversed: Russian Literature in the Times of Empires," in *Modern Intellectual History* 4, no. 3 (2007): 617–28.

[7] Stefan Tanaka, *Japan's Orient; Rendering into History* (Berkeley, CA, 1993); Ussama Makdisi, "Ottoman Orientalism" in *American Historical Review* 107, no. 3 (2002): 768–96.

have become increasingly sensitive to the subtle and often contradictory ways in which the "Orient" was invoked or read.[8] Finally, the last few years have seen the publication of careful new studies of particular branches of German *Orientalistik* such as Sabine Mangold's *"Eine weltbürgerliche Wissenschaft": Deutsche Orientalistik im 19. Jahrhundert* (Stuttgart, 2004), Indra Sengupta's *From Salon to Discipline: State, University and Indology in Germany, 1821–1914* (Heidelberg, 2005), and Pascale Rabault-Feuerhahn's *L'archive des origines: Sanskrit, philologie, anthropologie dans l'Allemagne du XIXe siècle* (Paris, 2008). My book is deeply indebted to all of this important new work.

But at present there is still no comprehensive treatment, in German or English, of modern German orientalism, the field Said himself knew to be a key exception to his claims.[9] Moreover, there are very few studies of modern orientalism that allow us to take seriously Hermann Brunnhofer's history of the field and that seek to understand the specific roles played by orientalist scholarship in the cultural histories of Europe's diverse states, comprehending the discipline's debts to and rivalries with theology and classics. Fewer still detail the local politics of orientalism – its educational institutions, disciplinary hierarchies, interpretive traditions, canons of evidence, divisions of labor, and the individual obsessions and innovations, religious longings and personal grievances, overweening ambitions and just plain hard work that shaped its practice. Let me be clear: in no way am I advocating a return to the pre-Saidian way of writing the history of oriental studies. We do not need more uncritical histories of oriental scholarship – there are *Festschrifts* and heroic biographies enough – that deny that orientalism had a politics. We need, instead, a synthetic and critical history, one that assesses oriental scholarship's contributions to imperialism, racism, and modern anti-Semitism, but one that also shows how modern orientalism has furnished at least some of the tools necessary for constructing the post-imperialist worldviews we cultivate today.[10]

That is what this book seeks to offer. It is a critical history of the *practice* of oriental scholarship, one that treats the politics of the field, but does so without presuming that those politics were primordially and perpetually defined by imperialist relationships. It is not a book about "orientalism" in the wider sense of "the image of the Orient" all Germans possessed or the "discourse on the Orient" they purportedly all shared; whether such things existed is something I very much

[8] See, for example, Bradley L. Herling, *The German Gita: Hermeneutics and Discipline in the German Reception of Indian Thought, 1778–1831* (New York, 2006); Todd Kontje, *German Orientalisms* (Ann Arbor, MI, 2004); Nina Berman, *Orientalismus, Kolonismus und Moderne; Zum Bild des Orients in der deutschsprachigen Kultur um 1900* (Stuttgart, 1997); Andrea Polaschegg, *Der andere Orientalismus. Regeln deutsch-morgenländischer Imagination im 19. Jahrhundert* (Berlin, 2005), and the older, but still useful, René Gérard, *L'Orient et la pensée romantique allemande* (Nancy, 1963).

[9] Of course, there are many specialized studies, in addition to those just cited, upon which I draw heavily. To cite just a few: Ludmila Hanisch, *Die Nachfolger der Exegeten: Deutschsprachige Erforschung der Vorderen Orient in der ersten Hälfte des 20. Jahrhunderts* (Wiesbaden, 2003); Wilhelm Halbfass, *India and Europe: An Essay in Understanding* (Albany, NY, 1988); Stephen Vernoit, ed., *Discovering Islamic Art: Scholars, Collectors and Collections, 1850–1950* (London, 2000).

[10] Of course, the multi-cultural worldviews common in European and American academic circles surely still retain Eurocentric elements, as Tomoko Masuzawa has recently demonstrated in *The Invention of World Religions: Or, How European Universalism was Preserved in the Language of Pluralism* (Chicago, IL, 2005).

doubt. Whether or not we could access such an image or discourse by cobbling together statements by a colonial official here and a novelist there is, to me, even more dubious, and I have decided, for theoretical as well as evidentiary reasons, not to try to create such an entity. My evidentiary reasons for rejecting the idea that German "orientalism" was a single, shared discourse are on display throughout the book. But the theoretical underpinnings of my work require a bit of elaboration here, especially as the rest of this book seeks self-consciously not to wear its theory on its sleeves. I do want to make a generally important contribution to European intellectual and cultural history, and my readers should know what sort of contribution to the study of knowledge-making this book purports to be.

Perhaps most provocatively, this book calls into question the widely used method of discourse analysis, at least as it has been applied to the study of European "orientalism." All too often, it seems to me, those who have followed Said's lead and adopted the Foucauldian tactic of analyzing only the surfaces of the texts they study end up simply reiterating what we know, namely that people make representations for their own purposes; too rarely do they ask about the *variety* of those purposes, or about the rootedness of those representations in weaker or stronger interpretations of original sources. Too frequently, discourses are identified by selectively assembling lines and phrases from disparate texts, and in the attempt to make power relations paramount, modern commentators are led to pick out metaphors or generalizations that have more to do with our own interests than with the authors' original ideas. This is not really Foucault's fault; his primary purpose was to offer a philosophical deconstruction of the identities we have unreflectively assumed, and his work has helped us to gain critical purchase on the institutions, sciences, and thought-structures of both past and present. But the re-elaboration of his philosophical critiques as historical methodology regularly results in tendentious bricolage, and when applied indiscriminately, this method frequently produces distorted and present-oriented pictures of hypostatized entities such as "orientalism."

When applied to the study of "the Orient" this method is particularly pernicious, delivering a definition of identity which presumes a primordial, binary distinction between "Europe" and "the Orient." We find ourselves believing that all Europeans – whether women or men, aristocrats or peasants, classicists or orientalists, Czechs or Scots – were actually cognizant of and bound by this reified "discourse," no matter who these individuals were, what they did or did not know, and what the context was in which their statements were made. Perhaps the distinction between European and Oriental was crucial for some individuals; but where is the proof that this binary distinction *actually* was what mattered most to all or even the majority of nineteenth-century inhabitants of the landmass we are calling "Europe"? Surely at least some Europeans defined themselves by means of other sets of distinctions – male and female, Christian and Jew, academic philologist and on-the-spot diplomat, German and Frenchman?[11] When scholars take up the subject of "orientalism," they seem to forget that many of those they lump together as "Europeans" did not inhabit this identity exclusively, or without

---

[11] Billie Melman's wonderful *Women's Orients: English Women and the Middle East, 1718–1918* (Ann Arbor, MI, 1992), suggests the importance of gender for the western travelers' interpretation of eastern cultures.

discomfort; there were plenty of self-critical Britons, Bavarians, and Hungarians who were worried enough about Europe's own warts – its history of intolerance, its materialism, its erasure of traditions, its tendency to treat others as means to an end – that they emigrated, converted, or risked destroying their own careers, or even lives, by publicizing their grievances. Some lived their lives in borderlands like Sweden, Estonia, or Croatia where they themselves felt "orientalized"– and believed the ultimate "other" sat in Rome, St. Petersburg, or Vienna, not in Istanbul, Cairo, or Dehli. We cannot *start* with the belief that Europeans found the categories "European" and "Oriental" primordial or totalizing and hope to discover how complicated these cultural relationships might really have been.

In what follows, I will show that the variable mix of identities inhabited by even the subgroup of Europeans studied here *did* make for different relationships to Asia and its cultures. Some, of course, did despise "mysterious India" and "decadent Persia," and thought the West wholly untainted by "oriental" values and vices. But as Brunnhofer suggested, every Christian certainly knew that he or she shared the "Holy Land" and some of their holy scriptures with eastern peoples, and professional students of the Orient were perhaps even more aware than most laypersons that the Orient had been continually linked to Europe from the earliest times. The peoples of the Near East, at least, were known to inhabit places with languages, cultures, and histories, which were both shared and not shared with post-Renaissance Christian Europe – and Central Europeans especially knew that the Ottoman Empire continued to cast a long shadow across the Bosphorus. Even some forms of racial thinking, fleshed out by specialists but widely popularized, were founded upon linkages between East and West, as was the case in speculative reconstructions of "Aryan" and "Semite" origins. It is far too simplistic to say that nineteenth-century Europeans always thought of themselves as a united group, over and against "the oriental other." In some contexts, the peoples of Asia were rendered "others" – but in other contexts they were treated as kin: relatives, wayward brothers, long-lost fathers, or sons in need of tutelage, but family members, just the same. We need to appreciate the richness and complexity of Europeans' relations with the Orient in order to see just how much imposing that binary distinction distorts our understanding of the lives of "others," by whom I mean, this time, the eighteenth-, nineteenth-, and early twentieth-century Europeans whose worldviews differed so much from those we now hold.

The foregoing explains why this book focuses on the *practice* of oriental studies in Germany rather than on "the German image of the Orient." It seems to me that this is an important way, if surely not the only one, of finding what Bradley Herling has called "a third way," a means to understand orientalism which does not become merely a critique of ideology (à la Said) or a hermeneutical defence of scientific progress.[12] The study of practice is an important way in which historians of science have tried to get beyond the constructionist/progressivist impasse, and it

---

[12] Bradley Herling has kindly allowed me to cite here his very important methodological mapping of this terrain, "'Either a Hermeneutical Consciousness or a Critical Consciousness': Renegotiating Theories of the Germany-India Encounter." His paper was originally presented at the German Studies Association Conference in Saint Paul in September 2008. Kris Manjapra is also seeking a "third way"; see his "'Ecumenical Thinking': Gadamer's Hermeneutics and the Critique of Post-colonial Theory," forthcoming in *Journal of the History of Ideas*, 2010.

is an approach early modern intellectual historians have used to good effect; but it has been slow to catch on amongst students of modern ideas. In my case, I focus on the knowledge-making practices of those individuals who counted as "orientalists" in their cultural milieux, namely the men (and they were mostly men) who invested time and effort in actually learning to read and/or speak at least one "oriental" language. This means that it is heavily a book about academics, though it also contains extensive treatments of travelers and diplomats, popularizers and missionaries, pastors and rabbis. These are the people who chose "knowing the Orient" as a career, and they were, after all, the individuals nineteenth- and early twentieth-century German society believed most worthy to write and speak about eastern cultures; even after Imperial Germany entered the colonial race, it was chiefly to them that Germans looked to explain the religious, historical, and cultural significance of Asia, and to understand its complex linguistic, artistic, and ethnographic relationships with Europe. Sometimes they also helped rule or exploit it – and those instances too need careful elaboration. By trying to understand why these individuals wrote or did certain things at certain times I hope to be able to illuminate the ways in which the techniques they pioneered were used to explore new areas or to shore up old prejudices, to advance ambitions, and to undermine conventions, to exploit others or to attempt to liberate them. I am not writing this book to resurrect "orientalism" or to bury it, but out of the profound conviction that we need a critical history of its practice and its practitioners in order to understand our more recent efforts at writing postcolonial and global history as part of a much longer, and much more complicated, trajectory.[13]

For the purposes of this book, then, "orientalism" is defined as a *set of practices*, practices that were bound up with the Central European institutional settings in which the sustained and serious study of the languages, histories, and cultures of Asia took place. Many, but by no means all, of the scholars treated in this book actually did call themselves "orientalists" – some would have described themselves as theologians, classicists, historians, geographers, archaeologists, or art historians. Their designation as such became increasingly conventional as academic specialization drove disciplinary development and increasingly divided those who studied the so-called *Naturvölker* of sub-Saharan Africa, Australasia, and the New World from those who studied *Kulturvölker*, people of high culture, refined spirituality, and (critically) readable ancient texts. Beginning about 1800, further divisions were made, at least in the philosophical faculty, between those who studied Greek and Roman texts and those who studied other ancient texts (there were as yet few academic posts for the study of modern European history or languages). This meant that institutionally speaking, an entity called "orientalism" was created under which virtually all non-classicizing humanists, from

---

[13] The general understanding of the origins of postcolonial thought divorces it from older forms of scholarship in ways that make it seem almost a deus ex machina, a sudden and entirely salutary development dating to the last decades of the twentieth century. I do not wish to invalidate subaltern criticism, which has contributed so much to the decentering of Europe; nor do I wish to criticize the institutionalization of world history – I am, after all, one of seven authors of a world history textbook (Robert Tignor et al., *Worlds Together, Worlds Apart*, vol. 2, 2nd ed. 2008). On the contrary, I simply want to show that today's conceptions and preoccupations were foreshadowed, and in some ways, prepared for, by the orientalists of the later eighteenth and nineteenth centuries. For more on this, see the Epilogue, herein.

Assyriologists to Sinologists, were thrown together, like the diverse animals of a single continent housed in one particular section of a zoo. Societies, journals, and institutes defined themselves as "oriental" often in the same way, meaning, essentially, the study of *Kulturvölker* beyond the classical world. It is this institutionally defined subject position, above all, that holds this book together, rather than an "ism," a political stance or the intellectual coherence of "*Orientalistik*." Even so, I should also note that some of those who made important contributions to what by the end of the century began to be called *Orientforschung* continued to identify themselves primarily as theologians, archaeologists, comparative linguists, or even classicists. Practices and subject matter were shared across institutional divisions, perhaps even more than in today's universities.

Oriental studies in German-speaking Central Europe certainly was different from British and French "orientalism," for reasons that have to do with Imperial Germany's late leap into the colonial race, but also with other cultural factors, such as the Austrian Habsburgs' long and usually "hot" border with the Ottoman Empire, the power of the tradition of Christian Hebraism in German Protestant territories, and the cultural dominance of Germandom's state-sponsored universities. How different its practices really were from those of others – including not only the French and British, but also the Russians, Dutch, Italians, and Swedes – is something that deserves further comparative study. Here, however, I will argue that the cultural politics of *Orientalistik* were defined much less by "modern" concerns – such as how to communicate with or exert power over the locals – than by traditional, almost primeval, *Christian* questions, such as (1) what parts of the Old Testament are true, and relevant, for Christians? (2) how much did the ancient Israelites owe to the Egyptians, Persians, and Assyrians? (3) where was Eden and what language was spoken there? and (4) were the Jews the only people to receive revelation? The German Reformers' attempts to clean up God's Word had involved orientalist knowledge from the first – and indeed sixteenth-century humanists had already struggled with many of the philological and chronological questions that would plague their descendants 300 years later. Although new sources were added, the old ones – particularly the Old Testament, the church fathers, and classical authors – continued to exert a powerful effect on the imaginations of even the most cutting-edge scholars long beyond the Enlightenment.

In addition to cultural factors, numerous a priori points of departure shaped individual perspectives on Asian culture and history: does humankind progress, or is what we see the result of a fall from a more perfect state? Can people borrow and learn from one another peacefully, or are conquest or racial mixing the only way cultures really affect one another? Are humans essentially monotheists, or nature-worshiping animists? Is religion the foundation of stable societies, or an opiate elites use to suborn the masses? It will be my job in this book to appreciate the persistence of such questions, sources, and orientations, while also showing how these were, over the course of the last 200 years, posed in ever more specialized terms, complicated by new evidence, and voiced to an ever-larger public. It will also be my job to show how various forms of racial speculation arose in the course of these debates and how Germany's quest to bask in imperialist sunshine, after 1884, contributed to, but did not wholly transform, these older debates and traditions.

Thus if this book seeks, in new ways, to provide an answer to a question posed by Edward Said, it is not ultimately a book framed by a Saidian, or an anti-Saidian, theoretical structure, and as grateful to him as I am for putting this highly important field on the map, Said's work will, from this page forward, scarcely be mentioned. To the extent that his framework insisted on a totalizing, global view of European–oriental relations, it simply does not help me understand what the German scholars were actually saying and doing.[14] As I became more and more interested in finding out what German orientalism, as a cultural phenomenon, actually was, I became less and less convinced that it was about European culture "setting itself off against the Orient" or that its leading ideas were informed by the imperial experience.[15] I would certainly agree with Said that European orientalism was enabled by the exerting of imperial authority over the East – how else can we explain the flood of manuscripts, artifacts, and specimens that gave library-bound scholars in the West the ability to claim themselves to be world specialists in medieval Persian poetics or Sanskrit literature?[16] And I would also agree that European orientalism "has less to do with the Orient than it does with 'our' world."[17] But unlike many of the recent commentators on Europe's "culture of imperialism," I do not think that all knowledge, orientalist or otherwise, inevitably contributed to the building of empires, or even to the upholding of Eurocentric points of view. In general, I find presumptuous and rather condescending the conception, so common to these readings of cultural history, that all knowledge is power, especially since the prevailing way of understanding this formulation suggests that power is something sinister and oppressive, something exerted against or over others. Of course, knowledge can be used in this way, but knowledge as understanding can also lead to appreciation, dialogue, self-critique, perspectival reorientation, and personal and cultural enrichment. Oriental studies did

---

[14] Said's rich readings of individual texts sometimes undercut a theory which demands that imperial politics is always *the* structuring element. Like Bernard Porter, I recognize that empire might have been structuring the cultural institutions and mental operations of nineteenth-century actors in ways that have not left traces in their texts, but I am rather dubious about depending on the proverbial "argument from silence," all too often invoked by those who wish to claim that European culture in this period was completely suffused with dreams or fantasies of empire. See Porter, *The Absent-Minded Imperialists: Empire, Society and Culture in Britain* (Oxford, 2004). I agree with Dorothy Figueira that one of the main problems with Said's method is that it imposes a primarily political authorial intention onto texts, "disregarding the testimony of a work's language, reception and character as narrative, poetry, translation, scholarship or artistic performance. By consigning to a secondary position the work of individual artists, a text becomes a commentary on a political situation rather than an expression of the motivations and desires that inspire the individual artist or scholar." Dorothy Matilda Figueira, *Translating the Orient: The Reception of Sakuntala in Nineteenth-Century Europe* (Albany, NY, 1991), p. 5.

[15] Cf. Said, *Orientalism*, p. 3.

[16] We have only to think of the situation the other way round to see this. Imagine hundreds of scholars in Isfahan, Cairo, Tokyo, Calcutta, Beijing, and Istanbul reading, writing, and publishing vast quantities of material about the Germanic tribes, Anglo-Saxons, and Gauls – but almost never doing so in German, English, or French. Imagine the same group of scholars collecting multitudes of medieval European manuscripts, and taking them off to libraries in Baghdad and Shanghai; picture Iranian scholars excavating the castles of the Teutonic knights, while Chinese archaeologists tackled Stonehenge – both groups telling Europeans how the reconstructions should look, and pilfering, buying, or otherwise extracting artifacts to fill the museum basements in Teheran and Beijing to overflowing. Surely the Germans, English, and French would have found this intolerable? On the other hand, one might well ask, would the Russians or the Portuguese have minded?

[17] Said, *Orientalism*, p. 12.

partake of and contribute to the exploitation and "othering" of nonwesterners, to be sure; but it also has led to positive outcomes of the type just listed, and I cannot subscribe to a philosophical stance that suggests that such things do not motivate or characterize the pursuit of knowledge.

Before we leave the theoretical realm, I would like to invoke another series of critical assessments of western orientalism with which I am in rough agreement. This position, first roughed out by the nineteenth-century Indian philosopher Ramohan Roy, but recently restated by Amartya Sen, underlines the West's tendency, at least since the Enlightenment, to contrast the East's spirituality or "imaginative irrationality" with western rationality.[18] Characteristic of William Jones's Indophilia as well as the Indophobia of James Mill, this parceling out of talents, as Sen argues, has led to the undervaluing of India's materialist and rationalist traditions; the same critique could be applied to discussions of the special talents of the Semites, who have repeatedly been praised for their soulfulness but damned for their failure to create secular institutions or beautiful works of plastic art.[19] As Partha Chatterjee also notes, this division of the western material world (including technology, science, economy, and politics) from the eastern spiritual world reproduced itself in anti-colonial nationalisms, which regularly recommended accepting and imitating the former (seen as culturally inessential) while insisting that cultural core identities lie in the spiritual realm.[20] Both those who loved the East, and those who despised it, tended to play down its materiality and even its quotidian forms of existence, a tendency exacerbated in the German scholarly world in which ancient and religious texts remained central to the study of the Orient.

But two important corollaries to this claim have been overlooked. First of all, if European intellectuals tended to spiritualize the East, they also tended to find distasteful material engagements with "others"; nineteenth-century academics in particular evinced little interest in the East's modern economic, military, or political conditions. To assess or address any of these topics was a job for the journalist, official, or businessman, none of whom had the same sort of cultural respectability as did the academic. That is to say, the intellectual work, which was most closely related to the real practices of colonialism, or pre- or postcolonial exploitation, was something the scholars did not think worth their time or worthy of their training (though some of their students did end up in such jobs, and during the Great War, many credentialed academics did do some of this sort of work). Of course this does not mean that the scholars did not endorse colonial endeavors (most did), but it does mean that they recognized that there were different ways of speaking about the Orient, and that they chose to speak about things of less utility and more permanence rather than about, for example, the price of land in Egypt or how to draw up a contract in China. If they focused on the ancient Orient and its

---

[18] Bimal Krishna Matilal, "On Dogmas of Orientalism," in K. K. Das Gupta, P. K. Bhattacharyya, and D. K. Choudhury, eds., *Sraddhanjali: Studies in Ancient Indian History* (Delhi, 1988), pp. 17–18; quotation p. 18. Amartya Sen, *The Argumentative Indian: Writings on Indian History, Culture and Identity* (New York, 2005), pp. 139–160.

[19] Kalman P. Bland, *The Artless Jew: Medieval and Modern Affirmations and Denials of the Visual* (Princeton, NJ, 2000); Margaret R. Olin, *The Nation Without Art: Examining Modern Discourses on Jewish Art* (Lincoln, NE, 2001).

[20] Partha Chatterjee, *The Nation and Its Fragments* (Princeton, NJ, 1993), p. 6.

religions – and they did – this surely suggested that they thought modern eastern cultures static or degraded and of incidental interest; but many members of the educated elite thought the same was true of their own culture, which is why the study of classical antiquity was dominant in educational institutions and why religious reformers emphasized the virtues of Jesus and the apostles, rather than those of contemporary Christians.

Students of orientalism seem too often to forget that all western scholars and intellectuals since the time of Alexander the Great, or even since Napoleon's Egyptian escapade, have not taken the part of the European would-be conqueror or the orthodox churches, and that, inevitably, other sorts of truth seekers appear who look to the East when the West faces critical challenges and despairs of its own answers.[21] The East has often offered iconoclasts a trump card to play in religious or cultural conflicts in the West, as demonstrated by the case of Giordano Bruno, the great champion of the Egyptian philosopher-prophet Hermes Trismegistus, or more recently, by Martin Bernal, author of the incendiary *Black Athena*.[22] Though generated by thoroughly western rivalries and concerns, invoking the Orient has often been the means by which counter-hegemonic positions were articulated; "orientalism" then, has played a crucial role in the *unmaking*, as well as the making, of western identities.

The foregoing discussion clarifies, I hope, the ways in which this study is informed, but not structured, by recent critiques of "orientalism" as a whole. Let me now clarify how it diverges not only from the Saidian grand narrative, but also from conventional disciplinary histories, which actually share with the critical school some interesting common assumptions. Both of these share, for example, a secularization story and a rough chronology – beginning in about 1780 and concluding more or less in the present day. I have found neither of these to be very helpful. The secularization story and the chronology are linked, for the presumption is that just about 1780, the preoccupations of the Renaissance and Reformation (biblical criticism and classical antiquity) disappear from orientalists' horizons, and at the same time, conveniently for Said, real European colonization in Asia begins. This narrative – underwritten by Raymond Schwab's insistence that an "oriental Renaissance" begins in Europe with Anquetil Duperron's publication of the Zend Avesta in 1771[23] – then draws on various romantic figures to demonstrate a purportedly new European interest in the Orient. The later nineteenth century, in Schwab's view, elaborated this romantic paradigm in various ways; but in fact, nothing important really changes. In the discipline's own histories, once scientificness sets in, ideology, error, rivalries, generational

---

[21] Nina Berman shows, interestingly, how crusading enthusiasm wore off in the Germanys in the wake of disillusionment with the actual conduct of warfare and the straying of German Christianizing ambitions from the Holy Land to the Slavic East. Friction between German secular leaders and the Pope also contributed to the increasingly widespread criticism of the Crusades in the later twelfth century, criticism which, she shows, took the form of admiration for the nobility of Muslim leaders and warriors and/or attacks on the brutality or decadence of their Christian counterparts. See Nina Berman, "Thoughts on Zionism in the Context of German Middle Eastern Relations," pp. 137–40.

[22] Bruno was burned at the stake on orders from the Pope in 1600. See Chapter 1.

[23] Raymond Schwab, *The Oriental Renaissance: Europe's Rediscovery of India and the East, 1680–1880*, trans. Gene Patterson-Black and Victor Reinking (New York, 1984), p. 11. Schwab's book was originally published as *La renaissance orientale* (Paris, 1950).

conflicts, joblessness, poor libraries, and religious convictions are written out; the positivistic cold shower that doused romantic orientalism's flames seems to wash away all externalist sins, and although knowledge grows, again, no fundamental changes occur. The conclusion for both is in one way or another the present, with both parties claiming we are in some way the product of the revolution of the 1780s, for better (the disciplinary historians) or worse (the Saidians).

There are many ways in which my story conflicts with this one. First of all, inspired by my readings and colleagues in early modern studies, I think 1780 is a problematical opening date. Critical changes were already underway in Europe's understanding of "the other" in the seventeenth century, and many of the claims made and questions asked in the later nineteenth century have even older roots in the Renaissance and Reformation. Consistently, too, scholars working in the nineteenth century returned to texts produced in the Hellenistic era and to problems articulated already by the Church fathers (and their "heretic" antagonists). The longer I study the subject, the more struck I am by the continuities and/or recurrent themes that have characterized European study of the East over this very *longue durée*. In many ways, this book sees itself as a continuation of the rich early modern literature on humanistic orientalism rather than as a study of the origins of the modern disciplines we now inhabit.[24]

Secondly, I cannot share the presumption that secular scholarship entirely displaced theological studies at the eighteenth century's end. Over the course of this long book, we will have ample opportunity to observe the various ways in which *Orientalistik* was not a fully secular science, perhaps especially in the German-speaking world, but elsewhere, I would wager, as well. Hand in hand with this assumption has been the notion that oriental studies in the nineteenth and early twentieth centuries were primarily concerned with the modern world, and with India and/or with Islam; I think this book will demonstrate the narrowness of that view. *Orientalistik* was, as Brunnhofer said, a field propelled forward by Reformed *Bibelforschung* – note that even in the passage from 1907 quoted earlier he makes no mention whatsoever of studies of modern Asia. It is my argument that this tradition, while modified in some respects and richly enhanced by a

---

[24] The study of early modern orientalism is enjoying something of a Renaissance these days, provoked especially by the work and encouragement of Anthony Grafton and by renewed interest in the history of classical philology and biblical criticism. See, for example, Grafton, *Joseph Scaliger: A Study in the History of Classical Scholarship* (Oxford, 2 vols., 1983), and *Defenders of the Text: The Traditions of Scholarship in an Age of Science, 1450–1800* (Cambridge, MA, 1991), as well as other titles; Jürgen Osterhammel, *Die Entzauberung Asiens* (Munich, 1998); David Sorkin, *The Berlin Haskalah and German Religious Thought: Orphans of Knowledge* (London, 2000); Debora K. Shuger, *The Renaissance Bible: Scholarship, Sacrifice and Subjectivity* (Berkeley, CA, 1994); Jonathan Sheehan, *The Enlightenment Bible: Translation, Scholarship, Culture* (Princeton, NJ, 2005); Wilhelm Schmidt-Biggemann, *Philosophia perennis: Historical Outlines of Western Spirituality in Ancient, Medieval and Early Modern Thought* (Dordrecht, 2004); Paula Findlen, ed., *Athanasius Kircher: The Last Man Who Knew Everything* (New York, 2004); Peter N. Miller, *Peiresc's Europe: Learning and Virtue in the Seventeenth Century* (New Haven, CT, 2000). There are also older, very rich works to draw on here, including Donald Lach, *Asia in the Making of Europe*, 9 vols. (1965–1993); Frances Yates, *Giordano Bruno and the Hermetic Tradition* (Chicago, IL, 1979); D. P. Walker, *The Ancient Theology: Studies in Christian Platonism from the Fifteenth to the Eighteenth Century* (Ithaca, NY, 1972); Hans-Joachim Kraus, *Geschichte der historisch-kritischen Erforschung des Alten Testaments von der Reformation bis zur Gegenwart* (Neukirchen, 1956); Frank Manuel, *The Broken Staff: Judaism through Christian Eyes* (Cambridge, MA, 1992); David E. Mungello, *Curious Land: Jesuit Accommodation and the Origins of Sinology* (Wiesbaden, 1985).

massive increase of new source materials, especially after 1880, was still very much alive, at least as late as 1914. Understanding the powerful shaping force of the tradition of Christian humanism will be one of the main missions of this book, and its centrality reminds us – as have so many recent works in German social and political history – that being modern does not necessarily entail being secular.

Thirdly, while I emphasize the continuities that link oriental studies to earlier ideas and practices, I also pay careful attention here to institutional, intellectual, and political changes over the course of the nineteenth and early twentieth centuries. There is a familiar conceit that Europe's conception of the Orient was formed in the 1780s or 1820s and then remained unchanged until the present; from that time on, it is argued the romantic and/or imperially subordinated Orient had become a central part of European cultural and scholarly life. Getting to know the East better was simply a matter of perfecting the already existing understanding of its peoples, languages, and histories, or of ratifying preexisting prejudices. But in light of the reading and research I have done, this Whiggish disciplinary history is simply untenable. The worst part of this disciplinary emplotment is that it makes the struggle to obtain *Wissenschaftlichkeit* – and in some cases, to avoid being labeled a heretic – seem easy and the attempt to sketch cultural history fruitless. It also offers a very distorted view of the study of the Orient in nineteenth-century Germany, giving pride of place to philosophy (for Hegel plays all too central a role) rather than to the disciplines that really sustained and transformed the study of the East, namely, philology, theology, and, to a lesser extent, geography. And it does not take stock at all of extremely important changes at the fin de siècle, or during the Great War. I have sought to plunge the reader into the world of those who labored, largely unsung, at orientalism's philological face over the course of the eventful era between about 1750 and 1918 in order to understand not only how indebted they were to past traditions, but how much, decade by decade, their world changed.

I should clarify at the outset that I am writing this book as a scholar of German cultural and intellectual history. In no way can I claim to be a professional orientalist; indeed, I believe I may be unusually impartial in my recounting of the history of the field simply because I was not trained as an expert in any part of it. I have tried to understand the subfields' parameters and protocols – and consulted experts on a number of subjects – but I have not learned the Orient's many languages, something that by 1830 was already a remarkable feat and that, thanks to subsequent discoveries and decipherments, would be humanly impossible today. I apologize in advance for errors specialists might find in this book; but I hope my status as outsider, as well as my familiarity with the evolution of German cultural and political institutions more broadly, will help rather than hinder the goal of understanding the significance of orientalist scholarship for modern German cultural history. I hope that specialists will read the book, not only to gain new perspectives on the history of their own fields, but also to better understand how orientalism as a whole evolved over the course of two centuries of its development. There are always dangers involved in writing the history of a discipline from the outside, but I hope they will be offset by my desire to understand in broad historical terms what it meant to be a German orientalist.

If the book will, I hope, interest practicing orientalists, I am also hopeful that it will appeal to nonspecialists, theologians, classicists, and historians. I am reasonably sure that the first two groups will appreciate the importance of the subject matter, and early modern historians too will probably share my interest in many of these questions. Modern cultural historians may find the book's preoccupations rather arcane, in part, I think, because we all too often fail to take seriously the nineteenth century's absorption in the ancient world and its range of knowledge about the past. I would like to convince my fellow modernists that the topic I have chosen is by no means a narrow one and that in fact the topic deserves more study in the future.

In the chapters of this book I cover in some detail Assyriology, Egyptology, biblical criticism, Indology, Persian studies, Arabic linguistics, Islamic studies, Sinology, and Japanology. I should also note that each of these subfields was actually pursued in multiple ways, by scholars primarily interested in pure philological work, or by those specializing in comparative mythology and linguistics, history of religions, art history, history, geography, or archaeology. Each of these fields had a slightly different dynamic owing to the major texts upon which it relied (and how many of them were, at any point in time, accessible and comprehensible to Europeans) as well as to the particularities of individual practitioners and institutional locations. Different fields, too, aspired to different sorts of culture–political significance. For example, fin de siècle Assyriology played a highly significant role in debates about the veracity of the Old Testament, whereas contemporary Sinology had little to do with these religious debates and entangled itself much more in colonial questions. This diversity necessitated dividing chapters into subsections, but I have also tried to emphasize the ways in which individuals and institutional developments fit together and form part of the larger culture. There is a significant amount of detailed information in this book, on subjects ranging from Saint Paul's debts to Persian philosophy to the supposed proto-Kantianism of the Vedas. But I hope to convince readers that the developments and debates I survey have implications for many wider questions in German intellectual and cultural history, and deserve to be far better understood than seems to be the case at present.

The size and complexity of this book's subject have made it imperative that I limit my investigations in several important ways. First of all, I have chosen to focus not on the conceptions of the Orient held by "great men" such as Hegel, Schopenhauer, Nietzsche, Max Weber, and Freud, but rather to detail the careers and ambitions of lesser-known figures like Justus Olshausen, Theodor Nöldeke, Paul Deussen, Adolf Erman, and Leopold von Schroeder. I have done so in part because the men in the first list were not, by the standards of their contemporaries, "orientalists" – though some may have known a little Hebrew, they were not skilled in the reading of oriental languages, and did not (to my knowledge) read nonwestern texts in their original forms. An additional reason to exclude the big names is that a considerable amount of ink has already been spilt in explicating their ideas, whereas the work of the men on the second list is practically unknown, at least outside small circles of directly descended experts. Though I hope sketching this galaxy of minor figures will help some of intellectual history's fixed stars to shine with new light, I also think our notions about whose ideas mattered in the nineteenth century are woefully narrow and it may well be time to train our telescopes elsewhere.

By omitting coverage of some of the "great" men, I have prevented the book from becoming even longer than it is. But it still includes a mass of long-forgotten names, from Walter Andrae (Assyriologist of an esoteric sort) to Bartholomaus Ziegelbalg (author of a Tamil dictionary and translator of the New Testament into Tamil). Overwhelmed by the number of such obscure men, some readers might find it hard to believe that many, perhaps a majority of, German oriental experts of the period are not even mentioned in my index. I have had to make choices and have selected some for their recognized innovations, some for their typicality with respect to other scholars in the field, and some because they played important roles as provocateurs or popularizers. I had to curtail my investigations even of those, like C. F. Andreas, who had what might be called "interesting" lives; Andreas, for example, whose parents were German-Malayan and aristocratic Armenian, spent some time as postmaster general of Persia before landing his job in middle-Persian philology at the University of Göttingen; he played an important role in deciphering the manuscripts brought back to Berlin by the Turfan Expeditions (see Chapter 9), but is better known to intellectual historians as the long-suffering husband of that most notorious of neoromantic muses, Lou [Andreas] Salomé.[25] I cannot hope to do justice to Andreas here – in fact, he is only mentioned once again briefly in this book. I can only apologize in advance for the cursory treatment he and many of his fellows receive here and hope that other scholars see fit to excavate more thoroughly territory I can only survey.

Selection is not the only difficulty, of course, connected with inquiries into the everyday life of scholarship. Compared with that of Andreas, the lives of most of the other orientalists were not so "interesting" and as a consequence, finding detailed information about some figures, like the rather obscure Brunnhofer, has been difficult. Sometimes the volume of work is an issue (as in the case of the Austrian scholar Joseph von Hammer-Purgstall); sometimes the work is so narrowly positivistic that teasing out its ideological underpinnings requires specialized learning I do not possess. Sometimes, too, one needs to restore so many contexts at once – as for example in the quest to evaluate the contributions of the Islamicist, politician, and pundit Carl Heinrich Becker – that only a partial treatment of a career or a person can be attempted. There are, of course, many other things about the individuals, and their work, that specialists in the fields they represent will understand and appreciate much better than I can, though I have tried to pay close attention to the meanings, for example, of dating the Psalms in a particular way, or of attributing certain characteristics to Buddha at one or another point in time. In many ways, this book is simply an attempt to map this vast and sometimes treacherous territory. I can only hope that others expand on (and, as the logic of scholarship dictates, supercede) what I sketch here.

---

[25] There is some interesting material on Andreas in Rudolph Binion's old but wonderful *Frau Lou: Nietzsche's Wayward Disciple* (Princeton, NJ, 1968) (see esp. pp. 133–5); but it might be rewarding to follow this up, given the couple's long and close (but of course unusual) relationship, and Lou's intimate relations with a large number of influential intellectuals, including Nietzsche, Rilke, and Freud.

One of the things I want to know is what it was actually like to be an orientalist. Why did some well-educated Germans choose this field of study, especially when it was largely unfashionable, and usually unprofitable, to do so? For it was never particularly easy or popular to be an orientalist. One had to learn a battery of difficult languages, often with little assistance; it took a special sort of person to commit himself to such a field of study when resources, manuscripts, colleagues, and positions were much more numerous in classics. Often enough, one had to battle other peoples' prejudices on top of these material and institutional difficulties. Consider Simon Ockley's difficulties, as he saw them, in 1708: Ockley, as Jürgen Osterhammel explains, "not only had to deal with material that was linguistically extremely difficult and had hardly been touched by an editor's hands, with 'dusty Manuscripts, without Translation, without Index; destitute altogether of those Helps which facilitate other Studies'; in addition he had to attempt to understand, without western arrogance, a historical and literary consciousness that expresses itself in its own unique forms."[26] More than 200 years later, the Sinologist Richard Wilhelm explained to a friend the hardships involved in trying to interest Weimar Germans in Chinese cultural history. In the past couple of years, Wilhelm wrote, he had been living "the life of a vagabond," dragging slides and lectures everywhere, attending many *gemütlich* get-togethers "in which one has always to inform people that the Chinese do not eat earthworms and rotten eggs and only rarely kill their little girls ..."[27] Although many lived to over-ripe old ages, a not inconsiderable number of orientalists perished in the field, among whom we could list Eduard Schultz, who was killed by Kurds while copying inscriptions in Van, and five of the six members of the expedition sent to "Arabia felix" in 1761. More generally, however, we should recognize that in the context of the times, choosing to be an orientalist was, on the whole, not to choose a career with political influence or significant cultural clout.

What was "the Orient" for these men? German writers and scholars did believe in the existence of "the Orient" as a geocultural concept, and for the sake of expediency, I will often refer, as my subjects sometimes did, to the vast and diverse cultural territory east of Istanbul as "the East" or "the Orient," using the scare quotations only when it seems imperative to underline the derogatory or dismissive implications of the term's usage. But they also were perfectly well aware that *Asien* (used interchangeably, but much less often, than *Orient* or the more poetic *Morgenland*) was – like Europe itself – not politically or religiously uniform. They were indeed proficient at juxtaposing one part of "the" Orient to another, making China, for example, exemplary of rational ethics and ordered stability, while Judea is blamed for inventing irrational otherwordliness and inhumane intolerance. It is important, in fact, to see clearly the important changes in European conceptions and passions over time, as China, for example, lost luster at the same time interest in ancient India was waxing. Moreover, though there were cultural trends – encouraged and exacerbated by state or private patrons – interests and passions did differ among individuals. We should not expect even orientalists

---

[26] Quoted in Jürgen Osterhammel, "Neue Welten in der europäische Geschichtsschreibung (ca. 1500–1800)," in *Geschichtsdiskurs*, vol. 2, ed. Wolfgang Küttler et al. (Frankfurt, 1994), p. 208.
[27] Richard Wilhelm quoted in Salomé Blumhardt Wilhelm, *Richard Wilhelm: Der geistige Mittler zwischen China und Europa* (Düsseldorf, 1956), p. 347.

who were contemporaries to speak with one voice any more than American or European area specialists do today – they were, as we like to think ourselves, individuals driven by different desires, demands, interests, and tastes, though their choices were, as are ours, limited and shaped by the political and institutional horizons we inhabit.

One of the subjects on which this history of *Orientalistik* hopes to throw new light is the history of humanistic endeavor in the context of the changing cultural landscape of the later nineteenth century. The universities in the Germanys were the site of major cultural and political battles over the course of the nineteenth century, battles over control of Christian doctrine as well as over the nature of Germandom's past and the proper behavior of citizens in the present. Positioned, quite awkwardly, between the secular humanities (classics and *Germanistik*) and the still highly influential if embattled theological faculty, "orientalism" was right at the heart of controversies about the future of *Wissenschaft*, as well as being central to an issue neither of its brother philologies could easily address: the past and future of religion. Having modeled itself, as much as it was able, on secular classical philology in the early nineteenth century, orientalism was just coming into its own at the century's close, at which time, however, it had to struggle with both widespread crises of religious belief and the dissolution of the humanities' monopoly over cultural production. This, then, is not only a story about the lives and careers of the orientalists; it is also a story about the internal dynamics and demographics of cultural production, the collapse of older forms of *Bildung* and *Wissenschaft*, and the opening up of a new marketplace of ideas, and the often successful resistance mounted to the advent of this brave new world.

In this endeavor, I offer here an overview of the cultural politics of German "orientalism," focusing heavily, but not exclusively, on its academic manifestations. Offering first a short history of the field, I will emphasize its entanglement in German cultural politics and the field's formative relationships to the study of classical antiquity and Biblical exegesis (Chapters 1 and 2). I will then describe the changes in scale, in depth of research, and in the public accessibility of texts, which occurred as the nineteenth century wore on. In the period between about 1820 and 1880, specialization, new sources of patronage, and the waning of clerical power in the cultural sphere *as well as* colonial aspirations drove scholarly interests deeper into the East (Chapters 3–5). A chapter (Chapter 6) I did not anticipate writing – on the profound impact of oriental studies on interpretations of the New Testament – in the end had to be written; it is not a chapter that an orientalist, or a typical modern cultural historian, would write, but it nicely illustrates two things we have missed: first, the reconvergence of theology, classics, and oriental studies at the fin de siècle and second, the ongoing power of oriental studies to shape Christians' view of the scriptures. It is followed by a closer investigation of the relationships between race and religion in studies of the East (Chapter 7), and then by a long chapter, which treats directly the Second Empire's development of colonial sciences (Chapter 8), and a shorter one, which surveys the study of oriental art (Chapter 9). The final chapter (Chapter 10) takes up the critical question of German orientalists' relationships with nonwestern "others," and traces some of these relationships through the disastrous course of the Great War. The book ends in about 1918, as the imperial era (for the Germans, at any rate) comes to an end, as the philological-historicist tradition folds its tents and as non-Europeans begin to play an increasingly visible and important role in German "orientalist" pursuits and intrigues. But, as the epilogue suggests, I believe there are many legacies of the era I treat that lasted well into the twentieth century and I hope that others too will continue this story down to contemporary times.[28]

[28] There are fascinating other studies underway here, many of which can be cast as studies of the exchange of knowledge, and the transformations of relationships on both sides of the Europe/non-Europe divide precisely because the authors are able to work in two or more linguistic and historical contexts at once. Here I will mention only Kris Manjapra's dissertation, "The Mirrored World: Cosmopolitan Encounter between Indian Anti-Colonial Intellectuals and German Radicals, 1905–1939" (Ph.D. Dissertation, Harvard University, May 2007), and the recent *Modern Intellectual History* volume, "An Intellectual History for India," ed. Shrutli Kapila (April 2007), but I know there is much more work of this sort going on at present.

I

Orientalism and the Longue Durée

> In the beginning was the Word, and the Word was with God, and the Word was God....
>
> John 1.1

It seems fitting that this book opens with this line from the New Testament, for throughout this book we will be dealing with words, with origins or beginnings, and with gods. While many other factors came into play, European, and especially German, scholarly orientalism in the nineteenth and even early twentieth centuries remained powerfully rooted in humanistic traditions that reach back into the early modern or even the Hellenistic world and are rooted in the interpretation of Jewish and Christian scriptures. I did not begin this project with such a conviction, but as I read the works of the German scholars, I recognized that the issues of central importance to them were not ones that could be explained in any sensible way by limiting myself to the Wilhelmine era or to the modern, secular study of India, the Islamic world, and China. German-speaking Central Europeans have taken up a variety of positions with respect to the peoples, cultures, and histories of the ever-shifting geographical entity known to the nineteenth century as "the Orient" – but I discovered that for those who devoted serious study to the subject, what mattered most was the *ancient* Near and Middle East, the birthplace of most of the world's religious texts. The key debates revolved around questions most students of "orientalism" ignore, seemingly obscure questions such as how to date the Zend Avesta or to assess the authorship of the Pentateuch. For the most part, my research brought me face to face not with policy makers but with the descendants of those often rebarbarative and iconoclastic theologians and philologists featured in such masterpieces of early modern intellectual history as Anthony Grafton's *Defenders of the Text*, Frances Yates's *Giordano Bruno and the Hermetic Tradition*, and D. P. Walker's *The Ancient Theology*. I have been forced to conclude that German orientalism – defined as the serious and sustained study of the cultures of Asia – was not a product of the modern, imperial age, but something much older, richer, and stranger, something enduringly shaped by the longing to hear God's word, to understand the meaning of his revelation, and to propagate (Christian) truths as one understood them. But I have also concluded, and will attempt to persuade my readers as well, that this legacy was by no means a simple one, and endowed German orientalism with a cultural ambivalence we have yet to appreciate.

Several very venerable Christian traditions played an important role in shaping the study of eastern languages and cultures in western Europe, most prominent among which were biblical exegesis and what we might call informed evangelizing. Biblical exegesis, or *critica sacra*, the critically informed drawing out of the meaning of sacred scripture, was born with the first efforts to collate and translate the scriptures themselves, and was similar in many ways to textual traditions practiced by the other "peoples of the book," Muslims and Jews. Christian theologians from the church fathers forward were well aware that textual divergences, internal contradictions, and obscure passages offered grounds for heresy or schism, and were anxious to create stable, defensible readings. They regularly performed various kinds of exegesis, applying reason and refined linguistic skills to elucidate God's words. Already in the third century, the learned Origen sought to demonstrate the plenitude of God's word by offering parallel, but non-identical, Greek and Hebrew versions of the Old Testament in his *Hexapla*. Like his near contemporaries Jerome and Augustine, Origen knew that non-Christians were also engaged in critical readings of scripture; their criticisms too needed to be taken into account if Christianity's truth were to be universally convincing.[1] European scholars who followed in the church fathers' traces knew that this sort of textual work was both necessary and a bit dangerous; those who practiced it used their skills to shore up Christian belief, but often, too, their immersion in the languages and cultures of non-Christians laid them open to charges of heresy. Compelled again and again to tackle the crucial theological question, what did Christianity owe to Judaism? They presumed a supercessionist relationship, but acknowledged, in one way or the other, Christianity's profound debts to the ancient Israelites, whose history was clearly rooted in the Levant.

In the medieval Christian world, there was already another important role for the scholar of Near Eastern languages, or "orientalist": – to understand the non-Christian cultures to whom the gospel could be preached. Informed evangelization, like *critica sacra*, was a very old task that required unusual linguistic skills in the effort to defend and spread Christian faith. Even in the centuries in which Christian states were far weaker and less wealthy than the Ottoman, Chinese, Moghul, and Safavid Empires, evangelists presumed Christian superiority – that was, of course, doctrinally non-negotiable. Those who learned foreign languages were charged with understanding non-Christian cultures so that infidels and heathens could more easily be converted. But along the hermeneutical path, there are many dangers, for who is to say exactly *how much* and *what kind* of

---

[1] On Origen's quite risky exegetical model, see Peter N. Miller, "Making the Paris Polyglot Bible: Humanism and Orientalism in the Early Seventeenth Century," in Herbert Jaumann, ed., *Die europäische Gelehrtenrepublik im Zeitalter des Konfessionalismus* (Wiesbaden, 2001), pp. 60–1, 74–5. Modern historians have perhaps underestimated the extent to which the exchange of polemics, especially between Jewish, Muslim, and Christian scholars, has, since medieval times, pushed forward the art of interpreting scripture – or the penchant for criticizing it. See Edward Breuer, *The Limits of Enlightenment: Jews, Germans and the Eighteenth-Century Study of Scripture* (Cambridge, MA, 1996), pp. 78–9; also, Amos Funkenstein, *Theology and the Scientific Imagination from the Middle Ages to the Seventeenth Century* (Princeton, NJ, 1986), and Martin Mulsow, *Moderne aus dem Untergrund: Radikale Frühaufklärung in Deutschland, 1680–1720* (Hamburg, 2002).

understanding is necessary? In the course of this study, we will meet many an orientalist who began by seeking to defend his or her own faith, and ended by discovering new problems or points of view, many who thought they might be useful to clerical or political authorities, but ended up complicating received wisdom. Again, traditions that began as Christian ones shaped post-Enlightenment practices; but again, too, these were already ambivalent traditions, with unpredictable applications and outcomes.

Of course, the study of the East in the West was shaped by other traditions too, perhaps especially by the study of another of Europe's special peoples, the Greeks. The specialness of the Greeks was not something introduced by J. J. Winckelmann in the eighteenth century; arguments for and against Greek specialness already appear in ancient texts such as in Herodotus, Plotinus, and Iamblichus, and we should recall that the first great philhellenists were the Romans, not the Germans. Interest in the Greeks was again partly theological; the world of the church fathers was one suffused with questions about relations between the Greeks and the Jews – after all, the earliest extant version of the Old Testament – the Septuagint – was in Greek, as were the writings of Saint Paul, and Greek is the language of the New Testament.[2] But there was considerable interest in the "secular" side of Greek culture as well. Greek art, literature, and philosophy were respected even in medieval times. It was possible to look upon at least some Greeks and Romans as noble pagans, and to acknowledge the cultural achievements of the Byzantine Empire. But the real breakthrough came with Byzantium's fall, and the flooding of western Europe with Greek scholars and eastern manuscripts; and then came the Renaissance, which made it acceptable for learned men and women to devote sustained attention and affection to the works of the classical, pre-Christian world. One of the stories we will be following throughout is the story of paganism's rise to respectability, something that not only helped classical scholarship achieve its dominant status in the nineteenth-century humanities but also made possible an increasingly non-perjorative and historicist study of Asian cultural history. Most disciplinary histories of oriental studies ignore the not just parallel but interconnected history of classical scholarship and thus fail to appreciate how differently specialization and secularization affected fields that were, even in the late eighteenth century, sister-sciences. But to understand orientalism as its nineteenth-century practitioners did, we cannot omit this part of the story.

There are also less fusty and formalized traditions that informed oriental studies from ancient times and which further complicate the claim that orientalism has always been about creating "others." One of these was Neoplatonism, a Hellenistic school of thought, which looked to eastern wisdom as well as Platonic reason to understand the deepest truths of existence. Alexandrian, Gnostic, or Manichean ideas were, in varying ways, mixed with and often preferred to classical or Christian

---

[2] This is not to say, however, that all "Greeks" were understood to belong ethnically or culturally to Europe, Christendom, or the West, all of which are concepts that cannot be applied transhistorically. It was well known, for example, that the Septuagint had been rendered into Greek for the use of Alexandrian Jews, and that large Greek communities could be found throughout the Ottoman Empire. But the Christian attempt to assert the superiority of New Testament ideas over those of the Old Testament did inflect, and after the eighteenth century help to shape, an opposition between Greeks and Jews.

ones. Neoplatonism experienced a Renaissance-era revival in late fifteenth century, thanks in part to the location of Horapollo's *Hieroglyphica*, a late Greek treatise, which purported to explain the allegorical secrets of the hieroglyphs. The text, we now know, contained many misleading attempts at symbolic readings, but it was long regarded, Erik Iversen argues, "with something like a sacred awe." From the fifteenth to the early nineteenth century, scholars depended upon it in their attempts to understand the supposedly mystical language eastern priests had employed in order to reserve special truths for the elite.[3] On the heels of this discovery came Marsilio Ficino's translation of the writings of the great Egyptian priest-cum-philosopher Hermes Trismegistus, who was rumored to have possessed knowledge later elaborated by Socrates and even Moses. Ficino's *Pimander* – the first part of what we now know as the *Corpus Hermeticum* – appeared in 1471, making it one of the first printed books in Europe. Esoteric though it was, the *Pimander* would go through sixteen editions before the end of the sixteenth century.[4]

The man who brought together the older Neoplatonism and the newer Egyptizing texts was the Italian humanist Pico della Mirandola. Pico also drew on his knowledge of a third source of mystical wisdom, the Jewish Kabbalah. In his *Conclusions* (1486–7), Pico sought to demonstrate in 900 propositions that the world's major theologies and philosophies – Christian, pagan, Jewish, and Muslim – set forth the same truths. By resolving apparent contradictions and dissimilarities between the faiths, Pico hoped to create a universal system to which all rational men could subscribe.[5] Thus was born the idea of the *philosophia perennis* and a long tradition of esoteric attempts to reconcile pagan philosophies with Christianity.[6] Here, we meet a strain of western thought which saw Asian religious and philosophical ideas as compatible with Christianity and which recognized the possibility of extremely ancient oriental ideas as foundational for western ones. It has had a long and formative effect on oriental scholarship, from the Kabbalist Johannes Reuchlin to the romantic poet Friedrich Rückert, and from the Catholic polymath Athanasius Kircher to the theosophical impresario Madame Blavatsky. It is an iconoclastic tradition, one that produced Giordano Bruno, burned at the stake in 1600, and Guillaume Postel, convicted of heresy by the Venetian Inquisition, imprisoned for four years, and then confined as a lunatic in St. Martin's Priory near Paris. And its patrons, from Cosimo di' Medici to the eighteenth-century Masons, were often iconoclasts as well. But as we will see, iconoclasm was by no means unusual among later orientalists even during the staid and sober mid-nineteenth century.

The Hermetic tradition may seem strange and even a bit silly, but the study of Egyptian priestly secrets actually had a very powerful effect on scholarship, for

---

[3] Erik Iversen, *The Myth of Egypt and its Hieroglyphs in European Tradition* (Princeton, NJ, 1993; reprint of 1961 edition), pp. 47–9, quotation p. 49.

[4] Frances Yates, *Giordano Bruno and the Hermetic Tradition* (Chicago, 1979), p. 14.

[5] Frank Manuel, *The Broken Staff: Judaism through Christian Eyes* (Cambridge, MA, 1992), p. 40.

[6] For a magisterial treatment of this intellectual tradition, see Wilhelm Schmidt-Biggemann, *Philosophia perennis: Historical Outlines of Western Spirituality in Ancient, Medieval and Early Modern Thought* (Dordrecht, Netherlands, 2004).

early modern fascination with eastern wisdom helped to broaden the range of cultures to which primeval revelation, of some sort, might have been available.[7] The newly available texts seemed to explain a passage in Acts (7:22) in which it was said that Moses was "well versed" in "all the wisdom of Egypt." As Jan Assmann has written, this set in motion a process of identifying biblical and ancient oriental parallels and propelled forward the process of ennobling – or at least treating more respectfully – pagan ideas. In this era, Assmann writes, ". . . the wall of intranslatability collapsed and Egypt began to appear as the origin, rather than the 'other,' of Biblical monotheism."[8] We will see the collapse of many more of these "walls of intranslatability" over time; for the present, it is sufficient to note that what we now call Egyptology did not begin (or end!) with Champollion but has its proper origins in Pico's esoteric "science" as well as in his late antique sources.

Hermeticism and Neoplatonism were long-lasting forms in which Westerners paid tribute to eastern wisdom; but there were other images and stereotypes which were equally ancient and enduring. Donald Lach has shown, for example, the image of India as mysterious and monstrous and that of the Brahmins as wise, simple, and pure was already current in Hellenistic Greek literature.[9] Jesuit characterizations of China were much younger, but just as lasting and that of fanatical Islamic infidels even more so. Images generated by the spice and silk trades were extremely influential and remarkably durable.[10] But, like Wolfgang Schivelbusch, I am not convinced that the images and associations created as a result of this trade were exclusively derogatory ones; Europeans did admire eastern craftsmanship and covet Chinese and Persian luxuries, even if they often polemicized against them. Of course, Europeans treated non-Christians at least in part as "others" – though Montesquieu, for example, meant his *Persian Letters* (1721) to show that they were not all that different, and that France, perhaps, was the less civilized country. In point of fact, Montesquieu surely had more in common with Mughal courtiers than with the peasants of Languedoc – and I believe he knew that, too. "Othering" then is neither new nor is it consistent or internally coherent, and did not create a set of immutable and mutually exclusive European and oriental identities.

This survey of intellectual traditions over the *longue durée* offers a provocative opening, but more important to this study is an understanding of the individuals, institutions, and practices that shaped early modern studies of oriental cultures. The first portion of this chapter tries to offer some insights into individuals and institutional arrangements and to underscore, in this context, the importance of chronological questions for oriental studies. We begin with a brief

[7] Similarly, early missionaries to China wondered if similarities between Confucian and Christian ideas might point to an *ur*-international revelation, one that perhaps preceded God's special, historical revelation to the ancient Israelites. See D. P. Walker, *The Ancient Theology: Studies in Christian Platonism from the Fifteenth to the Eighteenth Century* (Ithaca, NY, 1972).

[8] Jan Assmann, *Moses the Egyptian: The Memory of Egypt in Western Monotheism* (Cambridge, MA, 1997), p. 55.

[9] Lach, *Asia in the Making of Europe*, vol. II, *A Century of Wonder*, book 2, *The Scholarly Disciplines* (Chicago, IL, 1977), pp. 85–7.

[10] Wolfgang Schivelbusch, *Tastes of Paradise: A Social History of Spices, Stimulants and Intoxicants*, trans. David Jacobson (New York, 1992), pp. 3–14.

discussion of *Orientalistik*'s long history of ambivalent relationships with the orthodox churches and with the state. We then investigate the ways in which Enlightenment scholarship transformed older traditions, a critical subject, which is often the end point of early modern studies or the point of departure for modern ones, but too rarely the critical bridge that allows inquirers to traverse the full distance between the Renaissance and the Great War. Also, it was in the course of the eighteenth century that already existing differences in Europe's reception of individual oriental cultures began to generate many of the parameters within which nineteenth-century specialized fields would operate. Thus, one portion of this chapter will be given over to surveying what each of the major "Orients" meant to their western interpreters. The next section treats "the peculiarities of German orientalism"[11]; here, we return to a discussion of the centrality of Reformation-era Christian humanism in laying the foundations for *Orientalistik* and also underline the importance of Frederician tolerance and the diversity of Germandom's numerous university cultures in enabling the development of more extensive and intensive studies of Near Eastern texts. And finally, we turn to two of the most influential eighteenth-century German readers of God's words, J. D. Michaelis and J. G. Herder, for whom the orientalists' *ur*-text, the Old Testament, was the starting point for a new sort of *Kulturgeschichte* as well as the enduring foundation for Christian faith.

INDIVIDUALS, INSTITUTIONS, ICONOCLASMS

There never seems to have been a time during which Europeans did *not* want to know about Asian cultures – perhaps, because for so long, European "civilization" remained a backwater, its states comparatively barbaric, small, and poor. Herodotus, it should be recalled, was deeply interested in Persia and Egypt and the first major translation project we know of – the rendering of the Hebrew Bible into Greek by "the seventy" – involved the translation of oriental texts. The church fathers were very knowledgeable about oriental religions (they had to be, if for no other reason than to define the "heresies" around them), and though relations between Christians and Muslims in Spain as well as Central and Southeastern Europe were usually tense, and often much worse, there were also moments of peaceful coexistence and individuals who successfully crossed religious or political borders. As Donald Lach has shown, throughout the Middle Ages, Europeans read reworkings of the Alexander romance and of Indian parables; later, medieval readers delighted in the travelogues of Sir John Mandeville (ca. 1371) and Marco Polo and constructed fabulous stories about India and "Cathay."[12] Pilgrims and Crusaders brought back relics, stories, and manuscripts. But most Europeans' interest in the Orient was superficial or passing, while the individuals we have

---

[11] German historians will recognize this, rightly, as an attempt to engage the debate begun by David Blackbourn and Geoff Eley's seminal book, *The Peculiarities of German History* (Oxford, 1984).

[12] Donald F. Lach, *Asia in the Making of Europe*, vol. II, book 2, *The Scholarly Disciplines* (Chicago, IL, 1977), pp. 91–116, 330–1. See also Nina Berman, "Thoughts on Zionism in the Context of German Middle Eastern Relations," pp. 138–9.

to deal with in this book were of a different sort – men and women who learned to read and sometimes speak oriental languages or who made the effort to travel to the East and to study its cultures intensively. Their relationships with other Europeans – patrons, colleagues, readers, and rivals – and with non-Europeans structured the work that they did, as did the intellectual traditions they drew upon and the institutional structures they inhabited. In this section, we sketch some of these pursuits, passions, and patronage relationships, hoping to understand what it meant to devote oneself to oriental studies before the Enlightenment, and what those who made this choice contributed to European cultural history as a whole.

There were, of course, various ways to be an early modern orientalist and various Orients one could study. The most common and culturally acceptable kind of orientalist was the Old Testament scholar, for the simple reason that theology was a steady line of work; one could seek a job as a priest, a pastor, a translator, a missionary, or a professor of theology, for there were as yet no academic jobs for "secular" orientalists. Before the Reformation, there were few theologians with oriental language skills at the universities, for demonstrating the plenitude of God's word, as had Origen, could be a rather dicey business. The first professors of oriental studies, appointed by the Council of Vienne (1311–12) to propagate Catholicism among the Jews, Muslims, and eastern Christians, were regularly accused of siding with the infidel; before the sixteenth century, students of Arabic and Hebrew were often labeled heretics. The field's importance began to grow as the Protestant and Catholic Reformations spread, demonstrating to scholars the importance of reading Old Testament Hebrew and convincing the Popes of the need to draw eastern Christians back into the Church Universal. Once the utility of learning oriental languages became clear, Catholic and especially Protestant princes and clerical authorities were willing to countenance the spread of orientalism.

Europe's fragmented power structures and religious divergences spurred the proliferation of new forms of oriental scholarship. Bible translations and editions, studies of biblical "antiquities" and philologically informed commentaries abounded, their authors intending not to destroy the credibility of the scriptures but to validate and clarify them and to defend particular doctrinal positions. Many church officials began to fear that biblical interpretation was falling into inappropriate hands, and creating new heresies rather than healing schisms; but the rapid spread of the printing press made controlling the marketplace of ideas impossible; already by the 1530s, Frank Manuel argues, so many European presses were able to produce Hebrew characters that the Inquisition could not keep up.[13] More fonts were introduced as Jesuits, opposed to strict Latinity, began to push for the printing of religious literature in non-European, as well as European, vernacular languages. Printers, some of them specializing in travel literature, vocabularies, or exotic miscellanies, played an essential role in introducing Europeans to a vast number of new languages over the course of the sixteenth century, a process Donald Lach described as the "rebabelization" of the continent.[14]

---

[13] Manuel, *Broken Staff*, p. 31.
[14] Lach, *Asia in the Making of Europe*, vol. II, *A Century of Wonder*, book 3, *The Scholarly Disciplines* (Chicago, 1977), pp. 525–43.

Of course, there were plenty of scholarly orientalists outside the colleges and courts; learned Jews, importantly, produced many studies Christians read and used, whether or not the latter acknowledged their sources. Among Christians, there were also private scholars, knowledgeable travelers, booksellers and traders, diplomats, and above all missionaries, whose relationships with political and church officials varied widely. It would be a mistake to ignore the missionaries' contributions to scholarship as well as their essential collecting and disseminating roles. They went to places no other Europeans would or could visit and often stayed for a long time. They collected large numbers of manuscripts and sent home detailed reports. To preach the gospel effectively, they often found that they had to learn languages other Europeans did not know, and to help both their parishioners and missionaries who might follow them, they sometimes wrote their own grammars or dictionaries or translated scriptures into native languages. The Lutheran missionary Bartholomaus Ziegenbalg (1682–1719), for example, spent his career in India, where he produced the first Tamil dictionary; in addition to translating Luther's catechism and parts of the Bible into Tamil, Ziegenbalg also moved in the opposite direction, translating Tamil moral texts into German in the belief that these demonstrated that the Indians were once monotheists.[15] Although, for understandable reasons, the collections missionaries sent back often focused on religious matters – or on rituals or philosophies they took to be the nearest equivalents to Christian practices and beliefs – they, like the diplomats, also often had considerable amounts of free time on their hands, which they used, according to their personal druthers, to collect plants or bugs or to worry about irregular verbs or local marriage customs.

What they usually did not have, at least while "in the field," was access to a good European library, nor did they have, by virtue of their employment, the ability to proclaim their work "disinterested." In fact, Ziegenbalg's description of Hindu practices, written in 1713, was too "objective" for his era; when the text of his *Mythologie* reached August Hermann Francke in Halle, the redoubtable Pietist refused to publish it, insisting that the point of his mission was to root out paganism, not to spread it in Europe.[16] All of these factors would make it easier for nineteenth-century academic scholars to label missionary work "unscientific." And yet, missionary reports and collections would continue to serve as the basis for many fields of oriental study right through the nineteenth century, and even long into the twentieth. Thus, to be an early modern orientalist, at least by the early seventeenth century, was to be a person in the middle of debates and with a set of skills – for example, the ability to read ancient oriental languages – that made the person increasingly interesting, though perhaps still rather threatening, to clerical patrons. For even those orientalists most devoted to serving the churches' purposes often ended up in doctrinal difficulty. Jesuit missionaries in

[15] Walter Leifer, *Indien und die Deutschen: 500 Jahre Begegnung und Partnerschaft* (Tübingen, 1969), pp. 50–2.

[16] Ziegenbalg's text finally appeared in 1791, but anonymously, and appeared under his own name, only in 1867. Glasenapp *Das Indienbild deutscher Denker* (Stuttgart, 1960), pp. 167–9; Partha Mitter, *Much Maligned Monsters: A History of European Reactions to Indian Art* (Oxford, 1977), p. 59.

China, for example, found traces of monotheism in the Chinese classics, offering ground upon which conversions might be attempted but also awkwardly subverting the singularity of God's revelation to the Jews.[17] Or, one might take the case of the learned French bishop Pierre-Daniel Huet, whose huge *Demonstratio evangelica* (1679) drew on his knowledge of Syriac, Hebrew, and Arabic sources to confirm the historicity of Old Testament passages, which could then be matched up with their New Testament fulfillments. But this attempt to answer Spinoza's challenges to biblical authority, like so many others to follow, led not to the certainty that Huet longed for, but, inevitably, to more disputes about the authenticity and accuracy of his sources.[18] The English scholar John Dee used his Hebrew to converse with angels[19] – nice work, but not exactly a dogmatically defensible use of one's gifts. Thus, orientalism – in the form of biblical criticism, apologetics, and Jesuit reportage – already in the early modern period became an acceptable, and even valued, form of humanistic learning and of propagating the faith, but not one that necessarily offered the practitioner a stable career or an easy conscience.

As for orientalism's relationships to state power before 1750, the situation was rather analogous. As we saw in the theological realm, here too both patrons and practitioners had their ideas about how oriental scholarship could advance their own aims; orientalism was never a "disinterested" science. Sir Thomas Roe was sent to see the Great Mughal in 1615 in the interest of expanding English commercial privileges; Louis XIV agreed to send French Jesuits to China in 1685, not for the sake of either Christian missionizing or pure astronomy, but to improve the quality of French navigational charts. In this case, Louis hoped that the imprimatur of the Académie des Sciences would deflect the opposition of the Portuguese.[20] But patrons in the early period did not always know what they wanted, much less what they would get, from funding – as did the Catholic church – Athansius Kircher's studies of Chinese religions or Sebastião Mantique's stay in Bengal. And sometimes what they got surprised or vexed them. Some scholars worked for and pleased the state; others were thorns in its side. Ogier Ghiselin de Busbecq, who served as emissary of the Holy Roman Emperor in Istanbul from 1554 to 1562, was in general helpful; he did manage to forestall renewed Habsburg–Ottoman warfare after the Turks' victory at Mohács in 1526. But he was successful, partly at least, because he stayed so long and humbly adapted himself to local conditions. His long, newsy letters (in Latin) to a well-placed friend during his stay include a famous, rather admiring account of Suleiman the Magnificent, a man who was, Busbecq recognized, much more in control of Europe's destiny than vice versa.[21] Nor did politics, by any means, exhaust

---

[17] Walker, *The Ancient Theology*, pp. 200–3. Ricci's views were discussed in the introduction to the first Latin translation of Confucius (Paris, 1687). See also David E. Mungello, *Curious Land: Jesuit Accommodation and the Origins of Sinology* (Wiesbaden, 1985).

[18] April Shelford, "Thinking Geometrically in Pierre-Daniel Huet's *Demonstratio evangelica*," in *Journal of the History of Ideas* 63, no. 4 (2002): 615–16.

[19] Deborah Harkness, *John Dee's Conversations with Angels: Cabala, Alchemy and the End of Nature* (Cambridge, 1999), p. 165.

[20] Mungello, *Curious Land*, pp. 32, 36–7.

[21] These letters appeared in print already in 1589. See the new edition, *The Turkish Letters of Ogier Ghiselin de Busbecq*, trans. Edward Seymour Forster (Oxford, 1927; reprint Baton Rouge, LA, 2005).

Busbecq's interest in and contribution to the study of things eastern. The slow-moving pace of early modern diplomacy also afforded him plenty of time to attend to his collections, and he is credited with having brought to Europe some 240 classical manuscripts, a large number of coins, and sundry exotic animals, as well as the lilac, and possibly even the most highly prized oriental commodity of the seventeenth century, the tulip.[22] The Habsburgs did not particularly want any of these things – but they got them, and their circulation in Europe changed thought patterns in ways that went far beyond the satisfaction of Austria's political or economic interests.

If orientalism was never "disinterested," it was also a science that used from the beginning whatever resources it could muster in order to achieve its ends. Over the course of many centuries, scholars, confronting unfamiliar cultures, employed essentially the same tactics: utilize people over whom one has power or influence to help force open recondite textual secrets. Just as Saint Jerome depended upon learned Jews to help him create the Vulgate, Ramón Lull, in the thirteenth century, purchased his own Arabic Moorish translator in the form of a slave. In medieval Toledo, scholars wishing to read Arabic texts often needed two intermediaries: educated Jews, who had Spanish and Arabic but probably no Latin, to render the text into old Spanish, and Spanish priests who could make crude Latin drafts; the more widely educated scholar would then be responsible for making an elegant Latin translation.[23] Similarly, Pico, Johannes Reuchlin, Johann Buxtorf, Isaac Causabon, and many others learned their Hebrew from Jews or Jewish converts; the Jesuits learned their Chinese and their Chinese geography from local mandarins, on whose sufferance they depended. Of course, the Chinese were also extracting information from the Jesuits. Another means to obtain knowledge of "others" was kidnapping, from which Columbus and his men did not shrink – but the Ottomans did it too, on a regular basis. Modified forms of kidnapping – such as the importing of Africans for exhibition and study or the hiring of indigenous language teachers at pitifully low salaries – were practiced by ethnographers and linguists right through the nineteenth century. As suggested by the Ottoman and Chinese examples above, we should recall that nonwesterners have also, from time to time, adopted similar tactics, employing Europeans as teachers, doctors, engineers, catalogers, map-makers, and military advisors, often without much acknowledgment of their contributions or commensurate compensation. And there have been cases in both places, especially in recent times, of something more like reciprocal learn-ing. When we conclude this book with Richard Wilhelm, taught by Confucian scholars and devoted to his Chinese students, we begin to glimpse the founda-tions being laid for the new forms of exchange that have flowered since the 1970s.

If it is a mistake to overestimate or ignore early modern orientalism's interests, patronage structures, and entanglements in power relations, it is also a mistake – propagated by nineteenth-century self-promoters – to see early modern orientalism

---

[22] Karl A. Roider, "Foreward," in *The Turkish Letters of Ogier Ghiselin de Busbecq*, pp. xii–xiii.

[23] A. Bausani, "Notes on the History of Arabic and Islamic Studies in Italy during the Middle Ages," in *Journal of the Pakistan Historical Society* 3 (1955): 176.

as ahistorical or non-critical. As an important part of cartographic, military, medical, ethnographic, lexicographic, commercial, historical, natural scientific, and poetic practices, reading eastern texts or visiting the Orient was an essential part of European education both on the individual and the collective level. Both missionaries and secular travelers took reportage seriously and even armchair readers and writers at home, by the seventeenth century's end, had at their disposal a wealth of material about the particularities of Kyoto and Lahore, the different types of Buddhism and Islam, the geographical diversity of the Philippines and Palestine. Not all of this material was easily accessible; nor were there so many omnivorous consumers in this period as would be the case in the later eighteenth and nineteenth centuries. Most of it was not sorted in any clearly chronological or even geographic way. And yet, the early modern genres of universal history and *historia literaria* recently described by Tamara Griggs and Michael Carhart were an extremely productive form of gathering together materials for what would later be called archaeology and "cultural history."[24] In multiple ways, the "antiquarian" sciences of the Baroque era prepared the way for the "scientific" philology, cultural history, and comparative mythology of the later eighteenth and nineteenth centuries and should not be seen as merely dilettantish dabbling.[25] But before we get to these latter legacies, we must examine one of the most difficult and consequential questions orientalists and universal historians alike had to address in order to demonstrate the importance of their studies to western readers, namely the question of chronology.

THE DISCRETE CHARM OF CHRONOLOGY

One of the keys to demonstrating the Orient's relatedness to western ideas has always been the greater antiquity of its cultures. Chronology, thus, has often been the East's trump card, one played too by western iconoclasts to undermine European self-satisfaction. Scooping the Greeks, in particular, is a rather old game, and it is one that continues to raise passions, as the recent flap over Martin Bernal's *Black Athena* clearly demonstrates. Already in Hellenistic times, Near Eastern writers like Berosus or the Jewish scholar Josephus, in the words of Anthony Grafton, "tried to avenge in the realm of the archive their defeat on the battlefield, using documents and inscriptions to show that Babylon, Israel, and Egypt were older and wiser than Greece."[26] Early on, Christian euhemerists tried to show that the Greeks had stolen their ideas from Moses; this game would be revived with the appearance of Annius of Viterbo's forged *Antiquities* in 1498. In this work, Annius offered texts purportedly written by ancient authorities such as Berosus;

[24] Michael C. Carhart, "Historia Literaria and Cultural History from Mylaeus to Eichhorn," in Peter N. Miller, ed., *Momigliano and Antiquarianism: Foundations of the Modern Cultural Sciences* (Toronto, 2007), pp. 184–206; Tamara Griggs, "Universal History from Counter-Reformation to Enlightenment," in *Modern Intellectual History* 4, no. 2 (Aug. 2007): 219–47.

[25] See the essays in Peter N. Miller, *Momigliano and Antiquarianism: Foundations of the Modern Cultural Sciences* (Toronto, 2007).

[26] Grafton, "Traditions of Invention and Inventions of Tradition in Renaissance Italy: Annius of Viterbo," in idem, *Defenders of the Text: The Traditions of Scholarship in an Age of Science, 1450–1800* (Cambridge, MA, 1991), p. 76.

his work appealed to early modern thinkers such as Sir Walter Raleigh who were eager to show that Babylonian, Egyptian, and Greek mythologies were all rooted in misunderstandings of humanity's most venerable religious text, the Pentateuch.[27] It was ever one of the tricks of the iconoclast's trade to push dates for, say, the *ur*-revelation or the origins of music and the arts, back as far as possible in order to give priority to less hallowed peoples. And, of course, it has always been the Eurocentric's response to question high dates and hyper-diffusionist claims.

Chronological battles were so very passionate and consequential because long into the modern era, as in antiquity itself, it was assumed that "priority in time implied superiority in doctrine."[28] If the Egyptians or the Babylonians had developed, for example, complicated forms of astronomy or geometry – and many classical texts said they had – it was assumed that the Greeks had borrowed, and perhaps confused or erased this knowledge. This was a position held, for example, by the influential logician Petrus Ramus, and one that Joseph Scaliger in the sixteenth century passionately refuted, arguing that the Greeks had improved the sciences, so much so, in fact, that they deserved to be called the founders. It is worth quoting Anthony Grafton's summation of Scaliger's assault on the *prisca theologia* presumptions of his contemporaries here, as Scaliger's position strongly foreshadows the nineteenth-century philhellenist view of cultural relations in the ancient world: "In astronomy and astrology, it had been the Greeks, not the Babylonians and the Egyptians, who performed most of the observations and, above all, tabulated and systematized the results. The ancient Near East had been not a world of gold, populated by calm sages, but a world of iron, haunted by superstitious fears and only fitfully illuminated by the work of certain science-minded priests – themselves prone to spin out unfounded speculations."[29] But Scaliger's preference for the Greeks – and the systematizers – enjoyed neither immediate nor, as we shall see, universal triumph.

More common, in fact, was Walter Raleigh's presumption that the ancient Israelites were the earliest people and that Hebrew in some form was the "language of paradise," from which all other languages had descended. Speculation on these subjects was wide-ranging and long lasting; if the publication of Herbert of Cherbury's *De religione gentilium errorumque apud eos causis* (English: *The Ancient Religion of the Gentiles, and the Causes of Their Errors*, 1705) marked the beginning of the end of etymological and mythographic quests to find the ancient Israelites behind all other religions and national cultural histories, by no means was this the last of these quests. In the course of this book, we will trace various endeavors to find the origins of religion, the birthplace of all gods and myths, and the primeval forms of human languages. Certainly, some enlightened thinkers and nineteenth-century comparativists thought, like Cherbury, that religions might have naturalistic origins; but the large majority of religious believers, and of our orientalists, found such an idea atrocious – which is perhaps

[27] Don Cameron Allen, *Mysteriously Meant* (Baltimore, MD, 1970), pp. 61–5.
[28] Anthony Grafton, *Joseph Scaliger: A Study in the History of Classical Scholarship*, vol. 1 (Oxford, 1983), p. 211.
[29] Ibid., p. 212.

why Cherbury's remains were repeatedly exhumed and desecrated.[30] One can discern here two historical narratives, one a tale of the decline and corruption of ancient wisdom, and another, Scaliger's story, that of the gradual perfecting of modern knowledge. It is a grand generalization to say that the first tale-type is the Orientophilic one and the second the Graecophilic one (for some lovers of the classical world, like Gibbon, saw decline setting in with the founding of the Christian Church and this is also true of some radical Protestants). But throughout this book, we will see the power of the Orient – whether China, Babylon, Persia, or India is in question – linked time and again to its antiquity and those most defensive of the East underscoring its priority in time as a central argument for its proximity to forgotten or destroyed truths.

Indeed, the dating of the East's texts, its religious leaders, and cultures is a subject that will recur perpetually throughout this book. Chronology, sometimes by other names, remained just as crucial in nineteenth-century Europe as it was in the seventeenth century, even though later scholars tended to focus on particular linguistic or national entities. Perhaps we can trace a new set of chronological contests to the eighteenth-century's final third, as August Ludwig Schlözer's suggestion caught on that all ancient dates be integrated to form a composite timeline, counting backward from the birth of Jesus.[31] This innovation, in any event, made cross-cultural comparisons much more feasible and gave relative depth – or shallowness – to events or developments described. After 1800, in particular, newer, borrowing nations were prized less than the supposedly autochthonous, lending ones; both the scholarly and affective kudos went to those nations who were first to develop one thing or another, perhaps the secularized version of proximity to revelation. It is no accident that as the eighteenth-century's early dates for many eastern cultures were challenged in the mid-nineteenth century, European reverence for the East flagged and when, toward the nineteenth century's end, dates for particular cultural events were revised upward once more, the presumptive order of influence, and therefore the prestige of various cultures changed. For example, the revising of the date for the cave temples of Elephanta to about 1000 C.E. in 1819 from early modern dates that made them contemporary with the Egyptian pyramids completely altered Europeans' attitude toward the temples. As Partha Mitter has argued: "At one stroke the whole myth of [Elephanta's] remote antiquity was demolished as it was brought within a conceivable historical era."[32] Later in the century, however, dates for Indian, Persian, and Assyrian artifacts and religious texts were again pushed backward – this time with the primary consequence that the once revered "oldest" peoples, the Hebrews and the Egyptians, were left looking less

---

[30] Allen, *Mysteriously Meant*, pp. 75–8, quotation p. 78, n. 70.

[31] This was by no means a new idea; its origins lie in the thirteenth century. But early modernists tended not to use it because it lacks a year 0, often using instead Scaliger's system, which counts forward from an arbitrary date for creation. Grafton, personal communication, and *Joseph Scaliger*, vol. 2 (Oxford, 1993), p. 64.

[32] Mitter, *Much Maligned Monsters*, p. 157; on earlier dating, see pp. 119–20. To give another example: in the later eighteenth century, the law book of Manu was thought to be datable to 1,000 B.C.E.; by 1900, it had been dated to 400 C.E. Brunnhofer, "Die heiligen Bücher des Orients," in idem, *Östliches Werden*, pp. 34–5.

original than before. The most crucial and controversial dating involved, not surprisingly, the scriptures, for on such dates hung deeper questions about the chosenness of the Israelites, the true nature of Jesus and the originality of his message, and the proper content and interpretation of the Bible. As we shall see, these debates remained extremely important to the shaping of oriental studies, and indeed, many studies of oriental cultures were undertaken with the aim and purpose of contributing to these culturally significant battles over time.

The ancient, medieval, and early modern study of eastern texts and territories left deep traces on post-seventeenth-century practices, institutions, and ideas. But the eighteenth century and especially the century's second half witnessed a series of important transformations we must study in detail. These changes included a shift toward secular, prosaic, and nationally focused histories, an increased willingness to take non-Christian authors seriously – meaning new attempts to translate their texts – a wider distribution and larger number of exotic texts and travel reports in circulation, and finally by the century's close, a real diminution of interest (especially in Germany) in the cultures of the modern East.

All of these phenomena can be related in some way to Europe's expanding control of colonial territories; as political and economic interest in places like India, Java, and Japan grew, Europeans also made deeper incursions into the cultural history of others. Central Europeans also found new opportunities for making money or for learning new things appealing; closer to home, their quasi-colonial ambitions were also stimulated by the receding of the Turkish threat to the East, which was apparent by the 1690s, and especially after 1717, when the Austrians managed to defeat the Ottomans and retake a large chunk of territory in the Banat and Wallachia. By the 1780s, the Turks had become less feared than sought after, by the Austrians and Prussians, as alliance partners against the rising Russians or against each other.[33] In Christian literature, "the terrible Turk" had given way to the ineffectual, corrupt, and oversexed Ottomans of Mozart's *Abduction from the Seraglio* (1782).[34] Increasingly, one could now study, or simply delight in, eastern culture without seeming to offer comfort to the enemy or having to explain oneself to clerical authorities.

Still, changing conditions both internal to scholarly life and externally with respect to politics did not do away entirely with oriental philology's strong linkages to biblical criticism and to the esoteric tradition, nor did the shifting balances of power necessarily make oriental studies more culturally relevant for Central Europeans. As we examine departures from the era of high Christian humanism – and most intense Turkish pressure – we will also observe many continuities across the period between about 1700 and 1800, known more generally as "the Enlightenment."

---

[33] For a comprehensive study of Austrian–Ottoman relations in the eighteenth century, see Karl A. Roider, *Austria's Eastern Question, 1700–1790* (Princeton, NJ, 1982).

[34] See Fichtner, *Terror and Toleration*, pp. 96–110.

ORIENTALISM AND THE ENLIGHTENMENT

The great social, political, and especially the cultural revolution that we call the Enlightenment marks an enormous increase in Europe's pursuit of knowledge about the East. While older traditions continued, the eighteenth century witnessed data collection on a new scale; it saw the creation of new institutions, or institutional roles, for philological scholars, especially in the places where the study of pagan cultures became more socially and culturally acceptable. There were large numbers of new travelogues and translations of nonwestern texts and more armchair readers able to read them. Of course, capitalist commerce also greatly expanded, as did, accordingly, the European consumption of oriental commodities such as coffee, tea, opium, and porcelain. In the Germanies, the production of homemade porcelain began in Dresden and Meissen after 1708, making this oriental luxury more affordable, and by 1711, Antoine Galland's extremely popular *Mille et une nuits* (1704–7) was available in German. Theater pieces and operas played on Turkish themes; Egyptian forms were used for clocks and grave markers; Chinese figurines abounded. Images of the East, and the East itself, had never been so accessible without being threatening to Europeans, and by the century's end, the latter knew more about Asias's history, people, languages, monuments, literature, religions, and even music than ever before. This is not to say, of course, that what they knew was accurate with respect to the real histories or the cultural conditions of the countries to their East, but simply that the scale and density of discussion was rising and offering new opportunities for assessment, appreciation, critique, and utilitarian application.

The new knowledge about the East was enabled by swiftly changing global political relations, which made Asian countries – including the once-feared Ottoman Empire – easier to access and to represent. It made possible the more systematic employment of the collective term "Orient" to add India, Anatolia, and the Far East to the traditional "Orient," the biblical lands which lay to medieval Christendom's East. Never used consistently, exclusively, or without conjuring shades of the older religious definition, "the Orient" became widely used to designate all territories ruled by cultured non-Christians and lying, for the most part, to Christendom's East. What Europeans learned, imagined, or believed about their neighbors could be, and was, used for conquest, missionization, theological polemic, and diplomatic intrigue; but it was also put to other ends, including biblical exegesis, historical understanding, aesthetic pleasure, and self-criticism. We should not forget that for European intellectuals, the Enlightenment was an era in which older ideas, tastes, and, most importantly, beliefs came under fire; enlightened monarchs like Frederick the Great and Joseph II permitted open discussion of unconventional religious ideas, and radicals attacked corrupt and tyrannical clergymen and aristocrats. Though one can see, as Nina Berman suggests, recurrent recourse to stereotypical scenes of oriental decadence, violence, despotism, and sexuality in eighteenth-century representations of the Turks,[35]

---

[35] Nina Berman, *Beyond Orientalism: Germany and the Middle East, 900–2000*, forthcoming, Chapter 3 (cited with permission of the author, who has kindly allowed me to read some chapters in the manuscript).

it should also be said that many Europeans were saying the same sorts of things about their own leaders. Of course those who wrote in European languages about eastern cultures were representing the Orient to, and largely for, themselves. But some at least were also trying to decipher and learn oriental languages so that they could hear the East speak for itself. Not all representations were the same, and the newer ones were actually based on deeper encounters with Asian texts and peoples, some of them exploitative and some not. Again, we must recognize that "Europe" like the "Orient" was not monolith, and the presumption that the two were inexorably opposed will simply lead us to overlook the messy conditions of historical reality.

Some Europeans also appreciated the craftsmanship of Near Eastern artists and found their intricate patterns and rich colors more appealing than local products. The same, in essence, could be said of oriental poetry, which gained in popularity after the success of Galland's *1,001 Nights*. It appealed to the imagination, in part as an antidote to formulaic Latin verse; translations of it were not intended to be literal, but rather to revel in unfamiliar forms of human expression, which were considered beautiful. The flourishing, in this period, of European enterprises making "oriental" pottery, carpets, or poetry for the home market is perhaps indicative of a rather more eclectic and open artistic playing field than we have allowed. Although stereotypes were often reiterated, one might well think of this less as an attempt to "other" the Chinese or the Turks than as an exploration of the imaginative and aesthetic possibilities of escaping western norms for the purposes of stimulating the imagination and delighting the senses – or of combining East and West, as did Fischer von Erlach in building the Karlskirche in Vienna, a Baroque masterpiece, complete with "minarets."[36]

But this is not primarily a book about popular, literary, or artistic borrowings from the East – all subjects that need far more study. More important for oriental scholars in the eighteenth century – most of whom, incidentally, were still Old Testament exegetes – was the new zeal the century displayed for the art of translation. As we have seen, the translations of Arabic and Hebrew texts in the fifteenth and sixteenth centuries – and the attempts to translate Egyptian ones – had a major impact on early modern culture and ideas, though some of these "translations" were forgeries, pastiches, or bowdlerized excerpts. Long into the eighteenth century, there were indeed many translations that walked a fine line between forgery and paraphrase, translation and imaginative reconstruction. Galland's embroidered, expurgated, and recast *1,001 Nights* is one example; Montesquieu contributed a parodic "translation" in his enormously popular *Persian Letters* already in 1721. These were followed by the so-called *Ezourvedam*, which Voltaire read in manuscript in 1760. This false Veda, probably conceived by the Jesuits as a means to convert Hindus, convinced the philosopher and probably many others that India was home to the most ancient and pristine form of religion. A French text was published in 1778 and a German translation followed in

[36] This is a suggestion A. L. Macfie also makes; see his *Orientalism* (London, 2002), p. 71. In 1721, Fischer himself published a history of architecture, which contained drawings of unfamiliar buildings in China, Persia, and even Japan. John Sweetman, *The Oriental Obsession: Islamic Inspiration in British and American Art and Architecture, 1500–1920* (Cambridge, 1991), pp. 58–9.

1779 – and when after about 1782, the *Ezourvedam* became widely suspected of being a forgery, many Indophiles despaired, fearing that the true origins of Indian religion would never be discoverable.[37] Alexander Dow's translation of the early seventeenth-century Islamic historian Firishta appeared as *History of Hindostan* in 1768–72, though the text was suffused with Dow's own philosophical and cultural perspective. Edward Gibbon quipped that in this translation, "the style of Ferishta has been improved by that of Ossian."[38]

Evidently, taste for and interest in translations grew as the century went on, peaking in 1770s and 1780s; another wave of translations, which emphasized accurate rendering of the form and flavor of the East, followed after about 1810.[39] Portions of the Qur'an had been available since the mid-seventeenth century in Latin or French, despite the fact that the Muslim holy book remained on the Papal Index; in the 1690s, Leibniz had encouraged multiple efforts to produce a supra-confessional German translation, but the paucity of Arabic commentaries available to northern scholars and the short lives of early modern German Arabists foxed his plans.[40] The eighteenth century was far more successful; a full translation of the Qur'an reached Germany, first by way of an English translation (German version, 1746) then in two versions directly from the Arabic, in 1772 and 1773.[41]

In 1754, another would-be French translator, A. H. Anquetil-Duperron, traveled to India, hoping to learn Sanskrit. He would pass the next seven years there, unable to persuade the pandits – who were forbidden to teach the holy language to non-Hindus or even Hindus of lower caste – to teach him Sanskrit or sell him manuscripts.[42] He did, however, learn Persian, and was able, with the assistance of some Parsi priests, to obtain what he thought might be an ancient Vedic text. He took it home and translated it, apparently poorly, but well enough to recognize it as a Zoroastrian text. Anquetil's Zend Avesta appeared in 1771, and German translations followed in 1776–83. Anquetil's text was a scholarly sensation – although knowledge of Indo-Iranian languages and cultures was so fragmentary at the time that it was only in the 1830s that scholars recognized Anquetil's original text to be a Pahlavi translation of the Zoroastrian scriptures (the original of which is in Avestan).[43] Controversies over the authenticity of the text did not

---

[37] Halbfass, *India and Europe*, pp. 46, 57–8. Dorothy M. Figueira, "The Authority of an Absent Text: The Vedas, Upangas, Upavedas and Upnekhata in European Thought," in *Authority, Anxiety and Cannon: Essays in Vedic Interpretation*, ed. Laurie L. Patton (Albany, NY, 1994), pp. 201–16.

[38] Jürgen Osterhammel, *Die Entzauberung Asiens* (Munich, 1998), pp. 171–2.

[39] Andrea Polaschegg, *Der andere Orientalismus: Regeln deutsch-morgenländischer Imagination im 19. Jahrhundert* (Berlin, 2005), pp. 146–56.

[40] See Alastair Hamilton, "A Lutheran Translation for the Quran," in *The Republic of Letters and the Levant*, ed. Alastair Hamilton et al. (Leiden, 2005), pp. 197–221.

[41] Dominique Bourel, "Die deutsche Orientalistik im 18. Jahrhundert. Von der Mission zur Wissenschaft," in *Historische Kritik und biblischer Kanon in der deutschen Aufklärung*, ed. Henning Graf Reventlow et al. (Wiesbaden, 1988), p. 124, n. 53.

[42] It is instructive that Anquetil sailed for India carrying only two western books, Montesquieu's *Spirit of the Laws* and the Bible. James Darmesteter, *Essais Orientaux* (Paris, 1883), p. 9.

[43] Stefan Arvidsson, *Aryan Idols: Indo-European Mythology as Ideology and Science* (Chicago, 2006), p. 64.

prevent Anquetil's Avesta from being widely read and eagerly discussed by a large number of Europe's poets, philosophers, and theologians.

Things went more smoothly for William Jones, who was posted to India in 1783 with the intention of learning Sanskrit to understand Indian laws and thus to check the power of native lawyers.[44] Jones and other British scholars were able to use the East India Company's influence to recruit native teachers, and soon they were able to intervene in the administration of justice as well as to apply their expertise to the translating of religious and literary texts. In 1785, Charles Wilkins published an English translation of the *Bhagavad Gita*, and four years later, Jones's rendition of Kalidasa's sentimental drama *Sakuntala* appeared, followed by his translations of the *Gita Govinda* and *Laws of Manu* (1792, 1794). It was not really very much original material; even the major Sanskrit epics and religious writings (such as the *Mahabharata* and the *Rig Veda*) were, until the second half of the nineteenth century, available to European readers only in excerpts. But, as we will see, *Sakuntala* alone was enormously influential, inspiring numerous intellectuals to take a keen interest in things Indian and convincing some that an "Oriental Renaissance" had begun.[45]

Another sign that non-theological orientalist knowledge (and European influence) was expanding was the upswing in state-financed expeditions to the East; seeking a northeast passage and/or fur-trading outposts, Peter the Great and the St. Petersburg Academy sent out two Great Northern Expeditions in 1725–30 and 1733–43; when Catherine came to the throne, she sent expeditions to the Caucasus and to Siberia. Then followed the highly influential Carsten Niebuhr expedition of 1761–7, the Macartney expedition to Southeast Asia in 1792–4, and Bonaparte's Egyptian adventures of 1798–9.[46] We should add to this the French explorer Jean-Pierre Bougainville's round-the-world travels (published in 1771) and the Cook voyages of the 1760s. Few of these expeditions were so grand, so imperiously conducted, or so easily executed, as they may seem in retrospect; Bougainville had to make numerous detours to avoid hostile natives; Cook famously met his end on a Hawaiian beach. Niebuhr was only one of six original team members who returned from the expedition alive, and as Roger Guichard has shown in an elegant study of Niebuhr's stay in Egypt, the young man had to make his maps surreptitiously, hiding his instruments for fear that the Egyptians would seize them and/or execute him as a spy.[47] However, all of these expeditions brought home drawings, data, and artifacts in abundance, making

---

[44] Javed Majeed, *Ungoverned Imaginings: James Mill's The History of British India and Orientalism* (Oxford, 1992), pp. 18–19.

[45] Coined by Friedrich Schlegel, this term was used by Raymond Schwab to characterize the whole of the period beginning with Anquetil and lasting until about 1875.

[46] There were, of course, numerous individual travelers visiting the East. Their occupations and motivations differed. Jean Chardin, author of a widely read *Journal du Voyage en Perse* (1686), was a jeweler; the other renowned visitor to the seventeenth-century Moghul and Persian courts was François Bernier, a physician. By the later 1680s, Europeans had several more popular oriental travelogues to digest, of which Jean Baptiste Tavernier's *Nouvelle relation de l'interior du Serraill du Grand Seigneur* (1675) is just one example. Destinations became increasingly exotic; by the mid-1680s, Jean de Thévenot had visited Agra, and in 1691, Simon de Loubère made his way to Siam.

[47] Roger Guichard, *The Egypt of Carsten Niebuhr, 1761–1762*; unpublished manuscript; quoted with permission of the author.

them seem even more successful than they had seemed to their members at the time. Some of the team members understood and endorsed the political purposes to which their work was being put – this was surely the case for Cook and probably for many in Russian employ. Others, like Niebuhr, whose mission was more theological than political, expressed skepticism about the expeditions' ultimate purposes. There were obviously linkages between power and knowledge collection, but again this does not mean that all the outcomes were predictable or that the results would contribute directly and unproblematically to empire building, or even to Eurocentric modes of thought.

From the standpoint of the later nineteenth century, there was something not authentically "oriental" about these carpets and tea sets, these reworked poems, and poorly staffed expeditions. But, thanks to increased travel and trade, eighteenth-century scholars and collectors did build a much richer and more diverse database of materials than the one accessible to their forerunners a century before. When Immanuel Kant sat down to write his lectures on geography and anthropology, he was able to draw on *Allgemeine Historie der Reisen* (published in twenty-one volumes between 1747 and 1774), as well as an enormous English *Universal History* (fifty-one volumes; 1736–66).[48] His contemporary August Ludwig von Schlözer began lecturing on world history at the University of Göttingen in 1769; the subject had grown so huge by the 1780s that Schlözer's attempt to contain and guide its study ran to two volumes.[49] There were still – from the viewpoint, again, of nineteenth-century scholars – mixed motives and unscientific commitments here; the will to translate precisely, but the insistence on making oriental poetry, for example, sound beautiful to western ears; the desire to "normalize" revered texts coexisting with the longing to preserve their normativity; the cultivation of special fields of knowledge, combined with the confidence that one might profitably speak with and to non-expert readers; and perhaps most imponderable, the ease with which scholars moved from biblical to classical, and from modern to ancient subjects, without worrying too much about the credibility of the informants or the inconsistencies of the texts. We can see, then, important changes underway in oriental studies by the late eighteenth century; but we will also locate other important transitional moments in this history. This was not a renaissance accomplished once and for all in 1757 with the battle of Plessey, in 1771 with Anquetil's Zend Avesta, or in 1799 with the location of the Rosetta Stone.

The data collection and the new philology of the later eighteenth century did, however, put pressure on older chronologies and family trees, most obviously those derived from the Old Testament. This is not to say that Old Testament chronologies had not been challenged before – or that after 1786, a completely new chronology was accepted by all Europeans. William Jones's discovery that Sanskrit was the elder sister of Latin, Greek, and modern European languages had been foreshadowed by earlier claims that Hebrew could not be the *ur*-language,

---

[48] Osterhammel, *Entzauberung*, p. 202. A reworked German version of the English series was published in seventy volumes between 1744 and 1804 under the title *Allgemeine Welthistorie*.

[49] August Ludwig von Schlözer, *Weltgeschichte nach ihren Hauptteilen im Auszug und Zusammenhange* (Göttingen, 1785–9).

that Adam was not the first man, and that Eden probably lay east of the Caucasus. Importantly, Jones did divide the languages descending from Sanskrit from what he called "Arabian" languages – and Schlözer, in 1781 called "Semitic" tongues. And Jones pushed this branching of the human family tree back into prehistorical times.[50] But Jones, as Thomas Trautmann has shown, did not share the heretical and/or Hermetic ambitions of some earlier iconoclasts. On the contrary, he subscribed to a "Mosaic ethnology," which sought to defend the Bible against the assaults of radicals like Voltaire. He believed in the unity of humankind before the Flood and regretted not only the loss of Noah's *ur*-language but also the fall of the sons of Ham and Japhet into idolatry. So too did Friedrich Schlegel retain his faith in the basic historicity of the Old Testament; as late as 1828, he was still trying to verify the venerable ages reported for the Hebrew patriarchs by claiming that humankind, especially in Europe, had degenerated, just as modern elephants were degenerate compared to recently found mammoth remains.[51]

Schlegel's anti-evolutionary view, of course, was framed by an Ussherite chronology and would soon come under attack from the natural sciences. But what made it already antiquated by the 1830s was that it was generated by a reading of the Old Testament in which that text's testimony was consistently preferred to that of other sources. Thanks to changing attitudes toward conventional sources and to Europeans' widening tastes and enhanced contacts with the rest of the world, late eighteenth-century scholars began to be convinced not just that the older sources need critical scrutiny but that newer sources might be found to create a clearer, and more evenhanded, history of ancient civilizations. Schlegel himself participated in this development, as did his older contemporary J. G. Herder – though both struggled with the possibilities and problems unleashed by the contextualization of holy scripture. In 1774, bowled over by Anquetil's Zend Avesta, Herder described his generation's experience of the "unveiling" of pre-classical religious history, which even Thomas Hyde – whose study of Persian religions was based on European and Arabic sources – had lacked. "Anquetil takes us gently by the hand and leads us, without pedantry, citations or speeches, behind the curtain and shows us more ancient, perhaps the most ancient, writings of the sect [Zoroastrianism] itself."[52] Chastened by William Jones's critiques of Anquetil, Herder later voiced his suspicion that the Zend Avesta might be a forgery and despaired, for a time, of discovering Persia's secrets.[53] But Europe's newfound power – and the new texts appearing virtually every day – offered hope to many that the

[50] Thomas R. Trautmann, *Aryans and British India* (Berkeley, CA, 1997), pp. 42–61.

[51] Friedrich Schlegel, "Philosophie der Geschichte: In achtzehn Vorlesungen gehalten zu Wien im Jahre 1828," in *Kritische Friedrich-Schlegel-Ausgabe*, ed. Ernst Behler and Ursula Struc-Oppenberg, vol. 9 (Munich, 1975), pp. 31–49, esp. 47; 150–2.

[52] J. G. Herder, "Älteste Urkunde des Menschengeschlechts," vol. 1 (1774), in *Herders Sämtliche Werke*, ed. Bernhard Suphan, vol. 6 (Berlin, 1883), p. 492; Herder's collected works hereafter cited as *SW*.

[53] By 1804, however, Herder's confidence in Anquetil was restored. One of his last writings attempted to sort out, in detail, what was and what was not yet knowable about Persia and Zoroastrianism. Herder, "Persepolitanische Briefe" (written 1798, published 1805) in *SW* 24, pp. 465–564. On Anquetil, Herder, "Morgenländische Literatur" (1804), in *SW* 24, pp. 353–4.

Orient's legendary wisdom might finally be accessed directly and used to create a secure, all-embracing, and unprejudiced universal history. There were so many of these – many of them calling themselves "history of mankind" or "philosophy of history" – that already in 1774 Herder would title his first foray into the field *Yet Another Philosophy of History*.[54]

I will soon turn my attention more fully and directly to German *Orientforschung* and try to describe some of its peculiarities, most of which have to do with the complex religious landscape of Central Europe. But at least as important to the shaping of the discipline and its subfields in this era was the religious, political, artistic, or poetic content (real or imagined) of the cultures studied and the accessibility of their ancient texts and artifacts. Differences here always were and always would be critical to the development of the different branches of oriental studies. Indeed, throughout this book, I will often need to treat individual area studies separately; Old Testament criticism was never bound by the same rules and prejudices as the study of China or of India, and vice versa. Although Europeans regularly referred to the Orient as a cultural collective, they did appreciate differences between cultures; in this they could not have been much different than Ottomans who called Europeans "Franks," but surely understood that there were differences between the non-Muslims who lived to their West. In both worlds, those who traveled, learned foreign languages or made closer cultural studies naturally appreciated these differences even more than did laypersons. An accounting of which cultures' fortunes rose and whose fell, as stricter chronologies and deeper source criticism developed, as trade and travel increased, and as religious precepts changed will help us chart the fortunes of the various branches of *Orientalistik* in the decades to follow. Readers are reminded that this a very crude overview; diverse opinions about these cultures were expressed by different writers – often, in fact, diverse impressions of a particular oriental culture were expressed by the same writer, sometimes even in the same text. We will not get away here or anywhere else in this book with the presumption that everybody on the diverse continent of Europe, over the eventful period between 1780 and 1960, thought the same thing about the equally diverse cultures of the East.

ORIENTAL CIVILIZATIONS IN THE ENLIGHTENMENT

We might begin our survey by noting the changing representations of China and India over the course of the eighteenth century. Early in the century, the Chinese were certainly the most popular, thanks to the widely circulated *Lettres édifiantes et curieuses écrites des Missions étrangères de la Compagnie de Jésus*, published in thirty-four volumes between 1702 and 1776, and to Jean Baptiste Du Haldes's *Chinese Encyclopedia* (1735). As Jürgen Osterhammel has shown, many mid-eighteenth-century thinkers found China a model of non-absolutist monarchy – the Emperor's powers restrained by the bureaucracy – though many also deplored

---

[54] See Michael C. Carhart, *The Science of Culture in Enlightenment Germany* (Cambridge, MA, 2007), pp. 1, 240–3.

China's tendency to descend into "oriental despotism."[55] There are many individuals who might be mentioned here – from Leibniz and Christian Wolff, down to Frederick the Great, who in 1760 wrote a set of Chinese letters from Rome, employing the model of Montesquieu's *Persian Letters* to ridicule the Pope and the Jesuits. Frederick's friend Voltaire, of course, was important in spreading this passion and Madame de Pompadour in patronizing it. Chinoiserie was all the rage, expressing itself in monuments like the pagoda in Kew Gardens and Frederick's Potsdam tea house. But after 1770, the "China fad," especially in the Protestant Germanies, died a sudden death, and China's associations with the Rococo, the French, and the Jesuits made it anathema for early romantic writers. Herder was one of the first to proclaim China "an embalmed mummy" and to complain of its self-willed isolation and childish inability to develop.[56] Also eighteenth-century Sinophiles had few easily datable and unmediated ancient texts (for the Chinese "classics" had been studied and repackaged by centuries of East Asian scholars), and these did not bear on classical and biblical history in any direct way. The rapid demise of German Sinophilia left few traces in intellectual history, but it was a very important intellectual event, both because it left room for other passions and because it meant that very few Germans studied Chinese until the turn of the twentieth century and that East Asian studies as a whole lagged far behind other oriental subfields in its institutional and intellectual articulation.

After the 1760s, Indophilia, on the other hand, was on the rise. Here, as in Egyptian studies, there were numerous classical and especially Hellenistic sources which spoke of primeval Indian wisdom and the debts Greek science and philosophy owed to their eastern neighbors. Drawing on ancient authorities such as Iamblichus, Plotinus, and Porphyry, numerous seventeenth- and eighteenth-century histories of philosophy continued this discussion of Greek thought's debts to the East and many an enlightened missionary too sought a "natural light" in the Hindu world – which might be merged with the light of Christian revelation.[57] In 1761, under the spell of the *Ezourvedam*, Voltaire added a section to his *Essai sur les moeurs* in which he lavishly praised the Brahmins for establishing a religion based on universal reason – unlike, in his view, Christianity. This passage resonated powerfully, especially for enlightened German readers like Herder, Lessing, and Friedrich Schlegel. But it was the publication of Georg Forster's translation – of William Jones's translation – of the Sanskrit play, *Sakuntala*, in May 1791 that really ignited German Indophilia, offering romantics hope that they might find in ancient India a lyrical and lovely lost world unencumbered by bourgeois conventions, religious hatreds, and political polemics. Herder, who wrote the preface to the second edition of Forster's translation in 1803, described it as a sublime poem, which conveyed "the highest beauties of the drama."[58] But, as Wilhelm Halbfass rightly notes, there were also Enlightenment thinkers who

[55] Osterhammel, *Entzauberung*, pp. 300–04.
[56] See Willy Richard Berger, *China-Bild und China-Mode im Europa der Aukflärung* (Cologne, 1990), on Frederick, pp. 153–7, on Herder, pp. 120–7.
[57] Halbfass, *India and Europe: An Essay in Understanding* (Albany, NY, 1988), pp. 3–19, 146–9, 36–50.
[58] Herder, "Vorrede zur zweiten Ausgabe von G. Forsters "'Sakontala,'" in *SW* 24, p. 577.

ridiculed Indian wisdom and despised what they believed to be Buddhist nihilism, and even many admirers of ancient India lamented the eclipse of its "natural light" brought on by superstition, passivity, and lassitude – and completed by its Islamic and English conquerors.[59]

It is surely the case that the status of Persia also improved over the course of the seventeenth and eighteenth centuries. The Safavid and successor states had the advantage of being politically and militarily impotent with respect to Europe, while posing a threat to the *ur*-oriental enemy on Europe's border, the Ottoman Empire. Persia's ancient empire was still subject to heavy critique – good readers of Herodotus could not forget the overweening pride of Cyrus and Xerxes. But Thomas Hyde's major work on the religion of ancient Persia (*Historia religionis veterum Persarum*, 1700) managed to make the Persians more appealing to contemporary Christians by claiming they were monotheists and had foretold the coming of Christ. Hyde's work, argues Jacques Duchesne-Guillemin, would shape subsequent discussions of Zoroastrianism, both those which aimed (as did Hyde's) to defend Christian doctrine and those which sought (as did Voltaire's) to undermine the church's monopoly on truth.[60] Persia gained status too as European delegations increased their visits, seeking a share of the lucrative silk trade. One of these ventures resulted in Adam Olearius's detailed and popular *Offt Begehrte Beschreibung der Newen Orientalischen Reise* in 1647.[61] By the 1770s, there were two more major works, which enhanced Europeans' appreciation of ancient Persia: Carsten Niebuhr's publications on Persepolis and – for those who credited its authenticity – Anquetil's Zend Avesta.

In the seventeenth century, Persian carpets, silks, weapons, and illustrated manuscripts were widely respected – and Persian poetry took on new appeal. After 1654, readers could consult Olearius's translation of Sa'di's *Gulistān* (based in turn on a Latin version of 1651), which was reprinted four times before the end of the seventeenth century. By this time, an increasingly large number of travelogues were available, offering insights of various sorts into the Safavid courts. August Bohse's German translation of Galland's *1,001 Nights* followed in 1711, delighting a wide audience with its exotic tales of love, adventure, and courtly intrigue. Also highly popular were Hungarian diplomat Karl Revitzky's edition and translation of selected poems from the *Divan* of Hafiz (Vienna, 1771, in Latin) to be followed by Joseph von Hammer-Purgstall's more complete *Der Diwan von Mohammed Schemsed-Din Hafis* (1812–13).[62] Together these two texts created a fad for Persian poetry, which lasted long into the nineteenth century and spurred the fabrication of two of the best known works of European orientalizing literature, Goethe's *West-östliche Divan* and Edward Fitzgerald's *Rubaiyat of Omar Khayyam*. But as Andrea Polaschegg has argued, by the later eighteenth century, as the Ottoman threat dwindled, Europeans gradually

---

[59] Halbfass, *India and Europe*, pp. 57–61.
[60] Jacques Duchesne-Guillemin, *The Western Response to Zoroaster* (Oxford, 1958), pp. 10–15.
[61] Polaschegg, *Der andere Orientalismus*, p. 197.
[62] Arthur J. Arberry, "Persian Literature," in *Near Eastern Culture and Society: A Symposium on the Meeting of East and West*, ed. T. Cuyler Young (Princeton, NJ, 1951), pp. 68–9, on Hafiz, pp. 70–1.

lost respect for modern Persian courtly life, and interest in "the Persians" now focused on the contemporaries of Zoroaster or Cyrus.[63] Here, as in other philological subfields, European elites redirected their affections away from the living Orient, reinvesting them in the ancient one.

For early modern Europeans, the interesting Egypt was already the ancient one, central to the Old Testament and extensively described in classical and Hellenistic texts. As we have seen, Egyptian hieroglyphics had puzzled but enchanted Europeans since the discovery of the Hellenistic *Hieroglyphica* of Horapollo on the Greek island of Andros in 1419. Horapollo's garbled discussion seemed to confirm Plotinus's notion that hieroglyphics were endowed with symbolic powers and revealed to initiates not ordinary knowledge but an insight into the essence of things.[64] Although the Genevan-born scholar Isaac Casaubon proved the Hermetic texts post-Christian in 1614, the cult of Egyptian wisdom persisted in occultist and Rosicrucian circles in the seventeenth century and was strikingly revived in 1731 with the publication of Abbé Jean Terrasson's *Séthos, histoire ou vie tirée des monumens anecdote de l'ancienne Égypte, traduite d'un manuscrit grec.* As Darius Spieth has shown, this fictive translation of a newly discovered Greek manuscript was in fact an Egyptizing *Bildungsroman*, an attempt to imitate and critique Fénelon's enormously influential *Télémaque* of 1699. Hugely popular in France, Terrasson's *Séthos* was translated into English and German by 1732. The novel not only inspired many with appreciation for ancient Egypt's commercial, scientific, and artistic splendors but also revived interest in Egyptian cultic practices and the mysteries concealed by hieroglyphic symbols.[65] Among those impressed by Terrasson's ideas – and his willingness to celebrate Egyptian paganism over corrupted Christian society – were the eighteenth-century Masons who found in the Egyptian practices he described universal, non-Christian symbols and a suitably nonsectarian but still ritualistic culture of initiation. For some, the antics of the charlatan Count Cagliostro discredited this tradition; Catherine the Great, as well as Goethe and Schiller, penned satires of the man who claimed to "the Grand Copht" and specialized in Egyptizing potions and séances.[66] But long after Cagliostro's arrest for heresy in 1789, and even after the decipherment of hieroglyphics, a "mysterious" Egypt, as well as the historical one, continued to enthrall educated Europeans.

On the other hand, many an eighteenth-century rationalist saw in Egypt's mysteries merely the conjuring of specters by priests eager to bamboozle the people, and in the pyramids, monuments to despotism and slavery. The Comte de Volney's extremely influential *Voyage en Syrie et en Égypte pendant les années 1783, 1784, et 1785* focused not on ancient Egypt, but on the Egypt of the present, one lodged inside the decaying Ottoman Empire. Volney identified modern Egypt's military weakness and its terrible susceptibility to disease and argued that the best interests of the Egyptian population would be served by a foreign takeover. Though he did not advocate French intervention, many later readers

---

[63] Polaschegg, *Der andere Orientalismus*, p. 200. European connoisseurs continued to admire Persian artistry, however, and the taste for Persian poetry diminished but did not die.

[64] Iversen, *Myth of Egypt*, pp. 45–9.

[65] Spieth, *Napoleon's Sorcerers: The Sophisians* (Newark, DE), pp. 50–3.

[66] Iversen, *Myth of Egypt*, pp. 122–3.

considered his travelogue an invitation to colonization.[67] It was easy enough to apply to Egypt the same sort of logic of cultural degeneration as was being applied to Greece, Israel, and India already in this era: the ancient cultures were wise, creative, and original. The succeeding ones were, in one way or another, "fallen." In the case of Egyptian history, it was even easier for Europeans to apply this logic, for the religion into which the Egyptians had fallen was the one they found most frightening – Islam.

From Luther's time forward, Islam had been drawn into debates between Catholics and Protestants; a long series of reformed writers contrasted the piety and abstemiousness of Muslims favorably with the alleged hypocrisy and corruption of Roman Catholics. A few free thinkers considered Muhammed to be simply one of the three great "imposters" who had distorted the true, universal religion – the other two being Moses and Jesus. But, as Paula Fichtner reminds us, early modern Europeans – and especially Central Europeans – lived "in deep and immediate fear of an enemy that closely identified itself with Islam and conquered in the name of the prophet," namely, the Ottoman Empire. Christians also had to persuade themselves, she notes, that their religion was the right one – often in the face of Ottoman conquests and inter-Christian polemics. Vilifying Turkish behavior, which often *was* brutal – was an easy way to do this.[68] Over the course of the seventeenth century, Europeans learned an enormous amount about Islam's internal diversities; they developed good relations with the Muslims of the Mughal Empire and also good opinions about them, but retained poor opinions of and relations with southeast Asian Muslims and Ottoman residents.[69]

As the threat of Muslim expansionism declined in the eighteenth century, Europeans, and especially the Austrians, would decide that well-informed diplomacy was a better way to deal with the Ottomans than going to war; in 1754, Maria Theresa authorized the creation of an "Oriental Academy" for the training of translators and diplomats in which understanding – linguistic and cultural – was strongly preferred to religious polemics. But as Alastair Hamilton has stressed, it would be a mistake to see the early modern history of Arabic studies as a linear process leading from intolerant and ill-informed studies to objective, scientific ones. Though medieval legends were shown to be baseless, some of the technically best scholars continued to be conservative Christians and some of the most popular studies of Islam continued to sow fear and loathing.[70] Enlightened writers, like Voltaire and Gibbon, sometimes praised the Prophet; but enlightened critiques of tyranny, superstition, intolerance, polygamy, courtly hypocrisies, and priest-craft also damaged Europeans' respect for the Muslim world they knew best, that of the Ottoman court. Even in the high romantic era, as condemnation of some other oriental cultures softened, there was no shortage of literature celebrating Europe's salvation from what the Austrian orientalist

---

[67] Spieth, *Napoleon's Sorcerers*, pp. 49–50.
[68] Fichtner, *Terror and Toleration*, quotation p. 17.
[69] Lach, *Asia in the Making of Europe*, vol. III, *A Century of Advance*, book 4 (Chicago, 1993), p. 1893.
[70] Alastair Hamilton, "Western Attitudes to Islam in the Enlightenment," in *Middle Eastern Lectures* 3 (1999): 69–85.

Joseph von Hammer-Purgstall called "the hooved invasion of Turkish barbarism and Ottoman tyranny."[71]

The Islamic world was handicapped by its relative youth compared to the ancient pagan cultures of India, China, Egypt, and Persia and by its relative proximity to Europe; it had little of the precious mystery or deep antiquity which attracted European scholars to other oriental subfields. It did have commercial attractions – especially for Central and Eastern Europeans – but it also had armies, which continued to be used effectively in conflicts with the Russians, and the peoples of the Balkans, long into the nineteenth century. And it had minority populations – especially Greeks, Arab Christians, and Armenians – who were willing translators, traders, and go-betweens. The Austrians encouraged the learning of spoken Turkish and Arabic, and as a result, produced more effective diplomats than did the Russians or Prussians.[72] In the Germanies there were learned Arabists, but until the late eighteenth century, Arabic was taught exclusively as a theological *Hilfswissenschaft*, which did not, of course, make the field especially appreciative of Mohammed's ideas.[73] Outside the universities, J. J. Reiske was translating Arabic histories and poetry and opening a campaign – in so far as a man without a patron, job, or even a Sunday coat was able – for Arabic studies divorced from biblical philology.[74] But his successes were, unsurprisingly, limited.

Interestingly, one culture the later eighteenth-century enlightened elite did champion, especially against a purportedly degenerate and tyrannical Ottoman state, was that of the nomadic Arabs, who seemed not only the eastern equivalent of the noble savage but also, perhaps, the closest living relations to the ancient Hebrews – an idea, which was something of a slap in the face for modern Jews. This was the conception behind J. D. Michaelis's plan to send a scientific expedition to "Arabia felix"; another tradition, of comparing the ancient Greeks to the beduin, was born with Robert Wood's *Essay on the Original Genius and Writings of Homer* (1775).[75] Herder wrote glowingly of the Qur'an, which he envisioned as the great national epic of the Arabs; glancing enviously at a "nation" that, unlike modern Europeans, could still remember and recite its great ancient poetry, Herder even hoped, at one point, that Arabic poetry might help to rejuvenate European culture. Of course, as Ian Almond underlines, Herder romanticized the poetic, passionate, wandering Arabs at the cost of extruding them from history and imposing on them "a frozen primordiality."[76] Still, this positive image would endure; if, as Jürgen Osterhammel claims, the nomad lost much of his romantic allure in the course of the nineteenth century, the simple, unchanging, freedom-

[71] Joseph Ritter von Hammer, *Wien's erste aufgehobene Türkische Belagerung* (Pest, 1829), p. xvi.

[72] Fichtner, *Terror and Toleration*, pp. 117–61.

[73] Bourel, "Die deutsche Orientalistik im 18. Jahrhundert," p. 122.

[74] Robert Irwin, *Dangerous Knowledge*, pp. 127–8.

[75] Guy Stroumsa, "Homeros Hebraios," p. 98; though Wood's book was hugely popular in Germany, this comparison does not, interestingly, seem to have survived. On the "Arabia felix" expedition, see the section on Michaelis below.

[76] See Almond, "Terrible Turks, Bedouin Poets, and Prussian Prophets: The Shifting Place of Islam in Herder's Thought," in *Publications of the Modern Language Association* 123, no. 1 (Jan. 2008): 68–71, quotation p. 68.

loving sons of the desert would come again into their own in the neoromantic texts of T. E. Lawrence and Mohammed Asad.[77]

But if the study of the Islamic world did not much profit from eighteenth-century orientalism, certainly the bigger losers were the Jews. As Frank Manuel argued some years ago, in the sixteenth and seventeenth centuries, Protestant cultures in particular had celebrated the ethical superiority of the ancient Israelites and emphasized their descent from God's "chosen people." Enlightened thinking, on the other hand, tended to disenchant and nationalize the Jews, as well as to expose the more fabulous, violent, or legalistic parts of the Old Testament to criticism and ridicule.[78] By the mid-eighteenth century, it had become possible to express quite openly one's doubts about the ethical implications of some Old Testament passages. Voltaire, for example, glossing a famous passage in Exodus, where Moses commands that 24,000 of his countrymen be executed as a result of one Jew's dallying with a Midian woman, writes: "We must acknowledge, humanly speaking, that these horrid deeds revolt against reason and nature. But if we consider Moses as the minister of God's designs and vengeance, the aspect is entirely changed. He is not a man who acts as a man; he is the instrument of the divinity, whom we should not call to account. We should offer up silent adoration." What is striking in Voltaire's *Philosophy of History* is its focus not on the implausibility of the Old Testament, but on its pronounced failure to live up to "human" moral standards. Voltaire estimated that either through civil war, or by command of their God, the Old Testament Jews killed 239,650 of their own people; this cannot possibly be the right and natural religion of the future, he insists; we cannot embrace this God as our own.[79]

Voltaire's moral-rationalist critique was hardly the only, and surely not the most popular source of anti-Jewish feeling, even in the enlightened age; that infamous honor goes to the two-volume study of rabbinical writings titled *Jewry Revealed*, written by the Heidelberg Hebraist Johann Eisenmenger and published in Prussia, with the backing of King Friedrich Wilhelm I in 1711.[80] But Eisenmenger was drawing on traditional Christian attempts to vilify Jews as Christ-killers and Christ-deniers, while Voltaire, in downgrading Jewish history in favor of forgotten, or suppressed, pagan ancestors, was bringing to the fore ideas that had circulated underground since Giordano Bruno called the Jews "the excrement of Egypt" and accused them of stealing Egyptian ideas.[81] Voltaire's anti-Semitic ecumenicism drew on the writings of iconoclasts and skeptics, from natural scientists to Socinians to Spinoza, who had raised doubts about the Old Testament's miracles, rituals, and internal contradictions, as well as about the purportedly cruel, distant, and occasionally capricious God they saw articulated in it. As Jonathan Sheehan has elegantly argued, rationalist anti-Judaism was in many respects a by-product of a larger, pan-European conflict among Christians about

---

[77] Osterhammel, *Entzauberung*, pp. 261–70. For Asad, see the Epilogue.

[78] Manuel, *Broken Staff*, p. 164.

[79] Voltaire, *Philosophy of History*, in *Collected Works of Voltaire* (New York, nd), pp. 412–3; quotation, p. 416.

[80] Gotthard Deutsch, "Eisenmenger, Johann Andreas," on http://JewishEncyclopedia.com/.

[81] Yates, *Giordano Bruno*, p. 223.

the sanctity of the Bible, and the trustworthiness of traditional authority more generally. The Germans were by no means the only, or even the most rabid, eighteenth-century rationalists or anti-Jewish polemicists. But, as Sheehan notes, German Protestant culture did have a special, and especially fraught, relationship with the Old Testament[82] and its working out of the Enlightenment's legacy would cast a long shadow over the pursuit of oriental studies and over German culture as a whole.

THE PECULIARITIES OF GERMAN ORIENTALISM

It is not coincidental that this section on early modern German orientalism does not emphasize imperial envies, but rather focuses on Central European religious and political affairs, university building, classical philology, and Old Testament criticism. Central European intellectual life, after the Reformation, was primarily defined by these factors and by the paucity of secular, aristocratic patrons – or commercially oriented gentleman scholars – who might have provoked and paid for different sorts of scholarship. Political conjunctures are important here in explaining the development or the non-development of cultural institutions. Just as the Spanish and Portuguese were engaging in the first round of New World empire building, the German-speaking world was embroiled in the Schmalkaldic Wars; by the time things settled down, in the 1560s, the Spanish and Portuguese had monopolized the Atlantic trade and were making inroads into Asia. Central Europeans were also prevented from engaging in the second great round of British, Dutch, and French overseas expansion by the disastrous Thirty Years' War. For the critical period of 1618–48, and for many decades afterward, Central Europe's economies and polities were in chaos; its populations were decimated and its leaders, of necessity, focused on internal problems. Then there is the critical context – much more important for Central Europeans than for Britons or Frenchmen – of the long-lasting power of the Ottoman Empire. The Holy Roman Empire's capital city, Vienna, was besieged by the Turks as late as 1683, and long afterward, there were still fears of Ottoman invasions. Early modern Austrians, Prussians, Saxons, and Bavarians were also engaged in jockeying with one another, and with the Russians, for regional prominence. The relationship of the Germans to the "East" was not that of cross-oceanic commerce and colonization, but of powerful nations on one's own unstable borders.

As Nina Berman has correctly underlined, this does not mean that German interaction with the East was not "actual." From at least the fifteenth century onward, thousands of Germans assisted the Portuguese or the Dutch in their overseas endeavors, such as building metalworks for the ships, producing astronomical charts and excellent maps, and serving as deckhands and spice merchants. The period between about 1570 and 1618 saw new German involvement in the spice trade and the appearance of scores of new publications and translations by

---

[82] Jonathan Sheehan, *The Enlightenment Bible: Translation, Scholarship, Culture* (Princeton, NJ, 2005), p. 217, 89.

German scholars and missionaries; by no means were German scholars out of the loop in the reception and repackaging of Europe's new knowledge of Asia.[83] After 1648, many more Germans volunteered to serve the Dutch East and West India Companies, and a large number made their way eastward in the service of the Russian Czar. The Austrians, of course, had a long and bitter experience with their Ottoman neighbors, but they had commercial and diplomatic relations with them as well. But before 1750, the impact of this "actual knowledge" on what German-speakers wrote about the East seems to have been slight – as compared to the formative power of Sir John Mandeville's *Travels*, the Alexander romances, Ottoman captivity narratives, and the Old Testament. On the whole, the worldview of the early modern Central European educated elite can be said to have been far more continental than global and far more religious than "cultural."

Culture, in any event, was heavily bound up with the churches, for clerical callings were, for a very long time, the most viable means for talented but non-aristocratic German speakers to rise.[84] Theology was the most practical subject for non-aristocrats to pursue, for the confessionalized, state-supported *Landeskirche* needed a steady supply of pastors and priests. Rabbis were not supported by the state, but Jewish communities also needed well-educated religious leaders; schooled in Talmudic law and rabbinical commentaries, many of these men practiced what others called "oriental" scholarship, in their own institutions and for their own purposes. The diverse and contentious nature of the religious landscape of Central Europe produced many theologians, and also many theologically inflected conflicts; but it also produced a sort of interstate commerce in theological ideas, as scholars reacted to developments in neighboring territories. Students traveling from school to school in the course of their studies enhanced linkages between universities; competition between universities for faculty members, on the other hand, stoked institutional rivalries. The tradition of state support for unorthodox university professors – beginning with Luther – helped further to ensure that teachers who found clerical or political pressures too great in, say, Heidelberg or Helmstedt, might find a post in Giessen or Göttingen. This was a viable intellectual world in an early modern era in which, especially outside of the great Catholic states, there were few courts able and willing to support learning and a relatively weak world of secular arts and letters. From this matrix, a set of rich and diverse scholarly traditions developed. German university scholars emerged from the era of confessional conflict experienced in debating theological and philosophical questions and skilled in interpreting texts. As an intellectual community, however, German academe had its weaknesses, including little commerce between its members and the court or gentlemanly scholars; deficient libraries; and relatively little exposure to practical applications of the arts and sciences. All of these features would inform the critically important tradition of Christian humanism in the Holy Roman Empire and its successor states.

---

[83] Lach, *Asia in the Making of Europe*, vol. II, *A Century of Wonder*, book 2, *The Literary Arts* (Chicago, IL, 1977), pp. 324–53.

[84] See Anthony J. La Vopa, *Grace, Talent and Merit: Poor Students, Clerical Careers and Professional Ideology in Eighteenth-Century Germany* (Cambridge, 1988).

Of course, Christian humanism had Catholic as well as Protestant variants, and behind its practice lie Jewish, and even Muslim traditions of learning as well.[85] German scholars borrowed from Italian philologists like Lorenzo Valla, and from Frenchmen like Jean Morin and Richard Simon; developing the skill and the daring to challenge the Pope and the church over the interpretation of scripture, these Catholic humanists insisted that men in the present could clear away centuries of misunderstanding and misinterpretation of God's word if they used their own reason and their linguistic training to do so; in many ways, this notion made possible the career of Christian humanist and with it the long-subordinate career of orientalist. But the Church of Rome was at best unenthusiastic about most of this philological work, and after the seventeenth century, it would be in Protestant territories that it would flourish. Intellectually, too, we can say that without the Reformation's sanctioning and abetting of the idea of recovering the original meaning of God's word, it is doubtful that many specialized orientalists would have been needed, wanted, or welcomed in European society.

One of the things Reformed humanists contributed was the insistence that theologians should be able to read and clearly understand the Bible in its own languages, Greek, Latin, and Hebrew. We should note that theologians, and not all laypersons, were targeted here; this would be in keeping with Luther's view that some ideas and debates should be kept within clerical circles. But there was a persistent reformist and even democratizing drive built into this tradition by way of the Reformers' conviction that ordinary individuals should read the Bible in their own language; this conviction would open the door to the Pietists and other theological radicals who could always use it to argue for the importance of the Bible's accessibility to all. Though orthodox Lutherans and Calvinists were vexed by the Pietists' more sentimental and charismatic piety, doctrinally, they could not restrict access to the Word, nor were they able to slam the door on radical printers and underground book traders, not to mention varying interpretations of scripture. The Reformation's insistence on translating the Bible – and then the many disputes over the linguistically or dogmatically correct or era-appropriate translation – would also increase individuals' appetite for studying ancient languages and cultural remains, and fuel critical fires, which could not easily be quenched.

Indeed, the Reformation unleashed a philological-historical dynamism, which could never quite be contained though it threatened, repeatedly, to destroy the integrity and even sanctity of the scriptures. In the Protestant lands, humanist philology simply could not be divided from religious belief, as was possible in Catholic areas where the authority of the Church and of tradition could be invoked; the basis of the Reformation was, after all, *sola scriptura*, and humanist philology was the means by which Luther had discovered the errors of the Church and the means by which he had articulated his alternative vision of Christian truth.

---

[85] Joseph Scaliger, for example, drew on Catholic scholars' work on chronology; see Grafton, "Joseph Scaliger and Historical Chronology," pp. 158–62. Debts to Jewish scholars and scholarship are numerous and well known; Pico, Reuchlin, Richard Simon, Isaac Causabon, and John Dee, among many others, had Jewish teachers. On the interaction of Muslim and Christian scholarship in the late Renaissance, see Natalie Zemon Davis, *Trickster Travels: A Sixteenth-Century Muslim between Worlds* (New York, 2006), pp. 55–152.

Luther thought young theologians should learn Hebrew, in addition to Greek, in order to understand not just Saint Paul, but the prophets and Psalms on which he drew. Without language learning, the great reformer feared the original spirit of the scriptures could not be recovered and the message of the gospels could not endure: "And let us acknowledge," he argued, "that we cannot truly uphold the gospels without the languages. The languages are the sheath, in which the spirit's knife rests. They are the vessel, in which one grasps this drink. They are the storehouse which hold this [spiritual] repast.... Therefore it is certain that the place where the languages do not remain, there the gospel will in the end be lost."[86] The philologist, student, and lover of words and keeper of the linguistic flame, would be an essential member of the reformed Christian community.

Although, to put it very mildly, Luther did not like Jews, one of the consequences of his biblical criticism was the acceleration of a Hebraic Renaissance with its roots in the very late fifteenth century. In the Germanies, the first signs of the new learning came in Reuchlin's Hebrew grammar (*De rudimentis linguae Hebraicae*) in 1506 and his work on the Kabbalah (*De arte cabalistica*, 1517). After 1517, however, Reuchlin's esoteric side was played down in favor of a more theologically oriented emphasis on the learning of biblical Hebrew, encouraged in Dutch and German lands by the founding of positions for the teaching of the language not only in theological faculties, but in some cases also in philosophical faculties. Comparisons between the chosen and beleaguered Israelites and the righteous and persecuted Protestants abounded, making the ancient Jews (but not the modern ones!) the object of considerable Protestant sympathy. Calvinists, in particular, admired Jewish critiques of Christian idolatry, which could be easily turned into anti-Catholic polemics. By the seventeenth century, the Targums – third-century Aramaic paraphrases of some Old Testament texts – were widely read; the Hebrew Old Testament itself was much more easily accessible. In 1603, the Professor of Hebrew at the University of Basel, Johann Buxtorf, published his *Juden-Schul*, a learned and well-informed study of contemporary Jewish religious practices. Two decades later, Dutch scholars set about translating Talmudic tracts and some of the Misnah – the first rabbinic redaction of the Law – and by the middle of the century, great Hebraists like John Selden and Edward Pococke had perfected their skills and stuffed their libraries full of works by and about Jews.[87] The strong affinity Protestants felt for the ancient Israelites and the university positions and learned traditions established for the careful study of Hebrew texts would leave a lasting imprint on German theology and biblical philology, making the Old Testament a book of very special importance and resonance, as well as the object of intense scrutiny for several centuries of scholarship.

But as Luther himself was already aware, philologists, even the faithful ones, could also cause trouble. For Lutheran doctrine also depended on the doctrine of inspiration, according to which the scriptures in their entirety were inspired by God; rational explanation by men could assist in understanding the words God had given humankind, but it was not supposed to undermine their veracity. Luther assumed that interpreters of the Bible would already be believers; one read the

---

[86] Luther quoted in Kraus, *Geschichte der historisch-kritischen Erforschung*, pp. 9–10.
[87] Shuger, *Renaissance Bible*, pp. 33–4.

scriptures knowing that they were the word of God rather than reading them as skeptics seeking proof of God's truths. He did not worry about the possibility that the Pentateuch drew on pagan traditions or that some Psalms probably were not written by their putative authors. But some of his followers, and worse, some of his enemies, did worry about such things, and as Christian Hebraism dug more deeply into the world surrounding the Old Testament, a series of uncomfortable questions were raised, which made the founding of faith "on scripture alone" increasingly difficult.

The most consequential of these questions had to do with the Masoretic redaction of the Old Testament (brought together between the seventh and tenth centuries C.E.), the version accepted as authentic by Jews and used by Luther in his Pentateuch translation of 1523. In 1538, the Jewish scholar Elias Levita (1469–1549) pointed out that as diacritical marks had not existed in the time of Ezra, the Masoretes' rendering of the texts were open to challenge (as written Hebrew has no vowels, many unpunctuated words can be read in various ways, and the Masoretes had added "vowel points" to stabilize their readings). Many Christian scholars read Levita's work, but the vowel point debate did not become intense until some decades later when Catholics began to recognize that the instability of the Masoretic text made it more difficult for Protestants to defend scripture alone as the basis for faith. Hoping to embarrass the Protestants, some Catholic polemicists accused Lutherans and Calvinists of favoring Jewish, rather than Christian, beliefs and insisted on the greater authority and antiquity of the Vulgate or even the Septuagint.[88] Richard Simon, who had studied Talmud with Jona Salvador, a learned Jew in Paris, suggested more modestly that the errors in the Masoretic text could be overlooked and improved by comparing other versions. Some bits of the Old Testament, Simon argued, were of "authentic" and others of "secondary" importance; the book of Genesis, for example, contained material from other cultures and written by other hands.[89] For Simon, of course, this was not a problem because tradition could fill in where scriptures were imperfect or vague and the church itself could help individuals decide which bits of the "word of God" were authentic and which were of secondary importance. But for Protestants, this was no easy doctrinal matter and it continued to roil the learned world for more than a century afterward.

The mainline response was a vigorous, erudite defense of the self-sufficiency of scripture – that the text was itself, and entirely, the Word of God and by itself was clear enough for all believers to understand without assistance. Germandom's professors of Hebrew played a central part in this defense from the seventeenth to the mid-eighteenth century. In the 1620s, Johann Buxtorf the elder, professor of Hebrew at the University of Basel, undertook extensive studies of the Masoretic schools in order to show that they did have ancient evidence for their readings, and in 1648, his son, Johann Buxtorf the younger, took up the same cudgels.[90] We will

---

[88] See Edward Breuer, *Limits of Enlightenment*, pp. 78–107, esp. 80–2; Miller, "Making the Paris Polyglot Bible," pp. 75–81.

[89] Henning Graf Reventlow, *Epochen der Bibelauslegung*, vol. 4, *Von der Aufklärung bis zum 20. Jahrhundert* (Munich, 2001), pp. 88–91.

[90] Ibid., pp. 79–82.

see, below, members of the Michaelis family endeavoring to make the same case as much as a century later. Perhaps it was all this learned philology or perhaps it was the relative isolation of Central European Protestant scholarship from other, more worldly studies, which resulted in the fact that German scholars held fast to vowel points and to their faith in the perfection of the scriptures much longer than did English, French, and Dutch scholars. Not until after 1750 did their confidence really begin to crumble, though in the next three decades, German criticism would more than make up for its slow start.[91] By this time, however, the theological challenges were all on the table: how to admit that there might be errors in the Word of God without ceding to the Catholics the right to remedy them with tradition or admitting – to the advantage of Jews, Deists, or non-believers – that the Christian Bible was in fact the work of fallible men? How could belief be reconciled with reason and with the findings of the new sciences (including theology's important ancillaries, classical and oriental philology)? This would be a problem that would dog Protestant scholars for centuries to come.

One of the implications of the vowel point debates – and the one conclusion orthodox Protestant theologians were loathe to draw – was that the Old Testament, was not a fixed, unambiguous text. Even more dangerously (for Christians), scholars had also been tinkering with the New Testament in the attempt to improve Erasmus's *editio princeps*, which had been based on unreliable Byzantine manuscripts. One of these efforts, that of Elzevier of Leiden, produced in 1624 an edition subsequently known as the *textus receptus*, which was widely accepted by European Protestant churches. Over the course of the eighteenth century, there would be important challenges to the *textus receptus* in England, France, and the Netherlands, and pioneering work on biblical manuscripts by Johann Albrecht Bengel. Stretching *critica sacra* as far as it would go, scholars added textual variants at the bottom of the page, but resisted changing the text as they would have changed a classical one; even though the material needed for historicizing the Bible grew, biblical scholars delayed applying the full force of humanist criticism to the scriptures until pressed by Enlightenment radicals – and permitted by enlightened officials.

Thus, as late as the 1730s and 1740s, the German-speaking world showed little movement in the direction of what would become, in the 1770s, the critical study of the scriptures or Higher Criticism; Lutheran and Catholic theologians absorbed themselves in doctrinal debates or tried to combat other, more radical challenges to biblical authority underway in the forms, respectively, of Spinozan philosophy and Socinian rationalism, which made their way into the Germanies through underground channels.[92] Before 1740, state officials helped the churches root out these dangerous ideas; in 1723, the philosopher Christian Wolff, in praising Chinese "natural" ethics, raised fears that he was a Spinozist and was stripped of his chair at the University of Halle and banished from Prussia – though he managed to get a chair next door in less orthodox Marburg. But Spinozism was increasingly intermixed with other varieties of Deism and Anglican appeals for toleration, with the new sciences' insistence on universal laws and empirical

---

[91] On the English, Dutch, and French critics, see Breuer, *Limits of Enlightenment*, pp. 80–97.
[92] Mulsow, *Moderne aus dem Untergrund*, pp. 85–93.

observations, and in such circumstances, it was hard to keep the Enlightenment from creeping into the universities, and in some cases, offering radical challenges to orthodox interpretations of the Bible. Between 1735 and 1737, Buddeus's former student, Johann Lorenz Schmidt issued his "Wertheim Bible" (1735–7), a German translation of and commentary on the Pentateuch, which, Jonathan Israel writes, "was obviously a systematic attempt to dilute, or explain away, everything miraculous in the Five Books, substituting uncompromisingly naturalistic explanations." On its heels came J. C. Edelmann's *Moses mit aufgedecktem Angesicht* (1740), which denied the sanctity of scripture and existence of sin.[93] It should also be noted that H. S. Reimarus's *Apologie oder Schutzschrift für die vernünftigen Verehrer Gottes* was written about 1740, though it lay unpublished, and the author's radical views on the historical truth of the scriptures unknown to all but his most intimate friends until made public by Lessing in the *Wolffenbütteler Fragmente eines Ungenannten* (1774–8).

Once Frederick the Great came to the Prussian throne (1740), radical views could be openly expressed; indeed, one of the new King's first acts was to give Christian Wolff back his Berlin chair. Frederick himself would host Voltaire at Sanssouci between 1750 and 1753. By this time, the first German Masonic lodges were up and running, and the more daring among the biblical exegetes were dipping their pens in ever more radical inkpots. It is against this background of increasing, and increasingly publicly debated, radical ideas that we should understand the work of J. S. Semler, who, on beginning his career as a scholarly theologian in the 1750s, felt the need to invoke Dutch or French scholarship or, better, to return to the church fathers in order to separate "the historical explanation, which really appertains to those times, the first centuries, [and treats] the content and extent of the imaginations of contemporaries; and the present-day use [of criticism] for the edification of today's Christians...."[94] For a time Semler pursued, rather quietly, his historical studies at Halle. But, by the 1770s, Semler had gone far beyond Luther or even many of his Dutch contemporaries. In his pathbreaking *Abhandlung von freier Untersuchung des Canon* (published in four volumes, 1771–5), he argued forcefully that the *textus receptus* was an accidental collection of texts and called for critical differentiation of the historical and theological value of the pieces.[95] Semler was lucky enough to possess one of the few copies of Richard Simon's *Histoire critique du Vieux Testament* which had survived destruction, and in the year that saw the appearance of Adam Smith's *Wealth of Nations* and

[93] Jonathan I. Israel, *Radical Enlightenment: Philosophy and the Making of Modernity, 1650–1750* (Oxford, 2002), pp. 544–58, 660–1, quotation p. 553.

[94] D. Johannes Salomo Semler, *Lebensbeschreibung von ihm selbst abgefasst* (Halle, 2 vols. 1781, 1782), vol. 1, pp. 208–9. Also vol. 2, pp. 127–8. It is not quite fair to present Semler's critique of the "doctrine of inspiration" as having no German antecedents. His teacher Siegmund Jacob Baumgarten had begun to work out the principle of accommodation, which codified an idea Catholics, Jews, and Protestants had been hinting at for some time, namely that the Bible's authors were divinely inspired, but spoke in the language of their times; their knowledge was dependent on their milieu. Sorkin, *Berlin Haskalah*, p. 69.

[95] John D. Woodbridge, "German Responses to the Biblical Critic Richard Simon: From Leibniz to J. S. Semler," in *Historische Kritik und biblischer Kanon in der deutschen Aufklärung*, ed. Henning Graf Reventlow et al. (Wiesbaden, 1988), pp. 65–88.

Thomas Jefferson's Declaration of Independence (1776), he published a German translation. With Simon's assistance, Semler now put forward claims that flew in the face of the traditional Lutheran doctrine of inspiration, arguing that though the Bible *contains* the word of God, it is not *equivalent to* God's word.[96] As modest a claim as that may now seem, for an eminent professor of Lutheran theology to adopt such a position was indeed a revolutionary act.

Semler's school of thought was known as neology; the aim of this rationalizing, non-dogmatic, Protestant line of thinking was to reconcile reason and revelation by means of historicizing the Bible's message. Semler wanted to produce what David Sorkin describes as "a critical-historical method that scrutinized the contents of revelation and Scripture while maintaining belief."[97] For Semler, the Old Testament, in particular, needed scrutiny, for much of it was of much lower "moral-religious" significance than the New; its truth, as the apostles already understood, was allegorical rather than literal.[98] But Semler's rationalizing drive would not allow for allegorical readings either, and the Protestant scholar could not depend on church tradition to fill voids created by the disenchantment of scriptures, as had Simon, or on oral tradition as the means by which knowledge of God's message was preserved, as did Moses Mendelssohn.[99] In fact, Semler's school would end up trying so hard to explain the human factors – and errors – that shaped the writing of the Hebrew texts that very little of the Old Testament's sacred content, not to mention its literal truth, was left over.

Like his colleague Johann Griesbach, Semler also concluded, again in the 1770s, that the time for fiddling with Erasmus's footnotes was over: the *textus receptus* had to be junked and a new one created on the basis of the systematic use of manuscripts.[100] But Semler would not be willing to historicize the New Testament so deeply or dangerously, for in his view, this portion of Christian scripture articulated the universal and eternally true religion, rather than a provincial and time-bound faith. It is striking that at the same time as Semler was publishing Simon's critique of the Old Testament, he was attacking Lessing for publishing Reimarus's assault on the sanctity of the New Testament. As Hans-Joachim Kraus has argued, Semler reiterated and modernized a powerful Christian tendency that would be carried forward into nineteenth-century historical-critical scholarship. In effect, his answer to the Enlightenment's challenge to the Bible would be to do away with the Old Testament as inspired scripture, a reversion to the "Marcionite"

---

[96] Thomas A. Howard, *Religion and the Rise of Historicism: W. M. L. de Wette, Jacob Burckhardt and the Theological Origins of Nineteenth-Century Historical Consciousness* (Cambridge, 2000), p. 35.

[97] Sorkin, *Berlin Haskalah*, p. 67; Peter Hans Reill, "Religion, Theology and the Hermetic Imagination," in *Antike Weisheit und kulturelle Praxis: Hermetismus in der frühen Neuzeit*, p. 221.

[98] Semler, *Lebensbeschreibung* 2, pp. 135–42; see also "Semler, Johann Salomo,' in the Biographisches-Bibliographisches Kirchenlexikon, http://www.bautz.de./bbkl/s/s2/semler_j_s.shtml.

[99] Sorkin, *Berlin Haskalah*, pp. 96–8.

[100] Reventlow, *Epochen* 4: 201 makes Griesbach the first to throw out the *textus receptus*; Sebastian Timpanaro rejects this. See Timpanaro, *The Genesis of Lachmann's Method*, ed. and trans. Glenn W. Most (Chicago, 2005), pp. 60–70, esp. p. 70, n. 34. On English and German challenges, see Sheehan, *Enlightenment Bible*, pp. 87–240.

heresy that would appeal powerfully to German philosophers and radical religious thinkers from Schleiermacher and Hegel down to Adolf Harnack.[101]

Semler's critique would be especially important for the philosophically oriented theologians who followed in his wake; but there were, of course, other biblical scholars at work in the Germanies, the most prominent of whom was J. D. Michaelis, professor of oriental studies at the University of Göttingen. Michaelis will be profiled below, but here it is worth noting that, like Semler, he was a university professor and hence an employee of the enlightened state, with at least some independence from clerical authorities. Indeed, Michaelis insisted that he be made a professor of philosophy rather than theology, insuring thereby his independence from the orthodox Lutherans in the theological faculty, who were deeply opposed to his historicizing approach. It is worth noting that the university administration agreed to this and allowed Michaelis to rise to a position of cultural leadership; he was appointed editor of the hugely influential book-reviewing organ the *Göttingische Gelehrten Anzeigen* (1753–70) as well as secretary and then director of the Göttingen Society of Sciences.[102] Just as Semler, thanks to the support of the Prussian bureaucracy, maintained his position as head of the theology faculty at the University of Halle despite vociferous clerical protests, Michaelis was protected, and even encouraged, by those who favored deconfessionalization, or, to put it in another way, those happy to see the power of the churches diminished. Among the orientalist careers sketched below, we will find many similar stories of men able to use the power of the state to defend themselves and their iconoclastic religious ideas against persecution by orthodox clerics.

In 1786, Frederick the Great died and Prussia began to take a more conservative turn; two years before Bavaria had shut down the Illuminati and even Joseph II in Austria was, after 1785, slowing the pace of Enlightenment. The year 1785 was also the year during which Friedrich Jacobi unleashed what has become known as the *Pantheismusstreit* – a bitter debate over the religious views of the recently deceased Gotthold Ephraim Lessing. Jacobi claimed that Lessing had confessed to him his commitment to the philosophy of Christian orthodoxy's archenemy, Spinoza, an assertion that identified the great spokesman of the German Enlightenment as a pantheist and an atheist. As Bradley Herling has argued, Jacobi meant for his pamphlet to tar other rationalists, including Kant and Moses Mendelssohn, with the pantheist brush – and did succeed in making many philosophers and scholars run for theological cover (though Herder, as we shall see presently, moved in a different direction).[103] Semler and Michaelis found themselves moving to the right; Semler went so far as to side with the Prussian edict of 1788, which sought to bolster Lutheran orthodoxy, even though privately he continued to hold a number of heterodox positions, including the possibility that a secret, Hermetic

---

[101] Kraus, *Geschichte der historisch-kritischen Erforschung*, pp. 99–107; 175–9; Wolfram Kinzig, *Harnack, Marcion und das Judentum* (Leipzig, 2004).

[102] Anna-Ruth Löwenbrück, "Johann David Michaelis' Verdienst um die philologisch-historisch Bibelkritik," in Reventlow et al. eds., *Historische Kritik*, p. 160.

[103] Bradley L. Herling, *The German Gita; Hermeneutics and Discipline in the German Reception of Indian Thought, 1778–1831* (New York, 2006), p. 89.

chemistry might yield knowledge about nature's *Urstoff*.[104] Moses Mendelssohn too took up a defensive project, a five-volume edition of the Hebrew Pentateuch (*Sefer Netivot ha-Shalom*, 1780–3) intended to preserve Jewish readings of scripture against Christian-enlightened criticism.[105]

Semler, Mendelssohn, and Michaelis were by no means the most radical thinkers of their age; indeed criticism in their hands was, as Michael Carhart has characterized enlightened criticism more generally, "an antidote for religious skepticism and historical pyrrhonism. The critic analyzed a text's vocabulary, grammar, and extra-textual references to demonstrate that the text was actually of the age and provenance that it purported to be."[106] In response to more radical critiques of the scriptures, Semler and Michaelis tried to strip the Old Testament in particular of its irrational or morally objectionable portions, hoping to make it more credible. Recognizing the danger of this stripping operation to his community, Mendelssohn reacted differently – giving up some of his faith in the universality of reason in order to defend the particular truths of Jewish tradition. But both of these moves paved the way for more disputes about the authenticity and accuracy of the scholars' sources. Moreover, the tacit or occasionally explicit legitimacy given academic biblical criticism by the enlightened state bureaucracies, and the circulation of criticism to wider educated audiences further weakened the churches' ability to impose orthodoxy; debates now came out of seminaries and private studies and filled the pages of journals and pamphlets. The open application of stricter philological and historical methods to the Hebrew Bible made returning to older notions of revelation and divine authorship deeply problematical. Once the scriptures were put in historical and ethnographic context, it was very difficult to extract them again – though the aim, for many decades, would be that of reconciling reason and revelation, not of choosing between the two.

It is not quite correct then to claim, as did one commentator in the 1920s, that after the devastation wrought by Kant's *Religion within the Bounds of Reason Alone*, "the philological 'dustmen' had simply carried away the historical foundations of Christianity, stone by stone, whether they believed in the truth of the historical Jesus or not."[107] The "philological dustmen," among whom scholars trained in oriental languages were prominent, were working in this direction both before and after Kant, and historicist biblical criticism continued to matter deeply down to the 1910s. In many respects, enlightened philosophy and orientalist biblical criticism did complement one another at least with respect to their effects on traditional Christianity, just as both appealed to members of the enlightened bureaucracies eager to break the power of conservative clerics. Enlightened reason, and increasingly specialized oriental studies, put an end to *critica sacra* in the traditional sense. But on the French Revolution's eve, German oriental studies

---

[104] Reill, "Religion, Theology and the Hermetic Imagination," pp. 219–33.

[105] See Edward Breuer, *Limits of Enlightenment*, pp. 147–222.

[106] Carhart, *Science of Culture*, p. 5.

[107] Richard H. Grützmacher, "Die christliche Weltanschauung und die Geschichtsphilosophie Spenglers," in *Oswald Spengler und das Christentum: Zwei kritische Aufsätze*, Karl Heim and Richard H. Grützmacher, eds (Munich, 1921), pp. 52–3.

continued to be embedded in older traditions of Christian humanism, guided at least as much by the spirit of Luther as by that of Kant.

HERDER AND MICHAELIS: THE FATE OF THE ENLIGHTENED
OLD TESTAMENT

This chapter closes with an examination of two scholars critical to the fashioning of modern German orientalism, the Göttingen professor of oriental languages J. D. Michaelis and the Lutheran pastor and polymath J. G. Herder. Their positions were by no means identical, as we shall see, but both were deeply concerned with the problem of reconciling enlightened reason and Christian scripture and both looked to "primitive" history to find their solutions. For both scholars, language was a central concern; it is no coincidence that both wrote prize-winning essays on the question of the origins of language. Though deeply interested in the ancient Orient, neither cared much for modern Asian cultures – Herder, because he preferred simple, unspoiled cultures, and Michaelis, because he thought them – and especially the modern Jews – fallen and in need of reform. Both were avid consumers of the new oriental and orientalist texts and were powerfully influenced by new tendencies in classical scholarship. They were actively aware of French and English enlightened ideas, though neither liked to think the Germans behind in the production of critical thought. Finally, both were driven by the need to understand the truths of the scriptures – though each conceived these truths rather differently from their forefathers and from one another. In one way or the other, their orientalist work was aimed chiefly at elucidating the world of the Old Testament; but of course, new scholarship is often the result of digression from the subject at hand, an observation that explains more in oriental studies than perhaps in any other discipline.

Descended from a family of orientalists and exegetes, Johann David Michaelis was, like Herder and J. J. Wincklemann, the joint product of Pietist schools and enlightened ideas. Born in 1717, Michaelis was trained, as his student Johann Eichhorn later noted, in a generation in which education still meant learning ancient languages by rote rather than with an eye to "the enduring cultivation of taste."[108] Taste, indeed, had less to do with his choice of careers than his family, which was already committed to the study of oriental languages in the service of biblical exegesis. His great uncle Johann Heinrich Michaelis had long presided over Halle's Collegium Orientale Theologicum, where students could learn Syrian, Arabic, Ethiopian, Turkish, Persian, Chinese, Polish, Russian, and Italian, and his father, Christian Benedikt, was a Syriac expert with a professorship at the University of Halle. Both believed, as did other Halle Pietists, that oriental philology could help to correct errors of translation or unclear passages in Luther's Bible;[109] but they did not foresee how fully and confidently their heir would depart from the traditional practices of text reading and seek to evade theology's shadow.

[108] Johann Eichhorn, "Johann David Michaelis: Einige Bemerkungen über seinen litterarischen Character," in *Allgemeine Bibliothek* 3, no. 5 (Leipzig, 1791), p. 833.
[109] See Sheehan, *Enlightenment Bible*, pp. 59–62.

Though he exhibited considerable linguistic talents, the youthful Johann David did not promise to break his ancestors' mold, producing, in the year of Frederick's accession (1740), a rather run-of-the-mill defense of the infallibility of the Masoretic text and the authenticity of Hebrew vowel points. But thereafter, a series of travels and encounters would transform his pursuit of his calling. The first of these was his sojourn in England in 1741–2, during which time he heard Robert Lowth's famous lectures on Hebrew poetry; Michaelis would later annotate these lectures, creating an authoritative edition popular even in England. The next crucial event was his appointment in 1745 to an unsalaried lectureship in Göttingen, where George II – in his capacity as Elector of Hanover – had recently entrusted the project of university reform to the foresightful minister Gerlach Adolph Freiherr von Münchhausen. In the 1740s, Michaelis also met Albert Schultens, one of the first to group Hebrew and Arabic together as Semitic languages and even to foreground Arabic, making its grammar the means to understand Hebrew grammar rather than vice versa. Under Schultens's influence, Michaelis embraced Benjamin Kennicott's publication of variants from the Masoretic manuscripts and gave up his literalist attitude toward the Hebrew Bible. But, as Michael Legaspi argues, Michaelis in the 1740s also met and befriended the classicist J. M. Gesner, whose neohumanist ideas helped to shape the young orientalist's conception of Hebrew antiquity.[110] By the early 1750s, Michaelis was expressing his increasing dissatisfaction with *Orientalistik*'s tendency to avoid hard theological questions and modern perspectives by burying itself in language study; nor was its overly philological orientation helpful in winning humanistic interlocutors. "This field of scholarship," he lamented in 1755, "has the misfortune that because of the machines that have been designated 'Professores Linguarum orientalium' it has become uninteresting in the eyes of all the lovers of the humanities."[111] It would be his goal, in fact, not only to make the Orient interesting to humanists but also to make oriental studies itself a branch of the humanities.

Michaelis hoped, Legaspi claims, to use philology, as did his classicizing friends, to revive the "dead" language of Hebrew and to make it possible and desirable for his contemporaries to enjoy the company of the great and noble eastern sages as they might enjoy that of Plato or Euripides. Importantly, he selected pre-exilic Israel as his "Golden Age"; after this period, Hebraic literature and culture, in his view, had fallen into decline.[112] Accordingly, he defined Old Testament Hebrew as the language to be revived in this Renaissance, in the process delegitimizing rabbinic Hebrew and robbing modern Jews of special rights or skills in this endeavor. But this in turn produced an evidentiary problem. If Old Testament Hebrew was the language worth knowing, if the Golden Age was so brief, and if furthermore one should throw out rabbinical commentaries – the Jews' account of their own tradition – what could one use to compensate for the

---

[110] Michael Chris Legaspi, "Reviving the Dead Letter: Johann David Michaelis and the Quest for Hebrew Antiquity" (Ph.D. dissertation, Harvard University, 2006), pp. 34–70; Eichhorn, pp. 863–73.

[111] Michaelis quoted in Goldziher, *Renan als Orientalist*, trans. Peter Zalan (Zürich, 2000), p. 33.

[112] See Legaspi, "Reviving the Dead Letter," pp. 95–151.

paucity of texts and the distance between eighteenth-century Germans and the ancient Israelites? Here Michaelis made another bold move, prepared for and conditioned both by Schultens' emphasis on Arabic study and surely also by his forefathers' wide-ranging linguistic talents. As he argued in a 1757 treatise, one could use cognate languages – especially Aramaic, Syriac, Ethiopic, and Arabic – to develop a better understanding of ancient Hebrew; the latter could now be seen to be a "normal" language spoken by a distinct group of past individuals. If sacred things were expressed in biblical Hebrew – and Michaelis thought they were – it was not a sacred language whose comprehension was impossible for mortals or restricted to rabbis and theologians.[113]

A corollary to Michaelis's commitment to use cognate "Semitic" languages to understand ancient Hebrew was his conviction that the geography, botany, and zoology of contemporary "Arabia felix," along with the languages and customs of his Arab inhabitants, might help to explain some of the supposedly miraculous events or the *hapax legomena* of the scriptures. In 1756, he approached the Danish foreign minister, J. H. von Bernstoff, with a plan to send a scholarly expedition to this part of the world. Bernstoff persuaded Frederick V, King of Denmark, to foot the bill; again, an enlightened bureaucrat offered an innovative orientalist a helping hand. Michaelis's announcement of the planned expedition in the *Göttingische Gelehrte Anzeigen* yielded a large number of suggestions from across Europe; from these, Michaelis worked up a list of 100 questions that the team was supposed to answer in the course of its travels. The six scholars were also supposed to buy useful books on secular subjects, collect seeds, minerals, and if possible, animals.[114]

The team of six scholars set off in 1761, but only one, the young Danish cartographer Carsten Niebuhr, returned in 1768. Niebuhr could not answer many of Michaelis's original questions, but his detailed maps, drawings, and diary accounts were invaluable sources of information about the biblical world – as Eichhorn put it, their content was so rich as to be worth as much as "half a library of other travels to the same places."[115] What Michaelis and Eichhorn learned, in particular, from Niebuhr's travels was that the Holy Land, which Europeans were accustomed to treat as a familiar home, was in fact quite alien, remote, and primitive. It was understandable in its own terms, but what about it might make it relevant, much less normative, was hard to fathom. Between 1769 and 1785, Michaelis used materials gleaned from Niebuhr and other travelers to produce a multi-volume, extensively annotated translation of the Old Testament which demonstrated in detail how to read the scriptures in the context of their times. If Michaelis himself remained convinced that the ancient Israelites possessed a comprehensive sort of natural wisdom and universal religious significance, the upshot of his biblical scholarship was precisely to render the Hebrew scriptures a purely historical artifact.

In 1753, Michaelis began editing the *Göttingische Gelehrte Anzeigen*, which quickly became the most important scholarly book-reviewing journal in Central

---

[113] Ibid., pp. 132–6.
[114] Carhart, *Science of Culture*, pp. 31–44; Sheehan, *Enlightenment Bible*, pp. 186–211.
[115] Eichhorn, "Johann David Michaelis," p. 856.

Europe; in 1771, he began publishing a journal exclusively concerned with orientalist knowledge, the *Orientalische und exegetische Bibliothek*.[116] In addition to editing and writing for these journals, teaching and writing numerous other grammatical works, in the early 1770s, Michaelis produced his masterpiece, a six-volume study of Jewish Law. This was not only an exercise in erudition; Michaelis's *Mosaisches Recht* (1770–5), like John Locke's *First Treatise*, sought to delegitimize biblical justifications of divine-right absolutism and to push for the enlightened modernization of the Central European criminal justice system.[117] But to do these things, Michaelis made Jewish Law seem a very provincial and parochial sort of justice, one not at all befitting modern times, a set of claims that gave succor to critiques of orthodox piety – Jewish and Christian – and deepened the association of the Jewish nation with absolutist arbitrary justice and irrational legalism. That was probably not Michaelis's aim; but as the deconstructionists have taught us, texts often offer readings their authors do not anticipate. Ironically, in his attempt to bring orientalism in line with contemporary intellectual currents and to defend the scriptures against modern-day skepticism, Michaelis helped to validate a kind of orientalism in which texts were strongly preferred to living people, and post-Christian histories of the Orient were simply stories of decline.

In this presumption, he was certainly not alone, for which changing external political circumstances can partly be blamed. Though before 1780, there had been some interest in modern Asia, as Dietmar Rothermund and Jürgen Osterhammel have shown, after this time, Germans – and Europeans in general – lost much of their previous interest in and respect for modern Asian societies.[118] This was, perhaps, an especially attractive move for Germans, who were already beginning to feel themselves falling behind in colonial commerce, as the English made further inroads into India and the French made new profits in the West Indies. Indeed, Jonathan Hess has argued that Michaelis in particular was very much aware of new imperial endeavors and even advertised the superior quality of German scholarship as being free from these practical interests and prejudices.[119] This opened the way for Germans to borrow French and British materials while claiming to use them in a more impartial way. This rhetoric of "disinterestedness" also fits nicely with Herder's critique of colonization as the destruction of humankind's cultural diversity and Indologist Peter von Bohlen's

---

[116] This journal lasted until 1785 – a much longer run than most journals of the age enjoyed. Indeed it was succeeded by the *Neue orientalische u. exegetische Bibliothek*, which survived until 1793, two years longer than Michaelis himself. Though largely devoted to exegesis, and to Michaelis's view of the same, the journal did, importantly, report on and translate William Jones's work very soon after its publication in English and was apparently widely read by non-theologians as well as by enlightened exegetes. Ursula Freise, *Die Entwicklung der orientalischen Zeitschriften in Deutschland von ihren Anfängen bis zur Gründung der "Zeitschrift der deutschen Morgenländischen Gesellschaft"* (1847) (Cologne, 1967), pp. 22–5.

[117] Carhart, *Science of Culture*, p. 47.

[118] Osterhammel, *Die Entzauberung Asiens*; Dietmar Rothermund, *The German Intellectual Quest for India* (New Delhi, 1986).

[119] Jonathan M. Hess, "Johann David Michaelis and the Colonial Imaginary: Orientalism and the Emergence of Racial Antisemitism in Eighteenth-Century Germany," in *Jewish Social Studies* 6 (2000), p. 79.

later denunciation of the tyrannical practices of the British East India Company (EIC). The EIC, he claimed, had generated a highly prejudiced view of India, which could only be corrected by the intervention of an unbiased reader of the "national" language, Sanskrit.[120]

But external politics cannot entirely or even best explain the processes of historicization and professionalization underway in later eighteenth-century orientalist circles. We need to look again closer to home, to the ideas and institutional structures prevalent in our German scholars' particular contexts. It is interesting and important to note that Michaelis, if still a believer in biblical authority, was not at all an orthodox believer or an orthodox scholar; he did not like theology and fought ceaselessly with the members of the Göttingen theology faculty. In fact, it is doubtful if he could have been the sort of orientalist that he was if his appointment had been in theology – where clerics had much more sway over appointments and practices – or if it had been anywhere other than in English-influenced Göttingen, where Münchhausen's policies included an attempt to purge the faculty of dogmatic believers and "heresy-hunters" in order for calm and concentrated research to proceed.[121] If Michaelis catalyzed a "revolution" in biblical scholarship, as his student Johann Eichhorn claimed,[122] this was a revolution enabled by Frederician tolerance and the emergence of enlightened bureaucracies, at least in some German states. The willingness of princes and bureaucrats to patronize scholars who seemed to rise above confessionalism or at least to defend their usually iconoclastic views by reference to secular history or reason, rather than by reference to orthodox doctrine, is not something seventeenth-century scholars could have counted on. But this continued, with interruptions, especially in Prussia, Hanover, and Saxony for decades to come; the calling of W. M. L. de Wette to the newly founded University of Berlin in 1810 despite his well-known theological radicalism is another case in point.[123] In seeking to move beyond confessional polemics, enlightened bureaucrats too helped to lay the foundations for the treatment of the scriptures as man-made documents, what Eichhorn would call "the Higher Criticism," and for modern oriental studies as a whole.

And, as for the appeal of "disinterestedness," this too can be explained in other ways than as colonization by other means. Not being too "interested" made one seem rather more like a gentleman, as Steven Shapin has shown for seventeenth-

---

[120] Bohlen, *Das alte Indien, mit besonderer Rücksicht auf Ägyptens*, vol. 1 (Königsberg, 1830), pp. 49–60.

[121] See Legaspi, "Reviving the Dead Letter," pp. 32–45; Münchhausen quoted ("Ketzermacher") p. 45.

[122] Eichhorn, "Johann David Michaelis," pp. 868, 877, 860–1. If there was such a revolution – which our survey of early modern Bible criticism from Simon to Semler suggests is an overstatement – Eichhorn himself helped make it a permanent one; his highly important *Introduction to the Old Testament* (5 vols., 1780–3) sought to understand the textual history of the Mosaic Pentateuch – treating it essentially as just another man-made text, and he would continue his teacher's legacy at the University of Göttingen until his death in 1827.

[123] As we will see, it was a political mistake, not a theological one that caused de Wette to be dismissed in 1820.

century English scientists; it made one's findings harder to dispute and less problematical for men of differing political or religious backgrounds to accept.[124] A stable and lasting theology, Richard Simon had already realized, would have to be founded on honest history.[125] Claiming disinterestedness also set scholars apart from the emerging business community, for whom many of the humanistic elite had nothing but contempt. Trust in the individual scholar's credibility became more important as scholarly emphasis shifted from the teaching of old truths to the discovery of new ones. But humanists, of course, were not students of Nature, but of Culture, and they could not really design experiments or technical implements which would entirely strip their pursuits of subjective factors. What they could do was to play down as much as possible inter-confessional disputes and personal rivalries to seek the best – which usually meant the oldest – possible texts upon which to perform their operations and to perfect their linguistic skills. They could also focus attention on subjects distant enough in time to be of little current political import and ancient enough to seem noble and pure. Internal academic circumstances, then, as well as enlightened challenges and romantic sensibilities, inclined orientalists to more and more critical scrutiny of primary sources and specialization in ancient languages. Here, we find the roots of full-fledged source criticism and historicism, tangled up in attempts to escape confessional strife, humanistic specialization, romantic affection for pristine ancient cultures, and the building of enlightened, proto-national bureaucracies. It was this mixture of incentives and initiatives that we find most clearly exhibited in the work of J. G. Herder, to whom we now turn.

Johann Gottfried Herder did not quite naturally consider himself a professional orientalist – not only were there few such beasts in his day, but he was formally employed as a pastor and wrote extensively on many other things. But he did read Hebrew and read it well, and kept company with those who knew other eastern languages, including most significantly J. G. Hamann. Hamann in fact deserves the title "orientalist" in spades, having studied Hebrew, Aramaic, Arabic, Armenian, Turkish, and Tibetan, but he too would probably have preferred to be called a poet or a theologian, for he pursued language study not to know about eastern cultures for their own sake, but in search of sparks of God's long-obscured revelation.[126] Herder also kept up to date in the literature, and as the decades passed, his conception of *Orient* or *Morgenland* correspondingly widened eastward. It is instructive that in his day, it was still possible for a philosopher-theologian to intervene in these debates; he was not yet really outside the circle of professional linguists, as subsequent orientalizing philosophers – such as Schopenhauer or Nietzsche – would distinctly be. Herder's work on the "folk poetry" of the ancient Israelites would have an enormous impact on the scholarly study of the Orient, and especially of the Old Testament, right through the nineteenth century and indeed has often been blamed directly or indirectly for some of its anti-Semitic

---

[124] Steven Shapin, *A Social History of Truth: Civility and Science in Seventeenth-Century England* (Chicago, 1994).

[125] Stroumsa, "Richard Simon," p. 97.

[126] Tuska Benes, "Comparative Linguistics as Ethnology: In Search of Indo-Germans in Central Asia," in *Comparative Studies of South Asia, Africa and the Middle East* 24, no. 2 (2004): 49.

tendencies. There may be something to this, but in the following section, we will seek to understand him chiefly as an eighteenth-century figure and as a Christian humanist caught between his desire to preserve the universal significance of ancient Jewish history and culture and his expanding appreciation of the pagan Orients beyond.

Herder's major works on the Old Testament stretch from about 1769 to 1783, a period in which he was greatly concerned both with folk poetry and with the integrity of the scriptures, a combination that, Dieter Gutzen has argued, led to the sacralization of the former and the secularization of the latter.[127] He was, as is well known, fascinated by young cultures – Slavic and Celtic as well as Arabic – juxtaposing them to the overly decorative and rule-bound cultures of his day. And, following Hamann, as well as Diderot, Herder rejected the notion that words could be made a transparent "reading" of the world, insisting instead that languages reflected the souls of the peoples who spoke them and that great national literatures were the means by which these souls expressed their unique forms of genius. This crucial innovation made it possible to focus on the history and national character conveyed in languages, without worrying about the extent to which each transparently rendered an external referent. Herder's claims also reiterated Hamann's enthusiasm for the earliest forms of expression, the ones closest now both to revelation and to the autonomous soul of each folk. In some ways, Herder's appreciation of early Israelite culture sprang from this same romantic affection for autonomous, unself-conscious, natural poetry; he was also, especially after his trip to France in 1769, disillusioned with rationalizing universal histories, which ran roughshod over the cultural differences Herder thought central to deep humanistic understanding.[128] Throughout his later career, Herder would write effusively about the imaginative power of many eastern cultures, criticize Eurocentric norms, and from time to time denounce imperialist expropriations.

But Herder, we must not forget, was also a committed Christian and a Lutheran pastor writing during a period of radical challenges to the faith. In the 1770s and 1780s, Herder had to come to grips with Reimarus's *Wolffenbütteler Fragmente* and with his teacher Immanuel Kant's first great work, *The Critique of Pure Reason* (1781), which "left room for faith" – but none, in Herder's view, for the magnificent variety of human culture and thought, past and present. Lengthy works such as *Älteste Urkunde des Menschengeschlechts* (1774), *Briefe, das Studium der Theologie betreffend* (1780–1), and *Vom Geist der Ebräischen Poesie* (1782–3) show that Herder felt it necessary to mount his own sort of defense of the divinity, as well as the poetry, of the Old Testament against the excessive and desiccated rationalism of some of his late enlightened contemporaries. And, though Herder's writings on India and the Islamic world would be influential for some specialists, it is his Old Testament work that would be most important in framing the discussions of the East in the decades to follow.

Herder could not leave the interpretation of the Old Testament to the philological professionals; though he respected Michaelis's scholarship, the orientalist's

---

[127] Dieter Gutzen, "Ästhetik und Kritik bei Johann Gottfried Herder," in Reventlow et al. eds., *Historische Kritik*, p. 283.

[128] Herling, *The German Gita*, pp. 47–54.

attempt to sort out the irrational and rational aspects of Hebrew Law seemed hubristic to him. For Herder, history had happened and it was not up to mere mortals to impose their judgments upon it. But like Michaelis, he realized that the battle against modern skepticism was a serious one; his generation, he claimed, was being asked to choose between a modern form of revelation typified by the natural sciences, and divine revelation, between, as he put it succinctly, "Moses and Maupertius, Fontenelle and Isaiah." The battle could only be won with hard evidence of the truth of revealed religion, and in *Älteste Urkunde des Menschen-geschlechts* (1774), he claimed to have found it. The "oldest document" here is, of course, the Old Testament; but Herder also used Anquetil's recently published Zend Avesta, as well as the Kabbalah and the Qur'an to get as close to the *ur-*revelation as possible. His argument in this little-read text is that God reveals himself to the ancient Near East first as light "all of religion and philosophy and morality clothes itself in primeval light."[129] The number 7, he also argues, appears too frequently in the oldest human documents not to be a remembrance of the Creation. For Herder, it is critical that modern readers not expect the truths of the Orient to be voiced in our language, nor should they expect that all the events reported in ancient Near Eastern documents actually occurred as reported; he fully acknowledged that much of the Old Testament's contents was "myth-ical." But for Herder this did not mean that it was not, in a higher sense, still true. "Thus, finally, the spirit of these texts is also true, for it is nothing but the spirit of the people and its history," he wrote a few years laterthe;[130] the scriptures were "true" because in them breathes the soul of the Jewish people, who were, Herder had no doubt, God's chosen people and the carriers of pre-Christian Truth.

We should pause here to underline Herder's positioning of the Jews in the context of other, to his understanding spiritually inferior, oriental cultures. God's symbolic way of speaking, he claimed, was understood by all the peoples of the East – and Herder repeatedly refers to the "Spirit [*Geist*] of the Orient," character-izing it as childlike and poetic and juxtaposing it to the overly rational and stilted *Geist* of the modern world. He concedes – and this is no minor theological matter – that the Truth had been revealed to other oriental cultures as well as to the Jews. But he explains that soon thereafter, the other cultures spun out their own partic-ular religious forms, which Herder, the great fan of diversity in language and culture, does not fail to term "ignominy and idolatry" (*Schande und Abgöt-terei*).[131] These other cultures did develop religions before Moses – but these were all forms of Gnosticism, elitist priestly wisdom cut with magic, numerology, and radical anti-materialism. The exception, of course, was the Jews – though some of this rubbed off on them too – whom God chose to retain the Word; thereby the Jews earned the hatred of the "Gnostic" others (this is Herder's explanation of the origins of anti-Semitism!).[132] The oldest trustworthy document of humankind, as Herder repeats in his *Ideen zur Philosophie der Geschichte der Menschheit*, is the

---

[129] Herder, "Älteste Urkunde," pp. 202, 450.
[130] Herder, "Briefe, das Studium der Theologie betreffend," part 1, in *SW* 10, p. 140.
[131] Ibid., p. 465.
[132] Herder, "Älteste Urkunde," pp. 468–75. For Herder, Christianity was built both by fathers who swam in the Gnostic stream and by those revolted by it. Ibid., pp. 477–80.

Old Testament; Lessing would call it humanity's "primer," its expression of truth hampered by all the limitations of such a text.[133] The other texts now coming to light may well give us a wider picture of humankind before the Fall, of what we once were and of the home to which, with the Second Coming, we will return; but they are not of equal theological, or even historical, value.

But in addition to his *historical* defense of the religious priority of the ancient Israelites, Herder also felt it necessary to defend their aesthetic achievements. Here, the argument was not so much, of course, with the proponents of the natural sciences, but with the increasingly numerous fans of the Greeks. It is by no means accidental that part one of his long essay, *Vom Geist der Ebräischen Poesie. Eine Anleitung für die Liebhaber derselben, und der ältesten Geschichte des menschlichen Geistes* (1782–3; second edition 1787), takes the form of a Platonic dialogue – or, as he himself claimed, a catechism. The argument pits a jaded, Graecophile former theology student (Alciphron, or "stout-hearted") against a clearly older and more widely educated lover of Hebrew poetry (Eutyphron, or "right-minded"). It is instructive that Eutyphron's first move is to convince Alciphron that Hebrew really is a poetic language, or was one before its degradation in the diaspora. The teacher concedes that we may find Greek more pleasing to the ear, but attributes this to familiarity, not to aesthetic superiority: "Nothing is more national and individual than what is pleasing to the ear, just like the characteristic curvatures of the organs we use to speak." Hebrew poetry "is the soul's full breath: it does not ring out like Greek, but it breathes, it lives."[134] The Greeks, in effect, cannot be beat in human terms; but the Hebrews hold the divine trump card – they speak from the soul; God is, as Hamann claimed, the *ur*-poet. The text then demonstrates in detail, interspersing scriptural passages and Herder's own Hebraicizing poetry, the power and beauty of the older biblical texts, most notably Genesis, Job, and Psalms.

Vom Geist is heavily, but not exclusively, an aesthetic text, for it also pursues a host of historical and theological issues; what does the widespread dream of an *ur*-paradise indicate (that there was one); did the Jews borrow the idea of immortality from the Egyptians (no); does the poetry of the Old Testament simply provide "an opiate for the soul" such that humans are deceived about the realities of things (of course not).[135] Herder concludes part one by addressing his friend J. G. Eichhorn's claim that the Pentateuch represents a compilation of texts, perhaps transmitted – like the Homeric poems – orally before being written down (rather than being written at one go, and exclusively by Moses). Herder assures his readers that if Genesis has multiple sources, it is nonetheless the product of one source, the Hebraic oral tradition, through which speaks the voice of God.[136]

Part two (1783) continues in rapturous praise for the beauties of Hebrew poetry – but here Herder adds an interesting and highly significant temporal set of

[133] Toshimasa Yasukata, *Lessing's Philosophy of Religion and the German Enlightenment* (Cambridge, 2002), p. 103.
[134] Herder, *Vom Geist der Ebräischen Poesie: Eine Anleitung für die Liebhaber derselben und der ältesten Geschichte des menschlichen Geistes*, part 1 in SW 11, pp. 230–2, quotations pp. 231, 2.
[135] Ibid., pp. 324, 375–7, 383–5.
[136] Ibid., p. 448.

qualifications to his picture. He segregates an early, truly childlike period – ending with Moses – from a period of pre-exilic efflorescence, lasting from Moses to the reign of Solomon, and adding finally a period of decline.[137] Naturally, much of his evidence for this chronology is drawn from the Old Testament itself; it makes sense that the Israelites would themselves label the period of exile as one of cultural decline, in which believers had to be constantly reminded of the greatness of their history and the wonders of their past civilization. It is instructive that Herder's analysis rarely extends beyond what he conceived to be the oldest part of the Old Testament, the Pentateuch, plus the book of Job, the Song of Deborah, and the Psalms. The age of the prophets is, for him, of not much interest; the simplicity and beauty of youth is gone, though he does not, as later scholars will, dwell on the desiccation of the post-Solomonic era, or separate the vital era of Moses from a period of Hebraic rigidity, during which the Law was codified.

Finally, it is important to take notice both of Herder's enlightened hermeneutics and of his ultimate desire to give God, history, and nature, rather than natural law and present-day interpreters, the upper hand. The Old Testament, he writes in his letters on theology, should be read "menschlich": "You could also certainly believe, that the more humanly (in the best sense of the word) you read the word of God, the closer you come to the goal of the Author, who created man in his own image, and treats us as humans in all the works and deeds in which he shows himself to us as God."[138] This was clearly a departure from *critica sacra*, as was his answer to those – like Hume – who found biblical miracles offensive to human reason. Herder writes: "I have nothing against the idea that one seek to render natural, what allows itself to be treated naturally." But his follow-up lines qualified this position in a critical way: "The miracles in Egypt and in the desert . . . will never be made natural, and why should they need to be? God's goal in the whole series remains clear and certain: all the miracles merely serve it. Therefore," he tells the putative recipient of his letters, "you should not worry if many circumstances or so-called knots cannot be fully explained."[139] A special sort of hermeneutics, he argues in a latter passage, must be applied to God's book:

You see, my friend, how holy these books are to me, and how much I (according to Voltaire's ridicule) am a Jew, when I read them: for should we not be Greeks and Romans, when we read [the works of] Greeks and Romans? Every book must be read in its own spirit, and so too the book of books, the Bible; and since this one contains, from the beginning to the end, the revealed spirit of God . . . we cannot do anything more perverse than to read God's texts with the spirit of Satan, that is, to embellish the oldest wisdom by invoking the most recent stupidities, [or to explain] heavenly simplicity by means of today's roguish witticisms.[140]

The proper stance, it seems, is to make enlightened reason give way when God is the one speaking. Though the later readers would be widely conversant with Herder's Old Testament texts – during the nineteenth century, *Vom Geist* stood

---

[137] Herder, *Vom Geist der Ebräischen Poesie*, part 2, in *SW* 12, pp. 1–308.
[138] Herder, "Briefe, das Studium der Theologie betreffend," p. 7.
[139] Ibid., p. 45.
[140] Ibid., pp. 143–4.

second in popularity among Herder's texts[141] – this was one of Herder's convictions that his otherwise loyal heirs among the liberal Protestant critics would largely forget.

Here we see, in condensed form, the ways in which Herder both relegates the Jews to humanity's past and uses them against his decadent age, both renders them irrational and uses them to critique western rationality in the name of a higher Truth. It is undeniable that Herder's work represents an aestheticization and historicization of Jewish history and scripture, one which, as Frank Manuel and Hans Frei claimed some years ago, would eventually make it possible to claim them irrelevant to Christian truths. Furthermore, it has been argued more recently that *Vom Geist* can be seen as part of a larger, fully historicized, Protestant project of sketching "world literature" which Herder seems to have been developing in his later years and that already by the mid-1780s he was unconcerned with establishing Hebrew's divinity or absolute primacy.[142] But Herder did not see himself as leaving behind theology for philology. In one of his last writings, he clearly put himself among Protestant, non-sectarian biblical critics who believed, in his words, that "in grammar and hermeneutics, there are no classes, no sects; only healthy reason, together with sincerity of heart, and knowledge of nature and languages, unites minds, eras, and peoples." Herder does not say the task of exegesis is over; indeed, later in the piece, he praises other exegetes, Semler and Eichhorn most notably, and suggests that Lowth and Michaelis have by no means exhausted the study of the sacred poetry of the Hebrews. The aim of learning Persian and Arabic languages, he now concludes, is not exclusively to understand the Bible, but it remains partly that too.[143] There is no need for (Protestant) theologians and philologists to part, for all "healthy exegetes" are brothers.

Thus, we might agree with H. J. Kraus, that while Herder played a crucial role in launching a certain kind of historicism, his Hebrew humanism is also to be thanked that the Old Testament was not entirely swept away in the maelstrom of late Enlightenment philosophizing.[144] It was Herder's work, for example, which W. M. L. de Wette credited with having saved him from the through-going rationalism of the University of Jena, and interested him in the "divine epic" of the human race, namely the Old Testament. De Wette's *Beiträge zur Einleitung in das Alte Testament* (two volumes, 1806–7) was deeply Herderian, insisting even more forthrightly than did Herder that the Old Testament's literal truth was unimportant, but that as Jewish folk poetry, it beautifully reflected the ancient Hebrews' worldview.[145] Herder convinced de Wette, and de Wette convinced the next generation of scholars, of the necessity of hermeneutics, of living and thinking with the people of the Old Testament.[146] In many respects, this hermeneutical tradition cut across the source critical one, allowing for a kind of sympathetic

[141] Robert Clark, *Herder: His Life and Thought* (Berkeley, CA, 1955), pp. 294–5.
[142] See, e.g., Herling, *The German Gita*, p. 56.
[143] Herder, "Morgenländische Literatur" (1804), in *SW* 24, pp. 352–6, quotations pp. 352, 356.
[144] Kraus, *Geschichte der historisch-kritischen Erforschung*, p. 176.
[145] Howard, *Religion and the Rise of Historicism*, p. 26.
[146] Kraus, *Geschichte der historisch-kritischen Erforschung*, p. 110.

understanding of the early Israelites and appreciation of the literary beauty of their texts in spite of mounting criticism of the Old Testament's irrationalities and questionable authorship. We should not forget that this tradition was still alive in the much later worlds of Julius Wellhausen and Hermann Gunkel, both of whom, though they historicized ancient Judaism, also prized its early vitality and were deeply committed to trying to think themselves into its forms. But it is also thanks largely to Herder that these sympathetic hermeneutical exercises were almost entirely restricted to Judaism's early forms and that the Hellenistic Jews, in particular, were consigned to what was thought to be an unpoetic and theologically unimportant sensibility. And it may also be thanks to Herder that this tradition was identified so powerfully with liberal, especially German Protestantism, for the way in which his orientalist humanism was structured virtually forebade its use by Catholics, or by those concerned with contemporary oriental cultures.

Imperialist hubris might have played a role in Herder's primitivist treatment of "oriental" *Geist*: but if we attend to his words, we can also see a strong strain of anticolonial sentiment and enlightened opposition to missionization. In his later work, in particular, he voices considerable animus against British colonization in India; in his 1803 preface to a new edition of Forster's *Sakuntala*, he says that "English rhyme schemes suit Indian poetry as searing-hot water acts on the sweet blooms of the Mallika, which singe and destroy them (as the English do the Hindus themselves),'" and deplores the fact that "this cultural and spiritual treasure of the most peace-loving nation of our earth" has been entrusted to "the most commerce-driven nation of the globe."[147] In an essay of 1802 entitled "Conversations about the Conversion of the Indians by Our European Christians" he is even more vehemently critical. The non-European asks hard questions of the European: now that Europe has "subjugated, robbed, plundered, and murdered" the Indians, do they want to convert them? "If someone came to your land and explained your holy of holies, laws, religion, wisdom, state organization, etc. in an arrogant manner, with the most vulgar person in mind as an audience, how would you greet him?" The European weakly responds: "This case is different. We have power, ships, wealth, cannons, culture."[148] Similarly, Herder rages against Jesuit attempts to convert the Chinese, which have resulted, reports, in the persecution of perhaps as many as 300,000 Chinese Christians. "And for how many banishments, imprisonments and beatings of converted mandarins are the foreign proselytizers guilty! And why do the converted suffer? For foreign words and customs."[149] As Bradley Herling notes, Herder does think Christianity and western ideas can be good for others if not imposed arrogantly or by force (or by Jesuits!);[150] the passage above shows that he was sensitive too to the ways in which translations can be a form of colonization and worried about Europeans' use of oriental languages for "deception and repression."

[147] Herder, "Sakontala," pp. 579, 580.
[148] Quoted in Herling, *The German Gita*, p. 261.
[149] Herder, "Unternehmungen des vergangenen Jahrhunderts zu Beförderung eines geistigen Reiches" (1802), in *SW* 24, p. 8.
[150] Herling, *The German Gita*, p. 262.

In the end, the principal aim of Herder's Old Testament work was less to downgrade the Jews than to explicate sympathetically one of humanity's richest cultural documents. Herder was less radical than his contemporary Lessing, whose *Nathan the Wise* (1779) announced the brotherhood and the equivalent truth-value of Islam, Judaism, and Christianity; but then again, Lessing was one of the most radically tolerant men of his day and the performance of his play was prohibited during his lifetime. In Herder's day, one in which pogroms still periodically occurred and vicious polemics against Jews – not to mention Muslims – still circulated widely, his Christian humanism was remarkably progressive; if it might still be argued that Herder saved the Old Testament by dejudaizing it,[151] it is rather perverse to blame this "orientalist" for later evils.

Herder's Christian quasi-universalism, however, was not what we would describe as full-on cultural relativism. If Herder maintained the poetic truthfulness of the Old Testament, like his fellow exegetes, he argued for a higher kind of truth for the New Testament: if some of its testimony might be disputable or contradictory, if the Gospels, too, were written in the language of the Orient, they nonetheless did contain a few real historical truths, namely that Jesus, the son of God, was born, lived, and died as a man.[152] Herder's 1775 essay, "Erläuterungen zum Neuen Testament aus einer neueröfneten Morgenländischen Quelle," attempts something like damage control. He admits that the images and expressions used in the New Testament were powerfully shaped by the oriental contexts in which its writers lived and that many of the words it uses are replicated in the pagan religions of the East. But the question is, he asks, what did these words mean in their context? Unlike the faithless critics Herder calls "bad naturalists and Socinians," the German pastor intends to show that terms like Christ, savior, salvation, and the son of God, meant something entirely different to the pagans than they meant to John and to the other gospel writers. Moreover, God did choose some nations to bring enlightenment and progress to the world; "in the areas as yet untouched by the Jewish and Christian revelations," he wrote, "self-actualizing human reason still lies in slumber."[153]

The New Testament did come under historicizing fire in the eighteenth century, and in Protestant, scholarly circles lost its claims to be uncorrupted by human interventions. But because it – and virtually it alone – narrates the story of the Christian savior, it remained the document Christians could not treat as just a book of historically interesting fables. For nineteenth-century liberal Protestants – who will be central to the story to follow – however, an increasing number of testimonies about the ancient Near East made it possible, and even some thought necessary, to relativize and historicize Moses and his followers; that they could do this and still remain respectable members of society reminds us that they lived in a still overwhelming Christian society, but that this Christian society was no longer that of the Augsburg Confession, but rather one trying to reconcile its scriptures with abundant and troublesome new data. The lopsided historicism these scholars

---

[151] Gérard, *L'Orient*, p. 54.

[152] See, e.g., Herder, "Briefe, das Studium der Theologie betreffend," pp. 157–66.

[153] Herder, "Erläuterungen zum Neuen Testament aus einer neueröfneten Morgenländischen Quelle" 1775, in *SW* 7, pp. 341–70, quotation p. 370.

chose contributed much to the oft-expressed nineteenth-century liberal conviction that Christianity could be saved in the modern world by jettisoning its Old Testament baggage, a conviction, as we will see, with numerous doctrinal difficulties and disastrous cultural consequences.

In the wake of *Vom Geist*, Herder began a period of deep engagement with the non-biblical East and especially with India. The *Pantheismusstreit* inspired him to think more deeply about and perhaps even to embrace a Christian form of pantheism, and to produce some rapturous passages about ancient India, perhaps even relocating Eden to the Ganges.[154] But Herder knew very well that his knowledge was fragmentary and unlikely to replace Europeans' Christian and classical cultural preferences. In light of claims that he left behind him a fully historicized world, conversant now with all the cultures of the ancient Near (and Far) East, it is worth listening to his opening remarks in Book 13 of his *Ideen zur Philosophie der Geschichte der Menschheit* (1784–5):

> With the regret of a traveler, obliged to leave a country before he learned to know it as he wished, I take leave of Asia. How little we know of it! What we do know comes from such late periods and from such dubious authorities! The eastern part of Asia has become known to us only recently through religious or political parties, and in the hands of scholars in Europe has become so confused in parts that we still see great stretches of it as a fairytale land. In the Near East and in neighboring Egypt everything from all periods appears to us as a ruin or a vanished dream; what we know from written sources we know only from the mouths of passing Greeks, who were partly too young and partly of too foreign a way of thinking to understand the deep antiquity of these states; they were only able to grasp what interested them. The archives of Babylon, Phoenicia, and Carthage are no more: Egypt was in its decline, almost before a single Greek visited its interior. Everything has been shrunk down to a few faded pages, containing fables of fables, fragments of history, a dream of the prehistorical world.

Herder then announces the subject of the next chapter, in words that make clear why we cannot presume that an age of cultural relativism is about to begin: "With Greece the morning breaks, and we joyfully sail forth to meet it."[155]

Over the course of the eighteenth century, an important reversal had begun in oriental studies; though the field was still primarily lodged in the theological faculty, and primarily still concerned with biblical exegesis, the interpretive task at hand, as Hans Frei pointed out some time ago, was increasingly to fit the biblical story into another world with another story rather than to incorporate that world into the biblical story.[156] Human history was breaking free from a chronology defined exclusively by the Old Testament – though that document remained absolutely central to orientalists' pursuits and views of the ancient past. It was already customary to accuse European theologians and travelers of making pious, ignorant, or intentional errors in the transmission of evidence and

---

[154] Herling, *The German Gita*, pp. 90–106.
[155] Herder, *Ideen zur Philosophie der Geschichte der Menschheit*, in *SW* 14, p. 90.
[156] Hans W. Frei, *The Eclipse of Biblical Narrative: A Study in Eighteenth and Nineteenth-Century Hermeneutics* (New Haven, CT, 1974), p. 130.

judgments of other peoples; but now it became increasingly possible to check western accounts against the "most ancient documents" of other civilizations and to do so in the comfort of one's own library. New vistas were opening. But unlike Frei, I do not see this as the end of the tale. For even "secularized" orientalism – insofar as Bible studies and other forms of philology had broken with *critica sacra* – still bore powerful traces of its late eighteenth century birth and carried with it numerous elements of the Christian humanist tradition. Nor would this change even when faced, in the nineteenth century's opening decades, with the challenges of combating philhellenism and philological specialization.

2

Orientalists in a Philhellenic Age

... [I]f, in the last decades, an overly one-sided and simply frivolous preoccupation with the Greeks has distanced us too much from the solemnity of the ancient world, or even from the sources of all higher truth, the totally new knowledge and appreciation of oriental antiquity is able, the more deeply we immerse ourselves in it, to lead us back to the knowledge of the divine and to that power of conviction, which first gave life to all art and all wisdom.

Friedrich Schlegel, *On the Language and Wisdom of the Indians*, 1808[1]

By dint of a curious periodization, Raymond Schwab claimed that the "Oriental Renaissance", which started with Anquetil's Zend Avesta of 1771, "marked the close of the neoclassical age just as the Classical Renaissance had marked the close of the medieval age...."[2] But those who know their German cultural history will recall that in 1771 both *Sturm und Drang* romanticism and Graecophilia were just getting underway; to go back just a bit further, 1754, the year Anquetil-Duperron went to India, was the year before J. J. Winckelmann published his epoch-making *Reflections on the Imitation of Greek Works in Painting and Sculpture* and 1791, the year in which Georg Forster published his hugely popular translation of the Sanskrit play *Sakuntala*, came two years before Friedrich Schiller's Graecophilic *Aesthetic Letters* was published. The same Goethe who wrote the *West-östlicher Divan* also worshiped the Winckelmannian Greeks; Johann Voss translated (from French) *1,001 Nights* (1781–5), turning rapidly, then, to Homer's *Odyssey*.[3] Friedrich Schlegel, who championed the "wisdom" of the Indians in 1808, had been an ardent Graecophile just a few years earlier; and, at the same time he devoted himself to Sanskrit studies, Schlegel was also writing rapturously about medieval art. Friedrich Creuzer, widely famed, and blamed, for locating the origins of classical (and Christian) myths and symbols in India, was actually a classicist who specialized in Hellenistic literature. In the romantic era it was possible, as Goethe said in another context, for "two hearts to beat in one breast"; the eclectic bibliographies of the most famous writers of the days – Goethe himself,

---

[1] Friedrich Schlegel, "Über die Sprache und Weisheit der Indier," in idem, *Kritische Friedrich-Schlegel-Ausgabe*, ed. Ernst Behler and Ursula Struc-Oppenberg, vol. 8 (Munich, 1975), pp. 315–16. Hereafter cited as *KFSA*.

[2] Schwab, *Oriental Renaissance*, p. 11.

[3] See Ernst-Peter Wieckenberg, *Johann Heinrich Voss und "Tausend und eine Nacht"* (Würzburg, 2002).

Wilhelm von Humboldt, Friedrich Novalis, and Friedrich Schelling – testify that love of the Greeks did not rule out appreciation for the East.

For eighteenth-century writers, as we saw in Chapter 1, the Orient had stronger claims when it came to questions of the origins of peoples, languages, and religions; especially after William Jones rooted the Indo-European family tree in Sanskrit, a kind of Romantic primitivism conveyed on the ancient East the exemplary virtues of purity and originality, the mythical qualities of the childhood home to which jaded Europeans ought someday to return.[4] Especially as long as one focused on the ancient world, the Orient had many virtues: simplicity, courage, charismatic leaders, and cultural autonomy. It retained its reputation for the production and consumption (sometimes in excess) of luxury goods: spices, silks, perfumes, and jewels, and it was renowned for its love poetry and its diverting tales. These positive values could be turned into negative ones, and oriental luxury and love caricatured as decadent sensuality; the power of eastern armies was often attributed to their "barbaric" manners. But the Greeks too had their negatives – pagan polytheism, homosexuality, military weakness, and all too unstable forms of democracy. A few daring eighteenth-century writers gave these features positive spins and employed them as critiques of Christianity's inhumane God, loveless European marriages, or continental tyrannies; but there were plenty of enlightened Europeans who did not particularly like the Greeks, especially before the 1790s. Even after this time, it remained hard to narrow down one's ancient exemplars and ancestors, and as long as chronological questions were not pushed too hard or made too pivotal by either side and as long as cultural institutions were flexible and decentralized enough to allow many flowers to bloom, fascinations with both the Orient and with classical antiquity (as well as interest in the early Germans or Celts) could, and did, coexist.

This chapter begins by underlining the simultaneity of eighteenth-century Germandom's oriental and neoclassical renaissances, something modern cultural historians rarely emphasize. Perhaps this is because historians have tended to focus, heretofore, simply on one field or another rather than to juxtapose the two. But recalling the mixed passions of men like Novalis and Friedrich Schelling underscores the fact that like their French and British counterparts, the German enlighteners felt they could appreciate many beauties; in fact, before theological radicals like Friedrich Schleiermacher began to suggest the dispensability of the Old Testament and partisan philhellenes like Friedrich Wolf began to suggest that humanness was bound up with achievements in the secular arts, it probably did not occur to German humanists that one could appreciate the ancient world without appreciating the Orient. Before intense specialization set in, it was possible for men like C. G. Heyne or Friedrich Schlegel to make contributions to classical and orientalist scholarship; and when this era ended, rather abruptly, in the 1820s, it stranded many a poet and many a scholar on new, and to their minds, rather barren beaches.

---

[4] Thomas Trautmann describes this era in his *Aryans and British India* (Berkeley, CA, 1997) as one of "Indomania," whose duration, however, was rather short, giving way by the 1820s to "Indophobia."

One reason for the simultaneity of these renaissances was that those who undertook the serious study of languages and cultural histories in the eighteenth century were, socially and culturally speaking, virtually interchangeable. They tended to be well-educated, middle-class, and politically liberalish men – though there were probably many more women active in these circles than were know about at present. Practitioners and consumers of works on classical antiquity and on oriental subjects (excluding the more conservative biblical exegetes) seem to have been similarly attuned to archetypical late Enlightenment themes – the nobility of the savage, the primeval unity of all religions, the stupidity of superstition, and the bungling and dogmatism of the clergy. Moreover, most of these figures knew one another, studied with the same teachers, and read the same highbrow periodicals; a large number were even related by marriage. Thanks to the founding of journals such as the *Göttingische Gelehrte Anzeigen* and the *Allgemeine Deutsche Literaturzeitung* in the second half of the eighteenth century, the idea-sharing function of the early modern epistolary "republic of letters" was being widened, letting intellectuals across the German landscape know what they should be reading and which new directions scholarship, art, literature, and philosophy were likely to take (and which booksellers or lending libraries might have the right texts). But the scholarly world was still very small and access to its treasures limited to a handful of readers, something we will contrast to developments later in the century.

But perhaps an even more compelling reason for the "two hearts" phenomena was that studies of the ancient world, whether classical or oriental, were born from common humanistic and Christian roots, and during the eighteenth century had been reshaped by common supra-confessional and rationalizing drives. Encouraged by enlightened rulers and bureaucrats, the intellectual elite began to dream of spiritual and cultural renewal, over and against the landed aristocracy, Frenchified Baroque culture, and the orthodox clergy. Many of their hopes lay in some form of German national rebirth, whether conceived in cultural or political terms, and many looked to ancient models to shape a new Germanic destiny. A quite remarkable contingent of young scholars – including the brothers Grimm, Humboldt, and Schlegel – were captured by Herder's work on folk poetry and sought in the rewriting of universal cultural history a narrative that would explain and validate German-Christian culture's world-historical mission in the present.[5] These universal histories could not do without the Orient, because Christian and Neoplatonic ideas and texts were still so fundamental to these teleologies and because they all held, in one way or another, to the idea of a primeval, universal revelation, shared language, and common Eden, a garden to which humankind ought eventually to return (at a higher level of consciousness).[6]

The German romantics became some of the Orient's biggest champions in the period between about 1800 and 1820 – in addition to the wide-ranging studies of Josef Görres, K. L. Windischmann, and Friedrich Creuzer, a relatively large

---

[5] On Bunsen's youthful plans, see John Edward Toews, *Becoming Historical: Cultural Reformation and Public Memory in Early Nineteenth-Century Berlin* (New York, 2004), pp. 69–71.

[6] This is M. H. Abrams's argument in his classic study of romanticism, *Natural Supernaturalism Tradition and Revolution in Romantic Literature* (New York, 1971).

number of intensive studies of oriental languages, texts, landscapes, and myths were launched. But they did not invest this new energy in the East for altruistic or purely scholarly reasons. Rather, they found useful for their own purposes the Orient's traditional associations with the origins of humankind, language, and culture, with spirituality, mystery, and sensuality, with magical, iconoclastic, and esoteric forms of wisdom. Drawing deeply on Baroque universal history and Renaissance perennial philosophy, romantic orientalism was shot through with Christian messianic and German nationalist longings; if it was supposed to produce universals, its ideals and symbols were constructed from European perspectives and based largely (as Herder himself had noted) on Greek texts – and it had primarily domestic, not international, cultural, religious, and political ambitions.

Their romantics' efforts were bolstered by the evolution of new kinds of state patronage, much of which was linked to the extension of European influence – diplomatic, economic, and political – in the East. This was happening of course not only in Central Europe, where Maria Theresa established an Oriental Academy to train *Sprachknaben* for the Ottoman diplomatic service in 1754, but also in France, where the Convention founded the *École des langues orientales vivantes* in 1795, to replace a less exalted dragoman training school. Would-be British orientalists could now engage in on-the-ground research in India, thanks to the East India Company (EIC). State patronage for travel, as we saw in Chapter 1, was now available, and some, like the scholars and painters who traveled to Egypt with Napoleon, jumped at the chance to venture out on the state's (or in this case, the army's) dime. For Germans, the expanding Russian empire offered an especially attractive place to work.[7] Whether or not scholars bought into state objectives, bureaucratic backing made it less risky and more financially attractive for students of the East to go more places, extract more stuff, and ask a wider range of questions.

New institutions – the joint product of the rise of secular nation-states and of the opening of the age of high imperialism – offered new opportunities, and over the course of this chapter, we will see how the world of specialized oriental studies evolved in the period between about 1810 and 1870. We should not, however, overemphasize the parity of classical and oriental passions in this era or fail to note some important aspects of romantic orientalism, which were critical in shaping the career trajectories of German orientalists in the longer run. If interest in Egypt and ancient India was keen, affection for East Asians and modern Persians was scant. There was too much residual hatred for the Turks, resentment toward the Jews, and indifference toward all the other cultures of the East to ground an orientophilia that would have resembled Winckelmannian philhellenism; it is even harder to imagine young Germans volunteering to fight for Egyptian independence from the Ottoman Empire, as many did for the Greeks. And we should recall that alongside and interwoven with the evolution of orientalist passions and institutions there were other cultural developments underway, developments such as the creation of the classicizing Gymnasium, the post-1819 return to conservative paternalism, and the rise of a new canon of scientificness, all of which made

---

[7] See Bahodir Sidikov, *"Eine unermessliche Region": Deutsche Bilder und Zerrbilder von Mittelasien (1852–1914)* (Berlin, 2003) for examples.

romantic, universalist speculation less and less respectable by the mid-1820s. The list of new orientalist institutions and opportunities above sounds impressive – but if we put developments here in the context of the more general explosion of jobs, organizations, patronage sources, and publications for non-theological scholars (and especially for classicists) after 1810, it becomes clear that the mixed passions of the romantics did not lead to post-romantic institutional parity.

It is hard to guess how the direct involvement of the German states in the colonial race at this early date might have affected German orientalism. It might have heightened interest in the contemporary Orient, and it might have shifted the institutional basis for the Orient's investigation from the universities to other, more utilitarian, sorts of state institutions. For several decades, the German world relied on the citizens of other imperial regimes to learn modern languages and extract texts for them, something that put the Germans behind in the development of non-biblical oriental studies. In 1815, A. W. Schlegel still thought founding a chair in Indian languages and literatures in the German-speaking world was premature, as the Germans had neither Sanskrit manuscripts nor a large corpus of missionary reports to work from (not to mention, which Schelgel did not, the lack of German colonial presence in the East).[8] The *Deutsche Morgenländische Gesellschaft* was founded only in 1845 and its *Zeitschrift* two years later. Collections of oriental artifacts were almost unknown before the 1850s. But already by this time, the Germans had become the world's leading orientalists. As Theodor Benfey noted of Indology in 1869, much of the great progress made in German *Orientalistik* between 1820 and 1870 was made despite scanty collections and meager travel funds for scholars;[9] and he might have added, despite Germany's continued colonial abstinence. But this abstinence did shape the kind of oriental studies German scholars developed, allowing older romantic interests in folk poetry, ancient religions, originary languages, and universal revelations to form the enduring core of scientific inquiry.

Finally, there is another cultural-political contingency that shaped German oriental studies in its formative years, and that is, ironically, the inability, or unwillingness, of Central European states to control the spread of radical religious ideas. Had the Protestant churches been able to contain the spread of the Higher Criticism or to exert more power over university appointments, the text-threshing power of philological-historical criticism might have been broken and oriental studies might have been sidelined entirely. But the churches failed. Thanks to the support of enlightened bureaucrats, scholars in many German Protestant territories found it relatively easy to evade doctrinal discipline imposed by clerical officials; indeed, the radical opinions theology professors at German universities were able to voice after the 1770s often struck outside observers as scandalous. Their radicalism was both philosophical (à la Schleiermacher) and exegetical (à la de Wette), but for our purposes, the exegetes are the more interesting, as they were

---

[8] Schlegel quoted in Herling, *The German Gita*, pp. 168–9, quotation p. 168. Indeed, German libraries had no Sanskrit manuscripts until the late 1820s, and in 1840, the University of Berlin library still owned only thirty-one manuscripts.

[9] Benfey, *Geschichte der Sprachwissenschaft und orientalischen Philologie in Deutschland* (Munich, 1869), p. 418; on manuscript collections, ibid., pp. 686, 396–7.

the ones who insisted on the need to understand the scriptures in their original forms and contexts, something that entailed training students to read ancient oriental languages. Not surprisingly, then, the new orientalist centers grew up in places where Protestant liberal theology was strong, such as Göttingen, Bonn, Berlin, and Tübingen, and not in Munich, Vienna, and Cologne, and the development of oriental studies continued to be interwoven with liberal Protestant attempts to make biblical study scientific. In 1853, the German-born secretary of the Société Asiatique, Jules Mohl, credited the progress of oriental studies in the Germanies not just to the Humboldtian reorganization of its universities, but especially to "the learned education which the clergy receives there,"[10] and indeed German orientalists for decades continued to be trained as theologians – but by no means as orthodox preachers or believers.

In tracking the passage of ideas, institutions, and scholarly practices from the romantic to the positivist age, this chapter seeks to illuminate the affective, intellectual, and institutional forces which shaped the lives and careers of nineteenth-century German orientalists. The opening sections focus on the works of two key romantic philosopher-scholars, Friedrich Schlegel and Friedrich Creuzer, whose studies of the West's linguistic and religious debts to the East laid the foundations for the pursuit of *Orientalistik* right through the nineteenth century. But, as we demonstrate, these romantic histories also provoked intense reactions from those who wished to retreat from such grand – and some said, mystical and reactionary – worldviews in favor of more secure research projects and less universalist cultural models. Modern German orientalism was a product both of romantic visions and of the post-romantic narrowing and professionalizing tactics taken to make the field conform to an evolving academic world, one in which theology was increasingly giving way to a new master discipline, philology, and in which classical scholars increasingly defined what counted as *Wissenschaft* and, even more, as *Bildung*. Thus, a chapter, which begins in the high romantic realm of Friedrich Schlegel's master text *Über die Sprache und Weisheit der Inder* concludes with an intensive set of discussions of the challenges facing orientalism in the philhellenic and positivistic age, and the ways in which the discipline tried to come to grips with the brave new institutional and cultural world of the 1820s–1870s. Chapter 3 covers essentially the same time span, from about 1820 to 1870, but focuses on the individual fields, and on the individual scholars, who chose to devote their working lives not to what Schlegel in our epigraph called the "one-sided and frivolous preoccupation with the Greeks," but instead to "the still totally unknown territory" of oriental antiquity.

FRIEDRICH SCHLEGEL: RENAISSANCE AND REVELATION

In the 1790s, Friedrich Schlegel was a classicist and a Graecophile; a decade later, he was still a philhellene, but the Greeks had to share space in his heart with the medieval Germans and the ancient Indians. Schlegel's passions are important not

---

[10] Mohl, "Année 1852–3," *Vingt-Sept Ans d'Histoire des Études Orientales: Rapports faits à la Société Asiatique de Paris de 1840 à 1867*, vol. 2 (1854–1867) (London, 2003; reprint of Paris 1880 edition), p. 478. Hereafter cited as Mohl, *Rapports*.

only because the timing of their onsets tells us a great deal about the intellectual worlds in which he traveled but also because they left so powerful a legacy for the orientalists who followed him. We can specify even further the context for Schlegel's critical text, *Über die Sprache und Weisheit der Inder* (1808): it came on the downslope of Schlegel's Indomania, as the poet-philosopher began to move toward the Catholic conversion he underwent just days before the publication of the text. Precise timing explains a great deal about the content of this compli- cated and multi-directional text – and about the ways his contemporaries reacted to it.[11] We will need to understand Schlegel's *Sprache und Weisheit* from at least three angles, corresponding to the text's three major sections; firstly, as a contri- bution to the methods and prejudices of *Orientalistik*; secondly, as a contribution to debates about the origins of religion and a defense of Christianity's historical truth against Kantian rationalism; and thirdly, as an attempt to decenter the Greeks in the interests of promoting a Germanic, Christian cultural history of humankind. Only then can we see clearly what kind of foundations Schlegel laid for the study of the Orient in general and India in particular.

Schlegel's quite sudden embrace of the Orient at the century's turn was born just as the poet was despairing of his self-appointed mission of becoming the Winckelmann of Greek literature – and coming under the influence of some new acquaintances and friends. One of these was Friedrich Majer, a student of Herder, who began to offer courses about Indian philosophy at Jena in 1796. Another important instigator, for Schlegel, was his friend Friedrich Novalis, for whom the Orient represented a lost, organic "golden age," in juxtaposition, espe- cially to the fallen, mechanistic present. Schlegel was bowled over by *Sakuntala* and may have read English translations of other Indian texts. But René Gérard is right; no set of eighteenth-century texts or translations explains the romantic passion for the East that caught fire so suddenly around 1800; Neoplatonic phi- losophy and Renaissance Hermeticism had never really died, and both the libertine and the occultist traditions almost inevitably inclined esoteric inquirers toward the Orient.[12] Once Schlegel had begun to despair of idealism and natural philosophy as keys to the new religion and mythology he longed to create, for a person of his milieu and his increasingly anti-revolutionary sentiments, the path eastward was virtually irresistible.[13] But it is instructive that Schlegel, at this historical juncture, chose India – and not Egypt, China, or Judea – to represent oriental wisdom; generalize as they might, for Schlegel, as for all other Europeans of his class, all Orients were not created equal.

During the years Schlegel was working toward *Sprache und Weisheit*, British Indomania was at its peak – and, having supposedly purged itself of corrupt officials, the EIC had begun to make new conquests.[14] Schlegel drew heavily on English expertise; his Sanskrit teacher was a British naval officer, Alexander

---

[11] For more specifics, see Figueria, *Translating the Orient*, pp. 206–8. Also Herling, *The German Gita*, pp. 129–63.

[12] Gérard, *L'Orient*, pp. 76–85, quotation p. 82.

[13] On the romantic quest for a new mythology and its collapse, see Williamson, *Longing for Myth in Germany*, pp. 56–71.

[14] See Nicholas B. Dirks, *The Scandal of Empire: India and the Creation of Imperial Britain* (Cam- bridge, MA, 2006).

Hamilton, who had been caught in Paris at the renewed outbreak of war in 1802 and put to work cataloging Sanskrit manuscripts at the Bibliothèque Nationale. But Friedrich Schlegel and his brother August Wilhelm also had a rather ambivalent relationship to the "actuality" of empire, for their elder brother, Karl August, who had gone to India as a soldier in the EIC's employ, had died of disease in Madras in 1789. It is possible, as Bradley Herling has suggested, that this traumatic event deeply shaped the Schlegel brothers' fascination with India, sharpening their need to understand this distant and dangerous world.[15] Moreover, it was not the actuality of empire that inclined Friedrich away from things Persian and toward things Indian; instead, he was enraptured by ancient India, which promised to hold deeper, darker secrets than an Islamicized Persia.[16] Schlegel was also attracted to India because, despite conquests by European traders and Mughal emperors, India seemed not to have broken with its ancient spiritual and poetic traditions as the Persians more clearly had. As a true cultural revolution, in Schlegel's view, could only be generated from a spiritually unified cultural matrix, India was the right place to seek the sources for an "Oriental Renaissance."

Aside from Hamilton, the Schlegels too largely received their British learning through French mediators and during a period in which French universalism and rationalism seemed to be triumphing; eager for reform, the brothers knew that the collapse of Central Europe's old regimes offered exciting new spiritual and cultural opportunities, but also worried that particularities, ancient customs, and spiritual depth were being lost. In the years just after 1800, Friedrich was particularly concerned about hyper-rationalism and mechanical thinking, and like many other romantics, began to blame Kant and the high Enlightenment for Europe's fragmentation and loss of cultural continuity. Even the ancient Greeks, before their Hellenistic makeover, seemed to be too purely rational. In this context, India appeared the proper antidote to an alienated, rootless, materialistic West.

Combined with Schlegel's interest in India, it should be noted, was a perhaps even more powerful interest in the medieval world, and in the use of "primitive" styles as a means of reviving German poetry. When he went to Paris in 1802, he spent the first months absorbed in medieval poetry and painting and enraptured by Gothic architecture.[17] In the German Middle Ages, in particular, he found the persistence of stable hierarchies, folk traditions, and a spiritual message still in touch with primeval revelation; he would, interestingly, find many of the same cultural attributes in ancient India. But we should recall that Schlegel was – like most romantics – very serious about poetry, and it was surely also the high repute of Persian and Sanskrit poetry in his day that led him into the study of these languages. Indeed, at least at the outset, his objective in studying Sanskrit seems to have been to learn the rhyming patterns of the *Sakuntala* in order to create a new, direct German translation of this extremely popular play. At one point during his studies, Schlegel announced his desire to produce a chrestomathy, or an easy-to-read anthology for beginners, based on *Sakuntala* and a couple of other texts already in circulation; and the selection of Sanskrit poetry in translation he

[15] Herling, *The German Gita*, pp. 130, 117.
[16] Gérard, *L'Orient*, pp. 89–90.
[17] Ibid., pp. 87–8.

appended to his longer philosophical text would prove the most popular part of his *Sprache und Weisheit*.[18] In the end, Schlegel did not want to conquer India or to help rule it; he simply wanted to consume it intellectually, to see what richness it might add to European culture and then move on to new passions. He did not devote himself to India exclusively or for very long – but he did try to read its poetry and its "scriptures" in their original form, and in doing so, left his mark.

In spite of its primarily poetic and philosophical aims, Schlegel's essay, subtitled *Beitrag zur Begründung der Altertumskunde*, helped to guide the methods, goals, and one might say the self-conceptions of non-biblical *Orientalistik* for decades to come. Most important were the opening chapters on language. Here Schlegel modified William Jones's claims, arguing that Greek, Latin, and related Europeans languages were not just *related* to Sanskrit, but were in fact *descendent* from Sanskrit. Without giving these languages a collective name, Schlegel did divide them off from other language "families," including the group Jones called "Arabian" languages (Arabic, Hebrew, and Egyptian). But Schlegel's next move was more innovative and consequential, and that was the dividing up of all languages into two groups, those with inflection and those with affixes. The line he drew, importantly, cut right across the collective term "oriental", which others sometimes used to designate non-classical and non-Christian languages, dividing what Schlegel's heirs would call "Indo-European" or "Indo-German" languages from what would become conventionally referred to as "Semitic" languages. Though he claimed not to be raising one group above another ("Who would be able to deny the high art, the [great] worth and the sublime power of the Arabic and Hebrew languages?"[19]), it was quite clear that he was making an argument for the superior poetic and philosophical qualities of the inflected languages. Languages that lacked inflection, he claimed, were barren and uncreative;

only something like a heap of atoms, which the winds of chance can easily drive apart or push back together; the relationship [between them] is nothing but a purely mechanical one made by external attaching. These languages lack in their original form a germ from which life can unfold; the derivations always remain lacking, and when afterwards their artificiality has increased so much because of the appending of more and more affixes, the difficulty of achieving true, simple beauty and lightness is exacerbated even more. What appears to be richness is in fact poverty....[20]

Schlegel did not take the next step and argue for the static and inflexible racial characters of speakers of affixative languages; as a good romantic, he believed in the *ur*-unity of humankind, as well as in the great civilizations' inevitable decline and fall. As is abundantly clear in another essay of 1808, he shared William Jones's "Mosaic ethnology," believing that the story of language's diversification could be reconciled with the Old Testament account.[21] But Schlegel, unlike his eighteenth-century predecessors, was not really interested in using this history to

[18] Ursula Struc-Oppenberg, "Einleitung," (for "Über die Sprache und Weisheit der Indier") in *KFSA* 8: cxciii–cxcv.

[19] Schlegel. "Sprache und Weisheit," p. 163.

[20] Ibid., p. 159.

[21] Friedrich Schlegel, "Friedrich Leopold Graf zu Stolberg, 1808," in *KFSA* 8: 101–3.

uncover the origins of language as such – he was interested in pursuing comparative grammar for the sake of reconstructing historical relations between post-diluvial peoples, and of understanding, exclusively, it turned out, the history of those who spoke the inflected languages. This is what made his work useful for those who wanted to employ philological methods to understand *European* origins, and what made it deceptive as a means for plumbing *human* prehistory.

What made grammatical developments interesting and valuable to Schlegel was that they could fill in historical blanks, accounting for the movements of peoples for whom no documents survived. This was one way to write the history of each *Volk*, perhaps correcting speculation or accounts written exclusively by the conquerors. Another way to write this history, Schlegel noted, was to use racial features – though he thought race was a much more slippery form of evidence. Another narrative, he argued, might hinge on human use of metals.[22] We should pause to note the – from our point of view – admirable and not-so-admirable aspects of this endeavor. On the one hand, Schlegel was looking for firm evidence to tell the histories of peoples otherwise left off the record; on the other hand, he was laying the foundations for a sort of exclusionary philology in which the speakers of Sanskrit and its Indo-European spin-off languages are credited with all humankind's great achievements. It took both of these elements, a scholarly raison d'être and a means to pander to nationalist pride, to get comparative philology off the ground.

For Franz Bopp, the real founder of comparative linguistics, Schlegel's first chapters were of monumental importance. But for Schlegel himself, what was at stake in elaborating the grammar and defending the wisdom of the Indians was something much more than the foundations for a paltry academic field. The romantic poet-philosopher had in view a grand vision for cultural renewal, the reuniting of poetry, religion, science, and philosophy. The point of the second part of Schlegel's text, the portion which tackles the "wisdom" of the Indians, is not to suggest that the mythology and philosophy of India, as far as it was known in his day, was particularly admirable; Schlegel himself observed that much of its content was grotesque, confusing, and – it is essential to follow his logic here – wrong (only the Christians got it right). From an *ur*-monotheism, Indian religion had fallen into pantheism, one that only dimly betrayed signs of its primeval purity. Most of Indian history and culture displayed this degenerate pantheism. What was crucial to Schlegel were India's earliest texts, such as the *Laws of Manu* (available to him in William Jones's 1794 translation), which he believed bore signs that the writers still remembered something of the truth divulged to humankind in some kind of primeval revelation. The ancient Indian ideas of emanation and of the transmigration of souls suggested some understanding of immortality; the unique standing of the god Brahma in the *Laws of Manu* seemed to suggest an original monotheism: "... seen as the natural evolution of reason," he writes, "the Indian system of emanation is thoroughly unintelligible; as misunderstood revelation, everything in it is completely comprehensible."[23] The idea of an *ur*-revelation was one, as we have seen, entertained both by Jesuit missionaries and by

---

[22] Schlegel, "Sprache und Weisheit," pp. 265–71.

[23] Ibid., pp. 203–5, quotation p. 207.

Neoplatonic and Hermetic philosophers, and it might be argued that Schlegel here belongs less to the world of Bopp than to that of Pico della Mirandola.

But Schlegel's engagement with Indian religious beliefs clearly had contemporary opponents in mind. Linked to the European nations by language and probably also by blood – remember, Jones's model already invoked genealogical descent – mythologies descendent from Indian forms (Greek, Celtic, Germanic, Slavic, and Roman) carried with them too sparks from this divine torch, which were never fully extinguished. Indeed, he argued all ancient oriental – as well as European medieval – wisdom rested on divine miracles and revelation; the latter offered far better grounds for a real moral philosophy than did modern pantheism, which he clearly identified with "the system of pure reason." Pure reason, he claimed simply ruled the Eternal ["Unendlich"] out of bounds and sucked everything up into "reason-wisdom." "... [T]hus [the question] needs no further pursuing and researching; everything which is known or believed by other means is merely error, trickery and weak understanding, thus is all change and all life an empty illusion."[24] The critical part for oriental wisdom to play in the modern world, then, was to answer Kantian rationalism with an *historical* defense of religion in all its non-rational, sublime diversity.

As this suggests, Schlegel was a long way from being a modern historian of religion, committed to giving all faiths their due; the separation of truth from error, he insists, "surely no one will find outside of Christianity, which alone gives us access to truth and knowledge that is higher than all of reason's erudition and delusions."[25] He had given up neither the basic historicity of the Old Testament nor his strong prejudice in favor of the ancient Hebrews; of all the peoples who received the *ur*-revelation, he argues, they were the only ones to preserve the pure truth, while all the others, even the highly cultivated Indians and Persians, corrupted it. Appreciating these developments, Schlegel claims, should make critics appreciate the Hebrew prophets' strictness and isolation from others. Similarly, Schlegel was no relativist as concerns cultural or aesthetic achievements; ancient Greece remained for him an ideal moment torn out of human time. But he did fear that the Greek "lotus flower" had induced men to forget the deeper source of art, knowledge, light, and life: religion. It is one-sided and dangerously frivolous, he argues, for Hellas to provide the *only* norms for Germandom's cultural development in the future.[26] Remarkably, Schlegel already in 1808 saw the projected "oriental Renaissance" as a means to redress Graecophilia, a fetish he had shared, but now felt distracted his contemporaries from deeper spiritual truths. Schlegel's Indians were to be an answer both to Kantian rationalism and to Winckelmannian aestheticism in the name of *ur*-Christian Truth; they were not to be imitated or even admired in and for themselves.

The aim of the final section of *Sprache und Weisheit der Indier* – titled "On Oriental and Indian Studies, in General, and their Value and Purpose" – is to try to stop a scholarly train Schlegel fears has already left the station. Part of the problem

[24] Ibid., p. 243.
[25] Ibid., pp. 297–9; quotation p. 301.
[26] Ibid., pp. 315–16.

with cultural history today, he argues, stems from the growing tendency to divide classical from oriental studies:

One presupposition, which in this matter has been of great harm and continues to do harm, is the separation between oriental and Greek studies and [the Greek and oriental] mind; [this] is increasingly concocted and arbitrarily applied, as if this grand difference had foundations in reality. In the history of humankind the inhabitants of Asia and the Europeans are to be seen as members of one family, whose history ought never to be divided, if one wants to understand the whole.

He then, perceptively, denounces his contemporaries' tendency to create caricatures of the "Orient" based on only a few texts: "But what in the literature is commonly referred to as oriental style and spirit is based only on a few Asiatic peoples, especially on the Arabs and Persians, and on a handful of passages of the Old Testament, insofar as they can be considered poetry; for the other peoples, [these descriptions] do not fit at all."[27] The cure, he thinks, lies not only in the appreciation of oriental diversity but also in returning to the universalistic erudition of the fifteenth and sixteenth centuries when linguistic prowess was combined with historical knowledge and deep studies of philosophy; too often nowadays, he laments, "mere knowledge of languages gives one the right to the title of scholar."[28] What Schlegel could not foresee in 1808 was that his model of erudition, though still academically viable for a few more years, was doomed, and his would be one of the last attempts to save it.

There is one final point to be made. In attempting to save this Christian universalist model of scholarship, Schlegel hitched it to another, in 1808 highly pressing, bit of business: the now vigorous search for a "German" collective history and national identity. His text alludes numerous times to the import of oriental studies for illuminating "our" prehistory, meaning the prehistory of the Germanic tribes. He links the German language backward through Latin and Greek to Persian and Sanskrit and suggests a common home for Japhet's sons in northern India – though he does not dare to date the departure of the *Germanen* from their second Eden or even really to sketch their trek after passing the Caucasus (did they prefer mountains or riverbanks?).[29] Schlegel was not the first to seek a Germanic *Urheimat*, and his search was undertaken less in the service of understanding one race or linguistic group than in understanding a portion of the history of humankind. As we have seen, his whole argument rests on the presumption of a primeval, universal revelation; as is clear especially in his other works, the ancient Hebrews, not the Indians or the Germans, are the one incomparable people, for they alone had the willpower to preserve the divine spark offered to all.[30] But Schlegel's essay, which devoted little attention to the descendants of Shem and less to those of Ham, more clearly than any works of Herder or William Jones,

[27] Ibid., p. 311.
[28] Ibid., p. 309. Schlegel here is probably taking a shot at the linguistically-oriented classicist Gottfried Herrmann.
[29] See, e.g., Schlegel, "Sprache und Weisheit," p. 293.
[30] He reiterates this view as late as 1828. See his lectures: "Philosophie der Geschichte," in *KFSA* 9: 114.

offers the foundations for an exclusionary prehistory, and for a major division *within* oriental studies, which would have a long and tragic history.

Friedrich Schlegel's essay was widely circulated and read, but for his contemporaries, it could not be understood outside the context of his simultaneous conversion to Catholicism. Such a move by a well-known and widely admired cosmopolitan intellectual at a time that Prussian fortunes were at their nadir created a sensation. Heady with hope for a post-sectarian future – and perhaps an Austrian-dominated "big" Germany –Schlegel announced his conversion and called on all confessions to end sectarian strife as a means to salvage the cultural unity of the Holy Roman Empire in the wake of Napoleon's ravages. "The noble German nation, suffering so long from internal division, must not be totally destroyed in spirit, and must rather finally achieve a united, inner peace and a unified outlook [Gesinnung]."[31] But of course the German Confederation was not made up exclusively of Catholics – and among these, liberals were hardly a majority.[32] The moment in which Schlegelian universalism came to the fore, inspiring and inspired by works by Friedrich Graf zu Stolberg, Joseph Görres, and René de Chateaubriand, would prove intense and passionate, but, in the end, brief.

For there were also Protestants, as well as Kantian rationalists and Graecophiles, who reacted powerfully to Schlegel's *Sprache und Weisheit* – and for them, his simultaneous conversion also mattered deeply. As Bradley Herling argues, Schlegel's text made so central an issue of Indian pantheism – and compared it so obviously to Deism and Kantian idealism – that he rekindled the decades-old *Pantheismusstreit*. Philosophers and scholars who liked Spinoza, the Greeks, or Kantian rationalism all found Schlegel's text offensive and they used his conversion as a convenient means to condemn the essay to the philosophical rubbish bin. Goethe, for example, dismissed *Sprache und Weisheit* simply as veiled Catholic apologetics. Even A. W. Schlegel, who may well have shared Friedrich's belief in an Indian *ur*-revelation, would focus, in subsequent years, on linguistic issues rather than the big, provocative theological and philosophical questions his brother had raised; but the philhellene rationalist Johannes Voss called him a "mystical Pope-worshiper" nonetheless. Perhaps Hegel would not have been so scathing about India's "flower religion" and degenerate art had Friedrich Schlegel, and after him, Friedrich Schelling, not lavished so much attention on it.[33] This assault took its toll, and in the next generation, Indologists would allow the associations Schlegel created between India, romantic anti-Kantianism, and Catholicism to lapse, but both for linguistic and for political reasons, the link he forged between Germanic and Indian ancestry would, regrettably, endure.

---

[31] Friedrich Schlegel, "Friedrich Graf zu Stolberg," p. 87.

[32] The "liberalism" of these Catholics is moreover open to question. In his excellent chapter on the Creuzer *Streit* George Williamson shows that the orientalism of men like Creuzer and Görres ultimately played into the hands of the reaction. See Williamson, *Longing*, pp. 121–50.

[33] Herling, *The German Gita*, pp. 151–3, 172–83, 223–4, quotation p. 199.

ORIENTALISM AND CLASSICISM IN THE WAKE
OF THE CREUZER *STREIT*

As suggested in his chapter's opening pages, Friedrich Schlegel was by no means
the only intellectual of his day to gravitate eastward. In the period between about
1800 and 1820, there were numerous German publications on matters oriental;
writers clustered especially in Heidelberg, but there were also German scholars or
orientalizing poets in Vienna, Berlin, St. Petersburg, Paris, and Göttingen. There
were travel accounts and anthropological disquisitions; there were histories of
philosophy and a bumper crop of inquiries into the history of mythology, which
opened the way for investigations of such favorite romantic subjects as folkloric
legends, epic poetry, golden ages, pagan gods, natural religions, and the hidden
meaning of symbols. As in the case of Friedrich Schlegel, interest in the East arose
remarkably quickly; Schelling perhaps saw similarities between his work and that
of the Greek mysteries as early as 1802, but only in 1805–6 did he decide this pre-
rational Greece had oriental origins.[34] As his *Bruno* (1802) suggests, Schelling too
came to his iconoclastic conclusions by way of the Neoplatonic, western images of
the mystical and wise East, rather than by reading eastern texts directly. Christian
Bunsen may have learned *Mythenforschung* from the elderly Heyne, but he took
his ardent devotion to Sanskrit and Persian from Friedrich Schlegel; by 1814,
Bunsen was determined to integrate the study of these oriental languages into
German culture so thoroughly that "even the devil would not be able to tear it
out!"[35] The romantic geographer Carl Ritter leaned heavily on William Jones and
Friedrich Creuzer, but his remarkable *Die Vorhalle europäischer Völkergeschichten vor Herodotus* (1819) fleshed out an *ur*-Indian diffusionary history that
was even more ambitious than were their models. We will come back to Ritter in
Chapter 3; suffice it to note here how quickly late romantic universalists adopted
the writing of diffusionist histories, which located both human and cultural
origins in India and the Near East, and how shallow a foundation in authentic
nonwestern text these histories had.

For the history of German orientalism, the most influential product of this
vein – after Schlegel's *Sprache und Weisheit* – was the four-volume *Symbolik
und Mythologie der alten Völker* (1810–12), a massive study of the origins and
development of the West's myths and symbols, published by the iconoclastic
classicist Friedrich Creuzer. Or perhaps it was ultimately the German Protestant,
classicizing *reaction* to Creuzer's insistence on the oriental origins of those symbols and myths, which would exert the longest lasting effects. Indeed, the outcome
of this *Streit* was hugely influential, for German orientalists and classicists alike,
and strong echoes of it can be heard in the 1890s, in the 1920s, and even in the
Black Athena debate of recent years. The genesis of the book is telling and underscores the intertwined nature of Greek and oriental renaissances; as Creuzer told
his friend Friedrich von Savigny, the project evolved naturally out of his work
on Greek historiography (not clearly separated in Creuzer's mind or in the
current literature from mythography); as Creuzer described the project in 1808, it

---

[34] Gérard, *L'Orient*, pp. 212–13.
[35] Letter, Bunsen to Becker, March 6, 1814, quoted in Toews, *Becoming Historical*, p. 71.

was "an explanation of the most ancient philosophy and history of the Greeks and the sources that are relevant to this, and also an accentuation of one branch of philosophy and mythology that has up to now been neglected."[36]

What was "neglected" of course was the Orient, something Creuzer felt he knew a great deal about, ironically, because of his deep immersion in late Greek literature. Creuzer was a classicist, but he did not like Winckelmannian philhellenism, which seemed to him a kind of aesthetic hedonism, bound up with dangerous forms of political radicalism.[37] The Greeks Creuzer loved were not Socrates, Thucydides, and Phideas, but Iamblichus, Pausanias, Plotinus, and Strabo, scholars who wrote in times of relative Greek insecurity vis-à-vis the Orient and who not only appreciated their debts to the East but also, however dimly, realized that the perfect clarity of their Olympian culture was in some sense superficial compared to the mysterious profundity of their eastern neighbors.[38] Creuzer used these sources heavily in the *Symbolik*, splicing them with heavy doses of Herodotus, known for his philo-orientalism. Creuzer also knew much of the seventeenth- and eighteenth-century literature on comparative religion and was surely aware of its tendencies to iconoclasm, anti-clericalism, and libertinage, tendencies he himself shared. He openly cited C. R. Dupuis's twelve-volume *Origine de tous les cultes* (1795), a hugely popular survey of the history of priestly deceptions – though Creuzer turned Dupuis's anti-clerical claims upside down, turning his opiates, as it were, into culture-historical evidence. Interestingly, though the Heidelberg professor had read Anquetil's Zend Avesta (in German translation) and some of the new texts produced by the English Indologists, when Creuzer said "Orient," he mostly meant ancient Egypt whose primeval wisdom and originality he cherished. In the end, of course, he far preferred Greek art, philosophy, and literature to that produced by the East; but then again, in his view, no real lover of the Greeks – especially those of the Hellenistic age – could have failed to understand Greece's debts to or even dependence upon the East.

From his self-critical western sources, Creuzer learned that the history of ancient achievements was not simply a Greek story; there were universal truths to be found. One of those, he thought, was that humankind was not originally barbaric and nature worshiping, as his contemporary Christoph Meiners had argued; instead, as Anquetil's work had shown, monotheism was the original form of spirituality, and polytheism was a degenerate later development. It was this subject, Creuzer later claimed, that brought him into contact with romantic philosophers and poets. This was not a question that would go away; in fact, the subject of religion's primeval origins is one that continued to fascinate philosophers, philologists, and anthropologists for more than a century to follow.[39] But

---

[36] Creuzer to Savigny, January 29, 1808, in *George Friedrich Creuzer, Briefe Friedrich Creuzers an Savigny (1799–1850)*, ed. Hellfried Dahlmann (Berlin, 1972), p. 229.

[37] Eva Kociszky, " 'Khalepa ta kala': Das Konzept und die Rolle des Orients in Creuzers Werk im Vergleich zu Görres," in *200 Jahre Heidelberger Romantik*, ed. Friedrich Strack (Berlin, 2008), pp. 302–6.

[38] Creuzer, *Symbolik und Mythologie der alten Völker, besonders der Griechen*, vol. 1 (Leipzig, 1810), pp. xi–xv.

[39] Creuzer, *Aus dem Leben eines alten Professors* (Heidelberg, 1840), p. 364; Suzanne Marchand, "The Counter-Reformation in Austrian Ethnology," in *Worldly Provincialism: German Anthropology in the Age of Empire*, ed. Glenn Penny and Matti Bunzl (Ann Arbor, MI, 2003), pp. 283–316.

Creuzer was also a product of his age and its aspirations; like Friedrich Schlegel, he was seeking a supra-confessional history of religion, and his combination of Neoplatonic sources and romantic ideas allowed him to craft a story of the western migration of myths and symbols, mysterious puzzles created by a small elite, who hoped to transfer true knowledge only to those intellectuals suited to understand it. That Creuzer's argument dealt centrally with the Eleusinian mysteries, perhaps the most irrational, mystical, and overtly sexual aspect of the Greek cultural tradition, was certainly noted by his audience, which included liberal Protestant classicists as well as Catholic romantics; that it challenged F. A. Wolf's conception of scientific philology as well as Winckelmann's sharp divide between Greek and Egyptian cultures gave the text even more polemical valence. It is also instructive that Creuzer permitted his student Franz Josef Mone to add two additional volumes to the second edition of the *Symbolik* in 1819–23; these volumes traced the evolution of German prehistorical symbols and mythology. This was clearly a Schlegelian means to hitch the Orient to Germanic history and to make both seem more relevant to modern cultural life than was the study of the strange and short-lived world of the ancient Athenians.

Creuzer entered the debate about the origins of religion, myths, and symbols at a critical moment, one in which a question of central importance (for Europeans) was being directly and indirectly debated as the Catholic church attempted to recover from the revolutionary era: did European culture rest on religious foundations, or not? Some eighteenth-century historians had already claimed that Europe's cultural achievements had nothing to do with Christianity; Edward Gibbon famously had suggested that Christianity had actually destroyed much of what was great in Europe's classical heritage. But now, on the continent, the stakes were even higher: as Napoleon's armies occupied more and more of Europe, seizing church property and scattering clergy, those who had chafed under the churches' restrictions began to see secularism as the means to ground a more progressive, liberal society, and classical antiquity as an alternative foundation for European culture. In this context, for political and economic liberal nationalists, and for classicists and modern historians, it made sense to bracket or trivialize religion as a factor in European cultural history – and to see those who continued to defend its importance as handmaidens of the Pope and the old regimes.

Creuzer's attack on classical prejudices, then, was about more than whether one preferred Greek or oriental poetry; like Schlegel's *Sprache und Weisheit*, Creuzer's *Symbolik* argued for the central importance of the unfolding of Christianity in human history; told teleologically, this narrative required the linking together of eastern and western cultural developments. Even more than Schlegel's text, Creuzer's *Symbolik* was indebted to Neoplatonism and to the work of Dupuis and other libertines, from whom the Heidelberg professor took the narrative of the westward passage of eastern esoteric knowledge and the understanding of erotic forms as symbols for mystical wisdom. The East, Creuzer thought, deserved to be considered the fount of civilization; he considered its literature, religions, and arts extremely ancient and the source for classical and Egyptian cults and for modern moral truths. To this more or less conventional Neoplatonic trajectory, Creuzer added something else, applicable especially to the study of art, and that was a contrast between the "translatable" language of Greek art and the ever mysterious or "untranslatable" symbolism of eastern art, the purpose of which was to incite the spectator to meditate on the infinite and to warn the viewer that profound truths lie beyond the sensuous realm. This opened the way, as Partha Mitter has argued, for Hegel's insight that since art represented not reality but some ideal of it, different cultures might have different ideals, and ultimately, much later, for Heinrich Zimmer's contrast between the seductive but superficial beauty of the Greeks and the more profound religious aims of Indian forms.[40]

Creuzer did create a following, inspiring romantic and religious thinkers from many fields; mythology was a subject keenly pursued by philosophers at the time, but also a crucial one for classicists, theologians, and historians, for as Creuzer well knew, myths comprised much of the earliest testimony cultures offered about themselves. Herder had offered the cultural secularizers a way out, and after 1810, many philologists and philosophers took it, insisting on interpreting myths as pure products of the national poetic imaginary and discounting the importance of borrowed or imposed customs, fables, and beliefs. Theologians like F. C. Baur resisted and followed Creuzer, insisting instead on a universal diffusionary history with its roots in the Orient. In his own two-volume *Symbolik und Mythologie* of 1824–5, Baur argued that world history was at once "a revelation of the divine (*der Gottheit*)" and "the evolution of Consciousness," and neither of these processes had begun in Europe. Using Creuzer, Genesis, and the Zend Avesta, Baur traced the formation of the first mythologies back to a "primeval seat" [*Ursiz*] in "the Edenic highlands of Central Asia" between the Jaxartes and the Oxus, Tigris and Euphrates rivers.[41] Stressing the similarities between religious ideas across cultures, Baur readily admitted Europe's dependence on the Orient for its population and "a great portion of its culture." This also allowed him to lay the foundations for what he believed to be a scientific history of religious one philosophy, one which would put the evolution of Christianity into proper perspective – without compromising its unique truth.[42]

Rather more idiosyncratically, the geographer Carl Ritter published a Creuzerian study of Europe's peoples before Herodotus in which he suggested that the true source of religious ideas and of "civilization's seeds" was not Egypt or South Asia but northern India.[43] Here, all had shared a Buddha cult, one that included "a common belief in a single, highest God, a God of peace, and a belief in immortality, together with many dogmas, priestly teachings and priestly institutions,

---

[40] Mitter, *Much Maligned Monsters*, pp. 203–8; on Zimmer, see Marchand, "Philhellenism and the Furor orientalis," in *Modern Intellectual History* 1, no. 3 (Nov. 2004): 331–3. As it happens, Hegel turned this possibility for cultural relativism into a means of denouncing the Indian "spirit" (lacking in objectivity and barbarically sensuous) and Indian art (baroque, wild, formless, and repulsive).

[41] Baur, *Symbolik und Mythologie, oder die Naturreligion des Alterthums*, vol. 1 (Stuttgart, 1824), pp. v, 223; following Genesis 2:10–14, Baur situates Eden between four rivers. He also notes that the inhabitants of his area, the Medes, were also called the "Arier" by Herodotus, p. 223.

[42] Ibid., pp. 236, vi–viii.

[43] Carl Ritter, *Die Vorhalle europäischer Völkergeschichten vor Herodotus, um den Kaukasus und an den Gestaden des Pontus: Eine Abhandlung zur Alterthumskunde* (Berlin, 1820), p. 33.

such as reincarnation, rebirth, the Flood, the final salvation....."[44] Religious
sectarianism, however, had forced a Babel-like dispersal of this culture, provoking
the wandering of Indian priests throughout Europe and Central Asia; they brought
the Buddha cult with them, laying the foundations for a shared Graeco-oriental
mythology – and also clearly laying the foundations for a later, Judeo-Christian
revelation. Drawing heavily on Creuzer, as well as on the latter's beloved late
Greek sources, Ritter explicitly sought to decenter a Roman view of Europe's
prehistory by substituting one that insisted upon a shared primeval monotheism
and the "common roots" of the ancient Thracians, Germanic tribes, Indians,
Greeks, Scythians, and Persians.[45] It was this debate, which called forth Karl
Otfried Müller's *Prolegomena zu einer wissenschaftliche Mythologie* (1825),
which attacked comparativism and speculation about the preliterate past, effectively warning "scientific" scholars against interpretations of Greek myths, which
sought origins or explanations beyond Greek borders.

George Williamson has elegantly sketched the wider cultural background
against which Protestant liberals like Müller began to think Creuzer's work not
only philologically flawed, but politically dangerous.[46] The formation of the Holy
Alliance in 1815 and the issuing of the Carlsbad Decrees in 1819 convinced liberal
Germans that their governments were beating a hasty, conservative retreat. Metternich's opposition to the Greek War of Independence after 1821 enraged philhellenes as well as some Christians, and increased liberal hatred of both "oriental"
and domestic despotism. In this era, Heinrich Heine denounced the Schlegels'
work on India because it smacked of Catholic mysticism; Goethe praised one of
Creuzer's opponents, Gottfried Hermann, by calling him: "critical, Hellenic, and
patriotic" – precisely what Creuzer's work, in the eyes of the increasingly powerful
liberal Protestant classicists, was not.[47] Instead, critics argued that Creuzer's book
gave succor to "Romish" priests, conservative Christian mysticism, and dilettantes. Johann Voss, translator of the Homeric epics, led the charge against
Creuzer, calling him "an agent of the Jesuits" and deploring his sinking of the
ideal Greeks into the sexual swamp of the Orient. In an 1821 letter to his friend
Joseph von Hammer-Purgstall, Creuzer described the vehemence of Voss's
polemics, for him comparable to the condemnation of Giordano Bruno by the
Inquisition: "You must read Voss's review of the *Symbolik* to learn how entirely
misguided and crazy we are to believe that before Homer and in addition to
this great hero, there were actually other people in the world. Yes, we must be
burnt, along with all others who think anything of the Orient, and of Moses,
Zoroaster, Buddha and whatever else the liars are called. We are mystagogues and

---

[44] Ibid., p. 32.
[45] Ibid., pp. iv, 23. Clearly here, the language families articulated by Friedrich Schlegel are being
   articulated as ethnic groups as well. See the section on Ritter in Chapter 3.
[46] There are interesting parallels here to the way James Mill read romantic orientalism in Britain. See
   Majeed, *Ungoverned Imaginings*, pp. 123–200.
[47] Williamson, *Longing for Myth*, pp. 137–50; quotation p. 137. On Heine, John Pizer, "Heine's
   Unique Relationship to Goethe's Weltliteratur Paradigm," in *Heine-Jahrbuch* 41 (2002):
   26–7.

seducers of the young. In a word, we should renounce the devil and embrace Voss's *Mythologische Briefe* as the book of books."[48]

In the pivotal years of the early 1820s, it was unclear who would win the *Streit*. Creuzer could boast influential admirers, including Hegel, Hammer-Purgstall, Friedrich von Savigny, and Friedrich Schlegel. Jacob Grimm was persuaded, but thought Creuzer overargued his case, and hoped the controversy would force him to strengthen his claims.[49] But gradually, the anti-Creuzerians gained the upper hand; Voss drew in the rationalist theologian H. E. G. Paulus, and then, by April 1824, after Voss's violent polemic, the *Antisymbolik*, began to appear, more and more professors quietly began to take Voss's side. In November, key members of the Prussian Academy of Sciences, including Friedrich Schleiermacher, officially declared their support for Voss and Creuzer suspected that Georg Niebuhr too had joined the antis. By 1826, Goethe told a friend that he could not be nice about "the Symbolikers" – they were fundamentally "anti-classicists and have contributed nothing positive to art and antiquity ... yes, they have thoroughly damaged that which I, in my own way, have promoted."[50] In 1829, another critic, August Lobeck, ridiculed Creuzer's treatment of the Greek mysteries so voluminously (his two-volume book exceeded 2,000 pages) that respectable academics did not dare to raise the subject again until the fin de siècle.[51] Creuzer felt he and his allies were being "persecuted" (*verfolgt*), but refrained from rejoining the attack. In an 1825 letter to his friend Friedrich von Savigny, he lamented the narrowing of the concept of "classical philology" he had witnessed: "Philology, especially in Germany," he wrote dejectedly, "no longer partakes of the larger perspectives on scholarly inquiry as a whole."[52] Theologians and orientalists too narrowed their fields of vision. F. C. Baur forsook the writing of comparative mythological studies in favor of writing narrowly focused studies of the early Christian churches; Carl Ritter wrote no more speculative prologues. Even Franz Bopp, who was a Catholic, gave up his youthful affection for Creuzerism in exchange for a highly technical and outsider-unfriendly form of linguistics; despite the progress he made in Sanskrit studies, he was still frequently ridiculed by the classicists, who, he claimed, believed the study of anything but Greek to be a sin against scholarly criticism.[53] Creuzer's quest to give Neoplatonic mythography a scientific basis had failed.

---

[48] Creuzer to Hammer-Purgstall, December 3, 1821, in Joseph Freiherr von Hammer-Purgstall, *Erinnerungen aus meinem Leben, 1774–1852* (Vienna, 1940), p. 543.

[49] Grimm quoted in Creuzer to Savigny, May 15, 1821, in *Briefe Creuzers an Savigny*, pp. 335–6, n. 8.

[50] Johann Wolfgang von Goethe, *Gedenkausgabe der Werke, Briefe und Gespräche*, vol. xxi, *Briefe der Jahre 1814–1832*, ed. Ernst Beutler (Zürich, 1951); Goethe to Karl Friedrich von Reinhard, May 12, 1826, p. 686.

[51] Lobeck, *Aglaophamos sive de theologiae mysticae Graecorum causis libri tres*, 2 vols. (Königsberg, 1829); on the study of mystery cults, see Marchand, "From Liberalism to Neoromanticism: Albrecht Dieterich, Richard Reitzenstein and the Religious Turn in Fin de Siècle German Classical Studies," in *Out of Arcadia* (British Institute of Classical Studies Supplement, 79, 2003), ed. Martin Ruehl and Ingo Gildenhard (London, 2003): 133–4.

[52] Creuzer to Savigny, August 17, 1825, in *Briefe Creuzers an Savigny*, p. 351.

[53] See the section titled "Positivism and the Origins of the Aryan-Semitic Divide" in Chapter 3.

TO BE A GERMAN ORIENTALIST, 1820–1870

During the years of the *Streit*, the German states, led by Prussia, were undergoing cultural overhaul based on ideals championed by Kant, F. A. Wolf, and Wilhelm von Humboldt, all of whom envisioned the world of higher learning as one led by the philosophical, and not the theological, faculty. As Cultural Minister in 1809–10, at a time that the scholar-diplomat was entranced by the ancient Greeks, Humboldt was especially influential. By the 1820s, the educational institutions he promoted to central prominence, the philosophical faculty of the University of Berlin, the *Gymnasien*, the Academy of Sciences, and the Altes Museum, were all giving special attention to classical languages and cultures and promoting the idea that the imitation of the rational, secular, masculine, and above all beautiful Greeks was the means to German cultural greatness.[54] The aristocratic, secular, aestheticized wisdom of the Greeks became the basis for *Bildung*; the knowledge of Latin and Greek was understood to be the sine qua non of the educated man. Though Humboldt himself found reading the Bhagavad Gita in the late 1820s an earthshaking experience, this experience came too late to have much impact on Prussian institutions, and neither he, nor anyone else, suggested making Indian wisdom or Hebrew poetry the basis for the modern German educational system.

As universal history gave way to "scientific" history, treatments of oriental origins by non-orientalists – as in Creuzer's *Symbolik* or Hegel's *Philosophy of History* – were increasingly frowned upon. In the 1820s, Leopold von Ranke could still be counted among the orientalists on the strength of his work on Ottoman history in the Venetian archives, despite knowing no oriental languages. In this decade, Ranke did devote extensive attention in his lectures on world history to the early eastern empires, but by 1833, he had cut his "oriental" coverage back considerably. He did not lecture at all on ancient history between 1834 and 1848, and when he returned to the subject, he bracketed the Indians and Chinese, whose chronologies he now called fanciful, dismissed the use of ethnographic inferences to reconstruct early cultures, and played down the usefulness of comparative linguistics to historical studies.[55] Disappointed by the small splash made by his history of the Hellenistic world, J. G. Droysen too gave up writing about the Near East after 1843 in favor of producing Prussophilic modern histories. If the defections of men like Ranke and Droysen gave orientalists hegemony in interpreting Asian cultures, this also enabled classicists and European specialist to dismiss the question of Eastern origins; Greece, every Gymnasium boy's specialty, now became the conventional starting point for histories of art, science, and philosophy.[56] This allowed a host of historians of philosophy, for example, to sidestep the genetic questions that had absorbed western philosophers since Hellenistic times as J. F. Fries claimed in 1837: "Our history of philosophy can only be

---

[54] See Anthony La Vopa's careful deconstruction of the motives behind this change; La Vopa, "Specialists against Specialization: Hellenism as Professional Ideology in German Classical Studies," in *German Professions, 1800–1950*, ed. Geoffrey Cocks and Konrad H. Jarausch (New York, 1990), pp. 27–45.

[55] Ernst Schulin, *Die weltgeschichtliche Erfassung des Orients bei Hegel und Ranke* (Göttingen, 1958), pp. 155–79.

[56] See Halbfass, *India and Europe*, pp. 148–59; Marchand, *Down from Olympus*, pp. 46–7.

the Greco-Roman-Christian one. We know neither the time of formation nor any kind of history about other, Asian philosophemes. Moreover, the simple beginnings of Greek philosophy, which developed from mythology, makes it unimportant for our purpose to ask whether this mythology did or did not have a foreign origin...."[57]

Speculating about origins, in general, was out; that was one of the central lessons of the Creuzer Affair and it was not lost on most members of the next generation, classicists and orientalists alike. Of course, there were some, like Friedrich Rückert, a student of Creuzer, for whom this was impossible; even before learning oriental languages, he had seen in Hammer-Purgstall's translation of Hafiz "sparks of authentic religious poetry" and continued to believe that:

> Poetry in all its tongues
> To the initiated is but one language.[58]

Rückert, thanks to having learned his languages and adapted himself, at least in part, to the new scientific culture, was able to hold his head up among the specialists and did write a significant number of scholarly papers and book reviews. Other notable romantic Indophiles like Friedrich Schlegel were largely ignored by the philological community, who increasingly found them embarrassing. Schlegel and Hammer-Purgstall, Rückert's son Heinrich wrote in 1866, "are now both antiquated in the eyes of scholarship," the latter now appearing at best "as one of its subordinate servants ... who are only fit to serve up the raw material to the masses...."[59]

Citing the founding of the first chairs in *Germanistik* and Sanskrit in 1812 and 1818, respectively, scholars of the post-romantic period often claim that the period saw the development of a full-on cultural relativism, a historicism that truly made (as Ranke claimed) all nations equally close to God. But those who lived through the period knew very well that this was not the case, and Ranke notwithstanding, by the mid-1820s, within the world of *Wissenschaft*, the playing field the orientalists and classicists shared was anything but level. The classicists were quick to specialize and secularize their field, a set of maneuvers that meant avoiding, as much as possible, Hellenistic, Byzantine, and modern Greek texts and questions about Christianity's debts to the ancient world. Defining their rigorous attention to Greek texts as pure science, they ridiculed those who retained older polyhistorical erudition and aspirations. In the early modern period, oriental philologists had pioneered many of these text-critical skills, but nineteenth-century orientalists almost by definition could not concentrate on one language; nor could they secularize their field with equal alacrity. Creuzerian searches for oriental origins were abandoned in favor of pursuing subjects that one could research in the original language of the sources, which meant, for most, Greek or Romanones, and scholars began to feel the need – surely informed by the Greek War of Independence

---

[57] Quoted in Halbfass, *India and Europe*, p. 152.

[58] Rückert quoted in Andrea Fuchs-Sumiyoshi, *Orientalismus in der deutschen Literatur* (Hildesheim, 1984), pp. 107, 108.

[59] Heinrich Rückert, "Friedrich Rückert als Gelehrter" [1866], in *Friedrich Rückert im Spiegel seiner Zeitgenossen und der Nachwelt*, ed. Wolfdieterich Fischer (Wiesbaden, 1988), p. 209.

as well as by Hegelian conceptions of history – to emphasize Greek cultural autonomy. By the 1830s, with the exception of a few archaeologists, Ernest Renan recalled, scholars had all united in defending "the originality of Greek mythology against M. Creuzer. All agreed in rejecting that blasphemy, that Greece was ever a province of Asia, that the Greek spirit, so free, so objective, so limpid, could contain any element of the vague and obscure spirit of the Orient."[60] Of course, this was something of an overstatement; Creuzer's work continued to have a powerful underground effect and would later be reborn. But change was clearly underway – with consequences the next sections will try to illuminate.

THE LONG ROAD TO *WISSENSCHAFTLICHKEIT*

John Toews has recently described the period between about 1815 and 1840 as one in which the intellectual pacesetters were chiefly liberals inspired by the experience of German national unity in 1813, but chastened by Metternichian reaction; dreaming of grand universals, they settled for the gradual achievement of lesser goals.[61] Assessing the modest diligence of this generation's scholars, a man close to their values, Lord Acton, wrote: "By extreme patience and self-control, by seeking neither premature result nor personal reward, by sacrificing the present to the far-off future, by the obscure heroism of many devoted lives, they looked to prepare the foundation of the kingdom of knowledge."[62] Both Toews and Acton emphasize the scaling back of this generation's ambitions, the giving way of romantic, pantheistic faith in the workings of the spirit in favor of focusing on how things actually happened in the past. The post-romantic era was one that preferred facts to systems and feared that conjectures would undermine the legitimacy of those who did seek truth.[63] This was an age of specialists and one in which classicists, in particular, were able to convince the bureaucracy and the well-heeled public that focusing on the languages and cultures of the ancient world was the proper way to train the mind and enrich German cultural output. It was the period in which the foundations were laid for modern German cultural institutions and the scholarly practices and norms set for most of the modern disciplines, including *Orientalistik*. And its reverberations can still be felt, down to the present day.

By focusing on the complicated motivations and diverse personalities that characterized "the obscure heroism" of this era, the remaining sections of this chapter seek to restore richness and contingency to the practice of oriental studies in the early nineteenth century by emphasizing, again, the field's rootedness in the traditions of Christian humanism and informed evangelization. Facing new pressures and opportunities, orientalists in the early nineteenth century revised these

---

[60] Ernest Renan, "Des religions de l'antiquité et de leurs deniers historiens," in *Revue des deux Mondes* 23, no. 2 (1853): 835.

[61] Toews, *Becoming Historical*, pp. xix–xx.

[62] Lord Acton, "German Schools of History," in *The English Historical Review* 1, no. 1 (Jan. 1886): 27.

[63] "In history, everything must be proved," wrote Julius Klaproth in 1826, "and suppositions are almost on the same level as errors ...," Klaproth, *Mémoires relatifs à l'Asie, contenant des recherches historiques, géographiques, et philologiques sur les peuples de l'Orient*, vol. 1 (Paris, 1826), pp. 396, 411, 413.

traditions in the hopes of finding patrons and obtaining scholarly respectability as an era of reactionary governance and academic specialization set in. New institutional structures offered some people – especially Protestant men – many more choices and opportunities; others, women, Jews, and many Catholics, were left out in the non-*Wissenschaftlich* cold. The kind of orientalism made in this era was heavily made by male Protestants, and was peculiar to those who came of age between about 1820 and 1870; their scholarly practices need to be understood neither as pure fact-finding nor as pure power-seeking, but as the product of their attempts to define what it meant – in the post-Napoleonic world – to be the Europeans whose job it was to understand the Orient.

In what follows, I will refer to this mid-century generation's methodological-epistemological stance as positivist historicism or simply as positivism. I am well aware that there are many definitions of positivism and that a strict, Comtean one (according to which theology is left behind when society enters the "scientific" stage) does not meet our needs; but we do need some shorthand to describe this post-romantic, fact-seeking, theory-adverse stance. For our purposes, positivism represents the belief that only those facts which have been produced through the strict application of scientific methods (here, usually philological ones) constitute real knowledge, and the conviction that adding a brick to the edifice of knowledge is a sufficiently satisfying goal of scholarly endeavor. Philological positivists did not ask why writers had written as they did or (usually) decide whether or not what was said was true or false; they did not feel the need to admire or to agree with the sentiments expressed in their texts, but simply to emend, translate, decipher, or annotate them correctly. Critics often ridicule positivism's fact-fetishism; but we should also note its fruitfulness, for these fact-seekers produced many of the foundational grammars, lexicons, and translations still used in oriental studies today, doing so in ways that, for better and worse, effaced their subjective intervention.

As Acton's characterization suggests, this positivist-historicist orientation was the response of a rather modest generation, one not yet fully willing or able to break with its old chronologies and beliefs or its classical and biblical sources, but cognizant that this would probably happen in time; and it was a response shaped by the essentially liberal presumption that all well-intentioned and appropriately trained inquirers will ultimately agree on the same truths. It was clearly a reaction to the overweening ambitions of the romantics – and the dangers their systems posed to enlightened political, religious, and scientific ideals. This generation did not want to dream; rather, it wanted to make itself uncontroversial and to draw too few conclusions rather than say too much.

But positivist historicism was also the product of domestic religious contexts. In the 1820s, the post-Napoleonic Restoration states were seeking to shore up political authority by enforcing religious orthodoxy; in Prussia, Friedrich Wilhelm III insisted on unifying Lutheran and Calvinist churches and designating the Prussian sovereign *summus episcopus*. At the same time, in the now vastly enlarged Prussian state, the upper classes were swept by a Pietist longing to return to the original teachings of the Reformation and to purify Protestant belief.[64] In this context,

---

[64] Warren Breckman, *Marx, the Young Hegelians, and the Origins of Radical Social Theory* (Cambridge, 1999), pp. 44–6.

pursuing Higher Criticism – at least for Protestants – was relatively unproblemat-
ical, especially if one kept quiet about politics. W. M. L. de Wette made the
mistake that proved this rule; while his radical Old Testament criticism earned
him a job at the newly created University of Berlin in 1810, de Wette was fired in
1819 after Prussian authorities confiscated a letter in which he seemed to condone
the murder of August Kotzebue.[65]

Indeed, the Higher Criticism's appeal for Protestant scholars in this era was
that it claimed that scripture too could be tested and verified; unsatisfied with his
arguments about poetic truth, Herder's successors wanted to know exactly which
parts of the scriptures could stand up to "scientific" tests, believing, perhaps
naively, that good scholarship could never really endanger faith. As Peter von
Bohlen wrote in his 1835 commentary on Genesis, "[Christianity] is not founded,
we should hope, on so insecure a basis, that it must stand or fall with the mythology of the Jews; and a popular teacher, we may add, will always be able to
extract some religion and moral meaning even from a popular fiction."[66] The
important thing was to know all the facts; the individual would then have a secure
basis on which to base his or her faith. This stance made it possible to claim that
theology was not dilettantish preaching or wily deception, but science, of the most
profound sort.

To understand the evolving cultural profile of nineteenth-century German orientalism, it is crucial that we appreciate how much it was already, by the 1820s,
bound up with the Higher Criticism, something that allied it not only with Protestant forms of belief but with radical or at least liberal forms of Protestantism. As
Richard Simon's early efforts showed, the Catholic church would not tolerate
Higher Criticism; for that matter, orthodox Protestants and Jews too condemned
it. The Jews and Catholics did not really need it; not bound by "scripture alone,"
they could clarify meaning or emend textual errors with commentaries or encyc-
licals or by reference to tradition. Protestants, however, could not do these things
and thus saving the faith for those not content with orthodox blandishments
turned out to be the same thing as making the text clear, credible, and authoritative. In the process, something one could call orientalist-liberal Protestant syn-
ergy (or less charitably codependency) was created, and the older tradition of
critica sacra reformulated to suit nineteenth-century needs. Not surprisingly, a
very large number of the early "scientific" orientalists were trained initially as
theologians at the notorious Tübingen Stift, which produced, in the high romantic
years, Hegel, Schelling, and Hölderlin; and many orientalists, even those trained
elsewhere, shared with these often philosophically radical theologians a commitment to purifying the scriptures. Shared concerns led to cross-disciplinary
exchanges of ideas and information. In fact, the way in which oriental studies
made itself scientific in the Germanies was so strongly marked by this Protestant
purification project that more than virtually any other field, it became identifiable
as culturally Protestant and its practitioners inclined to adopt the stance that came
to be known as *Kulturprotestantismus*.

---

[65] See Thomas Howard, *Religion and the Rise of Historicism*, pp. 7ff.
[66] Bohlen, *Die Genesis historisch-kritisch erläutert* (Königsberg, 1835), p. 27.

Kulturprotestantismus was a middle-class conviction which embraced sober scholarship and artistic achievement as the truest expressions of faith; it drew strength from the irenic and semi-meritocratic belief that scholarship or art should succeed without appealing openly to coreligionists, who were presumably already on one's side. It was usually coupled with the certainty that secular teachers rather than clerics were best suited to further the interests of ethical self-formation.[67] Naturally, this meant that those who did wear their convictions on their sleeves – especially evangelical Christians, Catholics, and Jews – were accused of producing unscientific polemics. Indeed, after the Creuzer *Streit*, Protestant orientalists rarely cited contemporary Catholic scholarship, and Catholics increasingly pursued their own lines of inquiry in specifically Catholic institutions. Similarly, until very late in the century, Jewish scholars who did not convert remained ensconced in separate rabbinical schools and published their work in specifically Jewish journals.

Kulturprotestantismus made possible the purely secular public stances of Egyptologist Richard Lepsius, for example, who left all the charitable and religious work to his wife, and of Sinologist Ferdinand von Richthofen, whose dining room walls, his favorite student Sven Hedin was shocked to find, were covered with murals of the last supper, the apostles, and Maria and baby Jesus.[68] It made possible the favoring of Johannes Gildemeister for a Sanskrit chair in Berlin because he had helped to expose the "Holy Coat of Trier" as a forgery and Catholic swindle.[69] But it also meant that there was some opening of the academy's door to outsiders willing to adopt *Kulturprotestantismus*'s worldview; trained in seminaries, or at home, by fathers who were rabbis, Jews already had a leg up in a discipline that valued Hebrew skills so highly and were probably more esteemed in this discipline than in any other of the time.[70] Conversion was still necessary for full acceptance, but it is a mark of some progress that former Catholics like Franz Bopp could be accepted into Prussian scholarly institutions and assimilated Jews like Gustav Weil and Theodor Benfey could get jobs, albeit after long waits.[71]

The intense pursuit of textual purity and the ecumenical, historicist commitments of *Kulturprotestantismus* helped to give German orientalism a unique and

---

[67] On *Kulturprotestantismus* in the century's second half, see Gangolf Hübinger, *Kulturprotestantismus und Politik: Zum Verhältnis von Liberalismus und Protestantismus im wilhelmischen Deutschland* (Tübingen, 1994), pp. 7–17.

[68] M. Rainer Lepsius, "Richard Lepsius und seine Familie. Bildungsbürgertum und Wissenschaft," in *Karl Richard Lepsius (1810–1884)*, ed. Elke Freier and Walter F. Reineke (Berlin, 1988), p. 54; Sven Hedin, *Meister und Schuler: Ferdinand Freiherr von Richthofen an Sven Hedin* (Berlin, 1933), p. 14.

[69] Ulrich Sieg, *Deutschlands Prophet: Paul de Lagarde und die Ursprünge des modernen Antisemitismus* (Munich, 2007), p. 84.

[70] In some respects, this was simply a continuation of traditional Hebraist practice. Heinrich Ewald, Franz Delitzsch, and Hermann Strack all worked with Jewish scholars in the hope of improving their understanding of the texts; faithful Christians, however, these men also hoped to convert Jews, and were certainly capable of making derogatory remarks about Jews, Jewish scholarship, and Judaism as a whole.

[71] Benfey's wait was very long indeed; it took him twenty years after finishing his studies to receive an *Extraordinariat*, which he occurred in that liberal year 1848, and another 14 to obtain a chair – not surprisingly, at the University of Göttingen. See Pascale Rabault-Feuerhahn, *L'archive des origines: Sanskrit, philologie, anthropologie dans l'Allemagne du XIXe siècle* (Paris, 2008), pp. 296–7.

lasting shape. This was a tradition much different from that of the French; in France, orientalist scholarship in the revolutionary and Napoleonic eras was largely agnostic and laid the foundations for an increasingly anthropological understanding of religious communities. English and Dutch academic orientalism might have followed the German Protestant model more closely – but these nations' involvement in actual colonial rule in the East expanded the numbers and types of non-academic scholars working on secular, modern subjects.[72] We have much more to learn about Russian oriental studies, but these endeavors seem to have been almost wholly related to empire-building and with little connection to theology. The German tradition was imbued with exegetical aims and with suppressed romantic longings, both of which made German scholars ill-suited to apply their knowledge to the real-existing Orient. German orientalists, A.W. Schlegel claimed in 1819, were not suited to be missionaries or colonizers: "... on the other hand, they are all the more ideally suited to appreciate the world-historical, philological and philosophical insights the study of Indian monuments can offer. For the kinds of research that sharpen the eye for these sorts of perspectives on the unknown, prehistorical world are already deeply rooted in Germany, and foreign scholars cannot even imagine many of the concepts which the Germans already thoroughly comprehend."[73]

What the foreigners could not imagine – according to Schlegel – was that German devotion to the study of the treasures of the ancient oriental world could possibly be so serious, without being in any obvious way, useful. But as Schlegel well knew, it was also going to be hard to sell his own culture on the idea that Indology was a respectable and necessary science. Overt praising of pagans had to be avoided; that was clear. Some orientalists could still be useful as exegetes. But what about those whose work – like Schlegel's – was taking them away from Hebrew antiquity as well? They clearly would not fit in even the more radical Protestant theological faculties, and, lacking jobs in the colonies or private wealth, would need to find a home in university philosophical faculties where they could enjoy the patronage of enlightened state bureaucrats. Separating philology from theology – without necessarily giving up one's faith – was a tricky business in a culture shaped so profoundly by the tradition of Christian humanism; but by the 1820s, the orientalists had before them and sometimes against them a successful model to draw on: classics.

CLASSICS-ENVY AND ITS INTELLECTUAL CONSEQUENCES

Once upon a time, classical philology, like oriental philology, had been an auxiliary science whose chief function was to assist theologians in understanding Christian texts. But by about 1810, classics had become an autonomous, highly respected, and culturally influential discipline – it was, in fact, increasingly the

[72] On English oriental and biblical studies, see Sheehan, *Enlightenment Bible*, pp. 27–53; 241–58; and Eitan Bar-Yosef, *The Holy Land in English Culture, 1799–1917* (Oxford, 2005), as well as Bayly, *Empire and Information*, and Bernard S. Cohn, *Colonalism and its Forms of Knowledge* (Princeton, NJ, 1996). On the Netherlands, see Grafton, *Scaliger*, as well as Laffen, *Islamic Nationhood*.

[73] Schlegel, "Ueber den gegenwärtigen Zustand der Indischen Philologie" (1819), in *Indische Bibliothek* 1 (1820), p. 4.

model for what a modern *Wissenschaft* should be. F. A. Wolf had both broadened and narrowed the field of Greek studies, insisting that one include the study of whole cultures – institutions, rituals, everyday life, as well as literature, art, and language – but that one use and trust exclusively Greek sources and focus on Greekness, not on diffusionary issues. Wolf's student August Boeckh separated philologists from Christians, arguing – against the foundations of Lutheran exegesis – that philology was just as secular and universally accessible – as mathematics or chemistry. "As, in fact most men are Christians without being philologists," he continued, "and [as] Jews and Muslims have become excellent philologists, [it is clear that] one should not mix all these things up."[74] By the 1830s, the classicists had successfully colonized university philosophical faculties, which now teemed with secular classical philologists; they also seized control of elite secondary educational institutions, driving out clerical instruction at this level, at least in the largest German states.

The classicists' institutional successes were not lost on orientalists, some of whom, as we have seen, had been trying in various ways to escape the theological faculty or to gain new clout within it. Accordingly, orientalists in the 1820s and 1830s often looked to some of the same pacesetting scholars, as did classics, heroizing their achievements and imitating, as far as was possible, their strict methods of source criticism. Two scholars stand out here: Karl Lachmann and Barthold Georg Niebuhr, who were both trained in classics. Let us treat Lachmann first, for he was perhaps most influential and the impact of his philological model longest lasting.[75]

For mid-nineteenth-century scholars, Karl Lachmann epitomized "scientific" philology and Germanic *Sitzfleisch*; he worked so hard, in fact, that even the prodigiously diligent Theodor Mommsen thought it absurd.[76] Lachmann made his fame in the wake of A. W. Schlegel's 1815 critique of Jacob Grimm's undisciplined, "wild philology," offering a rigorous approach to medieval German literature by applying principles developed to explicate the Pentateuch and the Homeric epics to the *Nibelungenlied* (1826).[77] A few years later, Lachmann would also apply F. A. Wolf's ideas to the New Testament, placing the holiest of Christian texts under an exclusively philological magnifying glass.[78] Wolf, in his 1795 *Prolegomena*, had contrasted the thoroughgoing inspection of sources required to produce a recension with the commonly practiced, but "frivolous and

---

[74] Boeckh quoted in Giuseppi Veltri, "Altertumswissenschaft und Wissenschaft des Judentums: Leopold Zunz und seine Lehrer F. A. Wolf und A. Böckh," in idem, *Friedrich August Wolf: Studien, Dokumente, Bibliographie* (Stuttgart, 1999), p. 45.

[75] Sebastian Timpanaro's important articles on Lachmann, first published in 1959 and 1960, demonstrated, however, that Lachmann's method was in fact the culmination of centuries of biblical and classical scholarship and that Lachmann never applied his own "method" with care and consistency. Glenn Most, "Editor's Introduction," in Sebastian Timpanaro, *The Genesis of Lachmann's Method*, p. 11.

[76] Eduard Schwartz, "Rede auf Theodor Mommsen" [1904], in idem, *Vergangene Gegenwärtigkeiten*, vol. 1 of *Gesammelte Schriften* (Berlin, 1938), p. 295.

[77] Todd Kontje, *German Orientalisms* (Ann Arbor, MI, 2004), p. 113.

[78] Timpanaro rightly underlines Lachmann's debts to J. A. Bengel, and to the English critics. Timpanaro, *Genesis of Lachmann's Method*, pp. 84–9.

desultory" method of emendation: "... when the witnesses require it, a true recension replaces attractive readings with less attractive ones. It takes off bandages and lays bare the sores. Finally, it cures not only manifest ills, as bad doctors do, but hidden ones too."[79] Good "doctor" Lachmann applied these ideas to the New Testament, building a new edition by comparing a set of "oriental" and "occidental" codices rather than using them – as had his eighteenth-century predecessors – to correct the *textus receptus*. This method was both more conservative and more radical; it was less hubristic, because the critic did not allow himself to change the text to make it more coherent or elegant, and more daring, because scientific demands were given priority over theological concerns. And it was precisely this mixture of modern trust in philological science and conservative respect for the sources – what Lachmann called "the duty of modesty" – which characterized the practice of oriental philology by the 1830s and 1840s.[80]

Let us stay with Lachmann a little longer, for his view of the philologist's task with respect to that of the theologian was highly influential and tells us much about the milieu in which he operated. Though Lachmann conceived his New Testament project as a strictly "scientific" one, it was not without theological and ideological implications. Lachmann's work had been inspired by Friedrich Schleiermacher – a friend and colleague at the University of Berlin in the 1820s – and he himself hoped that the return to a purer, earlier text would help to shore up Christianity against critical attacks. But identifying the authentic New Testament would not be easy. Criticizing the eighteenth century's careless and incomplete critique of the gospels, Lachmann, in defending his edition of 1831, plotted for the nineteenth century a difficult course, involving careful comparisons and the search for missing pieces, personal restraint, and confidence in the unhindered, free progress of criticism. This whole project was evidently one intended for the Protestant elite and one hostile to clerical, and especially Catholic, attempts to stabilize the text: "It is not my job to judge whether one might find it expedient to make, uncritically, a text purified of difficulties, to cover up its weaknesses; [it is not to identify] a single unchangeable [text] but rather only differentiate between varieties of subjective readings."[81]

Lachmann believed he could (and should) simply print divergent readings of the texts he studied, selecting only those which agreed with the oldest and most widely attested sources and otherwise not pass judgment on which texts were authoritative.[82] This was the ultimate positivist answer: print all the texts, inscriptions, and commentaries; include in the travel account all the ethnographic, botanical, political, and artistic details; and let somebody else later choose the *ur*-text or write the

---

[79] Wolf, *Prolegomena to Homer*, trans. Anthony Grafton, Glenn W. Most, and James E. G. Zetzel (Princeton, NJ, 1985), p. 44.

[80] Lachmann, "Rechenschaft über meine Ausgabe der Neuen Testaments," in *Theologische Studien und Kritiken* (1830), p. 819.

[81] Ibid., p. 821.

[82] On Lachmann's New Testament criticism, see Léon Vagany, *An Introduction to New Testament Textual Criticism*, rev. and ed. Christian-Bernard Amphoux, trans. Jenny Heimerdinger (Cambridge, 2nd ed., 1991), pp. 146–7.

definitive history – and resolve all remaining disputes. But many theologians – including interestingly the trenchant critic of the Old Testament, W. M. L. de Wette – did not appreciate Lachmann's meddling, and over the course of the next two decades, the philologist was repeatedly attacked and his faith questioned. While the application of his method to old Germanic, Greek, and Latin authors brought the philologist fame and wide-ranging respect, his New Testament work remained highly controversial and long unappreciated – except, of course, among biblical critics with similar views, for whom Lachmann became a hero. Others made contributions, wrote Martin Hertz in 1851, just after the philologist's death: "But in the history of theological criticism Lachmann appears as the fire-bearing Prometheus, even though no one now remembers the eagles which tore at his liver ..."[83]

Lachmann was not an orientalist – he worked with Greek, Latin, and later German, not Hebrew or Syriac, texts. But his careful scholarship and his systematic application of the principles of recension made his skeptical stance with respect to all "received" texts hugely influential and appealing to the philologists, classical, Germanic, and oriental, of the 1840s–1870s. He traveled in influential circles; he knew the Grimm brothers, the architect Leo von Klenze, and the diplomat-scholar-patron C. J. Bunsen, and was closely bound up with virtually all members of the anti-Hegelian (and also anti-Creuzerian) historicist world, Schleiermacher, B. G. Niebuhr, Gottfried Hermann, and August Lobeck. In his methodology-oriented seminar, he taught large numbers of the next generation of philologists, including Paul de Lagarde, who would take on Lachmann's search for the earliest biblical texts with an aggressive zeal, mastery of oriental languages, and bad temper that divided him from his mentor. Lachmann, who apparently insisted on cleanliness, clarity, and order in all aspects of his life, believed carelessness (and, apparently, bodily comforts) of any sort to be a sign of commonness and immorality and saw himself as a man devoted entirely to the pursuit of exact truths, keenly concerned with getting the details right and reining in those who overreached their competence.

"Every sort of guessing, groping for and arguing about half-baked facts was an abomination to him," Lachmann's admiring biographer wrote in 1851,

The question he posed almost every time, "Do we really know that for sure?" always created a beneficial fright, for it usually made the facts seem very dubious. Quite frequently the end of the discussion was his conclusion, "Then we don"t actually know that." If anyone was unhappy that all that effort had resulted only in recognition of one's not knowing, he would receive an explicit rebuttal [reminding him] what an achievement it was to clearly recognize what one needed to investigate in order to achieve [real] knowledge.

The great man was often criticized for not telling his students what he knew. "But he believed that this was true discipline, that one could now investigate for oneself, that which one had learned ought to be researched."[84] He had (liberal nationalist)

---

[83] Martin Hertz, *Karl Lachmann: Eine Biographie* (Berlin, 1851), pp. 157, 165–6, quotation p. 167.

[84] Ibid., pp. 83–4.

political views, but he kept them to himself.[85] These were the great positivist's lessons, instilled in his students, and it should now be clear why this approach was so fruitful for the production of fundamental research – and why the students of the fin de siècle, eager to understand the big picture, found it so frustrating. We will see below in detail how this model of careful philological inquiry and resistance to sweeping claims shaped the practice of *Orientalistik* in the post-romantic era.

There were similar lessons to be learned from the Roman historian Barthold Georg Niebuhr. Niebuhr, the son of the Near Eastern traveler, produced an immensely influential *Roman History* (1827–32) in which he sought to understand the practical operations of Roman society (such as taxation, class conflicts, and institution building) rather than to derive moral lessons from traditional authorities. He discovered, edited, and used new manuscript sources for his work, and his high standards for establishing veracity, together with his personal history of loyal state service and unimpeachable honesty, made him a model scholar. His *Roman History* exemplified the fact-crunching, nationally focused style of history-writing descendants like August Boeckh, Ranke, and Mommsen would perfect.[86] Following this model, Peter von Bohlen claimed in 1835, the historian of the Orient must treat all people equally: "... he must learn to regard the wonders, which belong to the very spirit of the ancient legends, as an inviolable national inheritance, neither setting them aside by forced interpretations, nor proscribing them as the offspring of pure imagination or intentional deception, but simply endeavoring to discover the original nucleus of fact. ..." Moreover, he continued, the historical critic must strive, "unbiased by preconceived opinion, fully to understand and fairly to estimate the individual character of every people, according to their own standard of perfection, their peculiar turn of thought and their mode of action. ..."[87] Bohlen's Rankean advice nicely illustrates both the impulse toward de-theologizing and the inclination toward thinking in national histories that would characterize much of nineteenth-century orientalism, as well as classical scholarship after the romantic era.

Niebuhr's example seemed to promise to orientalists not only that gains could be made by applying strict tests to their sources but also that it might be possible to establish a kind of parity between national histories.[88] Those who could read the new texts, like the Indologist Peter von Bohlen, celebrated their liberation from classical and biblical sources and bruited the possibility of using instead the literature of "the *Volk* itself."[89] But which *Volk* would one study? In the era of positivist historicism, it became more and more necessary to focus one's interest on one people or, at the very least, on one linguistic family. This was no easy trick for

---

[85] In 1815, the young Lachmann had fought in the last battles of the Napoleonic wars as a volunteer; a proponent of unification in 1848, he was evidently greatly disappointed by the King's refusal to accept a constitutional monarchy. Hertz, *Lachmann*, pp. 21–32, 252–3.

[86] See Acton, "German Schools of History," pp. 10–13; Gerrit Walther, *Niebuhrs Forschung* (Stuttgart, 1993).

[87] Bohlen, Genesis, p. 12.

[88] This is evidently the reason C. J. Bunsen chose Niebuhr – also a close friend and mentor – to be the "guiding star" for his history of Egypt. See Bunsen, *Ägyptens Stelle in die Weltgeschichte*, vol. 1 (Leipzig, 1845), dedication page.

[89] Peter von Bohlen, *Das alte Indien, mit besonderer Rücksicht auf Aegypten* (Königberg, 1830), pp. 71–80, quotation p. 80.

orientalists, for even their *ur*-text, the Old Testament, interwove the histories of many Near Eastern peoples, and in other fields, such as *Arabistik* or Sinology, interest in the subject was too weak and paying positions too scarce to support such a specialization. Thus, in an era of increasing specialization, it remained typical for academic orientalists in this era to embrace *l'Orient totale*; two of the most prominent scholars, Heinrich Fleischer at Leipzig or Heinrich Ewald, professor at Göttingen and Tübingen from 1823 to 1867, for example, wrote, taught, and patronized scholarship in an amazing variety of fields. Ewald taught not only classical Hebrew (his specialty) and Arabic but also Sanskrit, Persian, Coptic, Turkish, and Armenian. Fleischer, a great linguist whose students were more famous than his publications, would doctor-father leading scholars in Old Testament criticism (Julius Wellhausen), Arabic literature (Theodor Nöldeke), Islamic Law (Ignaz Goldziher), Assyriology (Friedrich Delitzsch), Ethiopian linguistics (August Dillmann), Indology (Walter Roth), and ancient history (Eduard Meyer). Friedrich Rückert was apparently able to learn a new language in eight weeks or less; one scholar who studied his massive *Nachlass* claims that he mastered more than fifty languages.[90] Under such conditions, it was hard to claim any one of the orientalists' subfields had become fully "scientific."

By 1830, parity between classicists and orientalists remained a distant prospect – one cannot even really call it a "dream," for this generation did not really expect to achieve such a thing or even want to replace the Golden Age Greeks with oriental exemplars. But the gradual acquisition of linguistic virtuosity did give the orientalists new confidence in their superior scientificness with respect to the "oriental" cultures themselves. The change since the eighteenth century is clear if we juxtapose William Jones's statement of 1792: "The nations of Asia know more about themselves and about each other than we European scholars and travelers,"[91] with the mid-nineteenth century's insistence that Asian sources could not be trusted – at least so far as "the facts" were concerned.[92] As we have seen, the notion that European orientalism was ever autonomous was self-deception, for European Arabists learned their skills from Syrian Christians, Christian Hebraists employed Jewish teachers, and even the stay-at-home Indologists depended heavily on generations of Indian grammarians.[93] Though Gustav Weil's elegists generally describe him as a student of Silvestre de Sacy, his deep philological knowledge and familiarity with original Arabic texts was undoubtedly gained during his four years in Egypt, where he studied with the Arabic philologists

---

[90] Herman Kreyenborg, "Friedrich Rückert als Interpret orientalischer Dichtung," p. 262.

[91] Jones quoted in Osterhammel, *Entzauberung*, p. 169.

[92] We must be careful not to make too much of this claim; as the following passage suggests, there were many debates about which sources to trust for which purposes. Here is Jules Mohl, arguing with those who criticized the Vedas for not containing facts. It is true, he wrote, that they do not contain information on battles, famines, "ni de tout ce catalogue de calamités qui forme le fond des chroniques; mais on y voit le tableau des origines de la société civilisée, on y trouve les premiers essays de la pensée humaine, on y observe le germe et la première forme des idées que l'Inde et la Grece ont élaborées plus tard, et qui sont devenues la règle de l'esprit humain. Ce sont là des faits plus considérables que tous les faits materiéls; ce sont des faits moraux qui ont exercé une influence plus grande et plus durable que tous les événements politiques." Mohl, "Année 1848–9," in idem, *Rapports* 1: 359.

[93] Osterhammel, *Entzauberung*, p. 173.

Muhammed Ayyad al-Tantawi and Ahmad al-Tunsi.[94] An outgrowth of older forms of Christian hubris – according to which Christians could draw on other peoples' traditions to convince them of the truth of their own – this self-deception was nonetheless important for a culture that increasingly believed that Europe alone had developed real science. For "real science," like "true faith," gave one the right to tell one's stories "objectively," and, it seemed, for the "orientals'" own good.

THE GLASS HALF EMPTY: ORIENTALISM AS A CAREER

To understand what it was to be a German orientalist at mid-century, we must first accustom ourselves to an academic world far different from that of our own era and even from that of the better known fin de siècle German mandarins. Acton again paints the most evocative picture:

Those were the days in which the familiar type of the German scholar was generated, of the man who complained that the public library allowed him only thirteen hours a day to read, the man who spent thirty years on one volume, the man who wrote upon Homer in 1806 and who still wrote upon Homer in 1870, the man who discovered the 358 passages in which Dictys has imitated Sallust.... Primarily, he was a Greek scholar, bounded by ancient horizons.... More rarely he carried the dry powder of philology into the early Christian conflicts, or the chaos of the first, the Teutonic, middle ages. On the modern world, with its unsettled and unsettling questions, and its inaccessible information, he sternly turned his back. He loved to settle on a space he could hope to exhaust by giving his life to it.... Like Hegel, who comfortably finished his book at Jena during the battle, and, starting for the publisher's in the morning, was surprised to observe that the streets were full of Frenchmen, he did not allow the voices of the striving world to distract him. Often he had risen, by mere energy and conduct, from crushing poverty, had gone barefoot to school, or had begged his way like [Jena theology professor Karl] Hase across the Fatherland; and he remained frugal and austere, cultivating humble obscurity and the golden gift of silence....[95]

Though meant to sketch German scholars generally, this portrait is so resonant for the orientalists in this chapter that it deserves to be put first; in what follows, we will meet many such hard-working, self-effacing scholars, most of them still "bounded by ancient horizons" and often willing to ignite their philological powder in religious conflicts alone. Acton treats them as heroes – for the "furious orientalists" we will profile in Chapter 5, they were anything but. Naturally, here, our task is neither to praise nor to bury them, but to understand why they operated as they did and believed what they believed, and then to sketch some of the consequences of the kind of "orientalism" they made.

Let us begin by assessing, in a general way, what sort of individuals chose to become orientalists – for it is important to remember that to become an orientalist in the way I have defined the term involved individual choice and the investment of

[94] Jewish Encyclopedia, "Gustav Weil," http://www.jewishencyclopedia.com/view.jsp. Tantawi was famous enough in Europe to be called to a professorship in St. Petersburg in the late 1830s; he was still there in 1856. Mohl, "Année 1855–1856," in idem, *Rapports* 2: 75.

[95] Acton, "German Schools of History," p. 26.

a great deal of time and capital as well as the taking of some kinds of risk. One can often identify affective qualities as well as educational peculiarities in the making of the German orientalist, particularly after the passing of the first self-taught mavericks in each subfield. Owing to its relative outsider status with respect to cultural institutions and its nearer proximity to religious concerns and organizations, orientalism attracted even more pastors' sons than did classics and many more converted Jews. Although it also drew many sons of Gymnasium teachers and bureaucrats, a significant number of orientalists hailed from the *Besitzbürgertum*, something rare in classicist circles. On the other hand, aristocrats were more common here than in classics – and for good reason; the diplomatic corps remained almost exclusively noble and diplomats stationed in the East often took up orientalist scholarship to fill their hours and occupy their minds. Books were very expensive and travel essential, at least to libraries in Paris, Leiden, and London. Non-Europeans continued to be enormously important as language teachers, guides, intermediaries, and provisioners of source materials, but their perspectives (and even their names!) rarely appear in print. Before 1884, a few German women travelers wrote books for a popular audience (most notably Ida Pfeiffer and Ida Hahn-Hahn) and a few non-European women – like Machbuba, Hermann von Pückler Muskau's favorite concubine – played intermediary roles, but women were not on the whole admitted into the orientalists' world.[96]

It was not easy to become and remain an orientalist in this era; Justus Olshausen, for example, found that the only Semitist at the University of Berlin in 1819 was an *Extraordinarius* named G. H. Bernstein, who refused to lecture to an audience of one. Olshausen next tried the Persian scholar Friedrich Wilken, but he was too busy with his job as head librarian. J. I. Ideler finally agreed to help the prospective orientalist (who, thanks to his pastor father, already knew Hebrew), but Olshausen's elegist admits that he was on the whole self-taught. Luckily, while studying in Paris, Olshausen met and impressed Alexander von Humboldt, who would prove instrumental in furthering his career, as he did for many another orientalist. Appointed to a lectureship at the University of Kiel even before he had finished his doctorate, Olshausen published his first book in 1826, titled (rather predictably) *Emendationen zum Alten Testament*, an attempt to free the scriptures from the "slag" [*Schlacken*], which had covered them in the course of centuries. Olshausen's great ambitions, one elegist noted, were "... first, to establish the essence of Old Testament Hebraism on the basis of a text purified and fixed in this way, and then [to establish] its linguistic relationships, that was already then his aim [in *Emendationen*] – and it remained [his aim] until his death."[97] Like many another orientalist, Olshausen married into the field; his first wife, was a great niece of J. D. Michaelis, and his second wife, Marie Michaelis, was the great Göttingen professor's granddaughter.

---

[96] On Machbuba, see Eckart Klessmann, *Fürst Pückler und Machbuba* (Berlin, 1998).
[97] Schrader, "Gedächtnisrede auf Justus Olshausen," in *Abhandlungen der Königlichen Akademie der Wissenschaften zu Berlin 1883* (Berlin, 1884), pp. 1–21, quotation p. 9.

Olshausen's work proceeded well despite having few students and few colleagues with whom to discuss his evolving interest in Persian and Babylonian studies – until he made a political mistake. Fired by enthusiasm for the liberal revolutions of 1848, he was elected representative to Holstein's constitutional assembly and sent his decorations back to the Danish government. When the revolutions ended, he lost his university post – though Alexander von Humboldt helped him get a library job and then a post in the Prussian Cultural Ministry. Typically for his age, Olshausen lectured on and wrote about both Semitic and Indo-Aryan antiquity and gradually, but only gradually, moved away from Old Testament studies. Typically his plans for large-scale studies were deferred until he could complete the foundational linguistic work he thought incumbent on the real scholar. "Even in the last weeks before he became fatally ill he occupied himself ... with a study of sound-shifts in Pahlavi" wrote the Assyriologist Eberhard Schrader admiringly in 1883.[98] This was what it meant to be a mid-century German orientalist.

Like Olshausen, at the turn of the nineteenth century, most academic orientalists were still trained as theologians and held their professorships in the theological faculty – though their relationships to the orthodox clergy and official churches were often tense. Some tried to obtain jobs in the philosophical faculty, hoping to liberate themselves from teaching exclusively would-be pastors and Old Testament exegesis and to free themselves from the churches' oversight and intervention. But there were also good reasons for orientalists to remain in the theological fold. Theology was considered a scientific subject and was at mid-century still a vibrant one, full of charismatic teachers, from the romantic Pietist August Neander to the Protestant historicist F. C. Baur. In 1830, theology still accounted for 38.5 percent of the student body enrolled at German universities.[99] Though this figure would steadily decrease over the course of the next seventy years, in part in reaction to the declining number of pastorships, theology would continue to be a major cultural force as well as a highly visible, valued, and respected university discipline at least until 1914.[100] For orientalists, theology continued to be the training ground and usually the community into which they fit best. Individuals continued to be believers, for the most part, and even to bounce back and forth between academic and clerical, philosophical and theological careers. August Dillmann (1823–94) was trained like his father as a theologian, but preferred philological-critical study of Ethiopic to scriptural interpretation; called from his first teaching position in Tübingen's theology faculty to a professorship for Semitic languages and Sanskrit in Kiel's *philosophical* faculty, he completed his career back in the *theological* faculty at the University of Berlin.[101]

[98] Ibid., p. 15.

[99] John Edward Toews, *Hegelianism: The Path toward Dialectical Humanism, 1805–1841* (New York, 1980), p. 213.

[100] On theology's important cultural role at the fin de siècle, see Friedrich Wilhelm Graf, "Rettung der Persönlichkeit," in *Kultur und Kulturwissenschaften um 1900*, ed. Rüdiger von Bruch, Friedrich Wilhelm Graf, and Gangolf Hübinger (Stuttgart, 1989), pp. 103–31.

[101] Littmann, "August Dillmann, 1823–1894" [1940], in idem, *Ein Jahrhundert Orientalistik: Lebensbilder aus der Feder von Enno Littmann und Verzeichnis seiner Schriften* (Wiesbaden, 1955), pp. 1–4.

We should note that European scholars have often been wary of commenting on contemporary political and religious affairs; rising above polemics and ongoing events is always safer for one's reputation than taking sides, at least in the longer term. But mid-nineteenth-century German orientalists showed a remarkably strong disinclination to invest time and effort in the study of modern Asia. Between about 1820 and 1880, modern oriental languages were rarely taught and little respected; those who did earn the respect of their colleagues were those who specialized in the ancient Orient, especially the ancient Near East. A few orientalists were employed by the Foreign Ministry – but only those, like Johann Gottfried Wetzstein (1815–1905), who could pay their own way. Wetzstein's position as Prussian consul in Damascus was unpaid, which motivated him to write anonymous articles for newspapers and to conduct a lively business in selling Arabic manuscripts to German universities in order to supplement his income. He stepped down in 1861, following the massacre of 6,000 Christians in the Syrian city the previous year. Afterward, he continued to publish articles and taught for a few years as a *Privatdozent* at the University of Berlin. In 1870, he was sent to Tunis, apparently to help raise the natives against French rule, diverting thereby French African troops away from the Franco-Prussian front.[102] His career was a colorful one; but most mid-century scholars preferred scientific prestige to governmental service – which was, in any event, still largely in the hands of the aristocracy – and stuck to a kind of historicist positivism. For men like Franz Bopp or C. A. Lassen, Heinrich Ewald or Karl Lachmann, eastern policy was something for the Foreign Ministry, the missionary societies, or the business community to deal with; the orientalist had other, more historical or theological, fish to fry.

It was rather easier, of course, to be uncontroversial about ancient political or cultural history than about the scriptures, and orientalists, like their classicist fellows, accordingly moved in this era both toward a more exclusive focus on the ancient past and toward the study of secular history.[103] Increasingly, getting out from under the thumb of the clerical authorities, who still had considerable power over appointments in the theological faculties, became a major goal for the less than orthodox orientalist. In fact, movement in this direction was already palpable in the later eighteenth century; but the pace accelerated thereafter, and especially after 1820. In 1809, the Austrian orientalist (and Mason) Joseph von Hammer-Purgstall founded a journal, *Fundgruben des Orients*, which included philosophy, poetry, history, astronomy, and travel literature, but excluded theology. It folded in 1818, when its aristocratic patron left Vienna to settle his affairs in Poland.[104] When, in the 1840s, a group of eminent orientalists wanted to found a scientific journal, they imitated Hammer-Purgstall's model (though they denounced the dilettantish tone of the *Fundgruben*); the *Zeitschrift der deutschen morgenländischen Gesellschaft* (ZDMG) founded in 1847 explicitly excluded

---

[102] Ingeborg Huhn, *Der Orientalist Johann Gottfried Wetzstein als preußischer Konsul in Damaskus (1849–1961)* (Berlin, 1989), pp. 1–7, 53–6.

[103] Lachmann's New Testament work was easily his most controversial; his work on classical and Germanic texts, on the other hand, brought him nearly universal acclaim.

[104] Hannes D. Galter, "Fundgruben des Orients: Die Anfänge der Orientforschung in Österreich," in *Joseph von Hammer-Purgstall: Grenzgänger zwischen Orient und Okzident*, ed. Hannes D. Galter and Siegfried Haas (Graz, 2008), p. 99.

theology and published only pure philology, though most members of the society still had been trained as theologians and spent most of their time in biblical criticism.[105]

The first order of business, for scholars trained as Christian humanists, had to be getting their translations right. As the idolization of Lachmann and Niebuhr suggests, for mid-century scholars, models of scientificness were overwhelmingly those generated by philology – for language, not physiology or biology, was to be the means to create verifiable genealogies of early peoples. Artifacts (aside from coins) were not considered reliable testimony, especially as it was well known that collections were idiosyncratic and incomplete, and that techniques for dating minor objects remained controversial. Recalling his experiences in the Berlin Egyptian Museum in the 1880s and 1890s, Adolf Erman claimed that while he and his team learned quickly how to date important items, "the minor artifacts, the pearls, amulets, and so forth made terrible difficulties for us, for at that time, no one understood anything about them. We did what we could, and thought in general that the technically worst pieces must belong to times of decline...."[106] Thus, for most scholars, language continued to be, in Bunsen's words, "[t]he greatest prehistorical fact"[107] and the key to understanding any and all civilizations.

Not surprisingly, then, a great part of the scholarly energy in this era was spent, indeed had to be spent, simply in trying to clean up (or beschmirch) existing grammars, dictionaries, and lexica. This was no easy matter; as Raymond Schwab beautifully describes: "In hacking his way through the underbrush, the pioneer had to stop at each step to reinvent the ax."[108] The credulity of the romantic generation – epitomized in its enthusiasm for the supposed Celtic Homer, Ossian – now gave way to acts of stunning skepticism; in Mommsen's first foray into epigraphy, he rejected 1,003 Neapolitan inscriptions.[109] The same skepticism was applied to the new decipherments. Champollion's first breakthrough came in 1822 and many histories of Egyptology treat this date as a watershed, after which scientific Egyptology immediately commenced. In fact, it took Champollion an additional two years to clean up his work sufficiently to convince the well-disposed classicist K. O. Müller, and numerous German scholars continued to withhold their approval for many years afterward. Julius Klaproth completely rejected the French scholar's decipherment, as did Egyptologist Gustav Seyffarth. Seyffarth was appointed associate professor of archaeology at the University of Leipzig in 1830; the fiery Christian also served as the afternoon preacher at the University's church. In a sympathetic elegy, Georg Ebers would explain Seyffarth's virulent resistance to Champollion's method as the kind of mistake first-comers could hardly avoid:

---

[105] Carl Brockelmann, "Die morgenländischen Studien in Deutschland," in *ZDMG* 76, Heft 1 (1922): 10–11. For the journal's predecessors, see Freise, *Entwicklung der orientalischen Zeitschriften*, pp. 62–82.

[106] Adolf Erman, *Mein Werden und meine Wirkung: Erinnerungen eines alten Berliner Gelehrten* (Leipzig, 1929), pp. 195–6.

[107] Bunsen, *Ägyptens Stelle* 1: 20.

[108] Schwab, *Oriental Renaissance*, p. 90.

[109] Acton, "German Schools of History," p. 21.

As the only representative of his discipline in Germany, advised and warned by no one, provoked into defensiveness by many who knew him only as a diligent worker, but were not able to follow him into the realm of his Egyptological research, he soon learned to overvalue his finds. But which young scholars would not have had the feeling in the course of their own first independent discovery that he has accomplished something world-shattering?[110]

Unfortunately, Seyffarth never accepted his rival's correct insights and, unhappy with German scholars' failure to appreciate his work, left Leipzig for America in 1856, taking up a post at Concordia College in St. Louis. Though he lived to be 89 (he died in 1885) and witnessed the translation of numerous documents, including *The Book of the Dead*, the publication of grammars and dictionaries, and the beginning of large-scale excavation in Egypt, he never visited "the Orient" – nor admitted Champollion had been right.[111]

Surely much of Seyffarth's discontent was the result of the successes of a Leipzig student, Karl Richard Lepsius, the epitome of the successful orientalist. Unlike Carl Ritter or Franz Bopp, Lepsius had no romantic youth to reject and came to Egyptology with no apparent interest in *ur*-revelations or priestly secrets. Indeed, one commentator has gone so far as to call him a "technocrat," who treated Egyptology as "a bit of business to be accomplished without emotion."[112] Lepsius's dissertation had treated a Latin/Etruscan text and his feet seemed planted on the path to a classical career until he was introduced to the well-connected Christian Bunsen. The two differed in temperament; Bunsen was openly seeking a means to prove the truth of the Bible and to find the common home of the Hamitic, Semitic, and Japthetic peoples; Lepsius was considerably more reticent about elaborating grand religious or historiographical claims. But they complemented one another; Lepsius helped Bunsen with his Egyptian studies and Bunsen helped Lepsius secure the patronage of his friend, the Prussian King Friedrich Wilhelm IV. In 1842, Lepsius extracted from Friedrich Wilhelm large sums for a scholarly expedition to Egypt, the most successful – and virtually the only – excursus into oriental archaeology made by the Germans before 1900. Returning in 1845, Lepsius offered a series of popular lectures; the letters he wrote during his travels went into several editions and translations. The Egyptian Department of the Berlin Museums, stocked with artifacts acquired by Lepsius's expedition, was immediately a success on its opening in 1850. Friedrich Wilhelm IV also appointed Lepsius *Extraordinarius* at the University of Berlin in 1842, even though the faculty insisted they had no need for an Egyptologist.[113]

Lepsius was, then, the founder of Egyptology in the Germanies. But he was not fully "modern" in orientation; in pitching his expedition to Egypt, he made sure to mention "what extraordinary importance the misrepresentation of Egyptian chronology and history ... has for the understanding of biblical [history and

---

[110] Georg Ebers, "Gustav Seyffarth, sein Leben und seiner Versuch einer gerechten Würdigung seiner Thätigkeit auf dem Gebiete der Ägyptologie," in *ZDMG* 41 (1887): 207.

[111] Ibid., pp. 205–16.

[112] Dietrich Wildung, "Prioritäten der Ägyptologie, 1884–1984," in *Karl Richard Lepsius (1810–1884)*, p. 213.

[113] M. Rainer Lepsius, "Richard Lepsius und seine Familie," pp. 34–40; Marchand, *Down from Olympus*, pp. 47–9, 62–5.

chronology]," something the much more secular Napoleonic team would not have done.[114] His museum was modern in design; indeed, as he told Museum Director von Olfers, his exhibit was unique, "because in no other nation can the date of each individual monument be so precisely and surely presented."[115] Lepsius was right; his work was considered cutting-edge science at the time. But in retrospect, Lepsius's crude techniques for dating (simply using royal cartouches, which could be then correlated with Manetho's list of kings) limited both the objects collected and those displayed in the Museum. Lepsius was also willing to compromise history and authenticity for the sake of aesthetic appeal and frequently restored or perfected deficient original artifacts – once again heresy for the next generation of archaeologists.[116] Still convinced of the truth of scripture, he could not credit the full independence of Semitic and Indo-European languages or the presence of Stone Age civilization in Egypt.[117] One of Lepsius's early works ("Lettre à Mr. Le Professur H. Rosellini sur l'alphabet hiéroglyphique," 1837) is often cited as the work which completed Champollion's system; but not everyone – as the Seyffarth example above shows, was convinced. As late as 1848, Friedrich Creuzer remained skeptical of many particulars.[118] It took even longer for scholars to learn to read hieroglyphics easily and to make Egyptian sources central to their studies, especially since biblical and classical sources were so well known and so much more easily accessible. In a letter of 1867, Lagarde expressed his opinion that "insofar as it goes beyond names and dates, hieroglyphics today is nothing more than a great humbug."[119]

Nor was Egyptology an area of unique complexity and contention. Thomas Hyde had produced a learned treatise on the ancient history and religion of the Persians in 1700, but his evidence, as Martin Haug pointed out in the 1860s, was derived from later Greek, Roman, Arab, and Persian writers; Hyde had possessed some manuscripts of the Zend Avesta, but was unable to read them. Anquetil deserved great credit, Haug continued, for giving Europeans an inkling of that work's content, but his wretched philological work led to the "gravest errors and mistakes, which gave rise to wrong conceptions, not only of subordinate points, but of such as were of the highest importance to those interested in the Zoroastrian religion." William Jones decided Anquetil's Avesta must be a forgery, since its contents contradicted common sense – the ancient Persians, they presumed, were wiser than that![120] The first critical

---

[114] Lepsius, "Denkschrift über die auf Befehl Seiner Majestät des Königs Friedrich Wilhelm IV zu unternehmende wissenschaftliche Reise nach Ägypten," May 24, 1842, in B-AWA, Kap. VIII, II–VIII, 260.

[115] Lepsius to Olfers July 11, 1845, in Lepsius, *Letters from Egypt, Ethiopia and the Peninsula of Sinai*, trans. Leonora and Joanna B. Horner (London, 1853), p. 324.

[116] Erman, *Mein Werden*, pp. 192–7.

[117] Richard Lepsius, "Über die Annahme eines sogenannten praehistorischen Steinalters in Ägypten," in *Zeitschrift für ägyptische Sprache und Altertumskunde* 8 (1870): 89–97, 113–21; also Erika Endesfelder, "Der Beitrag von Richard Lepsius zur Erforschung der altägyptischen Geschichte," in *Karl Richard Lepsius (1810–1884)*, pp. 244–6.

[118] Creuzer, *Aus dem Leben*, pp. 153–4, 103–4.

[119] Paul de Lagarde to Heinrich Rückert, June 18, 1867 in Lagarde, *Erinnerungen über Rückert*, p. 31.

[120] Haug, *Essays on the Sacred Language, Writings and Religion of the Parsis* (London, 1878), pp. 16–19, quotation p. 19.

study of ancient Persian texts, Émile Burnouf's *Commentary on the Yasna*, appeared in 1833–5, but the great linguist died a few years later. His book was too expensive for German students anyway and the field languished for decades. Assyriology too developed slowly. Though the first steps in what proved to be the right direction were taken already in 1802, it was not until 1857 that French and British translators agreed on how the Akkadian script should be read. It took longer for the Germans to be convinced, and even in the 1870s, many professional orientalists still considered Assyriology an inexact, and negligible subfield (see Chapter 5).

The niceties of the language aside, there were further problems involved in extracting "factual" information from eastern literary and religious texts, and juxtaposing this to the much more extensive and better known classical and biblical texts. Competition between orientalists to raise their favorite nation's texts above those of the other oriental nations also made for vicious denunciation of the trustworthiness of the new documents and of the reliability of non-traditional oriental sources. In 1826, Julius Klaproth complained that the religious practices and dogmas of the Hindus "seem to have consumed all of their intellectual faculties, in a way that nothing could rescue them from their mental impotence, or make them open to anything that concerns the events of the human race." "It is necessary to see," he continued a few pages later, ". . . that the hope of drawing from the narratives of the Asians more material for the ancient history of mankind than what is found in the books of Moses, or from the Babylonians, the Egyptians and the Greeks, is too presumptuous."[121] "The reasons for the lack of clarity [in European explanations of Japanese culture]," wrote the official chronicler of the Prussian trade mission of 1860, "lies in our imperfect knowledge of Japanese language and texts and the [foreign] moral and religious foundations of its culture, the difficulty of mastering which [lies in] the closedness of the Japanese."[122] Though there might be some hope, from the vantage point of 1860, that Japan would "open itself" culturally as well as commercially, the report's emphasis on Japanese hostility toward Europeans makes this seem unlikely. Writing a history of Indian science or even a history of India based on Indian sources, Theodor Benfey argued, might not be feasible due to Indian "lack of respect for the subject"; historians simply could not tell how or often when traditions were begun or modified.[123] By no means did the positivist generation believe it had unraveled all the "mysteries" of the East – though most were hopeful that time and serious study would ultimately lift its veils.

It did not make things any easier that older sources too had come under increasing suspicion. This was certainly true of the Jewish and Christian scriptures, at least for Protestants; and we have seen Adolf Erman waxing skeptical about the reliability of Herodotus. Missionary accounts and early travelogues too now came under increasing scrutiny. Peter von Bohlen advised great caution in using missionary accounts; though some older accounts, like that of Abraham Roger, were carefully prepared, others were characterized by disdain for Indian

---

[121] Klaproth, *Mémoires relatifs à l'Asie*, pp. 396, 411.

[122] "Einleitendes zum Verständnis der Japanischen Zustände," in *Die Preussische Expedition nach Ost-Asien, Nach amtlichen Quellen*, vol. 1 (Berlin, 1864; reprint, London, 2001), p. 3.

[123] Benfey, *Geschichte der Sprachwissenschaft*, pp. 401–2.

religion and culture. And even the reliable accounts usually reported only on local linguistic and cultural patterns and could not be taken as reflective of "Indian" culture as a whole.[124] The Prussian trade mission report criticized "tendentious" Jesuit treatments of Japanese history "which had much less to do with the truth than with the glorification of the church and the order...."[125] Not everyone felt this way, or even felt they had to overcome traditional knowledge; as Jürgen Osterhammel argues, for his information about China, the geographer Carl Ritter depended heavily on seventeenth-century Jesuit studies (themselves dependent on Chinese scholarship) and still took Marco Polo's accounts seriously. Ritter's student Ferdinand von Richthofen also used the Jesuit reports to good advantage; as Osterhammel argues, countenancing this older scholarship helped the German scholars cut through the superficial and derogatory literature written by later, less well-informed traders.[126] And while Burnouf and Christian Lassen, in their essay on Pali, stressed their own superior, systematic findings, they admitted that they were building on the admirable instincts and suggestive wordlists made by seventh-century Catholic scholars.[127] Yet the general trend identified by Arnaldo Momigliano for ancient historiography holds here as well; gradually oriental studies began to shape itself exclusively around modern authorities and contemporary, European models of "science."[128]

What enabled the forming of new canons of scholarship and ultimately, though gradually, the breaking with traditional authorities and texts was unquestionably Europe's new economic and political status in the world. Imperial power made it possible for Europeans to travel, collect, and interact with indigenous intellectuals on an unprecedented scale; European wealth made feasible both the sending out of an increased number of scholars, travelers, and collectors, and also the bringing home to Europe of many eastern texts, artifacts, plants, and animals for further study. In 1855, Jules Mohl remarked on the large number of Europeans at work in eastern libraries or collecting manuscripts and artifacts for European use: "Once upon a time, when civilization had its center in Baghdad, the caliphs sent missions to Europe to buy the Greek manuscripts which the barbarian Occident was neglecting, and now Europe sends literary missionaries to save the remains of the ancient literature of the Arabs, which these same caliphs had sought out and reunified."[129] It was on the stuff acquired in these imperious trawling actions, as well as on the rhetoric of "saving

---

[124] Bohlen, *Das alte Indien*, pp. 77–80.

[125] "Geographische Lage und Beschaffenheit: Mythologie, Geschichte," in *Die Preussische Expedition nach Ost-Asien*, p. 17, n. 15.

[126] Osterhammel, "Forschungsreise und Kolonialprogramm: Ferdinand von Richthofen und die Erschließung Chinas im 19. Jahrhundert," in *Archiv für Kulturgeschichte* 69, Heft 1 (1987): 166, 182.

[127] Eugene Burnouf and Christian Lassen, *Essai sur le Pali, ou Langue Sacrée de la presqu'ile au-dela du Gange* (Paris, 1826), p. 8.

[128] Arnaldo Momigliano, "The Place of Ancient Historiography in Modern Historiography," in idem, *Settimo Contributo alla Storia degli Studi Classici e del Mondo Antico* (Rome, 1984), pp. 28–33.

[129] Mohl, "Année 1854–55," in idem, *Rapports* 2: 13.

civilization from barbarism," that all modern European-oriental studies, German orientalism included, were built.

But this does not explain why certain individuals devoted themselves to the study of the Orient, particularly at a time in which there were few jobs in the field and little prestige connected with its pursuit. Glancing generally at individual career narratives, it seems that what gave scholars additional inspiration to pursue often recondite, hard-to-access, and hugely complicated orientalia was the confidence that the scholarly world would value new information, as, often haltingly, it did. By no means were all of the field collectors Mohl mentioned Germans – though, owing to Germandom's relative lack of oriental materials at home, many were; no academic world so cherished the filling in of gaps as did the German. This is what led Eduard Schultz to Van, where he was killed by local Kurds while copying cuneiform inscriptions; it is what (in addition to the missionary impulse) led Isaac J. Schmidt to make such passionate inquiries into Tibetan, Kalmuck, and Mongolian that he went blind in 1842.[130]

Some, like Constantin Tischendorf, did make their fame by finding new stuff. In 1844, Tischendorf, a *Privatdozent* at the University of Leipzig, found forty-three pages of Greek Old Testament (Septuagint) texts on a heap of moldy papers at Saint Catherine's Monastery on Mount Sinai; he brought them back to Leipzig and dubbed his find (published in 1846) the Codex Frederico Augustanus after his patron, the King of Saxony. In 1854, he published the first critical edition of the oldest extant manuscript of the Vulgate, the Codex Amiatinus (which Tischendorf worked through in Florence). This work gave the exegete additional prestige and on his third trip to Mount Sinai in 1859 (this time funded by Czar Alexander II), he was shown the text now known as the Codex Siniaticus, a fourth-century Greek manuscript, which included parts of the Old and the entire New Testament. At that point, Tischendorf stole the manuscript, borrowed it, or got the monks to agree to give it to the Czar as a gift; in any event, the Russian Imperial Library ended up with one of the most precious documents for the study of the Bible. Tischendorf got his Leipzig chair and the right to use "von" in his name, conferred on him by Czar Alexander. On the basis of this discovery Tischendorf produced a critical edition of the New Testament and several popular accounts of his travels.[131] Tischendorf's story read to his fellow Germans something like the Horatio Alger stories to contemporary Americans; in a still relatively static social world, one could rise to the top, not by making money, but by finding and reading new texts.

Those who did manage to find their way to *Orientalistik* experienced both the benefits and costs of a small, highly interdependent world. Luckily for the Norwegian student Christian Lassen, his mentor A. W. Schlegel valued his work on the *Ramayana* sufficiently to fund it himself until he could get Lassen a stipend from

---

[130] On Schmidt, Tuska Benes, *In Babel's Shadow: Language, Philology, and the Nation in Nineteenth-Century Germany* (Detroit, 2008), p. 92.

[131] Matthew Black and Robert Davidson, *Constantine Tischendorf and the Greek New Testament* (Glasgow, 1981), pp. 8–14. In 1933, the Soviets sold the Codex Siniaticus to the British Museum for £ 100,000. Ibid., p. 14.

the Prussian Cultural Ministry and then a job at the University of Bonn. But this had the consequence that Lassen – despite having helped compose a treatise on Pali of immense importance – had to endure Schlegel's chiding about his expenditures and even permit his *Doktorvater* to audit his finances.[132] And orientalists were also dependent on foreign scholars and colonial officials for access to relatively arcane sources. For Lassen, the problem was working around the French scholar Léonard de Chézy, who was notoriously jealous as well as increasingly ill-disposed toward German scholars and who kept crucial library books at home in order to restrict the channels of scholarship.[133] Numerous orientalist projects were made possible or impossible by this question of access; in the early 1850s, Paul de Lagarde, for example, was forced to shelve his planned edition of the New Testament based on oriental sources when he was denied access to the Syrian manuscripts held by the British scholar William Cureton.[134] The same scholar was so desperate to get his hands on manuscripts held in Paris that a week after Prussia's victory at Sedan, he requested that the Prussian Cultural Minister force the French to lend Lagarde the texts indefinitely.[135] Cost also was a factor; some of the early, essential grammars were very expensive and not available to scholars in far-flung places, like Peter von Bohlen in Königsberg. Friedrich Rückert responded by writing out, by hand, copies of such works as H. H. Wilson's massive Sanskrit dictionary.[136]

In some respects, positivist historicism actually worked to the cultural disadvantage of orientalists compared to classicists; rarely permitted to specialize in just one language, oriental philologists usually could not make claims to perfect hermeneutical understanding of so many "others." For one thing, new texts and artifacts were being discovered virtually every day; no self-respecting positivist would have presumed himself yet able to write a comprehensive history of Indian literature or Armenian art. Then too many orientalists were still closer to the "linguistic machines" Michaelis had described than they were to synthetic scholars on the model of Theodor Mommsen or Ernst Curtius. Consider, for example, the labors of the Austrian scholar August Pfizmaier, who translated some 6,500 pages of Chinese and Japanese texts, more or less at random from the Habsburg Imperial library's shelves. The son of an innkeeper, Pfizmaier was trained as a medical doctor and taught himself Chinese and Japanese – as well as a host of other languages; he wrote essays on the languages of Greenland and translated Russian and Ainu poetry. Thanks to his publication of a Turkish grammar, in 1848 he was hired to teach at the Oriental Academy and organized in 1850 the funds for the Imperial publishing house to procure Chinese and Japanese fonts.[137]

Though it was widely accepted that the route to scientific progress was through linguistic virtuosity, this was, for non-Hebraists rather rare. Wilhelm

[132] See *Briefwechsel A. W. von Schlegel/Christian Lassen*, ed. W. Kirfel (Bonn, 1914), pp. 181–99.

[133] Lassen to A. W. Schlegel, July 2, 1825, in *Briefwechsel A. W. von Schlegel/Christian Lassen*, p. 138.

[134] Alfred Rahlfs, *Paul de Lagardes wissenschaftliches Lebenswerk im Rahmen einer Geschichte seines Lebens dargestellt* (Berlin, 1928), p. 42.

[135] Sieg, *Deutschlands Prophet*, p. 103.

[136] Heinrich Rückert, "Friedrich Rückert als Gelehrter," p. 220.

[137] R. L. Walker, August Pfizmaier's Translations from the Chinese," in *Journal of the American Oriental Society* 69 (1949): 216–17.

Schott, who earned a lectureship for Chinese, Tatar, and East Asian languages in 1838, had, according to one of his colleagues, learned Chinese from "two common fellows from villages in the administrative district of Canton ..., one of whom worked as a cook, both of whom had forced themselves on a prospector in order to show themselves for money like wild animals in Europe."[138] None of this amateurism, of course, impressed German university scholars, and despite their enterprising spirit and numerous publications, Schott and Pfizmaier earned little respect from their contemporaries and are now forgotten figures in the history of oriental studies.

Despite all such hardships, the profession did grow; when the Deutsche Morgenländische Gesellschaft (DMG) was founded in 1845, it had fifty-four members, most of them full professors, diplomats, or state officials and the others Gymnasium professors or high-ranking pastors; there was also one prominent bookseller. By 1880, the organization had named its 976th full member and was allowing in rabbis and *Privatdozenten*, non-Gymnasium teachers and ordinary pastors, librarians, military men, and private scholars – and many overseas members.[139] But we must look carefully at what forces caused *Orientalistik* to grow, rather than assume that this was the result either of the Germanies' expanded colonial ambitions or of the natural progress of specialized scholarship, for as usual, contingencies and individual idiosyncrasies create history too.

ON PATRONS AND THE PUBLIC

It is often noted, as further proof of the victory of romantic orientalism, that chairs in Sanskrit philology were created in Bonn in 1818 (for A. W. Schlegel), in Berlin in 1821 (for Bopp), and in Erlangen (Rückert), Königsberg (von Bohlen), and Munich (Othmar Frank) in 1826. What is less often noted is that chairs in other orientalist subdisciplines evolved more slowly and that these chairs were, for the most part, created by royal fiat, not by the general approbation of the faculties. In fact, we can trace the founding of the Sanskrit chairs to the lobbying of one influential man, Wilhelm von Humboldt, and the founding of positions in geography – the other great orientalist discipline of the mid-century – to that of his brother, Alexander von Humboldt. Together with another close friend of Friedrich Wilhelm IV, C. J. Bunsen, these are the men who gave orientalism its pre-1848 legs; and even after that time, the latter two played highly important roles in pushing and patronizing orientalists, a partial list of which includes Franz Bopp, Richard Lepsius, Paul de Lagarde, Julius Olshausen, and Max Müller.[140] In the later cases of Arminius Vambéry and Paul Deussen, too, either royal fiat or the

---

138 Klaproth quoted in Benes, *In Babel's Shadow*, pp. 93–4.
139 See *Die Deutsche Morgenländische Gesellschaft, 1845–1895: Ein Überblick* (Leipzig, 1895), pp. 42–85.
140 On Bunsen as Lepsius's great patron, see Ursula Kaplony-Heckel, "Bunsen – Der erste deutsche Herold der Ägyptologie," in *Der Gelehrte Diplomat: Zum Wirken Christian Carl Josias Bunsens*, ed. Erich Geldbach (Leiden, 1980), pp. 79–82; on Lagarde, Rahlfs, *Lagardes wissenschaftliches Lebenswerk*, pp. 40–1.

intervention of a single bureaucrat explains the creation of new positions in oriental studies.[141]

Many survived by using the German universities' convention of allowing those certified as *Privatdozenten* to offer unpaid courses on subjects of their choosing. Indeed, this practice is surely a fundamental reason for Germandom's far better ability to create specialists than any other university culture of the time. By using these unsalaried young scholars to teach specialized language courses – often for long periods of time – German universities were able to diversify their students' skill sets with no cost to themselves. But once produced, most could not be employed, and many ventured abroad to seek their fortunes. Jules Mohl and Julius Oppert made distinguished careers in Paris; many others made theirs in the Netherlands, Russia, or the United States. Max Müller spent his life in England where the English EIC funded his long-simmering edition of the *Rig Veda*. A few remained in Asia; having been sent (by Prussia) to Egypt, then Persia, then back to Egypt, the Egyptologist Heinrich Brugsch spent only three years as professor in Göttingen (1868–70) before being invited back to Egypt by Ali Pasha to run the School of Egyptology, which he did until British and French pressure forced its closure in 1879. His younger brother Emile came to Egypt in 1870 and spent the whole of his career there, first at the School and then at the Boulak Museum.[142]

If not for Bunsen and the Humboldts, it is hard to imagine non-biblical orientalists getting much of a foothold in German academia; certainly, student interest would not have merited the creation of new posts. Friedrich Rückert, for example, who specialized in the translation and imitation of oriental poetry, did manage to train a few Sanskritists at Erlangen (including, regrettably, Paul de Lagarde); but his clientele dwindled appreciably over the years, from seven students in 1827, to six in 1828, to one in 1830. Made professor for Arabic at the University of Berlin in 1841, he enjoyed the favor of Friedrich Wilhelm IV, but not of his colleagues, and he resigned in 1849, embittered and isolated.[143] As late as the 1860s, Paul Deussen was the only student in Indologist C. A. Lassen's courses at the University of Bonn, and there were still no Sanskrit books available to work with; Deussen, who would go on to be the great popularizer of Indian philosophy (and Schopenhauer), felt guilty in these years for indulging in the "luxury" of studying Sanskrit (see Chapter 7).[144] This can only be understood in the context of the cultural hegemony of the classics by the mid-century; all university entrants (including aspiring bureaucrats, experimental scientists, doctors, and lawyers) had to pass through

---

[141] Arminius Vambéry owed his to the kind heart of Franz Josef, who gave the daring traveler a position at the University of Budapest in recompense for his sufferings; Vambéry's colleagues were outraged at the appointment of a Jewish convert who specialized in spoken oriental languages. Lory Alder and Richard Dalby, *The Dervish of Windsor Castle: The Life of Arminius Vambery* (London, 1979), pp. 242–9.

[142] G. P. Gooch, *History and Historians in the Nineteenth Century* (Boston, 1959), p. 423.

[143] Ernst Windisch, *Geschichte der Sanskrit-Philologie und indischen Altertumskunde*, part 1 (Strasbourg, 1917), p. 90; Lagarde says he was Rückert's only visitor in the winter of 1847–8. Paul de Lagarde, *Erinnerungen an Friedrich Rückert/Ueber einige Berliner Theologen, und was von ihnen zu lernen ist* (Göttingen, 1897), p. 17.

[144] Deussen, *Mein Leben*, ed. Erika Rosenthal-Deussen (Leipzig, 1922), p. 87.

the *Gymnasien*, and partake of their intensive diet of classical languages; in turn, these higher secondary schools provided the major means of employment for those, like Deussen, who took university degrees in philology. As a student in the 1820s, 1850s, or even 1860s, it would have taken maverick intellect or personal idiosyncrasy to opt for a different set of values than those propounded by one's Gymnasium and university professors, most of them staunch philhellenes.

But there were some iconoclasts in this mix, and for them, there were various ways to cobble together a career. As Ulrich Sieg has pointed out, to get a paying academic position in these decades, it was usually necessary to have private means and powerful supporters in the bureaucracy, court, or the faculties – and some orientalists were able to satisfy these conditions. Paul de Lagarde, for example, used his inheritance to publish his own books and his connections with men like Bunsen, Rückert, and Jacob Grimm to wrest recognition from academia. Unluckily for him, these friends did not have much influence by the time he was job-seeking in the 1850s. Lagarde had to bide his time, serving as a "maid of all work" at a secondary school while waiting for a full-time position to turn up.[145] The theologian-orientalist persevered, finally getting his big break after several things fell his way: he received a stipend from the Prussian Academy of Sciences and then a fellowship to work on his Septuagint studies from the King of Prussia. Finally, in 1867, the holder of the Göttingen chair for oriental studies, Heinrich Ewald, was fired after refusing to swear loyalty to the King of Prussia (Prussia having annexed Hanover in 1866). Lagarde, already well known for his conservatism and rabid German nationalism, got Ewald's job in 1869, which many saw as a politically motivated appointment (though few Prussian professors opposed Bismarck's wars).[146] Getting a job and finding funds to complete one's research was not always the painful, difficult, and political struggle Lagarde so bitterly resented; but, among orientalists, his experience was more typical than not.

Once credentialed, even without real jobs, these young scholars were encouraged to publish their work, and publications on specialized topics abounded – paid for, in large part, by their authors themselves or published in the proceedings of the various academies of science. Once specialized journals got up and running, they not only lent the field new prestige but also provided a major source of dynamism. The DMG's journal, the *ZDMG*, first appeared in 1847, replacing several short-lived publications. The *ZDMG* was edited by a series of important orientalists, but most diligently sustained down to 1879 by the wide-ranging Leipzig linguist Heinrich Fleischer. The beneficiary of the boom in specialized, positivist scholarship of the mid-century – there were few other venues until the 1870s and 1880s – *ZDMG* volume 1 comprised 370 pages; but after volume 8, the journal regularly exceeded 700 pages. It was published by F. A. Brockhaus (Leipzig), who would prove to be one of the most influential publishers of both scientific and popular *Orientalistik*.[147]

---

[145] Rahlfs, *Lagardes wissenschaftliches Lebenswerk*, pp. 51–2.

[146] Sieg, *Deutschlands Prophet*, pp. 38–9, 89–103.

[147] From the beginning, the society and journal received governmental subsidies, from Prussia and Saxony, and later from other state governments as well. *Die Deutsche Morganländische Gesellschaft 1845–1895*, pp. 35–7.

What passed for "popular" orientalism in this day was largely religious literature, most of it written by non-scholars. Travelogues did sell and some orientalists tried to supplement their incomes in this fashion; but at mid-century, the
market was much better in England, and Arminius Vambéry was well advised to
publish his Central Asian travels there first, before attempting German, French,
and Hungarian editions.[148] It took some time to find a popular audience even for
distinguished travelers. Though Helmut von Moltke's letters from the Orient were
first published in 1841, the first edition did not sell out until 1870; between 1870
and 1893, they went through four editions.[149] Ferdinand von Richthofen's travel
diary, composed during his visit to China between 1868 and 1872, was published
only in 1907, after the great geographer's death. But Brockhaus Verlag had
reasons – beyond the financial – to publish orientalist work; early on, Friedrich
Brockhaus had shown iconoclastic tendencies, printing Arthur Schopenhauer's
iconoclastic and Indianophilic *World as Will and Representation* in 1819; his
son Hermann Brockhaus would become professor of Indology at the University
of Heidelberg in 1841 and marry Ottilie Wagner, the eccentric composer's actress-
sister.[150] As this suggests, the audience for orientalia in the mid-nineteenth
century era was small, and a bit strange, and its consumption patterns cannot
be explained exclusively – if at all! – by political ambitions.

Even those bureaucrats who did promote orientalism, it should be noted, had
little interest in overseas trade or in colonization. Indeed, thanks to his intimate
knowledge of French, British, and German scholarly worlds, Jules Mohl was able
to recognize, as too few of our contemporaries have done – that, as colonizing
progressed, imperial governments actually seemed to *lose* interest in oriental studies.[151] Meanwhile, the Germans by the 1850s had become the most proficient,
respected, and numerous orientalists in the world despite having no colonial
Empire. Indeed, some state officials probably realized, as did Clemens von Metternich, that individuals with too much knowledge of the East might be tempted to
take independent action. Though the great scholar of Ottoman history Joseph von
Hammer-Purgstall tried repeatedly to get a diplomatic post in Constantinople,
arguing that he knew the languages and the territory better than any other candidate, Metternich was equally insistent that the scholar – whose political liberalism he distrusted anyway – would be throwing away his literary and scholarly
talents by taking on such a post: "Among the subalterns I appoint to ministerial
posts I can use neither superior intellect nor special knowledge; I need character-
less machines."[152]

As this instance suggests, at least some German and Austrian scholars were
interested in making themselves politically useful; at least in public appeals, lack of
German presence on the ground was a perpetual complaint. Halle professor Emil

[148] Vambéry, *The Life and Adventures of Arminius Vambéry* (London, 9th ed., 1914), p. 292.
[149] Gustav Hirschfeld, "Moltke und der Orient: Einleitung zu Moltkes Briefen aus der Türkei," in
Helmuth von Moltke, *Briefe*, p. xiii.
[150] After his father's death in 1823, the press was run by Hermann's two brothers. http://www.refer-
enceforbusiness.com/history/Be-C/Bibliographisches-Institut-F-A-Brockhaus-AG.html.
[151] See Mohl, "Année 1854–1855," in idem, *Rapports* 2: 72–3.
[152] Metternich quoted in Joseph Freiherr von Hammer-Purgstall, *Erinnerungen aus meinem Leben,
1774–1852*, ed. Reinhart Bachofen von Echt (Vienna, 1940), p. 236.

Rödiger, in his memorandum advocating the founding of the DMG in 1845, held out the hope: "that it [the DMG], perhaps in the not too distant future, to which events seem to be tending, will appear a useful vehicle, to support Germany's increasing relationships with the Orient. For if it is a purely scholarly association, it will also, by its nature, hardly be able to endure without direct contacts with the Orient. . . ."[153] Promoting the creation of a paid consular position in Damascus in 1852, J. G. Wetzstein outlined the economic, diplomatic, religio-political, and scientific benefits of such a position for the Prussians; in addition to providing a real training ground for orientalists – German professors now were characterized "often by ignorance and charlatanism and almost always by pedantry" – Prussian presence might help link Protestantism to the cause of the Druse, with significant but not entirely foreseeable consequences for Syria.[154] But, for the time being, the Foreign Ministries remained uninterested in such blandishments; Wetzstein received no pay and the DMG only modest publication subsidies.

Particularities of patronage, institutional development, and internal prestige contributed to the forming of important disequilibria in the cultural salience of the orientalists' subfields. Thanks to several decades of Indological study and to links forged to the study of *Germanistik*, by the 1860s there was a growing and increasingly respected community of Sanskrit specialists in the German states. Fleischer's school at Leipzig was turning out well-trained Arabists at a regular rate – though their studies, as in the case of the Indologists, focused almost exclusively on the ancient, not the modern, cultures, and on languages, not on *Realien*. The editorial staff of the ZDMG also contributed heavily to the further-ing of these two linguistic specialties. Although the journal officially welcomed contributions in six major areas of study (Semitic, Indo-German, Malaysian, Mongolian and Turkic, Tibetan, and ancient Egyptian), contributions in the first two categories vastly outnumbered the rest. The ZDMG saw itself primarily as the venue for cutting-edge work in Arabic and Sanskrit, "the two, equally deserving, classical languages of the Orient."[155] In addition to these more secular subfields, Hebraists continued to be plentiful, for they were essential members of theological faculties and seminary staffs, and, moreover, continued to practice – in increas-ingly modern, scientific ways – the essential art of Old Testament exegesis.

By the 1860s, in these three fields – *Arabistik*, Indology, and Old Testament studies – orientalism's public and institutional profiles were growing. There were other areas about which the public was almost wholly uninformed: East Asia, oriental art, and southeast Asia being outstanding examples. Sinologist August Pfizmaier's lectureship at the University of Vienna began in 1843, but in 1848, the position was canceled; thereafter, most Austrian China experts before 1918

---

[153] Rödiger to Cultural Ministry, January 16,1845, on founding of DMG in B-GSPK, I, 76Vc, Sekt 1, Tit. XI, Teil I, Nr. 10, Bd. 1.

[154] Wetzstein predicted Syria would soon break away from the Ottoman Empire. See his "Motivirung der Nothwendigkeit einer Vertretung Preußens in *Damaskus* durch Errichtung eines besoldeten Consulats daselbst," reproduced in Ingeborg Huhn, *Der Orientalist Johann Gottfried Wetzstein*, pp. 353–84 [full text], here pp. 354–8, quotation p. 359.

[155] *Die Deutsche Morgenländische Gesellschaft*, pp. 28–30, quotation p. 30.

completed their projects not as academics, but as private scholars, as members of the diplomatic service, or as curators of library collections.[156] There were a few minor posts for Sinologists in the Germanies, but no chair until 1908. Though numerous German intellectuals were brought to Japan after 1868 to aid the Meiji modernization plans, there was no full professorship for Japanese in Germany until 1914. Specialists in modern languages of the East, in particular, were hard-pressed to find work; as studies of early Arabic began to gain respect, Turkish continued to be considered a decadent late language, undeserving of specialized academic study.

Thanks to the field's philological penchants, histories of the Orient, especially after Droysen turned to writing Prussian history in the mid-1840s, were thin on the ground; Hammer-Purgstall continued to produce massive tomes (his ten-volume *Geschichte des osmanischen Reiches* appeared in 1827–35), but his works came under increasing fire from philologists, who thought his translations far too loose and his critical methods dubious. The Fleischer school ridiculed Hammer's scholarship, making his name synonymous with philological dilettantism.[157] So thoroughly sick of philological niceties and Graeco-centered values was Droysen by 1844 that he wished fervently for some broad-minded readers to appreciate the significance, past and present, of his history of the Hellenistic world: "Philologists and other sorts of vermin have no notion of the missions of the day or of the future."[158] Even in the era of high historicism, it was not a good time to be an historian of the Orient.

Thus, just as Ranke and Droysen began attracting large crowds to their lectures on modern Europe,[159] an opposite tendency was taking hold in *Orientalistik*. Knowledge about the modern Orient had not been extensive in the German-speaking world before the 1820s, but after this time, it would grow even more scarce. Some of those trained before historicist positivism came to the fore – like Lassen, Benfey, and Karl Koeppen – did take their research and their stories into modern times. But their works would be the last scholarly histories of modern India written in German until after 1918.[160] In Islamic studies, similarly, Hammer-Purgstall would be virtually alone in devoting attention to modern history and literature. Most of the field was left to travelers, some of whom conveyed a great deal of ethnographic information, but very few of whom could speak the native languages. One of those who could, Arminius Vambéry, only exaggerated a little when, after giving a lecture to the Geographical Society in Leipzig in 1864, he reported to his English publisher that "the President and the public have as much notion about Central Asia as the Khan of Khiva has about Germany."[161]

---

[156] See Berhnard Führer, *Vergessen und verloren: Die Geschichte der österreichischen Chinastudien* (Bochum, 2001).

[157] Sabine Mangold, *Eine "weltbürgerliche Wissenschaft": Die deutsche Orientalistik im 19. Jahrhundert* (Stuttgart, 2004), p. 87.

[158] Gustav Droysen, *Johann Gustav Droysen*, vol. 1, *Bis zum Beginn der Frankfurter Tätigkeit* (Leipzig, 1910), p. 220.

[159] Droysen had 200 students attending his lectures in 1841. Droysen, *Johann Gustav Droysen*, p. 237.

[160] Windisch, *Geschichte der Sanskrit-Philologie* 1: 158–61, 187–9.

[161] Quoted in Lory Alder and Richard Dalby, *The Dervish of Windsor Castle: The Life of Arminius Vambery* (London, 1979), p. 241.

In sum, those who made orientalist knowledge at mid-century were, for the most part, either moonlighting theologians or at least partial iconoclasts; they shared many values with the classicists they envied and imitated, but they did not share, for the most part, the cultural prestige or academic clout of the latter. Most, like August Boeckh, were probably more given to speculation and enthusiasm in their lectures than in their publications,[162] which were carefully scrutinized by other experts in the field for dishonoring philological errors. In these publications, they still drew heavily on traditional texts – especially Herodotus and the Old Testament – but the supply of indigenous and accessible texts was growing and beginning to complicate the use of such testimonies. Most subfields had now, to a greater or lesser extent, embarked on the road to *Wissenschaftlichkeit*. But the trip would, for quite a long time, remain a lonely one.

[162] See Acton's comment on Boeckh in "German Schools of History," pp. 11–12.

3

The Lonely Orientalists

For who, beyond a very small number of specialized scholars, is willing or able to care about oriental studies?
– Heinrich Rückert, 1866[1]

Who indeed would or could devote themselves to the Orient in the age of high philhellenism and German nation-building? This question, posed in the popular magazine *Die Grenzboten* in 1866, was particularly poignant, for it was posed by Heinrich Rückert, son of the great orientalist and poet Friedrich Rückert, who had himself opted to become ... a classicist. The answer is, there were some willing to take on the still considerable challenges of studying oriental languages and cultures, but they did so either presuming they were continuing in time-honored Christian humanist traditions or realizing that what they were doing was frankly a bit odd. The most natural and reliable a career an orientalist could make remained that of the theologian or well-educated pastor, though the job market in both sectors continued to decline as fewer Germans made their way to church. The absence of a German colonial empire in these years meant that there was no argument from utility to be made. Gradually, specialization and historicization were making the newer branches of *Orientalistik* more respectable; but this was a slow process, especially if one wanted a salary-paying professorship and not just a license to teach in exchange for fees. One might decide that money was to be made in lively travel writing, as did Arminius Vambéry, or become an orientalist by accidents of location or opportunity, like Ferdinand von Richthofen. But most did not see themselves as linked in any important or lasting way to real-existing oriental countries or peoples. What German orientalists continued to be, for the most part, were scholars of the ancient world and interpreters of the scriptures, especially of the most important "oriental" scripture for Christians and Jews alike, the Old Testament.

Perhaps what is most striking about German orientalists between about 1820 and 1870 is how much their careers, and career prospects, continued to be determined by older patterns of academic respectability and cultural significance. Their contributions to biblical exegesis were important; indeed, as it became more and more acceptable to place the Old Testament in the context of other Near Eastern cultures and chronologies, Central European theological faculties valued them

---

[1] Heinrich Rückert, "Friedrich Rückert als Gelehrter" [1866], in *Friedrich Rückert im Spiegel seiner Zeitgenossen und der Nachwelt*, ed. Wolfdieterich Fischer (Wiesbaden, 1988), p. 207.

more than ever before. Decipherments of languages hitherto unreadable for Europeans and archaeological finds complemented the expansion of exegetical practices, and on occasion brought oriental studies into the public eye. But we should recall that before the 1870s, the university-educated public in the Germanies remained quite small, and even within this group, there were signs of *falling* interest in the East, such as Rückert's early retirement and Ranke's abandoning of his lectures on world history after about 1834. The chapter that follows will provide ample examples of the difficulties, intellectual and institutional, involved in being a German orientalist in the middle of the nineteenth century. This is deliberately to depart from the usual mode of disciplinary history, in which achievements and successes are usually the focal point. The aim is not to diminish the industry or originality of these scholars, but rather to underscore, firstly, the slow-moving nature typical of most academic cultures in the absence of intrusive state steering and/or massive influxes of money and, secondly, to reiterate the unique place of oriental studies in German academia and German culture as a whole.

As we saw in the previous chapter, the study of the Orient was changing in the later eighteenth century; between about 1820 and 1870, it underwent further, usually quiet, changes. In this period, *critica sacra* was increasingly left behind, and specialized, historicist study came to the fore – though this did not mean that German orientalism's focus on religion in general and the Old Testament in particular was lost. The period saw the decipherment of hieroglyphics and cuneiform (though both took some time to set in); Buddhism, largely mysterious to eighteenth-century scholars, became well known and its variants understood. Specialization increasingly divided Indo-German comparative philology from the study of Semitic and East Asian languages; the scholarly elite, at least, evinced considerably less enthusiasm for oriental poetry. The era saw the application of Lachmannian criticism, mythological interpretation, and historical positivism to the Bible. And of course it saw the expansion of European – though not yet German – imperialism.

The impact of European imperialist politics on oriental scholarship in this era is certainly palpable, but in some ways counter-intuitive. This is the period in which the one major European power not engaged in colonizing in the East became the undisputed international pacesetter in orientalist scholarship, above all as a result of the Germans' intense dedication to the philological study of the ancient Near East. Perhaps this was the result of a semi-conscious division of labor: the English, British, and Dutch were to enjoy the fruits of present-day colonization, while the Germans profited by enhancing their *Wissenschaftlichkeit*. This they surely did, benefiting from the large new manuscript and, to a lesser extent, artifact collections thrown into the market or discovered as a result of more invasive European penetration, especially in India, but also in East Asia and the Ottoman lands.[2] Germans themselves contributed to this increased presence, as new consulates

---

[2] It is worth noting that there had never been a dearth of Ottoman Turkish sources and printed materials in European libraries, and Austrian and Venetian archives, in particular, were filled with documentation of Ottoman history. But few, other than Joseph von Hammer-Purgstall, were interested in using this all-too-modern material.

were founded and more travelers, missionaries, and businessmen ventured eastward, a Bavarian prince was appointed king of the new Greek state and Prussian military advisors were sent to the Ottoman Empire and Japan – but they did not yet have overseas holdings. The new availability of source materials and, thanks to revolutions in printing and the building of libraries at home, their increasing diversity and accessibility, were certainly consequences of Europe's enhanced economic and political power. German scholars also benefited from a new sort of hubris, a real expectation that Europeans could know the Orient and its history better than its current residents. But the German states' relationship to the modern Orient differed from that of their colonizing counterparts, who *did* need to put soldiers, judges, and bureaucrats on the ground. Having no such needs, the Central European states had no cause to propel academic philologists and/or Protestant Bible scholars into modern studies – and German orientalists remained free to focus on the religious and historical questions that had long defined scholarly inquiry.

In defending the importance of their studies at home, orientalists faced difficult questions: What did the Orient have to do with the Germans, past and present? What moral or aesthetic good was served by studying the East? Rather than answering such questions directly and positively, mid-century orientalists tended to fall back on older answers (the Orient was relevant to religious questions or to the general history of ancient civilizations), a set of rhetorical moves which suggests appropriately that in this period orientalists rarely saw themselves as providers of *Bildung* or contributors (at least qua orientalists) to the nationalist cause. Though they tended to religious radicalism and political liberalism, most mid-century orientalists did not, as had Montesquieu and Voltaire, contrast rational oriental sages with western intolerance and cruelty – though there were a few philosophers, like Arthur Schopenhauer and Marx's friend Karl Friedrich Koeppen, who continued this tradition. A few picked up Friedrich Schlegel's suggestions about affinities between medieval Germans and Indians or Persians, and speculation intensified on the question of the "Indo-German" homeland. Arminius Vambéry tried to interest his Hungarian countrymen in the "Turanian" origins of their language. But mid-century orientalists rarely tried to play the nationalist card. Joseph von Hammer-Purgstall even dedicated his ten-volume *Geschichte des Osmanischen Reiches* (1827–35) to the Russian Czar, who, he said "had encouraged and inspired him to write the truth."[3] German orientalists occasionally criticized British (or French or Dutch) imperial ventures, occasionally applauded them, but mostly ignored modern international relations. One can see, in this era, foundations being laid for later forms of secular cultural engagement. But orientalists' attempts at secular cultural relevance in this era were, for the most part, diffuse, idiosyncratic, or fleeting, and on the whole not particularly successful.

This chapter, then, tries to illustrate some of the ways orientalists inserted themselves into the academic and cultural debates of the day and to assess the

---

[3] Hammer, *Geschichte des Osmanischen Reiches*, vol. 1 (Budapest, 1827), dedication page. Hammer meant to dedicate it to Alexander I, but as he had died by the time Hammer finished his project, he dedicated it to Nicholas I instead.

impact they had. I recognize that I will not be doing justice to all the subfields, much less to all the individuals who contributed to *Orientalistik* between about 1820 and 1870. I have divided the chapter into three parts, with the first two treating studies in the field of *Semitistik* (including biblical criticism) and developments in the study of Indo-European languages and cultures. The third part of the chapter covers the more popular, modern, and non-philological face of oriental studies insofar as it had one; it opens with short sections on orientalizing poetry and geography and concludes with a longer section on travel literature to suggest some of the ways in which scholarly and more popular worlds occasionally did overlap. All these sections are designed, too, with subsequent chapters in mind: section one (on biblical criticism) lays the foundations for many of my explorations of orientalism's impact on the study of the Old and New Testaments; Chapters 4 and 5 continue the story begun here of Islamic studies in the age of high positivism. Chapter 7, on Aryans and Jews, picks up where this chapter's section on Indo-Germanic linguistics leaves off. Developments during this period in some other subfields – such as art history – will be considered elsewhere in the book. In some cases, I have tried to highlight mind-sets that disappear later – like the countenancing of female scientific travel displayed by Carl Ritter or the left-wing critique of Brahmanic religion by Karl Koeppen – or forms of inquiry that later become unscientific – like Friedrich Rückert's "Nachdichtung" or F. C. Baur's study of oriental religions based exclusively on western texts. Elsewhere I have tried to lay the foundations for lines of thought that will have long histories – Heinrich Ewald's romanticization of the Hebrew prophets or Albrecht Weber's dedication to the Vedas. I will start with the most visible and important part of orientalism in the period, namely biblical criticism, and attempt there an overview of this wide field, populated by men of quite diverse character, convictions, and interests.

BIEDERMEIER BIBLE CRITICISM OR HOW TO STUDY JEWS – AND GREEKS

Chapter 1 argued that eighteenth-century orientalists and biblical critics, while adopting the latest scientific techniques and willing to take a hard look at the canon, were by no means the most radical critics of Christianity in their day. The same can be said, on the whole, for nineteenth-century orientalists. Until the century's last two decades, the vast majority of specialists in oriental languages considered themselves Christians (I will take up the case of Jewish scholars in the section to follow); some were even recruited or recruited themselves to orientalism precisely to defend the faith by adapting it to science. They were defending Christianity, or at least a Herderian version of it, against radical philosophy, but also against post-Enlightenment tendencies to view theology chiefly as a present-oriented form of moral philosophy and to sideline the ever-problematic Old Testament. For orientalists, the Old Testament remained, at the very least, a key literary, historical, and anthropological text. They saw it as their job to assess what sort of truth the scriptures contained and how properly – that is, scientifically – one could extract it.

This task was not exclusively in their hands – philosophers and theologians without language training were concerned with these matters as well. But in the era of Ranke and Lachmann, it increasingly became necessary to give historical scrutiny of the scriptures over to those who could read the works in the original and contextualize them properly. The Old Testament was especially concerned here, firstly because its original language was Hebrew (while the New Testament was compiled first in Greek); as we saw in Chapter 1, after Reformed scholars adopted the humanistic principle of *ad fontes* (interpretation based on original sources), this textual fact provided the foundations for the development of orientalism as a separate scholarly specialty. Early modern scholars knew Hebrew to be related to other languages of the Levant such as Syriac and Arabic, and by the seventeenth century they were already evolving an embryonic understanding of the ways in which the other "oriental" cultures and languages might be used to explain the scriptures. Michaelis and Herder showed how this might be done in detail, and showed too that it could be done without being persecuted for heresy. Their descendants, among whom one can count W. M. L. de Wette, Johann Eichhorn, Wilhelm Gesenius, and Heinrich Ewald – all trained as Christian Hebraists – followed very much in this tradition. None of these men wanted to throw out the Old Testament, and thanks to their scholarly efforts and to the conservative reaction characteristic of the Restoration era, the Old Testament after 1820 was rehabilitated as a truth-containing text.[4] Even more than in Michaelis's day, however, the truths it contained increasingly became historical, not theological ones, and truths specific to the Jewish people, not to all peoples.

It is crucially important to understand that the Jews who were the objects of orientalist research in the nineteenth century were overwhelmingly the Jews of the Old Testament, not those of the Hellenistic, medieval, or modern world, and that they were inevitably juxtaposed to that other great culture-creating people, the Greeks. Both Greeks and Jews, at this point, had qualities mid-century liberal scholars appreciated: the Jews were pious, non-materialist, and law-abiding; the Greeks were creative, aesthetically minded, and scientific. The former had willpower and soulfulness; the latter had good taste, healthy bodies, and an admirable love of individual liberty. But the very fact that these groups were increasingly seen and studied in isolation from one another laid the foundations for a lopsided sort of biblical criticism, in which the Old Testament was much more historicized than the New; the differentiation of Greeks and Jews also set the stage for the caricaturing of the Orient as a whole, for the Jews were so much a part of what this generation associated with that term. If, at base, the Jews represented spirit and faith, as against the rationality and progress of the Greeks, even when the first set of values were preferred to the second, a formula for East/ West comparisons was invented that would be very hard for later scholars or "orientals" themselves to shake.

In the work of Heinrich Ewald, one can see how Herderian ideas were reshaped and put into new scientific forms. Ewald was a wide-ranging philologist and extremely learned about all aspects of ancient Jewish life. He was an advocate

---

[4] Klaus Beckmann, *Die fremde Wurzel: Altes Testament und Judentum in der evangelischen Theologie des 19. Jahrhunderts* (Göttingen, 2002), pp. 57–9, 330–1.

of *Kulturprotestantismus*, one who insisted that history should be told as it was – and that believers had nothing to fear from the unembellished truth.[5] But he emphatically believed that the history of the ancient Israelites was a special history. As he wrote in the introduction to his eight-volume *Geschichte des Volkes Israel bis Christus* (1843–59),

The history of this ancient people is essentially the history of the self-cultivation of the true religion, through all the steps towards its perfection, [a religion] which, in this narrow community and through all these struggles raised itself to the highest levels. Finally in all its majesty [this religion] revealed itself, to spread from then on irresistibly and through its own power, never to be lost again, but to become the eternal possession and blessing of all peoples.[6]

The universal importance of ancient Israel justified focusing on this nation, even though it was hardly the most powerful in the ancient world and had borrowed ideas from elsewhere – though, Ewald averred, what was borrowed the Israelites quickly made their own. This universal import also justified Ewald's intense focus on Israelite prehistory as related in Old Testament stories; even if the "sagas" reported did not have the same truth value as pure historical writing, they could be used to understand much about the culture's history. The Israelites could be trusted even further than other ancient peoples, as they had always had a higher sense for truth, more modesty, and a sincere revulsion to playful fantasizing. The high seriousness of the Israelites was what had prevented them from developing their own mythology, for the true religion shrinks from false or sensual representations of the divine.[7]

Ewald's *Geschichte des Volkes Israel* painted a vivid, heroic picture of the Jewish kings and prophets – but Ewald was much less interested in, or attracted to, later periods of Jewish history. Though he did work with and respect Jewish colleagues and students and read rabbinic texts, in his view, at the birth of Christ, Jewish history was over as was too the East's contribution to western culture. Early Judaism, for Ewald, was far more interesting and admirable than "late" Judaism, that is, Hellenistic Judaism, with all its legal restrictions, its priests, and its unwillingness to embrace new prophets (like Jesus). But still, as Hans Liebeschütz noted many years ago, the fact that Ewald in his New Testament writings emphasized the life and teachings of Jesus as fulfillments of Old Testament prophecies, rather than focusing on Christ's death and resurrection, offered an opportunity to underline Jewish-Christian continuity.[8] Ewald continued Herder's tendencies to "primitivize" the Israelites – but he did not create a great gap between the two religions, a gap later Christian ideologues and students of other oriental religions would be tempted to create and fill with their own, often tendentious, content.

---

[5] Ewald, *Geschichte des Volkes Israel bis Christus*, vol. 1 (Göttingen, 3rd ed., 1864), p. 12.

[6] Ibid., p. 9.

[7] Ibid., pp. 48, 63–8. Ewald was answering here Renan's claim that the Semites were insufficiently imaginative to have a mythology.

[8] Liebeschütz, *Das Judentum im deutschen Geschichtsbild von Hegel bis Max Weber* (Tübingen, 1967), p. 253.

Generations of German Hebraists after Ewald would preserve his affection for early Judaism, and essentially ignore Hellenistic Judaism, or simply take their accounts of it directly from the Gospel writers who had, we now recognize, their own peculiar take on the religion of their (rejected) fathers. The Hebraists retained this Old Testament focus partly for theological reasons – in their eyes, Hellenistic Judaism was a spiritual dead end. But partly, too, they excluded "late" Judaism for philological reasons; according to deeply rooted humanistic divisions of labor, the world of Greek-speaking Jews (like Saint Paul) should belong to Greek scholars. In fact, classical scholars after Creuzer generally disdained the study of "late" Greek and especially Hellenistic religious texts. Thus, the application of the new scientific methods to the New Testament texts was left chiefly to theologians, and especially to radical theologians who came from the Tübingen Stift. Despite being theologians, these men tended to share the classicists' image of Greekness, believing the real Greeks were the fifth-century Athenians; New Testament Greek, on the other hand, was a sacred language, largely unrelated to the secular Greek cultures of the Mediterranean. They also shared the orientalists' notion of the Jews as fanatically religious primitives who degenerated into legalistic provincials. The attempts of both parties to make sense of biblical history thus reproduced and refined these essentialized nations, the Greek and the Jew. This was, of course, a schematization of the Old–New Testament relationship, which had always been central to Christian doctrine and to doctrinal debates. But now that both sides had their philological specialists, now that historicist thinking was increasingly stacking whole cultures in evolutionary order, it was all the more possible for those who came to be known as "liberal Protestants" to open up gaps between the two cultures or even to create two cultures where, as in late Hellenistic Palestine, there was one.

We must begin with F. C. Baur, professor at the Tübingen Stift from 1826 to his death in 1860. Baur's first substantial work (*Symbolik und Mythologie, oder die Naturreligion des Altertums* [1824–5]) was, like many other works of the early 1820s, a reaction to Creuzer's *Symbolik*, in this case a rather positive one. Baur admired Creuzer's comparativism but wished to overcome the disorganized clutter of the classicist's work by turning discussion away from the *ur*-origins of monotheism toward a discussion of the mytho-philosophical truth of Christianity. Baur hoped to develop systematically the young F. W. Schelling's notion that it is not the aim of philosophical myths "that one believes that these stories are history itself, but that through them one is convinced of the truth they symbolize."[9] But after publishing his *Symbolik*, Baur retreated from comparativism into historicism and devoted himself to the study of the evolution of Christian dogma, something he believed had to be understood in the context of the languishing ancient (and Jewish) worlds. Christianity, for Baur, was a product of the struggle between Pauline ("Greek") Christians and Petrine ("Jewish") Christians in the first two centuries CE. The struggle was won by the former, but only gradually, a conception which allowed Baur to offer a new understanding of the historical order in which the Gospels were composed – Matthew, Luke, Mark, and lastly John – according

---

[9] See Gotthold Müller, *Identität und Immanenz: Zur Genese der Theologie von David Friedrich Strauss* (Zürich, 1968), pp. 192–4, 240. Quotation from Schelling (1793), p. 193.

to the degree of anti-Judaism and Christian-Greek autonomy they displayed. Though understanding Christianity as an "overcoming" of Judaism, which was characterized in his work as narrow, nationalist, and legalistic, compared with Pauline universalism, Baur did not doubt Jesus' Jewishness; indeed, one of the difficulties he bequeathed to later scholars was that of the transition from Jesus' ideas to those of the founders of the church, most critically Saint Paul. Though Baur may have given scientific imprimatur to a view of Hellenistic Judaism's legalistic narrowness that would prove disastrous in later liberal theological discourse, he neither invented this view nor took it to its extremes.[10]

One Tübingen scholar who did run to extremes was Baur's student D. F. Strauss, whose *Das Leben Jesu, kritisch bearbeitet* created huge controversy on its publication in 1835 and for decades afterward. Strauss's *Leben Jesu* took off from Baur's Schellingian notion that myths contain symbolic truths; thus, though he was writing a "mythological" account of Christ's life, Strauss did not believe himself to be destroying Christian belief. He was rather trying to save it, not so much from ordinary believers – innocent faith was, in Strauss's eyes, acceptable for most laymen – but rather from rationalist critics, who were rapidly undermining their own arguments and would soon be left with neither a historical nor a divine Savior. In volume 1 of his very long book, Strauss completed the destructive task begun by the rationalists, arguing that the internal evidence for the life of Jesus recorded in the New Testament was so contradictory and fragmentary as to make the texts, as documents, historically worthless. It has become clear, he noted, that none of the Gospels are eyewitness accounts; thus, they cannot be presumed to be any more historically reliable than Homer or the books of the Old Testament.[11] Volume 2 then attempted to apply to the whole of the New Testament the "mythological" interpretations applied to the Old Testament by de Wette and worked out philosophically by Schelling and Baur. Strauss argued that the New Testament was in essence no different than the Jewish scriptures, the Qur'an, or the sacred texts of the Hindus, and it mattered rather little if it described real historical events. Still, the New Testament did convey *philosophical* truths, truths higher and purer than those of other nations, he implied, and thus it remained a book of universal significance and value.

These were, of course, very radical things for a theology professor to say, especially as conservatives and Pietists, after the death of Hegel in 1831, began to exert new influence on the cultural ministries, the church synods, and the theology faculties in Central Europe's Protestant states. Strauss was immediately fired – he was too radical even for the Tübingen Stift – and would never obtain another academic position, though his book would long continue to be a popular best-seller. In the course of the furious polemics over his *Life of Jesus*, one of Strauss's former teachers would describe his book as an example of "the Ischariotism of our time," and Heinrich Ewald, no conservative or Pietist himself, would accuse Baur, Strauss, and the whole Tübingen School of blotting out the light of

[10] On Baur, see Horton Harris, *The Tübingen School* (Oxford, 1975); Joseph B. Tyson, *Luke, Judaism, and the Scholars: Critical Approaches to Luke-Acts* (Columbia, SC, 1999), pp. 12–29.

[11] Strauss, *Life of Jesus*, pp. 47–9. For more on Strauss's interest in myth, see Williamson, *Longing for Myth*, pp. 155–73.

the Gospels and – through their ignorance of the Bible – causing harm to German science.[12] Interestingly, the huge reaction to, and official rejection of, Strauss's "mythical" interpretation did not prevent another of his arguments – that the synoptic Gospels are less theologically polished and contain more miracles, and so must be earlier than the more literary gospel of John – from stimulating new debate. Indeed many found that they could throw out the Hegelian bathwater and keep the text-critical baby, or putting it differently, scholars recognized that Strauss's philological and rationalist critique of the Gospels had merit, even if they rejected his notion that the historical Jesus was a fictitious and dispensable figure.

Most influential in the evolution of "liberal Protestantism" was an erstwhile pupil of Baur's, Albrecht Ritschl, who defended the Marcan hypothesis in an important essay of 1851, but sought to identify the uniqueness and superiority of Christianity in a most un-Straussian way. Moreover, in defending his faith, Ritschl turned the creative "Jewish" elements Baur had adumbrated as essential to the early movement into the remnants of a foreign faith, which Jesus and his followers sought to strip away. Ritschl's influential writings helped to push Protestant theology, at least in the universities, further away from Judaism and Jewish scholarship and into (said his critics) Greek, pagan arms.[13] Adolf von Harnack would continue this tradition by perfecting his knowledge of Greek texts and culture and emphasizing the linkages between Christian and Greek universalist, as opposed to Jewish provincial and national, ways of thought. Abraham Geiger and other Jewish writers would challenge Ritschl's line of thought by insisting, instead, that Jesus' teachings were simply a continuation of the ideas of the Pharisees. As polemics deepened and publications reached a broader audience, liberal rationalists, Christian and Jewish, forced the foundational question for Christians (What does Christianity owe to Judaism?), once again to the fore; by the nineteenth century's final third, this question, one of the West's most profound questions about its debts to the East, became again a question of profound cultural significance.[14]

For our purposes, the most interesting thing about the Tübingen School and its liberal descendants is that their quest to understand the history and development of the Church and Christian dogma, like Baur's work, was based almost exclusively on internal scriptural evidence; the sources to which they looked were, at this point, rarely "oriental" – and little if any attention was paid to rabbinical texts or to the larger world of the pagan Orient. W. F. Albright, attributing the

---

[12] *Der Ischariotismus unserer Tage* was the title of C. A. Eschenmayer's book, published in Tübingen in 1835; see Leander E. Keck, "Editor's Introduction" in David Friedrich Strauss, *The Christ of Faith and the Jesus of History*, ed. and trans. Leander E. Keck (Philadelphia, 1977), p. xvii. Ewald, "Ursprung und Wesen der Evangelien," in *Jahrbücher der biblischen Wissenschaft* 1 (1848): 113–54; William R. Farmer, *The Synoptic Problem: A Critical Analysis* (Dillsboro, NC, 1976), pp. 25–9. Ewald did not invent the Marcan hypothesis and indeed probably got his idea from Herder. But this was decidedly a minority opinion in his day – the Tübingen School itself still preferred to think of the book of Matthew as the earliest and most authentic gospel.

[13] See Heschel, *Abraham Geiger and the Jewish Jesus* (Chicago, IL, 1998), pp. 123–6 and Claude Welch, *Protestant Thought in the Nineteenth Century*, vol. 2: *1870–1914* (New Haven, CT, 1985), pp. 1–30.

[14] See Uriel Tal, *Christians and Jews in Germany: Religion, Politics, and Ideology in the Second Reich, 1870–1914*, trans. Noah Jonathan Jacobs (Ithaca, NY, 1975), esp. pp. 16–22.

Tübingen School's radicalism to incomplete sources, noted that in the era of the school's flowering:

Nothing was yet known about the chronology of Greek pottery or Hellenistic-Roman architecture, and papyrology had not even come into existence as a discipline. There was little but "common sense" to check the excesses of the Tübingen or the early Dutch school of [A. D.] Loman and [W. C.] van Manen which followed it along equally radical lines. Almost nothing was then known about the background of rabbinic Judaism, though most of the extant sources had been published. Even more serious was the fact that the language of the New Testament was in large part so different from any other Greek known ... as to seem like an undatable foreign body.[15]

Baur did work on Gnosticism, and laid the foundations, in his *Über das christliche in Platonismus, oder Socrates und Christus* (1837) for a great deal of fin de siècle work on comparative religion; but after his *Symbolik*, he did not range far to the East for his sources. The same would be true of Adolf von Harnack, who returned to Hellenistic religion and philosophy later in the century. Liberal theology's avoidance of "oriental" material thus left the field open for orientalists to deal New Testament criticism a series of devastating blows, when at last the time came for it too to be fully historicized and placed in the cultural and social context of its time (see Chapter 6).

But, at mid-century, progress along these lines was hampered by the fact that beyond the Baur School, there were few scholars willing to devote themselves to the study of the Hellenistic world. This was a world that fit uncomfortably into the national history paradigms so beautifully articulated by Ernst Curtius (for Greece) and Theodor Mommsen (for Rome); it was moreover a field that required a kind of sensitivity for religious piety, something alien to the positivist historicists and liberals of the generation of 1848. It required crossing disciplinary borders, from theology to philology and secular history, something philologists in particular found discomfiting, as it also required the study of "silver age" Greek and/or mixed and "late" oriental languages. And it required crossing the oriental/Greek divide, something made more difficult by specialization and less attractive by the combination of mid-century philhellenism and positivist rejection of romantic speculation. After Lachmann, wrote Eduard Schwartz – a member of the fin de siècle generation better suited to the challenges of studying the Hellenistic world – this sort of study languished, "because the philologists who followed him had neither desire nor courage" to continue his New Testament cleanup.[16] Droysen himself was unable to write the planned volume of his Hellenistic history treating the rise of Christianity, and though he recognized by the 1840s that Jewish Hellenism did deserve a place in his portrayal of the post-Alexandrian world,

[15] W. F. Albright, *History, Archaeology and Christian Humanism* (New York, 1964), pp. 36–7. Loman and van Manen were Dutch New Testament scholars whose claims – including their challenges to the authenticity of Paul's four major epistles – were even more radical than those of the Tübingen School.

[16] Eduard Schwartz, "Rede auf Hermann Usener" [1906], in idem, *Vergangene Gegenwärtigkeiten*, p. 308.

he never managed to integrate it into his history.[17] Theodor Mommsen struggled to write volume 4 of his *Roman History* in part because the anti-clerical liberal felt ill at ease with theological questions and source materials; as Schwartz noted, Mommsen misunderstood Cicero "because he did not understand Hellenistic ways of life" and judged all individuals by the standards of the classical Greeks. The Roman historian used much of the room in this volume that might have been devoted to another quintessentially Hellenistic figure, Jesus, to deal with a *Realpolitik* statesman clearly more comprehensible and intriguing to the great opponent of Bismarck: Julius Caesar.[18]

One of the few liberal-era scholars who did have a feel for the Hellenistic world was Mommsen's friend Jacob Bernays. Trained both in classics and in rabbinical Hebrew, Bernays was unusual in many ways; Jean Bollack calls him "a man between two worlds."[19] In addition to holding fast to his Judaism despite his immersion in Protestant academia, Bernays loved Hellenistic rather than classical antiquity and interested himself in the history of scholarship at a time that others were satisfied simply to boast of their escape from the dilettantism of the past. The son of Hamburg rabbi and Schelling fan Isaak Bernays, Jacob received his classical training at the Johanneum Gymnasium and then at the University of Bonn. He admired Lachmann – they both published editions of Lucretius in 1850–2 – and Friedrich Ritschl (later also Nietzsche's *Doktorvater*), who was extremely kind to him. Bernays completed his doctorate in 1848; thanks to the revolution's loosening of restrictions on Jews, he was able to habilitate and receive a *Privatdozent* position that same year. Hoping for a secular post, in 1849 he resisted attempts to appoint him rabbi of the Hamburg community to replace his just deceased father.[20] But, with the revolution's defeat, Bernays, who did not contemplate conversion, was out of the running for a chair. Christian Bunsen tried to help him – in fact, Bernays may have been his guest in England (1851) at the same time as was the notoriously anti-Semitic Paul de Lagarde. But to no avail; Bernays' religion was as much of a handicap in England as at home. Returning to the German states, Bernays first took a teaching position at the Jüdisch-Theologisches Seminar in Breslau, founded in 1852 (see below), and then returned to Bonn, as *Extraordinarius* and director of the University library. During his time there (1865–81), he found many Christian friends and admirers, among them Hermann Usener and Max Müller. He could not bring himself to enter into the debate over Heinrich von Treitschke's anti-Semitic propaganda, neither willing to side with Mommsen – who had

---

[17] See Momigliano, "J. G. Droysen between Greeks and Jews," in idem, *Essays in Ancient and Modern Historiography* (Oxford, 1977), pp. 315–18.

[18] Schwartz, "Rede auf Theodor Mommsen" [1904], in idem, *Vergangene Gegenwärtigkeiten*, pp. 291–2; Ernst Bammel, "Judentum, Christentum und Heidentum: Julius Wellhausens Briefe an Theodor Mommsen, 1881–1902," in *Zeitschrift für Kirchengeschichte* 80 (1969): 227.

[19] Jean Bollack, *Jacob Bernays: un homme entre deux mondes*, (Villeneuve d'Ascq, 1998).

[20] Jacob Toury, "German Jewry in Mid-Nineteenth Century, as Background to Jacob Bernays' Life," in *Jacob Bernays, Un philologue juif*, ed. John Glucker and André Laks (Villeneuve d'Ascq, 1996), p. 11.

projected the eventual conversion of the Jews – nor to take up the pen against his friend. Arnaldo Momigliano suspected the controversy killed him.[21]

What is most interesting, for our purposes, are Bernays' anomalous qualities, intellectual passions, and career moves, as well as his typical mid-century ones. Unlike his father, he was no romantic and admired instead the patron saints of mid-century positivism, Niebuhr and Lachmann. Although he also admired Mommsen and Gibbon, he did not attempt to write grand-scale narratives, as did they, and his major works were careful editions and narrowly focused studies. He both benefited from liberal policies and attitudes toward Jews and suffered from their incomplete institutional articulation as well as from liberalism's own blind spots. Perhaps most atypical of his classicist peers was his insistence that societies in their evolution required both "Athens" and "Jerusalem"[22] – here he was rather closer to Droysen, though unlike this liberal-nationalist Lutheran, Bernays did not see Christianity as the synthesis of "East and West," but rather as a corrupted form of Judaism. Bernays loved the Greeks, but could not study them in the "laique" mode characteristic of his generation; his Greeks were not always rational, nor was religion a negligible part of their history. He wanted the East to get its due, but he was not willing to devote his career exclusively to Jewish studies or to engage in the polemics carried out by his Jewish friends Abraham Geiger and Heinrich Graetz. An eighteenth-century-style polymath in a field (*Altertumswissenschaft*) increasingly inhabited by specialists, he did not learn the "newer" oriental languages, hieroglyphics, or cuneiform. In search of a soul mate, he wrote an admiring study of Joseph Scaliger, a man, in Bernays' portrait, vastly learned and philologically incisive, knowledgeable about things oriental and classical, and unappreciated by his age.[23] As Momigliano commented: "When he formulated his program in 1855 in his *Scaliger* he was in fact propounding a via media between the wild orientalizing speculations of Creuzer and the sound classical distrust of Lobeck."[24] In his era, this via media was at least as difficult and fraught with peril as the attempt to find a middle road between German liberalism and pious Judaism, between classical studies and orientalism – but as Bernays' career shows, it was, in the mid-nineteenth century, a possibility.

THE (EVEN LONGER) ROAD TO "SCIENTIFIC" JUDAISM

Jacob Bernays was certainly not the first nor the only German-Jewish scholar pursuing the study of the Orient. Although they would not necessarily have thought of Judaism as an "oriental" religion, Jews in religious schools had for centuries studied their own Hebrew texts and Talmudic commentaries. Those who inhabited the Mediterranean rim knew a great deal about the peoples around them and often spoke or even read Arabic, Turkish, and other "oriental"

---

[21] Momigliano, "Jacob Bernays," in idem, *Essays on Ancient and Modern Judaism*, ed. Silvia Berti, trans. Maura Masella-Gayley (Chicago, IL, 1994), pp. 144–70, esp. p. 161; Wilfried Nippel, "Jacob Bernays," in *Über das Studium der alten Geschichte*, ed. Wilfried Nippel (Munich, 1993), pp. 166–7.

[22] Bollack, *Jacob Bernays*, p. 61.

[23] Grafton, *Scaliger* 1: 1–3.

[24] Momigliano, "Jacob Bernays," p. 169.

languages. Most of their learning was put to use in their local communities, but some did interact with Christian and Muslim scholars. In the eighteenth century, some Jewish scholars founded German-language journals, and began the process Moses Mendelssohn would champion of breaking down barriers between Jewish and Christian learning. By the early nineteenth century, some of these barriers had been breached; Jews were allowed to attend universities and in some cases to teach as *Privatdozenten* – though not as regular staff members.

Thanks to Mendelssohn, Herder, Michaelis, and other enlightened Old Testament scholars, it became possible to integrate Jewish history more fully into the history of the ancient world and to debate the contributions of the Jews to the history of "civilization" – rather than discussing them purely as Christian ancestors. That this had become debatable was a sign that the Creuzerian insistence on religion as the foundation of civilization was losing out to classicizing secular history; and while we might cheer the secularization of scholarship, we should note that this change in the conceptualization of European cultural history was not altogether a happy development for the Jews. Battling conservative clerical forces within their own community and Christian prejudice outside of it, the Jews who launched the *Wissenschaft des Judentums* as a scholarly enterprise wished to walk a line between these two conceptions of European and world history, retaining religion as an important factor in civilization's development while also seeking to write history convincing and relevant to individuals of all faiths. Drawing on the work of the Jewish enlightenment, Hegel's student Eduard Ganz and F. A. Wolf's student Leopold Zunz instigated the founding of the Verein für Cultur und Wissenschaft der Juden in 1819. They hoped not only to initiate the construction of a non-sectarian, objective, cultural history that could be shared by all Jews, but also to create a field of Jewish studies, which would be – like classical studies – an indispensable component of European *Bildung*.[25]

In retrospect, the project appears both absurdly utopian and rigidly liberal-assimilationist; from the outset it was opposed from within the Jewish community by orthodox Jews, and Protestant positivists were never convinced that Jews could be objective narrators of their own (much less of Christian Europe's) history. But it survived and produced a remarkable outpouring of scholarship, published in scholarly journals such as *Wissenschaftliche Zeitschrift für jüdische Theologie* as well as more popular ones like *Der Orient: Berichte, Studien und Kritiken fur jüdische Geschichte und Literatur zunächst für Staatsmänner und Gesetzgeber, für höhere Theologie und Orientalismus, für Bibliotheken und Museen*, and by a network of Jewish publishing houses. The *Wissenschaft des Judentums* had religious-reformist ambitions to be sure – but much of its scholarship was just as deeply historicist, positivist, and philologically informed as that of Christian contemporaries, as just as deeply devoted to that supremely important liberal-rationalist virtue: *Wissenschaftlichkeit*.

To gain the respect of their liberal Christian peers without becoming apostates, the *Wissenschaft des Judentums* in this era sought to go beyond religious polemics

---

[25] See Veltri, "Altertumswissenschaft und Wissenschaft des Judentums," p. 47; Christian Wiese, *Wissenschaft des Judentums und protestantische Theologie im wilhelminischen Deutschland: Ein Schrei ins Leere?* (Tübingen, 1999), pp. 59–85.

by engaging in uncontroversial *Wissenschaft* (the model for which was, of course, classical philology). The intellectuals who founded *Der Orient* in 1840 did not envision having to give up their Jewishness to be scientific: "Science is a free gift," wrote editor (and Leipzig *Privatdozent*) Julius Fürst in the first issue, "like the love of life, which we breathe, like the rays of the sun, which warm us; science does not discriminate according to confessions, but between truth and lies."[26] Not surprisingly, one of the central aims for this group of scholars was the creation of (paying) university positions for the study of the history of Judaism; this would have offered Jewish scholars a position of authority outside the synagogue, where objective inquiries could be carried out, and individuals too radical (or too exclusively devoted to scholarship) for rabbinical careers could earn their livelihood – just as was the case in contemporary Catholic and especially Protestant theological faculties. But when Zunz approached the University of Berlin with a proposal for the founding of a chair for Jewish History and Literature in 1848, the faculty failed to understand Zunz's secularizing aims and answered that it was not the university's business to train rabbis.[27]

The failure of this movement to secure such posts at mid-century was certainly consequential. Without such secular posts – and without state funding – Jewish scholars were obliged to depend on private funding and to remain within seminary settings. Several reform-oriented institutions emerged in which those inspired by the movement flourished, including the Jüdisch-Theologisches Seminar in Breslau (founded 1854) and in 1872 of the Hochschule für die Wissenschaft des Judentums in Berlin. For most of the period covered by this book, German and Austrian university faculties refused to hire unconverted Jews for anything other than auxiliary posts. Thus, during critical decades in the evolution of orientalism and of German liberalism, those who were best suited to make the case for Judaism's cultural impact and scholarly traditions beyond the Old Testament were relegated to a sphere most Christian academics considered unscientific and of exclusively parochial significance.

That the "Science of Judaism" was compelled to develop outside the university system, while Catholic and Protestant theologies developed within it, certainly was the product of anti-Semitic prejudice and discriminatory treatment. But perhaps in the context of our other inquiries, we can understand this "failure" also as the result of the halting development of modern oriental studies more generally. The *Wissenschaft des Judentums*, in part as a reaction to deep and long Christian preoccupation with the world of the Old Testament, tended to focus on later periods – medieval Spain, for example – and to prefer cultural history to the political history so beloved to Ranke's generation.[28] As far as academic philologists were concerned, post-Hellenistic Jewish theology and history were subjects rather like post-Qur'anic Arabic literature or "modern" Indian religion – later, and far less interesting, chapters in the lives of peoples whose essence they had already captured. That private patronage was so critical in funding institutions and journals is interesting – but much of the study of the "modern" East until the

[26] Julius Fürst, "Vorwort," in *Der Orient* 1 (1840): vii.
[27] Ismar Schorsch, *From Text to Context: The Turn to History in Modern Judaism* (Hanover, NH, 1994), p. 352.
[28] Ibid., pp. 71–92.

very late nineteenth century was privately funded, as were the early archaeological ventures in Asia Minor.[29] It is certainly the case that Jews, as Jews, were excluded and the study of Judaism segregated, ignored, and even discouraged by the German states; but the struggles of the "Science of Judaism" for *Wissenschaftlichkeit* must be seen also in the context of a wider set of battles of modern history and nonwestern cultures for the respect of a humanistically-trained educated elite.

The *Wissenschaft des Judentums* has been extensively studied, especially by scholars wishing to critique what was perceived to be another sort of failure: its endorsement of assimilation or even conversion. Susannah Heschel, by contrast, has suggested that the movement should be seen as an early example of post-colonialist writing. "Nineteenth-century German-Jewish historians," she argues, "were the first to call into question accepted 'truths' about the history of the West and the respective roles played in it by Christianity and Judaism."[30] Abraham Geiger, one of the movement's leading lights, was not trying to Christianize Judaism, but rather to Judaize Christianity – and he incited a tremendous debate among Protestant scholars by claiming, in his *Urschrift und Übersetzungen der Bibel in ihrer Abhängigkeit von der inneren Entwicklung des Judentums* (1857), that Jesus was essentially just another Pharisee. Naturally, such a charge was deeply controversial. But Geiger was taken seriously, perhaps because, like Bernays, he had been trained in the academy, in his case, at the University of Bonn, where he studied history with Niebuhr and Arabic with Georg Freytag. Indeed, Geiger's dissertation, *Was hat Mohammed aus dem Judenthume aufgenommen?* (see Islamic section below), received a prize despite the fact that the author had become a rabbi (in Wiesbaden) by the time the prize was awarded. Geiger was respected outside the Jewish community, at least by important scholars such as Freytag, Heinrich Ewald, Theodor Nöldeke, and Alexander von Humboldt. That his more provocative biblical scholarship succeeded in unsettling old certainties, provoking wide-ranging debate, and opening new lines of research,[31] testifies to the willingness of both liberal Jews and liberal Protestant scholars to engage "the other," while also defending their existing prejudices.

Interestingly, one of the normative strains of thought mid-century Jewish scholars believed they needed to challenge, at least in part, was philhellenism. If the Greeks had bequeathed modern Europeans so many of their secular arts – philosophy, the sciences, the fine arts – it must not be forgotten, the argument went, that monotheism was a Jewish invention. The Greek nation did not possess a higher morality; as Heinrich Graetz put it, it lived "only for the present, not for the future, and lived only for itself, not for others."[32] It is worth quoting the introduction of Graetz's *Geschichte der Juden* (published in 1874; the multivolume project was begun in 1853) at some length to get a sense of the importance of this claim to Europe's rootedness in Hebraism as well as Hellenism, for liberal Jews as well as for their Christian counterparts.

[29] See Olaf Matthes, *James Simon: Mäzen im wilhelmischen Zeitalter* (Berlin, 2000), pp. 135–265.
[30] Heschel, *Abraham Geiger*, p. 3.
[31] Ibid., p. 59.
[32] Graetz, "Introduction to Volume One of the History of the Jews," in idem, *The Structure of Jewish History and Other Essays*, trans. and ed. Ismar Schorsch (New York, 1975), p. 186.

If you take away from the Latin, German, and Slavic nations of our day on both sides of the ocean that which they owe to the peoples of Greece and Israel, a great deal would be gone. But we can't even finish this line of argument; it is simply impossible to deprive these nations of that which was borrowed and to separate it from their very being. It has so permeated their blood and sap, that it constitutes part of the organism itself, which in turn has become its carrier and transmitter. It was the ladder by which these nations ascended to the top, or even better: it was the electrical current which unleashed the slumbering forces within them. Hellenism and Hebraism or – to speak without affectation – Judaism, have together created an atmosphere of ideas without which civilized nations would be unthinkable.

But Graetz then goes on to contrast the differing sorts of respect accorded to these two great traditions:

The part played by Hellenism in the rebirth of civilization is acknowledged freely and without envy. It dispersed the flowers of art and the fruits of knowledge. It unveiled the realm of beauty and illuminated it with an Olympian clarity of thought. And a regenerative power continues to pour forth from this literature and the legacy of its artistic ideal. The classical Greeks are dead, and toward them deceased posterity behaves properly. Envy and hatred are silent at the grave of the dead; their contributions are, in fact, usually exaggerated. It is quite different with that other creative nation, the Hebrews. Precisely because they're still alive their contributions to culture are not generally acknowledged; they are criticized, or given another name to partially conceal their authorship or to dislodge them entirely.[33]

Graetz's insights here deserve emphasis; he acknowledges the Greeks' contributions to the "organism" of European culture without "envy" – and he does not seek to scoop them by pointing out their late arrival in the course of the history of civilizations or by insisting on the debts they might owe to other oriental cultures. But he does ask for the equal appreciation of the contributions of the Hebrews, something posterity has not accorded them simply because (insofar as he is willing to specify a cause) the latter culture is still living. He says nothing, explicitly, about the utility of such a view of history – the purpose of revising our appreciation of the past is to rectify an imbalance in the understanding of shared, cultural ancestry. But redressing this imbalance would surely contribute to closing the gap between Jews and gentiles in the present.

If one can call Graetz's history a contribution to oriental studies, it is clearly one whose functions have little to do with conceptualizing external others and everything to do with trying to close the East-West gap at home. That this line of thinking was acceptable to some non-Jewish liberals is evident in the very similar formulations of both Ernest Renan and Matthew Arnold; though Renan, in particular, managed to essentialize the contribution of the Semites so as to all but negate this attempt at throwing bridges.[34] It should be noted, however, that none of these individuals really wanted to understand Judaism as an exclusively eastern phenomenon, nor were they eager to champion the autonomous achievements of

---

[33] Ibid., pp. 174–5, 176.

[34] To appreciate Renan's complexity, see both his "Prière sur l'Acropole" in his *Souvenirs d'enfance et de jeunesse* (Paris, 1973), pp. 73–9, and "Des religions de l'antiquité," pp. 821–48, as well as Dora Bierer, "Renan and His Interpreters: A Study in French Intellectual Warfare," *Journal of Modern History* 25, no. 4 (Dec. 1953): 375–89.

the Orient, as was the case for the neoromantic generation a few years hence. Together with liberal optimism, this all too Eurocentric and assimilationist orientation would become intolerable to the orientalists of the fin de siècle.

THE LONELY ARABISTS

The study of Arabic and other Semitic languages (*Arabistik* or sometimes *Semitistik*) was also, at mid-century, struggling to adjust itself to the Graecophile, but still deeply Christian cultural world of the German states. Though the Germans, like the other Europeans, had been interested in learning about the Islamic world at least since the Crusades, this part of the Orient did not inspire nearly as many romantic panegyrics as did India; the histories of the two rival faiths were too entangled and bitter for that. There had been some eighteenth-century interest in things Islamic – or better, in things that came from Islamic countries, like Persian poetry, noble beduins, or bloodthirsty conquerors. But even here, it was by no means easy to effect a full divorce between Arabic or Islamic studies and the theological faculty. In the mid-eighteenth century, J. J. Reiske – who refused to teach Hebrew and spent much of his career copying manuscripts in Leiden – attempted to make the case for the full separation of oriental studies and theology. But his aspirations were crushed by the opposition of Michaelis and the Dutch Arabist Albert Schultens and he took to calling himself a "martyr for Arabic literature."[35]

The German Arabists of the 1820s–1870s certainly suffered from continuing low levels of public interest and state support for their field; whether or not there was much personal passions involved in their "martyrdom" is another question. Aside from evincing interest in Persian and Arabic poetry and fables, the romantics did not much care for the religious life and secular history of the Islamic world – indeed, Friedrich Schlegel gave up his initial studies of Persian for Sanskrit precisely because too many Persian texts were overtly Islamic ones (see Chapter 1). Being a late-arriving religion, with respect to Hinduism, Buddhism, Judaism, and Christianity, Islam never really attracted the same sort of respect – and in fact the accusation that it was merely derivative robbed it of some of the appeal it might otherwise have had, given the long list of "civilized" achievements to which Arabs and Ottomans could point. Islam was not old enough to have contributed to Christianity, and Arab cultures and languages were not linked to European ones by way of William Jones's linguistic tree. Over the course of the century's first decades, the study of Arabic and Persian did grow; it was easier for students who already knew Hebrew to learn Arabic or Persian than to learn Sanskrit or hieroglyphics. And yet, at least until the 1890s, there was even less public interest in the field than in sub-specialties with more relevance to classically-educated German Christians such as Egyptology or Old Testament criticism.

---

[35] Mangold, *Eine "weltbürgerliche Wissenschaft,"* p. 33; Soubhi Nasser Hussain, "Die Bestrebungen der deutschen Orientalistik bis zum Ende des 2. Weltkrieges auf dem Gebiet der arabischen Literatur" (dissertation, Karl Marx Unversität, Leipzig, 1983), pp. 55–6.

Those Christians who did evince interest in the field tended to be even more liberal and enlightened than their counterparts in other fields of *Orientalistik*. If they continued to dislike Islam, they tended to have more friends across borders and especially to be more intimately acquainted with Jewish scholarship and more accepting of Jews in the profession. Ismar Schorsch estimates that twenty of the forty-nine people who attended the founding of the Deutsch-Morgenländische Gesellschaft – in its early days heavily dominated by Arabists – were Jews, and that one-third of the dissertations overseen by Heinrich Fleischer at the University of Leipzig between 1866 and 1886 were written by Jews. Though the career paths of talented Jewish Arabists like Moritz Steinschneider continued to be torturous, as Schorsch points out, Fleischer's courageous devotion to this cause did make a difference, both intellectually and in terms of institutional development.[36]

Still, the field, and especially its secular and modern branches, developed slowly, for its practice and especially its teaching were still dominated by its origins as an exegetical *Hilfswissenschaft*. Syriac was something of a bread and butter language, for theologians still needed to read it (many of the oldest remnants of New Testament texts were written in that language). Turkish was universally considered inferior to classical Arabic and Persian. After Syriac, these two languages were the most highly respected – if, that is, one studied them in their earliest, purest forms; virtually no one tried to teach modern spoken dialects. The reason for this was in part the widespread presumption that the earliest form of a language reveals the essence of the people who speak it. But scholars also hoped that Persian might help throw light on the world of the Zend Avesta and the early Aryans and believed that Arabic's earliest speakers might be the descendants of the ancient Israelites. As we have seen, this conceit was what drove Michaelis to conceive of the "Happy Arabia" expedition, and it was still alive and well in the work of Julius Wellhausen, who turned from Old Testament criticism to *Islamforschung* in the last years of the nineteenth century.

But before we get to Wellhausen, we must spend a little time with Creuzer's Austrian friend, Joseph von Hammer-Purgstall, who should be credited with the founding of modern *Arabistik* and Ottoman history despite the fact that he was trained as a translator and sustained as a Habsburg court translator, rather than as a professor of oriental languages. Paula Fichtner has done a marvelous job of sketching the education and career of this idiosyncratic and hard-working orientalist, so unlike most of the Protestant, professional orientalists of his day.[37] Hammer began to study spoken languages – not theology – as a boy, at the tail end of the Austrian reform era, at Maria Theresa's Oriental Academy. His Freemason father hoped that this unusual training would ensure him a bureaucratic career; and to some extent that was true, though Metternich would never give the

---

[36] Intellectually, Fleischer's commitment to Jewish scholarship led to his long-term collaboration with Rabbi Jacob Levy on his foundational *Neuhebräisches und chaldäisches Wörterbuch*, the first editions of which appeared in 1867. Ismar Schorsch, "Moritz Steinschneider," paper delivered at Dartmouth College, conference on orientalism and Judaism, August 2008, and quoted by permission of the author.

[37] Fichtner, *Terror and Toleration*, pp. 130–61.

adult Hammer what he wanted most, a diplomatic post in Constantinople. Hammer married a Jewish banker's daughter, and, flouting his iconoclastic tastes even more publicly, had Arabic inscriptions placed over the gate to his manor, and on his family tomb.[38] He was a highly idiosyncratic individual, and one who certainly should rate a fully researched biography.

Hammer had very mixed feeling about the Ottoman Empire. Like Busbecq before him, he certainly respected it and thought its history and culture of vital importance for Europeans, as well as being interesting in and of itself. Having kissed the soil of his "spiritual fatherland" when first he crossed the Bosphorus in 1799,[39] Hammer devoted his life to studying Ottoman history, languages, and literature; he spent large sums acquiring Turkish manuscripts and books and openly thanked his Ottoman friends for their assistance, intellectual and practical; in a concluding summary to his ten-volume *Geschichte des Osmanischen Reiches* (1827–35), he even responded, at length, to criticisms made by "my esteemed and learned friend... Melekpashasade Abdulkadirbeg"[40] – at a time when civil debates with nonwestern scholars were rare. He pressed the French hard to give back hundreds of oriental manuscripts Napoleon took from Vienna, and he chastised Eurocentric historians like Gibbon for depending on a narrow range of western sources; their works were not worth reading, he argued, not to mention those of "the legions of authors of pamphlets, with which European is flooded every time there is a war with the Turks."[41] Hammer was especially enamored of Ottoman poetry, which he understood as deriving from praises sung to God or in search of mystical reunion with Him – but he thought Ottoman statecraft, especially in recent years, despotic, and for this he chiefly blamed Islam, "the most intolerant of all religions, which strives for world domination, and thus for constant conquests."[42] The preface to his *Geschichte* spelled out his aspirations in a way that marks him as a man of the moderate Enlightenment: "... I seized my pen without prejudice (*Vorliebe*) and ill-will ... but with love for what is noble and good, with hatred for the shameful and bad, without hatred against Greeks or Turks, without prejudice for Muslims or Christians, but with love for restrained power and well-ordered governance, for the rule of law and the art of war, for public, benevolent institutions and the flourishing of scholarship, and with hatred for rebellion and oppression, for torture and tyranny."[43]

Hammer's work was encyclopedic, and where poetry was concerned, enthusiastic, but according to contemporary specialists, full of linguistic mistakes and overweening generalizations.[44] More scientifically respectable at mid-century was the work of the Leipzig School under the direction of the Arabic philologist

[38] Sibylle Wentker, "Joseph Freiherr von Hammer-Purgstall: Ein Leben zwischen Orient und Okzident," in Hannes D. Galter and Siegfried Haas von Leykam, ed., *Joseph von Hammer-Purgstall: Grenzgänger zwischen Orient und Okzident* (Graz, 2008), p. 7; Anabella Dietz and Rupert Werhart, "Schloss Hainfeld: Ort der ForscherInnen, Ort des Forchens," in ibid., p. 190.

[39] Hammer-Purgstall, *Erinnerungen*, p. 44.

[40] *Geschichte des Osmanischen Reiches* 9: xxix–xxxii.

[41] Ibid., 1: xxvi.

[42] Ibid., 9: xxxix.

[43] Ibid., 1: xxvii–xxviii

[44] Mohl, "Année 1856-7," in idem, *Rapports* 2: 133–8.

Heinrich Leberecht Fleischer, whom we met above. By dint of careful study of Fleischer's correspondence, Sabine Mangold has brought to life the values and achievements of this school, and so I will refrain from a detailed description of it. Suffice it to say that Fleischer, the most influential of Silvestre de Sacy's German students, was committed to painstaking, and non-theological, philological inquiry. He was also a partisan of the "linguistic philology" championed by the classicist Gottfried Herrmann against the conception of "the philology of things" pushed by August Boeckh. Fleischer did not publish much himself (positivist modesty, perhaps), but in the course of his career, he would train more than 300 students, including many non-Germans and Jews; he promoted the careers of the most talented among them, whether or not they converted or stayed in the German states.[45] Despite their methodical training, some of his students – like Martin Hartmann – would eagerly press beyond "pure" philology, while others insisted on the need to remain close to the texts; both groups recognized the importance of the foundations he laid for later scholarly advances.[46] Beyond his role as teacher, Fleischer would also serve his discipline in other ways, serving, most importantly, as lead editor of the *Zeitschrift der deutschen morgenländischen Gesellschaft (ZDMG)* for many of its formative years.

The Leipzig School's philological virtuosity and remarkable productivity had a very important and long-lasting impact on Arabic language studies; but that did not mean that it had much impact on Saxon, or German, culture at large. Its scholarship was devoted to older texts and written by and for a small number of specialists, very few of whom evinced any desire to understand the modern Orient, or even to visit it. I am rather loathe to credit any individuals with the pursuit of "scholarship for its own sake"; Fleischer and the Leipzigers certainly had their own penchants, prejudices, and goals. But they played their cards so close to the chest that it will take much more teasing (and careful reading of Arabic texts) to discover coherent ideological patterns to their usually hyper-empiricist publications. That the school did not provoke a public outcry despite an obvious bias toward religious ecumenicism, an openness to Jews and foreigners (but not women), and a relatively tolerant attitude toward Islam suggests the degree to which it kept its liberalism largely to itself.

Elsewhere, others were less diffident about their aims – which made them both less respectable as Arabists in their day, and in the longer run, more provocative. Most important here was Geiger's *What Did Mohammed Borrow from Judaism?*, which broke with the long tradition of Christian scholarship that labeled Islam a heresy. If Geiger's main aim was to sketch a family tree of religions, with Judaism firmly established as the roots and trunk, in using non-biblical Jewish sources, he also established an important (historicist) model for studying the confusing, syncretic world of early Islam and late antiquity.[47] Ten years after Geiger's book,

---

[45] Róbert Simon, *Ignác Goldziher: His Life and Scholarship as Reflected in his Works and Correspondence* (Leiden, 1986), pp. 36–8.

[46] Mangold, *Eine "weltbürgerliche Wissenschaft,"* pp. 94–5.

[47] Geiger's insistence on the Jewish roots of Islam and the positive portions of Christianity, however, did not appeal to all. After the 1870s, Christians like Wellhausen and Harnack began to insist on the influence of early Christian sources on Judaism and especially on the Greek sources of Christianity. Heschel, *Abraham Geiger*, pp. 53–61.

another scholar educated in Talmudic practice, Gustav Weil, published a biography of Mohammed – the first one, the author claimed, since Jean Gagnier's 1732 *La vie de Mahomet* to be based on original sources.[48] Weil's intention was to fill a gaping hole in the literature by sketching the life and teaching of this "extraordinary man," using not Christian but Arabic sources, including the biography of Ibn Hisam, which was not yet available in print. Well aware of the difficulties of using the Qur'an, Hadith, and hagiographic sources and conscious that in writing history, he was "stepping outside the sphere of my true profession," the philologist insisted that using these Islamic sources critically was the only way to write a truly "scientific" biography of this world-historical figure.[49] Weil's "scientific" orientation led him to offer a much more sympathetic picture of Islam and its founder than even Geiger had offered – though unsurprisingly Weil's assessment was still very much shaped by European norms and prejudices. Muhammed was not a true prophet, Weil concluded, because he had used force to spread his religion; but he had done much good for Arab society, including putting law in the place of arbitrary power, limiting blood feuds and polygamy, and protecting women against brutality. One might go so far, Weil concluded, as to say that "[Muhammed] still ought to appear to non-Muslims as 'God's emissary,' in so far as he planted the most beautiful teachings of the Old and New Testaments among a people who had never been enlightened by a single sunbeam of faith."[50] Weil's attempt to historicize Islam's founder also led him to apply western text-critical techniques to the Qur'an, and in the year following his biography, Weil published a *Historisch-kritische Einleitung in den Koran* (1844) – giving the Islamic holy book a "historical-critical introduction" equivalent to those given the Old and New Testaments by de Wette and Eichhorn.[51]

Let us conclude this brief section by noting that while Gustav Weil would earn scientific respectability on the basis of his histories and critical philological studies, his best-seller continued to be his first effort – his translation of the *1001 Nights*. His translation was far more authentically "oriental" than was Galland's French version, for Weil took his material exclusively from Arabic sources and did have an excellent command of the language – unusually, he had actually spent four years in Egypt, studying with Arabic scholars. Weil's first edition of 1838 was followed regularly by new ones throughout the next century and three-quarters; a new edition was published by Nebel Verlag in 2004. Thanks to the work of Weil, the translations made by Joseph von Hammer-Purgstall and Friedrich Rückert and the notoriety of Goethe's *West-östliche Divan*, the cultivation of Persian and Arabic poetry continued; indeed enough was known about it for Hammer-Purgstall to publish, between 1850 and his death in 1856, a history of Arabic literature, which ran to seven volumes.[52] One can smirk at such efforts, labeling them purely "exoticizing" – but were they more so than Grimm's fairy tales or the

---

[48] Weil, *Mohammed der Prophet: Sein Leben und seine Lehre* (Stuttgart, 1843), pp. vii–viii. Even that one, Weil argued, was only a hodgepodge of translated texts – and those riddled with errors.

[49] Ibid., pp. ix–xxiii, quotation p. xxiii.

[50] Ibid., p. 402.

[51] Later in his career, Weil would also write a *Geschichte der islamitischen Völker* (1866) and a three-volume *Geschichte der Chalifen* (1846–62).

[52] Hussain, "Bestrebungen der deutschen Orientalistik," pp. 51–95.

Nibelungenlied? Even considered as exotic objects for consumption, these texts were considered valuable enough to be worth rendering faithfully, and it was widely recognized that, unlike most ancient texts, these works could delight or inspire non-academic readers. As both the lonely Arabists and the equally lonely Germanic philologists of this era recognized, some forms of "orientalism" pleased the public, others bought one entry, if one were talented and fortunate, into the realm of Knowledge. One could work in both worlds without reducing the Orient to only one thing.

THE INDO-EUROPEANISTS

Having surveyed the pursuit of biblical criticism and *Arabistik*, it is time we pass on to the other great oriental field defined by the mid-century *ZDMG* – Sanskrit studies, which was, over the course of the 1820s–1850s, both losing some of its romantic luster and fragmenting internally. By the mid-1820s, Indological *Schwärmerei* was no longer fashionable; but this does not mean it disappeared entirely. Some champions of romantic India – including Schelling, Rückert, and A. W. Schlegel continued to write and teach students long after that date and romantic preoccupations – such as the desire to locate Eden or to find the *Ursprache* – still surfaced from time to time. A subterranean stream of esoteric literature kept Creuzerism alive, and in some circles, perhaps especially among Christian missionaries and Catholic liberals, the "ancient theology" also lived on. But, aside from the tiny circles around Schopenhauer and Rückert, the promotion of eastern priority, sagacity, or superiority was quite rare at mid-century. Even the esoteric Richard Wagner – whose brother-in-law Hermann Brockhaus was an Indologist – shelved plans made in the mid-1850s for a Buddhist opera, *Die Sieger*, in favor of the medievalizing *Tristan* and Ring cycle.[53]

Those who wanted to pursue Indology as a career did feel the need to distance themselves from romantic rhetoric, and they did so, not surprisingly, by embracing the same sort of narrowly-focused, philologically-exacting, and historically-minded scholarship embraced by their brothers in *Arabistik*. Eschewing the more flowery and speculative work of the older generation, which Jules Mohl called "erotic and emotional rubbish,"[54] the new professionals adopted new heroes, Thomas Colebrooke and Eugene Burnouf, in the place of older ones, such as Friedrich Schlegel. Philologically adept and wary of theological and political controversies, Colebrooke and Burnouf played the role for orientalists played by K. O. Müller for classicists after the Creuzer *Streit*, diminishing the role of genetic argumentation and focusing attention on researchable historical questions. This was especially clear in the group of literary-historical scholars descended from A. W. Schlegel, who made it his goal to apply the principles of classical philology to the study of things Indian.[55] But those who descended from the school of his

---

[53] Halbfass, *India and Europe*, pp. 155, 124.

[54] Douglas T. McGetchin, "Wilting Florists: The Turbulent Early Decades of the Société Asiatique, 1822–1860," in *Journal of the History of Ideas* 64, no. 4 (October 2003): 569–78; Mohl quoted in Schwab, *Oriental Renaissance*, p. 103.

[55] Schlegel, "Ueber den gegenwärtigen Zustand," pp. 14–15.

erstwhile Sanskrit teacher Franz Bopp made their own attempts to develop and apply rigorous philological principles – with, as we shall see, fateful cultural consequences.

Positivism and the Origins of the Aryan-Semitic Divide

The story of Franz Bopp's career path is important in and of itself – for Bopp would lay the foundations for the field of Indo-European linguistics, and for much of Sanskrit study in his day. But Bopp's story also tells us a great deal about his and his field's movement from romantic universalism to philological respectability, a not inconsequential cultural leap. Bopp began his studies in French-occupied Aschaffenburg, under the tutelage of the romantic Catholic philosopher (and former Illuminati) K. J. Windischmann. The world in which the two met was, as Bopp's student Salomon Lefmann noted, one suffused with the ideas of Friedrich Creuzer, Franz von Baader, and Friedrich Schlegel – and one, Lefmann added, despised or forgotten by the time of his mentor's death. But it was romantic idealism that inspired the young Bopp to go to Paris, where he was determined to find the truth of the Vedas; "The Truth is veiled in them, in order that it not blind the laity," he wrote to Windischmann in early 1815.[56] At the time, Bopp was also studying Arabic and Persian (he already had Hebrew), which he thought essential to drawing parallels between Semitic and Indian language groups. But the next years brought frustration; the University of Würzburg refused to hire him, as the theological faculty already had one orientalist (teaching Hebrew, Syriac, Aramaic, and Arabic), and thought a Persian and Sanskrit scholar would be a "literary extravagance," for he would have no students, and no relevance to biblical interpretation. Assisted by the Humboldt brothers, Bopp eventually got a post at the University of Berlin and focused his efforts on linguistic questions, looking back, as it were, behind Creuzerian cultural history to the eighteenth-century search for a "universal grammar." But as Bopp quickly realized, the time for universalism was over.

Bopp was a Sanskrit scholar, but, as his *Ausführliches Lehrgebäude der Sanskritsprache* of 1827 suggested, he was not interested in pursuing the historicist Indology of his erstwhile student A. W. Schlegel, now professor of Indology at the University of Bonn. Bopp also preferred the grammatical knowledge of Colebrooke and Charles Wilkins to that of the indigenous Indian tradition upon which Schlegel depended, and Germandom's first professional Sanskritists soon became antagonists rather than friends.[57] Increasingly, Bopp called himself not an orientalist but a scholar of comparative linguistics. But this supposedly all-embracing term concealed the fact that Bopp's new science was founded with his first love, Sanskrit, and his country's *Muttersprache* at the center of its concerns, reaffirming linkages that had been made for his own purposes by Friedrich Schlegel. Like Schlegel, Bopp was not really interested in linguistics as a whole, but in relations between Sanskrit, the great humanist languages, Latin and Greek, and German; the

---

[56] Lefmann, *Franz Bopp: Sein Leben und seine Wissenschaft*, vol. 1 (Berlin, 1891), pp. 9–31; quotation, Bopp to Windischmann, February 24, 1815, in ibid., 2: 18–19.
[57] Ibid., 1: 33–144.

science he articulated involved the sketching of the proper sort of tree, around which the other "Indo-European" languages could be arranged – and leaving the other language groups to fend for themselves.[58]

Though Bopp, by the end of his life, was an internationally respected and honored scholar, his was not a career without conflict. Reflecting much later on the difficulties his teacher faced, Max Müller recalled the period in the 1820s and 1830s in which scholars and especially classicists

would not believe that there could be any community of origin between the people of Athens and Rome, and the so-called Niggers of India.... No one ever was for a time so completely laughed down as Professor Bopp, when he first published his *Comparative Grammar of Sanskrit, Zend, Greek, Latin, and Gothic*. All hands were against him; and if in comparing Greek and Latin with Sanskrit, Gothic, Celtic, Slavonic, or Persian, he happened to have placed one single accent wrong, the shouts of those who knew nothing but Greek and Latin, and probably looked in their Greek Dictionaries to be quite sure of their accents, would never end.[59]

In general, Bopp seems to have reacted to criticism simply by making sure *his* diacritical marks were correct, but occasionally he did attempt to trump the classicists' objections by playing, as had Friedrich Schlegel, the nationalist card: "For what is more important and can be desired more urgently from the study of classical languages than the comparison of these with our mother tongue in its most ancient, most perfect form?" he asked in the introduction to his *Comparative Grammar*.[60] It was, of course, not too surprising that the classicists would remain hostile; as Wilhelm Corssen wrote in the widely circulated *Neue Jahrbücher für Philologie und Pädagogik* in 1853, "That classical philology received comparative linguistics with mistrust and doubt was very natural. The newborn younger sister threatened to pull the painstakingly prepared ground from under the feet of the elder, in giving her to understand, you have wandered in darkness up until now; I will enlighten you. Few trusted these voices at the beginning, many closed their ears to the sirens' songs..."[61] Perhaps they were won over, as they were eventually, as much by the Indo-Europeanist's modesty as by his sound scholarship. For Bopp and his students did do pioneering work on the languages of the Roma and of the Lithuanians, on Avestan and on Armenian, but they were not in the business of boasting about the mental or cultural attributes of the peoples whose tongues they studied; indeed, their works were (and still are) extremely hard for anyone outside the charmed circle of comparative linguists to understand. These scholars did not suggest replacing Gymnasium classicism with a more wide-ranging, comparative humanism – though in many ways, comparative *Sprachwissenschaft* would lay the foundations for such a move. Though they made comparative

---

[58] For a careful assessment of Bopp's role in founding the field, see Reinhard Sternemann, "Franz Bopp und die vergleichende indoeuropäische Sprachwissenschaft," in *Innsbrucker Beiträge zur Sprachwissenschaft, Vorträge und Kleinere Schriften* (Innsbruck, 1984), p. 33.

[59] Friedrich Max Müller, *India: What Can It Teach Us?* (London, 2nd ed., 1892), p. 28.

[60] Bopp, *Vergleichende Grammatik des Sanskrit, Send, Armenischen, Griechischen, Lateinischen, Litauischen, Altslavischen, Gothischen und Deutschen* (Berlin, 3rd ed., 1868) (1st ed., vol. 1, 1833), p. vi.

[61] Corssen quoted in Lefmann, *Franz Bopp*, 1: 292.

linguistics a science, they did not displace the culture of classicism; they were, in effect, sirens who opted not to sing.

Bopp made his brand of oriental studies scientifically acceptable. But the road to scientific acceptance Bopp plotted did have some significant cultural consequences. Already in 1823, Bopp told Windischmann that the comparative study of Sanskrit and Semitic languages he had planned had been put on hold: "I think it is better to juxtapose, again and again, individual points of grammar; this way allows one to go deeper."[62] After a break in their correspondence, owing apparently to Bopp's marriage to a Protestant and to sharp things Bopp said about the Pope,[63] Windischmann pled with his student to send him the results of his work on relations between Hebrew and Sanskrit: "I am now eagerly at work on the *History of Philosophy* in order to prepare the final edition. I beg you, therefore, urgently [to respond]," he wrote.[64] Bopp did not respond nor did Windischmann finish his encyclopedic history; the first four parts appeared as *Philosophie im Fortgang der Weltgeschichte* between 1827 and 1834, but treated only China and Japan, subjects about which Windischmann learned not from modern philologists, but from early modern Jesuit compilers.

This communicative failure was not the last time a close friend begged Bopp to seek common Indo-European and Semitic linguistic ground. In the last line of the last letter Wilhelm von Humboldt wrote to his beloved interlocutor Bopp, the Prussian nobleman mentioned that he had been reading a work by Julius Fürst on the connections between the Semitic and Sanskritic *Sprachstamme*: "When you've seen this publication, would you be so good as to give me your opinion of it?"[65] But Bopp never did venture onto this terrain; as his biographer commented, he already had taken on many languages and did not feel himself competent to embrace the Semitic ones as well, nor to risk his credentials on results generated by someone else: "In his scientific work, Bopp simply was unable to make the solution [to a problem] dependent on someone else's judgment or to let another determine the path of his own research."[66] And therein, one can see in retrospect, lies one of the heartbreaking moments in the history of scholarship: the birth of segregated Semitic and Indo-European languages from the spirit of philological positivism.

We cannot conclude from this that Bopp was a racist or that oriental studies were destined to develop purely along racial lines; but the period after about 1820 did see the fleshing out of the language groupings sketched by William Jones and Friedrich Schlegel, in ways that led to the writing of various sorts of self-aggrandizing and exclusionary prehistories. Quietly and unobtrusively, a process of mapping was going on, which kept a skeletal version of the speculative and sweeping trajectories of the romantics while also introducing deeper and sometimes racialized critiques of the post-biblical Orient. Lurking behind most of these

---

[62] Bopp to Windischmann, July 16, 1823, in ibid., 2: 75.

[63] Richard Harder insisted that Windischmann never forgave Bopp for his remarks. Harder, "Franz Bopp und die Indogermanistik," in *Nationalsozialistische Monatsheften* (Sonderdruck) 152–153 (Nov./Dec. 1942): 3.

[64] Windischmann to Bopp, March 3, 1824, in Lefmann, *Franz Bopp* 2: 76.

[65] Wilhelm von Humboldt to Bopp, March 12, 1835, in ibid., 3: 104.

[66] Ibid., 1: 352.

models, in one way or another, remained the account in Genesis of the dispersal of the sons of Noah and/or the collapsing of the Tower of Babel; but as European imperialist conquest continued and as catastrophism and climatic determinism lost persuasive power, the distance between descendants gradually increased. Whereas William Jones grouped together as sons of Ham all the ancient civilized peoples – Indians, Egyptians, Greeks, Celts, Persians, and Romans – and thought skin color differences were produced in a matter of a few generations by adaptation to climate,[67] it soon became harder for Europeans to accept short chronologies and all-too-close relationships with the "'darker" peoples of the East. Linguistic conclusions – such as the discovery that South Indian languages were not derivable from Sanskrit or that hieroglyphics were not related to Greek, while Lithuanian, on the other hand, was – pushed forward the project of lining up lighter peoples with Indo-European languages and casting darker peoples into cultural-linguistic outer circles. This was facilitated by Friedrich Schlegel's suggestion that differences between inflected (Indo-European) and agglutinative (other) languages pointed to differently constructed tongues and minds, and by a process we might call the racialization of paradise.

Despite the author's commitment to universalism, Carl Ritter's *Vorhalle* (1819) already looked in this direction. In this text, Ritter speculated that a prehistorical diaspora had pushed peoples from northern India westward, laying the foundations for European civilization. To demonstrate that the Black Sea kingdom of Colchis, mythical home of Medea and destination of the Argonauts, was not an Egyptian, but an Indian settlement, he depended partly upon physical characteristics, arguing that the Colchians' facial features and hair were different from those of the Egyptians, though both were, according to Herodotus, dark-skinned.[68] Ritter insisted that the Indians, Persians, Germanic tribes, Scandinavians, Greeks, and Scythians shared a "common root" as well as a kind of primeval monotheism, commonalities that made them more like one another than were some groups who shared spaces contemporaneously, like the Romans and Etruscans, or those who shared it over time, such as ancient and modern Indians.[69]

Ritter was not too worried about dark-skinned Indian ancestors, but as the British extended more and more control over the subcontinent, this relationship between modern – "fallen" – Indians and idealized ancient Indians began to become more problematic. Increasingly pervasive was the view that India was not the homeland of the Aryans, but rather the place where Aryans had mixed with darker others, instigating the cultural decline and weakness that would characterize Indian history ever afterward. Those who elaborated this view included A. W. Schlegel, Christian Lassen, Theodor Benfey, and C. F. Koeppen.[70] That these leading Indologists spent so much time, and spilled so much ink, in discussing this subject confirms the field's sense that this was not only a crucially

---

[67] Trautmann, *Aryans and British India*, pp. 169–70.
[68] Ritter, *Vorhalle*, pp. 42–3.
[69] Ibid., p. 23; on Colchis, pp. 35–48.
[70] Edwin Bryant, *The Quest for the Origins of Vedic Culture: The Indo-Aryan Migration Debate* (Oxford, 2001), pp. 20–1.

important issue, but also one for which a variety of difficult-to-interpret sources needed to be read to yield essentially the same results.[71] If these scholars used "race" in varying ways, clearly it was becoming a more prominent, and meaningful, part of the study of the ancient Orient.

The application of the term "Aryan" to a particular strand of European ancestry dates to this period, but it was not applied consistently or always understood in racial terms. Anquetil had used the Latin term "Ariens" and Ritter adopted "Arianen" sparingly to mean one of the peoples of northwest India together with the Bactrians and Medes.[72] In his *Indische Alterthumskunde* (five volumes, 1847–62), Christian Lassen used "Arier" to refer to the lighter-skinned, ruling people of northern India, the people who, he argued, were "the true subject of Indian history" – both, it seems, because they defined its high culture and because they were the ones to leave the records. Lassen praised this people for achievements that were the result of "the genius of the people, breathed [into it] at the creation."[73] But we should attend to some subtleties in the way Lassen deployed his terms. First of all, it should be noted that Lassen does not describe the "Arja" as a race (Rasse) – racially they, like the Semites and Deccan southern Indians, are all Caucasians – but rather as a people, species, or tribe (*Volk, Geschlecht,* or *Stamm*), and though he does indulge in typing and segregating of peoples, the contrast he makes juxtaposes *Indogermanen* and *Semiten*, not *Arier* and *Semiten*.[74] His derivations of the term are based on his readings of the ancient sources available to him. Various of these themselves designate as "Arier" the ancient inhabitants of the "Iranian lands": they are called *Airja*, in Zend, and Herodotus says that the Medes were originally called Άριοι and the Persians called themselves Άρταιοι, which shares a common root with *Arja*.[75] Trying to solidify an indigenous (*einheimisch*) definition of the term, Lassen begins with a term used in the *Mahabharata, Arjavarta,* "the precinct of the *Arja* or the noble men, the people of good breeding," whom he defines in opposition to the *Mlek'ha,* "the barbarians and despisers of the holy law." Thus, the *Arja* are "that part of the Indian people to whom the Brahmanical law was given and who differentiated themselves in descent and language from the others to whom it was later shown" – but two different forms of the word both meant also master or owner, implying economic rather than religious

---

[71] Sheldon Pollock's argument in his essay "Deep Orientalism" that some of the racism in the term "Arya" was already imbedded in ancient Indian texts has been modified by Bryant and Trautmann, who have shown just how much "reading in" was necessary to wrench a racial contest between higher, lighter people, and lower, darker ones out of the ancient Indian texts. On the soft evidence in Indian classical literature, especially the *Rig Veda,* and later racial readings of it (as well as contemporary Indian objections to these readings), see Thomas Trautmann, *Aryans and British India,* pp. 211–16; and Bryant, *Quest for the Origins of Vedic Culture,* pp. 60–2. Pollock's essay, "Deep Orientalism? Notes on Power Beyond the Raj," can be found in Carol A. Breckenridge and Peter van der Veer, *Orientalism and the Postcolonial Predicament: Perspectives on South Asia* (Philadelphia, 1993): pp. 76–133.

[72] Benes, "Comparative Linguists," p. 4; Ritter, *Vorhalle,* p. 20.

[73] For e.g., Christian Lassen, *Indische Altertumskunde,* vol. 1 (Leipzig, 1858), pp. 410–11; quotation p. 411.

[74] Ibid., 1: 414–16.

[75] Ibid., 1: 6–7. He also gives evidence from later Greek and Armenian sources.

or racial superiority.[76] Lassen concludes: "The result of this inquiry, which is presented here, is that *Arja* in part in itself, in part in forms derived from it, is proven to be the ancient, indigenous, honorable designation of the Iranian peoples and lands in its widest extension, as it also [designates] the three higher Indian casts and the Brahmanical constitution and the Sanskrit rhetoric of the Indian lands. It shows us the sense in which we are to differentiate the Aryan Indians from the rest. For the name seems not to apply to other peoples of the Indogerman family."[77]

One can see here, and in the pages following, possibilities for creating racial hierarchies and histories; what Lassen said about the Semites and the Indo-Germans surely informed Ernest Renan's claims that the former are a fanatical, intolerant people with no art or mythology, and the latter are the true makers of modern culture.[78] But one can also see that Lassen was working with economic hierarchies and religious differences and that he was trying his best to do what he announced he would do in the preface: use Indian sagas to try to tease out the earliest history of the subcontinent. He believed that ethnography and geography were central to understanding this history, a history which is important for a purpose quite different from that of establishing German racial purity. Lassen identifies this purpose later in the book in the section in which he divides Indian history into two halves (each with a further line down the middle): the period of a "free, independent India" and the period of "foreign domination." Overall he endorses British rule, but only as compared to the ravages of Muslim "foreign domination." There is an undercurrent here of longing for Brahmanical, independent days and of rooting failures of the project of uniting India in ethnic and religious differences.[79] Lassen here is speaking the language of liberal nation-building in a rather quietly but consistently anti-imperial vein; he predicts that the Brahmin will have a harder time battling Christians – who are using education and enlightenment rather than force and prohibitions to undermine Indian cultural foundations – than they had throwing off the "brutal, conversion attempts of Islam." But one can guess that he is nonetheless subtly encouraging the Brahmin, as the descendants of a great, ancient, independent India, to do so.[80]

All this is to underscore the fact that while language groups were coalescing and hierarchies and lineages were being formed using fragments of linguistic and ethnic data, we do not yet see, by the 1850s, fully racialized human histories. Many scholars continued to insist on the *ur*-unity of human languages and to preserve the possibility of a common "language of paradise" long after Humboldt's death. In 1830, the highly respected Christian Hebraist Wilhelm Gesenius claimed that similarities between many root words in Semitic and Indo-German languages pointed to a common origin; five years later, his student

[76] Ibid., 1: 5.

[77] Ibid., 1: 9, n. 1.

[78] Ibid., 1: 414–18; Stefan Arvidsson, *Aryan Idols: Indoeuropean Mythology as Ideology and Science*, trans. Sonia Wichmann (Chicago, IL, 2006), pp. 93–6.

[79] Ibid., 2: 353–9.

[80] Ibid., 2: 355.

Julius Fürst made a bid "to bring Semitic closer to the familial band of Indo-European languages" by giving both Aramaic and Sanskrit South Asian origins.[81] Christian Bunsen based his claims for human *ur*-unity directly on the purported derivation of both Semitic and Indo-European languages from ancient Egyptian or "Khamitic" language. This claim, elaborated at great length in his *Ägyptens Stelle in die Weltgeschichte* (five volumes, 1845–57), seems to have been pervasive among Egyptologists late in the century; it dovetailed nicely, for one thing, with their conventional racial history of the Egyptians (primarily Asians, who had mixed a bit with the Negroid southern Africans),[82] and it helped to underwrite the importance of Egyptological study. Others tried different schemes; in 1828, Heinrich Ewald constructed a conjectural timeline in which Chinese developed first, followed by Hebrew, and then by the Indo-European languages. In 1862, Ewald (who knew and taught both Sanskrit and Semitic languages) was still insisting that there had been a common *Urvolk*.[83] But by this time, scientific sentiment was beginning to lean against the common ancestor theories; not only had the latter become transparent attempts to save the credibility of the book of Genesis, but they did not suit the orientalists' scholarly need to specialize. These theories had also come under considerable pressure from new generations, for whom saving Genesis or universal origins was less important than recounting the history of a "higher" group, which was increasingly referred to as the "Aryans."

Stefan Arvidsson has recently argued that the Aryanism of the mid-nineteenth century needs to be understood in the context of liberal bourgeois attempts to modernize religious belief and to take Christianity out of the hands of ritual-loving conservatives. Seeing a "religion of light" in ancient Indian forms of worship, writers like Max Müller, Ernest Renan, and Christian Lassen happily contrasted this "light" with the qualities they thought of as darkness – Jesuits, urban industrialists, and Jews – though all of them, surely, would have been horrified by Nazi anti-Semitism. Unquestionably, non-liberals like Gobineau and Bachofen contributed just as much as the liberals to the rise of racialized Aryanism – as did physical anthropologists. Refreshingly, Arvidsson admits that we will never really be able to find a single origin for racial Aryanism or to exculpate any of these thinkers from having made statements that sound, and probably are, racist.[84] It is clear, as Maurice Olender points out, that lines drawn by philologists were, by the 1850s and 1860s, hardening into rigid cultural stereotypes with something like the force of biological boundaries and that traffic across the Semitic–Aryan divide had slowed to a crawl.[85] But it is also clear that race was not yet a stable concept, and oriental philologists were not all agreed about how or why one might want to deploy it.

---

[81] Benes, *In Babel's Shadow*, p. 104.

[82] See, for example, Georg Ebers, *Ägypten und die Bücher Mose's: Sachlicher Commentär zu den ägyptischen Stellen in Genesis und Exodus*, vol. 1 (Leipzig, 1868), pp. 40–54.

[83] Benes, *In Babel's Shadow*, p. 104.

[84] Arvidsson, *Aryan Idols*, pp. 63–123.

[85] See Maurice Olender, *The Languages of Paradise: Race, Religion and Philology in the Nineteenth Century*, trans. Arthur Goldhammer (Cambridge, MA, 1992).

Fetishizing the Vedas

By the 1840s, Bopp and his students were effectively working in an independent discipline, which they referred to as comparative linguistics or sometimes Indo-Germanic linguistics. Though this discipline was founded on Sanskrit studies and Sanskrit continued to be fundamental to it, gradually the field evolved away from the other fields of *Orientalistik*. Some of these scholars were not pure grammarians, but interested in comparing cultures and myths as well, as was the case for Max Müller, Adalbert Kuhn, and Heymann Steinthal. In the 1850s, a number of journals were founded, including Kuhn's *Zeitschrift für vergleichende Sprachforschung auf dem Gebiete des Indogermanischen Sprachen* (f. 1852) and Steinthal and Moritz Lazarus's *Zeitschrift für Völkerpsychologie und Sprachwissenschaft* (f. 1860),[86] and for a time comparative linguistics was all the rage. In a lecture of 1870, Max Müller swore that whereas in his student days in the 1840s, only one student (presumably himself) completed Hermann Brockhaus's Sanskrit course at the University of Leipzig, in the 1860s, Brockhaus had as many as fifty students, "who want to know at least enough Sanskrit to make it possible to engage in really fruitful studies of comparative grammar."[87] But by this time, even this subfield was breaking up. While many went on to specialize in what was typically called Indo-German philology, after Bopp's death in 1867, a number of the foremost comparativists, led by August Schleicher, formed a group known as the *Junggrammatiker*. Like the circle around Steinthal and Lazarus, this group moved closer to the natural and social sciences and away from colleagues who focused on reading and interpreting the cultural content of Indian texts. The social-scientific tradition would culminate in the work of Ferdinand Saussure, on the one hand, and Franz Boas, on the other; and move with them, in the 1880s, abroad. The Indo-Germanists would stay at home and move in increasingly nationalist and racist directions (see Chapter 7).

If the "young grammarians" moved in the direction of the social sciences, the study of Indian philology remained in the humanistic camp. And if comparative linguistics gained new credibility and institutional recognition, this was even more true of Sanskrit philology. Although on the publication of Bopp's first book in 1816 there was no scholar in Germany competent enough in Sanskrit to review it, over the course of the next fifty years, Indological chairs were established at a rapid rate, reaching a total of nine full professorships by 1877 – at a time, however, when there were 56 chairs in classical philology.[88] The number of chairs considerably under-represented the number of German scholars working in the field during these decades, as major contributions were made by untenured professors (Theodor Benfey), Gymnasium professors (Adalbert Kuhn), private scholars (Otto Boehtlingk), and scholars ensconced in jobs outside Germany (Max Müller, Theodor Goldstücker, Georg Bühler). The expansion was enough to

---

[86] See George Williamson, *Longing for Myth*, pp. 211–33.

[87] Müller quoted in Johann Figl, *Nietzsche und die Religionen: Transkulturelle Perspektiven seines Bildungs- und Denkweges* (Berlin, 2007), pp. 188–9.

[88] Rabault-Feuerhahn, *L'archive des origines*, pp. 434–42; Christian von Ferber, *Die Entwicklung des Lehrkörpers der deutschen Universitäten und Hochschulen 1864–1954* (Göttingen, 1956), p. 206.

astonish and, in some cases, worry outsiders. By the 1850s, the French and English were complaining bitterly about the German dominance of the field. Officially, German Indology had "made" it.

But in fact, the German scholars did not feel their battles for recognition had been fully won. In fact, many members of this generation were not entirely products of German *Wissenschaft*. More than a few had been trained, at least partly, by Émile Burnouf in Paris: Christian Lassen, Adolph Holtzmann (Heidelberg), Rudolf Roth (Tübingen), and Max Müller, among them. Others – like Müller himself, as well as Theodor Benfey – had their original training in classical philology or were taught Sanskrit by orientalists whose real specialty was something else (like Ewald, who introduced several theology students, including August Schleicher and Rudolf Roth, to Sanskrit). Long stays in England were still necessary for some, as manuscripts were scarce and dictionaries expensive; student numbers were small. Career trajectories were uncertain; Peter von Bohlen had been a tailor's apprentice, a jockey, and a clerk before becoming a Sanskritist.[89] A peasant's son, Martin Haug quit his job as an assistant schoolteacher and walked to Stuttgart with two florins in his pocket; he supported his Gymnasium education by giving private lessons in Hebrew.[90] Improvements were certainly being made, and in 1852, Hermann Brockhaus, professor at the University of Leipzig, was able to announce the dawning of a promising new age: "That era, the dilettantism which amused itself exclusively with Indian poetry, is past; serious science claims its rights, and I believe that in this field there is still much hitherto unused material from India which could be used for the history of the development of the human spirit."[91] As the scholarship of the next thirty years would show, a tremendous fund of new material was becoming increasingly accessible to "serious" scholars; whether or not they would be willing or able to integrate it into the "history of the development of the human spirit" was, however, another question, one that will be addressed in various ways in the chapters to follow.

Like the other mid-century orientalists we have surveyed, the post-romantic Indologists were hugely learned, vastly productive linguists; they too compiled massive dictionaries and multi-volume histories – such as Lassen's *Indische Altertumskunde* of 1847–62 or Otto Boehtlingk and Rudolf Roth's Sanskrit dictionary (1852–75), which ran to 9478 large folio, double-column pages. Most did not go to India, but profited greatly from the flood of new manuscript purchases, which made, according to an estimate made by Max Müller in the 1870s, approximately 20,000 Hindu texts known to Europeans.[92] For the most part, these were men not nearly so willing to flout bourgeois respectability as their predecessors. Unlike Peter von Bohlen, who had attacked the evils of English imperialism in his 1830 *Alte Indien*,[93] they said little about their politics or their religious beliefs – though many of them were active in political affairs, often on the liberal-nationalist side.

---

[89] Windisch, *Geschichte der Sanskrit-Philologie* 2: 210, 223–29; ibid., 1: 86.

[90] See entry under "Haug, Martin," in the *Encyclopedia Iranica*, available online at http://www.iranica.com.

[91] Brockhaus quoted in Windisch, *Geschichte der Sanskrit-Philologie* 2: 213.

[92] Ibid., pp. 238–5; Schwab, *Oriental Renaissance*, p. 93.

[93] Bohlen, *Alte Indien* 1: 55–60, 112–16.

As Ernst Windisch said of two typical members of this generation (Roth and Boehtlingk), they were "men of few words."[94] Though by 1860, the man who would be the fin de siècle Indologists' lodestar, Arthur Schopenhauer, was already dead, his work seems not to have touched the specialists' worldview. Karl Friedrich Koeppen mentions him only once in the course of his 1,000-page study of Indian religions – and then only in a paragraph about invocations of Buddhism "as mere affect, as a mood," rather than as a thinker to be taken seriously.[95]

From about 1850 on, in fact, what absorbed much of the attention of Indologists was their work on the oldest Indian texts, the Vedas. As Dorothy Figueira has shown, after the exposure of the *Ezourvedam* so prized by Voltaire as a forgery in the early 1770s, European scholars had presumed that the earliest Indian text, the *Rig Veda*, was lost forever; though it was presumed that ancient Indian religion had been based on an original, universal revelation, the texts sufficiently old enough to bear traces of this revelation were irrecoverable.[96] The romantic generation therefore, had focused on later texts, the *Sakuntala* and the *Bhagavad Gita*, while even Lassen depended heavily on the *Mahabharata*, something that would make his picture of Indian religion and society vulnerable to later critics. As early as 1805, H. T. Colebrooke had shown that it might indeed be possible to recover the Vedas – and that this Indian religion would be more to European tastes than was later Brahmanism. But as Figueria argues, it still took a quarter century for European scholars to give up *Sakuntala* and seek the absent texts. By the 1830s, hope for recovery of the *Rig Veda*, perhaps trailing sparks of divine wisdom and verifying Anquetil's belief in primeval monotheism, were revived.[97]

The best known of German Vedic scholars, Max Müller, was not the first into the field.[98] Friedrich Rosen got there first, with his 1830 *Rigvedae specimen*, a Latin translation of some manuscripts Colebrooke had purchased in India. Having received a professorship in London (as well as an appointment as secretary of the Royal Asiatic Society), Rosen began working on a full (Latin) translation of the text, but his efforts were stymied by an early death, at age 32, in 1837.[99] The next generation took up Rosen's project with alacrity, seeking to tackle at the same time the multiple chronological questions that still divided the experts. The main task was to differentiate between "early" (more pristine) and "late" (more likely to be the product of cultural mixing and hence less authentically "Indian") Vedas

---

[94] Windisch, *Geschichte der Sanskrit-Philologie* 2: 245.

[95] Carl Friedrich Koeppen, *Die Religion des Buddha und ihre Entstehung*, vol. 1 (Berlin, 1857), p. 213.

[96] Figueira, "Authority of an Absent Text," pp. 201–16.

[97] Ibid., pp. 215–17.

[98] In surveying the mid-century German Indological world, I have chosen not to focus much attention on the individual best known to outsiders (especially in India), Max Müller. Though Müller was trained in Germany and though his *Rig Veda* edition (1849–74) was very much a product of mid-century German philological positivism, his more famous essays on the history of language and on India were written largely for an English audience, and it is to Victorian cultural history that he really belongs. Moreover there is already excellent work on him – in, for example, Arvidsson, *Aryan Idols*, pp. 66–90.

[99] Patronized by the Oriental Translation Fund of Great Britain and Ireland, Rosen's translation of book 1 appeared posthumously under the title *Rigveda-Sanhita*, in London in 1838.

or fragments thereof, a task that called on the philological skills German classicists and Hebraists had been honing for some time. For a new set of "scriptures," there were now recognizably "scientific" means of dissection; this meant that European expectations for text formation and linguistic usage were imposed on other peoples' documents, literary texts, and religious observances, something that helped Europeans understand early Indian cultures with fewer prejudices than ever before, but which also contributed to new misreadings and to the eschewing of indigenous methods of commentary, compilation, and interpretation.

There were dialectical processes here that we should attend to, for Eurocentric as it might have been, philological exegesis did push scholars in the direction of better – more exact, but also more culturally authentic – readings of nonwestern texts. In the process of applying specialized philological techniques (which depended on the creation of grammatical and word-usage norms), Indologists began with classical forms, but gradually had to modify or even dispense with them, seeking to understand the Sanskrit texts from within, and often turning to indigenous scholars for assistance. Ironically, this process was underwritten by deeper imperialist penetration into India, which permitted the bringing home to Europe of more and more Indian texts; more Sanskrit texts, in turn, meant that scholars were able to depend less on conventional, classical, and biblical sources. As Ernst Windisch later said of Albrecht Weber, Indologist at the University of Berlin from 1856 to 1910: "from Robertson and Heeren to the time of Lassen, the reports of the [Mediterranean] ancients were a much beloved theme, which, however, receded, proportionally, as India became better and better known from its own sources. Weber was the last person who treated them comprehensively."[100] The next generation would depend on indigenous texts, and largely abandon western and classical accounts. Here we see the often unappreciated side of the grand collecting ventures of the mid-century and of the painstaking text-editing to which orientalists devoted so many hours; some westerners, in any event, were actually learning not to trust their own ancient authorities and seeking new ways to write the history of the ancient East.

Buddha and the Young Hegelian

Specialized philologists at the time saw men like Albrecht Weber – whose best known (and most highly regarded) works in his day were, tellingly, his three-volume edition of the *White Yajurveda* and his catalog of Sanskrit manuscripts in the Royal Libraries in Berlin – as the exemplars of scientific Indology. But in fact, there were others who could claim, equally, title to the legacy of Bopp and Friedrich Schlegel, men who invested their efforts in a field known as comparative mythology or, later, comparative religions. Here Max Müller is exemplary of the breed; but he was working now in the English context (where, we should remember, his work was for a long time not appreciated). In the Germanies too, comparative mythology was usually taught by orientalists, such as the Egyptologist Seyffarth, who taught it at the University of Leipzig, or Rudolf Roth, who taught it to Tübingen students. In the years after the Creuzer Affair, this was a tough field

---

[100] Windisch, *Geschichte der Sanskrit-Philologie* 2: 332.

to sell as "scientific" – after all, it involved dealing in multiple linguistic contexts and in generalizations vulnerable to endless challenges from experts. But it was a field of interest to mid-century students, both in theology and secular studies; and gradually, university faculties decided it was a useful one as well. After 1853, "the history of religions" even became a required course for students at the Tübingen Stift.[101]

Still, comparative religion in the Germanies tended to be a pursuit for iconoclasts, individuals who were not content with the cultural, and often political, status quo, and willing, as was Karl Friedrich Koeppen, to devote their attention to nonwestern religions. Koeppen's two-volume *Die Religion des Buddha* (1857–9) was an important and, with respect to later German studies, unusual study of Brahmanism and Buddhism, which appeared just in time to earn the ailing Schopenhauer's praise. It was a unique endeavor in its day, and many aspects of its argumentation will appear uncharacteristic of the German traditions we have been tracing. But like the work of Bernays, Koeppen's work says something about the possibilities still open at mid-century for German orientalism; again, we have here to do with a "lonely" orientalist, lonely in his day, and lonely too in the longer run of German cultural and disciplinary development.

Koeppen was not a philologist but a left-Hegelian philosopher, who had been friendly with Marx in the 1830s.[102] He had, however, evidently learned Sanskrit, Tibetan, and perhaps Chinese, and immersed himself in the literature on Brahmanism, Buddhism, and – again unusually – Lamaism, a late form of Buddhism usually eschewed by German scholars (Koeppen did not have anything nice to say about it either). Schopenhauer liked Koeppen's study and perhaps it was he who recommended it to Richard Wagner, who, however, found Koeppen's portrait of the Buddha insufficiently heroic.[103] Small wonder, for Koeppen's study was anything but romantic; rather, it was packed with sociological analysis as well as with anti-clerical and especially anti-Catholic vitriol. Leaning heavily on English and French scholarship, Koeppen deplored oriental indolence – and Brahmanical "despotism." *Die Religion des Buddha* was, in short, a work of left-liberal orientalism – and, perhaps because of the rarity of such books in German Indology, one still, in Max Weber's estimation, worth reading more than a half-century later.[104]

Koeppen's first volume opened with a racial history of the Aryans, drawing directly on Gobineau and reiterating the now widely accepted theory (in Europe) that the true Aryans must have come from outside India. Even once they arrived, the Aryans were, still, in Koeppen's view, "youthful, courageous, eager for adventures and battles, fearless and warlike," not yet "that divided sad-sack-religious, speculative, penitential breed, living only in vile fantasies and ghostly abstractions, despairing of all reality, unmanly and weary unto death, [that breed] which has declined more and more, thanks to the enervating influence of the climate of the

[101] Sengupta, *From Salon to Discipline*, pp. 161–2.

[102] See Warren Breckman, *Marx, the Young Hegelians, and the Origins of Radical Social Theory* (Cambridge, 1999), p. 261, 273.

[103] Roger-Pol Droit, *The Cult of Nothingness: The Philosophers and the Buddha*, trans. David Streight and Pamela Vohnsen (Chapel Hill, NC, 2003), p. 134.

[104] Weber, *The Religion of India: The Sociology of Hinduism and Buddhism*, trans. Hans H. Gerth and Don Martindale (New York, 1958), p. 377, n. 44.

Ganges valley, to the corruption of the reason and the imagination by priests and finally to the oppression of the Muslim and Christian conquerors...."[105] This was obviously in keeping with the high Enlightenment's disdain for priests and nobles – as were Koeppen's critiques of the caste system, and of the "superstitious" idea of reincarnation. The best thing about Buddhism and Lamaism, he remarked, was their ability to act as a civilizing force, rooting out a primitive "rudeness" so barbaric as to include cannibalism.[106] But it should be noted that this enlightened critique attributed the fallenness of the Orient not to racial inferiority or even to cultural differences (here, these were minimized), but rather to climate on the one hand and the despotic rule of priests on the other. Koeppen ceaselessly reminded his Christian European readers that there were strong parallels to be drawn between Brahmanism or Lamaism and medieval Catholicism, as systems skilled in oppressing and enervating the poor. Indeed, volume two ended by comparing the tutelage exerted over believers by the Catholic mother church and by Tibetan and Mongolian Lamaism, the only difference being that the latter had never used the "terroristic measures" the former had already exhausted and thus Lamaism was likely to last, "while the days of intellectual charlatanry in Europe seem to be numbered."[107]

Koeppen's study, as this suggests, was vehemently anti-Catholic and even anti-Christian – though he did defend the historicity of Christ, alongside that of Buddha, and his analysis is consistent with the sort of anti-clerical, radical Protestantism one finds amongst young Hegelians like D. F. Strauss and F. C. Baur. Much of the treatment of Buddhism, especially early Buddhism, is quite flattering; Buddha is said to be a person of exemplary ethics and the creator of the most rational of all religions. According to Koeppen, Buddha opposed the despotism and rigid hierarchy of the Brahmin priests; he preached a uniquely human religion, which did away with miracles and god-abstractions; and he exemplified the individual practice of virtue, rather than the churches' self-interested propagation of rituals and ceremonies.[108] Koeppen's Buddha was a revolutionary; indeed, the author argues: "There is really no question that if the Indian people had not already been completely stripped of their religion and robbed of all courage and zeal for life by theological-priestly vampirism and earthly despotism, the call of liberation and the preaching of the equality of all men which Cakjamuni [Buddha] unleashed would necessarily have led to a rebellion of the lowest classes just as Luther's preaching of Christian freedom [led to] the peasant revolts."[109] In fact, the main problem with Buddhism, in the author's view, is not its inferiority as a religion – but rather its "enslaving" effect in politics; a religion that forbids resistance "naturally preaches blind, passive, long-suffering subjection to the authorities, even in the face of the most depraved tyranny, and thus, despite its fundamental principle of the equality of all men, wherever it penetrates, [it] simply aids and abets despotism." Also problematic was Buddhism's failure to inspire

---

[105] Koeppen, *Religion des Buddha* 1: 2.
[106] Ibid., 1: 480–6; 2: 386–7.
[107] Ibid., 2: 388.
[108] E.g., ibid., 1: 121–36.
[109] Ibid., 1: 132–3.

creativity in the arts and sciences, teaching, "just like Pietism, that the world is nothing but a house of corruption, of sin and death, and that the secular arts and sciences are the work of Satan."[110] But, when viewed next to medieval Christian art, even Buddhist painting proved to be not so bad; we may not like the Buddhist monks' empty expressions of contemplation, Koeppen wrote, but at least the eastern painters avoided depicting holy men as "penitents so enervated and emaciated they appear to be skeletons," or imprinting them "with the stamp of that depraved martyrdom, of that theological pinchedness, of that revolting rolling of the eyes, which disgusts us in many Byzantine [icons] and in conventional Catholic images of the saints..."[111]

One last aspect of this – for the time – encyclopedic treatment of Buddhism and related religions should be underlined, for the field will look much different by the 1890s. Koeppen's book was really an exercise in the sociology of religion; the author returns again and again to the question of the social function of religion, not only in Brahmanism and Buddhism, but also in Christianity, Islam, and occasionally Judaism. In good left-Hegelian fashion, Koeppen clearly believed religions grew out of social, political, and climatic conditions – as well as made possible the melioration or perpetuation of such systems and conditions. Social practices were more often the result of economic conditions than of religious systems: polyandry, for example, was practiced in Tibet not because of Lamaistic perversity, but because the poverty of Tibetan peasants led them to try to consolidate households.[112] Koeppen recognized similarities between religious concepts and practices across time and across racial and cultural divides; but, and this should be emphasized, he had no desire to locate the point of origin for one or another ideal or practice, nor was he at all interested in the question of borrowing. He was not interested in cleaning up religions, including his own – though he was willing to offer a general critique, applicable to Christianity as well as to Buddhism and Islam: "Human religiosity can go far astray, when it is [articulated in the form of] a church."[113]

It should also be emphasized that race, though a prominent part of the analysis, plays no determinative role in Koeppen's book. Racial characteristics are used to describe sociological or regional differences between peoples – differences which matter really only because they are transformed into caste or class differences by political decision makers – but not as historical evidence which explains, for example, the intrusion of concepts, languages, or practices. There are Aryans in the book, but no Semites per se, and there is certainly no juxtaposing of the two as irreconcilable opposites. The Old Testament is not used as a source except in rare comparisons made between ancient Judaism and Brahmanism. Koeppen's sociological comparativism, as well as his religious radicalism, his climatological and sociological use of race, and, to a certain extent, his unwillingness to explore seriously the inner meaning and authentic expression of spirituality mark his book as a high liberal study of precisely the sort the next generation of scholars and believers would reject.

---

[110] Ibid., 1: 480.
[111] Ibid., 1: 507.
[112] Ibid., 1: 476.
[113] Ibid., 1: 533.

Poetic Wisdom's Last Proponent: Friedrich Rückert

If Franz Bopp and Karl Koeppen were individuals uniquely able to apply to oriental studies some of the most cutting-edge scholarly trends and ideas of their age, the same might be said, in the realm of poetry, about Friedrich Rückert. Rückert today is largely forgotten and was, even in his day, an almost uncategorizable individual. Was he a poet or a scholar, a writer or a translator, a German nationalist or a universalist, a Christian or a pagan? He did, in fact, inhabit all of these identities, often simultaneously, and it would take at least one very fat book to do his intellectual career justice. Though he was an extraordinary person, in what follows, we will consider him as in many ways symptomatic of his generation, one caught between romanticism and historicism, between its grand political and aesthetic dreams and its desire to be counted *wissenschaftlich*. Like Friedrich Schlegel, for example, the young Rückert idolized the ancient Greeks and the medieval Germans – and it was his fiery nationalist poems (*Geharnischte Sonette*) that first brought him to the public's attention. But he could not be satisfied with a purely literary career, or as his son Heinrich later argued, with the philological credo of the 1810s and 1820s that Greek represented the absolute perfection of language and poetry. Already in his 1811 dissertation (written at the radical University of Jena), he was arguing for the oriental origins of Greek culture – though his arguments, Heinrich insisted, were free from "all of that fantastical confusion, in which Creuzer and his followers lost themselves."[114] Inspired by Hammer-Purgstall's translation of the poetry of Hafiz, Rückert would begin learning oriental languages after 1818, beginning with Arabic and Persian (he already knew Hebrew), and then, sometime in the mid-1820s, adding Sanskrit. It is a tribute both to his talents and to the state of oriental studies at the time that he was made a professor of oriental languages and literatures at the University of Erlangen in 1826, even though his language skills were largely self-taught and his commitment to orthodox Christianity was widely suspected to be tenuous as best.[115] Hiring Rückert was indeed an adverturous move on the part of the Erlangen administration. They may have wanted a literary celebrity who could teach Hebrew, and, like August Schlegel, also dabble in the new field of Sanskrit studies. What they got was an orientalist uninterested in exegesis, and committed instead to composing pseudo-oriental poetry and pursuing an esoteric quest for the lost language of paradise.[116]

Rückert was an orientalist of a distinctively early nineteenth-century sort: the East he loved best was the poetic East, the East of Firdusi, Hafiz, *Sakuntala*, and the Psalms. And he was loved most for his least scholarly orientalism – his *Östliche Rosen* of 1822, his *Nal und Damajanti* of 1828, and his *Weisheit der Brahmanen* of 1836, all of them "Nachdichtung," that is, poetry composed in the oriental manner. These were not sloppy or ill-informed works, though in his early years he had to depend on seventeenth-century linguistic works, such as the Syriac grammar of Isaak Sklendarian (published in 1626) and Johannes

---

[114] Heinrich Rückert, "Friedrich Rückert," p. 212.
[115] Sengupta, *From Salon to Discipline*, p. 46.
[116] Benes, *In Babel's Shadow*, p. 76; also Rückert, "Deutsches Künstlerfest in Rom. Zum Anfang" in *Frauentaschenbuch für das Jahr 1823*, ed. Friedrich Heinrich Karl La Motte-Fouqué, vol. 9 (1823), pp. 3–10.

Buxtorff's rabbinical Bible and commentaries (1618–19).[117] By the later 1820s, English dictionaries and lexicons were easier to obtain and he was able to read his friend Franz Bopp's Latin translation of the *Mahabharata*. But Rückert was not after scientific authenticity; as he wrote in the preface to *Nal*, he wanted to render the Orient appealing to German-speakers' hearts, not just to scholarly critics:

What I offer here is not a translation; that would be superfluous. Rather, [I offer] an attempt to bring closer to us a beautiful foreign tale, through reworking it as German poetry ... I have attempted to reach this goal of nationalizing [the poem] by making the episodes stand alone, but also by dressing [them] in class-appropriate German costume, excluding everything foreign which is only understandable to us by learned means and is not immediately [understandable] through the feelings, while still retaining the local color, insofar as it does not destroy the poetic impression, but seems to strengthen it.[118]

Whatever one may say about the patronizing attitude of these lines, one should also note that Rückert clearly believed that "foreign tales" were beautiful, and could, if domesticated a bit, truly touch the hearts of Central Europeans. And, whatever one may say about the inauthenticity of his "oriental" voice, his readers were indeed touched. Though at first Rückert found it difficult to publish his *Nachdichtung*, once it caught on, *Nal* became, and remained, one of the best-loved and best-selling orientalizing books in the nineteenth-century Germanies, and even professional orientalists, including most recently Annemarie Schimmel, have marveled at Rückert's ability to evoke authentic styles.[119]

In addition to his *Nachdichtung*, Rückert used and improved his philological skills – in fact, Heinrich claims his father taught himself more than fifty languages, simply by immersing himself for six to eight weeks each in the relevant texts and thought-worlds.[120] But, when one looks more carefully at the translations he actually produced, as did Herman Kreyenborg, it is clear that they come mostly from the three major literary languages of the Near East, from Arabic, Persian, and Sanskrit, not from Armenian, Ethiopic, or Malayan.[121] He did translate some Hebrew texts – in fact, he was forced to teach Old Testament exegesis for many years – and not surprisingly, he chose a Herderian repertoire. He did not give up his religious belief, but his interest in Hebrew waned over years, in part because, according to Heinrich, the monuments of the Hebrew spirit did not offer as wide a poetic and linguistic range as did those of other oriental cultures.[122] For a time he worked on Coptic, Syriac, and Armenian texts – perhaps seeking, as

---

[117] Hartmut Bobzin, "Friedrich Rückert und die Universitätsbibliothek," in Bobzin, ed., *Friedrich Rückert an der Universität Erlangen* (Erlangen, 1988), pp. 122–8.

[118] Friedrich Rückert quoted in Herman Kreyenborg, "Friedrich Rückert als Interpret orientalischer Dichtungen" [1927], in *Friedrich Rückert im Spiegel seiner Zeitgenossen und der Nachwelt*, ed. WolfDieterich Fischer (Wiesbaden, 1988), p. 278.

[119] Annemarie Schimmel, *Morgenland und Abendland: Mein west-östliches Leben* (Munich, 2003), pp. 38–40.

[120] Heinrich Rückert, "Friedrich Rückert," p. 225.

[121] Kreyenborg, "Friedrich Rückert als Interpret," p. 267.

[122] Heinrich Rückert, "Friedrich Rückert," p. 221.

would his student Lagarde – oriental origins for New Testament ideas;[123] but he published little on this nor did he complete or publish in his lifetime his work on the Vedas and the Qur'an. He seems to have continued to believe in a kind of *Ursprache* (to which Sanskrit was the key) and in an original, universal revelation, the signs of which might be found in folk poetry. But he was wise enough not to spell out such Schlegelian beliefs in his post-romantic middle age, and so his poems could continue to be read by generations of bourgeois German schoolchildren without fear of imparting to them an unholy or Catholic-eccentric worldview.

Rückert did not give up poetry after his appointment to the professoriate, and produced historical dramas on the subjects of Emperor Heinrich IV and Christopher Columbus, as well as the heart-wrenching *Kindertodtenlied*, which Gustav Mahler would later set to music. In terms of volume, his scholarly output – when the unpublished manuscripts are counted in – easily outstrips his poetic work in this period in terms of sheer volume; his two-volume edition of early Arabic folk songs ran to more than 800 pages; between 1854 and 1856, he published a nearly 300-page review of Jules Mohl's edition of the Paris *Schahnameh*. When Georg Reimer published Rückert's own translation of Firdusi's epic after his death, it ran to nearly 1400 pages and three volumes (1890–5). Somehow, in between composing large numbers of lyrical poems, Rückert also found time to work on a comparative Semitic grammar, a Qur'an translation, a Persian Alexander legend, and a huge Hafiz manuscript. His *Nachlass* is said to be a treasure trove of fragments of Indian lyrics, Finnish epic, Albanian folk sayings, and texts in Lithuanian, Coptic, Hindustani, and Tamil.[124]

But in which field did his heart really reside? Learned verse of this sort hardly exists nowadays, and disciplinary historians looking back at his career often seem to think he wasted time on poetry that might better have been spent working up specialized journal essays. But Rückert was a true romantic, and it is quite possible that he never intended most of the translation fragments he left behind for publication, planning instead to use them for philologically-informed, atmosphere-creating *Nachdichtung*. Rückert was, after all, not only a close friend of Franz Bopp, but also of the Graecophile poet August von Platen and a great admirer of both Schiller and Friedrich Schlegel. The sentiments expressed by his oriental sage in one of his most famous poems, "Die Weisheit des Brahmanen," seem very much his own:

What separates art from science? The gift;
To it, proud knowledge must concede the crown.
Scholarship certainly knows how something ought to be
But it cannot create it – that you alone, art, can do.[125]

[123] Lagarde, "Einleitung," in idem, ed., *Der Pentateuch koptisch* (Osnabrück, 1867; reprint 1967), pp. v–vi; on Lagarde, see Chapter 4.

[124] See Herman Kreyenborg, "Friedrich Rückert als Interpret," p. 276.

[125] Rückert, "Weisheit des Brahmanen," stanza 2; reprinted in *Rückerts Werke*, ed. Georg Ellinger, vol. 2 (Leipzig, 1897), p. 63.

    Was unterscheidet Kunst von Wissenschaft? Das Koennen
    Dem muss der Vorrang doch das stolze Wissen goennen.
    Wohl weiss die Wissenschaft, wie etwas sollte sein,
    Doch machen kann sie's nicht, das kannst du, Kunst, allein.

Rückert did not doubt his "gift," and like Friedrich Schiller before him, preferred to sing to the heart than to write for the mind.

There are a few other aspects of Rückert's orientalism that should be noted before we let this elusive and influential character slip away. It is important to note, for example, that Rückert's Orient was a romantic, sentimental one, and an original home for all. There was a primitivism to it, but it was a Herderian primitivism – defined by the pervasiveness of folk poetry and the rich, earthy wisdom of simpler peoples. Its mysteries were not eternal and esoteric, but once linguistic niceties were out of the way could be rightly understood by all enlightened men of good will; it is no accident that Rückert, like his friend Hammer-Purgstall, belonged to the Masonic brotherhood. Rückert's Brahmin is wise despite having "read nothing but Nature's Veda," that is, he is steeped exclusively in the oldest religious poetry: that of nature.[126] He is wise because he understands that truth is one and lies beyond this world's appearances; on earth, we have only to struggle with incompleteness to be ever becoming. But this is not a cause for despair; rather, it is a spark of the eternal that presses us to look beyond. There may be some attempt here to understand Hindu philosophy – but the learned man's wise words might have been spoken by virtually any Mason or radical Protestant, or by Rousseau's Savoyard Priest, for that matter. There is no specificity here which tells us that these truths are meant merely for Indians or for non-Europeans; on the contrary, the whole poem (which he subtitled "A Didactic Poem in Fragments") is structured as a fatherly teacher's instruction to a young man and has universal intent. That it comes from a Brahmin simply gives the feel of a depth and antiquity and perhaps even wider applicability than might be ascertained from, for example, a Eurocentric French-Swiss tutor. One was not to learn from it how to be "oriental" – one was to learn from it, Rückert hoped, simply how to *be*.

CARL RITTER: ORIENTAL GEOGRAPHY IN WESTERN LIBRARIES

Of course, the kind of wise man one learned to be was a wise man of the *ancient* oriental type; Rückert never advised actually going to India to speak to modern Brahmin priests. As noted in Chapters 1 and 2, most mid-century German orientalists were philologists and most philologists did not travel, especially once European libraries began to acquire large numbers of Indian, Sanskrit, and Chinese manuscripts, and museums began to acquire cuneiform tablets. Numerous important German orientalists never ventured further East than Trieste; this includes Heinrich Fleischer and his student, the great Semitist Theodor Nöldeke, who died only in 1930. But these scholars did at least try to enter the Orient by way of its languages, while our next scholar, Carl Ritter, Professor of Geography at the University of Berlin, neither learned oriental languages nor saw much of the world beyond Europe. And yet, Ritter devoted a staggering fourteen volumes of his nineteen-volume *Erdkunde* to the Orient and was widely admired for his encyclopedic knowledge of the East. By our definition Ritter was not an orientalist, for he did not know, study, or even read any oriental languages. But he deserves brief

---

[126] Rückert, "Weisheit," stanza 1, line 1.

coverage here to underscore the foundational but ambiguous importance of his work for future, and especially non-philological, studies of the East. For his work was unabashedly Christian and awash in Eurocentric premises – and yet, it also offered readers a treasure trove of data that demonstrated the depth, complexity, and importance of Asia in world history.

Like many of our lonely orientalists, Ritter was essentially an autodidact; he spent his early career as a tutor in a progressive banker's household in Frankfurt, though he also spent time in Geneva in the company of August Schlegel and Madame de Staël, and in Göttingen, where he heard the lectures of Eichhorn, Blumenbach, and Heeren.[127] Most important to his formation were his readings of the pedagogical theorist J. H. Pestalozzi and of the Bible, which he began to read seriously in 1807, at the age of twenty-eight; together with his experience of Napoleon's conquests, these readings suggested to him the need to compose an organic, unified study of the entire earth – and of humankind's place and purposes on the planet. His method of doing this was one his contemporaries deeply respected, but we would find odd, to say the least. Rather than mapping the globe or traveling around it, Ritter dove into Europe's libraries and came out with a massive compendia of texts.

The texts Ritter used were of three sorts: ancient authorities (Herodotus, Strabo, and the Old Testament), medieval and modern European travel accounts, and modern orientalist scholarship, including translations of Indian, Chinese, and Islamic texts. He offered his readers very few maps, and those he did include, as even his admiring English translator admitted, were of very poor quality.[128] Over the course of his very long volumes, he reiterated Strabo's view of Europe's special-ness (the result of its temperate climate, mixture of plains and mountains, and men habituated to bravery); on top of this he piled eighteenth-century climatological determinism, insisting, for example, that Europe's emphasis on individuality and diversity was the result of its much longer coastline as compared to Asia's larger interior.[129] His teleological Christianity led him, especially in his late lectures, to sketch the crudest of universal histories, as the simplest continent, Africa (with the fewest natural ports) was succeeded by an Asiatic "nursery"; Europe then inherited Asia's culture and used its natural energy to push civilization forward.[130]

And yet, over the course of those fourteen massive volumes on the Orient, Ritter reiterated again and again the cultural importance of Asia for world history and insisted on its geographic, climatic, botanical, historical, and zoological inter-nal variations. He took the Indian philosophers' view of the world seriously enough to open his first volume on Asia with it, citing fragments from the *Ram-ayana*, the Puranas, the *Mahabharata,* and other original texts – in the interests of getting information from eyewitnesses.[131] In new editions, he added as many new

---

[127] For Ritter's biography, see Heinrich Schmitthenner, *Studien über Carl Ritter* (Frankfurt, 1951).

[128] William L. Gage, "Editor's Preface," in Carl Ritter, *The Comparative Geography of Palestine and the Sinaitic Peninsula*, vol. 1, trans. William L. Gage (New York, 187), p. ix.

[129] Carl Ritter, *Comparative Geography*, trans. William L. Gage (Philadelphia, 1865) pp. 186–7; 196–7.

[130] Ibid., pp. 198–201.

[131] Ritter, *Die Erdkunde im Verhältnis zur Natur und zur Geschichte des Menschen*, part 2, vol. 1, *Asien* (Berlin, 2nd ed., 1832), pp. 5–14.

sources of this type as he was able, partaking of the expansion of specialized scholarship over the course of the 1820s–1850s. Those who read only his lectures, or even the theologians who studied his volumes on Palestine and Sinai simply to understand the geography of the Holy Land would not have appreciated the extent to which Ritter made available eastern texts and specific details, reported usually with no prejudicial editorializing. It is certainly possible, even likely, that Ritter's *Erdkunde* supplied information to Europeans who wished to dominate and exploit the East;[132] but it is also possible to see this massive collection of facts as offering readers resources with which they might experience other worlds or challenge their own cultures' prejudices.

GERMANS ABROAD: NEITHER CONQUERORS NOR FRIENDS

Ritter did not get out much, but there were German scholars who left the library and got to know "orientals," humble and exalted, long before the colonial era. To take just a few examples: the Jesuit Heinrich Roth worked in India from 1650 until his death in 1668; his Sanskrit was good enough, apparently, to dispute with local Brahmins in their sacred language.[133] Julius Klaproth conducted fieldwork in Mongolia, China, Kazakhstan, and the Caucasus between 1805 and 1809. Heinrich Brugsch spent much of his career in Egypt and was responsible for helping Ismail Pasha set up a program there to train Egyptians to read hieroglyphics – though he was most famous back home for his *Demotic Grammar*, published in 1848.[134] Trained in medicine, Gerhard Rohlfs first joined the Austrian army and then the French Foreign Legion; for a time he served as doctor to the Sultan of Fez, but tired of his comfortable existence and took up cross-desert voyaging, some of it paid for by the Egyptian khedive. As this suggests, many traveling Germans did so in someone else's employ. Heinrich Barth joined an English mission to open trade routes into inner Africa; hoping to help end the slave trade and eager to travel, Barth did not bargain for a six-year, 13,000 mile trip, during which the expedition leader died crossing the Sahara.[135] The engineer Karl Humann began by planning roads for the Sultan – but ended by working for the German museums, helping to excavate and send home the Pergamon Altar among other treasures. The Russians sent German linguists to Central Asia to serve in the army or to teach languages; the English sent many a German Indologist to India, especially after 1857; this was perhaps testimony to the dearth of Englishmen trained in the sort of deep culture-historical hermeneutics thought proper to get a better grip on the subcontinent after the Indian Rebellion. Some Germans benefited from Dutch sponsorship, as did German missionary Karl

---

[132] Jens Ruppenthal, however, argued that academic geography had little impact on colonial research projects before about 1900. Ruppenthal, *Kolonialismus als 'Wissenschaft und Technik': Das Hamburgische Kolonialinstitut 1908 bis 1919* (Stuttgart, 2007), p. 25.

[133] Friedrich Wilhelm, "The German Response to Indian Culture," in *Journal of the American Oriental Society* 81, no. 4 (Sept.–Dec. 1961): 395.

[134] Donald Malcolm Reid, *Whose Pharoahs? Archaeology, Museums, and Egyptian National Identity from Napoleon to World War I* (Berkeley, CA, 2002), pp. 114–17.

[135] Behrmann, *Hamburgs Orientalisten* (Hamburg, 1902), pp. 99–101.

Gützlaff, whose translation of the Bible into Chinese helped to spawn the Taiping Rebellion, and Philipp Freiherr von Siebold, the medical doctor who returned to Germany with important collections of Japanese art and ethnographic materials. By no means is this an exhaustive list. Even in the pre-imperialist period, for Germans who wanted to travel, there was, usually, some way to do so.

For these travelers, the East was primarily a place to obtain experience, credentials or collections, which would make their careers successful back home – though some, like Heinrich Brugsch, never quite managed to turn the trick. While "experience" and "personal contact" counted in some areas, such as ethnography and to some extent in geography, this was not something scholars of history, religion, art, or languages needed to succeed, and as Arminius Vambéry discovered in the 1860s, German audiences were less impressed by sensational feats than were their more "practical" cousins across the channel: "Whereas the English have a particular consideration for the man who has made himself a name on the field of practical observations, or who has enriched any branch of science with new data collected on the spot, the French, and more particularly the Germans, have always a predilection for the theoretical investigator, for the man who, absorbed in his library, is able to write big books with numerous notes...."[136] Germany's early to mid-nineteenth-century travelers tended to be missionaries – with non-scholarly ends – or natural scientists, geographers, geologists, zoologists, botanists, and doctors, who recognized that finding something new was valuable and could be used to distinguish an ambitious young scholar from his fellow aspirants. A trip to an unmapped corner of the globe would certainly rate an essay in one of the increasingly popular geographic journals of the day – such as *Petermanns Geographische Mitteilungen* (begun in 1855) – or an appearance before the fashionable Gesellschaft für Erdkunde. Identifying new plants, animals, diseases, and not least *Naturvölker* was of interest for the purposes of filling in classificatory schemata, and also, as Darwin's *Beagle* voyage illustrated, for throwing light on evolutionary patterns. But, increasingly, humanists and theologians too valued the finding of new "stuff" and sometimes rewarded richly those who could haul it home and explain its significance.

The politics of our travelers was by no means uniform and was complicated by the fact that the Germans depended in large part on the assistance of local elites and of European colonial officials to do their work; the scholars were, on the whole, well treated by both sides and grateful for it. Hammer-Purgstall had numerous friends in Istanbul who helped him procure Turkish manuscripts and books; the proto-vitalist geographer Ferdinand von Richthofen developed a sort of romantic-ethnographic sympathy for indigenous, traditional elites, which would have a long and intricate history in the years to come. Some were invited to help Ottoman and Japanese elites; others (missionaries in particular) were neither invited nor especially welcome. A few Germans tried to make peace between English, French, or Dutch colonizers and the colonized, counseling the former, as did Carl Neumann not long before the Opium Wars, to tread more delicately for the sake of longer-term and more profitable relations.[137] Some made friends

---

[136] Vambéry, *Life and Adventures of Vambéry*, p. 310.
[137] Neumann, *Asiatische Studien*, vol. 1 (Leipzig, 1837), p. vi.

and/or economically useful alliances with locals. Others never strayed from European compounds.[138] These relationships with non-Europeans were idiosyncratic and usually fleeting; they were not fully woven into the carpet of *Weltpolitik*, first of all because no such policy existed before the 1880s and secondly because the German states in this era were insufficiently powerful for local leaders to see German travelers as either particularly useful or particularly threatening.

Helmuth von Moltke was rather an unwilling oriental traveler, though he did journey to Istanbul of his own volition in 1835. There he was cornered by the Ottoman Minister of War, who strongly desired Moltke to help reform his army. Encouraged to assist the Ottomans by the Prussian King, Moltke stayed for four years, some of it doing topographical work in Istanbul and some of it on Ottoman maneuvers. He was on hand for the battle of Nisib of 1839 and so had the opportunity to observe internal Ottoman strife at close quarters. He was certainly not an orientalist and probably spoke French to his interlocutors. But he came home with a rather positive picture of the Ottomans in the era of Mahmud II's reforms, and his letters home to his wife generally reflect the genial temper of an intrigued visitor, not a potential conqueror.

In the letters, Moltke lovingly describes his first Turkish bath and offers a positive picture of Istanbul. He dwells rather extensively on the plight of women – prisoners in their homes and wholly unlike the erotic creatures of the *1,001 Nights*. The locals, he argues, have no opportunity and probably insufficient imagination for these sorts of dalliances; if a Muslim woman has any contact with a Christian man, she is drowned and he is hanged without any further ado. Slavery here is much less onerous than, for example, in America; slaves in the Orient are more or less members of the household, treated well, and educated in the religion of the master. Moltke criticizes the tax system and the corruption of the bureaucracy, conscription measures, the disorganization of the army, and the persecution of Christians, but praises reform and Ottoman tolerance; his phrase "other places, other norms" nicely sums up his general attitude toward cultural differences.[139] Shaped by Gibbon's *Decline and Fall*, Moltke's historical narrative, however, is one very much of national decline, of internal fragmentation, and the weakness of the central state and army, and the concluding description of the Ottoman victory against the Egyptian challenger Ibrahim Pasha does not give him much confidence that this decline can be forestalled. But then again, Ottoman intellectuals had been discussing their culture's decline since at least the seventeenth century; Moltke might well have gotten his gloominess from his hosts. His letters occupy a space between Busbecq's admiring accounts of Suleiman's court and Martin Hartmann's attacks on Ottoman despotism and decadence (Chapter 8); they were meant to be informative, but not scientific, and they only sold well after the aristocratic leader's victories in 1870–1 made him a national hero. But by

---

[138] See Erwin Baelz's description of the European community in Japan in 1876; in Erwin Baelz, *Awakening Japan: The Diary of a German Doctor*, ed. Toku Baelz, trans. Eden and Cedar Paul (Bloomington, IN, 1974), p. 16.

[139] Helmuth von Moltke, *Briefe über Zustände und Begebenheiten in der Türkei aus den Jahren 1835 bis 1839*, ed. Gustav Hirschfeld (Berlin, 6th ed., 1893), pp. 15–17, 27, 1–7 (on Wallachia); on women, pp. 39–41; on slaves, pp. 35–6 on taxes, etc., pp. 294–9; tolerance, pp. 138–8; quotation p. 137.

1876, the editor of the second edition was calling Moltke's letters the equivalent for the Orient of Goethe's *Italian Journey*, suited "to make us at home in the Orient, whose fundamental sensibility they capture like the perfume of flowers."[140] That fundamental sensibility was one of backwardness with respect to Europe; but it was not dismissive either of the Ottoman Empire's strengths or of Turkish culture as a whole.

More popular than Moltke's travels in the pre-1848 era were those of Ida Pfeiffer, a tomboyish, middle-aged Christian woman who in 1842 finally realized her dreams to visit the Holy Land. Hers is a travel narrative overlooked by virtually all historians of orientalism – perhaps because her experience was too ambivalent, too unscientific, and too hedged around by Christian expectations to fit anyone's narrative. Several recent biographies, however, give a good sense of the complexities of Pfeiffer's experience – in addition to underlining her popularity (her book went through four editions and was translated into seven languages in its first decade).[141] Like Moltke, Pfeiffer found much to like in the East – she liked the Islamic world's simple manners and its ban on alcohol. Although she looked forward to reaching Christian Russia, when she got there, she was so rudely treated and living conditions were so poor that she longed to return to the land of the Hindu and Arab "infidels."[142] In a rather primitivist way, she imagined the harem women happier (because less sensitive) than their European counterparts, and she was thrilled at the opportunity to visit biblical sites, such as the riverbank where Moses was found in his basket among the bullrushes.

In her later travels, Pfeiffer set her sights on roads less traveled, visiting the Brazilian interior and venturing out on an Indian tiger hunt; she persuaded local guides to take her to visit headhunters in Borneo and was thrown out of Madagascar for plotting a coup against the island's tyrannical queen. Her relations with locals were uneven; she considered most of the tribesmen she met ugly and barbaric; on the other hand, as she pointed out, the Europeans who fought the early modern religious wars and who invented the Inquisition had little right to criticize: "Is not every page of our history filled with horrid deeds of treachery and murder?"[143] Pfeiffer expected locals, both Europeans and non-Europeans, to provide her with food and shelter. She stayed often with missionaries – but regularly criticized them for living luxuriously; she disapproved of the increasing practice of importing European wives for missionaries and officials. The latter too often fell ill or gave birth to weak children, she claimed, all of whom then had to return to Europe; it would be better for European men to take local wives, who would be healthier and stay on the job. Appalled by English treatment of Indians, she claimed that the Indians had a right to hate Europeans. On the other hand, she found the eastern cities dirty, the lack of education deplorable, and the need for Christian instruction urgent. Her reaction to traveling from Basra to Baghdad was

---

[140] Gustav Hirschfeld, "Moltke und der Orient: Einleitung zu Moltkes Briefen aus der Türkei," in ibid., p. lix.

[141] Eka Donner, *Und Nirgends eine Karawane: Die Weltreisen der Ida Pfeiffer (1797–1858)* (Düsseldorff, 1997), p. 73.

[142] Marion Tinling, *Women into the Unknown: A Sourcebook on Women Explorers and Travelers* (New York, 1989), p. 228.

[143] Pfeiffer quoted in ibid., p. 229.

predictable for a mid-century European: "... where once strong, well-ordered, flourishing empires stood, now rapacious hordes drift across desolate steppes."[144] Yet Pfeiffer made the same sorts of remarks about the decline and fall of the modern Greeks, who despite their lofty past now seemed to rank among the lowest of the world's peoples.[145]

Some aspects of her travels need emphasis to stand in contrast with later ones surveyed below. Above all, though Ida Pfeiffer had no intention of being a scientific traveler, she ended up, in a modest way, being forced into that mold. In her first book, she declared herself to be no *Altertumsforscherin*; she would be satisfied, she said, with studying the artistic and natural beauties of Egypt in her own simple way. After her first trip, she began forming a natural-scientific collection with an eye to selling it at home, and in consultation with August Petermann (cartographer and editor of *Petermanns Geographische Mitteilungen*), she decided even to forgo a visit to Australia – and instead to visit less charted territories, namely Borneo, Batavia, and North and South America.[146] Of course, by 1851 these places had been infiltrated by Europeans – and in fact, Ida depended on their hospitality, as she had little money and very limited language skills to support her travels. But she was thinking now in terms that would win her Carl Ritter's endorsement for an honorary membership in the Gesellschaft für Erdkunde and a gold medal for science and art, conveyed by the Prussian King and Queen. In seeking exotic, non-biblical, non-European ports of call, she was putting herself on the geographical cutting edge – or as close to it as her education and gender would permit. When she died of the after-effects of a fever contracted in Madagascar in 1858, she was more scholar than pilgrim, more scientific traveler than thrill-seeking iconoclast.

Ida Pfeiffer's acceptance by the scholarly community was certainly limited and condescending; but it is intriguing in several ways. It is no accident that she was ignored by the academic orientalists, but celebrated by the geographers Ritter and Alexander von Humboldt; for she had increasingly opted to visit territories little known to Europeans rather than to pay homage to older sites of western or Levantine "civilization." Pfeiffer was valued because she brought home not just religious experiences but new knowledge, new objects, and facts rather than feelings. This would prove an increasingly difficult enterprise for women after Pfeiffer, for they, more than men, were still expected to act the part of the pilgrim and discouraged from mixing with (male) merchants and local leaders; as European institutions and disciplinary structures became increasingly subject to specialization and professionalization, it became rather harder for female "scientific" travelers to compete. But in Ida Pfeiffer's day it was, at least briefly, possible to be a *Forschungsreisendin*.

Entirely different was the career trajectory of the German-Hungarian Jewish traveler Hermann Wamberger, better known as Arminius Vambéry or, in the Ottoman Empire, as Rashid Effendi. Vambéry was not, technically speaking, a

---

[144] Pfeiffer, *Eine Frauenfahrt um die Welt: Reise von Wien nach Brasilien, Chili, Ostahaiti, China, Ost-Indien, Persien und Kleinasien* vol. 3 (Vienna, 1850), p. 112.

[145] Pfeiffer, *Eine Frauenfahrt* 3: 321.

[146] Donner, *Nirgends eine Karawane*, pp. 70–153.

German orientalist; his university position was at the University of Budapest, and he exerted greatest political impact neither in Germany nor in Hungary, but rather in Great Britain and later on among Ottoman Turcophiles. And yet, his many books – and especially his travelogs and political manifestoes – were immediately translated into German and enjoyed some success. Seen as something of a buffoon by German academia – thanks to his sensationalism, his self-promoting endeavors, his political engagement, and his focus on things modern rather than ancient – Vambéry captures, nonetheless, qualities of the mid-century scientific traveler critical to our understanding of the uniqueness of this era.

Born to poor parents in 1831 or 1832 in a small town near Bratislava, Vambéry knew much of the Pentateuch, in Hebrew, by the age of eight, but opted not to become a rabbi and managed to obtain scholarships to finance study at Catholic schools. Like another poor boy from the German fringe areas of his age, Heinrich Schliemann, Vambéry then undertook his own extraordinary course of training. By 1852, he was able to speak not only his native Hungarian, German, and Latin, but also French, Italian, English, Greek, Turkish, Arabic, and Persian. His interest in Asia had been awakened, he later wrote, by the *1,001 Nights* as well as the knowledge that he was "by birth and education half an Asiatic himself." This delphic statement was the closest Vambéry, in his 1883 autobiography, got to admitting his Jewishness – and perhaps here he actually meant to allude to his Hungarian descent. In any event, the next passage was, for Vambéry, more revealing: "I knew Asia," he wrote, "as the land of the most fantastic adventures, as the home of the most fabulous successes; and ... being already in pursuit of some great good fortune, my yearnings after distant lands pointed already to Asia."[147] For Vambéry, Asia was the "wild East" and he intended to make his fame, as well as his fortune, there.

Vambéry's timing was fortunate, and his ability to charm potential patrons remarkable. In the mid-1850s, he met Hammer-Purgstall, who encouraged him to go into Turkology. In 1857, the liberal Hungarian writer and Cultural Minister Josef Eötvös called Vambéry to his office and arranged for a visa so that the struggling linguist and tutor might make his long planned trip to Istanbul. Penniless when he arrived that same year, Vambéry soon made friends and began participating in Islamic rituals; he earned his keep by tutoring Europeans in Turkish and Turks in European languages. Realizing that his thoroughly non-aristocratic background made appointment to a diplomatic post impossible, he turned to philology, publishing first a German-Turkish dictionary and then a Chagataic-Turkish dictionary.[148] He acquired modest support from the Hungarian Academy of Sciences for his travels in 1862–3 on the basis of his promise to seek out relations between the Turkic languages of Central Asia and Hungarian, whose linguistic origins remained mysterious and highly contentious. But in his case, it would be his face-to-face experience with non-Europeans, rather than his knowledge of their lost languages, which would define his orientalist career.

[147] Vambéry, *Life and Adventures of Vambéry*, p. 8.
[148] For biographical information on the young Vambéry, see Lory Alder and Richard Dalby, *The Dervish of Windsor Castle: The Life of Arminius Vambery* (London, 1979), pp. 12–61.

Vambéry was one of those remarkable nineteenth-century characters whose feats border on the implausible and many, including his student Ignaz Goldziher, believed some of his adventures little better than fiction.[149] But Vambéry does seem to have been a linguistic genius and to have actually undertaken – despite a lame leg – a two-year trip across the Ottoman Empire from Istanbul to Bokhara (and back) disguised as a dervish. The lectures given and books published on his return in 1864 made him a celebrity across Europe, and in 1867, he received a professorship for oriental languages at the University of Budapest. A lively writer, and after his initial successes, a passionate advocate for British colonization in Asia, Vambéry left behind his youthful romanticism; describing the horrors of his trip from Tabriz to Teheran, he opened his *Travels* with the warning: "How bitter the disappointment of him who has studied Persia only in Sa'di, Khakani, and Hafiz; or, still worse, who has received his dreamy impressions of the East from the beautiful image of Goethe's 'Ost-Westlichen [*sic*] Divan,' or Victor Hugo's 'Orientales'. . . !"[150] The picture Vambéry painted of the Orient was instead one of poverty, superstition, tyranny, and indolence. The sun had definitively set on the great eastern empires, he wrote several years later: "After the giants came dwarves, after millions empty voids, and the words 'Asia' and 'Asiatic' became identical with the concepts of bombast and hyperbole."[151]

As is clear from these passages, Vambéry was never in danger of being "seduced" by the East. Though he rather enjoyed some of his time as a dervish, he was supremely confident of the West's superiority and – despite his "half-Asiatic" origins – his own European identity. "My adopted Turkdom, my pseudo-Oriental character," he wrote, "were after all confined to external things, in my inmost being I was filled through and through with the spirit of the West."[152] He found it most difficult to reconcile his ambition to succeed in science – which required the careful collection of data – with his "oriental" habitus, one that prevented the taking of notes or asking of questions, lest the "dervish" reveal himself suspiciously interested in things of this world. While Vambéry refused to divulge how he managed to conceal even his "scanty notes" in his ragged costume,[153] his successor, Sven Hedin, would devise such dodges as gauging his steps to turns of his prayer wheel, in the hopes of accurately measuring the distance from the Tibetan border to the forbidden city of Lhasa.[154] Neither, apparently, felt uneasy about pretending to be holy men or divulging to wide European audiences personal or political details of the cultures they entered on false pretences. And neither, unusually, cared much about the *ur*-ancient world or about

---

[149] Goldziher, *Ignaz Goldziher: Tagebuch*, ed. Alexander Scheiber (Leiden, 1978), p. xxx; also Alder and Dalby, *Dervish*, pp. 244, 281–3.

[150] Vambéry, *Travels in Central Asia, Being the Account of a Journey from Teheran Across the Turkoman Desert on the Eastern Shore of the Caspian to Khiva, Bokhara, and Samarcand, Performed in the Year 1863* (New York, 1865), pp. 19–20.

[151] Hermann Vambéry, *Der Islam im neunzehnten Jahrhundert: Eine culturgeschichtliche Studie* (Leipzig, 1875), p. 7.

[152] Vambéry quoted in Alder and Dalby, *Dervish*, p. 62.

[153] See Vambéry, *Travels in Central Asia*, p. 120.

[154] Sven Hedin, *My Life as an Explorer*, trans. Alfhild Huebsch (New York, 1996 [orig. 1925]), pp. 342–51.

confessional questions. They imagined themselves supra-political pundits, thanks to their intimate knowledge of the East, and as such, were not men wont to speak lovingly or longingly of oriental *Geist*.

The opening pages of Vambéry's *Travels* offer interesting insight into his conception of the proper pursuits of the orientalist. The principal reason for his trip, he explained, was a philological puzzle; though Hungarian was known to belong to the Altaic stock of languages, whether it belonged to the Finnish or Tartaric branch remained "a burning question." He did not expect to locate lost ancestors, he explained in a note, but simply to seek "exact information about cognate idioms."[155] But he also expected, as he divulged in an 1863 letter to his patron Eötvös from Meschad, that philological positivism would bring him the fame he so richly merited. The Tartaric thesis, he claimed, would "throw a spark of light into the darkness in which the origin of my nation is surrounded; this spark does not yet shine but the future will set it aflame and posterity will not forget the *obscure limping Jew*."[156] Regrettably, however, this material, what he called the "real reward of a journey in which I wandered about for months and months with only a few rags as my covering, without necessary food, and in constant peril of perishing by a death of cruelty if not torture," was not yet ready for the press and would be put before the scientific world only "after maturer preparation."[157] Perhaps the ex-dervish already knew that the recognition he craved would not come from solving even the most "burning" of scholarly questions; as he passed through Istanbul on his way home from his travels, the elderly Austrian ambassador Prokesch-Osten had advised him to write a concise narrative for the English market "and particularly abstain from writing a book mixed with far-fetched argumentations or with philological and historical notes."[158] Another model was undoubtedly before his eyes, both in conceiving his journey and writing it up, namely that of Joseph Wolff, the son of a Bavarian rabbi who, having become an Anglican clergyman, set off for Bokhara in 1843 to find the lost officials Arthur Conolly and Charles Stoddart. First published in 1846, this best-selling travel account of a man so pious as to be known as the "Dervishi frengi" or foreign dervish, and so ill-treated as to have once been sold for a pair of trousers, was certainly known to Vambéry, who proved adept at imitating its mixture of condescending ethnography, self-inflicted suffering, and spy-adventure narrative.[159]

Vambéry did eventually publish "scientific" papers and books, but these never earned him the academic respect nor the popularity he craved, and obtained, by means of his non-philological publications; indeed, he earned relatively little respect among scholars, and like his student Goldziher, little respect in his native Hungary. He owed his professorship to the direct intervention of Austrian Emperor Franz Josef and was denounced as a "swindler" by many of his

---

[155] Vambéry, *Travels in Central Asia*, p. viii.
[156] Vambéry quoted in Alder and Dalby, *Dervish*, p. 179.
[157] Vambéry, *Travels in Central Asia*, p. viii.
[158] Prokesch-Osten quoted in Vambéry, *Life and Adventures of Vambéry*, p. 292.
[159] Alder and Dalby, *Dervish*, P. 73, 147; Lawrence I. Conrad, "The Dervish's Disciple: On the Personality and Intellectual Milieu of the Young Ignaz Goldziher," in *Journal of the Royal Asiatic Society of Great Britain and Ireland* (1990): 256.

colleagues at the University of Budapest; his few students were, as far as we know, all Jews.[160] Desperate to be accepted by polite, scholarly society, Vambéry was also desperate to secure his fortune, something understandable given his miserable youth, but not readily obtainable for non-chaired professors. He was thus greatly impressed by the warm reception he received in England after his return from the Ottoman Empire and was ever afterward vociferously and even ridiculously pro-British. This was yet another reason to opt for another style of orientalism than that of the German *Zunft*.

Thanks especially to his popularity and political influence in England, Vambéry gradually came to accept an identity as a non-academic orientalist – though he cherished his institutional post and became deeply jealous of his professionally respected student Goldziher. In a Russophobic tract of 1885, he addressed critics who disliked his meddling in politics by labeling himself not a philologist, "who spends his life in his library, viewing thing from a distance," but rather a

traveller [*sic*], who moves on the field of practical experience, and who, assuredly, is more vividly impressed by what he hears and sees around him. The traveller lives and breathes for a long time, if not during his whole life, with the peoples and nations he came across in his journeys, and whom he has made the special subject of his inquiries. He likes to indulge in speculations about their future; he is eagerly bent upon ameliorating their condition; and as the future of such nations is intimately connected with the daily question of European politics, the traveler is, so to say, dragged into the field of political speculation, and cannot help becoming a politician himself.[161]

Rather accidentally, Vambéry described here a difference between the "modern" or traveling orientalist and the philological scholar that warrants underlining. While it is certainly the case that the travelers and commentators on modern events tended to engage more directly in politics and to voice the most disparaging opinions about the Orient, some actually did care about the future of the continent in a way the stay-at-home scholars did not. They wanted to exert European control – both out of contempt for eastern societies and cultures and from more honorable motives of freeing the peoples of the East from oppression, ignorance, and poverty. Vambéry did not really want to understand the Orient, past or present, and this is one reason his protégé Goldziher came to detest him.[162] What he, like many of his high liberal counterparts in England and France, wanted to do was to *change* the Orient, an ambition which should be understood both as a humanitarian and as a grotesquely hubristic and self-serving aim.

In Vambéry's view, the West could not stand idly by and allow millions to slump into ever-greater decrepitude; Asia must be revived. The way to do this, however, was not to force Christianity upon it; for all his dislike of "fanatical" Islam and his praise of Christian superiority, Vambéry did not really believe that the key to

---

[160] Vambéry – who allegedly converted to Protestantism after hanging up his dervish costume – was the first non-Catholic professor at the University of Budapest, and despite his notoriety was originally hired as "lector," at a salary of only 1,000 florins (approximately a nurse's salary in England at the time). Alder and Dalby, *Dervish*, pp. 242–9; Conrad, "Dervish's Disciple," p. 256.

[161] Vambéry, *The Coming Struggle for India* (London, 1885), pp. 201–2.

[162] See Conrad, "The Dervish's Disciple," pp. 243–64.

eastern and western differences was religious. The difference instead was the West's possession of reason and science and its *escape* from Christian piety; "Europe began to think, and therefore stopped being Christian," he wrote in a remarkably forthright book of 1875.[163] Nor could it be expected that the peoples of the East would change overnight; western influence needed to be introduced gradually, especially in the easternmost areas where little had yet penetrated. For these reasons, Vambéry could not countenance the intervention of just any European power. While the French did not take their civilizing mission seriously enough, the Russians, he feared, would simply eradicate the peoples of Central Asia, for whom Vambéry, despite his crude caricatures and condescending rhetoric, did feel sympathy. He did not foresee or advocate Central European intervention; judging by his deep criticisms, voiced elsewhere, of Austrian domination in the Hungarian crown lands before 1867, he was unlikely to see the Habsburgs as the East's proper liberators.[164] It was the English who must shoulder the heaviest portion of the civilizing burden – for in addition to their reputation as the friend of Islam, they were also the nation with the widest experience of both personal and political freedom.[165]

Although he later explicitly denied that his Russophobia had its roots in the Czar's willingness to lend troops to help the Austrians suppress the Hungarian revolution of 1848,[166] it is clear that Vambéry was, in many ways, a product of mid-century liberalism. He had seen oppressive government in Europe itself – and appreciated both the British and the Ottoman Sultan for having harbored Hungarian fugitives from that conflict. In his *Travels*, he deplored eastern poverty and slavery, doing so much more openly than had Moltke and he became something of a hero to the Young Turks, despite his close friendship with the Sultan; it has even been said that he played an important role in the genesis of Pan-Turkism by convincing members of the Istanbul elite that their racial roots lay – together with those of the Hungarians – in Central Asia.[167] He denounced Russian treatment of the Turkic groups newly brought under their dominion and was especially critical of Shiite "fanaticism." But his colonizing jingoism eventually brought him into conflict with English liberals, who began to get cold feet about the Great Game by the 1880s, and his status as a not-so-secret secret agent at the Sultan's court grew rather uncomfortable as "Abdul the Damned" took to murdering Armenians in the 1890s. In another move signaling his departure from liberal cosmopolitanism, Vambéry in 1900 arranged for Theodor Herzl to meet Abdul Hamid in order to present his proposal to found an independent Jewish state in Palestine in exchange for forgiving Ottoman debts.[168] But even his friend Max Nordau admitted that Vambéry was

---

[163] Vambéry, *Islam*, p. 249.

[164] Vambéry, *Hungary in Ancient, Mediaeval, and Modern Times* (London, 2nd ed., 1907 [orig. 1887]), pp. 337–440.

[165] Vambéry, *Islam*, pp. 298–307; Vambéry, *Coming Struggle*, pp. 188–202.

[166] Vambéry, *Coming Struggle*, p. 201.

[167] This claim was made by Gotthard Jäschke in a 1941 essay, cited in Seçil Deren, "From Pan-Islamism to Turkish Nationalism: Modernisation and German Influence in the Late Ottoman Period," in *Disrupting and Reshaping: Early Stages of Nation-Building in the Balkans*, ed. Marco Dogo and Guido Franzinetti (Ravenna, 2002), pp. 133–4.

[168] On his relations with the Sultan and career as British secret agent, see Alder and Dalby, *Dervish*, pp. 359ff.

"by no means keen on the matter ... because he considered it likely to lead to nothing."[169] His only answer to Asia's woes was more and better European influence, despite his recognition of Europe's fissures and failures in the past.

FERDINAND VON RICHTHOFEN: AN EAST ASIAN ENCOUNTER

Voyaging to the Near East was one thing, but East Asian travel was, in this era, an even rarer experience for Central Europeans. Of course, Japan was officially "closed" down to the time of Commodore Perry's exploits, and China only accessible through a few port cities; there were some manuscripts in circulation, as well as the extensive collections of Jesuit letters from China and Dutch reports from Japan. There were few accounts in German available; the German doctor Engelbert Kämpfer (b. 1651) had worked for the Dutch in Japan, but his memoirs remained unpublished during his lifetime and only small parts were in print as late as 1928. While stationed in Japan in the 1820s, another doctor, Philipp Freiherr von Siebold (again in the employ of the Dutch colonial army) formed a series of intellectual friendships with Japanese officials. Siebold learned much from his friends – and apparently impressed many of them with his healing powers. But the reverie ended badly when one of his best informants, an astronomer at the court of the Shogun, was accused of making maps of Japan accessible to Europeans. Investigations led to the arrest of many of Siebold's Japanese friends, a number of whom had to pay for their relationship to the German doctor with their lives. Siebold himself was banished, ostensibly for life – though nearly thirty years later, in 1859, he did manage, briefly, to return.[170] Unlike Kämpfer, Siebold did publish his reflections on the country, *Nippon: Archiv zur Beschreibung von Japan* (in seven parts, 1832–52) – one of the very few well-informed works about East Asia to appear in German before the century's close.

It was very soon after Siebold's return to Japan, in fact, that Central European states began to evince interest in developing colonial holdings in East Asia, hoping to build on the network of German-speaking traders who plied the Chinese coasts. In 1859, the Austrians sent a ship to seek trade concessions and to scout the Indian Ocean for islands they might colonize, but they had to abort the mission when war in the Habsburgs' Italian territories broke out. As Bernd Martin has described, the Prussians stepped in, and quickly arranged their own expedition; the *bon vivant* diplomat Fritz Graf zu Eulenberg was appointed leader of the endeavor, despite the fact that he refused to sail the full distance on a Prussian naval vessel and traveled overland to meet the expedition in Singapore. Eulenberg's primary mission was to win trade concessions in China, Japan, and Siam, but the Admiralty also ask him to look for a spot in a moderate climate to found a Prussian criminal or emigrant colony. Though pressed by Prussian officials to act aggressively to establish Prussia's equal right to treat China and Japan as defeated powers,

---

[169] Max Nordau, "My Recollections of Vambéry," which was added to the ninth edition of *Life and Adventures of Vambéry* (1914), p. xxi.

[170] Even then, however, the Dutch (still his employers) feared that Japanese xenophobia would arouse violence, and in 1862 forced Siebold to leave. Felix Schottlaender, *Erwin von Baelz (1849–1913) Leben und Wirken eines deutschen Arztes in Japan* (Stuttgart, 1928), pp. 27–30.

Eulenberg found that he had little leverage. In addition to the weakness of the Prussian navy – the expeditions' ships broke down repeatedly – the Germans had no knowledge of East Asian languages or bureaucratic practices, and Eulenberg required French and American help to get commercial agreements with the Japanese and Chinese. The expedition's warm reception in Siam was less the result of the King's respect for the Germans than of his calculation that the Germans could be used as allies against more dangerous aggressors. Understanding his position, Eulenberg refused to obey a military order to invade Formosa, and headed home. He left consul Max von Brandt in Japan, with instructions to coordinate his work with the policies of other European nations. Given Prussia's weakness and Bismarck's disinterest (until the 1880s), this was less a choice than the only rational policy within Brandt's reach.[171]

Enhancing trade was the mission's major goal. But, in imitation of other contemporary trade missions, the expedition also took along a small scientific team, including one young geographer, Ferdinand von Richthofen, selected perhaps more for his illustrious family name than for his knowledge; he was, at the time, only a *Privatdozent* at the University of Vienna. As it happened, there was little time or opportunity during the mission for scholarly inquiries; but Richthofen did manage to do some important work after the trade officials left, and it is to his further travels that we now turn.

Richthofen's decision to stay in the Pacific was quite openly a career move. He wanted to take advantage of the new opportunities for European access to a formerly closed country as a means of obtaining "capital" with which to negotiate something better than "perhaps, at an undetermined time in the future, some expectation of [receiving] a badly-paid professorship."[172] Here he was following directly the model of the African travelers described by Cornelia Essner – the mid-century botanists, zoologists, geographers, and ethnographers who went to the "dark continent" precisely because they realized that the new knowledge available there might be the key to professional success.[173] But Richthofen, like many of Essner's travelers, had other motives as well: he was convinced that China harbored great natural resources and convinced that Europeans, and especially Germans, should help to develop them. And by the time he managed to launch his own expedition to the Chinese interior, his patrons too had to be satisfied – and the Anglo-American Shanghai Chamber of Commerce was above all interested in knowing the location and accessibility of China's coal deposits.[174] Ferdinand von Richthofen's pursuits were shaped by self-interests as well as larger political

---

[171] Richthofen diaries quoted in Jürgen Osterhammel, "Forschungsreise und Kolonialprogramm: Ferdinand von Richthofen und die Erschließung Chinas im. 19. Jahrhundert," in *Archiv für Kulturgeschichte* 69, Heft. 1 (1987): 171.

[172] On this expedition, see Bernd Martin, *Japan and Germany in the Modern World* (New York, 1995), pp. 4–14, 25–6.

[173] See Cornelia Essner, *Deutsche Afrikareisende im neunzehnten Jahrhundert* (Stuttgart, 1985).

[174] The Shanghai Chamber paid for three years of the expedition, the Bank of California for the first year. Richthofen had to bide his time before returning to China as a result of the internal turmoil of the 1860s, including the Taiping Rebellion. Traveling by way of Japan, he spent a few years in California, using his geological expertise to locate gold deposits. Osterhammel, "Ferdinand von Richthofen," pp. 170–2.

and economic interests, by prejudice, and by ignorance – for European sources on China's interior were weak and Richthofen knew precious little Chinese. But this does not mean that he did not learn from his experiences.

As Jürgen Osterhammel showed some years ago, Richthofen did not exactly "go native." He brought his own silverware, bedding, and red tablecloth despite the need to travel light; he refused to eat Chinese food and insisted that his hired "boys" prepare his favorite *Eierkuchen* in the wildest of places.[175] In fact, as Richthofen would note in his travel diaries, getting good "boys" was the most important of all travel preparations, for in cases of swindling or treachery, the local population was always on their side.[176] As Osterhammel shows, Richthofen – the European most traveled in China since Marco Polo – did not want to pick up any of the customs of the "lower race" in whose country he lived for four years, but he was not a racist brute or a wild-eyed imperialist; he was, ultimately, more "the development-oriented, and by the standards of the day, enlightened, administrative type." Although he certainly believed the Chinese to be inferior and backward with respect to Europeans, he also believed them capable of industrialization and cautioned Europeans against the counter-productive effects of violence and heedless exploitation. Unlike many Sinologists of twentieth century, he was unromantic about China's departure from traditional society.

As Osterhammel describes, Richthofen considered rigorous, scientific traveling a kind of personal test; his often absurdly ascetic exertions in pursuit of knowledge acted as a kind of proof of the superiority of the researcher and of European character as a whole, raising the foreigner above his less worthy milieu.[177] For Richthofen, a man of more reserved and aristocratic bearing than Vambéry, self-discipline, self-reliance, and self-control (usually in the face of extreme personal danger) were essential to European science's success abroad; one did not dress up or try to trick people. Nor did one tell "amusing" stories afterward. Sven Hedin, one of Richthofen's favorite students, noted that his mentor spoke about his travels in China only on very rare occasions.[178] As the geographer's very long and taxing instruction book for scientific travelers suggests, for Richthofen, facts and measurements were to fill the space other travelogs accorded to the self.[179] For Richthofen and many "scientific" travelers after him, a strange sort of stoical vitalism was not at all unreconcilable with a positivist scientific ethos; in fact, the two complemented one another and would underwrite European scholars' enormous productivity in the age of the "open door."

Although Richthofen, like Vambéry, believed European industrial society could help to bring progress to the "backward" East, the former was rather less idealistic about the prospects for this happening quickly and without strife. Perhaps that was because Richthofen, unlike Vambéry, was no Anglophile, but an increasingly

---

[175] Ibid., pp. 172–4.
[176] Richthofen, *Entdeckungsreisen in China, 1868–1872: Die Erforschung des Reiches der Mitte*, ed. Klaus-Dieterich Petersen (Tübingen, 1982), pp. 37–8, 66.
[177] Osterhammel, "Ferdinand von Richthofen," P. 191, 192, 174.
[178] Sven Hedin, *Meister und Schüler: Ferdinand Freiherr von Richthofen an Sven Hedin* (Berlin, 1933), p. 38.
[179] Ferdinand Freiherr von Richthofen, *Führer für Forschungsreisende: Anleitung zu Beobachtungen über Gegenstände der physischen Geographie und Geologie* (Berlin, 1886).

vocal proponent of German *Weltmacht*. On returning to his homeland, Richthofen not only became an influential professor of geography, reaching the University of Berlin in 1886, but also became highly active in the procolonial lobby. As longtime president of the Gesellschaft für Erdkunde and founder of the Geographisches Institut (1887) and Institut für Meereskunde (1901), he had numerous venues through which to articulate his conception of Europe's proper stance with respect to "the other." His *China* volumes were published, haltingly, but in lavish editions, heavily subvented by the Kaiser and Prussian Academy of Sciences. They were used not only for scholarly purposes, but also, it seems, were instrumental in identifying the geographical advantages of the port city to which the Germans would later lay claim (Qingdao) and heavily used by planners laying out China's railroads.[180] Richthofen joined the ranks of the orientalists in the field's lonely years, but he lived long enough to participate in the production of another kind of orientalism, one much more self-confident, more politically relevant, and much less willing to renounce its worldly aims. But as we shall see, the path from *Wissenschaftlichkeit* to relevance was by no means short or smooth, and there were many alternative routes available; we have many a life history to survey before we chart this portion of German orientalism's many-directional map.

It is often difficult, scholars have found, to get inside the heads of mid-century figures like Richthofen, Jacob Bernays, or Gustav Weil; though some – like Droysen or Rückert – had sons able and willing to recount their lives, even those biographers often found it hard to put the fragments together and form a whole. This was not a generation that wanted others to "feel their pain" – or even to celebrate too vociferously their accomplishments, which many insisted on reckoning as minor contributions to the later, greater achievement of full Knowledge. In a codicil to his will, the great Roman historian Theodor Mommsen insisted that the public not concern itself with his person, in part because he had, somehow, disappointed himself: "Despite outward successes my life has fallen short of its fulfillment. External accidents placed me among historians and classical scholars, although my training, and also, I suppose, my talent, was not sufficient for these two disciplines. The painful feeling of the inadequacy of my achievement, of seeming to be more than I was, has never left me in life and is neither to be veiled nor brought to light in a biography."[181] How much more painful must this feeling have been for his contemporary orientalists, who, in addition to being swamped with new materials that could not easily be spun into scientific gold, had few institutional achievements to point to. We have seen, in this chapter, flashes of state or public interest in orientalism – in Ida Pfeiffer's travels in the 1840s, for example, or in Richthofen's appointment to a chair; we have seen moderate support develop for projects like Lepsius's Egypt expedition and for positions in Indo-German linguistics. But these were, for the most part, only flashes – in the world of biblical criticism alone were orientalists kindling real cultural fire. A more profound public and state engagement in things "Asiatic" would await the next generation – or even the next century.

---

[180] Vorstand, Gesellschaft für Erdkunde to Kaiser April 2, 1906, plus "Denkschrift, betreffend Ferdinand von Richthofens Chinawerk und seine Vollendung" in B-GSPK, I, 76Vc, Sekt I, Tit. XI, Teil VB, Nr. 20.

[181] Theodor Mommsen, "Last Wishes," in *Past and Present* 1 (Feb. 1952): 71.

4

The Second Oriental Renaissance

It cannot be my task to describe to this assembly how following one step after another has led to the fact that a certain amount of knowledge of Babylonian culture now belongs to a general education; [Babylon] is discussed everywhere, from the King's castle to the elementary schools. Nor should I attempt to recount how in parallel with the study of Mesopotamia culture, new discoveries about ancient Egyptian culture have proceeded, how light has been carried into the dusky forest of Indian antiquity, how China and Japan have been opened, how that most important monument of oriental writing [the Old Testament], which has been the object of diligent study for almost two millennia, has been traced to its origins. I cannot, in short, enumerate [the deeds of] all the fields of oriental scholarship. So allow me to synthesize it all by saying: in a never dreamed of way, the darkness of antiquity has been illuminated, all the boundaries of the knowable have been pushed back a quarter millennium, and if once upon a time we only carefully groped our way beyond the borderlands of the Mediterranean to the Far East and South, science has now conquered Asia, as far as the furthest ocean, and Africa is being crossed and its innermost parts [conquered] not only by the clever pioneers of commerce, but also by the servants of science, working in silence. That has been the nineteenth century's achievement. . . .

– D.G. Behrmann, 1902[1]

As Hamburg Senator D. Georg Behrmann pointed out in this opening address to the International Congress of Orientalists in 1902, "the work of the nineteenth century" was Herculean. It was, as his rhetoric unashamedly averred, a kind of conquest, an illumination of the "dark" corners of Asian and African history so that Europeans could peer into them and snatch up whatever treasures came to hand. That these intellectual "conquests" were enabled by Europe's greater penetration into eastern economies and territories was something Behrmann would surely have acknowledged – without, of course, regretting the costs of both political and cultural domination to the cultures in question. He was well aware that even before the German Empire joined the great games in Asia and Africa, German scholars were emboldened and enriched by the intrusions and extortions of other Europeans. Those conquests allowed them to travel newly opened routes and stay with colonial officials stationed abroad, to consult oriental texts bought cheaply when indigenous elites were compelled to sell, or robbed of their cultural goods,

---

[1] Behrmann in *Hamburgische Correspondent*, Sept. 5, 1902, in B-GSPK, Rep. 76 Vc, Sekt I, Tit XI, Teil VI, Nr. 3, Bd. 4.

and to learn new languages and sacred secrets from local religious figures no longer able to sustain their practices in the modernizing and Europeanizing world. But Behrmann also drew explicit attention to something Raymond Schwab and most students of the history of oriental studies miss, and that is that Europe's great leap forward in oriental studies was one that had happened, for the most part, long *after* Champollion and Silvestre de Sacy were dead and buried; it was a product not of the era of imperialism's onset, but of its post-1850, or even post-1880 intensification. Just as importantly, it was a product of new access to sources, of the declining cultural power of the established churches, of the waning of neohumanist forms of *Bildung*, and of new forms of patronage made possible by German unification and the Reich's increasing economic dynamism. Together, these processes generated a second great leap forward in oriental studies, one which deserves to be called a Second Oriental Renaissance.

Indeed, if there was a first Oriental Renaissance, fostered by Anquetil-Duperron, William Jones, Herder, and Friedrich Schlegel, there was even more clearly a second one, enabled by Germany's increasingly wealth and world power. In the period under consideration in this chapter – roughly 1871–1900 – German culture and politics changed a great deal. Bismarck turned on the National Liberals, and destroyed their ability to guide the national agenda; he tried to destroy Catholic political power by launching a *Kulturkampf*, and attempted to keep socialism at bay by banning the Sozialistische Partei Deutschlands; neither of these plans worked, and by the 1890s, both Catholics and socialists were important political players. Bismarck also tried to resist being drawn into the Eastern Question, and for a time refused to countenance those who wanted to create an overseas empire. But Germany's unavoidable alliance with the Austro-Hungarian Empire gradually drew the Reich into negotiations over the fate of southeastern Europe, and after Bismarck's departure in from office in 1890, Kaiser Wilhelm II aspired, increasingly, to extend German influence throughout the Ottoman Empire. In 1884, Bismarck capitulated on the empire question, and the Kaiserreich began actively to acquire colonies in Africa, in the Pacific, and in China (Qingdao). At the same time, German industries boomed, commercial shipping flourished, and private wealth surged. All of these developments remade German cultural institutions in a variety of ways, offering orientalists in particular new forms of patronage and new opportunities to travel and to fill museums and libraries with the world's treasures. This age of "open-door science" would prove highly productive, in scholarly terms; but we should recognize that most of the scholarship produced actually concerned the *ancient*, rather than the *modern* Orient, and had little direct relevance to Germany's very real colonizing efforts on the ground. It will explain something of the context and the preconditions, but little of the practice or cultural salience of the Second Oriental Renaissance to link it to the Wilhelmine Empire's global "conquests."

Perhaps it is useful here to recall that renaissances usually require not only "open doors" and new wealth; they also follow on the heels of changes in relations between spiritual and worldly authorities. Though Behrmann did not mention it, early Wilhelmine orientalism flourished as the result of the relaxing of censorship and the lapsing of clerical influence over schools and other cultural institutions, replaced by the growing influence of the secular states. In such circumstances, orientalists could study pagan cultures and nonwestern religions without fear – though they were still very much aware of, and often embroiled in, theological debates, and their domestic culture-political impact continued to be almost wholly limited to discussions about Christian history and the truth of the scriptures. They could continue to distance themselves from theological faculties, and to expand the scope of secular learning because they had established their philological bona fides, and because state-sponsored universities now found room for scholars whose work was not immediately scripturally relevant – as well as for those who challenged orthodox interpretations. This was a continuation of the enlightened patronage role played in Chapters 2 and 3 by individuals like Christian Bunsen and Alexander von Humboldt, but the new scope and scale of this support was crucial in ushering in Behrmann's "never dreamed of" rethinking of the oriental (and European) past. In promoting this rethinking, the Second Oriental Renaissance – in which the Higher Criticism played so central a role – may have helped to produce the fin de siècle "crisis of faith" so many church leaders decried. But it could not have done so had immense changes not already occurred, as the state (especially in Protestant areas) took over a broad range of the cultural functions that had once belonged to the established churches.

For practicing orientalists, perhaps the most exciting aspect of the Reich's new worldliness was its greatly increased ability to acquire its own artifacts, and especially its own texts. Unlike its cash-strapped predecessors, this generation was able – at the end of the period under consideration – to haul home spectacular pieces of ancient Near Eastern architecture, like the Ishtar Gate from Babylon and the Mschatta Gate from present-day Jordan. But ancient texts continued to be what scholars wanted most, and the brisk trade in manuscripts underway by the 1830s only accelerated after the mid-century. The number of new manuscripts acquired by European libraries is hard to estimate, but it was surely high. In one collecting trip, Heinrich Brugsch acquired a cache of more than 2,000 manuscripts in Greek, 120 in Arabic, and 60 in demotic and other languages from beduin tribesmen.[2] The University of Berlin library had only eight Sanskrit manuscripts in 1827 (pity poor Franz Bopp!), but some 2,000 by 1886.[3] Moreover, by this time, many more of these items had been edited and printed (sometimes by on-site scholars, in Calcutta or Cairo), and purchased by state or university libraries, and were thus accessible to scholars without independent means. It is perhaps useful to recall that whereas early nineteenth-century scholars like Joseph von Hammer-Purgstall or C. F. Neumann were compelled to buy their own libraries of Ottoman, Sanskrit, or Chinese manuscripts from indigenous intellectuals or intermediaries, by 1905, German scholars could avail themselves of Max Müller's fifty-volume series of edited and translated *Sacred Books of the East*, leaf through the pages of any number of specialized journals, and immerse themselves in original oriental manuscript collections without leaving home.

But texts and artifacts do not interpret themselves, and this era's advances in *Orientalistik* were made by well-trained linguists who continued the "lonely"

---

[2] Zedlitz to Kaiser, August 27, November 12, and December 24, 1891; Bosse to Kaiser, June 23, 1894, in B-GSPK, I, 89, 21366. Brugsch's money came partly from a private source – Jewish publisher Rudolf Mosse (30,000 M) – and partly from the Kaiser (22,273 M).

[3] Sengupta, *From Salon to Discipline*, pp. 121, 135.

generation's internalist source criticism, perfecting its attempts to take texts apart from the inside, and to determine their authenticity, date, and authorship. Combined with "external" testimony (from, inevitably, the Old Testament and classical authors), these findings could be, if one dared, used to recreate lost worlds. Though this sounds like an arcane and narrow process and was completed mostly by Eurocentric scholars in European libraries, the lasting beauty of it was that at least in principle, one listened to the texts themselves, speaking in their own tongues, and even sometimes trusted their testimony over and against that of traditional authorities. It was a novelty, and a triumph, that, by 1852, as Jules Mohl announced, thanks to the new work on Persian cuneiform and inscriptions, "we are able to check Herodotus and Ctesias against the autobiographies of the great kings and the descriptions of their empires which they engraved on their monuments."[4] This happened, of course, at different rates in different fields; having begun with the Hebrew Old Testament in the sixteenth century, this sort of hermeneutical operation was still underway in East Asian studies in the mid-twentieth century.[5] But the reading and, increasingly, the trusting, of original oriental sources constituted, in important ways, a Renaissance – even if this Renaissance was less a passionate search for normative models than a diligent attempt to recover world-historical facts.

I will return to this question of passions, for it is central to the way I have split the material in this chapter from that in the next; both chapters treat more or less the same time frame, 1871–1910, with this one, however, looking backward to the 1840s–70s, and focusing on individuals who were, by the 1880s, mostly mature or even senior scholars. The next looks forward from 1880 and deals almost exclusively with younger men. What is characteristic of the individuals highlighted in this chapter is that they tended to retain older text preferences – for classical texts and the Old Testament, most especially – even as they expanded their knowledge of original oriental literature; this is to say nothing of their aesthetic preferences, which still ran heavily to the Greek. Moreover, trained in the era of high positivism, they found it hard to adapt to the fin de siècle's taste for synthesis and speculation. Some still thought of themselves more or less as *Hilfskräfte*, providing useful material to the higher pursuits of classical scholarship or biblical criticism. Despite the intellectual progress orientalists had made, by the 1870s, the oriental-classical playing field was still not level; but few German orientalists, even in this generation, expected, or even desired, that it should be.

In any event, it would have been rather odd for a nineteenth-century scholar to think of himself as personally and passionately involved in his subject – aside from the world of Greek scholarship, where aestheticizing was conventional, one was supposed to study things because they were important, not because one liked them. In the autobiographies of the sober and severe men surveyed in this chapter, one rarely comes across admissions of personal interest in the material they spent so many of their hours studying. Few offered few explanations for their choice of careers – with the great exception of those who took to oriental studies in order to

---

[4] Mohl, "Année 1851–2," in idem, *Rapports* 1: 464 (emphasis mine).
[5] Franke Fritz Jäger, "Otto Franke (1863–1946)," *ZDMG* 100 (nf 25) (1950): 30–1, 35–6.

clear up the Bible or their own doubts about Christianity's truth. One could hardly say they were "othering" the Orient; they were, in their view, simply trying to get the historical facts straight, facts that might well affect the ways in which Europeans conceived their own cultural history or religious development, but which had very little to do, positively or negatively, with the real-existing people of the East.

We cannot, of course, accept this positivist credo at face value; even if establishing ancient facts was the only object, all of these in-depth studies of the ancient East were implicitly if not explicitly critiques of the Orient's modern "backwardness," which permitted or even required non-Asians to set the norms for what could be considered scholarly work. And, especially by our period's end, numerous orientalists expressed the keen desire that their *Wissenschaft*, despite its disinterestedness with respect to modern affairs, would boost German prestige in Europe and abroad; a few even began to agitate for the Reich to extend its economic, political, and cultural power over others. But what is interesting is this: trying to get the facts straight, on the humanist model, required one to read the indigenous texts and in the indigenous languages, and to think oneself into other minds. Though German orientalists certainly did not want to *become* ancient Israelites or Assyrians – as generations of young men claimed they wished to *become* Greeks – their positivist-historicist practices delivered the materials necessary for scholars to see new worlds from the inside – while making older research, based on traditional classical and biblical sources, or on French intuition, look increasingly suspect and superficial.

The hopes of this generation were still fixed on the achievement of academic positions, the numbers of which they believed would increase once dilettantism was rooted out. Part of this effort was focused on pushing out, or at least getting around, the aristocrats, missionaries, and diplomats who still contributed much to oriental studies, men like Joseph von Karabacek (1845–1918), an aristocrat who became *Privatdozent* at the University of Vienna in 1869 – that is, before Austria's Second Oriental Renaissance had really gotten underway. Karabacek was made full professor in 1884, and director of the Imperial library in 1899, despite being in Carl Becker's words "more courtier than scholar" and more antiquarian than professional historian.[6] Becker's obituary for Karabacek – the only one, the author argued, which told the truth about the dilettantish aristocrat, for his colleagues "clenched their fists in silence" – described the ways in which this "fortune-hunter cum scholar" spun wild theories out of erroneous readings of inscriptions, coins, and artifacts, and jealously sat on unpublished material so that better scholars could not use it.[7]

Karabacek was a roadblock, particularly in his field (*Arabistik*); but more generally embarrassing were new anthropological attempts to reconstruct the religions of prehistorical times. Speculation here had drawn scholars – especially in Britain, France, and Switzerland – into studies of ancient sexuality and maternalism, topics that discomfited the typical straightlaced *Bildungsbürger*, and

---

[6] Becker, "Joseph von Karabacek," in idem, *Islamstudien* 2: 491.
[7] Ibid., pp. 491–8.

moreover, smacked of Creuzerian romanticism. More and more, after the 1860s, German scholars shied away from comparative mythology – and indeed from the notion that the religions of the *Naturvölker* might help to explain the world-historical religions sacred to the *Kulturvölker* of Europe and the Orient. It was safer to stick to philological historicism and to leave comparisons either to the anthropologists or to the scholars of the future, who would be able to say something scientific once all the specialized studies had been completed. Perhaps most promising was to dedicate oneself to newly discovered texts or not yet deciphered languages – the scholarly equivalent of planting one's flag – in virgin territory. It was this quest to fill the gaps and to increase national prestige, rather than passionate admiration of eastern wisdom or proto-imperialist ambition, which generated the Second Oriental Renaissance in Germany.

ORIENTALISM AS A CAREER, 1871–1900

Orientalist scholarship, as we have seen, evolved from the tradition of Christian Hebraism, and made itself *wissenschaftlich* at mid-century by adopting itself to models provided by classical philology. Iconoclasm and specialization increasingly drove orientalists to seek institutional homes outside of the theological faculty, and specialization, in turn, created internal disciplinary divergences that became increasingly difficult to bridge. By the 1870s, orientalists were no longer compelled to teach Old Testament exegesis (unless they specialized in Hebrew); nor were Hebraists expected to learn Sanskrit. Many orientalists, in fact, had more in common with their colleagues in theology or in classics than they did with one another. Disciplinary histories play this down, but in practice, studying the ancient Orient was and is unthinkable without some poaching into these two territories. There were many friendships and working relationships across the faculties, and one has only to examine the footnotes of some of the works of this era to see a great deal of cross-reading going on. But institutions think in specialized boxes, and especially as the trans-linguistic theological faculties faltered, it was in the interest of oriental linguists that they underline the autonomy, and if possible, the coherence, of *Orientalistik*.

It helped, certainly, in this quest for institutional and intellectual autonomy that both classics and theology were facing new threats to their cultural hegemony. The theological faculty, in particular, was rapidly losing students and prestige; by the 1880s, some secularist reformers were advocating excluding theology from the university entirely. Classics, too, had its critics; the linguistic focus and deep specialization of mid-century classical philology began to irk students and aspiring scholars, some of whom – like Richard Lepsius and Theodor Nöldeke – would decide that orientalism offered a freer sphere for investigation, and more opportunity to stand out from the crowd. By the 1890s, though the classicists retained considerable cultural and academic clout, their forcing-houses (the *Gymnasien*) had begun to lose their monopoly on university admission. Both threatened fields responded aggressively; Protestant theologians developed what Friedrich Wilhelm Graf has called a "cultural" defense of the centrality of Christian faith to German national character and the integrity of the individual personality; classicists rallied to forestall too much modernizing school reform. But, as archaeological excavations, sensationalist travel writing, imperialist rivalries, and expanding global business opportunities drew attention to the East, it looked increasingly like *Orientalistik* might well be the beneficiary of these disciplines' losses; or, at the very least, find itself more "relevant" than ever before.

In one respect, at least, orientalists continued to be disappointed; though universities established new chairs – there were a total of fifty chairs in *Orientalistik* by 1905 – this was by no means enough to absorb into paying positions the ever-increasing number of *Privatdozenten* seeking academic employment. These were now being produced in every conceivable subspecialty – though there were glaring and telling discrepancies. The numbers of students and positions in East Asian studies or in the more modern fields were still miniscule; George Jacob was virtually the only academic to specialize in things Turkish – and even he focused on medieval writers and travelers. It was still possible for a professional diplomat without specialized university training to be offered a chair in Sinology in 1908 (Germany's only chair too), something that by this time would have been unthinkable in fields like *Arabistik* or Indology.

In the 1880s and 1890s, it was still much riskier to devote oneself to *Orientalistik* than to classics or to theology – as parents of this generation of orientalists repeatedly pointed out. Even the most talented spent time in limbo; in 1901, Enno Littmann grudgingly accepted a position at Princeton while he waited for a German chair; appreciating Littmann's quality, his mentor nonetheless advised the young scholar to secure his future by marrying a Vanderbilt.[8] Nor was one assured that specialized training would in fact prepare one for the "oriental" careers available. In some cases, there was no career ladder. Digging in Samarra in 1913–14, Ernst Herzfeld began to despair of ever finding a position; despite the Reich's great excavations in Asia Minor, there was no chair for oriental archaeology in Germany and no prospect for founding one.[9] As it happens, Herzfeld's employment worries were almost immediately deferred by his deployment to the western front. He would spend most of the rest of his career working in Persia, until forced to return to Princeton in the 1930s.

Getting a job was one thing; but publishing one's work was another, and that was getting easier and easier. There is much work still to be done on the book trade in imperial Germany, but it is clear that the production both of academic monographs and of illustrated travel and picture books was expanding enormously by the later 1880s. It seems apparent that presses like B. G. Teubner, which had formerly focused on classical texts, followed academic trends toward diversification; by the century's end, they were producing journals and monographs devoted to Egyptology and Byzantine studies. In 1898, Teubner took on the *Archiv für Religionswissenschaft* and published thereafter a great many of the pathbreaking works on ancient esoteric religions by scholars such as Franz Cumont, Richard Reitzenstein, and Albrecht Dieterich.[10] Brockhaus in Leipzig continued publishing extensively in Indology, but expanded its list to other

---

[8] Littmann to Nöldeke, November 11, 1901, B-SB, Nachlass Nöldeke, K. 1.

[9] Herzfeld to C. H. Becker, November 30, 1913, and July 2, 1914, in B-GSPK, Nachlass Becker, M. 4023.

[10] Reinhold Merkelbach, "Die Altertumswissenschaft bei Teubner," in *Wechselwirkungen: Der wissenschaftliche Verlag als Mittler: 175 Jahre B. G. Teubner, 1811–1986* (Stuttgart, 1986), pp. 16–24.

oriental subjects too. The Georg Reimer Verlag had published Ritter's massive *Erdkunde*: this feat established Reimer's reputation for publishing maps, which the Dietrich Reimer branch continued after 1847. Ernst Vohsen, who took over Georg Reimer Verlag in 1895, had actually studied at Berlin's Seminar für Orientalische Sprachen; this, together with his energetic support for German colonization in Africa, inclined this press to take on many a grand-scale orientalist publication, including Ferdinand von Richthofen's lavish atlas of China and Friedrich Sarre's four-volume *Archäologische Reisen*.[11] By 1900, Emil Felber in Weimar was offering a wide selection of inexpensive Midrash text editions and studies with titles such as *Die altchinesische Reichsreligion*; F. A. Bruckmann was profiting handsomely from the proceeds of Sven Hedin's oriental travelogs.[12] Aside from the travelogs and popular Christian literature, it is hard to believe that any of these publications made money. But printers and publishers, occupying a critical niche at the crossroads of the *Besitz-* and *Bildungsbürgertum*, often play pivotal roles in cultural politics, and it may well be that we should give men like Friedrich Bruckmann and Ernst Vohsen, in addition to scholars like Eberhard Schrader or Theodor Nöldeke, credit for launching the Second Oriental Renaissance.

Many of these presses published not only monographs, but also journals, and here too, we see rapid proliferation after 1870, generated by specialization, and by factional hostilities. A brief list of a few of these new periodicals, accompanied by the year of their founding, should suggest some of the dynamism and specialization underway: *Zeitschrift für ägyptische Sprache und Altertumskunde* (1863); *Zeitschrift des Palästina Vereins* (1878); *Zeitschrift für Keilschriftsforschung und verwandte Gebiete* (1884, vol. 2, 1890); *Die Buddhistische Welt* (1905); *Der Islam* (1910); and *Ostasiatische Zeitschrift* (1914). The order in which these journals were founded indicates generally the order in which these scholarly fields came of age, Egyptology preceding Assyriology, the study of Palestine preceding that of East Asia. *Buddhistische Welt* was a minor and not a very scholarly publication, but it is on the list to remind us that the study of Buddhism did not die with Koeppen; in 1905, it was just beginning to take on wider appeal. Similarly, though there were numerous scholarly studies of the Islamic world before the debut of *Der Islam* in 1910, this marks the point at which both political and business communities really began to pay attention to this literature – and at which the literature began to address present-day concerns. Of course there were plenty of orientalist journals being produced outside of Germany, and German scholars and lay readers were also eager readers of the *Journal of the Asiatic Society* and the *La Revue des deux Mondes*. The orientalist of the 1890s lived in a quite different world than did, for example, Franz Bopp, in 1812; far from being lonely, orientalists were now beginning to feel they had rather too much company (and competition), not to mention reading matter.

---

[11] Christoph von Wolzogen, *Zur Geschichte des Dietrich Reimer Verlags, 1845–1985* (Berlin, 1986), pp. 22–63.

[12] Advertisement for Emil Felber following text of Richard Pischel et al., *Die Deutsche Morgenländische Gesellschaft, 1845–1895: Ein Überblick* (Leipzig, 1895). This book was itself published by F. A. Brockhaus.

Already by 1898, Assyriologist F. E. Peiser was complaining about "Zersplit-terung" and the difficulties of paying for and reading the twenty-odd journals in the field, especially as many still did not have enough good new material or a sufficiently competent and unbiased editorial staff to be worth the candle.[13] His solution was to found yet another journal, the *Orientalistische Literaturzeitung* (OLZ), which was to publish brief editorials on topics of current, general interest, critical book reviews, and notices about the activities of the new private and public associations springing up all over Europe. One of the main goals of the OLZ was to promote the relatively new field of Assyriology, but its founders envisioned its purview as had mid-century orientalists, that is, as covering all things Asiatic, from prehistorical Japan to modern Morocco. Though they published no schol-arly articles and kept most book reviews very short, the OLZ's editors were quickly overwhelmed by the enormity of specialized production. As they admitted in 1904, the OLZ was having trouble comprehending all of the new oriental material and would have to dedicate itself primarily to the study of the Eastern Mediterranean to the exclusion of Central and eastern Asia.[14] The *Zeitschrift der Deutsch-Morgenländische Gesellschaft* (ZDMG) experienced even more severe problems of this sort. Every issue increased in length, even though the editors tried to direct articles of more specific interest to new, more specialized journals (some of which the Deutsch-Morgenländische Gesellschaft itself subsidized); and the journal and the society evolved increasingly into "umbrella" organizations, which oversaw the activities of a rising number of subgroups, many of which had virtually nothing in common with one another.

As this suggests, the internal dynamism of the discipline was part and parcel of changes in the larger cultural world, the onset of the imperialist age, the coming of an age of mass readership of specialized and/or illustrated journals, the decline of older models of *Bildung*, and of conventional forms of religious faith. Oriental-ism's practitioners were growing in number and their works finding new readers and patrons; we have left behind the era in which the discipline was essentially dependent on the patronage of the Humboldt brothers and Christian Bunsen or on the sufferance of the theological faculties. Increases in support came both from private organizations and from state-funded ones.[15] To take the latter first: although those theological faculties – and in particular, the Jewish seminaries and the Tübingen Stift – would continue to be central in the production of aca-demic orientalists, philosophical faculties increasingly felt the need to hire not just one but several orientalists (though most new positions remained unsalaried). The enormous expansion of museums all over Germany – like university expansion, driven in part by inter-regional competition – and the hefty increases in their budgets after 1871 allowed for an impressive and intellectually highly significant enlargement of Germany's nonwestern collections, and also for the hiring of

---

[13] Peiser, "Was wir wollen," OLZ 1, no. 1 (1898): 4.

[14] [Peiser], "Altertums-Berichte aus dem Kulturkreis des Mittelmeers," OLZ 9, no. 5 (1906): 283–4.

[15] Under "state funding" I am subsuming both funding from the separate German cities and states (for they paid for the universities, museums, and academies), and imperial funding, supplied by the Kaiser or by other agencies of the Reich.

experts able to sort and catalog them. The academies of science, so important in promoting, circulating, and paying for early nineteenth-century scholarship also expanded their coverage of oriental subjects, as more and more experts qualified for admission to their ranks. Finally, after 1884, state agencies founded several explicitly utilitarian institutions designed to serve Germany's colonial empire (see Chapter 8). But before these came into being, other sorts of institutions were developing as well, and it is worth a paragraph or two to describe the role these played in putting orientalism on Germany's cultural map.

The great leap forward in state funding for oriental studies was critical to the discipline's efflorescence. But perhaps just as important was the coming of age of the *Vereine*, the private, leisure-time associations devoted to every possible cause from prison reform to gymnastics to the study of East Asian ethnography. These sorts of organizations had been around for a long time, but flourished in at the fin de siècle and played central roles in organizing German cultural as well as political affairs. In the cultural sphere, they were often founded and led by university professors; the Gesellschaft für Erdkunde, founded by Carl Ritter and presided over by a series of chaired geographers, is a good example. The size, prominence, and wealth of each of the *Vereine* differed greatly, of course; but many did provide patronage for cultural projects, like research trips and archaeological digs, and sometimes sponsored the acquisition of artifacts or manuscripts. They often published their own journals and their meetings offered scholars young and old, credentialed or not, the opportunity to address wider audiences than available at the universities. Associations could also be helpful in pressing state officials to patronize projects, and they played a highly important role in attempts to increase Germany's cultural presence overseas. Like the publishers, these organizations do not get much credit in disciplinary histories, but they undoubtedly deserve more, if for no other reason than for integrating specialized orientalist scholarship into the wider cultural sphere. As the *OLZ* observed at the founding of the high-profile Deutsch-Orient Gesellschaft (DOG): "We orientalists can always find cause for cheer when laypersons are taught that they should no longer treat our field, as now so often occurs, as superfluous amusement."[16]

Founded only in 1898, the DOG was certainly not the first *Verein* devoted to patronizing and popularizing oriental studies; it has earlier antecedents in the geographical and biblical archaeology societies founded in the 1830s–1850s. By the 1870s, these had become more explicitly interested in promoting national studies and funding German, not Christian or European scholarship. When the Deutsche Verein zur Erforschung Palästinas was founded in 1878, for example, its president Hermann Guthe asked the Prussian Cultural Ministry for support in light of the fact that it was devoted to getting German youth to work together in the study of biblical areas, "... and thereby to introduce the German nation as a self-sufficient collaborator in this endeavor, to work alongside the other nations active in this field."[17] The DOG was even more obviously and determinedly nationalist in its rhetoric and in its aims; a lay and scholarly society composed

---

[16] [Peiser], "Die Deutsch Orient-Gesellschaft," in *OLZ* 1, no. 2 (1898): 38.

[17] Hermann Guthe to Cultural Ministry, July 20, 1878 in B-GSPK, Rep. 76Vc, Sekt I, Tit. XI, Teil 1, Band 11, 1.

of wealthy patrons, pastors, politicians, businessmen, and scholars, the DOG not only wanted to give Germany new scholarly and museological prestige vis-à-vis the French, the British, and the Americans, but also sought to impress upon the German public the cultural and political importance of oriental studies. It aimed explicitly at acquiring artifacts, both because this would give Germany's museums new prestige and because, its founders argued, Germany needed to enhance its philological supremacy by conquering the world of things as well. The more nationalistic and imperialist attitudes adopted by many *Vereine* made them more efficient and useful patrons than were university administrations, whose research and travel funds were limited. The DOG was particularly obliging as it generally let academics and museum officials guide its decisions about where funds should be directed and who should be hired to take on new projects. Of course, these newfangled patronage relationships were never perfectly harmonious;[18] but in general they worked to the great benefit of scholars and scholarship, especially in this era of rapid diversification, "open door" exploitation, and rather indiscriminate acquisition.

Having offered a general survey of the cultural ecosystem into which German orientalism adapted itself at the fin de siècle, we now need to say something about the individuals who took part in the Second Oriental Renaissance. As a group, they were more conservative than their predecessors – in this they followed the trajectory of the majority of post-unification German liberals. But most were outspoken Bismarckian nationalists – that is to say, not 1848 nationalists or pan-German racists (with the important exception of Paul de Lagarde). Clear descendants of the tradition of *Kulturprotestantismus*, as a group, they were even more religiously radical than their fathers and probably, thanks to the *Kulturkampf*, even more anti-Catholic. Without indulging in hagiography, I think it still can be said that some of the individuals treated later in this chapter were intellectual giants; it is hard not to be astounded still by the enormous and wide-ranging productivity of Theodor Nöldeke or by the discipline-transforming power of Adolf Erman. Of course, many were less remarkable and some of those thought to be giants in their day have either lost their reputations entirely (like Lagarde) or have been totally forgotten (like Eberhard Schrader). But their productivity or quality is hardly the issue here; what we want to know is, what kind of scholarship was produced by these unique persons, working in the institutional setting of the early Kaiserreich, and with a specific and selective set of source materials? How did they transform oriental studies, and what were the cultural consequences of their work? Those questions will guide us as we survey some of the most significant contributors to the Second Oriental Renaissance.

THREE AGAINST THE CHURCHES: PAUL DE LAGARDE, THEODOR NÖLDEKE, AND JULIUS WELLHAUSEN

We begin by profiling three scholars who played crucial roles in pushing forward internalist critiques of the best-known scriptures, the Hebrew Bible, the New Testament, and the Qur'an. One could say they were instrumental in historicizing

---

[18] See for example, Marchand, *Down from Olympus*, pp. 209–20.

and secularizing the study of the Near East – especially if one considers "secularizing" as does Owen Chadwick, as a halting, and sometimes reversible process, and one that often affects institutional structures before it permeates the hearts and minds of individuals.[19] We must be careful here, for most mid-century orientalists were less proponents of secular culture than heirs to that very long tradition of religious iconoclasm, which so often in the sixteenth, seventeenth, and eighteenth centuries led intellectuals to oriental subjects. Most studies of modern *Orientalistik* make too much of the secularization story not only because they presume this tradition to be, after the romantic era, dead, but also because so many of them focus on the history of *Arabistik* and *Islamforschung*, where older forms of Christian humanism had less purchase, and modern concerns more urgency.[20] Here, however, the focus is less on a generalized secularization story than on this generation's peculiar antagonisms toward orthodox religious ideas and institutions; we shall see, in any case, how deeply embroiled even these individuals were in questions of theological significance. And in the next chapters, readers will see quite clearly why secularization is not emphasized here; for though there were important institutional and intellectual movements in this direction, the fin de siècle would bring in its train not only a return to the Protestant project of cleaning up the Bible, but also a deepening of occultist, Buddhist, and "Aryan" quests to purify the soul.

Paul de Lagarde: The Orientalism of the Future and the Positivism of the Present

Paul de Lagarde was one of those for whom secularization was never an option or a desiratum, and for whom the consolidation of the German nation was far more important than the establishment of a German empire. Born in 1827, in many ways he remained a late romantic, and composite of his mentors, Christian Bunsen and Friedrich Rückert, and his heroes, Jacob Grimm, J. G. Fichte and Karl Lachmann. Lagarde remained, as his disapproving younger contemporary Julius Wellhausen claimed, "in his religious views, trapped in the orthodoxy of Friedrich Wilhelm IV, a degenerate, clerical form of romanticism. In his scholarly practice," Wellhausen continued, "he was dominated by the then common comparative method, a rather wild mania for comparison."[21] In fact, Lagarde was to turn his strange, late romanticism in theologically and even philologically more radical directions than would Wellhausen, and his work will carry us forward into the neoromantic and *völkisch* world of the early twentieth century.

As Ulrich Sieg has recently emphasized, Lagarde's linguistic positivism fit uncomfortably with his outspoken political apocalypticism, and it is largely as a

---

[19] See Chadwick, *The Secularization of the European Mind in the Nineteenth Century* (Cambridge, 1976).

[20] Typical here are Mangold, *Eine "weltbürgerliche Wissenschaft"* and Irwin, *Lust for Knowing*.

[21] Wellhausen quoted in Sieg, *Deutschlands Prophet*, p. 12.

political thinker that we know him today.[22] A hater of epic dimensions, Lagarde despised Jesuits and Lutherans, bureaucrats, and academics. As a young man, he opposed the 1848 revolutions; he hated the school system's cosmopolitanism; and most famously was revolted by Bismarck's unification, which had created a soulless, artificial state untrue to the real Germandom of the little people. He saved, however, his most poisonous bile for the Jews. Wellhausen, like many of his contemporaries, detested the viciously anti-Semitic Lagarde, calling him in a letter to his friend Theodor Mommsen "a rascal and a liar."[23] But Wellhausen did praise Lagarde, after his death, for waking up theologians and showing them how fruitful (and explosive) oriental studies could be. And there, too, Wellhausen was completely correct.

Lagarde's popular political and religious writings have been scrutinized by many historians; far fewer, however, have been willing to tackle his philological work, which was for the most part highly specialized and narrowly focused. For our purposes, however, we must try to understand Lagarde the philologist and exegete, and to appreciate the fact that, misanthrope and ideologue that he was, he did earn respect for his work in oriental philology. In 1869, indeed, he obtained Ewald's professorship at the University of Göttingen.[24] Contemporaries who knew Lagarde as a scholar did not necessarily like his politics or agree with his findings, but they knew him to be a vehement and influential practitioner of Protestant positivism, passionately committed to the notion that a true faith could only be founded on secure, scientific evidence. This commitment underwrote not only his own scholarly work, but explained, in part, why he hated many of his peers: he believed them to be backpedaling on their commitment to science. His version of divine justice was one that had severe implications for fainthearted philologists: "... [E]veryone who does wrong will be ruined [geht unter]," he wrote, in an otherwise highly technical essay on the Greek Psalter; "and those who will not seek truth should be destroyed [vernichtet warden]."[25] Though laced with typically Lagardian vitriol, this was a conviction that many of his contemporaries shared.

Lagarde's important essay, "Über das Verhältnis des deutschen Staates zu Theologie, Kirche und Religion: Ein Versuch, Nicht-Theologen zu orientieren," published first in 1873, opens with a kind of credo, which may help us comprehend his view of the proper way to practice theological and oriental *Wissenschaft*:

[22] Ulrich Sieg's excellent *Deutschlands Prophet* confirms in beautiful detail many of the views I had formed independently, and, which were also laid out in embryo in Fritz Stern's classic treatment of Lagarde in *The Politics of Cultural Despair: A Study in the Rise of the Germanic Ideology* (Berkeley, CA, 1961), pp. 3–94.

[23] Wellhausen to Mommsen, October 3, 1889, in Ernst Bammel, "Judentum, Christentum, und Heidentum: Julius Wellhausens Briefe an Theodor Mommsen, 1881–1902," in *Zeitschrift für Kirchengeschichte* 80 (1969): 247.

[24] There were, however, numerous critiques of Lagarde's philology during his lifetime: Friedrich Spiegel continuously criticized Lagarde's Iranian philology, and Heinrich Brugsch attacked his Coptic philology. Sieg, *Deutschlands Prophet*, p. 53. For the politics behind Lagarde's appointment, see Chapter 2.

[25] Lagarde, untitled essay on the Greek Psalter, presented to royal society of sciences (Göttingen) February 7, 1891, in idem, *Septuaginta Studien* (Göttingen, 1891): 77.

"Everyone ... who understands science knows that it has its goal exclusively in itself and that therefore it seeks its methods for itself and takes no instructions, laws or conclusions from any powers in heaven or on the earth. It wants to know, nothing but know, and only in order to know. It knows that it knows nothing where nothing has been proven."[26] He continues: "One can easily deduce that this description of science is not applicable to the discipline we in Germany call theology, and that therefore the theology we actually have is not a science."[27] The major reason for this, he contends, is that theologians today, Catholic and Protestant, liberal and conservative alike, refused to ask the really hard questions about the New Testament that the work of Lachmann and the Tübingen School had raised. The questions remained: how was Christianity's most important text put together? Who collected the material? What were the principles guiding its inclusions and exclusions? When did it emerge as a full text? Were there inauthentic pieces that should be excised? Only those willing to risk answering these questions, in Lagarde's view, deserved to be called scholarly theologians.

A product of the orthodoxies of the world of Friedrich Wilhelm IV, Lagarde might have been, but the 1870s had a radicalizing effect on the cantankerous philologist; by the decade's end, he was theologically much more radical than Bunsen or Schelling. By this time, he was no longer recognizable as a Christian and became a vicious and relentless critic of all the religious institutions of the Reich, condemning not only the spiritual disunity of the new state but also its spiritual backwardness. The New Testament, Lagarde argued, had no historical value; it was simply the product of the Catholic Church's struggles with Judaism and with heresy; it was especially, he argued later in the essay, influenced by the Jewish rituals and principles introduced into the new faith after Jesus' death by the apostle Paul. This departure from F. C. Baur's interpretation – and from that of the other great liberal biblical critics, including Renan, Nöldeke, and Wellhausen – was especially telling. Paul was for them the great Greek thinker, the man who had broken with Judaism in favor of founding a universal Church. Paul was also central to Luther's thought, his doctrine of grace having been derived chiefly from the apostle's letters to the Romans. This Lagarde knew, of course; but he despised Luther for making the absurd mistake of thinking that he and his friends could clean up and renew Christian faith by going back to the Bible, and for trusting Paul, the man Lagarde believed to be the chief perpetrator of the whole swindle known as "Christentum."

Borrowing his terms from Richard Wagner's *Zukunftsmusik*, Lagarde in 1878 penned an important essay on "the religion of the future," which, he argued, would have to be built on the presence of God in the here and now. Creating it would require throwing out all foreign elements and recognizing the real proof of immortality in God's plans for individuals and peoples. Belief in *something* was

---

[26] Lagarde, "Über das Verhältnis des deutschen Staates zu Theologie, Kirche und Religion: Ein Versuch, Nicht-Theologen zu orientieren" (1873), in idem, *Deutsche Schriften* (Munich, 4th ed., 1940), p. 45.

[27] Ibid., p. 46.

crucial; "Piety exists, for individual men and even for the people as a whole, to push forward consciousness, in times of tempest and storms and of sunshine and mild dew, and throughout it all to drive to completion the goals that God has set for the nation and the individual: piety is the consciousness of the highest health."[28] But belief in the historical Jesus was not necessary. Like his friend Ernest Renan, Lagarde considered Jesus chiefly a charismatic individual – though the German scholar took care to separate the Savior as much as possible from his Jewish milieu and "Jewish" followers. But for Lagarde, what was important to establishing Germany's spiritual well-being for the future was simply the "Evangelium," which we might translate as the Gospel incarnate. This abstract entity would give Germans courage and the will to work. It had virtually no ethical or ritualistic content, and perhaps consequently, was the only facet of Lagarde's theology *not* to be historicized.

Quite clearly, Lagarde's theological radicalism was linked to the history of biblical criticism, which had moved in increasingly radical directions during Lagarde's lifetime. Lagarde himself had been sufficiently mesmerized by the Higher Criticism (in which his pastor father also dabbled) to learn Hebrew, Greek, Arabic, and Syriac before the age of sixteen in order to prepare for a career in the field.[29] Thereafter, his obsession with the scriptures and their sources never wavered. His first great project as a theologian-philologist, formulated in the early 1850s, was the editing of the New Testament based on oriental sources. This was neither a new nor an obviously ideological project; one of his mentors, Karl Lachmann had published the first New Testament based on original documents, not on emendations of the *textus receptus*, in 1831. As we have seen, after several years of wheedling, in 1859, another German theologian, Constantine von Tischendorf, extracted from the monks at Mount Sinai the so-called Codex Sinaiticus, which contained parts of the Greek Old Testament (Septuagint) as well as the earliest extant Greek New Testament; but that dated to the fourth century, and it was widely known that earlier, "oriental" translations of the New Testament into Syrian, Ethiopian, and Coptic existed in widely scattered manuscripts, and might have been used to generate a more authoritative version of what was still presumed to be a Greek *Urtext*. This was not, it turned out, a vain hope; between the 1860s and the 1890s, many new manuscripts of this type were indeed found by American and British as well as German scholars.[30] But the editing of a whole new New Testament in this way was far out of Lagarde's reach; not only were the sources fragmentary, hard to find, and hard to date, but Lagarde was denied access to one of the main pieces of the puzzle then available, the Syrian texts collected by the British scholar William Cureton. By the 1860s, Lagarde had given this up, in favor of an even more grandiose plan: the production of a pre-Christian Septuagint.

Cleaning up the Septuagint was no easy job, even for a scholar with Lagarde's language abilities (he added Coptic, Armenian, Sanskrit, Arabic, Persian, and

---

[28] Lagarde, "Die Religion der Zukunft," in idem, *Deutsche Schriften*, p. 286.

[29] Sieg, *Deutschlands Prophet*, p. 29.

[30] One example is the Diatessaron of Tatian, a Syriac sequence of direct quotations of the gospels in circulation by 172 C.E., found in an Arabic translation, and published in 1888. See Christopher de Hamel, *The Book: A History of the Bible* (London, 2001), pp. 305–7.

several other safely dead languages during his college years), and Lagarde devoted many decades to the project. His attempts to recreate the original text must be seen in the context of exegetical and theological debates that had been raging for centuries. One might call two of the foremost positions the philo-Judaic and the anti-Judaic positions; the latter was represented, for example, by the second-century theologian Marcion, who thought Christianity should do without the Hebrew Bible, and Dutch scholar Isaak Vossius, who believed that the Septuagint was superior to the Masoretic redaction of the Old Testament, and even that the latter was a forgery.[31] Though he never said as much in public, Lagarde was inclined in the direction of Vossius. Had he simply wanted philosophical justification for this view, he could easily have found it in Fichte or in Schleiermacher; but Lagarde, the great admirer of Lachmann, wanted more: "All investigations of the Old Testament remain foundationless if they are not based on the earliest credible text," he wrote in 1863; "Science demands more than opinions and provisional remarks: method is its essence."[32] The mid-century philologist in him told him he had to start with a stripped-down, original Septuagint if he wanted to end up with a wholly discredited Masoretic text.

Lagarde's project may seem arcane to us, but his contemporaries found it exciting, and it was on the basis of this project that he first earned the support of Wilhelm I. The Septuagint project would have significant support not only from the Hohenzollerns, but also from the Prussian Cultural Ministry and Academy of Sciences for most of Lagarde's lifetime; after his death, in 1908, Lagarde's own house and library became the basis for a Septuagint research center.[33] In retrospect, it is fortunate that Lagarde did not complete the stripping down of the Masoretic text; enough Germans gravitated toward Marcionism based simply on prejudice, and a Lagardian edition would have offered "scientific" grounds for Christianity's full divorce from Judaism. If Lagarde was personally unpopular and his politics highly controversial, his linguistic virtuosity gave him considerable prestige (and not just in Germany!), and his positivistic approach veiled the ideological operations he was seeking to perform on this extremely important text. Only a few Jewish scholars protested his neglect of rabbinical texts and of recent Jewish scholarship, which was, in any event, a time-honored Christian practice.[34] It would have taken another Isaac Casaubon to detect Lagarde's sleights of hand.[35] And Casaubons are not, regrettably, all that common.

---

[31] By no means was this a widely accepted view; Semler, for example, did not buy this. See Semler, *Lebensbeschreibung von ihm selbst abgefasst* 2: 128–9.

[32] Lagarde, "Anmerkungen zur griechischen Übersetzung der Proverbien" (1863), in idem, *Mitteilungen* 1 (Göttingen, 1884), p. 20.

[33] Sieg, *Deutschlands Prophet*, pp. 89–112, 273–91.

[34] One of these was Prof. Dr. David Kaufman, who pointed out Lagarde's deficiencies, but who was also humane enough to express sympathy for "Prometheus Lagarde, chained to the rocky cliffs of Jewish literature, while his eager hatred for the Jews hacks apart his liver." David Kaufman, *Paul de Lagarde's Jüdische Gelehrsamkeit: Eine Erwiederung* (Leipzig, 1887), p. 44.

[35] On Casaubon's solving of the Hermetic puzzle, see Anthony Grafton, "Protestant versus Prophet: Isaac Casaubon on Hermes Trismegistus," and "The Strange Deaths of Hermes and the Sibyls," in idem, *Defenders of the Text* (Cambridge, 1991), pp. 145–61, 162–77.

But what is even more significant for our purposes is the second, even more incomplete stage of Lagarde's project. Lagarde seems to have had in mind a corpus of other sources for the Septuagint and ultimately for Christianity. These sources were oriental ones – drawn primarily from what his contemporaries were beginning to call "Aryan" cultures, works written in Armenian, Coptic, Sanskrit, and especially Persian.[36] Lagarde consistently sought to push back the dates of these "pagan" texts and seems too to have been seeking linkages between them (and between them and the medieval German world), an exercise whose outlines surely owed to the work of nationalist romantics before him, but which he, again, sought to raise to the level of pure science. That is, just as Julius Wellhausen was *lowering* dates for Hebrew texts (thus dating Jewish innovations to later periods than previously thought), Lagarde was *raising* dates for pagan oriental texts and traditions (making these earlier than previously appreciated). His work here, again, was fragmentary, rarely fleshed out, and accessible only to a very small number of fellow orientalists. But it would lay the foundations for future, more consequential and controversial, efforts in this direction.[37]

Finally, to understand Lagarde's orientalism, we need to invoke that old, esoteric, Hermetic tradition, which was, I am convinced, still in some way active in Lagarde's mind and was probably what Wellhausen had in mind in referring to Lagarde's "wild mania for comparisons." Lagarde's beloved advisors included Friedrich Rückert, who believed that all living languages held traces of their descent from a Babylonian *Ursprache*, and the Egyptologist Moritz Gotthilf Schwartze, a pioneer of Coptology and one of the translators (into Latin) of the only then known Gnostic treatise, the *Pistis Sophia*. Then too Lagarde was a protégé of Christian von Bunsen, who, as we have seen, thought traces of the *ur*-revelation might be discoverable in Egyptian or other oriental texts. Lagarde clearly conceived himself as belonging to the long list of victims of the Church militant, a list that also included Galileo, Copernicus, and Giordano Bruno.[38] One of the few projects he did complete was an edition of the Italian works of the latter – which included Bruno's most famously anti-Semitic text, the *Spaccio de la bestie trionfante* (1583), in which Bruno accused the Jews of having stolen Egyptian ideas. The Germans, the oriental pagans, and the truly courageous and innovative scientists, Lagarde believed, had always had to contend with the suppressive power of the church. He saw himself, that is, not only as Germany's only truly scientific theologian, but also as something of a Hermetic heretic-humanist, an association understood by at least two of his contemporaries: Ulrich von Wilamowitz Moellendorff, who quoted a poem of Bruno's in concluding his

---

[36] Lagarde's theses for his habilitation included a defense of the Aryan origin of Armenian; already at this time (1851) he was interested in emphasizing differences between "Indo-German" and "Semitic" languages. Sieg, *Deutschlands Prophet*, pp. 35–6. See also Chapter 6.

[37] It is no coincidence that Josef Strzygowski, for one, looked back to Lagarde with admiration. See Chapter 9.

[38] Copernicus was one of Lagarde's few heroes; more than once Lagarde compared the astronomer to Jesus (Lagarde, "Die Religion der Zukunft," p. 262; Lagarde, "Die graue Internationale" (1881), in idem, *Deutsche Schriften*, p. 367).

speech at Lagarde's funeral, and Houston Stewart Chamberlain, who popularized so many of Lagarde's ideas, including that of the Germanic martyr for science.[39]

Lagarde's critique of the construction of Christianity would surely have its echoes in Nietzsche's *Anti-Christ* and *Genealogy of Morals* – though, as Andreas Sommer has nicely shown, Nietzsche also drew on numerous other sources (including Wellhausen and Renan) and made some major modifications to Lagarde's theologically-driven picture of the early church.[40] It would also, as we will see, have profound echoes in the work of the "religious-historical" school after the turn of the new century. What is interesting here is to see how neatly Lagarde's scholarship fits into a larger literature whose mission was to reinterpret the well-known Orient of the Bible by using the fruits of secular philology and history – and how this program was driven by a desperate desire to make theology (and its descendant, *Orientalistik*) "scientific" – and by the perhaps even stronger desire to save German Christiandom from the now historicized clutches of Judaism.

Theodor Nöldeke: Liberal Semitist

Unlike Lagarde, Theodor Nöldeke was no romantic, but he was certainly an iconoclast. The son of a *Gymnasium* director, Nöldeke began with a deep classical education, and – as nineteenth-century scholars frequently did – picked up Hebrew during a quarter year's illness at the age of fifteen. As a boy, he read (also *de rigueur*) Galland's translation of the *1,001 Nights*. He enrolled in oriental as well as classical language courses at the University of Göttingen on his arrival in 1853. What drove him into the Orient's arms was first the charismatic Old Testament scholar and accomplished linguist, Heinrich Ewald, and second, his ambition to stand out from the scholarly crowd. Nöldeke, his friend Christiaan Snouck Hurgronje later underlined, wanted above all to obtain "valuable results," and classics by the 1850s, was already too crowded.[41] *Orientalistik*, as we know, was not, the downside of which was that Nöldeke was expected to learn Aramaic, Sanskrit, Turkish, Persian, and Arabic – which he did. He was not, however, expected to go to the Orient, and indeed the man who would be for nearly half a century Germany's most eminent Semitist never got farther East than the manuscript collections in Vienna. In 1856, he completed his doctoral thesis on a subject that typifies Europe's newfound confidence in its superior knowledge of oriental texts and traditions: the origins of the Qur'an.

---

[39] The poem describes the material universe's ever-frustrated quest for pure unity and the author's longing for an unmediated view of the sun. Wilamowitz, *Rede gehalten im Auftrage der Königl. Georg-August-Universität am Sarge des Geheimen Regierungsrates Professors Dr. Paul de Lagarde am 25. Dezember 1891* (Göttingen, 1891), p. 7. Judging from the title it does not appear that Wilamowitz was particularly honored to give this elegy nor was his tribute particularly laudatory.

[40] Andreas Urs Sommer, "Zwischen Agitation, Religionsstiftung und 'Hoher Politik': Friedrich Nietzsche und Paul de Lagarde," in *Nietzscheforschung* 4 (Berlin, 1999), pp. 169–94.

[41] Hurgronje here is paraphrasing Nöldeke; Hurgronje, "Theodor Nöldeke," in *ZDMG* 85, no. 3 (1931): 244.

How Nöldeke came to the topic is not entirely clear; in a letter to Ignaz Goldziher, written much later in life, he would call his choice simply the product of "fate":

It was the power of fate, in Allah's book it was written, that I should occupy myself first of all with [Allah's] revelation to his envoys. "Oh, it was not my choice!" How much more would I have preferred to occupy myself with the ancient wild beduin ... to reconstruct with the help of my own imagination the relations between the ancient peoples (the Amalekites, etc.), to investigate the ancient Israelites, not the pious ones of the book of Judges, and so on! What is tolerably good in my Qur'an book has very little to do with religion per se.[42]

Quite clearly, for Nöldeke, the Qur'an was a philological problem – like that of the Pentateuch or the Homeric epics. He had chosen it against his romantic longings because it seemed a suitable object upon which to practice the sort of Higher Criticism Ewald had taught him and a subject, which allowed him to display his already formidable knowledge of Arabic texts. Evidently, fate made a felicitous choice on Nöldeke's behalf, for his *Geschichte des Qorâns*, published in 1860, was widely acclaimed (in Europe) and proved to be the first masterpiece of his career.[43]

What was pathbreaking about the book was that Nöldeke was now not just *using* but often *trusting* Arabic and Islamic sources over Christian ones.[44] The Arabic sources, of course, were also subjected to philological-historical criticism – something Gustav Weil and Abraham Geiger had pioneered, but which Nöldeke carried much further.[45] He was quick to underline the impossibility of reading these sources, as it were, "straight": they focused too much on miracles and, worse, were slanted to elevate Muhammed and/or to defame his enemies.[46] But, like Weil, Nöldeke wanted to take the book, and even Muhammed himself, seriously and to avoid falling into the long Christian tradition of religious polemic against the great "imposter." Thus, Nöldeke took the radical step of arguing that Muhammed had to be understood as a prophet; it could not be denied, he argued, that Muhammed thought himself God's vessel.[47] That he conceived of himself in that way, Nöldeke continued, was the result of his exposure to Jewish ideas – probably not in the form of written texts, but by way of oral traditions, which remained powerful in the medieval Arab world. In making this argument, Nöldeke was again doing something quite radical: he was borrowing (*with* acknowledgment) from the insights offered by Geiger's *Was hat Muhammed aus dem*

---

[42] Nöldeke to Goldziher, August 13, 1913, in Richard Símon, *Ignác Goldziher*, p. 368.

[43] On Nöldeke's early life, see Hurgronje, "Theodor Nöldeke," pp. 241–51; Enno Littmann, "Theodor Nöldeke," in idem, *Ein Jahrhundert Orientalistik: Lebenbilder aus der Feder von Enno Littmann und Verzeichnis seiner Schriften* (Wiesbaden, 1955), pp. 52–5.

[44] Nöldeke, *Geschichte des Qorâns* (Göttingen, 1860), p. xvi.

[45] Islamic scholars could not contest the claim that the Qur'an had been revealed in its entirety to Muhammed, and thus were not permitted to discuss the question of the book's sources.

[46] Nöldeke, *Geschichte des Qorâns*, pp. xxiii–xxiv.

[47] Ibid., p. 2.

Judenthume ausgenommen? (see Chapter 3). Well-trained in rabbinic literature as well as the Hebrew Bible, Geiger had shown in detail the dependence of the Qur'an on Jewish texts and traditions, part of his larger project of demonstrating the rootedness of all the religions of the book in Judaism. Nöldeke cared little about the spiritual value of the Muslim holy book; what Geiger's work did for him was to open one avenue into the text's historicity. Weil's *Historisch-kritische Einleitung in den Koran* (1844), which tried to put the suras in rough historical order, had opened another. Nöldeke devoted much of his book to an even more incisive attempt to separate out the Medina-era from the Mecca-era suras, that is, to undo the work of redaction done by the first three caliphs after the prophet's death, work which Nöldeke described as a political, rather than a religious act.[48]

It might well be said that by writing its history, Nöldeke was robbing the Qur'an of its special spirituality and originality; but it can also be argued that his moves here had relatively little to do with his feelings for Islam per se. Nöldeke was, in 1860, a radical Protestant on his way to agnosticism, and he would remain through his life a man firmly ensconced in Enlightenment rationalism. This made him more critical of Islam than was Geiger; he suspected that Muhammed suffered from epilepsy and did not hesitate to claim that the Qur'an was full of all sorts of ancient superstitions and ethnographic curiosities. The book was interesting historically, but spiritually obsolete. We could, and should, read this as a dismissive, and Eurocentric, gesture. On the other hand, in the Old Testament work Nöldeke undertook in the 1860s, he would say many of the same things about the Hebrew Bible, further radicalizing the tradition we have traced through the eighteenth century down to de Wette and Nöldeke's mentor, Heinrich Ewald. Indeed, we can see the heavy hand of that tradition in Nöldeke's preference for "wild beduin" poetry to Qur'anic scripture, for the beauty of Genesis and the book of Job, and the wise leadership of Moses over the "the terrifying image of the desiccated "law" created by Ezra.[49] Though his two biting popular critiques of the Old Testament's sources would be largely forgotten in the wake of Julius Wellhausen's *Prolegomena*,[50] Nöldeke, in the later 1860s, was very much a Higher Critic, to whom few texts (if any) were sacred, and all of them fodder for purely historical studies.

Nöldeke called himself a Semitist and believed throughout his life in the unity of Semitic peoples and of Semitic culture despite his extensive knowledge of the constructed entity's disparate languages, histories, and ideas. The commonalities he saw (and commonalities he created, by applying Higher Criticism to Islamic texts) between the ancient Jews and the medieval Muslims are perhaps what have led Robert Irwin to call him a "racial bigot" – though for the reasons elaborated below, I think that is rather too harsh.[51] Although he taught introductory Sanskrit while at the University of Kiel (1864–72), Nöldeke focused his attention on the Semites, and indeed, after the 1860s, settled almost exclusively into linguistic studies, hoping someday to write a complete comparative grammar of the Semitic languages – though he was too ardent a positivist to ever compose one. Perhaps

---

[48] Ibid., p. 205. On Jewish sources, pp. 5–14; on Mohammed's epilepsy, p. 18.
[49] Nöldeke, *Die alttestamentliche Literatur* (Leipzig, 1868), p. 41.
[50] Ibid. and idem, *Untersuchungen zur Kritik des A. T.* (Kiel, 1869).
[51] Irwin, *Lust for Knowing*, p. 198.

the closest to a general statement he ever made was a popular essay of 1872, "On the Characteristics of the Semites,"[52] written chiefly, it seems, to try to negotiate a truce between the great French Semitist, Ernest Renan, and the equally renowned Russian scholar of Judaism, Daniel Chwolson.[53] Nöldeke politely disagreed with Renan, who had emphasized the negative traits of the ancient Jews (blood thirstiness, lack of imagination), and deplored Christianity's continuation of these practices. Nöldeke wished to temper this view with the perspective of Chwolson, who offered a much more sympathetic portrait of the moral courage, democratic instincts, and peaceful nature of the Israelites – though he could not accept all of Chwolson's picture either. He concluded by describing the ancient Semites as one-sided and their achievements as inferior to those of the Indo-German peoples, above all the Greeks; still, Nöldeke argued, "it would still be decidedly unfair to deny them the right to one of the highest positions among the human races."[54] Like his predecessor J. D. Michaelis, Nöldeke saw the modern Jews as entirely different beings than their ancient forefathers, but unlike Michaelis, Nöldeke liked Europeanized Jews and celebrated their incorporation into modern culture.[55]

Nöldeke's view of good "science" can certainly tell us a great deal about the culture in which he lived and worked. He was a firm believer in facts and in working them out for oneself; he insisted on reading texts in the original and fixing them when they erred. Above all, he cared about languages and about precision in reading, editing, and translating "oriental" texts. His letters to his friends are full of corrections to their manuscripts, published and unpublished, and queries about particular details, which might be better known to them – he asked Goldziher, for example, how to read certain Hebrew or Arabic words and the widely-traveled Martin Hartmann about modern Arabic turns of phrase. He was, by everyone's account, a deep-dyed rationalist, who hated mysticism; he had trouble, he once joked, finding the right place for an Arabic translation of Swedenborg on his bookshelves: "Unfortunately in my library, I don't have a section for insanity."[56] His distaste for "irrationalities" made the study of religious texts unpalatable to him and certainly hindered his appreciation of Islamic (and ancient Judaic) spiritual life; but he was able to recognize his own limitations and, moreover, to appreciate the work of those, like Goldziher, who worked in different ways. Of course, to also understand languages as thoroughly as he did meant mastering cultural history, economic life, literary history, and understanding customs (including medical practices, the uses of animals and plants, etc.); and

---

[52] Published first in the journal *Im neuen Reich* and then in a collection of Nöldeke's popular pieces, *Orientalische Skizzen* (Berlin, 1893).

[53] Chwolson, a convert from Judaism, was a professor of oriental languages in St. Petersburg and a member of the Russian Academy of Sciences; he spent much of his career defending the Jews and Jewish scriptures from attack.

[54] "Zur Characteristik der Semiten," p. 20.

[55] See, for example, his comments in "Zur Characteristik der Semiten," where he argues that the great humanitarianism of the modern Jews and their scientific successes cannot be used to argue for the same qualities in their early ancestors (pp. 11, 18). It should also be said that Nöldeke's criticisms of Semites notwithstanding, unlike most Christian theologians and even numerous Old Testament critics of his generation, he did not disdain Jewish scholarship and had many Jewish students.

[56] Littmann, "Nöldeke," p. 62.

by all accounts he did, though his texts rarely flaunt his expertise in the world of *Realien*. His diligence and his intellectual generosity were legendary and his production prodigious, amounting to more than 700 scholarly books and essays.[57] But he was not a compiler or secondary source gleaner, as a modern scholar with such a c.v. would surely be; as his friend Hurgronje noted, it was his nature to work independently; "the only results he could 'lay before the world' were those he achieved through his own researches, [and] had repeatedly tested."[58]

Nöldeke's political views are as indicative of his era as his religious and scholarly perspectives – though it is important to stress the diversity of opinions possible in his mid-century context. Though he shared a library at the University of Göttingen in early mid-1860s with two of the other great orientalists of his day, Heinrich Ewald and Paul de Lagarde, their political views were, explosively, at odds. Ewald, the eldest, was a pre-Bismarckian liberal; in fact, he had been one of the "Göttingen Seven," dismissed from the University in 1837 for refusing to swear an oath to the King of Hanover. After his return to Göttingen in 1868, Ewald vehemently opposed Bismarck's annexation of Hanover and the other German territories. Nöldeke dedicated his *Geschichte des Qorâns* to his teacher in 1860; but during the wars of unification, they broke, over politics and religion, and as a result of Ewald's overbearing personality. Nöldeke, by this time, had become not only an agnostic but a firm supporter of Bismarck; his enthusiasm for the cause of unification was great enough to accept a position in 1872 at the University of Strasbourg, the new German university intended to bring German *Wissenschaft* to the just-conquered French territories. Nöldeke would remain essentially a Bismarckian liberal throughout his life, supporting imperialist ventures, but not very enthusiastically, and endorsing national pride and progress, but not without restraint. Ewald's era was clearly over. The 1860s, 1870s, and 1880s belonged to the liberal historicists, to men like Nöldeke and to those like Julius Wellhausen, who would push the Higher Criticism to its logical and perhaps even self-immolating conclusions.

Julius Wellhausen: Hebraism and Realism

There has been uncertainty for many years about Julius Wellhausen's religious convictions; if he remained at heart a Christian, as is probable, still, the theology professor who gloried in reading Petronius with his classicist colleague Ulrich von Wilamowitz Moellendorff in the later 1870s would have been a strange one – in any other company, that is, than that of the scholarly Protestants of the Wilhelmine era. Certainly the orthodox clergy thought him an atheist; his fellow Hebraist (and *Kirchenrat*) Franz Delitzsch described his "speculations" as "merely applications of Darwinism to the sphere of theology and criticism."[59] A Lutheran pastor's son, Wellhausen certainly did not wear his beliefs on his sleeve; he detested organized

---

[57] Ibid., p. 61.
[58] Hurgronje, "Nöldeke," p. 277.
[59] Quoted in Rudolf Smend, "Julius Wellhausen and his Prolegomena to the History of Israel," in *Julius Wellhausen and His Prolegomena to the History of Israel*, special issue of *Semeia* 25 (1983): 14.

religion and anything – Christian, Jewish, or Muslim – that smacked of priestly incursions into the lives of free individuals. A perhaps apocryphal story has it that Wellhausen deliberately timed his Sunday swimming expeditions to coincide with the hour Göttingen's burghers went to church so that he might meet them with his bathing costume over his shoulder.[60] He was characterized, wrote his good friend Edward Schwartz, by "simplicity," "the taste for independence," a healthy peasant-boy appetite, and by his contempt for rhetorical pyrotechnics and self-advertisement.[61] Wellhausen was comfortable throughout his life playing the iconoclast; he did not mind taking unpopular positions or choosing controversial or unfashionable subjects for study. But we should not think of Wellhausen as a kind of Mephistophelian, nay-saying *agent provocateur* – for he did believe quite ardently in something. Julius Wellhausen believed in *Wissenschaft*.

In this, as in so many other things, Wellhausen was a man of his age; he admired and in many respects resembled his older contemporary Theodor Mommsen and his younger one Eduard Meyer. He shared with them a powerful dedication to realism, rather than idealism, and to factual history. Even though his histories often look rather Hegelian, Wellhausen in fact despised speculative philosophy and built his historical accounts less on the master philosopher's schemas than on the Young Hegelian versions of them formulated by Wilhelm Vatke.[62] More specifically, of course, Wellhausen sprang from a tradition of Semitic studies stretching back to Herder and running through de Wette, Heinrich Ewald, Theodor Benfey, and Wilhelm Gesenius. These earlier nineteenth-century scholars saw it as their task "to apply the same principles to the Jewish People and its development as we are accustomed to applying to other human developments"; but they also, in Benfey's words, displayed "the deepest recognition of the life-wisdom put forward in these works...."[63] They could still believe that scripture contained poetic and moral truths – even when its historical value was questionable. Wellhausen might well have believed that too deep down; but he was the product of a younger, *Realpolitik* generation, for whom these sorts of truth were not only problematical – for they could not be proved – but also rather too embarrassing to discuss publicly. We have to do, here, with not just a postromantic but even an antiromantic generation, one which for professing scientific theology meant to have one's philological ducks in order – especially at a time in which fundamental questions about the integrity and chronology of biblical texts were being debated more intensively and extensively than ever before.

Wellhausen was, first and foremost, a student of Ewald and carried forward many of his projects. He shared Ewald's affection for the prophets, for example, and also his interest in Arab civilizations; indeed, Wellhausen, as we will see

---

[60] Smend, "Julius Wellhausen," p. 4.

[61] See Schwartz, *Rede auf Julius Wellhausen* (Berlin, 1919), esp. pp. 29–30.

[62] Vatke's quite radical study, *Die Religion des Alten Testaments nach dem kanonischen Büchern entwickelt* (Berlin, 1835), was largely ignored on its issuing, partly because of its Hegelian jargon and partly because it appeared in the same year as Strauss's even more radical *Leben Jesu*. H. P. Smith, "Vatke's Old Testament Introduction," in *Hebraica* 3, no. 3 (Apr. 1887): 188.

[63] Benfey, *Geschichte der Sprachwissenschaft und orientalischen Philologie in Deutschland* (Munich, 1869), p. 702.

below, eventually gave up Old Testament research in favor of studying the early
history of the Arab world and became a much greater Arabist than was Ewald. But
Wellhausen was never the *Orient totale* sort of scholar Ewald represented; he did
not, for example, learn or teach Sanskrit or train students in Amharic. In many
respects, Wellhausen also shared Ewald's prejudices – he certainly saw the Jews as
one of God's two chosen people (the other being, of course, the Greeks).[64] But
their "chosenness," in Wellhausen's eyes, was not at all a matter of revelation but
simply a matter of historical foundation-laying; they were like all other primitive
peoples, if a bit more ardent (and he thought, more primitive); as he wrote in his
entry on "Israel" for the ninth edition of the *Encyclopedia Britannica*: "The
religious starting-point of the history of Israel was remarkable, not for its novelty,
but for its normal character. In all ancient primitive peoples, the relation in which
God is conceived to stand to the circumstances of the nation – in other words,
religion – furnishes a motive for law and morals; in the case of none did it become
so with such purity and power as in that of the Israelites."[65] Ewald, for all his
historicizing, was not ready to "normalize" the Israelites and/or to see religion in
so functionalist a manner. Perhaps that is why it is Wellhausen and not his mentor
who is usually credited with making the Higher Criticism not just dangerous to
Judaism and Christianity, but potentially lethal.

Wellhausen was, as Marco Frenschkowski describes in his entry for the *Biographisch-Bibliographisches Kirchenlexikon*, "one of the most significant German
scholars of the nineteenth century, [a man of] unsurpassed learning and immense
powers of innovation."[66] His work was, for its time, quite daring and highly
controversial. But it should be reiterated that his new chronology for Hebrew
scriptural fragments and his conceptions of all three religions of the book also
betrayed liberal Protestant prejudices characteristic of his day, and remained
hostage to the relatively circumscribed source base available in the 1860s. His
work also reflected the methodological caution typical of the mid-century German
positivist. Like his Scottish friend William Robertson Smith, Wellhausen drew
inspiration from English-inflected comparative anthropology, but he was much
less inclined to theoretical speculations. It was Smith, and not Wellhausen, who
made the subjects of ritual and sacrifice central to understanding the religious
practices of the early Israelites. Though Wellhausen would not die until 1918,
he did not keep current with finds or with new directions in comparative religion,
which enriched and complicated the familiar picture of Christianity's relationship
to ancient Judaism after about 1890. While it is certainly true that Wellhausen's
work helped to solidify a highly influential Protestant conception of desiccated
"late Judaism," like Ewald and de Wette before him, Wellhausen still very much
believed that (Protestant) Christianity represented the true and organic heir to
ancient Israelite monotheism. For better or for worse, Wellhausen did not move
with his times; his times caught up with him and, then rather quickly, sped past.

---

[64] Schwartz, *Rede auf Wellhausen*, p. 24.
[65] Wellhausen, "Israel," *Encyclopedia Britannica*, ninth edition, reprinted in idem, *Prolegomena to the
History of Ancient Israel* (New York, 1957), p. 437.
[66] See the entry on Wellhausen at http://www.bautz.de/bbkl/w/wellhausen/shtml.

Wellhausen's first book, *Die Pharisäer und die Sadducäer* (1874), made an important contribution to mid-century theological debates by refuting Abraham Geiger's challenge to conventional Christian readings of the two groups. Instead of portraying the Pharisees as hidebound hypocrites, Geiger had used Mishnaic sources to contend that the Pharisees actually represented a reformist, democratizing strain in Hellenistic Jewish thought and even that Jesus was, essentially, a Pharisee. Wellhausen insisted that Geiger's argument could not be upheld because it was based on rabbinic and Mishnaic sources – testimony that was in his view "too late" to be relevant. Ironically, as Susannah Heschel has shown, Wellhausen failed to apply this test to his own authorities, which were chiefly non-contemporary and mostly Greek Christian sources (such as the Gospels and the apocrypha).[67] But Wellhausen's interpretation carried the day: though heirs to a rich and complex tradition, the Pharisees, for this generation and too many to follow, represented the narrowing of Hellenistic Judaism into an unnatural, inorganic law-fetishizing cult.[68]

From 1874 forward, however, it was "early" Judaism that occupied Wellhausen and made his "literary-historical" school of biblical criticism infamous. By the 1860s, this field had moved beyond Ewald's Old Testament studies, as specialized Semitic philologists in Holland, Great Britain, and in the other German states intensified their studies of the Hebrew scriptures. In the summer of 1867, in fact, Wellhausen had already encountered the work of Karl Heinrich Graf, who had argued, unconventionally, that the books of the Torah might well *postdate* the time of the prophets. Wellhausen was undoubtedly prepared for such a suggestion by his work with Ewald, the great champion of the prophets, and by the deep-seated prejudice in the Protestant tradition against the formalistic and dogmatic qualities of the Law, as exemplified in the book of Leviticus; "... and almost without knowing the reasoning behind [Graf's] hypothesis," Wellhausen admitted, "I accepted it; I allowed myself to recognize that Hebrew antiquity could be understood without the book of the Torah."[69] Others before Wellhausen (and Graf) had questioned Mosaic authorship of the Torah and its historical veracity; they had turned its historical material into poetry. But to sideline it, to describe it, as Wellhausen did, "as a ghost that makes noises, but is not visible and has no real effects,"[70] was quite a radical step. What gave Wellhausen's inclinations real force, however, was that, by 1878, the biblical critics had fleshed out Graf's thesis and applied a hyper-critical, historicizing philology to the Old Testament's texts. In combination with an underlying theory about the evolution of religions and civilizations – in which polytheism must precede monotheism and primitive rituals and blood sacrifices must precede more abstract ideas and symbolic practices – Wellhausen's philological work seemed to offer proof for a new scriptural chronology, one which might yet resolve doctrinal debates through the application of *Wissenschaft*.

---

[67] Susannah Heschel, *Abraham Geiger*, pp. 209–13.

[68] Hans-Günter Waubke, *Die Pharisäer in der protestantischen Bibelwissenschaft des 19. Jahrhunderts* (Tübingen, 1998), pp. 197–226.

[69] Wellhausen, *Geschichte Israels*, vol. 1 (Berlin, 1878), p. 4.

[70] Ibid., p. 3.

In 1878, Wellhausen gave his new chronology its most important airing and, indeed, after the publication of what he originally called *Geschichte Israels*, volume I (retitling it *Prolegomena zur Geschichte Israels* in the second edition of 1883), Old Testament criticism would never be the same. Wellhausen's chronology was not, as the reference to Graf above suggests, completely new, and there is much in his picture of early Israelite culture that is reminiscent of Herder and de Wette. Even his conviction that the Torah must have more than one author had been anticipated by the eighteenth-century French doctor Jean Astruc. But Wellhausen's philological work demonstrated quite clearly that the language of the Pentateuch was not all of a piece; so many voices could be heard in it that, he argued, it must be the work of many hands and must contain fragments of documents composed in various eras, ranging from the eighth to the fifth centuries B.C.E. Wellhausen claimed, in fact, that one could deduce the existence of at least four proto-texts from which redactors had drawn to compose the Torah, and he gave each of these texts letter names: J (Yahwist text), E (Elohist text), D (Deuteronomic text), and P (Priestly text). This was the foundation for the so-called "documentary hypothesis," according to which the Torah is not a unitary composition with a single author (Moses), but a synthetic and – we would say – constructed text.

Wellhausen was not only able, but also willing, to offer his suggestions on how this construction had occurred, and what social, political, and religious purposes the Torah was meant to serve. He had shown, he believed, that the fragmentary and contradictory material in books like Samuel, Kings, and Judges predated the more narratively coherent pieces of the Law, in Exodus or Leviticus. The Law was not the *ur*-ancient, national history of Israel, but rather a product of the priest-dominated society of post-exilic Judaism; its fragments had been assembled by the Babylonian scribe Ezra and promulgated only in 444 B.C.E–though Ezra, and subsequent Jewish tradition, had claimed this version of Law to be much older, and therefore the true and binding form of belief and practice. In fact, Wellhausen argued, ancient Israel had been much freer and more individualistic than it was in Ezra's day; and as his repeated use of organic metaphors showed, the clear drift of his history was to separate the Israelites from the Jews and to endow the former with a vitality, authenticity, and innocence which the latter sorely lacked. The early Israelites had been, Wellhausen asserted, much like other heathen peoples and closer to nature than was possible for later cultures. "In ancient times," he wrote, "the cult can be compared to a green tree, which grows from the soil as it wishes, and where it is able; later it becomes a carefully hewed timber, ever more artificially shaped with square and compass." In the hands of the systematizers, the written Torah took the place of Moses' vibrant oral tradition: "The water which in old times rose from a spring, the Epigoni trapped in cisterns."[71] Even more powerful was Wellhausen's claim that, despite Moses' commandments and King Solomon's grandeur, the early Israelites had not – on the whole – been monotheists or seen the temple in Jerusalem as the center of the cult. All the things Christians thought they knew about Judaism were now seen as characteristic only of what Wellhausen and his fellows insisted upon calling "late" Judaism. "Late"

---

[71] Ibid., pp. 84, 426.

Judaism, in their eyes, was a sclerotic, law-fetishizing religion, which led not to Christianity but to rabbinic orthodoxy; for them, it was what contemporary anthropologists called a "survival" – that is, as an irrational custom or practice that lives on long beyond the time its actual social functions have ceased.

Not surprisingly, many of Wellhausen's contemporaries were shocked and angered to hear such things from a professor of theology; a large number of orthodox theologians too found Wellhausen's work irreverent or even heretical.[72] He was accused of Darwinism and, for conservative Germans, its logical corollary, atheism. The polemics engendered by the *Prolegomena* were small scale in contrast to those of the fin de siècle, but even so, they ensured the book a wide reception. Having at first promised Wellhausen no honorarium for his book, the publisher, Georg Reimer, enjoyed such great profits from the *Prolegomena* that he agreed to share his tidy profit with the author.[73] Perhaps the controversies about the book were what enticed Friedrich Nietzsche to read it; in Wellhausen's depiction of the constructed, life-denying nature of "late" Judaism, the young philosopher found much fuel for his own fires.[74] Strikingly, however, it was Wellhausen himself who chose to lay down his Greifswald theology chair in 1882, feeling he could not responsibly train pastors for the ministry, rather than the decision being made by the clerical and state authorities, as in the cases of D. F. Strauss and Bruno Bauer. But the world of the 1870s was a different one than that of the 1830s and 1840s. Both because the churches were losing cultural clout and because philological "science" was queen, it had become much harder to root out "heretics," even in the theology faculty. Less than twenty years after the *Prolegomena*, Wellhausen's "literary-historical" understanding of the sources of the Pentateuch had become at least liberal orthodoxy. Wellhausen himself accepted a demotion to a junior professorship at the University of Halle in order to join the philosophical faculty, but soon moved to a full professorship at Marburg (though the Cultural Ministry made him promise not to lecture on the Old Testament). By 1892, his reinvention was complete, and he came out of the process with a better job: a professorship of oriental languages at the University of Göttingen.

Wellhausen's New Testament research, which he began only after the turn of the century, ruthlessly pared down the number of statements to be credited to Jesus so that as little was left of the Savior as of Moses in his Old Testament criticism. In many ways, in fact, Wellhausen simply extended here his claims that world-historical religions were merely the products of sly and self-serving, if also genuinely pious, acolytes; just as the second temple Jews created Judaism, the

---

[72] Henning Graf Reventlow, *Epochen der Bibelauslegung*, vol. 4, *Von der Aufklärung bis zum 20. Jahrhundert* (Munich, 2001), p. 312.

[73] Schwartz, *Rede auf Wellhausen*, p. 18. Georg Reimer would, in fact, publish many of Wellhausen's later books, including *Israelitische und jüdische Geschichte*, which had gone through seven editions by the time of the author's death in 1918.

[74] On Nietzsche's engagement with Wellhausen's work, see Andreas Urs Sommer, *Friedrich Nietzsches 'Der Antichrist': Ein philosophisch-historischer Kommentar* (Basel, 2000), esp. pp. 258–66.

apostles created Christianity, and Muhammed's disciples invented Islam.[75] Statements like "To a certain degree, Reimarus may have been right"[76] seemed to ratify the radical's view that the apostles had concocted the idea that Jesus was the Messiah and fabricated all their accounts to prove it. It was this work, not surprisingly, that liberal academia could not stomach and that incited rebuttals from theologians like Adolf von Harnack and even from Wellhausen's old Petronius partner, Wilamowitz.[77] It was one thing to attribute devious text-dating to the Jews and quite another to attribute it to the apostles.

But by the 1910s, Wellhausen was only moderately radical, or better, only really radical in what he said about the New Testament, which was the least influential sphere of his scholarship. In the many critiques of his work that appeared in the 1920s, the ways in which Wellhausen continued to belong squarely in his mid-century context were made clear. If hyper-critical with respect to the texts at hand, Wellhausen, his later detractors pointed out, still focused exclusively on texts and especially canonical ones; he took rather little notice of the texts or artifacts unearthed by the Second Oriental Renaissance and looked askance at attempts to detach Jesus from Judaism. A consummate liberal historian, Wellhausen was able to criticize the canon and to draw attention to the manner in which it had been constructed – but he was not able to invent a new one, both because of his deep-seated skepticism and because of his inability to embrace new sources. He was extremely critical of some new strains of thinking, disapproving of racial anthropology and of some facets of *Religionsgeschichte* (see Chapter 6). Like other members of his generation, he expended most of his effort in demolishing old interpretations and cleaning up texts to prepare the way for new views, rather than actually articulating them; of his many books, only two, *Das arabische Reich und seine Sturz* and *Israelitische und jüdische Geschichte*, are positive histories rather than critical prolegomenae.[78]

Commentators have often overlooked the extent to which Wellhausen's work championed the liberal ideals of his era: individual liberty, freedom of conscience, and the virtues of national, political autonomy. The great age of Israel, for him, was the age in which individuals were free to choose their form of religious practice (and especially to mix local and "national" cults), and in which the tribes joined together to form one nation, able to rule itself. Israel's age of desiccation corresponded to the periods of priestly hegemony, and of the Jews' subservience to

[75] For Wellhausen's work on Islam, see discussion later in the chapter.

[76] Wellhausen, "Einleitung in die ersten drei Evangelien" (2nd ed., 1911), reprinted in idem, *Evangeliendommentare* (Berlin, 1987), p. 83.

[77] On Harnack's response, see Nils A. Dahl, "Wellhausen on the New Testament," in *Semeia* 25 (1983): 104–6; for Wilamowitz's view of Wellhausen, see his letter to Edward Schwartz, March 28, 1918, in William M. Calder III and Robert L. Fowler, eds., *The Preserved Letters of Ulrich von Wilamowitz-Moellendorff to Eduard Schwartz* (Munich, 1986), pp. 78–84; and also Momigliano, "Religious History Without Frontiers," in idem, *New Paths of Classicism in the Nineteenth Century* (Middletown, PA, 1982), pp. 49–51.

[78] This was noted already by Martin Hartmann, in his review of Wellhausen, *Die religiöspolitischen Oppositionsparteien im alten Islam* (1901), in *OLZ* 3 (1902): 96–104.

foreign rule (Assyrian, Persian, Seleucid, Roman). Indeed, it was political dependence that made Judaism a unique and uniquely powerful religion; after the state collapsed, the priests became the effective leaders of the nation, and since the political nation could never be reconstituted, a kind of moral uniformity had to be imposed on the Jews. The restrictive monotheism of post-exilic Judaism too, in the view of Wellhausen and theologian Friedrich Weber, entailed the worship of a remote and angry God, one who had no interest in individuals.[79] It is not surprising that mid-century liberals would balk at the imposition of religious conformity this process (as they described it) entailed nor that they would see the Jewish diaspora as a threat to existing states; Theodor Mommsen called the diaspora "an effective leaven of cosmopolitanism and of national decomposition."[80] It was perhaps a little more unusual for a liberal like Wellhausen not to share Mommsen and Ranke's affection for the Roman Empire and to admire so deeply the small warlike states of the early Israelites and the Arabs. But Wellhausen, who admitted to having read Jacob Burckhardt's *Weltgeschichtliche Betrachtungen* five times,[81] was already something of a late liberal – twenty-seven years younger than Mommsen and nearly fifty years younger than Ranke – as well as a fan of Bismarckian *Realpolitik*.

"Wellhausianism" was never accepted by conservative Protestant clerics (not to mention Catholics and Jews), and the fact that the great Hebraist hailed from Hamelin, hometown of the Pied Piper, gave rise to many parallels between the medieval figure and the modern one, who led not only the rats, but the theologians away from the Church.[82] This is clearly an exaggeration, and a misconception of how and why the European churches lost their cultural centrality – which, too, was not equivalent to individuals' loss of faith. To paraphrase one analyst of relationships between science and belief in Victorian England, we should not think that Wilhelmine Germans lost their religious faith as some people lose umbrellas[83] – and in any event, in Chapters 5 and 6 we will see faith in biblical texts persisting long after the Higher Criticism had run its course. Wellhausen has also been accused of being an anti-Semite or of providing the foundations for modern anti-Semitism. The former goes too far, though Wellhausen's portrayal of "late" Judaism and his sidelining of Jewish texts did prepare the groundwork for a new and disastrous reiteration of the theory that Christianity did not spring from Jewish roots and furthermore could do without Judaism in the future. Wellhausen surely applied hyper-skeptical methods too liberally, without considering counter-arguments, and presumed, like so many mid-century liberals, a unidirectional form of cultural evolution. But for iniquitous misdirection, Julius Wellhausen could never compete with Lagarde or with the Assyriologist Friedrich

---

[79] On Weber's picture of Judaism and its effects, see E. P. Sanders, *Paul and Palestinian Judaism: A Comparison of Patterns of Religion* (Philadelphia, 1977), pp. 36–8.

[80] Mommsen quoted in Wellhausen, "Israel," pp. 543–4, in note.

[81] Friedemann Boschwitz, *Julius Wellhausen: Motive und Masstäbe seiner Geschichtsschreibung* (Darmstadt, 1968), p. 74.

[82] Smend, "Julius Wellhausen," p. 5.

[83] James Moore, quoted in James Secord, *Victorian Sensation: The Extraordinary Publication, Reception, and Secret Authorship of Vestiges of the Natural History of Creation* (Chicago, 2000), p. 330, n. 81.

Delitzsch. And unlike most contemporary theologians, he was willing to devote considerable time and effort to the study of another of the Semitic peoples: the Arabs.

AN ISLAMIC RENAISSANCE?

If we recall the long-lasting centrality of Old Testament studies for *Orientalistik*, the linguistic relations between Hebrew and Arabic, and the influential parallel Michaelis and his contemporaries drew between the ancient Israelites and the Arab beduins, it might not be so surprising that two of the most influential students of the Islamic world in the post-1871 era were also major contributors to the Higher Criticism. In the previous section, I have already had occasion to describe Theodor Nöldeke's work on the Qur'an; though Nöldeke's *Geschichte des Qorân* did unleash a wave of scholarship whose purpose was to historicize Islam and the cultural world of the Arabs, his later work focused more narrowly on Semitic linguistics. More influential on a broader scale was the work of Julius Wellhausen, who used his linguistic skills to write a history of the Arabs, and a lay orientalist, Alfred von Kremer, who was, remarkably, not a theologian but a diplomat, heir to the Busbecq–Hammer-Purgstall tradition. Though Nöldeke and Wellhausen had something of a soft spot for the pre-Qur'anic tribesmen, neither their work nor Kremer's was generated by deep sympathy with the cultures under study. Enlightenment era critiques of Muslim superstitions, despotism, and excessive luxury consumption had left their marks too, especially on liberals already suspicious of mysticism, theocracy, and sensualism. All of these factors made it more possible in Islamic studies than in other fields of *Orientalistik* to consider the subjects of inquiry "others" – something that took some of the passion out of this field that continued to inhere in others (like Indology), and permitted, perhaps, more politics to fill the remaining space.

But the politicization of the field was not, of course, purely a matter of substitution; it came from external circumstances, the most obvious of which was the increasingly obvious decline of the Ottoman Empire and the inroads into the Muslim world being made by British, French, and Dutch colonists. German Arabists before the 1880s tended not to travel much, but armchair Arabists like Wellhausen or Heinrich Fleischer did know something about the real-existing Muslim world, especially by virtue of their connections with Dutch scholars like Christiaan Snouck Hurgronje, which were regular and extremely friendly.[84] Yet judging by their letters and occasional writings, German academics were not particularly interested, professionally or personally, in the events of the day. Some contemporary Central European travelers like Arminius Vambéry had plenty of firsthand experience abroad. But, as Vambéry's example suggests, on-the-ground experience did not win one many points with the academic elite of the 1860s–1880s, and even long after that time, being skilled in modern languages and modern history

---

[84] Hurgronje spent six months in Mecca (in disguise) in the 1880s, and then seventeen years as a Dutch colonial official in the East Indies. He also wrote extensively on modern Islam. On his career, see Michael Laffen, *Islamic Nationhood and Colonial Indonesia* (London, 2003), pp. 91–7.

continued to be far less valued in traditional institutions than was the study of the linguistic niceties of the distant past.

Wellhausen came to the study of Arabic and the history of the Arabs with several academic aces up his sleeve. First of all, he had a university chair, awarded on the basis of his Old Testament work, but as he was actually discouraged from continuing that, he had time to devote himself to other subjects. Second, he had already mastered the historio-critical study of a major religious text, and as Gustav Weil and Nöldeke had shown, there was much to be gained by treating the Qur'an and other early Arab sources in the same way. Third, his sub-Hegelian stage theory of civilized developments and his Ewaldin preference for the charisma and chaos of the period before the formalization of Islamic doctrine already convinced him that he could profitably focus on early history and still claim to know the essence of Arab civilization. And fourth, beyond the promise of breaking new ground in a rather fallow field, Wellhausen had hopes that his new studies would throw light on older ones. Of his decision to begin inquiries into the history of the Arabs he wrote: "I made the transition from the Old Testament to the Arabs with the intention of getting to know the wild seedling [Wilding], onto which the shoots of Jahwe's Torah were grafted. For I did not doubt that it was from the comparisons with Arab antiquity that one could most easily tease an idea of the original condition in which the Hebrews entered history."[85] Possessing both the proper methods and skills, and a plausible justification for making his leap into post-biblical orientalism, Wellhausen was well positioned to give the history of the Islamic world new credibility and interest.

Studying the Arab "Wildling," however, required reading almost exclusively Arabic sources and teasing out of them a political narrative involving events and figures known to very few readers in the West. Thanks to Dutch scholars, a full edition of al-Tabari's *Annales* was available to Wellhausen, and he depended heavily on this oldest – and thus to Wellhausen most trustworthy – source.[86] Applying his well-honed critical eye to this and other little-studied texts, he was able to separate out Syrian and "Iraqi" (*irakisch*) traditions, just as he had identified the sources of the Pentateuch. This made possible the writing of a new and clearer history of the Caliphate, a contribution to scholarship some specialists thought even more original and masterful than Wellhausen's work in Old Testament criticism.[87] Wellhausen's publications, including *Reste arabischen Heidentums* (1887), *Prolegomena zur ältesten Geschichte des Islams* (1899), and *Das arabische Reich und sein Sturz* (1902), focused on the Arabs and the Islamic world through the collapse of the Ummayid dynasty and on power struggles between and within ethnic groups during this era.

If Wellhausen and the other Higher Critics believed the history of the Jewish people ought to be understood as a history like any other, they also extended this normalizing principle to Islamic history – with the consequence that mere religious polemics were now no longer admissible. Wellhausen assumed that like other

---

[85] Wellhausen quoted in Boschwitz, *Julius Wellhausen*, p. 32.

[86] R. C. Ostle, "Foreword," in Julius Wellhausen, *The Religio-Political Factions in Early Islam*, ed. and trans. R. C. Ostle and S. M. Walzer (Amsterdam, 1975), pp. ix–x.

[87] Becker, "Julius Wellhausen," in *Der Islam* 9 (1919): 95–6.

histories, this one would be characterized by power struggles and interest groups; he drew few conclusions and did not take sides – but we can see, quite clearly (the effect of his account of Islamic history of his high liberal anti-clericalism and even of the politics of the Germanic world of his day). Islam, for him, was a "normal" religion – that is, it motivated some people, sometimes, but more often, it was manipulated by various groups for their own – non-religious – ends. He was keenly aware of internal dissension in the Arab world and in the Islamic world as a whole. In fact, for Wellhausen, Muhammed's chief achievement was his statecraft, his Bismarck-like unification of the Arabs, rather than his authorship of the Qur'an and creation of a new world religion.[88] But – painting a picture that might have been informed by the increasingly embattled position of the ethnic Germans in the contemporary Austria – Wellhausen described how Arab dominance was destroyed by minority groups (especially Shiites) who exploited Arab internal divisions to gain not only equality but even superiority. Interestingly, in describing the triumph of Iranian-inflected, universal Islam, Wellhausen drew on another set of analogies, creating a picture of empire that reflected Luther's view of medieval Catholicism. Here, he claimed, Islamic rule resulted in the suppression of "the general living interest in politics" and the institution of a kind of Caesaro-papism, complete with inquisition, executioners, and court astrologers. This was the system, Wellhausen implied, inherited by the Ottomans, in which an empire ostensibly held together by religion simply masked one group's suppression of the others.[89]

For historians and for Arabic philologists in his day, Wellhausen's work was pathbreaking, but it did not spawn public debates like those surrounding his *Prolegomena* in the 1870s. His tour de force, *Das arabische Reich*, appeared in the year of the great "Babel-Bibel Streit" – but perhaps even in a normal year, his book would not have been much noticed by the general or even the wider orientalist public. Wellhausen himself was shocked by how little resonance his hard work in a new field seemed to find; writing of the reception of *Das arabische Reich*, he lamented: "I knew that interest in and understanding of Arab history was weak, but I would not have believed that it is so minimal that no review of my book has appeared [a year afterward] ... the harvest here is rich, but the workers are too few. Everybody is fascinated with the Old Testament and cuneiform. No one wants to read through many-layered [*weitschictige*] Arabic literature; even most professors do not do it."[90] Whether or not Wellhausen might have done more in this field had interest been higher is questionable; but clearly the great iconoclast missed the thrill of combat. After 1902, he abandoned Islamic studies for a subject of much more general interest and greater controversy: the New Testament (see Chapter 6).

---

[88] Josef van Ess, "From Wellhausen to Becker: The Emergence of *Kulturgeschichte* in Islamic Studies," in Malcolm Kerr, ed., *Islamic Studies: A Tradition and its Problems* (Malibu, CA, 1980), pp. 92–3.

[89] Wellhausen, *The Arab Kingdom and its Fall*, trans. Margaret Graham Weir (Calcutta, 1927), pp. 556–66; quotation p. 560.

[90] Wellhausen quoted in Becker, "Julius Wellhausen," p. 95. Becker notes, probably rightly, that this silence was also the result of the reverence Arabists felt for Wellhausen's accomplishment.

Quite different from the work of Wellhausen and the Ewald school was that of Alfred Freiherr von Kremer, an independent scholar and diplomat who had actually lived for a long period in the Levant. This did not mean that Kremer was any more appreciative of Islam or of modern middle-eastern culture; indeed, Kremer's experiences inclined him away from romanticization of the deep past and toward ethnographic and even racial analysis. Kremer's view of Islamic history was essentially a liberal-enlightened one – though his narrative also betrayed its less-than-liberal debts in expressing considerable admiration for state power and fascination with Islam's ability to extract "unconditional obedience" from its followers.[91] Kremer respected the Arabic world for its great, progressive achievements in the medieval era (in science, law, financial matters, and even politics), which he compared to the civilizing power of the Romans, and he blamed its decline on decentralization, racial mixing, and (shades of Wellhausen) the petrifaction of religious dogma.[92] Often relying on racial categories – though race seems to have been in his view a product of habits and institutions rather than vice versa – Kremer gave the Arabs both credit for cleverness, courage, and manliness, and blame for greed, envy, and xenophobia.[93]

Kremer had little good or interesting to say about Islam as a system of belief; his interests lay in its social and political functions rather than in its teachings or its internal evolution. The reasons for its endurance, he claimed, had nothing to do with its truth or its ethical power, but lay simply in its ability to make its practices habitual. Indeed, Islam's successes here made its believers virtually impervious to Christian missionization: "What allows Islam to stand its ground vis-à-vis Christendom, which contains a far purer morality, is the strength of its ritualistic and dogmatic forms."[94] For Kremer, religious ideas were really only a function of political developments or of deep-seated racial characteristics. Though he did devote some attention to the leading ideas of Islam and to the phenomenon of Islamic mysticism, this was essentially a *Kulturgeschichte* of the Islamic world – with Islam left out.

We should pause, briefly, to take note of Kremer's understanding of cultural history, which he laid out carefully in the introduction to the major work, *Kulturgeschichte des Orients unter den Chalifen* (1875–7). For him, cultural history was not just the history of manners, ideas, and achievements, but centrally the history of the progress or decline of what he called "the organism of the state." The reason for this was that, at the end of the day, "The last and highest, but yet the most difficult task of cultural history is this: to try to grasp, by comparing an overview of the whole course of a nation's civilizing process with the developmental processes of other cultured people, those general laws which determine the course of the history of peoples, and direct it in just as lasting a way as natural forces guide the realm of matter."[95] The goal of identifying general and universal

---

[91] See, for e.g., Kremer, *Kulturgeschichte des Orients unter den Chalifen*, vol. 1 (Vienna, 1875), p. 10.
[92] Ibid., pp. iv, 470; on decline, *Kulturgeschichte*, vol. 2 (Vienna, 1877), pp. 44–6, 485–500.
[93] Ibid., 2: 136.
[94] Ibid., 2: 34.
[95] Ibid., 1: vii, ix.

laws marks Kremer not only as a mid-century positivist, but also as a forerunner of twentieth-century social scientists like Max Weber, who were not so crude in their assessments of various civilizations, but essentially aimed at the same goals.

I would like to make three remarks about Kremer's search for universal laws, which was, as we have seen, relatively rare in German orientalist analyses, but much more prevalent abroad, especially in England. First of all, this approach often inclined scholars to introduce race as a category – in order to explain variations in institutions and rates of development. And yet, the search for laws ultimately still made cross-cultural understanding possible and desirable, which was not necessarily the case for the more romantic-relativist approach to cultural history. Secondly, while liberal analyses of progress and decline made eastern empires look stunted or degenerate in comparison with Europe's most progressive states, analogies with Europe's *less* progressive empires were often made, and religious polemics, at least, were usually left aside. And finally, though often condescending or even hostile toward their subjects, these studies treated Asian cultures as ongoing, living entities, not as dead objects of philological-historical inquiry. It will not do to lay exclusive blame for racializing and "othering" the Orient on either the English enlightened critique of backwardness or on the German romantic tradition. Both had their sympathetic and unsympathetic aspects, and both contributed to European hubris and to critiques of the same.

NEW POWER, NEW SOURCES: THE FLOURISHING OF INDOLOGY IN THE ERA OF THE RAJ

Before about 1890, the escalation of European empire building had even more powerful effects on German Indology than it had on Islamic studies in large part because the extension of English dominion allowed an increasing number of German scholars to actually go to India. In South Asia they not only procured large quantities of manuscripts, but also came in contact with members of the indigenous elite. The opportunity for making such ventures was provided by the British colonial administration, which after the Rebellion of 1857 began to recognize its need for detailed, deep knowledge of Indian religions and customs (the Archaeological Survey of India, for example, commenced in 1861). Quite a number of German Sanskritists ended up in the employ of the Raj, including Martin Haug, who was posted to Poona College near Bombay in 1859; Georg Bühler and Franz Kielhorn also worked for the British, tracking down ancient manuscripts in Indian collections. The manuscripts would then be purchased and/or Indian pandits would be hired to make copies; originals, copies, or both were then brought back to Britain – though some also found their way into German libraries.

Some practical consequences of these endeavors are worth mentioning: first, the mid-century's focus on the Vedas was reduced as a more diverse set of manuscripts became accessible. Second, the increased volume of Sanskrit, Avestan, Middle Persian, Gujarati, and other manuscripts made possible wider and more detailed grammatical studies and helped to diversify the Indo-Aryan linguistic family trees. But, perhaps most important were the contacts that visitors to India made with traditional elites. Scholars, and especially German scholars, now found indigenous priests and pandits more friendly and forthcoming than they had been in the days of Anquetil – less, probably owing to "the progress of time and education," as Martin Haug explained it, than to shifts in power balances such that resistance now seemed futile. But interestingly, Haug was willing to "unlearn much that he had learnt in Europe" and to accept "the fact that European scholarship must often stand corrected before Indian tradition. . . ."[96] During their long years in India (1863–81), Kielhorn and Bühler, similarly, came to appreciate indigenous scholarly traditions, and their work would stimulate a return to A. W. Schlegel's insistence (against Franz Bopp) that the best way to study Indian literature was by examining it through the eyes of the Indian tradition itself. Indeed, beginning with Richard Pischel's 1889 *Vedische Studien*, the next generation would go Schlegel one better, junking his usage of methods derived from classical philology in favor of inquiries generated from the study of indigenous Indian grammarians.[97]

Both abroad and at home, religion continued to play a role in Indology; in the 1870s, there were still many German Indologists who continued the tradition of informed evangelizing described in Chapter 1, and for whom classical texts and biblical history were still the cardinal points of reference. Albrecht Weber apparently hoped advertising his potential role in Hindu spiritual awakening would appeal to the conservative Lutheran Prussian Cultural Minister Karl Otto von Raumer in 1855. He was right; he received an associate professorship at the University of Berlin, which turned into a full chair in 1867. Rudolf Roth, professor at the University of Tübingen, saw the significance of his Sanskrit studies in understanding the history of "Aryan" religions (of which Christianity was the culmination, and the true way). It is undoubtedly significant that after 1857, when "Allgemeine Religionsgeschichte" became a required course for Protestant theologians at the Tübingen Stift, Roth taught many more students about ancient India than did the linguists at Bonn and Berlin – though he did not, like his counterpart across the channel Max Müller, write for a popular audience.[98] We will see, in subsequent pages, the ways in which this tradition lived on.

But there was also some relaxing of the traditional Christian critique of Indian paganism and even some new cooperation between indigenous religious leaders and visiting European scholars. This seems to have been especially pronounced in cases where the Europeans felt themselves to be religious iconoclasts of one sort or another, and/or politically and personally alienated from their home cultures. Let us take the example of Martin Haug, one of a very few peasants' sons to obtain academic credentials. Largely self-taught, Haug funded his education and early career by teaching private Hebrew lessons; he studied with Benfey and Ewald, and in 1854 became a *Privatdozent* at the University of Bonn. In 1855, he established himself as the foremost expert on the Zend Avesta, publishing a seminal essay in which he isolated the "songs" written by Zarathustra himself from material that had been added later; he was, in effect, identifying a Zoroastrian equivalent to

---

[96] Haug, *Essays on the Sacred Language, Writings and Religion of the Parsis* (London, 2nd ed., 1878), pp. 45, 44.

[97] Sengupta, *From Salon to Discipline*, pp. 113–16; Windisch, *Geschichte der Sanskrit-Philologie* 2: 254–70.

[98] Sengupta, *From Salon to Discipline*, pp. 72–84. Sengupta rightly emphasizes differences between German schools of Indology; among them, the Tübingen school was much more theologically oriented than were the more linguistic programs centered in Bonn and Berlin. Ibid., p. 44.

Jesus' "Sermon on the Mount" and suggesting its origin in the deep past, as early as 2500 B.C.E., rather than contemporary with the actual date of the other texts of the Avesta and its collation (about 200–600 C.E.). In the essay, Haug attempted to speak the positivists' language, claiming modestly: "If I have succeeded in throwing one or two rays of light on these fragments of the true songs of Zarathustra, rescued from a 4,000 year-old past, ... I will be richly rewarded for the indescribable difficulty and the great sacrifices I had to make."[99] In fact, the "reward" Haug got was not a professorship, but rather the private patronage of our old friend Christian Bunsen; Haug acquired financial security only upon reaching India in 1859. His German colleagues seem to have found his nonbourgeois mannerisms distasteful, and only grudgingly gave him a job when he returned to Europe for health-related reasons in 1867. Small wonder that he felt so much better loved abroad, where he was able to travel, collect manuscripts, and to hobnob with influential Brahmins and Parsi *dasturs*.[100]

In India, Haug did not disdain the company of local elites, and in fact formed intimate relations with them; sharing their interest in Avestan and Hindu scriptures and rituals, he proved both a quick study and an effective teacher. Encouraged by his mentor, Haug's student Ramakrishna Gopal Bhandarkar would become one of the first Indians formally recognized by European contemporaries for his contributions to Sanskrit studies, as well as a leading champion of religious reform.[101] In 1862 Haug produced an influential series of *Essays on the Sacred Language, Writings and Religion of the Parsis*, published only in English and never translated into German. But by no means did the *Essays* endorse British colonization and modernization. Contrasting his warm reception by the Parsis in the 1860s with the ill-feeling occasioned by H. H. Wilson's publications in the 1840s, Haug noted that the learned men "were delighted to find a European scholar who understood so much of their religion as to appreciate its good points without dwelling too severely upon those which are doubtful or objectionable. With a feeling of growing confidence, the priests discussed their ceremonies and sacred books, and the laity were glad to receive, from a European scholar, explanations of their older scriptures which had hitherto been nearly sealed books to all." While we should be skeptical about the degree of confidence and gladness the Parsis actually felt toward a still obviously Christian European in the pay of the Raj, it is interesting to see Haug himself reveling in the exchange and downplaying unpleasantnesses. Writing of himself in the third person, he mentions the lectures – (in India) – and prizes – (for Indian scholars) – he offered "in pursuance of his schemes for encouraging Parsis in the study of their religious literature." The "History of the Researches into the Sacred Writings and Religions of the Parsis" that opens Haug's book of *Essays* concludes with a section devoted to Parsi writings – as if these are the wave of the future. Haug even dedicated his book

[99] Haug, "Die fünf Gâthâ's oder Sammlungen von Liedern und Sprüchen Zarathustra's, seiner Jünger und Nachfolger," pt. 1 in *Abhandlungen für die Kunde des Morgenlands* 1, no. 3 (Leipzig, 1858), p. xvi.

[100] See the entry under "Haug, Martin," in the *Encyclopedia Iranica*, available online at http://www.iranica.com; also Rabault-Feuerhahn, *L'archive des origines*, pp. 340–4.

[101] "Haug," in *Encyclopedia Iranica*, http://www.iranica.com.

to the Parsis of Western India "in memory of the old times of friendly intercourse."[102]

Haug's introductory section also includes what can only be described as a Lutheran humanist attempt to console indigenous text critics:

Let them not be discouraged if the results be not so flattering to their self-love as they anticipated. So far as their researches disclose what is good and proper in their religion, they must strengthen the belief in its divine origin; and so far as they disclose what is bad and improper, they merely indicate the corruptions introduced by human tradition. Such corruptions can be neither concealed nor defended with safety; but when discovered, they must be rejected as mere human inventions and superstitious errors. All religions have passed through human minds and human hands....[103]

Similarly, the Vedic scholar Albrecht Weber saw his mission as contributing to the "spiritual reawakening of the Hindus"; his critical editions of the earliest Vedas, he hoped, might "assume a role among the Indians, similar to Luther's translation of the Bible."[104] There remained, of course, tremendous hubris behind these two projects, as European scholars denounced the "decadence" of the religions of the present and offered to help the presumably less advanced Indians launch their own reformation. But indigenous intellectuals and religious leaders also found food for thought in liberal Protestant ideas, especially when voiced by individuals outside the British administration.[105] Forged in the high imperialist era, this tradition's valorizing of primeval religio-cultural purity and national autonomy could be turned against the British – or against western modernizers as a whole – in the decades to come.

In the end, Haug was something of a late liberal positivist; he remained rather reticent about drawing grand conclusions and although he would have liked to have had more recognition from his German colleagues, he clearly did not expect large readerships or monetary rewards. Similarly, though Albrecht Weber devoted his professional life to studying the Vedas, the only "popular" texts he wrote concerned the history of the Protestant churches in Europe. As orientalists, these men continued to pursue specialized philological studies and seemed more or less content to circulate their works to a small group of peers inside and outside Germany. Their valorization of linguistic virtuosity, their continuing emphasis on ancient religious traditions, their disdain for modern and "mixed" cultural products would live long beyond them and provide sources of resistance to "relevance," as well as resources others could deploy for their own purposes.

---

[102] Martin Haug, *Essays*, pp. 45, 47, dedication page.
[103] Ibid., p. 62.
[104] Quoted in Sengupta, *From Salon to Discipline*, p. 73.
[105] For detailed information on the intellectuals on the Indian side of these discussions, see M. M. Thomas, *The Acknowledged Christ of the Indian Renaissance* (London, 1969).

BEYOND THE BIBLE? ASSYRIOLOGY AND EGYPTOLOGY
IN THE HIGH LIBERAL AGE

As new, indigenous texts expanded the study of Indology, so too did external information, especially from newly discovered or decoded inscriptions and artifacts, offer a set of new contexts for understanding the scriptures. Scholars by the 1860s at least could read both hieroglyphics and cuneiform, and boxes of new tablets and papyri were regularly being delivered to museums and libraries. Museums began to fill up basements with Near Eastern artifacts, and to compete to obtain new masterpieces and/or digging privileges. By 1856, Jules Mohl wrote that there were sufficient cuneiform tablets in circulation to fill some 20,000 quarto-sized pages – should any scholar be able and any publisher willing to render them all in print.[106] But how much did casual visitors or readers really know? As we cautioned in the last chapter, it is a mistake to assume that total and accurate knowledge is instantly available to all the moment artifacts come out of the soil or that one scholar makes a breakthrough discovery. For decades after many decipherments or finds, even specialized scholars continued to argue about some aspects of the decipherments and to refine their interpretations of the texts. Those inclined to produce synthetic works did not have an easy job of it; it took time to work through all the materials making their way to Europe, and scholarly publications still, in the 1870s, tended to be quite narrowly-focused and directed to the philologically adept. There were still many mysteries surrounding the relations between Near Eastern states; it was only in 1880 that Oxford professor A. H. Sayce identified stones found in the Syrian city of Hamath with the Hittites mentioned in the Old Testament, and it would not be until 1915 that anyone could actually read these inscriptions.[107] Thus, for a very long time – much longer than the average history of orientalist scholarship suggests – what was popularly known or thought about these great empires continued to be based on the Old Testament and on classical sources, or on backward deductions from often unsympathetic European travelers. And even in the academy, the shift to the indigenous sources was fitful and fraught with peril.

Nor was this an entirely professionalized operation. Dealing with artifacts has always been, and perhaps will always be, an activity much more open to non-academics than the study of texts. The beauty of the Napoleonic expedition's Egyptian volumes and the enormity of A. H. Layard's winged bulls often give historians a false sense of the depth, sophistication, and funds applied to nineteenth-century archaeological work in the Near East; in fact, in the mid-nineteenth century, the collection and interpretation of new material, from sites primarily in Egypt and Mesopotamia, was often executed by individuals working on the margins of traditional biblical scholarship, and especially by travelers, and missionaries; one of the most important contributors to Assyriology, in its early days, was George Smith, a copperplate engraver. Down at least to the 1890s, excavation in

---

[106] Mohl, "Année 1855–6," in idem, *Rapports* 2: 104.

[107] That person was the Czech scholar, Bedřich Hrozný, whose *Die Sprache der Hethiter* appeared in 1917 – but had only just reached an American expert in 1920. Carl D. Buck, "Hittite an Indo-German Language?" in *Classical Philology* 15, no. 2 (Apr. 1920): 186.

Africa and Asia was mostly small scale and ill-funded and usually not much better than glorified tomb-raiding.

Systematic archaeological inquiry in the Near East – and the state funding to support it – really began only after 1890; though, once again, I would caution against claims that this era brought with it a sudden and dramatic shift to "scientific" excavation. There was still a great deal of grave robbing going on, some of it being done with the connivance of the "professional" archaeologists.[108] One can say that work begun after this time tended to be more secular in orientation, owing partly to the more positivistic attitudes of younger archaeologists like Flinders Petrie or Robert Koldewey, but perhaps more importantly in the involvement of secular state museums, now operating in subcolonial (antiquities-rush mode) in the Ottoman Empire. To out-compete their rivals, excavators wished to appear as "scientific" as possible, thereby securing their prestige amongst their academic colleagues and (it was hoped) camouflaging their museological cupidity and Christian cultural prejudices from Ottoman officials. But Friedrich Delitzsch, in the opening words of his first "Babylon and the Bible" lecture of 1902, let the old cat out of the new bag;

What is the object of these labors in distant, inhospitable, and dangerous lands? To what end this costly work of rummaging in mounds many thousands of years old, of digging deep down into the earth where no gold or silver is to be found? Why this rivalry among nations for the purpose of securing, each for itself, these desolate hills – and the more the better – in which to excavate? ... To either question there is one answer, which, if not exhaustive, nevertheless to a great extent tells us the cause and aim: it is the Bible. The names Nineveh and Babylon, the stories of Belshazzar, and of the Wise Men who came from the East, have been surrounded, from our childhood up, by a mysterious charm. ... With these recollections of our childhood, however, is associated in riper years the struggle for a conception of the world which shall satisfy equally the understanding and the heart – a struggle which in the present day occupies the mind of every thinking man.[109]

And though his interests and inheritance made him a less secular creature than some of his contemporary "thinking men," Delitzsch was not far from wrong: though new finds had begun to reduce its centrality, the Bible was still at the heart of Near Eastern scholarship, even as the Second Oriental Renaissance reached its peak.

This was particularly true for the newer science, Assyriology, whose development in the 1860s–1890s we track first. Egyptology, thanks perhaps to its long-term association with esoteric and pre- or non-biblical wisdom, found it easier to separate itself from theological concerns; though here too, as noted above, the divorce was by no means easy or fully effected. In the first section, I will profile, briefly, two major contributors: Eberhard Schrader and Friedrich Delitzsch – though Delitzsch's activities after the 1890s take us beyond the Second Renaissance and will need to be covered in the chapter to follow. A section on Egyptology

---

[108] Julia Hankey, *A Passion for Egypt: Arthur Weigall, Tutankhamun and the 'Curse of the Pharoahs'* (London, 2001), pp. 158–208.

[109] Friedrich Delitzsch, *Babel and Bible: Two Lectures*, ed., C. H. W. Johns (New York, 1903), pp. 2–4.

before the Great War comes next; here, I focus my attention on Germany's most important Egyptologist to date, Adolf Erman. In Erman and his historian-counterpart and friend Eduard Meyer, we really begin to see secular scholarship, based on indigenous, "oriental" sources, take hold.

Assyriology's Escape from Infancy

In Chapter 2 we noted the incomplete acceptance of Champollion's readings of hieroglyphic inscriptions in mid-nineteenth-century Germany; in the case of cuneiform decipherments, the process of acceptance took even longer. Though Georg Friedrich Grotefend had made progress in deciphering Persian cuneiform inscriptions early in the century, he was able only to read a few names – and in any event, the Persian script he worked on was vastly simpler than the older and more commonly found Assyrian-Babylonian script (which we now refer to as Akkadian); while the former had only about forty signs, the latter, Eberhard Schrader testified in 1872, had over 400.[110] Numerous scholars worked on these problems in the next decades, including Émile Burnouf, Lassen, Henry Rawlinson, Edward Hincks, and Julius Oppert, and the conventional date for decoding the script is usually given as 1857, when Hincks, Rawlinson, Oppert, and William Henry Fox Talbot produced, independently, similar translations of the inscription of Tiglath-pileser I, found at Assur, and submitted them to the Royal Asiatic Society.[111] They decided that Akkadian was a Semitic language, but one with structural and phonological differences, which might mean that it had originally been used to write another non-Semitic language – one about which nothing was known until Ernest Sarzec discovered what came to be called "Sumerian" culture in his excavations at Telloh, beginning in 1877. This period of discovery, and uncertainty, made possible much linguistic as well as theological and racial speculation.

Many orientalists responded negatively to the decipherment; the racial theorist J. A. de Gobineau wrote a 200-page book attempting an alternative solution by using Arabic roots; Heinrich Ewald and Ernest Renan announced themselves highly skeptical. In the course of the next twenty years, the work of French and British scholars such as Rawlinson, Oppert, and François de Lenormant largely satisfied scholars west of the Rhine. The excavations led by A. H. Layard and P. E. Botta at Nineveh, Nimrud, and Khorsabad – and the treasures they brought home – attracted significant public interest, especially in England, though they were ended in the early 1850s and not started again for decades.[112] Though the Germanies were, by the 1840s, home to the most respected orientalist philologists in the world at the time, they did not participate much in Assyriological research in this period. In fact, German scholars continued to greet work in the field with skepticism precisely because, Eduard Meyer explained, Assyriology's popularity in

[110] Schrader, *Die assyrisch-babylonisch Keilinschriften: kritische Untersuchung der Grundlagen ihrer Entzifferung, nebst dem babylonischen Texte der trilinguen Inschriften in Transcription sammt Übersetzung und Glossar* (Leipzig, 1872), p. 5.

[111] Svend Pallis, *The Antiquity of Iraq: A Handbook of Assyriology* (Copenhagen, 1956), pp. 160–1.

[112] Ibid., pp. 161–80; Frederick Bohrer, *Orientalism and Visual Culture* (Cambridge, 2003).

England offered so many dilettantes the opportunity to speculate wildly about the proper decipherment of its signs.[113] It took not only happenstance, but also daring, for one of Germany's leading Semitists, Eberhard Schrader, to jump on this particular bandwagon.

Eberhard Schrader was, like so many other orientalists of his generation, a student of Heinrich Ewald; but, as the leading orientalists in the Prussian Academy of Sciences insisted in a memo seeking Schrader's appointment to the University of Berlin in 1875, he was "not [Ewald's] toady." He was, instead, "a man of iron determination, of fundamental and multifaceted learning, of thoroughly sound criticism, free of illusions and of prejudices" – in short, everything a Protestant theologian of the high positivist generation should be.[114] Trained as a Hebraist, in 1863 Schrader had published a careful philological study of the first eleven chapters of the book of Genesis and taken a job at the University of Zürich.[115] His command of cuneiform had come to him rather accidentally; during his time in Switzerland, the Zürich Museum was given a collection of cuneiform tablets and Schrader was asked to catalog them. Having moved to Giessen and then Jena (always in the theological faculty), Schrader had then been commissioned by the board of directors of the Deutsch-Morgenländische Gesellschaft to study the linguistic foundations of Assyrian-Babylonian cuneiform and the differences between different scholars' decipherments. Schrader's highly detailed 392-page response appeared in 1872 and helped to refine the Assyriologist's art, insisting that as important as the trilingual inscriptions were, it was also essential to look to parallel texts inscribed on buildings and on cylinders, vases, and other vessels.[116] But the volume certainly was not meant for laypersons; its purpose was exclusively to put Assyriology on sound philological footing. Schrader was only partially successful here, and when he took his first Assyriological student, Friedrich Delitzsch, in 1873, there were still very few others able to read the language in Germany, little internal respect for the field, and no jobs. Delitzsch was able to complete his habilitation after only one year's work with Schrader; this was relatively easy, he said, "cuneiform study being in its infancy."[117] Assyriology was still very much an auxiliary science, whose importance was both linked to, and hampered by, its relationship to biblical scripture.

Long before cuneiform's decipherment, Assyria was connected with the Old Testament, where many of its sites and rulers are mentioned. Schrader, perhaps more than any other scholar of his generation, was prepared to put the new knowledge into this old context. In the same year as his DMG response, he published *Die Keilinschriften und der Alte Testament*, again a specialist's study. In the preface, Schrader insisted that he was simply laying the foundations for an

---

[113] Eduard Meyer, "Schrader, Eberhard," in *Biographisches Jahrbuch und deutscher Nekrolog* 13 (1908): 160.

[114] Memorandum written by Olshausen and signed by Lepsius, Mommsen, Droysen, and Max Duncker, quoted in Meyer, "Schrader, Eberhard," p. 159.

[115] Eberhard Schrader, *Studien zur Kritik und Erklärung der biblischen Urgeschichte, Gen. Cap. I–XI* (Zürich, 1863).

[116] Schrader, *Die assyrisch-babylonisch Keilinschriften*, p. 11.

[117] Delitzsch quoted in Jerrold S. Cooper, "Posing the Sumerian Question: Race and Scholarship in the Early History of Assyriology," in *Aula Orientalis* 9, nos. 1–2 (1991): 50, n. 21.

Assyrian-Israelite history, "upon which later a lasting building can be built." He wanted to give readers original texts and translations of cuneiform inscriptions relevant to the Old Testament. "It is not our intention to attempt, at any price, to do away with any sort of discrepancies between the Bible and the cuneiform inscriptions, or even to hush them up. If a way to resolve these without force presents itself, we will not stand in its way. But it would be a thousand times better to leave today's incongruences – for whose solution today's available material does not suffice – than for one to forcibly cover them up, thereby distorting the Bible or by doing violence to the monuments."[118] In the chronological section, Schrader discounted the chronology of Kings I and II, preferring inscriptions to biblical texts, "which, notoriously, have suffered multiple transformations in the course of centuries and millennia," but also found many areas of concurrence.[119] Organized as a series of commentaries on particular Old Testament passages, the book concerned itself chiefly with rectifying dates, events, places, and rulers' names; for Schrader, returning to a Scaliger-like study of biblical chronology, the Old Testament was history, not Herderian folk poetry – what was at issue was its accuracy vis-à-vis what he clearly saw as more trustworthy Assyrian documents.

Most of Schrader's work was narrowly focused and read only by field experts. But Assyriology, thanks especially to the efforts of an English engraver turned Assyriologist George Smith, also experienced a brief wave of popular attention. In 1872–6, Smith published a series of important books reporting his discovery of Assyrian flood tablets and comparing these and other Assyrian texts extensively to the book of Genesis. He also reprinted, in one of these, the already well-known Hellenistic accounts describing a lost Greek text of the Chaldean priest Berosus; Berosus's description of ancient Assyrian legends, including legends that spoke of a flood and of an *ur*-god, the fish Oannes, were preserved in texts of Josephus and Eusebius and had given rise to speculation on relations between Hebrew and Assyrian floods as well as to Voltaire's highly amusing parodies.[120] Smith was certainly convinced that his work ratified Berosus's claims that the Assyrians had recorded the flood first; he, however, took quite a moderate view of his findings and did not seize the occasion to denounce the Jews for borrowing from their betters. But for others, these texts seemed to confirm the need to decenter Jewish history and the Old Testament, something in the interests both of non-Hebraist orientalists and of Christian anti-Semites.

The pivotal figure here was a young Assyriologist just beginning his career in the 1870s, Friedrich Delitzsch. Friedrich's father, Franz, was also an orientalist, but of a rather different character than his son; father Franz was a Hebraist – celebrated for his Hebrew translation of the New Testament – and also a Lutheran pastor. Franz Delitzsch worked intensively with Jewish literature and with Jewish scholars, including Goldziher – though he was also famous for attempting to convert them to his hyper-Protestant point of view. In addition to possessing

---

[118] Schrader, *Die Keilinschriften und das Alte Testament* (Giessen, 1872), pp. iv–v.
[119] Ibid., pp. 297–305, quotation p. 297.
[120] Grafton, *Defenders of the Text*, pp. 95–100; Voltaire, "Zadig," for e.g., Chapter 12, in *The Portable Voltaire*, ed. Ben Ray Redman (New York, 1977), pp. 367–71.

cuneiform skills his father did not have, Friedrich seems to have been less willing to work with Jewish scholars and more critical of traditional Lutheran doctrine; he was, accordingly, much more intrigued and convinced by Smith's tablets than was Delitzsch *père*. Friedrich was in London when Smith's *The Chaldean Account of Genesis* appeared, in 1876, and considering it "an epoch-making book," convinced his brother Hermann to translate the text. Hermann did so quickly enough for the volume to appear in Germany in the same year. When it appeared, it contained a preface and afterward by Friedrich, as well as the young scholar's corrections of the Berosus section (Smith had used an English translation; Delitzsch went back to Eusebius's Greek). Most important for our purposes is this afterward, where Delitzsch categorically denies the possibility that the Assyrian and Old Testament flood stories might simply be parallel accounts – instead they derived from one source. This was also true, in his view, for the Tower of Babel story, and he expected that soon a Babylonian account of the Fall would be found; "For it is not thinkable that a so highly gifted people as the Babylonians, who also had so deep a feeling for sin and guilt ... would not have had a specific set of reflections and traditions about the origins of sin as they had about the origins of the world."[121]

Already in the early 1860s, the Jewish scholar Heymann Steinthal had begun to worry about a reversal going on in Christian scholarship, in which polytheism, rather than monotheism, was beginning to be seen as the source of European progress.[122] He was right to be concerned; by this time, the philhellenic love for the humanness and vibrant diversity of the Olympian gods began to be assimilated to an understanding of pagan, "Aryan" cultures as imaginative and creative, over and against Semitic cultures, depicted as inflexible and desiccated. The longer-term consequences of the Creuzer *Streit* were becoming clear as Christian identity was submerged and a secular, classicizing narrative took hold, one that opened the way for the elevation of more fully racialized forms of Friedrich Schlegel's linguistics. Steinthal's concerns led him to underscore the primeval polytheism of the Semites, something which made them more like *ur*-Aryans and less likely to have a racially determined "instinct" of any kind. Claiming that the legend of Samson had counterparts in other myths about solar heroes such as Hercules, he drew myth into the argument to suggest the existence of a primordial universal mythology.[123] But under the pressure of new, oriental evidence such as the flood tablets, this universalism was increasingly difficult to defend. And diffusionists like Delitzsch were doing their best to destroy it.

It is striking that it was a Jewish scholar and an admirer of Steinthal, Ignaz Goldziher, who saw immediately the implications of the new Assyriological finds both for the reputation of the Jews and for the universalist paradigm. Goldziher's 1876 study, *Der Mythos bei den Hebräern und seine geschichtliche Entwicklung*,

---

[121] Delitzsch, "Erläuterung und fortgesetzte Forschung," in George Smith, *Chaldäische Genesis: Keilinschriftliche Bericht über Schöpfung, Sündenfall, Sintfluth, Thurmbau und Nimrod ...* authorized trans by Hermann Delitzsch, introduction and additional material by Friedrich Delitzsch (Leipzig, 1876), p. 306.

[122] Williamson, *Longing for Myth*, pp. 224–5.

[123] Ibid., p. 225; on the association of solar gods with Aryanism, see Arvidsson, *Aryan Idols*, pp. 63–81.

also addressed itself to Ernest Renan's influential claim that the Semites had no mythology. Goldziher pointed out, first of all, that there were other sources than the Old Testament in which Semitic forms of mythology might be found, including the rabbinical Haggadah and Arabic folk literature.[124] Here the young Hungarian Hebraist neatly called Christian scholars on their perpetual prejudice against using rabbinical texts in painting their portraits of "Judaism." Goldziher also objected to Persian specialists' pushing back of dates into the foggy realms of prehistory in order to prove Hebrew dependence on Zoroastrian ideas.[125] Moreover, religion and mythology, in his view, were essentially to be understood in the context of various peoples' relationship to nature (farmers love sunshine; nomads find the unclouded night-sky inspiring) and the point they had reached in culture-historical evolution. This put Goldziher in the rather ticklish position vis-à-vis Jewish ortho-doxy of arguing that the Jewish monotheism was the product of evolution rather than revelation – but it had the advantage of keeping a sort of universalism intact. In the book's final pages, Goldziher incorporated the fruits of the new orientalism, including Smith's tablets, and acknowledged that the Hebrews probably had bor-rowed ideas and practices from the Babylonians as well as the ancient Persians. But borrowing, Goldziher insisted, did not vitiate the creativity and uniqueness of the Hebrews; it was possible, in his view, to assimilate the new findings and still retain the fundamental belief that Judaism was the common root both of Chris-tianity and of his new passion, Islam.[126]

Goldziher was, at this stage, a young man, but one full of enormous promise, and it is a matter of some significance that precisely in these years, his liberal patron in the Hungarian establishment died, and the chair that should have been his was given to a much less deserving candidate. Instead, the enormously talented Goldziher took a job as the secretary of the Jewish community in Budapest. One consequence of this institutional contingency was that Goldziher decided that he had to limit himself to Islamic studies rather than continue publishing broadly in *Orientalistik*; had he at this stage decided to learn cuneiform or to continue work-ing in early Israelite literature, perhaps he could have prevented a hyper-diffusion-ist philology from asserting dominance in this area. But as we shall see in Chapter 7, Goldziher would face challenges enough in pursuing his chosen branch of *Semitistik*, Islamic studies.

In the meantime, Friedrich Delitzsch continued his line of argument. In 1886, he published his first major book, *Wo lag das Paradies?*, in which he sought to determine definitively the original location of Eden, and the language that had been spoken there. Regrettably, for Delitzsch, Assyriological solutions were largely rejected by mainstream orientalists; Theodor Nöldeke, reviewing *Wo lag das Paradies?* in the ZDMG in 1886, warned readers not to be fooled by the Assyriologist's apparent certainty – Delitzsch's claims, linguistic, geographic, and ethnographic, were dubious, to say the least.[127] German scholars were

---

[124] Goldziher, *Der Mythos bei den Hebräern und seine geschichtliche Entwicklung: Untersuchungen zur Religionswissenschaft* (Leipzig, 1876), p. 34.

[125] Ibid., pp. 388–9.

[126] Ibid., p. 390. See also Símon, *Ignác Goldziher*, pp. 77–87, and Chapter 7, below.

[127] Nöldeke, review of F. Delitzsch, *Wo lag das Paradies?*, in ZDMG 36 (1886): 173–84.

prominent among those who, for a number of years, suspected that the huge cache of letters between the Egyptian and Assyrian kingdoms found at Tell el Amarna in 1886 were forged. But Delitzsch plodded on, devoting himself to writing specialized grammatical works, and in time his positivistic philology was rewarded with an appointment to the first full professorship in Assyriology in Germany at the University of Breslau (1893); in 1899, the University of Berlin gave him its first chair. Heinrich Zimmern got one at Leipzig in 1900, and by 1909, three more cuneiform specialists (Fritz Hommel, Carl Bezold, and Arthur Ungnad) were holding full professorships.[128] Unlike Schrader, these scholars were cuneiformists first and exegetes after – though they were all fully versed in Old Testament Hebrew and occasionally dabbled in theological debates.

Schrader had plotted the course, using Assyrian documents to check the reliability of the Hebrew Bible, and even preferring their testimony to that of the scriptural authors. But it took time, hard work, and a half-ideological, half-source inspired commitment to listening to the Assyrians' voices to establish disciplinary autonomy. We should pause, briefly, and note just how radical this consequence of the Second Oriental Renaissance was for the early Wilhelmine era. The ambitions of Schrader's exegesis ranged well beyond those of Wellhausen – who might have been the most hyper-skeptical of humanists, but who was, by comparing traditional texts to one another and applying to them tests of internal coherence and rational logic, still working in a recognizably Christian humanist manner. Schrader and Delitzsch helped open a new period of vast expansion of Near Eastern knowledge, one that scholars found even harder to get their heads around than the one ushered in by Napoleon's Egyptian campaign. In a 1908 elegy for Schrader, Eduard Meyer tried to describe the difficulty he and his fellows had in adjusting to this new era:

Today it is hard enough even for those who lived through the following development to call to mind what an enormous proportion of that which we now know of the history of the ancient Orient – which has now become almost an elementary common possession – was, but twenty years ago, still wholly unknown. Of the great political background against which the episodes recounted in the Old Testament took place, of the individual processes, from which the statements of the prophets were born, we knew pitifully little; and we were everlastingly engaged in the Danaiden task of trying to wrest an overview of the history of the ancient Orient from the information in Herodotus, Ctesias, Berosus, and the historical remnants preserved in the Old Testament. Then the Assyriological information arrived. Everywhere – that it was accessible – it brought unimagined data, but above all it came into flagrant contradiction with the conventional presentation of Israelite history (but in no way with the most important historical material which the Old Testament provides) as well as with the information given by the Greeks and the systems that had been constructed from it. Small wonder that one resisted accepting [this new information]: how much we had erred, how much of the Greek information in particular – apart from the fragments of Berosus – turned out to be historically worthless data, one could not until then have imagined. This explains why so many scholars lacked the intellectual elasticity to test and incorporate the new [evidence] without preconceptions . . .

---

[128] Mangold, *Eine "weltbürgerliche Wissenschaft,"* pp. 166–7.

Moreover, Meyer continued, old-school orientalists and theologians had attacked every tiny linguistic error the Assyriologists made, "and believed that with these errors they could justify throwing away, or at least casting suspicion on their discoveries as a whole."[129] This philological resistance entangled Schrader in a number of feuds with his colleagues and forestalled the incorporation of Assyriological information into Old Testament studies for some time. Though Meyer did not touch on the sociological effects of these debates, we should note here that these conflicts also gave Schrader, and especially his students, a set of grievances against the academy. As we shall see in Chapter 5, these grievances would make German Assyriologists, in particular, eager to expose the limitations and prejudices of liberal-era scholarship when, at the fin de siècle, their grammatical foundations grew firmer and their evidentiary base grew larger, and when the cultural climate shifted in their direction.

Studying the Assyrians made Schrader officially a Semitist – but that did not mean he was a philo-Semite. On the contrary, by the 1870s he had signed onto the Renanian conviction that Semites could not really have invented anything requiring mental agility. He concluded, for example, that the epic-like elements of the story of Ishtar must be the result of the Babylonians' contact with a non-Semitic, local people. The Northern Semites (Babylonians, Phoenicians, and Hebrews), he suggested in an 1875 essay, had migrated to Babylonia from Arabia with only the intellectual tools of the Arabs; writing, mythology, art, and perhaps even monotheism were the products of their contact with the indigenous "Turanians."[130] Schrader was not the only scholar to find the "Turanian" Sumerians more suitable fathers of civilization than the Semitic Assyrians, though the equally stubborn Jewish scholar Joseph Halévy attempted to refute these claims. In 1889, Friedrich Delitzsch agreed with Halévy that Sumerian must also be a Semitic language – though he had changed his mind by 1897. Down to at least 1905, other German scholars, including Eduard Meyer and Alfred Jeremias, took Halévy seriously; this was not an open and shut case, and there were sound linguistic reasons for not grouping the Sumerians with other Semitic-speakers.[131] But Schrader's sweeping racial-philological history helped to decenter an Old Testament whose historical value and internal coherence was already under heavy attack. In trusting the testimony of the Assyrian sources over the biblical ones, he prepared the way for a new vision of the ancient Near East to emerge and made an important contribution to the secularization and professionalization of Assyriology; but he also took the first steps down the road that would lead his student Delitzsch to his "Babel und die Bibel" lectures of 1902–3 and perhaps to his fiercely anti-Semitic polemic *Die grosse Täuschung* (1920–1) as well.

---

[129] Eduard Meyer "Schrader, Eberhard," pp. 159–60. The Danaides were the daughters of Danaus, king of Argos; as punishment for having killed their husbands on their wedding nights, they were sentenced to spend eternity pouring water into bottomless vessels.

[130] "Turanian" was a linguistic and ethnographic category used by Max Müller to group the non-Indo-European and non-Semitic languages of the steppes; it was adopted by those seeking an original and glorious homeland for the Hungarians and Turkic-speaking peoples in prehistorical Central Asia. There is too much ideological baggage—and too little linguistic commonality—for scholars now to use the term.

[131] Cooper, "Posing the Sumerian Question," pp. 52–3, 59–62.

Egyptology for Realists: Adolf Erman

Ancient Egypt too was an important site for biblical history, and knowledge about it had long been used in theological debates. It had, of course, been hoped that the decipherment of hieroglyphics would resolve these questions and/or provide the key to unlock the secrets of eastern wisdom. But the texts, it turned out, were largely pedestrian, and the archaeological evidence pointed in varying directions. This meant that the Old Testament and Herodotus continued to provide the most fleshed-out and detailed points of entry for Egyptologists – even those who could read the inscriptions and papyri easily. For some, like the Swiss scholar Edouard Naville, confirming the scriptures continued to be an aim and end; for others, like Richard Lepsius and Georg Ebers, this does not seem to be the case. Lepsius and Ebers did, however, continue to believe in some version of the Flood story and to depend on traditional authorities, while also stockpiling large amounts of new data for future researches. Both knew Egypt and its artifacts well; Lepsius spent three years there on a successful pillaging operation and ran Berlin's Egyptian Museum thereafter. Ebers, Lepsius's student, traveled to Egypt a number of times and wrote a very detailed coffee-table book as well as the first Baedecker guide to Egypt. Ebers also produced a series of highly popular Egyptizing novels, which aspired, in his words, "to clothe the hardly-earned results of severer studies in an imaginative form."[132] Ebers could read hieroglyphics, but neither he nor his mentor could persuade themselves to trust these texts over the conventional biblical and classical ones. It would be their joint student, Adolf Erman, who would fully effect Germany's Second Egyptological Renaissance.

It had taken a long time, Erman told the Cultural Ministry in 1900, for Egyptology to become a respected science. "In the first half-century of its existence Egyptology like all young sciences suffered from the fact that amateurs who lacked the necessary training flocked to it ... how far this went is shown by the lack of confidence German orientalists and historians had in Egyptology in the [18]60s, despite Lepsius's most serious endeavors. In the last two decades a change has occurred: the charm of the sensational, which captivated the dilettantes, has for the most part disappeared...."[133] Erman's memorandum, written in hopes that the state might help German archaeologists break the French-British stranglehold on Egyptian excavation sites, draws our attention, once again, to the slow process of *Orientalistik*'s rise to scholarly respectability; as Erman notes, as late as the 1860s, Egyptology in the Germanies was quite a modest and usually unrewarding career choice. There were some talented scholars about; at the age of sixteen, Heinrich Brugsch began putting together his demotic grammar; it was finished, and published, by the time he was twenty-one, in 1848. He founded the *Zeitschrift für ägyptische Sprache* and wrote extensively for it; he received a professorship at the University of Göttingen in 1867. But, like his younger brother Émile, Heinrich

---

[132] Ebers, "Preface to the Second German Edition," *An Egyptian Princess*, trans. Eleanor Grove (New York, 1880), p. iii.

[133] Erman, "Bericht über die Lage der deutschen Ägyptologie in Kairo," May 1900 in B-GSPK, I, 76Ve, Sekt. I, Abt X, Nr. 2, Bd. 2.

Brugsch Pasha chose to spend most of his career in Egypt, photographing, collecting, and conserving archaeological materials.[134] His extensive and important philological work was well known in Germany, but no one missed him – or his linguistic skills – enough to entice him to come home.

The highly successful popularizing efforts of Leipzig professor Georg Ebers have been treated elsewhere[135] and so shall not detain us here. What is important about Ebers for our story is to understand the relative ease of his transition from law student to Egyptologist; he finished his law degree in 1862, but, by 1865, had completed a habilitation in Egyptology – despite enduring a life-threatening illness and taking time out to write his first novel, *An Egyptian Princess* (1864). By 1875, he was a full professor and engaged in training students like Eduard Meyer and Adolf Erman as well as non-Egypt specialists like Goldziher, Fritz Hommel, and Ulrich Wilcken. Ebers' novels circulated widely – by 1900, *An Egyptian Princess* had reached its eighteenth edition and had been translated into fourteen languages, including Arabic.[136] The novels gave Egypt new vitality, obscuring the fact that the Germans, after Lepsius's trip in the 1840s, had been largely shut out of the trawling for Egyptian treasures. But Ebers' Orient was still a very mixed one; his popular travelog *Ägypten in Bild und Wort* combined images of Egypt's past and its present and his novels always included Greek and Jewish characters. Indeed, Erman would later describe Ebers' Egyptian characters themselves as "inauthentic and prettified; but," he continued, "one has to ask oneself, if the public would have found them so attractive, if he had left about them the smell of the Orient."[137] Jean Pierre Adolphe Erman, on the other hand, rather liked the authentic smell of the Orient, and though he loved and respected his mentor, he was not a man to pretty things up.

Born in 1853, Erman was younger than most of our protagonists in this chapter and unlike them found his Gymnasium education wholly unfulfilling and the philhellenic *Schwärmerei* of men like Ernst Curtius off-putting.[138] Unlike most of the lonely orientalists, too, he found a sympathetic mentor (Ebers) and enjoyed quite early institutional favor. Already in 1884 he was made Professor of Egyptology at the University of Berlin as well as Director of the Egyptian and Assyrian departments of the Royal Museums. By this time, he had already published an important linguistic study, *Neuägyptische Grammatik* (1880) and was well along in his work on a popular study of Egypt, commissioned in 1881 by the H. Laupp-schen Buchhandlung. The book was to address upper-level Gymnasium students – following the model of Hermann Bender's 1879 *Rom und Römisches Leben im Altertum* – but one can well imagine the publisher also had the successes of Ebers' novels in mind.

In the preface to the second edition of *Ägypten und ägyptisches Leben im Altertum*, Erman would admit that trying to write a synthetic book in the wake

---

[134] On the Brugsch brothers, see Donald Reid, *Whose Pharaohs?*, pp. 114–18.

[135] See Marchand, "Popularizing the Orient," *Intellectual History Review* 17, no. 2 (July 2007): 175–202.

[136] Hans Fischer, *Der Ägyptolog Georg Ebers: Eine Fallstudie zum Problem Wissenschaft und Öffentlichkeit im 19. Jahrhundert* (Wiesbaden, 1994), pp. 152, 101–2.

[137] Erman, *Mein Werden*, p. 257.

[138] Ibid., pp. 73–84; on Curtius, p. 120.

of the rising tide of new scholarship had forced upon him the realization that the old frameworks simply would not do:

I had no idea how little of the necessary legwork for my subject had been done, and I believed in all seriousness that in [J. G.] Wilkinson's old book, *The Manners and Customs of the Ancient Egyptians*, re-edited by [Samuel] Birch in 1878, I had a preparatory study which had only to be filled out a bit more. But as I got to know this famous book more intimately, I could no longer deceive myself that the "ancient Egyptians" as he portrayed them had ever existed. [Wilkinson] had juxtaposed, willy-nilly, pictures from all periods; he had uncritically thrown in much from Greek and Roman literature, and from the Old Testament too; all of that he had explained clearly and usefully and done so as well as one could in 1836, but what was produced was no better than if in a book on Greek life the heroes of the Iliad, the contemporaries of Pericles and the subjects of Justinian were treated together simply as "the ancient Greeks."[139]

Greek sources and the Old Testament, he pointed out, were both much too late to be very useful for characterizing ancient Egypt; even if the author of the books of Moses knew Egypt at first hand, trusting his testimony was like using medieval martyr legends to learn about Rome in the early imperial era. Using, instead, archaeological material and papyri, Erman wrote a wholly new book, one which sought to treat the Egyptians objectively, as an historically important people, but not as an especially mysterious or wise civilization. Cutting through the mystical "nimbus" that had surrounded the Egyptians since the time of the Greeks, Erman insisted that his subjects had not been privy to profound secrets and were, instead, normal representatives of their level of cultural development.[140]

In the brief history of the discipline included in the volume, Erman juxtaposed an era of esoteric dilettantism to the era after the publication of the *Description de l'Egypte*. "Since this time the mystical darkness, in which Egypt languished so long, has dissipated . . . ," he wrote.[141] But he knew full well that Egyptology had not become scientific overnight. Indeed, as he noted in the preface to the second edition, it was really the era *after* the publication of his *Ägypten* that saw the vast acceleration of Egyptological knowledge. He had completed the book in 1886, he wrote, in the wake of his first trip to present-day Egypt; "It was lucky that I finished the book then, for in the next years the huge wave of new knowledge began to deluge us, [a wave] I could hardly have worked through to completion. Then came Petrie's digs and those of his followers; then came the clay tablets from Tell el Amarna, which at the time had the effect of a revelation. The pyramid texts introduced us to the perceptions and language of the most ancient period. . . . Then came the numberless inscriptions and papyri – a truly endless [body of] material."[142] It was so "endless," in fact, that Erman handed over the production of the second edition to his student Hermann Ranke. "I could not myself take part in his difficult and tedious work," explained the busy professor.[143]

[139] Adolf Erman, "Vorwort des Verfassers," in idem, *Ägypten und ägyptisches Leben im Altertum*, revised by Hermann Ranke (Tübingen, 1923), p. v.
[140] Erman, *Ägypten und ägyptisches Leben*, pp. 5–6, 2–4.
[141] Ibid., p. 10.
[142] Adolf Erman, "Vorwort," p. vi.
[143] Ibid., p. v.

What came after the original edition of *Ägypten* was a spate of grammatical studies by Erman himself (*Sprache des Papyrus Westcar*, 1889; *Ägyptische Grammatik*, 1894) and his student Kurt Sethe (*Das ägyptische Verbum*, 1899–1902), as well as a series of important excavations led by Flinders Petrie, George Reisner, and Ludwig Borchardt. In the pursuit of scholarly progress, Erman was central; his influence on Egyptology has been described by scholars in the field as "cyclonic and the greatest since Champollion; he completely revolutionized the subject, especially the grammar and teaching of philology . . ."[144] But Erman was also central to the wider cultural politics of Egyptology and orientalism as a whole. He was a promoter of German national interests, leading the campaign to establish a German Archaeological Institute branch in Cairo (one was founded in 1907 after many years of pressure), and he was responsible for the modernization of Lepsius's Egyptian museum – which meant painting over the popular, but not historically accurate, murals. He did not stop writing for wider audiences after *Ägypten*, publishing in 1905 a history of Egyptian religion for laymen, in 1923, a popular *Literatur der Ägypter*, and finally, an accessible overview *Die Welt am Nil* (1936). He defended Egyptian uniqueness with vigor, but his lack of interest in claiming Egyptian origins for Jewish or Greek ideas made him acceptable to his colleagues in classics and Old Testament studies.[145] Like Nöldeke and Wellhausen, Erman was no fan of mysticism and would produce one of the late great exemplars of positivist philology, *Wörterbuch der ägyptische Sprache* (with Hermann Grapow), issued in five volumes between 1926 and 1931. His "cyclonic" contributions to Egyptian linguistics in particular mark him as one of the fathers, rather than sons, of the Second Oriental Renaissance. But in his self-conscious break with his forefathers' methods, in his championing of indigenous sources, in his willingness to write for the popular market, and in his interest in daily life, religion, and material culture, his work also pointed in new directions, some of which he, like most of his older contemporaries, would find deeply problematical.

EDUARD MEYER: UNIVERSAL HISTORIAN IN A SPECIALIZED AGE

The "liberal" careers sketched in this chapter should suffice for now to suggest the scale of changes underway in late nineteenth-century *Orientalistik*, changes sizable enough to constitute a second renaissance in the field. In the chapters to come, I will also be sketching the transformations made in this generation in the fields of art history (Chapter 9) and East Asian Studies (Chapter 8). But perhaps it is best to conclude this chapter with a short profile of liberal-era orientalism's most prominent synthesizer, Eduard Meyer. Meyer, born in 1855, would have one of the longest and most productive careers of any of these scholars, dying only in 1930, a life span that makes him hard to place in this study. Moreover, though trained as an orientalist (his dissertation was in Egyptology), he then became by general acknowledgment a *Universalhistoriker*, the first such since J. G. Droysen gave

---

[144] Warren P. Dawson and Eric P. Uphill, *Who Was Who in Egyptology?* (London, 1972), p. 99.

[145] In his autobiography, he remarked on his love for Greek, speculating that had he had the right introduction to the subject, he probably would have liked classical languages better than all the Orient had to offer. Erman, *Mein Werden*, p. 83.

up writing about Hellenism. Meyer was certainly more suited to "universal history" than was Droysen, for the former mastered the major oriental languages and did much to make familiarity with the political histories of oriental "high" civilizations essential to the man of true *Bildung*. But Meyer never entirely shook the mid-century's view of the ancient past, premised on classical literature and the Old Testament. He was, in this way, still a man of the nineteenth century, though he lived long into the twentieth, and a product of that hugely dynamic and innovative, but still cautious, Second Oriental Renaissance.

Meyer's father was a classical philologist, professor at one of Lutheran humanism's *ur*-institutions, the Johanneum (Gymnasium), in Hamburg; his post was sufficiently lucrative to allow the elder Meyer to amass an extensive library, in which young Eduard learned to love (Attic) Greek literature. It is not entirely clear how he made his way toward orientalism, but it may have been, as Ulrich Wilcken suggested in an elegy, by way of an interest in mapmaking, which led him to Strabo and thence to Hellenistic history.[146] Meyer cast his net broadly, studying Sanskrit, Arabic, Persian, Turkish, and hieroglyphics at the University of Leipzig, before settling down to write his dissertation on the Egyptian god Seth under the direction of Ebers; he would later learn cuneiform. He then spent some time as a private tutor in the house of the British general consul in Constantinople, during which time he was exposed to discussions about Ottoman political life in European diplomatic circles, and also visited a few ancient sites, including the newly located Troy.[147] He then returned to Leipzig, habilitating there in 1879.

Like Erman, Meyer was inspired to alter his career plans by a commission, in his case from Cotta Verlag, to write a handbook on ancient history for Gymnasium students. What happened to Meyer was precisely what happened to Erman — to whom, in fact, the second edition of Meyer's *Geschichte des Altertums* would be dedicated. Meyer read the syntheses of his predecessors, but with the exception of the works by Max Duncker and Henry Rawlinson, found them horribly out of date, or too popular, and lacking in critical foundations. "The history of the ancient Orient was until the beginning of this century a wholly dark realm, illuminated only by a rare ray of light," he wrote in the introduction. "Only the colossal discoveries of the recent years, the study of the monuments and literatures of Egypt, Assyria, Babylon and Persia have given us the potential to possess more exact knowledge."[148] Duncker and Rawlinson had begun the work of integrating the new literature into general histories, but Meyer, who had immersed himself in the cutting-edge and highly varied philological studies of his Leipzig teachers and friends, knew that more needed to be done. As Meyer's friend Wilcken would describe in an elegy, Meyer's greatest contribution lay precisely in reviving the genre of universal history after the post-Niebuhr decades of specialized research. Far surpassing Duncker, he was the first, Wilcken argued, who ". . . took on the challenge of putting together an ancient universal history in which the whole

---

[146] Ulrich Wilcken, "Gedächtnisrede auf Eduard Meyer," in *Sitzungsberichte der Preussischen Akademie der Wissenschaften*, Phil.-Hist. Klasse (Berlin, 1931), p. cxxxiv.

[147] Christhard Hoffmann, "Eduard Meyer," in *Classical Scholarship: A Biographical Encyclopedia*, ed. Ward W. Briggs and William M. Calder III (New York, 1990), p. 265.

[148] Meyer, *Geschichte des Altertums*, vol. 1 (Stuttgart. 1884), p. 24.

Mediterranean realm including Egypt and Asia Minor is made a unified field for study and the narrative is based on his own research."[149] But there was a price to be paid for his commitment to this project, which would make and define his career. In working through the *Geschichte des Altertums*, Meyer abandoned most of his plans for studies in religious history and grew increasingly interested in the particularities of each oriental culture and state.[150]

Meyer was able to give each of these states its due by dint of his remarkable linguistic talents, his prodigious capacity for hard work, and his peculiar generational position – which gave him access to and insight into all the new research at the point just before it became impossible to master. The first and last of these factors gave Meyer an advantage over Leopold von Ranke, who had published volume 1 of his own world history in 1881. Ranke, Meyer charged, by failing to include the ancient Orient in his supposedly global history, had ignored a half-century of scholarly research; though he knew Wellhausen's work on the Old Testament and Hammer-Purgstall's history of the Ottoman Empire, he had used neither. Ranke had ruled out the latter because Hammer had depended on Ottoman rather than European sources, and the Eurocentric Ranke had believed Venetian accounts were far more trustworthy.[151] Meyer's critique of Ranke would be one of the first in a long line of orientalists' critiques of this sub-Hegelian and cavalier treatment of the ancient Orient; the time had come, they argued, to give the Asian polities the independent value and organic integrity Ranke had insisted upon for the post-classical states of Europe.

Meyer criticized Ranke's failure to appreciate the civilizations of the Near (and Far) East.[152] But he had a lot in common with the Rankeans of his day. For both parties, history was a process of state development, and it was to their institutions that one should look for signs of progress; fundamentally, Meyer was a political historian, one who thought the highest aim of all human action was the developing and securing of the power and greatness of states.[153] Cultural greatness, in his view, was bound up with the development of individuality, which occurred in clashes between egoistic individuals and the power of tradition; where the latter force predominated – as in Egypt in classical times or in the Muslim world of the present – the developmental dialectic stalled, and there was no real history.[154] For Meyer, the greatest contributions to the self-consciousness of individuals were made by the ancient Jews and the Greeks; this gave him a secularized, and historicizing, justification for emphasizing these two "chosen" people. Interestingly, he thought Alexander, not Pericles, represented the summit of Greek civilization, and

---

[149] Wilcken, "Gedächtnisrede auf Eduard Meyer," p. cxxxiv.

[150] Christhard Hoffmann, "Die Selbsterziehung des Historikers. Zur intellektuellen Entwicklung des jungen Eduard Meyer (1855–1879), in Calder and Demandt, eds., *Eduard Meyer*, p. 241.

[151] Alexander Haridi, *Das Paradigma der 'islamischen Zivilisation' – oder die Begründung der deutschen Islamwissenschaft durch Carl Heinrich Becker (1876–1933)* (Würzburg, 2005), p. 98.

[152] Meyer also gave China credit for being a high civilization, with an elaborate and important history. But as he thought China had had virtually no impact on the forming of European cultural history, he did not learn Chinese nor did he give it much space in his texts.

[153] See, for example, Meyer, "The Development of Individuality in Ancient History" (1904), in idem, *Kleine Schriften* (Halle, 1910), pp. 227–8.

[154] Meyer, *Geschichte des Altertums* 1: 14.

like many of his fellows, liked the rule of law and even constitutional government, but did not like Greek "mob" democracy. Finally, even more than Ranke, Meyer believed that history had to be about events and people who left a trace, who had real impact on what came after them. He believed that without texts, one could not really have histories; linguistic, mythological, or archaeological evidence could be used in the absence of texts, but it could never really tell one anything definitive. The important figures were not the "good" men and women or even the most powerful among them: they were simply the "effectual" figures, the people who changed history's course. Of course, this had a tendency to justify the writing of history by the victors; but in Meyer's view, that was simply the reality behind the Rankean call to describe events "wie es eigentlich gewesen."

Meyer's theory of history and his influence, or lack thereof, on Max Weber have been the subject of a number of books and articles, so I will not delve deeply into these questions and controversies here.[155] Suffice it to say that Meyer was no knee-jerk positivist, as he argued "I do not know of any absolute knowledge, I only know the struggle for knowledge ... all science is an ongoing discussion of problems that can never totally be solved."[156] Nor, however, was Meyer a relativist, with a modern, anthropological view of cultural history. There has been much made of his "anthropological" method – the first edition of his *Geschichte des Altertums* in fact opened with a prefatory essay entitled "Anthropologie," which was expanded in his 1902 edition to form a volume on its own. The origins of this section are, however, interesting; Meyer himself said that he wrote it essentially to cover the "externalities," that is, the universal and prehistorical elements that were left out in the treating of the histories of each of antiquity's peoples independently of one another. And, in fact, what the section does is to explain his methodology, which owes much to cultural Darwinism (Meyer did not, however, acknowledge these debts, which would not have made him particularly popular in German academe). Societies developed from simple to complex, driven by a universal *Differenzirungstrieb* (drive to differentiation); but the first unit must be the state, for the articulation of individuals and families was, in his view, inconceivable without a defining and protective *Verband*. The origins of religion were obscure, but lay in man's response to nature; Meyer evidently did not believe in any sort of primeval revelation and repeatedly insisted that it was not the historian's job to speculate about the origins of humankind. Non-historical peoples entered history when they came in contact with historical peoples (that is, those trying to develop individuality); otherwise, their fates were unknown and of little interest.[157] One could say his historical method was shaped by his embrace of *Realpolitik*; everything was assessed with an eye to its effectiveness.

---

[155] See, for example, the excellent essays in Calder and Demandt, eds., *Eduard Meyer*, and Arnaldo Momigliano, "Max Weber and Eduard Meyer: Apropos of City and Country in Antiquity," in idem, *Sesto Contributo alla Storia degli Studi Classici e del Mondo Antico*, vol. 1 (Rome, 1980), pp. 285–93.

[156] Meyer, response to remarks after his lecture, printed together with his "Thukydides und die Entstehung der wissenschaftlichen Geschichtsschreibung," in *Mitteilungen des Vereins der Freunde des humanistischen Gymnasiums* 14 (1913): 103.

[157] Meyer, *Geschichte des Altertums* 1: 3–14.

As this suggests, if Meyer, like Herder, paid careful attention to cultural particularities, he had none of his predecessor's primitivizing romanticism. Missing
from his repertoire was the sort of sympathy for the Orient that the romantics
harbored, a sympathy born from the notion that the Orient might have represented, or still represent, a purer, more innocent childhood, which Europe might
profitably recollect. The Orient had no secrets – aside from some number of
unrecoverable facts – and offered no unique alternative map for modern Europeans to follow. Like Erman, Meyer happily embraced the post-decipherment
realization that Egypt, like the other civilizations of the East, had a unique but
not divinely inspired course of development.[158] Though he thought the Hebrew
prophets extremely important in their articulation of the importance of individual
conscience, he was not, like Ewald, a passionate admirer of them, nor was he
interested in, or apparently convinced of, the truth of their prophecies. The Orient
might be interesting as part of European ancestry, but, Meyer openly admitted, it
would never be as relevant to European concerns as the history of classical antiquity: "The history of the ancient Orient can never awaken the same sort of
interest as do Greece and Rome, and the same goes for the history of the many
Islamic dynasties and for the ephemeral and narrowly-circumscribed states created
in the middle ages and the first centuries of the modern era. . . . Not only is their
inner value small, but [small too] is their impact on history."[159] No wonder Meyer
never gave up writing on classical as well as oriental topics; his heart – like that of
the wider culture around him – belonged to the Greeks and Romans.

Far from being a critic of the establishment, Eduard Meyer was the ultimate
insider, and his institutional success tells us much about the kind of scholar who
flourished under the cultural conditions of the post-unification era. Meyer was
appointed professor at the University of Breslau already at the age of thirty,
followed by a call to Halle (1889) and two more offers (Tübingen and Munich),
which he declined. In 1902, he received the Berlin chair that marked the summit of
academic ambition for scholars of his day. From this time forward, he was an
important player in the Prussian Academy of Sciences, the Deutsch-Orient Gesellschaft, and in university politics more generally. He and his cohort – men and
women whose formative experiences predated the era of school reform, mass
politics, and hyper-imperialism – became ardent supporters of Bismarck and
champions of German national interests. Many of them were – like the trio profiled
in this chapter's opening section – were alienated from the churches, though few
were as seriously agnostic as Meyer and Nöldeke or as radical as Lagarde. They
had grown up with Graecophilia – but were not ready to junk it; they did not
particularly like the Jews or Judaism, but they still recognized the ancient Jews as
contributors to the history of European civilization. By drawing attention to new
material, they were able to convince their generation to accept a wider set of
oriental ancestors – though, ironically, their attempts to keep pace with the further

[158] Eduard Meyer, *Geschichte des alten Ägyptens* (Berlin, 1887), p. 3.
[159] Meyer quoted in Beat Näf, "Eduard Meyers Geschichtstheorie: Entwicklung und zeitgenössische
    Reaktionen," in Calder and Demandt, eds., *Eduard Meyer*, p. 302.

specialization of scholarship made their work less and less readable for general middle-class audiences.[160] Outstripping their "lonely" predecessors in terms of academic respectability, institutional infrastructure, and even scholarly achievements, these scholars gave German *Orientalistik* a series of new avenues to explore, from the Assyrian origins of biblical texts to the everyday lives of the Egyptians. They put enormous effort into reading the Orient's own texts – though for Meyer, as for most members of his generation, the Orient remained more career than calling. But very soon, a new generation of readers and scholars would come along for whom Meyer's mixture of philology, "anthropology," and facts would prove unsatisfying, and his *Realpolitik* and right-liberal presumptions vexingly narrow and old-fashioned. And, as new domestic and international concerns, new institutional conditions and new audiences developed, German orientalists would use the proceeds of their late nineteenth-century renaissance to force their way into broader cultural debates in unprecedented and highly significant ways.

---

[160] Whereas, for example, in the first edition of Meyer's *Geschichte des Altertums* of 1884, the section on the Egyptians ran to 116 pages, in the second edition of 1907 it ran to 298 pages, and in the third (1913) to 322 pages, the Babylonian material had expanded even more, rising from less than 50 pages in 1884, to 301 pages in the second edition, and to 352 pages in the third edition.

5

The Furor Orientalis

What [amazing] work has been completed in the last fifteen years! How unimaginably our knowledge has been, from all sides, enriched! What new perspectives have been opened for us in all, absolutely all, areas of scholarship! One is breathless and can hardly keep pace. We live in an era of electricity, even in scholarship!

Enno Littmann to Carl Heinrich Becker, September 7, 1913[1]

Writing to his fellow orientalist C. H. Becker on the eve of the Great War, Enno Littmann could hardly contain his excitement about the progress of oriental studies in the previous decade and a half. Strikingly, Littmann emphasized changes in perspective, in addition to the enriched content, the scholars' shared field had witnessed – it was not so much that those great positivist edifices had been completed, but that one now viewed the evolving structures in quite different ways. As successful and well-placed members of the post-positivist generation, Littmann (born in 1875) and Becker (born in 1876) were in a position to recognize the fundamental changes underway in their cohort's knowledge of Asian cultures. And Littmann was right – at least as concerned the ancient world; by 1913, not only was the ancient Orient much better known than it had been two decades earlier – it was also increasingly being conceived from new, non-biblical and non-classical, perspectives. Together with the increasing salience of matters eastern for German political and commercial interests, such changes gave orientalists like Becker and Littmann new confidence; though they knew very well that the Reich's institutions remained overwhelmingly Christian and classical, they saw themselves as cultural players, strutting and fretting upon a stage much bigger than ever before, and able perhaps to make a stronger case for the Orient's richness and relevance than ever before. For this generation of German-speaking orientalists, the fin de siècle was indeed "an age of electricity" – and they intended to administer shock treatment to a central European cultural world badly in need of new light.

New light came, in part, from new sources; and new sources there certainly were thanks to the processes we have described as the Second Oriental Renaissance. The literature on non-European religions and on the Hellenistic world, in particular, exploded. Even Theodor Mommsen, writing volume IV of his *Römische Geschichte*, found it hard to navigate the massive new literature on the origins of Christianity and had to ask for help in determining which works

[1] Littmann to Becker, September 7, 1913, in B-GSPK, Nachlass Becker, M. 4579.

to trust – a concession to the times the great historian of the positivist generation must have found difficult to make.[2] But the large-scale shift in oriental studies, which occurred between about 1885 and 1905, must be understood as much more than simply the result of new discoveries and better "science." What made for the "electricity" Littmann described was less the material itself than the individuals who took it upon themselves to read, interpret, and, for the first time, to successfully popularize it. Here we have again to do with affective as well as institutional changes and with another set of generational considerations and conflicts, one that remarkably looks rather like the 1820s in reverse.

If the last chapters focused on the scholarly achievements and institutional changes of the later nineteenth century, this one emphasizes the changed mindset of the orientalist, and especially the scholars born after about 1860. This was a generation born and educated during the Second Oriental Renaissance; their experience was shaped not, like that of the previous generation, by cautious institution-building and philological positivism, but rather by specialization, the gradual evolution of new patrons, positions, and publication venues and, in 1884, the Reich's entry into the colonial race. The intellectual achievements of their fathers too emboldened the new generation to claim general relevance for their fields of study; though the younger generation's grander hopes would often be disappointed and its ambitions frustrated by the shortage of academic positions for those coming of age after 1885. The students of Nöldeke, Wellhausen, Lepsius, and Schrader, moreover, for reasons that go beyond the crowded job market, were more daring and less respectful of disciplinary divisions than were their mentors; eager to find meaning in their studies, many were willing to advance grand-scale hypotheses without first mastering all the relevant languages or specialized literature. These younger scholars also often denounced their *Doktorväter* for their narrow source usage and old-fashioned chronologies; many began to incorporate material culture, psychological, or ethnological insights, and oral and folkloric traditions into their work. Confident that Germans needed and wanted cultural and spiritual overhaul, they were willing to challenge the methods and norms of their positivist "fathers."

Cultural historians long ago identified the unique qualities of the "generation of the 1890s" in Germany and beyond and have described its origins in socioeconomic, political, psychological, and intellectual terms.[3] We should keep in mind that the scholars and intellectuals subsumed under this "generation" still represented a very small slice of the male population of the Kaiserreich, the slice that attended elite schools, consumed large quantities of specialized literature (as well as, increasingly, modern art, philosophy, and literature) and sought academic jobs. These individuals were or wanted very much to be Germany's culture-makers, just as forebears like Theodor Mommsen, Ernst Curtius, and Albrecht Ritschl had been;

---

[2] Ernst Bammel, "Judentum, Christentum und Heidentum," pp. 221–30.

[3] H. Stuart Hughes, *Consciousness and Society: The Reorientation of European Social Thought, 1890–1930* (New York, 1961); Fritz Stern, *The Politics of Cultural Despair*; Fritz Ringer, *The Decline of the German Manadarins* (Cambridge, MA, 1969). For the classic analysis of sociocultural changes in the universities, see Konrad H. Jarausch, *Students, Society and Politics in Imperial Germany* (Princeton, NJ, 1982).

but all around them, the cultural marketplace was expanding and diversifying. Enrollment in higher education exploded after the 1870s – but university expansion did not keep up; academic jobs quite suddenly became more difficult to come by and waiting periods for good jobs longer. Added to this was an increasing sense that the Graecophile cultural world the liberals loved was nothing but a "plaster cast antiquity"; Greek individualism and rationalism boiled down to unhealthy egoism and superficial wordplay. Even Roman history began to seem short, shallow, and tediously well known. This generation, as a whole, was inclined to contrariness or even to revolt against the liberal, rational, and philhellenic culture of their forebears – which was a central reason why it found the Orient so very appealing and so very useful.

Both political and intellectual circumstances conspired to make the Orient more "interesting" to Germans than ever before. In the external world, both the Middle and Far East were, by the 1890s, in the news virtually every day, as the Kaiserreich increased its trade and expanded its political relations with the Ottoman Empire and began to seek territory in East Asia. This was the era of the Great Game, the race to reach Tibet, the Sino-Japanese War, and the Boxer Rebellion – during the course of which the German ambassador to China was murdered. After 1905, the modernization and industrialization of Japan also turned many heads. The Russo-Japanese War, the Indologist Leopold von Schroeder claimed, gave the Orient salience beyond the appeal of its religions, wisdom, discoveries, and art; "Now," he wrote, "it affects us through deeds – and these have a wholly different force and persuasive power." These sudden changes in the Orient's status, Schroeder thought, would mean big changes for orientalists:

Hereafter, we will have to reckon again and again with Japan, indeed, with the Orient as a whole. *Orientalistik* will become a practical field of study, no longer what it was previously, a scrupulously avoided domain of dry as dust pedants. A chair for Japanology will soon be created [actually, the first came in 1914]. But chairs are not the only thing – and they are not the most important thing in the world. In hundreds and thousands of canals the life blood of the peoples is flowing back and forth. From now on will it circulate in a totally different, powerful way, between the Orient and Occident ... and not only will the Occident act on the Orient, but the Orient will also act on the Occident.[4]

These were heady years for young orientalists, many of whom saw a revolution taking place in Europe's conceptions of history and humankind. By 1912, a specialist in East Asian art could boast in a major German newspaper that Eurocentrism was, effectively, dead:

The twentieth century has shown its face. The world has become wider in this last decade. Europe no longer is the globe. In the Far East, the first great struggle among peoples played itself out. The term "world history" now takes on a new resonance. Historians can no longer limit themselves to the narrow circle of European states, and touch on the world outside here and there with a few tentative words. The fate of the peoples of Europe is ever more intertwined with that of the peoples of other continents.

---

[4] Leopold von Schroeder, "Orient und Individualismus" [1905], in idem, *Reden und Aufsätze vornehmlich über Indiens Literatur und Kultur* (Leipzig, 1913), pp. 236–44, 237–8.

The concept of "humanity" itself is being widened. The inhabitants of the "fairyland" of Japan, whose great leaders silly operetta librettos like to parody, are energetically demanding their rights. The powerful mass of humanity in the Chinese Empire will press forward too. The name "pigtail wearer" has lost its meaning. The yellow race is awakening. Old Europe is no longer the middle of the world.[5]

Old concepts, the author continued, were no longer valid, challenged by the political and economic "awakening" of Japan; though he identified the racial otherness of the "yellow" East Asians, the iconoclastic reviewer almost reveled in the shifting of global power dynamics and with them the collapse of Eurocentric stereotypes. Where we once were horrified by ritual suicide ceremonies of the Japanese, he argues, today we admire the willing suicide of Field Marshal Nogi; where once we admired colorful porcelains and "droll mandarins" we now see art and wisdom.[6] Though well aware that shopworn prejudices continued to exist, this reviewer was strikingly confident that modern scholarship would trample them in its forward march.

The individual quoted in the earlier section, Curt Glaser, was collector of avant garde art, but his sense that he was experiencing the demise of a shopworn Eurocentric *Weltanschauung* was shared by many of the scholars and educated laymen who are the subject of this chapter. No name yet exists for this group – indeed no one seems to have identified the phenomenon, with the important exception of scholars of Jewish thought, seeking the origins of Zionism and the revival of Hasidic ideals.[7] Perhaps because so many studies of late nineteenth-century scholarship focus narrowly on individual disciplines, it has been difficult to identify trends such as this one that cut across many fields. To better understand these individuals, I have dubbed them "furious orientalists" – though by no means were all of those treated later in this chapter professors of oriental languages. In my view, the major characteristics of this cohort, whose disciplinary homes lay in theology, classics, and art history, as well as *Orientalistik* proper, lie in their vigorous championing of the claims of the Orient to historical, religious, philosophical, and/or artistic priority (and sometimes even superiority) over and against the dominant tendency to isolate and exalt ancient civilizations conventionally hailed as special, especially Greece and Israel. It was not a self-conscious movement or an entirely coherent strain of thought, but it had a recognizable set of enemies (classicizing Gymnasium and university professors; orthodox theologians). Prosopographically too, the "furor" has at least loose coherence; its proponents belonged largely to the generation that came of age in the 1880s and 1890s, as post-unification anxieties (including colonial ones) came to the fore, as

---

[5] Curt Glaser, "Ostasiatische Kunst," in *Der Tag*, October 6, 1912, reprinted in Hartmut Walravens, ed., *Die Ostasienausstellung Berlin 1912 und die Presse: Eine Dokumentation zur Rezeptionsgeschichte, Bibliographien zur ostasiatischen Kunstgeschichte in Deutschland*, vol. IV (Hamburg, 1984), p. 53.

[6] Ibid., pp. 53–4.

[7] See, e.g., Paul Mendes-Flohr's chapter, "Fin de Siècle Orientalism, The Ostjuden and the Aesthetics of Jewish Self-Affirmation," in idem, *Divided Passions: Jewish Intellectuals and the Experience of Modernity* (Detroit, 1990), pp. 77–132. Because Mendes-Flohr and others have done such excellent work in describing the consequences and internal contradictions in what might be called "self-orientalizing" in Jewish circles, I will leave that subject largely aside.

classical learning and scholarly positivism came under attack, and as new, more intensive bouts of collecting, editing, deciphering, and publishing made available a vast new "oriental" arsenal. Trained as specialized philologists, but often subjected to long delays before receiving paying academic jobs, a number of these young scholars exhibited frustration with cultural institutions that seemed outdated and unable to provide Germans with either a reliable account of their descent or an inspiring vision of their future. This frustration, and the attempt to further personal, intellectual, and ideological interests by flinging open the doors to a wider, deeper, and more powerful Orient represents what is called in this chapter the "furor orientalis."

Though retrospectively invented, this moniker might well have been coined by classicizing contemporaries, for whom the movement was quite clearly a new-fangled sort of barbarian invasion. More moderate orientalists too, who did not share the aspirations to cultural transformation so central to their more radical students and colleagues, generally cast a disparaging eye on the movement. The number of players, then, is relatively small, comprising only a subset of those trained in oriental languages at the fin de siècle and their names are now little known. But understanding both their challenges and their failings provides an important new context for the evaluation of better known figures such as Martin Buber, Max Weber, C. G. Jung, Aby Warburg, Ernst Troeltsch, Rudolf Bultmann, and Gershom Scholem, and for understanding the dynamics of fin de siècle German culture as a whole. What follows will describe, first in rather general terms, the generational dynamics and cultural context that enabled the launching of this form of what H. S. Hughes called "the revolt against positivism."[8] The chapter's second half considers one particularly important group of "furious orientalists," those who came to be known as the Panbabylonists. In the chapters to come, we will see strong echoes of "furious" orientalism in Indology and in art history – though I will also be arguing that in some fields, such as Islamic Studies and Sinology, involvement in the imperialist projects of the Reich blunted or redirected passions that might otherwise have been turned inward. For if the furor orientalis was, in part, about pushing forward the specialized study of nonwestern cultures in order to further German interests in the world, it was also about seizing humanistic and theological territory from liberal-era theologians and old-fashioned classical philologists. It was not simply a battle over the East; it was also a western civil war.

TO BE A (FURIOUS) ORIENTALIST

This section opens with some definitions and provisos – for in creating a category, giving it a generational profile, and focusing attention on it, I will be oversimplifying on the one hand and leaving out important contributors to oriental studies on the other. I also do not wish to draw hard and fast boundaries between the groups I will call "liberals," on the one hand, and "post-liberals" or "neoromantics," on the other, the latter being the larger contingent to which our "furious" orientalists belonged. Readers should also take stock of the longer term dialectics that, in

---

[8] Hughes, *Consciousness and Society*, pp. 33–66.

interesting ways, brought the "furious" generation back to many of the questions and some of the methods of their grandfathers, the romantics. The new directions taken by the 1890s generation were, in my view, both a logical extension of late liberal work and a reaction to liberal suppression of questions posed by the generation of Creuzer and Friedrich Schlegel; this is, in many ways, the story of three generations, not two, of the attempted, but not entirely successful, return of the repressed romantic narrative in the brave new world of the fin de siècle.

In defining the late "liberal" as against the "neoromantic" generation, I divide, for the most part, those who came of age between about 1850 and 1885 from those who published their first works after this time. Of course, there are some who do not fit this chronology and drawing lines is complicated by the fact that several members of what I have called the "liberal" generation, like Ulrich von Wilamowitz Moellendorff (1848–1931) and Eduard Meyer (1855–1930), lived long into the post-liberal era. Although products of the Bismarckian *Gründerzeit* rather than, as were their "sons," products of the age of mass parties and high imperialism, what makes these scholars "liberals," for me, is not really their politics; Eduard Meyer, for example, was politically farther to the right than Wilhelm Bousset, whom I group with the post-liberals. Rather, the "liberals" here are those who, by and large, maintained the tradition of secular humanism and *Kulturprotestantismus*; though increasingly historicist in orientation, they betrayed, at key moments, a residual attachment to aestheticizing Graecophilia, faith in the autonomy of Greek culture, belief in data collection (as opposed to intuition), and resistance to interdisciplinary or comparative endeavors. Some, like Julius Wellhausen, also had a hard time decentering the Old Testament; though Wellhausen lived to see a dramatic period of change in the study of the ancient Orient, his historical narrative had taken shape long before. As Ernst Sellin commented in 1925, Wellhausen's conception of the ancient Near East had formed "before the stones of Babylon, Assyria, Palestine, and other lands, began to speak. He was never able to adapt himself to the more modern and scientific way of contemplating the ancient Orient with which we are now so familiar."[9] To be fair, "liberal" attitudes were not merely the product of the inability or unwillingness of senior scholars to learn new philological tricks. Those who felt their generation was the first to fully emerge from theological and/or classical tutelage found the younger cohort's return to romantic questions and speculative syntheses deeply unsettling. And in a number of cases, their intellectual conservatism would prove well founded.

Indeed, looking at things in new ways is very hard, much harder than our garden-variety histories of scholarship suggest. Even after the publication of a pathbreaking book, many are left fumbling in the dark, without the proper resources or training to switch gears; many will have to finish old research projects even though they are now obsolete simply because they are too far along to

---

[9] Ernst Sellin, *Archaeology versus Wellhausenism* (Nashville, TN, 1925), p. 245. As an 1876 essay shows, Wellhausen actually knew a great deal about cuneiform and recognized that Akkadian cuneiform literature is much more extensive than ancient Hebraic writings. But he could not bring himself to trust the former above the latter. Wellhausen, "Ueber den bisherigen Gang und den gegenwärtigen Stand der Keilentzifferung," in *Rheinisches Museum für Philologie* 31 (1876): 153–75; p. 163. This was noted already by Martin Hartmann, in his review of Wellhausen's *Die religiös-politischen Oppositionsparteien im alten Islam* (1901), in OLZ 5 (1902): 96–104.

abandon them. In nineteenth-century *Orientalistik*, "keeping up" was not merely a matter of reading the big books and journals but also of having the proper linguistic skills and access to the latest troves of texts and inscriptions. Moreover, some members of the "liberal" generation did not want to entirely rethink the ancient past because those who did often clutched at disputable new evidence or had ideological axes to grind – not that the older generation had no axes of its own, but somehow, in the flux (intellectual and political) of the 1880s–1920s, the opportunities for tendentious reconceptualization seem to have expanded. Rules for the usage of new sources had not yet been agreed upon. Nor was everyone on the same interpretive page; how did one establish the origins of monotheism? What exactly constituted cross-cultural influence? Reading the literature of the period, one finds a pervasive feeling of "everything up for grabs" as a desperate search for stable and provable origins commenced.[10]

In some sense, the whole of antiquity and prehistory *was* up for grabs and changing day by day. We should remember that it took some years after Schliemann's excavations to work out a coherent periodization for the Mycenaean world, and this was again thrown into confusion following Arthur Evans' discovery of what he called the Minoan world after 1902. As we saw in Chapter 4, George Smith's translation of cuneiform flood tablets in the early 1870s coincided with the first uncovering of Sumerian artifacts and for quite some time, controversy raged over the relationship and dating of these two cultures. Much confusion reigned as to the proper dating of developments in ancient Persia, which in turn complicated understanding purported relationships between Zoroaster, Confucius, Moses, Mithra, Buddha, and Christ – each of whom, of course, had his own spokespersons and his own claim to *ur*-originality. Perhaps the sobriety of the generation of the Second Oriental Renaissance and its tendency to construct carefully and to hedge its bets should be seen as a kind of modesty in the face of all of this uncertainty; numerous members of the next generation considered it weakness or failure to promote the field properly. In the chapters to follow, we will see how this sobriety gave way to new forms of orientalist intoxication and deeper, but not necessarily more constructive or progressive, relationships to the East.

There are of course some individuals who defy neat characterization as "liberals" or "neoromantics." Notorious for their scathing reviews and political pronouncements, Paul de Lagarde and Heinrich Ewald exhibited some behaviors typical of the "furious" generation long before its coming of age. Early in his career, Eduard Meyer exhibited characteristics that might have classed him with the "furious" orientalists – he rejected his father's and his professors' emphasis on the study of language in and for itself, he wrote his dissertation on Egyptian religion. What set Meyer on a new, and more "liberal" path, as we have seen, was the commission that resulted in his signature publication, the *Geschichte des*

---

[10] As the Russian scholar Vassili Bartol'd commented in 1913: "The interpretation of the inscriptions that the civilized peoples of the ancient Orient have left behind still raises many doubts, and the question of the ethnographic origins of these peoples still remains contested." W. Barthold, *Die geographische und historische Erforschung des Orients mit besonderer Berücksichtigung der russischen Arbeiten* (Leipzig, 1913), p. 89.

Altertums (see Chapter 4), which perhaps says something more about the sobering effect of writing textbooks on ambitious young specialists than it does about Meyer himself. And, of course, some members of the 1890s cohort exhibited few signs of furor; the period between 1900 and 1930 produced a rich crop of scholars known, as were Enno Littmann and Carl Brockelmann, for their linguistic virtuosity. Their slightly older colleague Carl Bezold (born 1859) wrote in the vita at the conclusion of his dissertation, which was completed in 1880: "I consider the mission of my life to be the study of languages for their own sake and particularly for the furthering of studies of Semitic grammar."[11] There were plenty of others who felt the same way in all of *Orientalistik*'s sub-disciplines. But there are too many who fit the "furious" type to ignore; some of these, like Hugo Winckler and Josef Strzygowski, I will profile in detail, others, like Turkologist Georg Jacob, who opened his thesis with an attack on modern, decadent society's failure to appreciate the power of the East in the early Middle Ages, will have to remain peripheral to this study.[12] I am, of course, characterizing a particular and note-worthy type, not claiming that all scholars of this generation behaved or thought in the same way.

What a large number did, however, have in common was the longing to return to subjects left fallow by mid-century scholars, namely, the impact of eastern cultures on western ideas; the erotic life of the ancients; and the role of religion in pagan antiquity. Certainly, the liberal positivist generation had begun to feel some of these pressures by the time they achieved chaired status, but most were unable and unwilling to alter their research programs to suit the new opportunities and new demands; often, indeed, their reaction to the next generation was a kind of retreat from lines of inquiry they feared would cast them back into the pre-*wissenschaftlich* world of their romantic forbears. For them, to break with Greek sources, as also to break with the Old Testament texts over which they had labored so intensively, was to lose touch with history, a disastrous leap of faith into an alien and mistrusted modern world. Many members of the fin de siècle generation were unequally dubious about the modern world – but they were, with respect to the interpretation of the ancient world, much more inclined to be risk-takers and self-confident propagandists for the Orient's coming of age.

Despite their accomplishments and their institutional successes, orientalists by the 1880s still felt themselves to be peripheral contributors to the larger sphere of German and Austrian cultural identity, as indeed they were. Although the School Reform Conference of 1890 officially broke the Gymnasium's monopoly on university entrance, Gymnasium attendance was still essential for aspiring *Bildungsbürger* and Greek and Latin remained central to the higher schools' curriculum. Germany's Royal Museums were full of classical artworks and casts, purchased with state monies, while Indian, Chinese, Assyrian, and Islamic arts, insofar as they were exhibited at all, languished in museums of ethnography or decorative arts. Funding for things "oriental" was growing, but orientalists still depended on private organizations, while classical archaeologists extracted large sums from the

---

[11] Quoted in Franz Boll, "Carl Bezold," in *Sitzungsberichte der Heidelberger Akademie der Wissenchaften: Phil.-Hist. Klasse 1923*, no. 1 (Heidelberg, 1923), p. 6.

[12] On Jacob, see Enno Littmann, "Georg Jacob," in idem, *Ein Jahrhundert Orientalistik*, pp. 96–109.

museums and the Kaiser. The only place where credentialed academics taught the living languages of the Orient was Berlin's Seminar für Orientalische Sprachen; though by 1900, this Seminar did enroll a considerable number of students aiming at jobs in the colonial ministry, overseas trade, and missionary work, scholarly philologists continued to look askance at its all-too-modern and "practical" pursuits (see Chapter 8). University positions in *Orientalistik* were expanding, but many of them remained unsalaried, which meant that students without independent means, like the young Enno Littmann, still often trained themselves to be pastors in order to secure their careers as scholars.[13] All of these limitations on disciplinary autonomy and cultural relevance would provoke increasing vexation among younger orientalists, many of whom felt the time had come to escape their intellectual and institutional subordination.

Vexed by the indifference or hostility of outsiders, our "furious" orientalists were also frustrated by the narrow and overly modest practices of their teachers. As we will see in Chapter 8, specialists in modern Islam like Martin Hartmann thought oriental studies the key to German colonial success – and fulminated against *Arabistik*'s absorption in philological questions. Some younger theologians took up the study of oriental religions, believing that their new knowledge could be used to treat the pressing problem of Christianity's fitness and appeal for the modern world; for them, the older generation's hostility to contextualizing the New Testament as they had the Old represented both ignorance of the new scholarship and refusal to confront Christianity's life-threatening modern crises. Some members of the newer sub-specialties developed a loathing for the complacent, one-brick-at-a-time pursuit of specialized scholarship because it amounted to established scholarship's "killing with silence" of their epoch-making endeavors. In a 1907 review for the *Orientalistische Literaturzeitung* (OLZ), Wilhelm Erbt noted that though the Assyriologists had indeed discovered a new world, it was beginning to look as if no one would take notice of it until it started disturbing the peace of its neighboring fields and demanding – like the ever more aggressive German Empire in world politics – its deserved place in the sun. Instead of embracing the new field's enormous promise, Erbt argued, classicists as well as Old Testament scholars were still defending their bailiwicks against outside incursion and holding fast to claims for the autochthony of Israel, Greece, and Rome: "The natural consequence of the older [generation's] position is a fear-inspiring warning to the young people they are to educate against any exposure to oriental studies."[14] Erbt's review can be read as a transparent political and cultural grab for power on the part of the "sons" who were, in his view, being treated as disruptive, illegitimate children rather than as men who had earned their rightful "place in the sun."

One striking aspect of philistine ignorance against which many members of this generation rebelled was the still conventional belief that the aim of understanding "the Orient" was to explicate the Old Testament. Having now compiled libraries

[13] See Enno Littmann, "Autobiographical Sketch," in *The Library of Enno Littmann, 1875–1958,* ed. Maria Hofner (Leiden, 1959), pp. xiii–xx.

[14] Erbt review of Otto Weber, *Die Literatur der Babylonier und Assyrer* (Leipzig, 1907), in *OLZ* 10 (1907): 433.

and storehouses full of non-Judaic oriental texts and artifacts, the generation of the 1890s was eager to widen the sweep of ancient oriental history, not only for the purposes of specialist research but also for popular consumption. Their more sympathetic understanding of these cultures too led them to reappraise pagan religious and ethical traditions and to invoke them as possible parallels to or ancestors of Christian ideas. Though scattered attempts in this direction had already been made in the late Renaissance, by the end of the nineteenth century, lay and academic studies in comparative religion were exploding and changing thinking even within the universities' theological faculties. Here, as we have seen, Christian scholarship had for centuries emphasized Christianity's superseding of Judaism. But until the fin de siècle, it was hard for most Christians to get around the Jews' contribution to Christian history and doctrine. It was the furor orientalis that helped to supply essential tools for this severing operation; fascinated by new finds and the deciphering of new texts, it succeeded in pushing the histories of the ancient Indians, Assyrians, Persians, and, to a lesser extent, Egyptians to the fore, mostly at the cost of the ancient Hebrews. For Jewish scholars, some despairing of liberal-assimilationist *Wissenschaft des Judentums*, the furor led them too to emphasize the "oriental" aspects of their tradition and its uniqueness, not its commonalities with western rational Christianity; the intellectual history of Zionism too owes much to the furor orientalis.[15]

As the example of Zionism suggests, this generation was also rather more interested in interacting, in some way, with the real-existing land, people, and languages of the East. "Going there" was becoming a requirement for the career orientalist, even if one only went once; taking indigenous scholars seriously was also becoming more common, though most were still treated as language tutors and nothing more. It had long been the case that the excavators or procurers of material objects were not considered "real" scholars – real scholars were the ones who, like Linneaus, sat at home and made sense of the material. But by the turn of the century, discovery and ownership of the stuff, both for nations and individuals, increasingly gave one the right to claim a place at high table. "Stuff" was, in any event, more powerfully effective as evidence and as bargaining chips in an age of well-publicized, grand-scale archaeological excavations and of mushrooming national museums. If the Greeks and Italians had imposed restrictions on excavations and the export of antiquities, it was still possible to bring home impressive treasures from the Ottoman lands and from China's weakly controlled western provinces. In this context, knowing the "stuff" at first hand gave career boosts to orientalists like Albert Grünwedel, Ernst Herzfeld, Friedrich Sarre, and Walter Andrae, none of whom were renowned for their philological prowess.

As concerns this generation's relationships with nonwestern people, we would be hard-pressed to generalize. Some younger scholars were more condescending or racist than their forefathers, some were less so; some sympathized with the imperial regimes and some with the indigenous opponents of westernization.

---

[15] See, here, Mendes-Flohr, *Divided Passions*, pp. 77–132, and Peter Gordon's intriguing chapter on Franz Rosenzweig's attempt to "orientalize" the Hebrew Bible; "Facing the Wooded Ridge," in his *Rosenzweig and Heidegger: Between Judaism and German Philosophy* (Berkeley, CA, 2003), pp. 237–74.

Richard Wilhelm, for example, developed strong links to conservative Chinese mandarins and Paul Deussen befriended the Hindu nationalist philosopher Swami Vivekananda. But there were also those like the Arabist Karl Süssheim and the self-promoting journalist Ernst Jaeckh, who made friends with Turkish modernizers, and Bismarckian diplomats, like Friedrich Rosen, who socialized with local nationalists without buying into their political dreams.[16] There were some – probably a large number – who traveled less to get to know new people than to experience the geography and climate or to visit the monuments they planned to write about. But those who could call themselves Orient-experts by virtue of simply having read manuscripts in the libraries of Berlin, London, and Paris were a dying breed.

As for the relations between oriental scholars and Germandom's Jews, the situation was again mixed. The fact that some of the newer orientalist scholarship contributed to the decentering of the ancient Jews does not mean that all orientalists were anti-Semites; Hugo Winckler, who insisted on the Aryanness of the Hittites, was; the *Islamforscher* C. H. Becker was not – though he did hold racist views when it came to sub-Saharan Africans. In his autobiography of 1929, Adolf Erman traced his family heritage, which included, he emphasized, three Frenchmen and a Jew; he was no pure Aryan, and "was naughty enough not to believe in the superior qualities of 'pure races'...." Erman was, however, mistaken when he added: "[s]cience has long ago completely abandoned the 'races' of 'Aryans' and 'Semites'; the languages to which these names refer were spoken by the most diverse people, who had nothing to do with one another."[17] Some scholars had indeed given up racial thinking – or better, had never gone beyond the Boppian philological family trees. Others, however, had jumped on the bandwagon, and in 1929, in some fields, it was not so easy to get off.

But we run far ahead of our story and it is important to remind ourselves that in the late Wilhelmine period, *Orientalistik* was actually getting to be a *less* rather than a *more* exclusive club. As we noted in previous chapters, throughout the nineteenth century oriental studies had been rather more welcoming of Jews and especially of Jewish converts than was, say, classics or German philology, in part for the very good reason that they were the best Hebraists. *Kulturprotestantismus* too made for some degree of tolerance, as did linguistic positivism, which valued contributions to science if the contributors' political and personal qualities were rendered invisible (which was, of course, never entirely possible). By the century's final third, there were chaired professors in place who were fair-minded enough to recognize scholarly merit when their Jewish colleagues displayed it in impressive quantities, and sometimes even promoted their careers: a partial list of these enlightened professors would include H. L. Fleischer, Th. Nöldeke, Georg Ebers, Julius Wellhausen, Adolf Erman, Theodor Mommsen, and Franz Delitzsch. With their assistance, Jewish scholars began to receive appointments. By no means, of course, had anti-Semitic sentiments entirely disappeared; Marc Lidzbarski, Enno Littmann remarked in a 1904 letter to his mentor Theodore Nöldeke, had earned

---

[16] See Friedrich Rosen, *Aus einem diplomatischen Wanderleben*, ed. Herbert Müller-Werth (Wiesbaden, 1959), pp. 54–6, and Chapter 10.

[17] Erman, *Mein Werden*, p. 42.

the Strasbourg chair, "But I have already heard from many parties that in personal relations the characteristics of the Polish Jew – shall we say, euphemistically, tactlessness – have not been stripped away, and that in Kiel people have very little to do with him." Faculties must be careful, he warned, to hire a "member who is some use as a human being."[18] Despite such concerns, Lidzbarski did receive a professorship at the University of Greifswald in 1907 and in 1917 succeeded to the chair once held by Littmann – and before him by Lagarde! – at the University of Göttingen. Lidzbarski had converted to Protestantism as a student, but made no secret of his origins; in fact, in 1927 he published an autobiography, *Auf rauhen Wege*, which concerned almost exclusively his childhood in a Polish *shtetl*.

Jews were the most notable beneficiaries of orientalism's increasing openness, but they were joined now also by a few women and a few non-Europeans. In Prussia, women were able to audit university lectures only in 1897 and to matriculate only in 1908; once admitted, few gravitated toward orientalism. Perhaps, as Gerdien Jonker has argued, German orientalism's philological orientation made it difficult for women to break in (though one wonders about Jewish women); surely too, it matters that those who had actually lived in Asia, as wives of officials, businessmen, or missionaries, had little place in academia because of the universities' focus on the ancient, rather than the modern world. Nor were German women welcome in the theological faculty, for they could not hope to take clerical orders. But thanks to Jonker's careful work, we now know that there were some women at work on some of the larger scale projects generated by the positivistic aims and evidentiary superabundance of the Second Oriental Renaissance. Women worked, chiefly as "mechanical" assistants, on the Egyptian Dictionary project and sorting, cataloging, and preserving Asian materials in the museums. Some, like Elizabeth Morgenstern, devoted their lives to this barely recognized and poorly paid labor; Morgenstern, for example, began work on Erman's Egyptian dictionary in 1898 and was still helping to organize materials in 1926, twenty-nine years later, while her male counterparts had long since moved on to higher level jobs.[19] Scholars' wives had always been valuable assistants of one sort or another; but now a few, like Sanskritist Heinrich Lüders' wife Else, had university training too.

The Second Oriental Renaissance was also characterized by the increasing presence and influence, if sometimes veiled, of non-Europeans in the making of orientalist knowledge. With the founding of Berlin's Seminar für Orientalische Sprachen, numerous non-Europeans came to the Reich capital to teach language courses (as ill-compensated instructors) or to attend other university courses. Well-born visitors, like Swami Vivekananda, who stayed with Deussen in 1896, or novelist Rabindranath Tagore, were the subject of much curiosity, as too were the non-Europeans who were displayed at the world exhibitions and as part of traveling ethnographic tableaux. But some non-Europeans were intervening more

[18] Littmann to Nöldeke, Sept. 30, 1904, in *B-SB* Nachlass Nöldeke, K. 1.
[19] Gerdien Jonker, "Gelehrte Damen, Ehefrauen, Wissenschaftlerinnen: Die Mitarbeit der Frauen in der Orientalischen Kommission der Preußischen Akademie der Wissenschaften zu Berlin (1907–1945)," in *Frauen in Akademie und Wissenschaft: Arbeitsorte und Forschungspraktiken, 1700–2000,* ed. Theresa Wobbe (Berlin, 2002), pp. 132–3, 147–64.

directly in the making of orientalist knowledge, participating, for example, in the yearly international congresses of orientalists. As a condescending newspaper report described the 1894 meeting in Paris:

It was a mishmash of languages and peoples such as one is seldom able to observe. There one saw, to start with the Orient that lies furthest afield, intelligent-looking Japanese together with well-to-do Chinese, Egyptian Effendis with their harsh features, which, betray, in a single glimpse, their descent from the beduins, Algerian sheiks in their picturesque costumes, Turkish delegates with the highest decorations, Persians, Indians – even the newest French colony, Madagascar, was represented. And in addition to the orientals, the orientalists.

In suggesting that the "orientals" and the scholars of the Orient were two different groups, the writer was reiterating a Eurocentric stereotype – but he did, at least, note that the non-Europeans were there. What he also noted, however, was that among the Europeans, German was the language most frequently spoken; more than seventy of the approximately 400 participants, the paper reported, were Germans and Austrians, inspiring a French scholar to call it an "invasion allemande."[20]

Finally, one does begin to observe some new exchange going on between orientalists and what one might call the counter-culture. This was not entirely new either; Friedrich Creuzer had been associated with the romantic counter-cultural world of Heidelberg and it was widely known that his refusal to return the affections of Caroline von Günderode had resulted in her suicide in 1806. Mid-century orientalists, on the other hand, as we have seen, were not such flamboyant characters and largely kept their *Biedermeier* private lives to themselves. One important exception, however, would suggest future directions: in 1836, the Indologist Hermann Brockhaus married the actress Ottilie Wagner, then rather more famous than her composer brother Richard. The elective affinity Indologists later showed for Wagnerism would, in fact, be brokered by Schopenhauerians, mostly importantly Nietzsche's school chum Paul Deussen and Karl Eugen Neumann, son of the Austrian tenor and ardent Wagnerian, Angelo Neumann. There are other linkages; Lou Andreas Salomé, mutual friend of Nietzsche and Deussen and lover to Freud, Rilke, and a host of other counter-cultural figures, was actually married to a Persian philologist, Friedrich Carl Andreas, for more than thirty years. Johannes Paul Achilles Jung – a name that beautifully reflects the Christian-classical world into which he was born in 1842 – studied Hebrew and Arabic at the University of Göttingen and produced an heir (Carl Gustav) whose interests in religion were (a) hardly orthodox and (b) heavily oriental. A few orientalists (like the archaeologist Walter Andrae) were drawn to theosophy or anthroposophy – and participants in the notoriously unorthodox communities of Schwabing, Ascona, and Heidelberg were eager consumers of orientalist knowledge. All of this is to say that while most professional orientalists remained solid citizens, some of the younger generation began to dabble in matters and relationships anything but bourgeois.

[20] L. B., "Der Orientalistenkongreß zu Paris," *National Zeitung*, September 24, 1894, in *B-GSPK*, Rep. 76Vc, Sekt I, Tit XI, Teil VI, Nr. 3, Bd. 2.

The intrusion of new, less European texts and a wider array of artifacts, the onset of imperial politics, the greater inclusiveness of the set of practitioners, and involvement in new cultural contexts, overseas and at home: together these factors tended to destabilize older forms of orientalist knowledge and open the way for new searches for meaning. All of this suggests, once again, something like a return to the romantic era. What permitted this destabilization to occur on a broader stage than that of the romantics, however, was a change in the Reich's cultural institutions and audiences. In the previous chapter, we noted the expansion of the book and periodical market for works on oriental subjects; it should be underlined here that new patrons and the expansion of the semi-academic and popular press gave orientalists new opportunities to circulate their wares and ways to get around the philologists' near monopoly on orientalist knowledge. Having friends or relations in the publishing world in particular was a way to circumvent institutional blockages, and it was used to great effect, for example, by Wilhelm Bousset, brother of the business manager of Gebrauer Schwetschke Verlag, which undertook the publishing of the *Religiongeschichtliche Volksbücher* (see Chapter 6). Publishers like the maverick modernist Eugen Diederichs took interest in neoromantic themes and also sometimes commissioned work that broke with liberal paradigms.[21] Important too are advances in publishing technology, which allowed the faster and much cheaper printing not only of text but also of photographs, central to archaeology's new cachet as well as to the younger generation's love of images and its longing for authenticity.

One of the most revealing manifestations of *Orientalistik*'s newfound confidence and combativeness was a journal on which I have drawn extensively in this chapter: the *Orientalistische Literaturzeitung*. Founded in 1898 in imitation of the classicists' *Philologische Wochenschrift*, the OLZ was a monthly journal whose explicit purpose was to further the study of the Near East, and especially the discipline of its editor, Felix Peiser, Assyriology. Composed largely of trenchant book reviews, written by scholars with many disciplinary homes, the OLZ before the war devoted itself chiefly to criticizing old-fashioned scholarship that failed to keep pace with the explosion of Near Eastern *Kulturgeschichte*. The OLZ reviewed books on all the civilizations of the ancient Near East and over time gradually added coverage of the more modern Middle East, folklore, and East Asia. In addition to scholarly monographs, it also reviewed numerous popular books as well as new editions of older works; it often featured inflammatory lead articles on professional or political subjects such as the obsolescence of secondary-school textbooks, the paucity of resources for orientalist seminars, and the necessity of establishing German scientific outposts in the East. Published by Wolf Peiser – Felix's brother – the journal disapproved of purely positivist oriental studies and championed new ideas; for this reason, it offers especially good insight into the mentality of its mostly younger, mostly "furious," reviewers.

There were, of course, other popular media and contexts in which the Orient could be encountered. The oriental dancers who became fashionable in cabarets – and in

---

[21] The work on the Eugen Diederichs Verlag is exemplary of more studies that might be done here; see, e.g., the essays in *Versammlungsort moderner Geister: Der Kulturverlger Eugen Diederichs und seine Anfänge in Jena, 1904–1914* (Munich, 1996).

Expressionist art – entertained a wide circle of Wilhelmine viewers; Berlin's "Cairo" exhibit of 1896 drew more than two million visitors to Treptow Park and offered for their ethnographic scrutiny more than 400 native Egyptians, Syrians, and Nubians. Circuses, which drew millions of visitors, featured snake charmers and Arabian horses.[22] German and Austrian orientalist paintings had developed rather late – in the 1870s and 1880s rather than the 1830s and 1840s – but by the 1890s, this had become a robust and innovative genre, and sales of oriental carpets were soaring (see Chapter 9). Architects added orientalizing flourishes not only to places of entertainment – such as zoos, cafés, and theaters – but also to private homes, public buildings, and even factories.

The extent to which the "furor" did transform orientalism, and with it Germans' conception of the past, present, and future of East/West relations, is another question that this chapter and the succeeding ones will try to answer. The furor did not, of course, go unopposed – classicists, orthodox theologians (Jewish, Catholic, and Protestant), western-oriented art historians, and also many orientalists were convinced that the new methods and attitudes were reckless and irreverent or at least hubristic and one-sided. Sometimes opposition was self-interested, as in Egyptologist Adolf Erman's resistance to Assyriologists' claims to represent *the* great culture of the ancient Near East; and sometimes, even when self-interested, criticism was warranted to redress the floating of unproven hypotheses, such as many of those aired by Erman's antagonists. Often the positivist generation – as we have seen, convinced that the scholar had to know the material intimately to speak of it – found reprehensible the next generation's longing for synthesis and its exhaustion with painstaking philological practices. Through various forms of institutional shaming – refusing promotions, critical book reviews, failure to engage in debate – the orthodox made it difficult for the radicals to break in; but some did nonetheless, sometimes by means of back channels, sometimes by dint of discoveries that could not be obscured (such as the Mschatta Gate, the Turfan texts, or the Oxyrhynchus papyri), and sometimes by attaching themselves to sympathetic insiders. And their polemics would have a profound effect on *Orientalistik*, classics, and theology in the years before the war.

It is, however, probably most accurate to say that the furor orientalis damaged but did not destroy German philhellenism, orientalist positivism, and orthodox theology; most Christians did not substitute the epic of Gilgamesh for the Old Testament, become Buddhists, or abandon belief in texts and facts. If it lost prestige among academic orientalists, the Old Testament continued to be widely read and passionately defended. The Mschatta Gate was placed in a dark basement; the Turfan expeditions to Central Asia brought back literally tons of material – but the little that was displayed was on view only at the Ethnographic Museum; meanwhile, the Reich began building a grand new museum to showcase the (Greek) Pergamon Altar. Though press converge was extensive, the number of

---

[22] See Lemke, *Staging the Orient: Fin de Siècle Visions/ Representations de l'Orient: imaginaire populaire du fin de siècle* (Beirut, 2004), p. 47; Marline Otte, *Jewish Identities in German Popular Culture, 1890–1933* (New York, 2006), pp. 21–82; Jill Lloyd, *German Expressionism: Primitivism and Modernity* (New Haven, CT, 1991), pp. 89–95.

visitors to the Muhammedan and East Asian exhibitions was disappointingly small. Many of the specialized journals had to be kept afloat with state subsidies. If in 1905, Indologist Leopold von Schroeder proclaimed that Buddha was taking the place of Socrates in the minds of the cultural elite,[23] this was by and large wishful thinking.

Of course, the furor orientalis was not the only force transforming Wilhelmine intellectual life; bombarded by exotic influences and modernizing demands, the art world was undergoing its own break with traditional forms; the same could be said for literature, theater, law, social thought, and philosophy.[24] The initiative for school reform came not from orientalists, but from nationalists and pragmatists, from natural scientists and social reformers – and in fact, even the usually hotheaded *OLZ* was ambivalent about school reform, criticizing the exclusive and life-killing teaching of classics, but also arguing against the idolizing of "a purely technological paradise ... where the motto 'do it, don't know it' absolutely rules."[25] Women, Catholics, and Jews, so long shut out of participation in most of the Reich's cultural institutions, were now demanding the right to speak and be taken seriously. The socialist parties were flourishing, but so too were the industrialists. All of these modernist and/or modernizing ventures contributed to the decentering of classical aesthetics and *Kulturprotestantismus* in Wilhelmine intellectual and institutional cultures. But none of them were unmitigated successes, even in the Weimar era, and many of these causes lost ground (to say the least) in the Nazi era. And in this respect, the furious orientalists were part of a movement whose full realization we may not, even now, have seen.

RETURN TO DIFFUSIONISM, OR THE PROBLEM OF UNIVERSALISM IN A PHILOLOGICAL CULTURE

The furor orientalis was an interdisciplinary phenomenon, generated across and between the disciplines of theology, classics, and *Orientalistik* proper. It was also, at least to some extent, an international phenomenon, enabled by the flood of new oriental materials, school reform pressures, and the cultural politics of the "open door." In Britain, France, and the United States, many scholars also drew upon anthropological comparisons to make sense of these new materials, resulting in methodologically pathbreaking studies like Numa Denis Fustel de Coulanges's *La cité antique* (1864), William Robertson Smith's *Kinship and Marriage in Early Arabia* (1885), and James George Frazer's *The Golden Bough* (1890). In the German-speaking world, there were some early efforts in this direction, such as the work of Adalbert Kuhn and Wilhelm Mannhardt in the 1850s–1870s, and J. J. Bachofen's *Mutterrecht* (1861), but text-centered German humanists had never found material and universal explanations for the origins of cultural or religious phenomena particularly useful or convincing. For those like Wellhausen who wanted a pseudo-evolutionary scheme, some form of Hegelian thought

---

[23] Schroeder, "Buddha und unsere Zeit" [1905], in idem, *Reden und Aufsätze*, pp. 216–17.

[24] See the essays in Suzanne Marchand and David Lindenfeld, eds., *Germany at the Fin de Siècle: Culture, Politics and Ideas* (Baton Rouge, LA, 2004).

[25] [Peiser], "Alma technica militans," in *OLZ* 3 (1900): 44–5.

usually sufficed. It was not that Germany lacked anthropologists – of both the cultural and the physical sort; and some of them, such as Adolf Bastian, did attempt synthetic treatments of human development. But as Andrew Zimmermann has argued, German anthropologists for the most part considered themselves entitled to speak only about the "natural" peoples, and not the "historical" ones, who remained, of course, the preserve of the humanists.[26] And when, in the 1890s, cultural Darwinism began to crack under the weight of new evidence, the Germans found it rather easy to abandon this form of universalist thinking.

As Alfred Kelly pointed out long ago, one of the reasons for the weak reception of cultural Darwinism in German academe was that Darwinism was heavily associated with left-wing or even socialist thought, something anathema to most German mandarins.[27] But the Herderian-Humboldtian tradition was already one that favored the appreciation of cultural diversity and one that had developed linguistic means of intercultural linking and stacking before the era of evolutionary thinking set it. After the death of Wilhelm von Humboldt and the rise to prominence of Franz Bopp, Indo-Germanic linguistics in particular seemed the proper, *wissenschaftlich* way to ground comparisons and to suggest historical relationships. There were comparativists in *Semitistik* – but even the most wide-ranging of these, Theodor Benfey, thought Semitic languages more or less irrelevant for the development of comparative linguistics – and East Asian, Amerindian, and African languages even more so.[28] Another comparativist, Hans Conon von der Gabelentz (1808–74), was rumored to know eighty languages; his son Georg started with Chinese at age seventeen and actually got an academic job (unlike his father) at the University of Leipzig in 1876; but his work was little read outside Far Eastern studies. Comparativism went on, that is to say, long after Bopp's death, but usually remained within the Indo-Germanic world. In the meantime, intellectual exchange across rising linguistic boundaries virtually ceased. This made it even more difficult for anthropologists to make universalizing claims about human history and the fin de siècle's critiques of evolutionary *Kulturgeschichte* easy for most humanists to accept.

Space does not permit a full investigation here of the breakdown of liberal-universalist forms of thought, but fortunately historians of anthropology have already done marvelous work here. Some years ago, Woodruff Smith called our attention to what he called "The Diffusionist Revolt," spearheaded by the Leipzig geographer Friedrich Ratzel. For Ratzel, physical similarities between artifacts were proof of the migration of peoples and culture was, in essence, a collection of specific traits.[29] Ratzelian diffusionism made it possible to turn material evidence into history – but it also skirted several important questions, such as how many traits or artifacts constitute a culture? What place and meaning do specific traits have within cultures? As Smith contends, Ratzel's

---

[26] Andrew Zimmermann, *Anthropology and Antihumanism in Imperial Germany* (Chicago, IL, 2001).

[27] Alfred Kelly, *The Descent of Darwin: The Popularization of Darwin in Germany, 1860–1914* (Chapel Hill, NC, 1981).

[28] Benfey, *Geschichte der Sprachwissenschaft und orientalischen Philologie in Deutschland* (Munich, 1869), p. 420.

[29] Woodruff D. Smith, *Politics and the Sciences of Culture in Germany, 1840–1920* (Oxford, 1991), pp. 140–61.

work – beginning with his *Anthropo-Geographie* (1882) – was highly influential, not just for ethnographers, but for a wide variety of cultural scientists. German orientalists found diffusionism useful for two particularly important reasons. Promising to throw light on the history of world religions and of the migration of peoples, it offered them a means to demonstrate cultural contact using both linguistic and material evidence; and it gave them the chance to play the "higher antiquity" card against partisans of Rome, Greece, and as we shall see, of ancient Israel as well.

For orientalists, no matter how secularized their study, ethnography was most important for the light it might throw on the history of world religions. By the 1880s, a number of British and French scholars favored a sub-Darwinian account of the evolution of religion that traced its development from animism, to polytheism, and then to the most civilized form, monotheism. Wellhausen had managed to make this trajectory fit the history of the Israelites, but this theory had never found wide acclaim in German universities, perhaps because romantic declensionism still coursed so powerfully underneath German liberal positivist worldviews, or perhaps because radicals – like Friedrich Engels – who might have embraced such a view were not permitted to teach at these institutions. Thus, German scholars rejected the Humean notion that all religions had evolved from primeval forms of animism, and welcomed the Scottish ethnographer Andrew Lang's insistence that the notion was insulting to "lower" cultures and out of step with the mounting ethnographic evidence.[30] Lang, who, not incidentally, had recently re-embraced his own childhood faith, claimed that monotheism was much more prevalent and much more "natural"; and many of the German neoromantics, for their own reasons, were inclined to agree.

It is not surprising that it would be in the context of an appreciation of Bopp that German philologists like Richard Harder would describe their resistance to English universalism. In 1942, Harder looked back to the previous mid-century's "equating-frenzy" and described Germandom's subsequent revulsion to it:

Especially consequential [in the years after Bopp's *Comparative Grammar*, the era of Müller and Kuhn] was the extension of comparisons to the so-called primitives. It was a great surprise that many customs and institutions of Indo-Germanic protohistory were found to have apparent parallels in the cultures of primitive peoples. It seemed to prove the existence of a fundamental stock of common human traits. The vastness of this material flowing in was so impressive that even today a number of scholars, especially the Anglo-Saxons, are still of this opinion. Out of the difficult art of comparison arose, often, a colossal drawing of parallels. In the course of this, the fact was often obscured that, despite clever operations, the "paralleling" among the Indogerman peoples had already been given a historical foundation in earlier proofs of linguistic and thus ethnic relationship. The indiscriminate equating-frenzy unleashed a reaction, especially among German scholars, which ended in the passionate rejection of all comparisons.[31]

---

[30] George W. Stocking, Jr., *After Tylor: British Social Anthropology, 1888–1951* (Madison, WI, 1995), on diffusionism, pp. 179–232; on Lang, pp. 53–61.

[31] Richard Harder, "Franz Bopp und die Indogermanistik," in *Nationalsozialistische Monatsheften (Sonderdruck)* 152/153 (1942): 8–9.

Here, Harder (trained as a classicist) represents the culmination of a process of narrowing that began with Schlegel and Bopp, but was still incomplete in the 1890s. But his comments nicely reflect the fin de siècle's sense that what mattered were comparisons and parallels *within* and not *beyond* one's family tree. Diffusionist language was useful in defining the tasks of the patriotic prehistorian or orientalist and in demonstrating the utility of scholarship to the nation, even if that scholarship focused on the early history of the Persians or the *ur*-religion of the Vedas. Moreover, scholars really did believe that finding a *Volk*'s roots would offer insight into its destiny. The Germans were by no means the only group seeking their ancestral origins or their racial identity, but perhaps the swiftness of the new state's rise in the international firmament, coupled with continuing anxieties about what "Germanness" meant, resulted in peculiarly deep cultural investment in these quests. Or perhaps this deep cultural investment was simply a reflection of the greater density of linguistic specialists here, and Germandom's continuing focus on the textual traditions of the ancient world. In any event, cultural Darwinism – according to which nature prompted all cultures to develop similar institutions and to pass through the same stages, though at different moments in historical time – was never easy to square with the Germans' interests, passions, or scholarly traditions, and it is not too surprising that the moment for it passed rather quickly in favor of a return to more relevant, useful, and respectable ideas.

The diffusionist cause was helped by the fact that the comparativists were now dying (Wilhelm Mannhardt in 1880, Adalbert Kuhn in 1881, Max Müller in 1900, and Adolf Bastian in 1905), and that few of them had kept up with the further progress of the Second Oriental Renaissance. The increasingly out-of-date scholarship of ex-patriot Max Müller had a particularly powerful discouraging effect on German scholars. Even Leopold von Schroeder, himself an admirer of much of Müller's work, testified to German philologists' increasing revulsion toward comparativism in an elegy for Müller in 1900: "If it happened that serious scholars soon did not want to hear anything more about comparative mythology . . . then Max Müller, with his wide-ranging-dilettantish style of treating the subject, bears a large part of the blame."[32] An anonymous announcement of the launching of the important new journal, *Archiv für Religionswissenschaft*, described its endeavors accurately as a "[r]eaction against the Max Müller-Kuhn sort of comparative study of religions," resulting chiefly from that school's "lack of a sense of history and [its] tendency to deduce [its claims] from a few petitiones principii, which soon prove themselves untenable."[33] This was no way to do science or to treat faith.

The reaction to comparativism in the philological fields was in many ways part of the wider discussion of the applicability of natural scientific conceptions and laws to the *Geisteswissenschaften*.[34] The vehemence of the debate, as well as its practical consequences for institutional development, was reflected in the Berlin philosophical faculty's passionate rejection of Kurt Breysig's attempt to found a

---

[32] Leopold von Schroeder, "Max Müller" [1900], in idem, *Reden und Aufsätze*, p. 304.
[33] *OLZ* 1 (1898): 159–60.
[34] See, e.g., Roger Chickering, *Karl Lamprecht: A German Academic Life (1856–1915)* (NJ, 1993).

study for comparative history at the University of Berlin in 1909. Despite Breysig's insistence that such an institute would be enormously beneficial for colonial praxis and despite the Prussian Cultural Ministry's desire to pursue the plan, the faculty vociferously rejected the proposal. The official memorandum was written by none other than Eduard Meyer, who highlighted the faculty's fears that students of comparative history – which for Breysig included a heavy dose of ethnography – would be "half-educated" and fail to develop proper philological skills. Anthropology was all very nice, they wrote, but the study of "cultureless prehistorical peoples" could not be combined with the study of historical peoples, whose writings the scholar had to know at first hand.[35]

Prussian scholars were a bit more appreciative of the work of James George Frazer – though *The Golden Bough*, hugely popular in England, is strikingly little cited in the German literature. Though Frazer himself was made a corresponding member of the Prussian Academy of Sciences in 1911, his acceptance was tempered with a formal critique of his habit of comparing *Natur- and Kulturvölker*. The Academy chastised Frazer's less careful disciples, who saw totemism "as the primeval form of religious conceptions" but were glad of Frazer's clarification ". . . that true Totemism is only found in the brown and black races of South Africa, the South Seas and North America, and that by contrast, this phenomena does not present itself in the white and yellow races of Europe and Asia." *The Golden Bough*, noted the document, signed by Hermann Diels, Alexander Conze, Eduard Meyer, and Adolf von Harnack, among others, was not really convincing, though it might contain useful folkloric material that could be employed, for example, to illuminate "a series of superstitious survivals in the Old Testament. . . ."[36] Frazer's perpetual, if indirect references to the New Testament throughout his text were pointedly not mentioned by the German academics. When, at the end of his long life, Theodor Mommsen circulated a questionnaire to several of his expert friends, inquiring about oldest penal codes of the cultured peoples, Julius Wellhausen responded that he thought the question should be answered historically rather than anthropologically: "It seems to me that this [subject] can be treated without invoking Frazer. . . ."[37] And in general, "ohne Frazer" was the order of the day.[38]

But this left German scholars with a problem. The texts, inscriptions, and artifacts left behind by ancient cultures very often *did* look alike, in one way or another; similar phenomena, like dying and rising gods, fertility cults, or dragon-slaying heroes did recur, but it was not always possible to document the means by which symbols, ideas, or customs were transferred. In a purely historicist world,

---

[35] See the documents contained in B-GSPK, I, 76Va, Sekt 2, Tit X, Nr. 182, vol. I, including Breysig, "Denkschrift über die Begründung eines Seminars für vergleichende Geschichtsforschung an der Universität Berlin" (May 12, 1907); Philosophical faculty to Cultural Ministry, February 27, 1909, and "Separatvotum der Vertreter der Staatswissenschaften," February 27, 1909.

[36] William Calder III and Dietrich Ehlers, "The German Reception of J. G. Frazer: An Unpublished Document," in Calder, ed., *Men in Their Books: Studies in the Modern History of Classical Scholarship*, eds. John P. Harris and R. Scott Smith (Zürich, 1998), pp. 199–201.

[37] Wellhausen to Mommsen, February 24, 1899, in Bammel, "Judentum, Christentum und Heidentum," p. 251.

[38] Though a French translation of *The Golden Bough* was produced between 1903 and 1911, there appears to have been no German edition until a brief version was published in 1928.

one did not explain (or perhaps even acknowledge) cultural parallels across linguistic lines. But the "furious" generation did not want to tarry in positivist particularism, for they thought they now had the materials and expertise to tackle big questions. The biggest of these was the one ethnographers had failed to answer, classicists had ignored, and positivist orientalists had sidelined since the 1820s: that was, of course, Creuzer's classic question, the question of the geographical origins of all myths, religions, and symbols, or, put differently, the question of the West's cultural dependence on the East.

Importantly, however, Creuzer's classic question was now being posed in a new context, a context in which there were many more accessible oriental texts and many more scholars able to read them. The churches had virtually no power anymore to censor the book market or purge the university faculties. And in classics, *Orientalistik*, theology, and in anthropology itself, the declining tendency to privilege Christianity (and Judaism) opened the way for what one might call more relativist forms of historical study. Enlightened radicals had suggested that Christianity was, so far as ethical behavior went, actually inferior to various forms of paganism. Over the course of the nineteenth century, this inflammatory critique had been reiterated in various ways, especially with respect to the events and prescriptions in the Old Testament. Mid-century secularizers had often praised Greek philosophy for its ethical virtues and even for its quasi-monotheistic tendencies, but by the 1880s, it was possible to extend these courtesies to Vedic, Assyrian, or Buddhist beliefs and customs – though doing so still made one a recognizable iconoclast. As scholars began to interpret texts in indigenous terms too, dates for oriental achievements tended to be pushed backward into the still deeper past. All of this meant that by the fin de siècle, it was easier to entertain the idea that there might be such a thing as, to cite the title of one well-known work, *Eine Mithrasliturgie*, or some point returning to the *Corpus Hermeticum*.[39] Perhaps the *Symbolik* had something to teach after all.

One of the first scholars to suggest this openly was not an orientalist, but an unconventional classicist, Otto Gruppe. In 1887, Gruppe published (with B. G. Teubner Verlag) a long study of the relations between Greek rituals and myths and oriental religions that signaled the opening of a new, neoromantic, and one might say multicultural series of inquiries. In the book's opening pages, the young classicist explicitly invoked Friedrich Creuzer as a flawed, but insightful pioneer in the still incomplete scientific interpretation of myths. Creuzer's picture of Greek dependence on Indian and Persian religious ideas was, Gruppe claimed, riddled with errors – but only because the sources available to him were so limited and misleading. Regrettably, Creuzer had retreated from the fray as evidence and decipherments in the wake of the publication of the *Symbolik* undermined his big claims; but, Gruppe claimed, he should have stuck to at least some of his guns. Creuzer's emphasis on the shared culture of the Orient and Hellas was hugely

---

[39] Albrecht Dieterich was the author of *Eine Mithrasliturgie* (published by B. G. Teubner in Leipzig in 1903). On Dieterich and the revival of the Hermetic texts, see Marchand, "From Liberalism to Neoromanticism: Albrecht Dieterich, Richard Reitzenstein and the Religious Turn in Fin de Siècle German Classical Studies," in *Out of Arcadia* (British Institute of Classical Studies Supplement, 79, 2003), ed. Martin Ruehl and Ingo Gildenhard (London, 2003), pp. 129–60.

significant, as was too his overcoming of eighteenth-century suppositions "that mythology is a priestly deception or a falsification of history." Creuzer had, for the first time, Gruppe argued, "penetrated the thought-patterns of the myth-making, prehistorical age," and this was precisely the sort of sympathetic, hermeneutic task to which researchers now needed to return.[40] Gruppe confessed his own limitations – he did not know all the relevant languages and found it difficult to understand oriental literature; he openly admitted he feared being written off as a dilettante. But he was hopeful, he wrote, in a sentence that would have caused Karl Lachmann considerable pain, "that the overall usefulness of the publication will be greater than its overall damage."[41] It was time to be daring.

To be daring meant, here, not only to return to Creuzer's questions but also to move beyond pure philological inquiry. Gruppe indeed was already describing his "expanded" method as "religious-historical," which meant, he explained, adding to the study of texts the study of rituals. For Gruppe, this still meant the study of rituals as they appeared in texts (and mostly Greek ones, at that); he did not rely on ethnographic or archaeological material. But Gruppe did draw on newer Egyptological and Assyriological publications, and perhaps most importantly, he incorporated a vast number of Hellenistic Greek sources, many of them of the sort the previous generation would have deemed untrustworthy or opaque. He did so to underline the point that Greek mythology and philosophy were part of the religious landscape of the eastern Mediterranean, not just literary confections created by a thoroughly rational culture. The main task of the book, Gruppe insisted, was neither to show that the Greeks were unlike all others nor to show that they were just like the others, but rather to demonstrate "that the relationship between Greek and oriental cults and myths does not rest on accidental transmission, but on the existence of an unbroken and shared cultural community. . . ."[42] The return to Creuzer was to be by way of expanded historicism, not by way of psychological or anthropological universals.

Though Gruppe did not use it, included in this expanded historicism was increasingly material culture. The results of archaeological treasure trawls had been filling German museum basements for some time, and gradually they began to interest cultural historians. As New Testament scholars began to investigate the life-world of Jesus, they were drawn to archaeological material such as *ostraca* (potsherds), upon which common people had inscribed pious and not-so-pious remarks. After the recovery of so much material from the rubbish mounds of Oxyrhynchus, wrote Adolf Deissmann, the conventional picture of Jesus world, based on elite Roman sources, would have to change; for Europeans now had access to "countless bits of evidence about individuals from the middle and lower classes . . . documents that render popular dialect and documents that illustrate the little affairs of the little people."[43] All of this offered a much deeper and richer

---

[40] Otto Gruppe, *Die griechischen Culte und Mythen in ihren Beziehungen zu den orientalischen Religionen*, vol. I (Leipzig, 1887), p. 37 (both quotations).

[41] Ibid., p. viii, ix.

[42] Ibid., p. vi.

[43] Deissmann, *Licht vom Osten: Das Neue ed: hel-le-nisfischTestament und die neuentdeckten Texte aus dem hellenistisch-römischen Welt* (Tübingen, 1908), pp. 4–5, quotation p. 5.

picture of the world in which Christ and his disciples lived and worked. Deissmann was confident that archaeology would bear out the gospels; others were not so sure. What was certain, however, was that the "big digs" of the fin de siècle would turn up plenty of previously unknown material and that orientalists as well as theologians and classicists after Gruppe would have to take it into account.

Though paying jobs remained scarce, as their public stature grew, those trained to excavate and interpret artifacts exuded greater confidence and a greater willingness to criticize their teachers and colleagues. The fieldworkers took on the stay-at-home philologists, who dealt in mere words; the oriental specialists took on their nearest rivals (and in many cases their teachers and institutional superiors), the classical archaeologists. Writing to the *OLZ* from Smyrna in 1909, one orientalist claimed that it was high time classical archaeologists recognized that the era of their tutelage was over. Thanks to the flood of recent Near Eastern finds, "suddenly the roles are reversed: the teachers must now go back to school with the 'kids'."[44] Naturally, the classical archaeologists did not see the need for reeducation in the same terms; but more or less grudgingly, in an era that included Schliemann's Troy excavations, Arthur Evans' sensational Cretan dig, and Flinders Petrie's work in Egypt and Palestine, they came to accept the relevance of Near Eastern finds for their own field of study – though this did not occur swiftly or completely enough to satisfy many orientalist "kids."

There were risks involved in the elevation of material culture and the relaxing of philological discipline; the materials introduced to prove racial linkages were particularly subject to manipulation and abuse. But there were also big advantages in the eyes of contemporaries to using style, symbolism, and race to fill in the gaps in eastern history left by the fragmentary textual record. One could use existing evidence to create maps that demonstrated cultural (and/or racial) migrations, as did the Germanic prehistorian Gustav Kossinna, or as a means to trace the origins of myth-fragments or scientific ideas back to their original homes, as did the Assyriologist Hugo Winckler. The combination of a diffusionist mentality and the improved evidentiary status of artifacts made for the possibility of a much more global and democratic – but also a much less stable and more easily manipulated – cultural history of the ancient world.

Diffusionism allowed orientalists to make claims that anticipate those made regularly in today's world history textbooks. It allowed them to argue, for example, that modern western culture owes debts to both Greek philosophy and to Chinese gunpowder, to Roman law and Indian mathematics, to Christian ethics and Islamic design. But sometimes the argument could go further too, as in Georg Jacob's 1902 lecture "Eastern Cultural Elements in the West" in which the Turkish specialist not only made these claims but also insisted that oriental influences ran deeper than did classical ones: "While Hellenism never penetrated into the [life of] the people ... but essentially passed its existence in the confines of the school, the compass, for example, directly benefited the whole seafaring population; every soldier, at least, learns the advantages of explosives, and writing and printing can be seen as the common property of the nation."[45] The Orient's influence, Jacob

---

[44] E. Brandenburg, "Klein-Asiatische Untersuchungen III," in *OLZ* 12 (1909); 100.
[45] Georg Jacob, *Östliche Kulturelemente im Abendland* (Berlin, 1902), pp. 23–4.

was claiming, is deeper and more meaningful. Hellenism is a superficial phenomenon; orientalism lasts.

The new diffusionist history also permitted orientalists to argue, as did Jacob in the conclusion to his lecture, that in dispensing with this narrow, classicizing history, they would be preparing the way for a new, scientific, and political future:

Humanism, which once meant a considerable widening of the intellectual horizon, has become a petrified classicism.... We hope, however ... that our science ... once certain external obstacles which have in recent years impeded its rise have been removed, will be called too to play a prominent role in emancipating humanity from a one-sided worldview and in the restitution of humanity's appreciation of the beautiful in its vast multiplicity. And for the nations who cultivate [this science], practical achievements will go hand in hand with intellectual ones, since only the systematic reduction of [the diversity of] earlier periods has clouded our vision of the universal, has led us to abandon the world to other peoples and has nourished the kind of German naïveté whose unfortunate consequences have not yet today been overcome.[46]

To those who understood and appreciated the multiplicity of past and especially ancient civilizations would belong the non-scholastic, post-humanist future, and some "practical" goodies as well.

As Woodruff Smith wisely observed, there is an underlying elective affinity between diffusionism and procolonial politics, one observable in Ratzel as in Jacob, in Kossinna, and in Strzygowski (see Chapter 9)[47]; for emphasizing the spread of ideas from center to periphery offers the mother country the opportunity to advertise the benevolence of exporting its culture to its colonies. Diffusionism, too, was well-suited to Germany's pursuit of "peaceful penetration" in the Ottoman Empire and elsewhere, where the propagandists made much of the Germans' supposedly less invasive and more culturally sensitive overseas policies. But, of course, the liberal generation had its own justifications for imperialism and for Eurocentric hubris, as numerous studies of British and French anthropology have shown. And we should keep in mind that the orientalists most directly involved in colonial matters were those who specialized in the study of the Islamic world and the study of East Asia; and they tended to be less "furious" than the Assyriologists, Indologists, and Persian specialists surveyed in this chapter and the two to follow. Diffusionism was, first and foremost, a means to reopen Creuzerian questions and to undermine old classicist or orthodox Christian worldviews; it flourished less as the result of new externalist political ambitions and influences than as the result of a new generation's desires and opportunities to exploit their specialized knowledge for domestic, personal, professional, and they would have strenuously argued, scientific, national, and cultural gains.

German historicism and the preference for diffusionist interpretations had some benefits; it lent itself, in general, to a less presentist approach and to fewer speculations on the nature of "the primitive mind." Because the emphasis remained on understanding cultures in their contexts, and through their own

---

[46] Ibid., p. 24.
[47] Smith, *Politics and the Sciences of Culture*, pp. 151–4; Kossinna and Strzygowski were more interested in German expansionism in eastern and central Europe than in colonization overseas.

languages, it was often a less condescending method than the attempt to compare what Claude Levi-Strauss many years later called "hot" and "cold" cultures.[48] But the problem of parallels continued to create controversies – about the Greekness of New Testament ideas, for example, or the origins of the basilica form – and these seemed soluble only by plunging further backward in time and further eastward in space. The race was on to find the earliest, most original culture – something that led to a diminution of interest in better known and more accessible cultures like Egypt, Greece, and, of course, ancient Israel. For those trekking through Indo-German territory, the trail usually led back to Vedic India. This had its rewards and also its dangers (see Chapter 7). But after the mid-century, there was another contender for *ur*-cultural fame, a contender with explosive new texts and objects to offer, and one with the power to up-end and supplant the Hebraic narration that still formed the backbone of ancient Near Eastern history: Assyria.

PANBABYLONISM: AN ASSYRIOLOGICAL REVOLT AND ITS CULTURAL CONSEQUENCES

Like the more general accounts offered earlier in this chapter, this story begins with a transition from the positivist generation to the "furious" one – though, given the brief time between the decipherment of cuneiform and the emergence of the post-liberal generation, this time frame is somewhat foreshortened compared, for example, to Egyptology or Indology. The exemplary member of the positivist generation must perforce be the one great mid-century German Assyriologist who stayed in Germany (Julius Oppert and Fritz Hommel having left), Eberhard Schrader, whom we met in Chapter 4. Schrader was first and foremost a linguist, but he did not conceal his conviction that cuneiform reading was chiefly of interest to those wishing to better understand the Old Testament, as the title and content of his collection of inscriptions, *Die Keilinschriften und das Alte Testament*, shows. But, like so many members of this positivist generation, Schrader was rather hesitant to popularize or generalize his findings. Not so his students, a group which included Friedrich Delitzsch, Alfred Jeremias, Peter Jensen, and Hugo Winckler, all now obscure scholars, but once at the eye of the Assyriological storm.

More than perhaps any other orientalist sub-discipline, Assyriology was transformed by the developments of the fin de siècle. In the 1870s, George Smith's flood tablets had inspired a first wave of scholarly interest in cuneiform texts. But a more important series of inquires began after 1886, when a large group of tablets was found in Egypt, which – once accepted as authentic – would open new vistas on the history of the ancient Near East. The Tell el Amarna letters, as these tablets came to be called, would give Asssyriologists all the more reason to underscore both the historical and the biblical importance of their field, for, written in cuneiform, the documents demonstrated clearly that Assyrian influence had been extensive and long-lasting, even as far west as Egypt. In 1899, the Deutsch-Orient Gesellschaft managed to get permission from the Otto-man authorities to dig at Babylon, and with some fanfare, and high expectations,

[48] See Claude Levi-Strauss, *Tristes tropiques* (Paris, 1955).

a German team commenced what would be a fifteen-year excavation. The Germans were not alone in pursuing Mesopotamian artifacts; in 1901, a French team working at Susa uncovered the Code of Hammurabi, which showed striking similarities to the Law of the Torah. In museum basements and cramped offices, a small number of European and American Assyriologists worked hard to interpret these new materials, discovering in them extremely important new sources for the history of science, mythology, and theology. Especially as many of the texts predated their Greek or in some cases, Egyptian equivalents, it seemed to many of these scholars that they were laying the foundations for the wholesale rewriting of ancient cultural history. And yet, it would take Friedrich Delitzsch's hugely controversial "Babel und die Bibel" lectures of 1902–4 to put Assyria on the public stage.

The "Babel-Bibel Streit" is one of the few well-known episodes in the history of *Orientalistik*; less well understood is the broader inter- and intradisciplinary context from which this controversy arose. If it was the question of biblical parallels that aroused popular interest in (and disdain for) Delitzsch's Assyriological work, it should be noted that in academic circles, discussions about Babylonian inventions ranged far beyond theology. Assyriologists played a central role in debates over the origins of the natural sciences, in discussions of proper historical and philological method, and in anthropological arguments about the origins of monotheism. Several novels set in the ancient Near East – Alfred Döblin's *Babylonische Wandrung* and Thomas Mann's *Joseph* novels – drew heavily on materials generated in the course of these debates, and reflect the widespread sense many shared that the once familiar biblical world had been swallowed up by an Orient that was deeper and more strange.[49] Indeed, understanding the movement that came to be caricatured as "Panbabylonism" may even help us to better understand that most famous of excurses on the non-Judaic origins of the Old Testament, Freud's *Moses and Monotheism*.

Panbabylonism was a quintessential expression of the furor orientalis; it was produced not by Delitzsch alone or even most importantly, but by a generation of slightly younger Assyriologists who dedicated themselves to the field in the 1880s and 1890s, the period in which the field's ambitions and source materials were expanding, but being held in check by older orientalists and Old Testament scholars. The individuals who fit this profile include Fritz Hommel, Hugo Winckler, Felix Peiser, Eduard Stucken, Peter Jensen, Alfred Jeremias, Ferdinand Bork, and the less combative Heinrich Zimmern and Bruno Meissner – though this was never an entirely cohesive group.[50]

Although Delitzsch drew the most public attention – and criticism – to the group in his "Babel" lectures, the real leader of this pack was Hugo Winckler, a figure almost totally forgotten today except for his role in unearthing Hittite civilization

---

[49] One of the major sources for Mann was Jeremias's *Das Alte Testament im Lichte des alte Orients*, originally published in the heat of the Babel-Bibel Streit (1904), and in its fourth edition (1930) when Mann read it. See Thomas Mann, *Briefe: Thomas Mann*, vol. II, 1937–47, ed. Erika Mann (Frankfurt, 1962), p. 25.

[50] Hommel and Jeremias, e.g., as convinced Christians, were opposed to the more radical implications of the work of Winckler and Jensen. See Fritz Hommel, *Die altorientalischen Denkmäler und das Alte Testament* (Berlin, 2nd ed., 1903).

by way of his excavations at Boghazkoi (ancient Hattusa) beginning in 1906.[51] Winckler was at work developing his ideas before Delitzsch took the podium in Berlin, and contemporary commentators – including his friends at the *OLZ* – knew it was he, and not Delitzsch, who was leading the campaign to give Babylonian culture its historical due. The volume, importance, and sheer chutzpah of Winckler's work argue for the need for an in-depth scholarly study; but for now, a few paragraphs will have to suffice. We will then survey the work of some of his best friends and co-conspirators, Eduard Stucken and Peter Jensen. Their efforts testify to the inter-relatedness of themes spelled out above: the tendency to adopt a winner-takes-all approach to the study of cultural origins; the preference for oriental paganism over the more established cultures of the book; and a generational critique of positivist practices.

Hugo Winckler was, like Adolf Erman, a discontented and not particularly distinguished Gymnasium student, but his work in classical languages was strong enough to encourage him to go to the University of Berlin in 1881, at age eighteen, to study philology. Inspired by Schrader, Winckler threw himself into the study of cuneiform. Unlike Schrader and Delitzsch, Winckler did not have theological training; in fact, he was one of orientalism's few forthright atheists. Also unlike these two successful philologists, Winckler did not take to the study of pure grammar and began inventing plans to rethink the history of the eastern Mediterranean. His mentors disapproved of his "unmethodical" studies; perhaps they also disapproved of what Ludwig Curtius later described as his "petty bourgeois mannerisms."[52] In any event, by the late 1880s, Winckler had already developed deep resentments against the humanist establishment and the strident style that would characterize his entire *oeuvre*.

Getting his contemporaries to rethink their ancient history, he claimed in a study of ancient oriental history published in 1889, was tantamount to forcing a conversion, and despite the gradual acceptance of some of his ideas, Winckler would continue to treat the subject as one that required an evangelist. The "religion" from which Winckler had to convert his audience was not so much Christianity but the worship of classical civilizations, and he dedicated his efforts to encouraging the younger generation to abandon shopworn humanistic dogmas:

May these lines be useful to those who, in beginning to take part in the study of antiquity, can get it into their heads that only philistines can look down their noses at the ancient Orient, from which they have taken all high culture's achievements and that antiquity cannot be understood when one only understands a small fragment of it; may it finally be understood on all sides that a wall between classical antiquity and the "barbarians" should not exist for researchers, just as one never existed for the cultural and spiritual life of both areas.[53]

---

[51] Kurt Bittel, *Hattusha: The Capital of the Hittites* (New York, 1970), pp. 8–10.

[52] Alfred Jeremias, "Hugo Winckler: Gedächtnisrede," in *Hugo Winckler: Zwei Gedächtnisreden in der vorderasiatischen Gesellschaft zu Berlin, Mitteilungen der vorderasiatischen Gesellschaft* 20 (1915): 3–8; Ludwig Curtius, *Deutsche und antike Welt: Lebenserinnerungen* (Stuttgart, 1958), p. 202.

[53] Hugo Winckler, *Untersuchungen zur altorientalischen Geschichte* (Leipzig, 1889), pp. v, ix.

Here, in embryo, was perhaps the most influential and insightful part of the Panbabylonists' program, that is to say, their insistence on the necessity of understanding the ancient Near Eastern world as a whole without linguistic barriers and philhellenic (or orthodox Jewish and Christian) prejudices. This was something their contemporaries and even many of their critics eventually agreed was a useful perspective – though it was also one, given the power of academic traditions, that was never so easy to adopt in practice as to defend in theory.

Where Winckler's conception ran into much more severe difficulties was in its insistence on the dominant, and indeed, the original and all-pervasive role of things Babylonian in this Near Eastern cultural whole. Though Winckler emphasized the unified nature of the pre-biblical Orient, for his purposes, it was insufficient to treat the interaction between these cultures or describe the better documented but much later Assyrian Empire, where cultural mixing was known to have occurred. Rather, it was crucial for Winckler himself and his school to show that Assyrian ideas were already present in ancient Babylon, which was much more autonomous (and according to Schrader's view, less Semitic) than the weaker empires of the Neo-Assyrian and Seleucid eras – where too Greek scientific ideas were known to have been present. It was even more urgent to show that Babylonian gods and myths predated Egyptian or Old Testament equivalents.[54] Winckler might have spoken often of the need to break down "walls" between cultural histories, but at the end of the day, he too was not able to move past questions of origination and longings for cultural purity. He too had his favorite people, whose attraction stemmed largely from their primeval originality – or at least the fact that no one knew from whence *they* had borrowed their cultural goods.[55]

The diffusionist commitments of the group were neither accidental nor inconsequential; it would not have been terribly controversial to argue that Babylonian culture had simply contributed to Near Eastern development nor would such a position have justified the kind of institutional and cultural revolution the young Assyriologists wanted to make. To be fair, they did think that the evidence justified their claims and they were certainly right that others were reluctant to dispense with their old chronologies and source materials. Moreover, Babylon was certainly not the only culture lobbying for its day in the sun, and in an era of intense interdisciplinary competition, it is perhaps natural that the lobbyists put their case as forcefully as possible. In 1903, the theologian Karl Budde recalled that just a year or two earlier, he had received a manuscript claiming that everything in the Hebrew Bible was derived from Egyptian mythology. Not long before that, he had reviewed a manuscript in which the author insisted that the origins of Old Testament legends lay in ancient Irish folkore; a defender of more orthodox views, Budde thought Assyriological attempts to "scoop" the Bible were more of the same hocus-pocus.[56] Similarly, the French scholar Adolphe Lods attributed

---

[54] See, e.g., Alfred Jeremias, *Die Panbabylonisten: Der alte Orient und die ägyptische Religion*, in *Im Kampfe um den alten Orient* 1 (Leipzig, 1907).

[55] More than the other Panbabylonists, Winckler was a fan of race theory, and incorporated it frequently into his work. See, e.g., Hugo Winckler, "Die Völker Vorderasiens," in *Der alte Orient* 1 (1900): 6.

[56] Karl Budde, *Das Alte Testament und die Ausgrabungen: Ein Beitrag zum Streit um Babel und Bibel* (Giessen, 2nd ed., 1903), pp. 22–3.

Assyriology's enthusiasm to the discipline's youth and recalled that Egyptology had once claimed that "the civilizations of Thebes and Memphis could explain everything, in particular the religion of Israel.... Today Babylon replaces Egypt. Tomorrow – as all the signs show – it will be the inscriptions ... of South Arabia."[57] The Indologists too were seeking to claim ancient Indian origins for numerous Judeo-Christian ideas. But the Assyriologists could claim the newest and the most sensational finds, and they possessed a near monopoly on the ability to read cuneiform. And they also had the stars on their side.

Western scholars had long known about Babylon's special investments in the study of astrology; Greek writers had made much of this, so too had the anti-clerical author of *Origine de tous les cultes*, C. R. Dupuis. Some of Winckler's earliest work treated Babylonian astrology; indeed, it was such a large part of the culture that one could hardly ignore it. But the general historical significance of Babylonian star-gazing was given its most fervent statement in the early work of Eduard Stucken, a student and friend of Winckler, who also happened to be the nephew of the anthropologist Adolf Bastian. Serendipity, and the desire to become, like his uncle, a scholar of universal *Kulturgeschichte* led Stucken first to complete a course in *Sternkunde* or the craft of star-gazing, in Hamburg, and then to sign onto Robert Koldewey's 1890 expedition to the Hittite site Send-schirli (northern Syria). On returning to Berlin, Stucken began to study, together with Winckler, Hebrew, Arabic, Syrian, Coptic, Amharic, Akkadian, and Egyptian hieroglyphics, none of which he seemed to have mastered very well. In 1896, Stucken produced the first volume of his *Astralmythen*, a book swimming in philological detail. The point was nonetheless clear enough: the origin of all art, and all myths, and especially Old Testament tales, Stucken argued, lay in Assyrian observations of the stars. If the author recognized the dangers of "seeing Helen in every woman," he had felt the need, he argued, to "follow the hypotheses to their final consequences,"[58] that is to say, all western ideas to their oriental origins. His mentors were unimpressed, and refused him the title of *Doktor*; but this simply provoked Stucken to publish a second volume of *Astralmythen* in 1899. In volume 2, he explicitly rejected his uncle's ideas on independent evolution and universal "elementary forms of thinking" and insisted upon the diffusion of all myths from an *ur*-Babylonian form.[59] Though Stucken's books were too dilettantish to be cited even by most members of the "furious" generation, "astral myths" thereafter formed a central part of the Panbabylonists' repertoire.[60]

The story of Gilgamesh – based on tablets found by A. H. Layard at Nineveh – took some time to be raised to the status of an "epic." Gilgamesh's first great advocate was a now largely forgotten professor of Assyriology at the University of Marburg, Peter Jensen, whose first contribution to the field, in 1890, was a rather positivistic study of the cosmology of the Babylonians.[61] By 1906, however,

---

[57] Adolphe Lods, *Les découvertes babyloniennes et l'Ancien Testament* (Dole, 1903), p. 11.

[58] Stucken, *Astralmythen (der Hebräer, Babylonier und Ägypter)*, vol. I (Leipzig, 1896), p. 65.

[59] *Astralmythen 2* (Leipzig, 1899), pp. 189–90.

[60] Stucken, however, went on to write novels. See Ingeborg L. Carlson, *Eduard Stucken (1865–1936): Ein Dichter und seine Zeit* (Berlin, 1978).

[61] Peter Jensen, *Die Kosmologie der Babylonier: Studien und Materialien* (Strasbourg, 1890).

Jensen had become perhaps the most polemical and embittered Panbabylonist, thanks, it seems, to the cold reception his writings on the world-historical significance of the Gilgamesh story had received. He was ignored by the classicists and spurned by the theologians – not surprisingly, as Jensen also claimed that Jesus was not a historical figure at all, but simply an Israelite reworking of the Babylonian hero. Even the positivist orientalists found him an embarrassment; Theodor Nöldeke, in letter to Goldziher of 1910, could only manage to mention in passing the Marburg Assyriologist, "over whose wrongheaded stubbornness, by the way, I could weep."[62] Despite Jensen's insistence that Gilgamesh deserved to be called an epic hero, his contemporaries were by no means ready to admit him to the pantheon.

To understand Jensen's frustration and anger at the reception of his work, it is worth quoting at length the opening to his *Das Gilgamesh-Epos in der Weltliteratur*, as he offers here a telling parable. This story involves an orientalist traveler (obviously himself), who ventures beyond his borders to seek knowledge and assistance from a group of "great sages"; but the latter, who can be no other than the classicists of his day, react to the traveler's diffusionist precepts with indignation and ridicule, making communication impossible:

"Many of your beautiful streams," said the foreigner to many great wise men outside his borders, "arise in my fatherland, and I have come here to follow them to their source. Can you advise me? Will you help me?" But the wise men laughed at him, as over a dreamer; they shook their heads over him, as if he had come there directly from the moon; they even were scandalized by him. How in the world, then, could this romantic seeker from foreign parts teach the wise men? Could their divine rivers have had their origins in the land of the unspeakably horrible barbarians? No, that cannot, that ought not to have been possible. The gods would never have wanted that. And still, not one of all the wise men have seen the source of the rivers, even from afar. Against such know-it-all behavior even the strongest arguments are in vain. And so ended the quest to win over the great wise men beyond the borders, entirely unsuccessfully, even in many respects painfully, and the man had finally to renounce further efforts.[63]

That is how it felt to be a "furious" orientalist – laughed at by self-satisfied wise men, who refused to look beyond their narrow confines, who treated newcomers with new knowledge as absurd visitors from the moon. In many ways, Jensen's anti-acknowledgments remind one of the erring teenager's reproach to his or her parents: if I go too far, it is because you refused to listen to me, to meet me halfway. And, indeed, it may be that the inflexible "fathers" do deserve some measure of the blame.

Jensen would go on to contribute even more radical critiques of the canon, but it was perhaps two other members of the Panbabylonist tribe who were most influential in spreading its ideas: Alfred Jeremias and F. E. Peiser. Neither contributed much in the way of ground-breaking scholarship, but they were relentless propagandizers on Panbabylonism's behalf. Jeremias was a theologian, not a philologist, by training and continued to serve as a Lutheran pastor throughout

---

[62] Nöldeke to Goldziher, June 13, 1910 in Simon, *Ignác Goldziher*, p. 327.
[63] Jensen, *Das Gilgamesh-Epos in der Weltliteratur*, vol. I (Strasbourg, 1906), pp. vii–viii.

the fifteen years in which he taught (as a *Privatdozent*) at the University of Leipzig. Only in 1921 did he receive a special, unsalaried professorship for Semitic *Religionsgeschichte*; his full professorship came only in 1927. But it was to his credit, writes Kurt Rudolph, that the history of religions was established as part of the theological faculty's curriculum.[64] Before the war, Jeremias was extremely active in promoting and explaining Panbabylonism and also in softening its often-atheistic edges. He also helped to launch the widely read *Religionsgeschichtliche Volksbücher* (see Chapter 6), and in the 1920s, he would go on to write numerous other popular tracts on nonwestern piety, which inevitably had some similarity to Babylonian forms.[65] A large number of lay readers – including Thomas Mann – probably received their information about relations between Babylon and the Bible not from Friedrich Delitzsch but from Alfred Jeremias.

But it was perhaps Felix Peiser's innovation that most directly benefited the Assyriologists' cause. Peiser, like the others, was trained at the University of Leipzig under Eberhard Schrader; here he met Delitzsch and befriended Hugo Winckler, whose work he would never cease to promote. In 1898, as we have seen, Peiser founded the *OLZ* to promote orientalist scholarship generally. In reality, however, the *OLZ* under Peiser's direction devoted itself particularly to promoting the new field of Assyriology and the younger generation's view of Near Eastern history. The field's institutional as well as intellectual travails were covered extensively in the *OLZ*'s pages; already in the first issue, Peiser devoted an introductory editorial to the problem of Gymnasium textbooks, which, he argued, still gave Assyria extremely scant treatment, and depended almost exclusively on the Bible and Greek sources.[66] Though many new Assyriological chairs were created, the rate of the field's rise to respectability was too slow for Peiser, who frequently complained about the subject in his editorials. Adversity – or the perception of such – drove Peiser along with the other "furious" scholars to take their fight to the wider public. Inspired by his example, in 1907, Winckler established a journal explicitly dedicated to the cause, entitled *Im Kampfe um den alten Orient*.[67]

As this discussion suggests, what frustrated the furious Assyriologists beyond measure was the older generation's "wait and see" attitude, its smug insistence that the verdict on the trustworthiness of the newer sources and methods for handling them was not yet in. A typical expression could be found in Karl Budde's 1903 pamphlet "Das Alte Testament und die Ausgrabung," a reaction to

---

[64] See Kurt Rudolph, *Religionsgeschichte an der Leipziger Universität und die Entwicklung der Religionswissenschaft: Ein Beitrag zur Wissenschaftsgeschichte und zum Problem der Religionswissenschaft*, in *Sitzungsberichte der Sächsischen Akademie der Wissenschaften zu Leipzig*, Phil. hist. Klasse, Band 107, Heft 1 (Berlin, 1962), pp. 103–9.

[65] For example, Jeremias, *Buddhistische und Theosophische Frömmigkeit* (Leipzig, 1927); idem, *Muhammedanische Frömmigkeit* (Leipzig, 1930); also *Der Antichrist in Geschichte und Gegenwart* (Leipzig, 1930).

[66] [Peiser], "Die Verwertung wissenschaftlicher Ergebnisse," in *OLZ* 1 (1898): 65–8; [Peiser], "Die Völker des alten Orients im deutschen Geschichtsunterricht," in *OLZ* 1 (1898): 129–35.

[67] See Nittert Janssen, *Theologie fürs Volk: Eine Untersuchung über den Einfluß der Religionsgeschichtlichen Schule auf die Popularisierung der theologischen Forschung vor dem Ersten Weltkrieg unter besonderer Berücksichtigung des kirchlichen Liberalismus in der lutherischen Landeskirche Hannovers* (Göttingen, 1993), esp. pp. 156–7.

Delitzsch's lectures. Budde, full professor of theology at the University of Marburg, first took Winckler and his collaborator Heinrich Zimmern to task for their work on the third edition of Schrader's *Die Keilinschriften und das Alte Testament* (1902); in Budde's view, they had transformed Schrader's positivist reference book into a self-referential piece of Panbabylonist propaganda. The remainder of the text too was characterized by "father knows best" condescension. While Budde appreciated the "pride, even insolence" the Assyriologists felt toward the traditional scholars of the book, the wise scholar would wait out the period of "proteus-like changes, in which a modern Haggadah based on the actual or presumed insights that one wrests from the monuments is used to constrain and correct Old Testament testimony." On the following page, Budde continued: "As thankful as we representatives of Old Testament scholarship are to the excavations for every little contribution to our knowledge and for the great expansion of our view of the ancient world [they have enabled], we do not think the time has come to allow our beautiful town [the Israelite world] to be annexed by the metropolis [the Assyrian-inflected Orient] overnight, or even to seek incorporation into it."[68]

Undoubtedly many contributors to the *OLZ* found Budde's pamphlet fatuous and vexing – after all, it was here that the term "Panbabylonism" was coined.[69] But the editors were even more furious with the "big wigs" who sat on their hands throughout the dispute over Delitzsch's lectures, allowing the layman, who had "the sensitive skin of school children" to avoid everything "which reminded one even slightly of the school master's cane."[70] Even more frustrating to participants in the debate was the tendency of the established scholars not to mention the names of the Panbabylonists except when ridiculing them; credit for advances went to members of the liberal generation or reference was simply made to "the widening horizon of Near Eastern studies." It was as if, Wilhelm Erbt argued, the hard work of integrating *ur*-Israel into the wider Orient had already been accomplished by Wellhausen and Robertson Smith, as if there had been no battle waged and all the smug chair-holding theologians had simply and gratefully accepted the iconoclasts' findings.[71]

In the face of such claims, the Panbabylonists asserted their special talents – their ability to read cuneiform, their true appreciation of the uniqueness of the Orient, and their daring attempts at big-picture history. The real Orient was foreign and frightening, Winckler argued, and only those who really understood it (as opposed to old-fashioned grammarians) could comprehend the meaning of its texts.[72] Another *OLZ* reviewer raged at theologian Hugo Gressmann's condescending critique of hypotheses "springing up like weeds"; there were only four hypotheses about the relationship between the Old Testament and the ancient

[68] Budde, *Das Alte Testament und die Ausgrabung*, pp. 6–7, quotation pp. 39–40.
[69] Klaus Johanning, *Die Bibel-Babel Streit: Eine forschungsgeschichtliche Studie* (Frankfurt, 1988), p. 144.
[70] [F. E. Peiser], "Auf verlassenem Pfade," in *OLZ* 7 (1904): 250.
[71] Wilhelm Erbt, review of Hugo Gressman, *Altorientalische Texte und Bilder zum Alten Testament* (1909), in *OLZ* 14 (1911): 444–7.
[72] Winckler, "Der alte Orient und die Geschichtsforschung," in *Mitteilungen der vorderasiatischen Gesellschaft* 1 (1906): 18.

Near East, Erbt argued, laid out by Bastian, Gunkel, Jensen, and Winckler; "Other hypotheses that explain the facts of those parallels are impossible." One simply had to choose if one wanted to move science forward.[73] Like Adolf Erman, the younger Assyriologists disparaged the attempts of the Greeks and Romans to understand the essence of the East, and accordingly, the whole body of humanist scholarship that was based essentially on these sources.[74] Ferdinand Bork blasted the treatment of non-classical civilizations as "adiaphora"; ancient history, he insisted, had to be taken out of the hands of classical philologists or there would never be any progress. "Their understanding of world historical interconnections," Bork argued, "is destroyed by their predilection for Greekdom."[75] The work of Peter Jensen, Peiser argued, might have its flaws, but the positivists' criticisms were akin to the small-minded quibbling of the indignant journeyman, "who has lost the ability to see the whole in the course of his work on tiny pieces of mosaic...."[76] The menial mosaic-makers were standing in the way of real scientific progress, and the Graecophiles and orthodox Christians were suppressing historical realities; against such opponents, one had to wield the sharpest of weapons, including, ultimately, conspiracy theories and racial invectives.

BABEL UND DIE BIBEL REVISITED

Perhaps we can now return to the so-called "Babel-Bibel Streit" and see how this episode reflects the conflicts and projects at the core of the furor orientalis. I will not describe in detail the controversy or the content of Friedrich Delitzsch's lectures, but simply offer the briefest of summaries. In these lectures, Delitzsch, who held Germany's first and most prominent chair for Assyriology (at the University of Berlin), attempted to demonstrate Assyrian origins for Old Testament concepts such as the Sabbath and the belief in one high God. Until late in the previous century, he argued in the first lecture, "the Old Testament formed a world by itself" – but now the new oriental sources revealed that the Israelites were the youngest among the cultures of Asia Minor and that "Hebrew antiquity from beginning to end is closely linked to Babylonia and Assyria."[77] In this lecture, delivered before the Deutsch-Orient Gesellschaft and the Kaiser at the Singakademie in Berlin in late January 1902, Delitzsch focused on the Old Testament's debts to Assyrian culture, something orthodox believers (Catholics, Protestants, and Jews) found shocking and which the conservative press took to be proof of liberal Protestant scholarship's atheistic leanings.[78]

The controversy resulted in massive sales of the printed version of Delitzsch's lecture (some 60,000 by 1905) and in terrific anticipation of the second lecture,

---

[73] Erbt, review of Gressman, *Altorientalische Texte*, p. 447.

[74] Jeremias, *Die Panbabylonisten*, p. 32.

[75] Ferdinand Bork, "Die Weltgeschichte in der Schule," in *OLZ* 10 (1907): 3–4.

[76] Peiser, review of P. Jensen, "Kritik von Winckler's Himmels- und Weltenbild der Babylonier," in *OLZ* 7 (1904): 143.

[77] Delitzsch, "Babel and Bible: First Lecture," in idem, *Babel and Bible: Two Lectures*, ed. C. H. W. Johns (New York, 1903), pp. 6–7.

[78] Reinhard G. Lehmann, *Friedrich Delitzsch und der Babel-Bibel-Streit* (Göttingen, 1994), pp. 111–12.

which was delivered in April 1903, to a very large audience, including again the Kaiser. Delitzsch's second lecture went beyond his diffusionist insistence that the Babylonians had developed their ideas first; now he offered a vehement attack on the Old Testament itself. Yahweh, Delitzsch argued, is a cruel, primitive God, "who butchers the peoples with the sword of his insatiable anger, who has but one favorite child, while he consigns all other nations to darkness, shame, and ruin." How can such a God's outbursts provide proper moral guidance, he asked, for the Christian peoples of the modern West? The revealed character of the Old Testament, he concluded, "cannot be maintained, either in the light of science, or in the light of religion and ethics."[79]

In the wake of this lecture, the "Streit" broke out in earnest. The Kaiser, as titular head of the Calvinist and Lutheran churches, was forced to issue a letter distancing himself from Delitzsch's views. Theologians, pastors, rabbis, priests, laypersons, and even a few orientalists felt the need to comment on the lectures, and, for the most part, to denounce them, generating some 1,650 articles and twenty-eight pamphlets in just two years' time.[80] Yaacov Shavit estimates that German Jewish presses alone generated at least seventy pamphlets and response came as well from the wider Jewish community, from Warsaw to Buenos Aires.[81] The Babylonian texts "were the subject of a vast literature, which was discussed in the wardrooms of our warships and in the crowded debating halls of the trade unions,"[82] Adolf Deissmann recalled in 1908. Unlike the Creuzer *Streit* eighty years before, the "Babel-Bibel Streit" was a very public affair.

I would like to say something more about the *Streit* itself, what it tells us about the furor orientalis, and the wider contexts in which it occurred. First of all, one can see Delitzsch's outspoken defense of Babylonian monotheism as part of the larger debate about the origins of religion and a continuation of the post-Herderian tendency toward the upgrading of pagan mythologies. But Delitzsch's ability to make his claims rested, as he openly admitted, on the achievements of the Second Oriental Renaissance – and he was now convinced that the non-biblical sources, including the Tell el Amarna letters, the Code of Hammurabi, and Smith's flood tablets, should be trusted *in preference to* the scriptures. Second, one can see his accessibly written lectures – delivered not to the Academy of Sciences, but to the Kaiser and a well-educated lay public – as a reflection of the "furious" generation's interest in popularizing their knowledge. And one can see his dismay at the reception of his claims not with joy at the "rich harvest that Babylon is continually offering for the 'elucidation and illustration' of the Bible," but instead with "gall and bitterness by a prejudiced regard for dogmatic considerations"[83] as another reflection of this generation's disillusionment with established cultural authorities.

[79] Delitzsch, "Babel and Bible: Second Lecture," p. 149.
[80] Lehmann, *Friedrich Delitzsch*, pp. 50, 111–12; Delitzsch, *Babel und Bibel: Ein Rückblick und Ausblick* (Stuttgart, 1904), pp. 3, 50.
[81] Yaacov Shavit, "Babel und Bibel – The Controversy as a Jewish Event," in *Leipziger Beiträge zur jüdischen Geschichte und Kultur* 1 (2003): 268.
[82] Deissmann, *Licht vom Osten*, p. 3.
[83] Delitzsch, *Babel and Bible: Second Lecture*, p. 152.

Numerous commentators have described Delitzsch's strident assertions and the Kaiser's initial enthusiasm for them, and rightly underscored the anti-Semitic tendencies in Wilhelmine culture they reveal.[84] But we have perhaps overlooked the fact that Delitzsch quite clearly *lost* the debate in 1902–4; although he was not fired (nor burned at the stake), he was sidelined by 1904, and never regained the respect of his academic colleagues. So vehement and negative was the response to his second lecture that by the time of Delitzsch's third lecture (October 1904), he had lost his elite audience and the limelight; indeed, the third lecture was given at a joint meeting of the distinctly less exalted literary societies of Barmen and Cologne and the Society for Geography and Statistics in Frankfurt. His scholarly friends did not exactly run to his defense; Harnack distanced himself and even the *OLZ* remained rather subdued in its treatment of the affair.[85] In a 1908 tribute to progress in the study of the ancient Orient, Eduard Meyer mentioned the names of several respected "liberal" orientalists – Nöldeke, Erman, and Bernhard Stade – but neither Delitzsch nor any other Assyriologist, made his list; indeed, he devoted a long paragraph to debunking the wholly unhistorical "fantasizing of 'astral mythology'" and the "countless popular pamphlets" that presented as real scientific knowledge ridiculous speculation on the existence of a grand Babylonian worldview in very early times.[86] It would not have escaped the notice of the members of the Prussian Academy of Science – to whom Meyer's lecture was delivered – that Meyer was, rather openly, calling his colleague an unscientific popularizer.

If Delitzsch lost, it should be said too that those who won did so less by refuting the Berlin professor's claims than simply by reiterating Israel's uniqueness and accusing the Assyriologists of fantasizing. One critic, a pastor from the small town of Friedersdorf, mocked Delitzsch's diffusionism in the pages of the *Evangelische Kirchenzeitung*. A Babylonian statue in the British Museum, the parodist insisted, had been found to be wearing a cross that bore a remarkable similarity to a Prussian military decoration: "My, how our understanding of the significance of the decorations has been advanced by this newest discovery! Already in Babylon the Red Eagle, Fourth Class, was awarded! And since the origin of our decorations in Babylon has been established without a doubt, thus we can also prove that our modern culture is thoroughly suffused with Babylonian [culture]."[87] Though this send-up accurately identified the problematic leap Delitzsch made in moving from the identification of similar traits or words to the presumption of grand-scale cultural influence, it was hardly a carefully considered assessment of the professor's claims. Nor did the positivist Assyriologists of the day want to engage in a debate. As the *OLZ* recognized, the "clarification" issued at the Hamburg

---

[84] See, e.g., Johanning, *Bibel-Babel Streit*; Lehmann, *Friedrich Delitzsch*, pp. 122–251.

[85] Lehmann, *Friedrich Delitzsch*, p. 262.

[86] Eduard Meyer, "Die Bedeutung der Erschliessung des alten Orients für die geschichtliche Methode und für die Anfänge der menschlichen Gechichte "überhaupt," *Sitzungsberichte der Königlichen Preussischen Akademie der Wissenschaften, Gesammtsitzung vom 25. Juni 1908* (Berlin, 1908), p. 653.

[87] Pfarrer P. Wolff quoted in *Delitzsch*; "Schlusswort," in idem, *Zweiter Vortrag über Babel und Bibel* (Stuttgart, 1903), pp. 47–8.

Congress of Orientalists in 1902 defended the Bible's special status "not as would a scholar, who weighs [the evidence] but as a preacher, who uplifts."[88]

Of course, for orientalists this was the hottest of hot topics, and we can hardly blame them for avoiding the controversy, one that too surely stirred up old anxieties about the possibility of reconciling science and faith. But, as the Near Eastern scholar Jacob J. Finkelstein noted many years later, the long-term development of Assyriology was damaged by the specialists' ceding of the field to laypersons and to Old Testament scholars, most of whom could not read the cuneiform tablets. Delitzsch's critics were in such a hurry to dispense with Babylonian religion that they did not give the Assyriologist's arguments the careful, serious attention they deserved. Finkelstein concludes: "It was just this kind of refusal to appreciate the merits of Babylonian religious thought and literature on their own terms by biblical scholars that contributed to the violence of Delitzsch's reaction."[89]

Delitzsch certainly did react angrily to criticism, and like Lagarde was never willing to compromise with his critics. He insisted in the second lecture, and throughout the rest of his life, that neither the public nor scholars should fear that science's new discoveries would endanger faith. Invoking the long tradition of Protestant humanism, Delitzsch claimed that accepting scientific findings was vital to the purification of faith. As he argued in the conclusion to a lecture delivered in numerous places in 1906–7, the results of the latest excavations in Mesopotamia

... contribute powerfully to freeing us from ancient, firmly-rooted errors in our religious thinking; [and they] assist in that further development of religion, built upon the foundation of unshakable historical knowledge, to which our age is ever more inexorably driven. ... In such pursuits, science might also require us to separate, with pious hands, any human additions to the Old and New Testaments, in order to grasp tightly, all the more joyfully and unreservedly, the kernel of eternal truth.[90]

Methodologically, at least, Delitzsch had not gone all that far beyond Lachmann or Ewald; but for these two, liberation from error did not have the same radical and ultimately racist ends as it did for the benighted Assyriologist. For by 1907, Delitzsch was preparing to throw a bridge from the Higher Criticism to the lower anti-Semitism.

We have seen how the work of numerous Old Testament scholars, from Herder and Michaelis onward, reduced the uniqueness of the Jews and limited the truth-value of the Old Testament. Julius Wellhausen took this even further, ignoring the chronologies offered in the scriptures themselves in favor of creating a new model for Israelite development. And Wellhausen did something more; he suggested that the Torah's accounts were constructed after the fact, indeed even constructed with an eye to misleading the faithful as to the origins of the Law and the original nature of the cult. On to this Winckler, and ultimately Delitzsch, would graft something else: the idea that the ancient Israelites had knowingly borrowed, or

---

[88] F. E. Peiser, "Der XII. Internationale Orientalistenkongress zu Hamburg," part 2, in *OLZ* 5 (1902): 418.

[89] Finkelstein, "Bibel and Babel: A Comparative Study of the Hebrew and the Babylonian Religious Spirit," in *Commentary* 26, no. 5 (1958): 426.

[90] Delitzsch, *Mehr Licht: Die bedeutsamsten Ergebnisse der Babylonisch-Assyrischen Grabungen für Geschichte, Kultur und Religion* (Leipzig, 1907), p. 55.

stolen, their ideas from the Babylonians and Egyptians, but then refused to acknowledge their theft.[91]

The critique of the Jews' conscious theft had, of course, been trotted out long before by Giordano Bruno and suggested, rather more politely, by some enlightened Egyptophiles. But Delitzsch's *Die grosse Täuschung* – completed, the author claimed, in 1914, and published in 1921 – went much further in its assault on the Old Testament as a whole. The author was clearly fed up with a text in which "robbing and murdering nomads" passed themselves off as the chosen people – especially as "science" now demonstrated that the Old Testament itself was a vast, ingenious swindle, designed to claim Canaan for the Jewish *Volk*. The real fathers of history, the Sumerians, Chaldeans, and Galileans (of whom Jesus was one) had been too honest or naive to construct such a narrative, allowing the Jews to deceive humankind for millennia, but oriental philology and archaeology, Delitzsch argued, had at last demonstrated the Jews' deceptions. It was time, the Assyriologist raged, to tell the truth, no matter how painful: "For I have never understood why in such serious matters one ought not dare to speak the truth."[92] And it was time to take action: first of all, Zionists should not be allowed to claim Palestine. Secondly, German Christians should recognize that the Old Testament had absolutely no religious value, and that their children would be better off reading Babylonian myths and Germanic epics. The moral of the story was, finally, that "this conniving, stateless or international people represents a great, a fearsome danger for all the other peoples of the earth."[93]

That Delitzsch's final truth-telling should have as its focus the unmasking of the modern Jews as a danger to Germandom and of the Old Testament as the Jews' "great deception" points us back, once again, to *Orientalistik*'s long entanglement with theological questions and with the interpretation of the Old Testament. It also underscores the long tradition of radical Protestant thought, from Herder and de Wette, through Wellhausen and Lagarde, which focused its efforts on cleaning up the scriptures. And finally, with the addition of one small piece of biographical information, this finale should demonstrate the more than metaphorical level upon which the battle with the "fathers" was sometimes waged. Delitzsch's father, the famous Hebraist Franz Delitzsch, had been born in the house of a Jew, Lewy Hirsch, with whom his parents roomed. Hirsch had helped to support Franz, and the scholar was widely rumored to be his illegitimate son. Friedrich, who had been taunted as "der Judenenkel" [grandson of a Jew] was surely sensitive about his ancestry. He rarely referred to his father's work in his own, and when he did, in the second lecture, it was to stress his own greater willingness to adopt a critical position with respect to the Hebrew scriptures.[94] Both privately and intellectually,

---

[91] For Winckler's claims, see his *Abraham als Babylonier, Joseph als Ägypter* (Leipzig, 1903), and review thereof by Hermann Volgelstein, in *OLZ* 7 (1904): 67.

[92] Delitzsch, *Die grosse Täuschung: Kritische Betrachtungen zu den alttestamentlichen Berichten über Israels Eindringen in Kanaan, die Gottesoffenbarung vom Sinai und die Wirksamkeit der Propheten*, 2 vols. (Stuttgart, 1921), p. 6.

[93] Ibid., pp. 95–107, quotation p. 105.

[94] Cooper, "Posing the Sumerian Question," p. 56, n. 56; on Delitzsch's reference to his father, Bill T. Arnold and David B. Weisberg, "A Centennial Review of Friedrich Delitzsch's 'Babel und Bibel' Lectures," in *Journal of Biblical Literature* 121, no. 3 (2002): 456.

Delitzsch felt himself struggling to throw off the weight of the "liberal" past – a past that might, quite literally as well as theologically, have made him a Jew. Delitzsch was seeking liberation – from a mixed identity, a mixed religious heritage, and a mixed modern state, all things that his diffusionist science, his humanistic philological training, and his German nationalist friends had taught him to despise. It is *Die grosse Täuschung*, not the Babel-Bibel Streit, that represents the worst outcome of the furor orientalis.

AFTER THE "AFFAIR"

In the years after "Babel und Bibel," Assyriological material was drawn into debates on the New Testament as well as the Old, culminating in a debate about the Babylonian and Persian sources of the gospels. Once again, Jensen entered the fray, publishing in 1910 a book whose title says it all: *Moses, Jesus, Paulus: Drei Varianten des babylonischen Gottmenschen Gilgamesch: Eine Anklage und ein Appell.*[95] Though committed to Panbabylonism, Alfred Jeremias – who was, after all, a pastor as well as a scholar – responded unfavorably, bridling at Jensen's claims that Moses, Jesus, and Saint Paul were all mythological reworkings of Gilgamesch. Jensen's friend Heinrich Zimmern also took up his pen, convinced, he wrote, that as a specialist, he was duty-bound to make the Babylonian material accessible to a wide audience. Rather unusually for the day, Zimmern urged temperance and flexibility in the interpretation of such parallels; he did not think it necessary to decide in general whether or not such parallels were the result of independent evolution or of borrowing; perhaps, he argued, each case required a different set of explanations. As concerned the New Testament's debts to the East, Zimmern argued that most of what the New Testament said about Jesus "can only in a very limited way lay claim to historical verity," and pointed out that Parsism and Mithraism had very probably contributed at least as much as the Babylonians to the framing of New Testament stories. But, Zimmern concluded dramatically, the historicity of Jesus was perhaps not actually necessary for the future of Christian belief.[96] Ultimately, Zimmern was willing to step off the historicist cliff – to take a leap for faith, without the philological-historical evidence that had begun to seem not only elusive, but positively dangerous.

By 1910, Panbabylonism's furor was, in any case, fading. Winckler had managed to fund several seasons of digging at Boghazkoi, but to do so, the notorious anti-Semite and hater of classicists had to appeal first to wealthy Jewish patrons and then to the classical archaeologists who ran the Deutsches Archäologisches Institut.[97] Winckler died in 1913, much lamented by contributors to the *OLZ*, but not apparently by many others. But the theory continued to provoke interest and

---

[95] *Moses, Jesus, Paulus: Drei Varianten des babylonischen Gottmenschen Gilgamesch: Eine Anklage und ein Appell* (Frankfurt, 3rd ed., 1910).

[96] Zimmern, *Zum Streit um die 'Christusmythe': Das babylonische Material in seinen Hauptpunkten dargestellt* (Berlin, 1910), pp. 10–11, 56–7, quotation, pp. 5–6.

[97] Curtius, *Deutsche und antike Welt*, pp. 203, 205–7. Of the 1907 excavations, in which he participated, Curtius notes that Winckler though on site, paid no attention to the digging, and sat reading tablets the whole day in his study, trying to keep up with the massive quantities coming to light each day. Ibid., p. 207.

indeed to serve as something of an instructive extreme position, against which more moderate orientalizing diffusionist theories could be juxtaposed. In a series of lectures given in 1911–12, the great Belgian scholar of Mithraism and oriental paganism, Franz Cumont, who had more than a little in common with the "furious" orientalists, denounced Panbabylonism as being merely a newly tricked out version of Dupuis's Egyptian fantasies. The American Assyriologist Morris Jastrow, whose father had been a Talmudic scholar educated in Germany, used Panbabylonism as a jumping off point in his Haskell lectures in 1913 – but only so that he could refute or at least moderate the hyper-diffusionist program.[98] Two Catholic priests, Wilhelm Schmidt and F. X. Kugler, engaged seriously in attempts to refute Panbabylonist claims, Schmidt attempting to show that monotheism was a universal and independently developed idea, and Kugler, who was also an astronomer and Assyriologist, seeking to discredit Winckler's assertions about astral religion.[99] Recruited by positivist Assyriologist Carl Bezold, Franz Boll passed the period between 1911 and 1918 in collaboration with his senior colleague, in a largely successful endeavor to end Panbabylonist speculation in matters astronomical.[100] The culmination of the critique of Panbaylonism was in many ways Otto Neugebauer's classic study of mathematics and astronomy in the ancient Near East, *The Exact Sciences in Antiquity*; but Neugebauer's careful study was in no way a return to a Greece-centered account of the history of science. On the contrary, Neugebauer's central problem, "the origin and transmission of Hellenistic science," was a highly complicated one that balanced "oriental" and "occidental" borrowing and reworking and sought to document contacts, not to steal any nation's fire.[101]

Thus, when Max Weber opened his essays on *Ancient Judaism* (published between 1917 and 1919) with an attack on Panbabylonism, he was criticizing a movement whose days were numbered. But Weber characteristically added an insightful bit of analysis. While this form of thought called itself "culture-historical universalism," it was really the creation of diffusionist-minded philologists, and as such, it radically opposed the "ethnographic universalism" of British scholars like William Robertson Smith and the German transplant Max Müller. Moreover, if it posed in the sharpest terms the question of "the indubitable peculiarity of Israelite religious development," it tended to answer this question in anything but a neutral way.[102] These were not the foundations for a proper kind of cultural history, Weber knew, and in adding into his analysis

[98] F. Cumont, *Astrology and Religion among the Greeks and Romans* (New York, 1912), p. 1. Jastrow's lectures were subsequently published as *Hebrew and Babylonian Traditions* (New York, 1914).

[99] Morgens Trolle Larsen, "Orientalism and the Ancient Near East," in Michael Harbsmeier and idem, eds., *The Humanities between Art and Science: Intellectual Developments, 1880–1914* (Copenhagen, 1989), pp. 197–8.

[100] Boll, "Carl Bezold," pp. 9–10.

[101] Neugebauer, *The Exact Sciences in Antiquity* (Princeton, NJ, 1952), p. 1; on Panbabylonism, p. 132. Trained at the University of Göttingen, Neugebauer had already begun publishing papers on Assyrian science during the interwar era.

[102] Max Weber, *Ancient Judaism*, trans. Hans H. Gerth and Don Martindale (New York, 1952), pp. 427–8.

socio-economic factors, he showed how questions about the origins and uniqueness of ancient religions might be posed without plunging into philological or theological debates.[103] Regrettably, however, Weber did not live long enough to see his work taken seriously by his countrymen, all too many of whom continued the quest for *ur*-origins and purified faiths.

In the end, it must be said that the Panbabylonists did reopen debate on the eastern origins of western ideas and helped to popularize the fruits of the Second Oriental Renaissance in ways that were intellectually provocative as well as morally reckless. They went much too far and many were driven by racialist or religious purification projects that we can, with hindsight, only abhor. But perhaps the older generation deserves some measure of blame for rejecting or ignoring some of their exciting new findings and "big-picture" questions, and for failing to entertain the possibility, to return to Jensen's parable, that the rich rivers of western culture might have their sources, at least in part, in eastern climes. In an "age of electricity," after all, one cannot go on pretending that one can only see by candlelight.

We will see something of the same pattern as we now turn to the work of another cadre of fin de siècle scholars, a loosely connected group of theologians, classicists, and orientalists who pioneered the study of what they called "Religionsgeschichte." This group staged their generational revolt in a way that departed once again from enlightened forerunners and which reflected the inroads of the Second Oriental Renaissance. And, like the Panbabylonists, the German historians of religion by and large rejected the ethnographic universalism of their brothers across the channel. Their quest was, however, not the newer search for the Babylonian origins of western culture – but a much older one, for the oriental origins of Christian beliefs.

---

[103] Cf. the remarks of William H. C. Freund in "Die Bedeutung von Max Webers Ansatz für die Untersuchung der frühen christlichen Sektenbewegung," in Max Weber, *Sicht des antiken Christentums: Interpretation und Kritik*, ed. Wolfgang Schluchter (Frankfurt, 1985), pp. 466–85.

6

Toward an Oriental Christianity

> For several decades ... among our philosophers as among our empirical scientists,
> there has been a prevailing tendency to avoid entirely areas in which an exact,
> demonstrable conviction does not seem attainable. But what has this abstemiousness
> meant for our inner lives, for our spiritual patrimony, for our national *Bildung*? Into
> the empty space that Christian philosophy is no longer allowed to fill ... has stepped,
> for many, the philosophy of pessimism....
>
> Rudolf Seydel, "Buddha und Christus" (1883)[1]

From the days of Johannes Reuchlin to those of J. D. Michaelis, orientalists were
frequently condemned as heretics and enemies of the true religion – and long
afterward, those who challenged orthodoxies directly (like Julius Wellhausen
and Friedrich Delitzsch) still spent much of their lives fighting with members of
the theological faculty. By the third quarter of the nineteenth century, liberal
Protestant scholars had succeeded in wresting control over university appointments from clerical consistoria and in making the Higher Criticism seem the
proper, "scientific" way to treat the Bible; their anti-clerical, enlightened critiques
of rituals, miracles, and intolerant attitudes could be openly aired, as Germany
and Austria-Hungary now enjoyed a virtually free press, and many of their
criticisms had won acceptance among well-educated, middle-class readers. But
the incorporation into mainstream cultural discourse of what had once been
iconoclasm paved the way for all sorts of new "heresies" – from Ernst Haeckel's
monism to Paul de Lagarde's Germanic "religion of the future," from Marxian
socialism to Nietzschean nihilism. By the 1890s, some scholars began to fear that
criticism, and particularly biblical criticism, had gone too far, and was threatening
to undermine the liberal Protestant cultural world from which it had sprung. In the
context of widespread discussions of "the crisis of values" and Germany's lack of
"spiritual unification," many orientalists would decide, as did Leipzig philosophy
professor Rudolf Seydel, that the time had come to give up positivist "abstemiousness" in favor of a more forthright commitment to Christianity; the world had
changed, and now it was their duty not to propagate heretical ideas, but to subvert
them.

In many respects, late Wilhelmine culture was an increasingly secular one; but
cultural and intellectual historians have perhaps underestimated the extent to
which the fin de siècle "crisis" was understood by both liberal and conservative

---

[1] Rudolf Seydel, "Buddha und Christus," in *Nord und Sud* (Nov. 1883): 195.

Christians as a religious crisis, as middle-class believers began to fear that Christianity itself would collapse, opening the way for the domination of what they saw as atheistic social democracy, English materialism, and amoral, urban-commercial (read "Jewish") interests. Protestant-Catholic hostility had not disappeared either, but was in fact becoming better organized, as both faiths founded mass political parties and pressure groups.[2] As George Williamson has argued, educated Protestants in particular felt themselves being squeezed out, threatened by the rise of both a "Red" and a "Black" International, and alienated from conservative dogma and the clerical power of the established churches. "Whereas in France the default position of this class was a kind of secularism, in Germany competition with the Roman Church and a desire to maintain a distance from the socialist milieu ensured that most educated middle-class Protestants cultivated some form of religiosity."[3] In this context, a number of scholars, mostly Protestants like Seydel, but some Catholics as well, decided that deepening early Christianity's historical context might be the right way to revive Christian piety among the elite, even if it meant acknowledging that the New Testament, too, was an "oriental" book. The challenge was to create a form of Christian belief that could be squared with Near Eastern religious history without allowing the "light of Asia" to blind one to Christianity's superiority for the citizens of the present.

The theological defense of New Testament Christianity sought to enroll orientalists and oriental scholarship for its own ends; but impetus came from the opposite direction too, from orientalists who might have criticized Christian clerics, rituals, and dogmas, but who did not want to destroy German religious faith as a whole. The two groups – together with some maverick classicists – found common ground in the practice of *Religionsgeschichte*, a diffuse set of pursuits interlinked by the practitioners' conviction that comparison, contextualizing, and even some relativizing of Christianity were necessary both to science and to the renewal of faith (of some kind) for the future. The engagement of orientalists in often high-profile theological controversies, in turn, drew orientalist scholarship further out of its specialized foxholes and into the sometimes-harsh Wilhelmine sun. Its mobilization for these purposes had a powerful, perhaps even shattering, impact on Protestant liberal theology, but it also had a series of feedback effects on oriental studies, one of which was something one might describe as de-secularization, or at least, as the return of the repressed neoromantic narratives in the brave new world of post-liberal cultural politics.

Naturally, religious motivations did not drive all orientalists; there were plenty who stuck to plowing their philological furrows and others, as we will see in Chapter 8, seeking more practical forms of cultural relevance. But with respect to the place of oriental studies in Germany's wider cultural politics, this quest for a scientifically respectable, "oriental" Christianity was highly significant and had a series of effects not only on the development of the disciplines of theology, archaeology, Indology, Semitic studies, and Assyriology but also on the public's

---

[2] See Helmut Walser Smith, *German Nationalism and Religious Conflict: Culture, Ideology, Politics 1870–1914* (Princeton, NJ, 1995).

[3] George S. Williamson, "A Religious Sonderweg? Reflections on the Sacred and the Secular in the Historiography of Modern Germany," in *Church History* 75, no. 1 (2006): 11.

perception of its own religious and racial prehistory. Indeed, it was in the context of this discussion of religious history and Christian revival that the subject of race was raised most often, and mattered most to citizens of the Wilhelmine Empire. The escape from "Semitism" that many Christian writers sought was both a racial and a religious quest; it was driven both by the desire of some liberal Protestants to distance themselves from forms of piety that, for various reasons, they believed could not be reconciled with modernity and by the desire of xenophobes and old elites to rid the community of "foreign" elements. Thus, race, which became a matter of extensive discussion at the fin de siècle, will be treated here as part and parcel of other purification projects, the net effect of which for the history of orientalism was the construction of a flawed and prejudiced picture of Near Eastern history and Christianity's origins. In the chapter that follows, racial thinking itself will take center stage.

Imperialism played a role in all branches of fin de siècle orientalism and will be foregrounded in Chapter 8, which deals with the subdisciplines most thoroughly reshaped by Germany's entrance into the colonial race, *Islamforschung* and Sinology. Here, however, the focus is on religious motivations and texts, both because this aspect of the study of the East at the fin de siècle is so often overlooked in treatments of orientalism and because it is quite clearly the orientalism about which Germans themselves cared most. Though cultural and intellectual historians have largely overlooked it, the volume of turn-of-the-century literature on, for example, Christianity and Buddhism, or the eastern origins of the ideas of Saint Paul, is massive; not only were some publications reprinted numerous times, but there were whole series of booklets—such as *Biblische Zeit- und Streitfragen* (begun in 1905) – devoted to such issues. That the classicists, orientalists, and theologians of this era as well as numerous clerics, laypersons, and esoteric enthusiasts avidly took up their pens to treat these subjects is testimony to their deep investment in such questions and their faith that the cultural sciences could and should be used to steer Germany past its crisis of values. That so many publishers were willing to issue these books, journals, and newspaper articles in thousands and sometimes even hundreds of thousands of copies points, similarly, to widespread interest in these questions. We have here to do with a new scale of social acceptance and distribution of what had once been esoteric ideas.

There is a generational story to be told here too; and again it is a story about those who experienced the Second Oriental Renaissance and the breakdown of neoclassicist cultural hegemony early in their careers. The 1890s saw a reaction to mid-century Protestantism's focus on ethics, systematic theology, and modern social issues, something critics now saw as the generation's unwillingness to take both faith and history seriously. Moreover, many members of the younger generation felt, the leading liberal theologians had not taken on board the results of numerous investigations of nonwestern religions and editions of religious texts which had been underway since the 1840s. Christianity's origins, in their view, could no longer be conceived simply as a mixture of Jewish monotheism and Greek universalist philosophy. Finally, the liberal generation had too cerebral a view of religion as a whole; as Adolf Deissmann would later complain, the focus remained on the articulation of theological doctrines, rather than on the full religious and historical *Umwelt*, which gave birth to Christianity.[4] In Deissmann's seminal *Licht vom Osten*, as overwhelmingly in the work of the religious-historical school, this milieu was explicitly an "oriental" one, one that included ritual practices, folk piety, and everyday life and one that had to be grasped in its entirety, not just extrapolated from its theological texts.

In part, the directions in which this contrary generation of orientalists and theologians went were also shaped by possibilities inherent in their sources once the various walls of untranslatability – between the Greek world and the Near East, the Old Testament and Mesopotamia, the New Testament and the Hellenistic Orient – had been breached. The Greeks, and especially those of the Hellenistic age, readily acknowledged their borrowings from the Orient; this made the anti-philhellenist line of thought rather easy to pursue, though defenders of the Greeks continued to insist that borrowings were not meaningful. The one great ancient Jewish text, the Old Testament, on the other hand, is a religious text and a national history and Jahwe is, among other things, a jealous God.[5] Thus, the attempt to find *ur*-oriental sources for Old Testament ideas was already inherently an antagonistic one with respect to the Jewish texts and modern-day believers who could and did – as pagan Greeks could not – talk back. Similarly, as orthodox Muslims believe the Qur'an to be the word of God dictated directly to Muhammed, all attempts to locate the sources of the Qur'an were inherently polemical. Many Protestant scholars acknowledged this – but having made their own accommodations to allow for the construction of the Gospels (e.g., substituting the Gospel *according to* Mark for the Gospel *of* Mark), they could not tolerate the defensiveness of others.[6] To be fair, many were equally critical of orthodox Christians who held the same sort of protective stance with respect to the Bible. But it remains clear that those who were determined to open up a wider, more multicultural ancient Orient found it convenient and more appealing to emphasize the narrowness and the inauthenticity of Semitic cultures (Jewish, Arab, and sometimes Egyptian), and the originality, universality, and purity of Aryan ones (Persian, Indian, and for some Hittite and Sumerian). Here too, racial presumptions were increasingly evident and helped to structure both the historical and the theological interpretations of ancient texts and artifacts.

Like the other chapters of this book, this one will not dwell on canonical figures such as Nietzsche, Freud, Max Weber, or C. G. Jung. The literature on their "orientalisms" is already vast and shows, as a whole, that their knowledge of the cultures they were describing was not very deep and rather idiosyncratic. Freud was not particularly interested in the Orient in this time, and Jung, though he imbibed a vast quantity of the orientalist literature of the time, was too young to have written much before the war. The influence of Schopenhauer and Nietzsche on the

---

[4] Deissmann, *Licht vom Osten*, p. 278.

[5] Cf. Duchesne-Guillemin, *Western Response to Zoroaster*, p. 70.

[6] In the foreword to the second edition of his book on Hellenistic Judaism, Wilhelm Bousset says that he has paid attention to Jewish as well as Christian reviews of the first edition, even though the former "for the most part start from fundamental presumptions that can scarcely permit an agreement." Bousset, *Die Religion des Judentums im neutestamentlichen Zeitalter* (Berlin, 2nd ed., 1906), p. viii.

generation of orientalists and oriental enthusiasts (including Buddhists) after 1890 was considerable; but as we will see in Chapter 7, Schopenhauer's impact was filtered very much through his major orientalist popularizers, Karl Eugen Neumann and Paul Deussen. Nietzsche's debts to liberal-era Semitic studies are well known – but it is not clear that scholars in the field, even the younger, more radical ones, learned anything from his *Genealogy of Morals* they could not have gotten from Wellhausen, Renan, or Lagarde. Co-parented by Nietzsche's confidante Lou Salomé, the figure of "Zarathustra," may well have inspired and helped to shape the study of Persian religion and philosophy at the fin de siècle; in the case of Lou herself, it may have underwritten her urge to marry the half-Armenian, half-Malayan Persian specialist Friedrich Carl Andreas. But Nietzsche's yea-saying prophet – into whose construction so much Creuzerian romanticism was poured – could hardly have meant much to Andreas, a positivist so modest about his own pretensions that he never did finish his long-awaited study of middle Persian grammar.[7]

In focusing on less-studied writers, this chapter hopes to reconfigure our views of the late Wilhelmine intellectual context such that the debates to which Nietzsche, Jung, and others contributed are illuminated. I also want to bring the histories of orientalism, classics, and theology back into conversation with one another, for as we saw in the last chapter, their reconvergence at the fin de siècle had significant cultural consequences. An examination of fin de siècle German orientalism, which leaves out the interplay, competition, and interdependency of these fields, fails to do justice to the rich intellectual context in which each of discipline took a modern turn, but even more importantly also fails to appreciate the broader politico-cultural meaning of the Orient for the Wilhelmine Empire – and its successor states.

LIBERAL THEOLOGY IN CRISIS

As we have seen, over the course of the nineteenth century, liberal Protestant theologians gradually managed to curtail the clergy's influence in appointments to the theological faculty and to make the Higher Criticism respectable – at least among the educated elite. It is instructive that while in David Friedrich Strauss's day, an academic's answers to sensitive theological questions might result in dismissal, by the 1880s and 1890s, orthodox clerical opinion no longer really mattered to university scholars' successful pursuit of their careers – at least in German Protestant territories.[8] In large part, this reflected changes in the outer political world, in Germany as in France, and the willingness of the state to tolerate or even endorse scholars with unorthodox religious views. Under the Second Empire,

---

[7] On Lou Andreas Salomé, see Rudolf Binion, *Frau Lou: Nietzsche's Wayward Disciple* (Princeton, NJ, 1968), pp. 101–4, 133–5; on Nietzsche and Creuzer, Robert A. Yelle, "The Rebirth of Myth? Nietzsche's Eternal Recurrence and its Romantic Antecedents," in *Numen* 47, no. 2 (2000): 175–202. Other Persian specialists seem to have been equally impervious, but I happily admit there is much more research to be done here.

[8] Where churches had more control, however, there were efforts to crack down on unorthodox religious histories. In 1881, the Free Church of Scotland declared William Robertson Smith's views heretical and he was fired by the Aberdeen Free Church College (he ended up with a job at Cambridge). In a much more far-reaching proclamation of 1907, Pope Pius X condemned what he called "modernism" among Catholic scholars.

Ernest Renan had been attacked by the churches and had lost his position at the Collège de France; but he was reinstated after 1871 by the liberal anti-clerics of the Third Republic. Across the Rhine, as we have seen, though despised by orthodox Lutherans, Julius Wellhausen held onto his Greifswald theological chair until he relinquished it voluntarily in 1882. Wellhausen's slightly younger counterpart in New Testament theology, Adolf von Harnack, also made himself unpopular with the churches – and angered his own theology-professor father – but his careful philological work on Christian dogma made him respected in academia and the liberal Prussian Cultural Ministry. A showdown over his proposed appointment to a chair in theology at the University of Berlin in 1888 was won by the liberals, thanks to the Kaiser's intervention. And, as we saw in the previous chapter, though Wilhelm II did have to distance himself from some of Friedrich Delitzsch's claims, he did not ask Delitzsch to recant or consider removing him from his Berlin professorship (which was, in any event, not in the theological faculty).

The reduction of the churches' cultural clout seems to have emboldened an ever more trenchant critique of scripture not just from inside the Reich's institutions but from outside as well. Here again we must mention the proliferation of associations, newspapers, journals, and inexpensive books, as well as the democratization of concern over the future of Germany's spiritual life. In the face of new bouts of urbanization, industrialization, and working-class organization, many middle-class men and women decided that it was up to them to do something to save German *Geist*. And publishers, perhaps remembering the great successes of Strauss's *Leben Jesu* and Paul de Lagarde's *Deutsche Schriften*, were willing to put out a dizzying array of scholarly and semi-scholarly works on religious topics. Gradually, this work grew more radical, as some, including Strauss himself, in his *Der alte und der neue Glaube* (1872; in its seventh edition by 1874), proclaimed God himself dead and Jesus simply a good man.

The Higher Criticism had completed its work, the radicals argued; science had demonstrated even the thin Christian doctrine of the liberal Protestants untenable. Jesus, concluded the theologically educated hero of Gustav Frenssen's extremely popular novel of 1905, *Hilligenlei*, was nothing but "the most beautiful of humankind's offspring."[9] What gave Frenssen's conclusion even more force for bourgeois readers was that the author had himself been a pastor and had written a highly successful earlier novel (*Jörn Uhl*, 1901), which liberal Protestants had praised for its portrayal of simple, this-worldly piety.[10] In *Hilligenlei*, Frenssen not only acknowledged his own loss of faith but also listed at the back of the novel the scholarly sources upon which he had drawn; the list cited virtually every important liberal Protestant theologian of the day.[11] Dramatically, Frenssen

---

[9] Gustav Frenssen, *Hilligenlei* (Berlin, 1905), p. 570. The novel sold 120,000 copies in its first year.

[10] Andreas Crystall, *Gustav Frenssen* (Gütersloh, 2002), p. 226. Frenssen was also an intimate friend of Martin Rade, editor of the influential *Christliche Welt*, and brother-in-law of the left-liberal politician Friedrich Naumann.

[11] The list included most of the prominent Protestant theologians of the day: H. Holtzmann, Adolf Jülicher, Paul Wernle, Wilhelm Wrede, Wilhelm Bousset, Ernst Troeltsch, and Adolf von Harnack, as well as the *Religionsgeschichtliche Volksbücher* and the anthropological work of Catholic priest Wilhelm Schmidt. On the controversy, see Crystall, *Gustav Frenssen*, pp. 225ff; Frenssen, *Schlußwort zu Hilligenlei* (Berlin, 1906).

had his protagonist reject the New Testament, as well as miracles, masses, and saints: "Away with all of that! God, working through German science, has let all of that be judged and condemned to death."[12]

The *Hilligenlei* controversy marked a pivotal moment in which the Higher Criticism was publicly turned against itself. But this was hardly the only one; another was the dispute over Arthur Drews' *Die Christusmythe*, which appeared in 1909 and by the next year had sold over 10,000 copies, necessitating a second edition. Produced and promoted by the avant-garde house of Eugen Diederichs in Jena, Drews' book created considerable controversy, not only because of its conclusions (that the historical Christ was a fiction) but also because of its trenchant critique of liberal Protestant hypocrisies. For Drews, liberal Protestantism was simply a desperate sort of apologetics, which tried to fool itself into believing its conclusions were scientific. Not mincing words, the convinced monist denounced: "... this apathetic doctrine of salvation which fundamentally doesn't believe in itself, this sentimental, aesthetically-tinged cult of Jesus pushed by Harnack, Bousset, and the rest ... would not this so-called Christianity of well-read pastors have collapsed long ago of its own poverty of ideas, suavity and sleaziness, if only it was not thought that Christianity had to be preserved at any price, even if that was the total evacuation of spiritual content?"[13] Drews also denounced professional theologians for snubbing non-professionals (like himself) who entered the fray; as if, he argued, they themselves did not simply throw science and critical thinking out the window when it came to defending their last apologetic island, the historical Jesus. We will see in this chapter how Drews drew on orientalist literature to validate his exposure of the "Christ-myth," but it is useful here to underline the radical nature of some of the popular literature now circulating widely in bourgeois circles.

This was farther than even the radical Protestants had wanted to go, and by the later 1880s, some theologians began thinking that the Higher Criticism had gone too far and looking for new ways to reconcile science and religion. They had not given up on such a reconciliation; in fact, in their view, science and faith *had* to be reconciled if Germany's widely perceived "crisis of values" was to be overcome. Friedrich Wilhelm Graf has convincingly argued that this was a debate in which turn-of-the century Protestant theologians believed their voices should be heard, and heard above all others.[14] Though theology's student body and share of faculty chairs was declining relative to other fields, the field's leaders still thought themselves called to steer the culture clear of a crisis caused by the clash of their two most cherished principles, *Wissenschaft* and *Glaube*, the very clash, it should be noted, that nineteenth-century *Kulturprotestantismus* had been designed to avert or sublate. The question was, however, not only how to perform this reconciliation but also how to "steer" the population effectively. Over these two questions, there was again a generational schism, as the younger generation began to look

---

[12] Frenssen, *Hilligenlei*, p. 588.
[13] Drews, *Die Christusmythe* (Jena, 2nd ed., 1910), pp. 222–3.
[14] Friedrich Wilhelm Graf, "Rettung der Persönlichkeit," in *Kultur und Kulturwissenschaften um 1900*, ed. Rüdiger von Bruch, Friedrich Wilhelm Graf, and Gangolf Hübinger (Stuttgart, 1989), pp. 103–31.

back to the romantic world and to the fruits of the Second Oriental Renaissance in order to create a different kind of science and a different kind of steering.

The Religious-Historical School

The school with which we are concerned chiefly here is the one that came to be known as the "religious-historical school," whose deeper roots lie in the *philosophia perennis* of the Renaissance and the Baroque era's inquiries into religious comparativism. But the full flowering of religious-historical inquiry needed as its pretext and prologue both Friedrich Creuzer's recognition that myths and symbols were the keys that unlocked the religious belief systems of the ancients and the Second Oriental Renaissance's mass of trustworthy oriental data. The combination meant that firstly, one had testimony directly from the mouths of the oriental pagans themselves, rather than the accounts of their persecutors; and secondly, that one could use this material to understand, rather than simply ridicule, past systems of belief. It depended on the elevation of non-European belief systems (most importantly Hinduism, Confucianism, and Buddhism) to the status of "religions" – something that, as we have seen, was happening over the course of the nineteenth century. In addition, defunct religions of the ancient world – Zoroastrianism, Babylonian paganism, and Mithraism, for example – were now given greater substance and significance, and more scholars devoted themselves to the study of ancient sects, such as the Essenes, the Gnostics, the Galilean Jews, and the Manicheans. Here too, known but unsavory texts like the *Corpus Hermeticum* came back into usage and poaching on other disciplines became commonplace, if sometimes risky. Indeed, willingness to take new risks was perhaps the final ingredient needed for full-on *Religionsgeschichte* – it was dangerous, both for one's career and perhaps with respect to Christianity's stability, to embrace oriental syncretism and emphasize "irrational" factors. But many members of this generation had decided that "liberal"-era scholarship – in their case, the philological historicism of men like Wellhausen – had reached the end of its usefulness and the risk was worth taking.

Susannah Heschel dates the beginning of nineteenth-century religious-historical inquiry to 1857, when Adolf Hilgenfeld set out his claims that the Hebrew Bible was suffused with Buddhist and Parsee ideas, adopted by the Jews in Babylonian exile.[15] In Hilgenfeld's generation too were Albert Eichhorn and Albrecht Ritschl, as well as Paul de Lagarde and Julius Wellhausen, all of whom taught at the University of Göttingen and contributed in various ways to the launching of the new school. But it was in the next generation of students at the University of Göttingen that religious-historical thought really was born; among those who spent time there in the 1880s and 1890s were Wilhelm Bousset, Hermann Gunkel, Wilhelm Wrede, Ernst Troeltsch, Heinrich Hackmann, and Alfred Rahlfs, all of them pioneers in the field.[16]

[15] Susannah Heschel, "Quest for the Aryan Jesus: The Archaeology of Nazi Orientalist Theology," in *Jews, Antiquity and the Nineteenth-Century Imagination*, ed. Hayim Lapin and Dale B. Martin (Bethesda, MD, 2003), p. 72.
[16] For details, see Gerd Lüdemann and Martin Schröder, *Die Religionsgeschichtliche Schule in Göttingen: Eine Dokumentation* (Göttingen, 1987).

Elsewhere too, at the universities of Tübingen, Marburg, Leipzig, and Bonn, young theologians were forming religious-historical circles and becoming self-conscious of their generation's differences with the "fathers."[17] As they finished their degrees and began the increasingly difficult search for both academic and pastoral jobs, they also began to explore works in other disciplines and push the boundaries of their own.

In addition to its self-consciousness and sense of entitlement, what made this generation of historians of religion different was its deep interest in oriental paganism, its critique of pure historicism in favor of a wider, one might say more folkloric understanding of traditions, and its neoromantic return to the question of origins. It also differed from the previous generation in possessing even more manuscripts and artifacts, and in its willingness to combine different types of evidence and to borrow ideas from other disciplines. Strikingly, it drew much more heavily on archaeological finds than had its predecessors, believing, as did other Europeans of this generation, that excavated material might be used not simply to document the aesthetic life of the ancient world, but also to understand its religious practices. In this context, Germany's organization for topographical and archaeological study of the biblical world, the Deutscher Verein zur Erforschung Palästinas, gained some new respectability – though the largely amateur association was just making its real pitch for funding for large-scale excavations in 1913.[18] What is telling here, however, is not so much the increasing engagement with biblical *Realien*, but the ends to which the material was put; for increasingly, archaeology came to be seen as the means to plumb the deep and mysterious history of the human spirit, and to understand cultic practices that had escaped the notice, or fallen prey to the "abstemiousness," of the positivist generation.

This evidence could be used in a number of ways, simply to understand Mithraic, Egyptian, or Zoroastrian practices, or to engage directly in what was increasingly being described as "Christian archaeology." Already in the 1890s, enemies of the Higher Criticism recognized that archaeology might actually be used as a foil for skeptical philology, a position pioneered and popularized by Oxford professor of Assyriology A. H. Sayce, whose enormously popular *The Higher Criticism and the Verdict of the Monuments* first appeared in 1894.[19] In Germany, this position was vigorously defended by Ernst Sellin, professor at the University of Vienna. In the excavations underway in Egypt, Cyprus, Palestine, and Babylon, Sellin found cause for celebration; the excavations not only illustrated the accuracy of the Old Testament but also offered no evidence that Christianity owed anything substantial to any other culture. "In this sense," he wrote in 1905, a mere two years after the Babel-Bibel Streit, "one can say that the excavations form one of the most spectacular apologies for the Old Testament, and thus we ought to support them not only in the interest of scholarship, but even

---

[17] Nittert Janssen, *Theologie fürs Volk*, p. 186.

[18] Deutscher Verein zur Erforschung Palästinas to Kaiser, July 3, 1913, in B-GSPK, I 89, 21369.

[19] On Sayce, see Roshunda Belton, "A Non-Traditional Traditionalist: Reverend A. H. Sayce and His Intellectual Approach Authenticity and Biblical History in Late Victorian Britain" (Ph.D. dissertation, LSU, Baton Rouge, LA, 2007), and Mark Elliott, "Biblical Archaeology and Its Interpretation: The Sayce-Driver Controversy," published in *The Bible and Interpretation* (March 2003), available online at: http://www.bibleinterp.com/articles.

more importantly, in the [service] of religion."[20] Sellin himself would go on to perform small-scale excavations of Jericho, funded by wealthy Jewish private patrons (though he himself was no philo-Semite), and write attacks on Well-hausianism.[21] Most orientalists treated his Jericho findings (which included a large, ruined wall) as suspect, but nonetheless intriguing. The discovery of a huge cache of papyri – many of them documenting Jewish life under Persian rule – at Elephantine, on the other hand, was greeted with widespread hope that the findings would square with Old Testament accounts; the same could be said of Eduard Glaser's South Arabian inscriptions.[22] Archaeological finds like these were growing in number – as German institutions wrested new concessions from Ottoman officials – and for the younger generation in particular, they seemed to demonstrate the narrowness of Wellhausian internal text criticism as well as the imbeddedness of the cultural and spiritual history of Judaism and Christianity in the wider world of the ancient Orient.

By 1913, Wellhausen himself had moved from Old Testament criticism, through Islamic history to New Testament criticism – though his impact in New Testament studies would be minimal. He had also become entirely deaf and would be, until the end of his life in 1918, increasingly ill and isolated. Unwilling to accept much of the religious-historical literature, he fell off the pace; in a biographical entry on Wellhausen published in 1931, Hermann Gunkel explained his school's rise and fall:

[Wellhausen's] school succeeded in taking over a large portion of the Old Testament chairs and drawing the whole next cohort to its side, thanks in part to its remarkable talents, at least among its first generation, but thanks also to a series of favorable conditions: the lack of equally-talented opponents, the willingness at that time of the [state] governments, in [making] academic appointments in the field of theology, to give scholarly prowess first priority. Thus, for a long time, Wellhausen's assertions have been treated as fully certain. This scholarly situation has, since sometime around the beginning of this century gradually changed. The following objections have been raised, successfully, against W[ellhausen]: his

---

[20] Sellin, *Der Ertrag der Ausgrabungen im Orient für die Erkenntnis der Entwicklung der Religion Israels* (Leipzig, 1905), p. 39.

[21] Sellin's digs in Palestine were funded almost exclusively by the Jewish patron James Simon, who also contributed heavily to the Deutsche-Orient Gesellschaft's "secular" excavations in Mesopotamia; other DOG members apparently contributed little, however, to Sellin's cause. See Olaf Matthes, *James Simon: Mäzen im wilhelmischen Zeitalter* (Berlin, 2000), pp. 241–6. For Sellin's view of relations between Christianity and Judaism, see, e.g., Sellin, *Der Ertrag der Ausgrabungen im Orient*, p. 41.

[22] Eduard Meyer was moved to write an enthusiastic pamphlet on Elephantine: Meyer, *Der Papyrusfund von Elephantine* (Leipzig, 1911). Glaser made four trips to Yemen between 1882 and 1895, during which time he recorded numerous inscriptions and acquired large numbers of squeezes and artifacts, which are now held by the Kunsthistorisches Museum in Vienna. It took Glaser a very long time to publish his materials, and he was loathe to allow anyone else to see his stuff, which gave rise to much bitterness and also much speculation on their content. In 1889, Fritz Hommel predicted that when published, the South Arabian materials would offer Old Testament and Hebrew scholars "a mass of parallels, etymological explanations, etc., such as one could scarcely dream of now"; but the implication was that these would enhance the credibility of the scriptures, not diminish their originality. Fritz Hommel, "On the Historical Results of Eduard Glaser's Explorations in South Arabia," in *Hebraica* 6, no.1 (1889): 49–54, quotation p. 53.

overall vision was sketched without reference to the history of the other areas of the Orient of the time and cannot in all parts be made to concur with the ancient oriental discoveries, which have multiplied in such an unforeseen manner. The school – and especially its younger representatives – has buried itself in initially necessary and salutary but then increasingly fruitless literary criticism and has shown no serious comprehension of the literary history that has become more prominent in the last few years.[23]

As Werner Klatt has pointed out, Gunkel's scholarly practices actually owed a good deal to Wellhausen and he might have been a bit more generous in his assessment of the great philologist's legacy. But it was in keeping with the furor orientalis that Gunkel clearly considered himself not Wellhausen's heir, but his better.[24]

It should be noted that though it drew on the increasing numbers of nonwestern texts and artifacts accessible to Europeans, *Religionsgeschichte* was still chiefly about the West and especially about the future of Christianity; as Kurt Rudolph has pointed out, almost all the members of the religious-historical movement were in essence Old or New Testament scholars, not general comparativists or historians of non-European religions,[25] and many of them were sons of Lutheran clergymen or themselves professors of theology. But their attitudes toward the ancient Orient and its belief systems were much less dismissive and dogmatic than those of their liberal fathers. It is to their insistence on a new kind of inclusiveness that we owe much of the thinking that still informs the teaching of "world religions" in today's institutions – though it may also be the case that the backdoor defense of Christianity that has often characterized this field also owes a great deal to the ways in which this generation structured their new, comparative histories.[26]

New sources and inter-generational conflicts were crucial in expanding the study of the history of religion. But a series of entrepreneurial publishers, too, were instrumental in giving this movement its impetus – and its popular audience. One of the first efforts in this direction was the *Evangelisch-lutherische Gemeindeblatt für die gebildeten Glieder der evangelischen Kirchen*, founded in Leipzig in 1886; in 1889, this journal changed its name to the much more manageable

---

[23] Gunkel, "Wellhausen," in *Die Religion in Geschichte und Gegenwart*, vol. V, ed. Gunkel and L. Zscharnack (Tübingen, 1931), p. 1821.

[24] W. Klatt, "Die 'Religionsgeschichtliche Schule' in Giessen," in *Theologie im Kontext der Geschichte der Alma Mater Ludoviciana*, ed. Bernhard Jendorff et al. (Giessen, 1983), p. 119. It is rather amusing in this context to read Wilhelm Erbt's review of the third edition of Gunkel's Genesis book in the *OLZ*, 1914, in which Erbt writes: "For him, neither Amarna nor Boghazkoi existed. For him, Palestine was always an isolated island in a surging sea of peoples, as it was in the era of Wellhausen, when no one could have known better." *OLZ* 17 (1914): 70, 72. Like all other revolutionaries, the furious orientalists were willing to eat their children as well as their ancestors.

[25] Kurt Rudolph, "Eduard Nordens Bedeutung für die frühchristilche Religionsgeschichte, unter besonderer Berücksichtigung der 'Religionsgeschichtliche Schule,'" in *Eduard Norden (1868–1941): Ein deutscher Gelehrter jüdischer Herkunft*, ed. B. Kytzler et al. (Stuttgart, 1994), p. 87.

[26] Tomoko Masuzawa has recently offered a critical treatment of this legacy; she demonstrates nicely – though using primarily French and British examples – how this literature hangs on to a defense of Christianity, even while seemingly relativizing its uniqueness. Masuzawa, *Invention of World Religions*, pp. 309–28.

Christliche Welt and in 1892 it moved to Tübingen. It was followed by the *Theologische Rundschau*, founded in 1897 and edited for many years by two important members of the younger generation, Wilhelm Bousset and Wilhelm Heitmüller. The *Rundschau* was also based in Tübingen, and published by J. C. B. Mohr, which in 1896 also began issuing a *Sammlung gemeinverständlicher Vorträge und Schriften aus dem Gebiet der Theologie und Religionsgeschichte*; this long-lasting series printed its 188th and last number in 1945. In 1899, the same press would publish the Kautzsch-Weiszäcker *Textbibel des Alten und Neuen Testaments in Verbindung mit zahlreichen Fachgelehrten herausgegeben* (1899), a translation, with notes by scholars, but for non-scholarly Bible readers. Mohr was not the only house to ramp up its offerings in theology and religion in this era; Teubner Verlag, for example, longtime publisher of classical texts and specialized philological literature, followed Hermann Usener's school as it drifted into religious subjects, publishing the *Archiv für Religionswissenschaft* as well as numerous other works on the history of religion.[27]

Once begun, successful attempts to speak to the people through semi-popular publications were made by theological liberals and conservatives, as well as younger theologians; Harnack's *Essence of Christianity*, for example, sold 60,000 copies in three years' time.[28] But the younger generation remained much more outspoken in its backing for popularizing efforts and also more ambitious with respect to the size of audience it intended to reach. Often, in fact, its spokesmen accused the older generation of having failed to explain its scholarship to the public, and hence put Christianity in greater peril. The classic formulation of this critique was offered by Hermann Gunkel in *Die Christliche Welt* in 1900: "Dear God, if only I had a voice that would speak to the heart and conscience of every scholar of theology, I would proclaim, day and night, nothing other than this: do not forget your holy duty to your people! Write for the educated elite! Do not talk so much about literary criticism, text criticism, archaeology and all those other scholarly things, but talk about religion!.... Our people thirst for your words about religion and its history!"[29] But he was not alone. In the same year, Rabbi Felix Perles criticized generations of fearful scholars who, since Spinoza, had been convinced that in the hands of laypersons, the Higher Criticism would destroy Christian faith.[30] The crucial thing was not to defend the churches, but to reconfigure Christian ideas to fit modern consciousness and to do so before total cynicism, materialism, and atheism set in. Criticizing the liberals' failure to tackle the preservation of *Glaube* by speaking directly to the public (rather than letting the burden fall on the ill-educated provincial clergy), these men saw themselves not just as scholars but as educators with a crucial cultural mission.

Thanks to the dovetailing of its interests and ambitions with those of the publishing houses, the younger generation was, after 1903, able to expand its endeavors considerably. After delivering a series of popularly oriented lectures on

---

[27] Reinhold Merkelbach, "Die Altertumswissenschaft bei Teubner," in *Wechselwirkungen: Der wissentschaftliche Verlag als Mittler: 175 Jahre B. G. Teubner, 1811–1986* (Stuttgart, 1986), p. 24.

[28] Graf, "*Rettung*," p. 109; Janssen, *Theologie fürs Volk*, p. 150.

[29] Gunkel quoted in Graf, "*Rettung*," p. 108.

[30] Perles, review of Kautzsch-Weisäcker, in *OLZ* 3 (1900): 63–5.

"The Essence of Religion" in Hanover, Wilhelm Bousset, one of the leaders in religious-historical thinking, was approached by the Wilhelm Ruprecht Verlag with the intention of publishing them. What happened next, however, was more momentous. Instead of going with a relatively small and expensive edition, Bousset interested his brother Hermann in the venture. Hermann, who had just become business manager of the Gebauer-Schwetschke Verlag in Halle, sold the idea of publishing Bousset's lectures at an inexpensive price (4 Marks, 284 pages) and of beginning a series of similar tracts, addressed to a circle much wider than the professional theologians; though building on earlier publications, like Mohr Verlag's *Sammlung gemeinverständlicher Vorträge und Schriften*, this was really an effort to tone down the science in favor of reaching women, elementary school teachers, and the "middle bourgeoisie," and not just university graduates. The *Religionsgeschichtliche Volksbücher* series was begun; by 1913, it had succeeded far beyond the Boussets' dreams, selling some 500,000 copies.[31]

As Hermann Gunkel said of the popularization of theological work in 1913, "[s]ince then an extraordinary rich, even un-surveyable popular theological literature has, as if from a thousand sources, flowed forth! Pamphlets, essays in newspapers, whole journals and newspapers, books, larger works! All points of view are represented. In many cases a hundred or more pamphlets have appeared in the course of a couple of years on the very same subject, which are then accompanied by the small arms' fire of numberless newspaper articles...."[32] As this suggests, popular publishing proved to be one way to get the religious-historical agenda discussed widely, even when the group's members found institutional power difficult to wrest from their liberal "fathers."

But, as their tactics were quickly imitated both by their more conservative and by their more radical opponents,[33] popularization did not mean any group achieved anything resembling hegemony in religious thought. In addition to taking on the predictable conflicts with orthodox theologians, the religious-historical school soon found itself facing inflammatory contributions published by the esoteric Eugen Diederichs Verlag. Diederichs himself was deeply interested in the subject of oriental religions, but by no means did he want to publish garden-variety theology. Three of his books, Albert Kalthoff's *Das Christusproblem* (1902), Arthur Bonus's *Vom neuen Mythos* (1911), and Arthur Drews' *Die Christusmythe* (1909), would prove particularly controversial − but lucrative as well, sufficiently so that he would gradually expand his popular offerings on world religions, in 1912 commencing two new multi-volume series, *Religiöse Stimmen der Völker* and *Religion und Philosophie Chinas*.[34] For academics like Gunkel − "furious" as they might be − the widening outward of theological debates encouraged by organizations like the Diedrichs Verlag offered both new opportunities to reach readers − and the ever-present possibility that

[31] Janssen, *Theologie fürs Volk*, pp. 150–9.
[32] Gunkel quoted in ibid., p. 180, n. 96.
[33] Two examples of the defense in the popular realm were Johannes Nikel, *Alte und neue Angriffe auf das Alte Testament* (1908), and J. Rohr, *Der Vernichtungskampf gegen das biblische Christusbild* (2nd ed., 1908).
[34] On Diederichs, see Gary D. Stark, *Entrepreneurs of Ideology: Neoconservative Publishers in Germany, 1890–1933* (Chapel Hill, NC, 1981), pp. 70–4.

someone else would seize the culture's tiller, and never again let the "scientists" steer.

Conservative theologians, not surprisingly, dismissed the new school out of hand. But even many liberals, including Adolf von Harnack, did not approve of the new school and often found its publications lacking in rigor, reverence, and even significance. As Hermann Gunkel recalled in 1922: "The history of religions was for the 'positivists' a scandal and for the Wellhausians a form of stupidity."[35] Indeed, a number of highly talented graduates of this school did have to languish a long while in the wilderness before their work became academically respectable and their careers secure.[36] While chairs for comparative religion were founded in the Netherlands, France, Italy, and Sweden, and extensive work was underway in English, Scottish, and Belgian universities, the German system had no chair for comparative religion until just before the outbreak of the Great War. The explosion of studies of Iranian, Egyptian, Tibetan, Islamic, Assyrian, Chinese, and other religions made itself felt in public lectures and in seminars on "allgemeine Religionsgeschichte,"[37] but did not generate many paid academic positions, and in turn, little respect for specialists in the field. Bad feeling was generated in particular by Harnack's refusal to allow the University of Berlin to create a position in *Religionsgeschichte* in the theological faculty. In 1901, Harnack delivered a *Rektoratsrede*, insisting that there was no need to study religions other than Christianity. "He who doesn't know this religion [Christianity], knows none, and he who knows all of its history, knows all [religions]." "What is the significance of Homer, of the Vedas, of the Qur'an next to that of the Bible?" he asked.[38] Institutionally, at least, Harnack prevailed; when at last a chair was founded in 1914, it was placed in the philosophical faculty. In previous generations, of course, many scholars had been denied full institutional ratification and their new ideas quashed. But this was a more self-consciousness cohort, and from its sufferings, ideas and abiding grudges were born.

As in the study of ancient culture more generally, the history of religions in Germany tended to downplay the universal and anthropological aspects of religion so central to contemporary studies going on to the West (in England and France), to the North (in Scandinavia and the Netherlands), and even to the South (in Austria and Italy). What Max Müller, in 1890, called the "German style" of studying comparative religion[39] was one deeply imbued with philological methods and prerogatives; here it was presumed that differences between cultures and

---

[35] Gunkel quoted in Gunnar Sinn, *Christologie und Existenz: Rudolf Bultmanns Interpretation des paulinischen Christuszeugnisses* (Tübingen, 1991), p. 17.

[36] Gunkel, who started in New Testament theology, was strongly advised to move his iconoclastic mind to Old Testament work, where contextualization was a bit less controversial. But even here, he did not receive a full professorship until 1907, by which time he was 45. Alfred Jeremias held a *Privatdozent* position for fifteen years, until, in 1921, he received a *nichtplanmässig* assistant professorship at the University of Leipzig.

[37] For a sampling of this work, see Kurt Rudolph, *Die Religionsgeschichte an der Leipziger Universität*, pp. 79–111.

[38] Adolf Harnack, *Die Aufgabe der theologischen Facultäten und die allgemeine Religionsgeschichte* (Giessen, 1901), p. 11.

[39] Rudolph, *Religionsgeschichte an der Leipziger Universität*, p. 49.

languages were more important than similarities, that the divide between the literate and the non-literate cultures was uncrossable, and that cultures invented rather little and preferred to borrow from one another. As suggested in Chapter 5, in Germany after the 1880s, discussions of influence and dependence were pervasive, often bitter, and extremely consequential – despite frequent protestations that the significance and power of a phenomenon (such as Judaism) was not exhausted by demonstrating its partial dependence on earlier forms. The quest for origins tended to be played as a winner-take-all game, which meant that the order in which texts or artifacts were found and the dates given to them were extremely important.

In this respect, it is quite significant that the members of the religious-historical school focused so much of their attention on oriental paganism, applying to it what Gunkel called the "traditionsgeschichtliche Method." This method assumed that sacred texts represented the culmination of long periods in which religious ideas and practices were transmitted orally and informally; thus, one could read *backward* from them to learn about the earlier periods in which ideas had been borrowed and communities shaped. Gunkel's method – which he first applied to the book of Genesis in 1895 – represented essentially a reworking of Lachmannian song theory, according to which it was suggested that the texts that westerners now possessed (like the *Iliad* and the *Nibelungenlied*) were late arriving compilations of much older folk stories or songs and commonplace phrases, transmitted orally from one generation or group to the next. This made it possible to offer interesting suggestions about historical layers betrayed by the texts, and to suggest, just as in the case of the Panbabylonists reading backward from Assyrian to Babylonian culture, that rather recent texts might contain words, customs, or ideas that were much, much older.

That the dates pushed backward in the prewar period were chiefly those of non-Jewish oriental cultures and texts meant that Judaism, in particular, lost much of its originality and uniqueness, while previously the reviled pagan systems of Babylon, Egypt, and ancient Persia were accorded new respect. It is telling that in 1909, Carl Clemen, who would have to wait eighteen years between his habilitation (1892) and his acquisition of an assistant professorship at the University of Bonn (1910), was able to publish a lengthy, synthetic book entitled *Religionsgeschichtliche Erklärung des Neuen Testaments*, subtitled, significantly, *Die Abhängigkeit des ältesten Christentums von nichtjüdischen Religionen und philosophischen Systemen*. As the subtitle indicates, the book treated explicitly the dependence of Christianity on non-Jewish religions. Positioning himself as a moderate, Clemen spent many of its pages discounting the wilder claims of the "furious" orientalists – though he also berated the older scholars for lending their authority to unproven hypotheses rather than "warning against the improper application of new methods."[40] The methods in question were Gunkel's "tradition-historical" approach and diffusionist history-writing more generally; the most egregious and improper application of these methods, he thought, was their

---

[40] Clemen, *Religionsgeschichtliche Erklärung des Neuen Testaments: Die Abhängigkeit des ältesten Christentums von nichtjüdischen Religionen und philosophischen Systemen* (Giessen, 1909), p. 289.

use to divorce Christianity entirely from Judaism. Clemen admitted that it was normal, in the first stages of new discoveries, for people to be excited by similarities between ancient religious practices and ideas, but insisted that on closer examination, it was clear that no part of the "inner essence" of Christianity had been borrowed from non-Jewish sources. But that statement, as Clemen well knew, depended in turn on what one construed to be Christianity's "inner essence," how one identified similarities, and whether or not one thought borrowing constituted a creative act – or essentially boiled down to thievery. And by no means did all of those drinking from the ever-deepening well of *Orientalistik* answer those questions in the same way, especially when they were posed with respect to a Greek text many still considered sacred, namely, the New Testament.

THE ORIENTAL ORIGINS OF NEW TESTAMENT CHRISTIANITY

Though German historians of religion at the fin de siècle busied themselves with the study of numerous world faiths, the most visible and consequential of their pursuits surely lay in the excavation of the sources of the New Testament. In this field, as opposed to that of Old Testament studies, orientalists entered as relative novices, contributing to a new round of powerful and painful historicization that had already been started by late romantic theologians and philosophers.[41] Importantly, the Tübingen School, in the 1830s and 1840s had made vigorous and, for their members, dangerous moves in this direction; here, internal philological critique (Greek, Hebrew, and Syriac) and philosophical rationalism was used to fuel bitter and intense debates about the Gospels' chronology, veracity, and means of transmission. But the mental shift Wilhelm Bousset would describe as "the transition from Jerusalem to Antioch," the locating of Christianity's origins in the wider Hellenistic world *beyond* Palestine, was again the work of the fin de siècle.[42]

This is not to say that the liberal generations did not prepare the path to Antioch. Though New Testament criticism in the mid-nineteenth century had been heavily internalist, close philological study had made for revolutionary changes in understanding the order and authorship of various bits of the Gospels and Paul's epistles. At mid-century, D. F. Strauss had challenged the pervasive romantic-era view that the Gospel of John was chronologically the first and theologically the most authentic Gospel; in the decades to follow, a strong consensus emerged among liberal exegetes in favor of the Marcan hypothesis, that is, the theory that Mark's Gospel is the earliest and follows most faithfully a very

---

[41] Ever ahead of the pack, Herder had suggested in 1775 that the "broken" Greek of the apostles was not a special biblical language, but a Hellenistic patois suffused with ideas from Judea, Persia, Egypt, Chaldea, Greece, and Rome. Herder, "Erläuterungen zum Neuen Testament aus einer neueröfneten Morgenländischen Quelle," in Herder, *SW* 7: 359.

[42] Bousset, "Foreword to the First Edition" [1913], in idem, *Kyrios Christos: A History of the Belief in Christ from the Beginnings of Christianity to Irenaeus*, trans. John E. Steely (Nashville, 1970), p. 13.

primitive source (*Urmarcus*), used also by the other synoptic writers.[43] By no means were all textual problems solved, and indeed, William Wrede would destabilize New Testament criticism again in 1901 by showing that Mark's account of the life of Jesus too was a theological fabrication.[44] But after about 1880, agreement on the piecemeal construction of the synoptic Gospels made it seem logical that to solve the remaining mysteries and internal contradictions scholars needed to move *outside* the texts to the chaotic world in which they were produced.

This turn to context was also related to the attempt to clarify Jesus' message for modern Europeans. We have seen how important – and dangerous – this question was for mid-century liberals like D. F. Strauss and Ernst Renan and how effective Strauss's *Leben Jesu* was in provoking conservative reaction. The same could be said for Renan's *Vie de Jésus*, published in French in 1863, and translated immediately into German.[45] Composed during the French scholar's visit to Palestine, Renan's *Life* emphasized the geographical particularities of Palestine (the "fifth Gospel," in Renan's words) as well as Jesus' personal charisma. Liberal-era German scholars, though critical of Renan's aestheticism and apparent atheism, similarly emphasized the personality of Jesus, underscoring too his ethical work in the world. The next generation would see Jesus' charisma in a different, rather more vitalist light; their savior was less a teacher of proper moral behavior than an apocalyptic prophet. Similarly, though they would follow the liberals from the texts to the context, their view of "primitive Christianity" would be less circumscribed than that of the liberals, including Renan himself – for whom the two operative traditions were Greek philosophy and Jewish messianism. As we will see in the section on interpretations of Saint Paul at the end of this chapter, working out which other cultures had contributed to the formation of early Christianity became a matter of urgent importance.

For the "furious" contributors to the New Testament debates, the world of the New Testament was, more than ever before, an oriental world. That it was now possible to see the Hellenistic world in this way was again the product of our Second Oriental Renaissance. By the fin de siècle, there were new grammars – Gustav Dalman's *Palestinian-Aramaic Grammar* appeared in 1894 – and massive new syntheses – like Emil Schürer's *Geschichte des Jüdischen Volkes im Zeitalter Jesu Christi* (three volumes, 1886–90); there were topographical studies and new papyri from Oxyrhynchus and Elephantine. There were excavations underway at Hellenistic sites such as Ephesus, Baalbek, Palmyra and Pergamon, and massive new early Christian and late Roman finds in Italy, Croatia, and France. New caches of Gnostic and Manichean texts came to light, including letters, poems, Psalms, hymns, and apocryphal stories about Jesus and the apostles, written by philosophical iconoclasts whom the churches deemed heretics. For scholars of the period, it must have been at once a thrilling – or "electric," as Littmann put it – age

---

[43] This was the solution proposed by Adolf Holtzmann in 1863, building on previous work of C. H. Weisse and others, including Herder, who had suggested Mark as the earliest, precisely because of the "primitiveness" of the language and its non-theological qualities.

[44] Wrede's claims were made in his *Das Messiasgeheimnis in den Evangelien* (Göttingen, 1901). See Baird, *History of New Testament Research*, pp. 147–8.

[45] Indeed, an eleventh edition of the illustrated, popular edition of Renan's *Life* was published in Berlin in 1864.

and also a terrifying one; who knew if a series of deductions put forward one day would hold the next?

Of course, the orientalists were the frontline interpreters of this material, much of which had to be sorted, deciphered, and dated, and this role certainly enhanced *Orientalistik*'s appeal to theologians. But theologians now could also learn much from new departures in classics, where the Creuzer taboo was at last wearing off. The fin de siècle saw an astonishing increase in work on Creuzer's most infamous subject, oriental mystery cults, as well as rising interest in the Hellenistic world. Because the Greek spoken in this world was the feared and reviled "silver" Greek, and because so much inquiry here focused on the origins of Christianity question, this was an era that had largely been avoided by mid-century classicists. J. G. Droysen had lamented the unwillingness of historians and classicists to study the post-Alexandrian age in the first volume of his *Geschichte des Hellenismus* (1836),[46] but the period was still being ignored when Droysen's second edition came out in 1877–8. As late as 1907, Paul Wendland, professor of classical philology in Breslau, described the lingering "Atticist" prejudices which had dominated the field before the great excavations in Asia Minor began. But the new archaeological finds, he wrote, were forcing the classicists to recognize the narrowness of their conceptions of the ancient world. "The work of the spade," he wrote, ". . . has set before [classics] imperative new tasks and goals which the protests of aestheticizing connoisseurs – who don't care about historical problems – cannot drive away." Moreover, he added, theologians pursuing studies of "primitive Christianity" too now had recognized "the necessity of studying the history not only of later Judaism, but also the history of its roots in the culture which reigned at the time of Christianity's spread."[47] At long last, the disciplinary divisions that had inhibited the study of the Hellenistic world for the better part of a century were breaking down and allowing scholars to appreciate the world-historical importance of this crucial period.

One of the theologians most energized by new interdisciplinary studies of the Hellenistic world was Adolf Deissmann, author, in 1908, of a hugely popular study entitled *Licht vom Osten: Das Neue Testament und die neuentdeckten Texte aus dem hellenistisch-römischen Welt*. Deissmann confirmed that archaeology had come to the rescue of theology by providing scholars with papyri, inscribed pot-sherds, and other everyday artifacts from the time of Christ which made it possible to show that the New Testament was not an isolated work created by elite theologians, but rather a book written in the language of the Savior's humble contemporaries. For too long, Deissmann argued, the "primeval prejudices of the Atticizers," inculcated in Gymnasium-Greek, had prevented even theologians from recognizing that the Greek world had not ended with Alexander, and that popular religious sects of many types had continued to think and speak in Greek. The new finds allowed inquirers to appreciate "the embeddness of primitive Christianity in folk culture" [die Volkstümlichkeit des Urchristentums] and to understand the success of Christianity's message; the popular piety and cultic

---

[46] Johann Gustav Droysen, *Geschichte des Hellenismus*, vol. I (Hamburg, 1836), p. v.

[47] Paul Wendland, *Die hellenistisch-römisch Kultur in ihren Beziehung zu Judentum und Christentum* (Tübingen, 1907), p. 3.

practices of the East were the key to understanding what had been and should always be a book of and for the people.[48]

Deissmann also hoped that fellow students of the Gospels would have the chance, as he did, to travel in the Holy Land and to see familiar texts reanimated by the appropriate "eastern" light. After all, as he stated in the book's opening lines, "The Gospel was first preached beneath an eastern sky. Jesus and Paul were sons of the East."[49] It was by going East, by abandoning, at least to some degree, western scholarly strictures that one could actually understand what was for Deissmann the world's most significant set of texts. He wanted to plunge his contemporaries – laymen as well as scholars – into the oriental thought-world from which Christian salvation had come. Europeans had to face up to the fact that Jesus was, as Friedrich Naumann put it, "a foreigner from a past social world"[50]; the hope was that an oriental Jesus was not too foreign to speak truth to the alienated western soul.

BUDDHA VERSUS JESUS; OR, FIN DE SIÈCLE CHRISTIANS AND THE PROBLEM OF PARALLELS

But of course Jesus was not the only "oriental" sage to speak truth to the peoples of the ancient world; and at the fin de siècle, some Europeans began to think they might prefer a less conventional savior. Especially in the wake of the huge popularity of Edwin Arnold's epic recounting of the life of Siddharta Gautama, *Light from the East*, published in 1879, Buddhism began to seem less like a superstitious and nihilistic cult and more like a proper religion; the parallels Arnold suggested between Buddha and Jesus intrigued those seeking new forms of solace and enraged traditional Christians. The number of actual converts was very small; but counting them cannot help us understand the much broader effects of Buddhism's increasingly positive reception among the European elite. For Christian modernizers, Buddhism was an intellectual challenge; as a philosophical religion which clung to the here and now, it was – as its advocates never ceased to repeat – more easily reconcilable with modern natural science than was miracle-ridden Christianity. But even more threatening was Buddhism's historical priority and the similarities that could be identified between the lives of Buddha and of Christ. We will never take the measure of Buddhism's cultural importance for Europeans until we see it juxtaposed to Bible studies and New Testament theology – until, that is, we see how fin de siècle believers dealt with the problem of parallels.

Edwin Arnold was not the first to note similarities between the two great teachers; indeed, at mid-century, there were already some posing the question in its genealogical form: what did Jesus owe to Buddha? One of the most provocative was the French dilettante and colonial official Louis Jacolliot, author of *La Bible dans l'Inde, vie de Iezeus Christna* (1869). In this book, the Indophile descendant of Volataire claimed that Jesus had visited India and brought back all his important

---

[48] Deissmann, *Licht vom Osten*, pp. 39, 278, 282.

[49] Ibid., pp. vi–vii, quotation p. 1.

[50] Friedrich Naumann, *Asia: Eine Orientreise über Athen, Kontantinopel, Baalbek, Nazareth, Jerusalem, Kairo, Neapel* (Berlin, 7th ed., 1909), p. 120.

ideas from there. Jacolliot's book, together with the essays of Émile Burnouf (written 1864–8, published together in 1872), proved extremely popular and provoked an angry response from Max Müller.[51] If Jacolliot convinced neither professional orientalists nor orthodox Christians, his work did push some unsettling parallels to the fore and contributed further to the crumbling of another "wall of untranslatability," the one, that is, that had separated New Testament ideas and those of religious leaders further to the East.

We should recall that for German readers, the work of Arnold, Jacolliot, and Burnouf rode in on the heels of Strauss's *Der alte und der neue Glaube* and Paul de Lagarde's inflammatory essays, feeding an increasingly public discussion of the need for a new religion, one that did not contradict modern knowledge. This was the project pursued by Madame Blavatsky, also active in this era, and by Rudolf Steiner, who also looked to eastern traditions in pursuit of a truly rational and universal religion, which would at last reconcile science and faith.[52] Some looked to Brahmanism for inspiration, but for adherents of the tradition of *Kulturprotestantismus*, Buddhism seemed particularly attractive, for it was, as its adherents frequently pointed out, a religion without a transcendent sphere and thus one easy to reconcile with this-worldly natural (and philological) science. At the same time, Buddhism rejected the materialism of the purely scientific standpoint and offered individuals a means to overcome fatalism by self-willed action. It promised diminution or just rejection of the "struggle for existence" cultural critics found so pervasive in modern social and economic relations. And, as one of Germany's early converts to Buddhism Paul Dahlke argued, in a 1912 pamphlet titled *Die Bedeutung des Buddhismus für unsere Zeit*, in the absence of the "saving barbarity" that had rescued the European spirit after the fall of Rome, it was the only true source of new moral values, without which technological "Zivilisation" could not survive.[53]

We will examine in a bit more detail below those who actually converted to Buddhism, a quite small but culturally active group, but it would be premature to make them central actors in the cultural sphere of the 1880s and 1890s. For the first major German intervention into Buddhist studies was a quintessential product of high liberal thought, one that continued in many respects the rationalist criticism of Buddhism evident in Karl Koeppen's work of the 1850s – though it lacked Koeppen's Young Hegelian affection for Buddha's solidarity with the poor. This was Hermann Oldenberg's widely circulated *Buddha*, published in 1881. Here, Oldenberg, a twenty-six-year-old *Privatdozent* at the University of Berlin, presented Buddhism primarily as a sign of the Aryans' decline; it was the result of adapting to tropical conditions and of Indian disinclination for work, state-building, law, and freedom.[54] Though some of his prejudices were carried forward by the next generation, Oldenberg proceeded quite differently in his study than

---

[51] See Masuzawa, *Invention of World Religions*, pp. 246–53. For Jacolliot's influence on Nietzsche, see Dorothy Figueira, *Aryans, Jews, Brahmins: Theorizing Authority through Myths of Identity* (Albany, NY, 2002), pp. 52–3.

[52] For Steiner, see, e.g., his lectures of 1904–5, collected in Steiner, *Die Grundbegriffe der Theosophie* (Dornach, 1957), pp. 15–16.

[53] Dahlke, *Die Bedeutung des Buddhismus für unsere Zeit* (Berlin, 1912), pp. 7, 16.

[54] Oldenberg, *Buddha: Sein Leben, sein Lehre, sein Gemeinde* (Berlin, 1881), pp. 11–12.

would many German specialists afterward; his work was, one would have to say, sociological rather than genealogical; he pitched its importance as "the study of those everywhere-valid norms, which dictate changes in the religious thought of [all] peoples...."[55] Working directly from indigenous sources – and especially from the earliest Pali texts – he described Buddhism as a social and cultural system rather than attempting to discern where it had borrowed foreign elements or what dates to assign to texts. He did not compare it to Christianity, except insofar as both were religious systems, nor did he extract any lessons about modern spirituality, eastern or western, from his inquiries. In this accessible and widely read book, the liberal positivist tradition was alive and well, happily declaring its preference for the Greeks in things philosophical and the Jews in religious ideas and displaying a fundamental disinterest in ultimate meanings or the relevance of its findings.

On reviewing the sixth edition of Oldenberg's *Buddha* in 1914, one writer commented that the book "belongs to the most widely-circulated books in all of orientalist literature. In many circles, reading it is seen as the furthering of one's all-around cultivation."[56] As of 2009, it is still in print in German and in English, which should remind us of the enduring respectability of this study as compared with some of those generated by the debates I will describe below. The "liberal" tradition in Buddhist studies – just as in classical studies and Old Testament scholarship – was not destroyed by the threats to it at the fin de siècle, and indeed Oldenberg went on to a professorship at Kiel (1889) and then at the University of Göttingen (1908). But soon after his Kiel appointment, Oldenberg too began to feel the power of the religious-historical undertow and focused his later work on Vedic philology and religious life. Similarly, the question Oldenberg skirted in *Buddha* about the genealogical relations between Christianity and Indian religions soon would become troubling to Christian scholars. Here, one might even say, the idea that Buddhism might in fact be one of Christianity's precursors (rather than simply another pagan rival) had the same sort of effect as the Hermetic texts and the *Hieroglyphica* had on their predecessors in the Baroque era. To be sure, the "liberal" tradition and its prejudices endured; but for those who still believed faith and philological science should be reconciled, the problem of Buddhist parallels required taking seriously yet another set of "oriental" texts.

Our story begins the year after the publication of Oldenberg's *Buddha*, in 1882, when Rudolf Seydel, a now forgotten professor of philosophy at the University of Leipzig, felt himself compelled to publish a comparative study of Christianity and Buddhism. Seydel was a devoted student of the liberal biblical scholar Christian Hermann Weisse and no stranger to controversy.[57] But in the 1880s, he struck out on a new path, that of understanding the "religionsgeschichtliche Gesetze," which all religions followed. To this end, Seydel studied faith-founders and religious practices of all sorts, Egyptian, Buddhist, Native American, Assyrian, and

---

[55] Ibid., p. 6.
[56] J. von Negelein, review of H. Oldenberg, *Buddha*, in *OLZ* 17 (1914): 476.
[57] See Seydel's *Katholicismus und Freimaurerei: Ein Wort zur Entgegnung auf die vom Freiherr von Ketteler, Bishof von Mainz wider den Freimauerbund erhobenen Anklagen* (Leipzig, 2nd ed., 1865).

European pagan; he took the enlightened Lessing as his model, invoking *Nathan der Weise* and *Die Erziehung des Menschengeschlechts*, whose moral, according to Seydel, was "that the history of the religious evolution of humankind is the history of divine revelation."[58] Seydel believed this, but realized that compelling, detailed orientalist scholarship had made the problem of tracing this evolution more risky. For modern Christians, it was necessary to know that one's faith did not rest on ignorance of the *full* truth, and to do this, one had to take the fully scientific, historical path.

For Seydel, the most pressing question was, what did Christianity owe to Buddhism? To answer this, he offered a synthetic overview of such parallels, drawn from the recent translations and explications of Buddhism, for Seydel was no philologist and did not know Sanskrit at this time – though he later began to learn the language to defend his claims against philological critiques.[59] Together with a long section, which attempted to date the formation of the Buddha legends to the pre-Alexandrian age, the parallels formed most of the book. Seydel spent rather little time, on the other hand, trying to specify exactly how the life of the Buddha had been transformed into the apostles' accounts of the life of Christ; perhaps, he speculated that there had been a third source for the Gospels, along with the lost texts upon which Mark and Matthew had drawn, a "poetic-apocalyptic Gospel," which represented a Christian reworking of the Buddhist biographies. Pushing up to a later era Carl Ritter's romantic portrayal of Indian monotheism's dispersal, Seydel suggested that Buddhist missionaries might have traveled the trade routes between India and the Levant, bringing with them ideas that would be fruitful for the birth of the new religion.[60] In any event, the similarities between Buddhism and Christianity, and Buddhism's temporal priority, pointed directly to the latter faith's dependence on the earlier one. That did not mean, however, that Christianity was the inferior religion; on the contrary, Seydel argued, in typical liberal-era fashion, Christianity had absorbed universal and this-worldly, positive elements from "European Aryan" religions, endowing it with a less contradictory set of ethics and a greater scope for individual freedom than Buddhism permitted. Seydel concluded that Christianity was the most perfect and complete religion – but also warned against hubris; "It is, instead, the duty of Christians to renounce themselves, and not to slander the Holy Spirit where it appears as a 'guide in all truth' in other vestments as those to which we are accustomed."[61]

Philological and Christian theological criticisms provoked Seydel to work on a revised edition of *Das Evangelium*, but the Leipzig scholar died before it reached the printers. The new version, now titled *Die Buddha-Legende und das Leben Jesu nach den Evangelien: Erneute Prüfung ihres gegenseitigen Verhältnisses*, was published in 1897, by Seydel's son Martin, also a theologian-philosopher, and looked

---

[58] Seydel, *Das Evangelium von Jesu in seinen Verhältnissen zu Buddhasage und Buddha-Lehre mit fortlaufender Rücksicht auf andere Religionskreise* (Leipzig, 1882), p. 8.

[59] Martin Seydel, "Vorwort zu zweiten Auflage," in Rudolf Seydel, *Die Buddha-Legende und das Leben Jesu nach den Evangelien. Erneute Prüfung ihres gegenseitigen Verhältnisses* (Weimar, 2nd ed., 1897), pp. vi–vii.

[60] Seydel, *Evangelium*, pp. 304–14.

[61] Ibid., pp. 117–18, quotation, p. 319.

quite different from the original. We should recall that between 1882 and 1897, quite a lot of orientalist water had passed under the bridge. The period saw the integration of Schopenhauer into popular Indology, by Karl Eugen Neumann and Paul Deussen (Chapter 7), as well as the convening of the World Parliament of Religions and the impressive appearance there of Swami Vivekananda. This was the era in which Assyriology began its rise, in which archaeological expeditions expanded, and in which new patrons for oriental studies emerged (see Chapters 8 and 9). Domestic political and social changes of great magnitude and significance had also occurred. This was the period in which a large influx of Eastern European Jews, fleeing pogroms in the Pale, moved into Central Europe, inciting the anti-pathy in particular of the Germans of the Austro-Hungarian Empire. After being banned for twelve years, the socialist party was legalized again in 1890; its ranks swelled immediately and the Catholics recovered sufficiently from the *Kultur-kampf* to form their own politically powerful parties. Women had begun attending universities; soccer clubs mushroomed; bicycles became ubiquitous. Cabarets and cafés flourished; church attendance plummeted. And, of course, in 1884, Germany had joined the ranks of the colonizers. Internally and externally, German culture and Christian belief were being transformed, often in ways that the traditional Protestant elites found painful and perilous.

Seydel accordingly recast the problem of how to conceive Christianity with respect to Buddhism and did so in a strikingly *less* universalist manner. The problem of parallels was now a more pressing one, and Seydel, or perhaps his son the editor, was not as ecumenical as he had been in 1882. The rules for assessing borrowing were now stated more directly, as a "Canon of Logical Probability": "The probability of the independent origin declines in proportion to the increasing specificity of similarities and the increasing frequency of those specifics." Though Seydel continued to insist that the parallel elements and the chronology pointed to Christianity's heavy borrowing from Buddhism, he now claimed that the point of recognizing what he now called "pagan ornament" in the Jesus story was to liberate the Savior from his "husks" so that all could clearly recognize him. "We will more easily reclaim the true image of the master if the foreign origins of his disfigurement are clear."[62] Lessing and the remnants of "ancient theology" were now gone, and with them the Enlightenment's trust in universal religious truth and the injunction to admire other vestments.

Seydel was, of course, not alone in retreating from mid-century liberal theol-ogy, which had been willing to criticize some aspects of Christian history and doctrine. Mid-century scholars had done so, however, confident that they still inhabited a world which did not question the superiority of Christian ethics and ideas. But as secularization and socialism diminished church attendance, and as challenges to the New Testament's historicity and originality multiplied, this presumption seemed no longer supportable. Christian theologians began to feel the necessity of specifying what the "essence" of Christianity actually boiled down to; a proper definition, they hoped, would not only demonstrate what Ernst Troeltsch would call "the absolute truth" of Christianity but also convince con-temporaries of the need to preserve their faith. In his lectures entitled "What Is

[62] Seydel, *Buddha-Legende*, pp. 20 (emphasis in the original), 125.

Christianity?" Adolf von Harnack sought to reassure believers that Christianity was in no sense a derivative religion, mentioning in his list of the current purveyors of false truths both those who claim that "primitive Christianity was closely akin to Buddhism" and those who insist that Christianity "must be thought of simply and solely as a higher phase of Judaism."[63] The energy Harnack put into this quest for the essence of Christianity was surely a function of his anxiety about the survival of the faith in a rapidly modernizing world. But as he himself recognized, the debate itself had been generated by the logic of historicism. Theologically, Jesus had to be a real man, which, as Harnack explained, "means, in the first place, to possess a certain mental and spiritual disposition, determined in such and such a way, and thereby limited and circumscribed; and in the second place, it means to be situated, with this disposition, in an historical environment which in its turn is also limited and circumscribed."[64] The now numerous "lives of Jesus" in wide circulation and the falling of the second wall of untranslatability, between the New Testament and the oriental world, made this contextualization problem an acute one, so acute indeed that the young Albert Schweitzer argued, in his epoch-making *Quest of the Historical Jesus* (1905; originally titled *Von Reimarus zu Wrede*), that theologians should simply stop historicizing and opt for eschatology.

Professional Indologists were also made uncomfortable by the discussions about Buddhism's relationship to Christianity. On the one hand, they were quite happy to see the study of Buddhism obtain such prominence both in scholarly and popular realms. It was with real pride that Leopold von Schroeder, professor of Indology at the University of Vienna, wrote in 1899: "Every newspaper wants an essay, every *Verein* wants to have a lecture about the Buddha."[65] On the other, the actual adoption of Buddhism, especially by some of their former students, was deeply distressing to a group of men who, if unconventional in their beliefs, remained loyal to some sort of cultural Protestantism. In 1893, Schroeder, who had himself briefly flirted with Buddhism in the 1880s – and apparently forfeited a fiancée as a result[66] – warned that admiration of Buddha's moral character and toleration for others should not result in the playing of Indian ideas against Christian ones, or the crediting of Buddhism with all of Christianity's good ideas. The faiths were actually quite dissimilar; while Christianity offered redemption from sin, Buddhism preached salvation from life. One could learn about others without succumbing to their thrall, he argued; the classical Renaissance had not killed Christianity and there was no reason that an Indological one should do so either.[67]

Even more anxious to staunch a presumed flood of European attraction to Buddhism was Joseph Dahlmann, Indologist and Jesuit priest. In 1898, Dahlmann published three lectures under the title *Buddha: Ein Culturbild des Ostens*, which

---

[63] Harnack, *What Is Christianity? Lectures Delivered in the University of Berlin During the Winter Term 1899–1901*, trans. Thomas Bailey Saunders (New York, 1901), p. 2.

[64] Ibid., p. 12.

[65] Schroeder, "Indiens Geistige Bedeutung für Europa," in idem, *Reden und Aufsätze*, p. 181.

[66] Perry Myers, "Leopold von Schroeder's Imagined India: Buddhist Spirituality and Christian Politics during the Wilhelmine Era," unpublished paper, cited with author's permission.

[67] Schroeder, "Buddhismus und Christentum, was sie gemein haben und was sie unterscheidet" (1893; 2nd ed. 1898), in idem, *Reden und Aufsätze*," pp. 106–25.

might better have been titled: *Buddha: The Cause of the Culturelessness of the East*. Dahlmann opened by invoking the recently explored, decrepit ruins of the Buddha's birthplace, Kapilavastu, an appropriate metaphor, he argued, for the inner rot of Aryan Indian culture. In Dahlmann's view, Buddhism was the bastard son of Brahmanism; it represented neither a true program of religious and social reform nor an organic continuation of the great religious and cultural traditions of India (just as, by analogy, Protestantism was no authentic offspring of Catholicism). Brahmanism had been theistic and this had made possible the flourishing of art and architecture, science and religious thought, ethics and literature; but Buddhism, the "brotherhood of nothingness" had killed all of this.[68] Surely, the implication was Europeans would not want to embrace such a vampiric creed.

The pastor and later professor of *Religionsgeschichte* (at the University of Amsterdam) Heinrich Hackmann reached similar conclusions, though his work focused on contemporary Buddhism. Trained in Göttingen, Hackmann had served as a pastor in Shanghai and traveled widely in East Asia. He entered the debate in 1905 with a book entitled *Der Ursprung des Buddhismus und die Geschichte seiner Ausbreitung* in which he argued that the stagnation so many Asiatic cultures still suffered was mainly the result of the monastic principles of Buddhism. The religion itself was unnatural; it made man view the world as if he were an outsider and as if it had no positive value for him. History had proven the inadequacy of Buddhism; all civilizations that partook of it now lagged badly behind the Christian West. A promoter of progress rather than "reformation," Hackmann did not wish to see Brahmanism revived, and indeed argued that the purifying efforts underway in Ceylon were being generated exclusively by Europeans and were unlikely to appeal to the nonwestern masses. Though he did not explicitly endorse the Christianization of the East, Hackmann – who was by this time living and preaching in London – clearly thought this the best foundation for the articulation of individualism and for general human progress.[69]

As for the actual Buddhist converts, their numbers were very small, especially in the 1890s; the Buddhistischer Missionsverein für Deutschland, founded in 1903 and dissolved in 1907, had at most fifty members and the main prewar Buddhist journal, *Buddhistische Welt*, seems to have had no more than 500 subscribers.[70] The largest number of conversions seems to have come in the Weimar rather than the Wilhelmine era. Only two converts (Karl Seidenstücker and Karl Eugen Neumann) had been professional students of Indology, though several more learned Pali, Sanskrit, and other languages on their own, enabling them to publish translations and readings of original texts. Some had been Catholics (Anton Gueth and Georg Grimm), some Protestants, some Jews (Siegmund Feniger, a.k.a. Nyanaponika); many had shown early signs of fervent religiosity, but had then lost their traditional faiths and redirected their piety toward Buddhism. Quite a number

---

[68] Dahlmann, *Buddha: Ein Culturbild des Ostens* (Berlin, 1898), quotation p. 31.

[69] Hackmann, *Buddhism as a Religion: Its Historical Development and Its Present Conditions*, trans. unknown (though said to be a "well-traveled lady," p. ix) (London, 2nd ed., 1910), pp. 296–9; on European promotion of Buddhism, p. 125.

[70] Helmut Hecker, ed., *Lebensbilder deutscher Buddhisten*, vol I, *Die Gründer* (Konstanz, 1990), pp. 123–4.

came to Buddhism during or after years in bureaucratic or business careers; Paul Dahlke was forty-one when, in 1906, he gave up his career as a *Sanitätsrat* in Berlin to devote himself full time to propagating lay Buddhism; Georg Grimm was a criminal court judge until pensioned off, for medical reasons, at age fifty-two. Many German Buddhists traveled extensively in the East or lived abroad, especially in Ceylon, for extended periods of time – which meant that many suffered repeated bouts of detention, as did Gueth, who was interned by the Entente during the Great War, arrested as a suspected spy in Bangkok in 1920, and was back in Ceylon in 1939 in time to be interned again.[71] The Hungarian charlatan Trebitsch Lincoln converted to Buddhism in 1925 and remained an ardent advocate for the remainder of his life – though he did not lose his penchant for political intrigue.[72] Fragmented by infighting between monks and advocates of lay Buddhism, the movement, if it can be called one, had little prospect of wrenching large numbers of Christians away from their faith.

What made these converts worrisome to Indologists was not their numbers, but their enormous productivity; starting with K. E. Neumann, who began publishing translations of the earliest Buddhist texts in 1892, the group proved extremely prolific. Neumann, who had university training but remained a private scholar after his conversion, published eleven of his own books (some multi-volume), which appeared in numerous editions, especially after he signed on with Piper Verlag in Munich in 1904. In the 1920s, his translations of the sayings of the Buddha were extremely popular and his work lavishly praised by Hugo von Hofmannsthal, Hermann Hesse, Thomas Mann, and Edmund Husserl.[73] Seidenstücker, after studying Sanskrit, *Religionsgeschichte*, Chinese, and Indology, began translating in 1902 and served as editor and publisher of several short-lived Buddhist journals: *Der Buddhist* (1905–10), *Die Buddhistische Welt* (1905–10), and *Buddhistische Warte* (1907–11). He published seventeen of his own books (six under pseudonyms), translated fourteen books and brochures written by English Buddhists, and contributed nearly 100 articles to Buddhist journals. Dahlke contributed twenty-three books and pamphlets and 199 articles, and Gueth four multi-volume collections of Pali translations (in numerous editions), seventeen books treating Buddhist beliefs and practices, and fifty-five articles.[74] Though their means were slender, the Buddhists managed to find niche markets and sympathetic publishing houses as well as to get their issues aired from time to time in popular journals or newspapers.[75]

---

[71] Not surprisingly given this history, Gueth became a citizen of Sri Lanka in 1948. Hecker, *Lebensbilder*, pp. 60–2.

[72] See Bernard Wasserstein, *The Secret Lives of Trebitsch Lincoln* (New Haven, CT, 1988), pp. 222–90.

[73] Helmut Hecker, *Karl Eugen Neumann: Erstübersetzer der Reden des Buddha, Anreger zu abendländischen Spiritualität* (Hamburg, 1986).

[74] Hecker, *Lebensbilder*, pp. 103–9, 124–37; on Dahlke, pp. 16–30; on Gueth, pp. 64–73.

[75] In Breslau, the publisher Walter Markgraf – himself a Buddhist monk – devoted himself to bringing Buddhist light to Germany and did so by printing not only journals but also cheap Buddhist "catechisms." Review of Dahlke's *Buddhismus als Weltanschauung* by Dr. Ferd. Maak, originally printed in the *Hamburger Fremdenblatt*, August 4, 1912, appended to Dahlke's *Bedeutung des Buddhismus*, p. 23. An advertisement appended to Dahlke's text offers Markgraf's *Kleiner buddhistischer Kathecismus* for a mere 40 pfennig.

If worried by Christianity's travails at home, German Indologists were less insistent that the inhabitants of South Asia prefer Christianity to Buddhism, Hinduism, or Parsiism; some, like Paul Deussen, liked the idea of the subcontinent returning to earlier, "purer" forms of its own faiths. Other Indologists of this generation, however, continued to believe that India too needed a reformed and purified Christianity. Richard Garbe, in his *Indische Reiseskizzen* of 1889, made sure to preface his criticism of missionary operations with the following disclaimer: "In order to protect myself against the charge of expressing anti-clerical views, I note that I would greet a mass conversion of the Indian population to Christianity joyfully and would see it as the foundation for progress and prosperity."[76] In fact, like Ida Pfeiffer several decades before, Garbe simply complained that missionaries were not taking their jobs seriously enough. Garbe's important synthetic treatment *Indien und das Christentum*, published in 1914 after many more years of scholarly debate, opened by stating the author's hopes that the volume would be helpful to missionaries in India, "for those who seek to exert influence on the religious life of the educated Hindus can, in my opinion, link [their work] with nothing better than with the elements that already have found their way from Christianity into the teaching of the Hindu sects."[77] Garbe's religious-historical stance here betrays telling traces of its descent from the Jesuit version of "the ancient theology."

There are some other striking aspects of Garbe's *Indien und das Christentum* that point once again to the persistence of problems posed by diffusionist thinking for defenders of Christian truth. The volume opens with a discussion of Judaism's relationship to Christianity, averring that everyone now agrees that Christianity is a syncretic religion, formed from many oriental faiths. But Garbe had not been convinced by the work of Zimmern, Gunkel, and Jensen that ancient Babylonian ideas had a very significant role in shaping Christian practices. All of these "dilettantes" had in common a sloppy and self-serving method (the "traditional-historical" one), which could never properly establish real historical relations.[78] But Garbe thought there was something to be said for the influence of lives of Buddha on the narrative of the life of Christ in the gospels, and speculated that perhaps someday a "Buddhist-Christian missing link" might be discovered. In the meantime, one had to survey non-parallels as well as parallels and temper the desire to extrapolate ancient oral traditions from more recent texts. Garbe did find some parallels, but saw no reason why they should compromise the authenticity of Christianity any more so than did the already widespread conviction that the Greek world had powerfully shaped the gospels.[79] He concluded by running the stream of influences in the opposite direction to discover Christian influence on Krishnaism after the seventh century.

Playing K. O. Müller, rather than Johannes Voss, to the neo-Creuzerians, Garbe used both a well-tempered diffusionism and his devotion to Christianity

---

[76] Garbe, *Indische Reiseskizzen* (Berlin, 1889), p. 250.
[77] Garbe, *Indien und das Christentum: Eine Untersuchung der religionsgeschichtlichen Zusammenhänge* (Tübingen, 1914), pp. v–vi.
[78] Ibid., p. 12.
[79] Ibid., pp. 14–15, 31–61.

to shore up the sciences of *Religionsgeschichte* and Indology. Buddha's teachings did not make those of Christ any less valuable, nor did the Vedas' historical priority mean they were more sacred than Buddhist texts. But with the razing of the "wall of untranslatability," the reopening of questions about the primeval origins of religious ideas had been permitted, and even the efforts of Garbe and Schroeder could not halt further efforts at seeking and celebrating Christianity's earliest ancestors, especially in the absence of influential German versions of Frazer or Émile Durkheim.[80] And there was another, perhaps more ancient, and conveniently less living ancient oriental religion with which Christians also needed to grapple and another great founder-teacher-prophet who also threatened to steal Christ's – or even Moses' – fire; a figure known as Zoroaster, or in German, as Zarathustra.

PERSIA AND HELLENISTIC JUDAISM

Unlike Buddha and his followers, the ancient Persians, we should recall, show up prominently in texts foundational to European identity. They appear in the Old and New Testaments, where they are not particularly hostile "others" – the Persians free the Jews from their Babylonian captivity and the Magi bring the Christ-child presents. But they also appear in Herodotus's *Histories*, where they are the epitome of exotic (and hostile) others. For eighteenth-century Europeans, Persia was especially interesting for its modern love poetry – at least until Anquetil Duperron's Zend Avesta and Jones' articulation of the Indo-European language family. Interest in Persian poetry continued long after this period – it is central to Goethe's *West-östliche Divan* and to the work of Friedrich Rückert, for example – and in the century's second half, small fortunes were spent on Persian carpets, thought by many to be the summit of oriental art (see Chapter 9). But after the 1870s, century, German scholars focused primarily on Persia's religious beliefs and its linguistic and perhaps racial relations with Europe and India, and it was around these topics that the most passionate of debates revolved.

The development of Persian scholarship was rather slower than was the case for its "Aryan" neighbor, Sanskrit. For most of the nineteenth century, Iranian languages were not well integrated into or central to Indo-European scholarship. The big works in comparative philology were produced before Iranian languages were either discovered (Sogdian, the first Middle Eastern Iranian dialect to be investigated, was not discovered until the first Turfan expedition, and the first publication on it dates to 1904), or well studied; archaeological investigations also came very late to the region.[81] Progress was hampered by the small number of ancient Persian texts and the uncertainty of dates for various developments, including the separation from Brahmanism and the abandoning of the ancient "Aryan" homeland. The Zend Avesta itself clearly contained texts from various

---

[80] There was, however, an Austrian Catholic answer to this diffusionist literature: Wilhelm Schmidt's *Der Urpsrung des Gottesidee* (Münster, 1912), first published in French in Schmidt's journal *Anthropos* in 1908–10.

[81] Xavier Tremblay, "Iranian Historical Linguistics in the Twentieth Century," in *Indo-European Studies Bulletin* 11 (1) (2005): 2–4.

time periods and by different hands – thus working out from it toward a more general *Kulturgeschichte* of ancient Persia proved extremely difficult. The one period that was datable and for which there were historical texts was the period in which the Jews had been subjects of the Persian Empire; but this reliance on the Old Testament and the scant treatment therein of relations between the cultures left commentators with big questions about the meaning of this encounter. Beyond a number of reliable fourth-century B.C.E mentions, neither classical nor Indian texts could help much, though there was a long esoteric tradition based on Plutarch's dates for the founding of the Persian religion (5,000 years before the Trojan War), which made Zoroaster the author of the very ancient Chaldaic oracles. In the wake of Anquetil's translation, some radical critics gleefully credited Zoroaster with supplying ideas such as the immortality of the soul and Satan's revolt against God.[82]

In 1849, Rudolf Roth, professor at the University of Tübingen, tried to walk a middle course, declaring Plutarch's dates too high, but also insisting that the Persian reformer could not have been a subject of the Achamenid Empire (founded c. 550 B.C.E), as later Persian and Muslim sources maintained; he hailed from an era in which Iranian folklife was not oriented so much to the West and still showed strong signs of its ancient Vedic origin (Ormuzd, he claimed, originated in Varuna, the Vedic god of light). Like many at mid-century, Roth was interested in "natural" religions and suggested that Persia's Ormuzd-religion, like that of the Vedas, was based on the perception of nature and especially on contrasts between light and darkness. While the Vedic Hindus had developed a richer form of sensuous polytheism, the Zoroastrians had spiritualized light and darkness and given them ethical meanings. Roth found no trace of *ur*-monotheism in early Aryan religions (he claimed the "Zervanism" Anquetil found was a post-Christian development) and simply said that there were "great similarities" between many Ormuzdian ideas about last things and those the Hebrews developed after the Babylonian captivity.[83]

This view would change dramatically in the wake of Martin Haug's 1858–60 studies of the section of the Zend Avesta he called the "Gathas"; these poems or songs, he argued, were the only parts of the text directly attributable to Zoroaster. The Gathas, Haug claimed, proved the prophet's theology monotheist (while his philosophy was dualistic), while later parts of the Avesta, such as the Vendidad, were truly dualistic. To counter Roth's claims, he explained Zervanism as a monotheistic *return* to Zoroaster's original ideas. Haug insisted on an early date for Zarathustra, no later than 1000 B.C.E; there were good reasons, he argued, for "making him a contemporary of Moses."[84] Haug also maintained, against earlier writers, that the ideas of heaven and hell and the resurrection of the dead were held by the Magi from the earliest times and were not borrowed from any foreign source. His ideas were eagerly adopted in Persia by the Parsees, who believed

---

[82] Duchesne-Guillemin, *Western Response to Zoroaster*, pp. 4, 87.
[83] Roth, "Die Ormuzd Religion," in *Theologische Jahrbücher* 8 (1849): 282–90.
[84] Haug, *Essays*, p. 299.

Haug had demonstrated their primeval monotheism, and gradually adopted in Europe, where they would be dominant for the next seventy-five years.[85]

In the German-speaking world, scholars were at first slow to respond to Haug's work, but it is striking that the question of Jewish debts to the Persians resurfaced just at the time George Smith's lectures were posing similar questions about Assyria's religious legacy. In his three-volume *Eranische Altertumskunde* (1871–3), Erlangen professor Friedrich Spiegel suggested that the Hebrews had given the Persians the idea of God and the Flood legend and received from them the idea of paradise.[86] Spiegel did not push his conclusions very hard and his work did not attract much attention in the era of the *Kulturkampf* and Wellhausen's *Prolegomena*. But with the general acceptance (at least in German academic circles) of Wellhausen's periodization of Old Testament texts and characterization of early Israelite history by the late 1880s, it became possible to argue for a greater degree of Iranian influence on "late" Jewish thought. Wellhausen had shown that the early period was one of polytheism and this-worldliness, of little speculative thought and primitive rituals rather than well-developed ethical codes. His late dates for the prophets and some of the Psalms opened the way for the next generation to credit the Persians with having given Judaism the idea of the immortality of the soul, of salvation, and even of monotheism.[87]

Outspoken on the subject was, not surprisingly, Paul de Lagarde, whose *Purim* appeared in 1887. In this text, originally presented as a lecture to the Göttingen Academy of Sciences, Lagarde characteristically claimed that he had long ago discovered the origin of the rites of Purim in the Persian Fraverdian festival; it was one among many others – Pentecost, Christmas, Easter – which had deep roots in the soil of ancient pagan practices. "This is the way it is, in fact, whatever the rationalists and liberals say," he insisted, attacking in the course of his explication all the scholars, but especially the Jewish ones, Abraham Geiger and Heinrich Graetz, who tried to insist on the specific Jewishness of the ritual. One could not believe either ancient or modern Jews, he argued; they have always been bad at writing history, and in the documents pertaining to the establishment of the Purim rituals, "make things up."[88] The Persians, on the other hand, did not invent traditions.

Here we can see the Second Oriental Renaissance exacting some of its revenge on conventional theology, which tended to trust Jewish accounts and discount pagan ones; dates were being manipulated to the advantage of the iconoclast, a practice to which I drew attention at the beginning of Chapter 1. Lagarde's argument depended heavily on the pushing backward in time of Sassanid-era texts (especially the Avesta) to a much earlier period and the attribution of the ancient Persian calendar to Zoroaster. This made it possible, moreover, for Lagarde to speculate on the existence of a very early shared calendar, with traces in Aramaic,

---

[85] Duchesne-Guillemin, *Western Response to Zoroaster*, pp. 20–1; Haug, *Essays*, pp. 301–3, 311–14.

[86] Duchesne-Guillemin, *Western Response*, p. 24.

[87] For example, Deussen treats this as conventional knowledge, in his *Allgemeine Geschichte der Philosophie mit besonderer Berücksichtigung der Religionen*, 2, part 2, pp. 102–88.

[88] Paul de Lagarde, *Purim*, pp. 48, 50.

Persian, and Cappadocian texts, which led him in turn to suggest the possibility of *ur*-political or – religious unity in the Middle East, which could only have been rooted in Persian and/or Zoroastrian culture. Though written in classic Lagardian style – complete with an admonition to all German professors to actually read Jacob Grimm's *Deutsche Mythologie* – this text would find its way into the footnotes of many to come.[89]

Though it continued to be debatable whether Zoroaster had been the retrospective product of a later anti-dualist reform or the founder of the first form of monotheism, whether he had lived in eastern Iran (in which case he would have had little to do with the Jews), or in western Iran and where Zervanism and Mithraism fit into the picture, by the 1890s, the Persians as religious and not just political actors in the ancient Orient began to play a larger role. Intensifying this trend was the younger generation's more sympathetic view of religious mysticism, individual piety, and cultic practices. Though they continued to despise, as did Wellhausen, "late" Jewish desiccation and rule-boundedness, Wellhausen's students were more sympathetic toward apocalyptic pronouncements and syncretic philosophies. Like him, they did not care for the synagogue – but they were much more sympathetic toward the Church or at least the early Christian community and the small but influential group of iconoclasts who paved the way for it. They devoted considerable attention to the history of Gnosticism; and here importantly they tended to "orientalize" their subject matter, emphasizing Gnosticism's origins in Persian, Mandaen, and perhaps even Assyrian thought rather than in Greek sources.

One might date the opening of the neoromantic era in Persian studies to Lagarde's *Purim* or perhaps to the publication of Franz Cumont's *Textes et monuments relatifs aux mystères de Mithra* (1896–9), and the new edition of the Zend Avesta published by Karl Geldner (1895). The period also saw the appearance of Christian Bartholomae's *Altiranische Wörterbuch* (1905), and the multi-authored *Grundriß der iranische Philologie* (two volumes, 1896 and 1904). All of these publications set the table for a series of new investigations into things Iranian, both scholarly and popular. Movement in the direction of a "furious" Persianism is observable here too, beginning with Robert Eisler's 1910 cosmological study *Weltenmantel und Himmelzeit* and culminating with the Weimar-era promotion of Persian art by Josef Strzygowski and Persian theology by Richard Reitzenstein.[90]

All of these works attempted to give Persia its proper role in ancient cultural history – and as in the case of Strzygowski's work, some of the overexuberant diffusionism here met with challenges from classicists or art historians (see Chapter 9). But the most intense and controversial discussions of Persia's legacy at the fin de siècle revolved around the question of relationships between Persian ideas and Jewish ones. The book which provoked the most controversy was Wilhelm Bousset's *Die Religion des Judentums im neutestamentliche Zeitalter*, a hugely erudite and wide-ranging study that culminates with a chapter entitled "Das

---

[89] Ibid., pp. 36–42; on Grimm, p. 52.
[90] Duchesne-Guillemin, *Western Response to Zoroaster*, pp. 70–3; on Strzygowski, Marchand, "Rhetoric of Artifacts."

religionsgeschichtliche Problem." Here Bousset knew he was posing central questions: "if these powerful changes [the ones that led to Christ's appearance] in the
religion of the Israelites can still be conceived as a genuine development out of the
religion of the prophets and Psalms, or if we are dealing with a convergence of
multiple foreign religious elements."[91] In other words, was "late" Judaism a
coherent religion and was it still the same religion Moses founded? Was Christianity a product of Judaism or of oriental syncretism?

Bousset's answer was complicated and required that he review recent developments in *Orientalistik* and *Religionsgeschichte*. The whole character of the Hellenistic age, he argued, citing Eduard Meyer, was that of confluence [*Verschmelzung*]:
"Should Judaism alone not have participated in this milieu?" Having surveyed the
work of Delitzsch, Zimmern, Reitzenstein, Gunkel, Winckler, and Dieterich,
Bousset concluded that the impact of Babylonian and Egyptian religions on Judaism was slight; Hellenism too had made inroads, especially in shaping the worldviews of important individuals like Philo and Paul. But much more influential was
the "Iranian-Zoroastrian" religion, at least as it was practiced on Babylonian soil,
and although good, datable information about the organization of Persian religion
was lacking, one could raise the question, he argued, ". . . if it was not the case that
synagogue ritual, the suppression of the cult, the orderly, liturgically-formulated
prayers, the religious instruction of the young, synagogue poor-relief, the organization of monastic sects like the Essenes and the Therapeutae, and many other
things, do not have parallels and even their origins in foreign religions."[92] On top
of this came the influence of foreign and especially Persian legends and myths on
the Jewish conception of paradise and the creation of Adam, the figure of the
Messiah, the Flood, the story of Satan's fall, and other Old Testament figures and
stories. Numerous aspects of late Jewish cosmology and eschatology were borrowed, including the "central idea of Jewish eschatology" – the idea of a last
judgment.[93] Judaism in the age of the New Testament had been incoherent, suffused by a chaotic blend of foreign influences – it formed the "alembic" from which
Christian ideas, "through a creative miracle," were formed.[94] But it was not by any
means Christianity's only source.

Bousset's powerful argument for the syncretic origins of Christianity was
extremely controversial and hotly disputed, especially in the Jewish community.
Bousset claimed that the response of the rabbi Felix Perles – a frequent contributor
to the *OLZ* and normally not a defender of orthodoxy – was so intemperate as to
make engagement with it impossible.[95] But liberal Protestants too objected –
again, however, as in the case of the Babel-Bibel Streit, largely on the basis of
preconceived ideas and religious convictions. That was because Bousset's critics
did not, on the whole, know how to read or assess the "oriental" evidence – and
the Christians, at least, were largely unwilling to use later Jewish sources. Bousset

[91] Bousset, *Religion des Judentums*, p. 541.
[92] Ibid., pp. 542, 554.
[93] Ibid., p. 577. Though Bousset admitted that clear evidence for the formulation of this idea in Persia
was not available in the Gathas, but only in a very late work of the Sassanid era, he insisted that this
text was probably a true repetition of material that was much older.
[94] Ibid., p. 594.
[95] Bousset, "Vorwort," in idem, *Religion des Judentums*, p. viii.

had consistently assumed earlier dates for non-Jewish materials, but this was hard to recognize when on the one hand, Wellhausian chronologies still held for the Old Testament and on the other, dates for the Persian texts were so fluid. And of course, some of what Bousset and the other fans of ancient Persia were saying simply fit the racialized vision of Christian origins some Germans had begun to formulate. Few, regrettably, were willing or able to go to the hard work of sifting and weighing the evidence.[96]

Bousset's views did not find sweeping acceptance – though he did get a rather more sympathetic hearing than did Delitzsch. But together with the work of Reitzenstein, his work contributed to the reevaluation of a figure who stood precisely on the threshold between "late" Judaism and Christianity, a figure, moreover, cherished by Luther and central to the understanding of the origins of Christian dogma: Saint Paul.

ORIENTALIZING SAINT PAUL

In his *Quest of the Historical Jesus* (1905), Albert Schweitzer made Gustav Frenssen's just published *Hilligenlei* the logical conclusion of modern historical theology, the final making over of Jesus into a modern, German man. But the Jesus produced by this school, Schweitzer predicted, could not, as hoped, inspire the religious regeneration of the age. "Its Jesus is not alive, however Germanic they may make Him."[97] Perhaps it was Schweitzer's despair for the future of German theology that caused him, at this crossroads, to offer himself as an African missionary; in his letter to the Paris mission society, he noted with pride that he had given his *Antrittsvorlesung* at the University of Strasbourg at the quite young age (especially for his generation!) of twenty-seven, but insisted that neither art nor science had satisfied his thirst; "I felt that this is not everything, that it is nothing."[98] Given the parlous state of the field he had been hired to practice and teach, it seemed probable that he could serve Christ better in Africa than in a German theological faculty.

But Schweitzer was not yet done with theology or theology with him: his insistence that historicization be given up in favor of eschatology or social work marks a pivotal point in the history of Christian thought. While retraining himself as a medical doctor, Schweitzer felt compelled to undertake another historiographical excursion, one of greater significance to our subject. This was his *Geschichte der paulinischen Forschung*, published in 1911, the last and most

---

[96] Ernst Herzfeld did take on Josef Strzygowski's carefully crafted but far overreaching claims for the influence of Persian art on the West; but this took him thirty-eight closely argued pages in the *OLZ* – probably the longest review of a book the journal ever printed. Herzfeld, review of Max von Berchem and Josef Strzygowski, *Amida* (1910), in *OLZ* 13 (1910): 397–435.

[97] Schweitzer, *The Quest of the Historical Jesus*, trans. W. Montgomery (New York, 1962), pp. 309–11, quotation p. 311.

[98] Schweitzer to Alfred Boegner, July 9, 1905, in Albert Schweitzer, *Leben, Werk und Denken, 1905–1965, mitgeteilt in seinen Briefen* (Heidelberg, 1987), pp. 11–13, quotation p. 12. Though Schweitzer evidently came upon Boegner's article appealing for missionaries in 1904, he was moved to write this letter in the summer of 1905, that is, precisely during the period in which he was offering the lectures on life of Jesus research that later would become *Von Reimarus zu Wrede*.

important chapter of which treated Paul in the context of new religious-historical studies. This was a crucial subject, Schweitzer acknowledged, for after the Babel-Bibel Streit, and the life of Jesus debates, the next burning question for biblical scholars and theologians was the question of Paul's relations to Christ and to the early Church, a question which classical philologists and orientalists, as well as members of the religious-historical school, now felt competent and eager to answer.

How Paul became a figure fin de siècle Protestants felt they needed urgently to revisit requires a little explanation. Paul was, of course, Luther's great hero, the man who had articulated most clearly the centrality of belief and Christianity's freedom from the Law. But Paul was the maker of dogma and the seer of visions, the man who nurtured the first Christian cults, and the New Testament writer who dwelt most on Christ's death and resurrection. Indeed, it was always questionable whether Paul could be called a "disciple" of Christ – no meeting with the living Jesus is recorded in the New Testament and the Pharisee Saul's conversion on the road to Damascus occurred after Jesus had already been crucified. None of this particularly bothered Luther, but enlightened Deists found much to dislike in Paul. Voltaire, for example, had exempted Jesus from ridicule but skewered Paul, as well as the bungling and self-interested Gospel writers. Fichte went further, charging Paul with having Judaized Christianity.[99] As usual, moderate Protestants had resisted the philosophers' radicalism, and in the 1870s and 1880s, Paul was still chiefly a positive figure, whose Christian conversion was more important than his Jewish upbringing. Both Harnack and Wellhausen believed Paul had understood Jesus better than anyone else, and the former would continue to argue that the Church's fall into rigid Hellenized dogma occurred long after Paul's death, as a result, in fact, of the Church's reaction to the Marcionist and Gnostic heresies, which he considered essentially Pauline.[100]

But as new texts and new research bearing on the Hellenistic age multiplied, the liberal generation found itself caught on the horns of what Susannah Heschel has called "the dilemma of reconciling the Jewish teachings of Jesus with the Christian teaching of Paul."[101] Unresolved too was the question of the relationship between Paul and the apostles. Could a man whose only contact with the Messiah was by means of an ecstatic vision have understood the teachings? Where did his distinctively non-Jewish ideas come from? By the turn of the century, Protestant theologians were engaged in a vehement battle over the origins and meaning of Paul's worldview, which had come to seem less Greek or Christian than "Gnostic," "mystical," "syncretic," or, in short, "oriental."

The most radical, but in a way the most old-fashioned of these interpretations returned to enlightened anti-Judaism for inspiration. Ernest Renan, reviver of some of the worst bits of Deist polemic, portrayed Paul as a wild-eyed and perhaps epilectic fanatic as against the genial simplicity of Jesus. While, in the Frenchman's

---

[99] Voltaire, entry titled "Religion" in his *Philosophical Dictionary*, reprinted in *The Portable Voltaire*, pp. 187–95; Daniel Havemann, *Der "Apostel der Rache": Nietzsches Paulusdeutung* (Berlin, 2002), p. 78.

[100] Baird, *History of New Testament Research*, p. 128.

[101] Susannah Heschel, "*Quest for the Aryan Jesus*," p. 73

writings the latter was allowed to transcend figuratively and perhaps even biologically, his Semitic milieu, Paul became ever more deeply "oriental," by which Renan meant, as had Fichte, that Paul even after his conversion had somehow remained a Jew. This line of thinking was greatly to the taste of Paul de Lagarde, who happily revived Fichte's view that the task of the German *Volk* was to wrest Christianity from Pauline theology with its "Jewish" emphasis on sin, death, and a distant, angry God. Like Lagarde, the iconoclastic Basel theologian Franz Overbeck juxtaposed a supposedly Pauline-Jewish "world-collapse sensibility" to a this-worldly Greekdom, a picture Friedrich Nietzsche would make famous in *Genealogy of Morals*.[102] Here Christianity was simply Saul's world historical swindle. This picture of Paul is essentially the one Frenssen adopted in *Hilligenlei*;[103] but it could not work for most scholarly theologians who did, after all, have to defend the uniqueness of Christianity and its enduring truth.

Moreover, the theologians of this generation could not so easily chalk up all of Paul's idiosyncrasies to Judaism or fanaticism, nor could they return to the orthodox reading of his visions and his mission simply as divine inspiration. The tradition-historical method suggested that one needed to look beyond Paul's writings and perhaps even beyond the Greek elite of Hellenistic Tarsus to the pre-Christian Orient in order to understand the long-term gestation of his ideas. And when one looked, in the wake of so many "oriental" discoveries and publications, one now found abundant studies of mystery religions and Mithraism, Buddhism, and Babylonian beliefs, Zoroastrianism, and Germanic nature worship. At the same time as younger theologians like Johannes Weiss began to stress what we would call the "irrational" aspects of early Christianity, its apocalypticism and cultic practices, classicists like Albrecht Dieterich were publishing Mithraic "liturgies," and orientalists like Richard Pischel were probing the Buddha's preaching style (including his use of parables) and the development of an early Buddhist "parish community" [Gemeinde].[104] Paul's context (and his ideas) no longer seemed so unique or so explicable by traditional recourse to the Hebrew Bible and Greek classical texts.

This rich and exotic context weighed heavily on theologians trying to defend Christianity's uniqueness. Dying and rising gods, as Frazer's *Golden Bough* showed in exhaustive detail, were celebrated in cultic practices throughout the East; but were these redeemer-gods? What about the idea of the unity of the individual with the deity? From whence came Paul's insistence on universalism and his insistence on belief, rather than on fulfilling the Law? These were things that seemed to Christian thinkers of the time to lie outside the world of Jewish thought, and the search was on for their origins. Gnosticism, once presumed to be a post-Christian heresy, increasingly was pushed backward in time, and eastward geographically, making it possible for Albert Eichhorn to suggest it as the undergirding of Paul's conception of the transubstantiation at the Last Supper, and

---

[102] Havemann, *"Apostel der Rache,"* pp. 22–30, 65–8, 45–8.

[103] Of Paul, he writes "He made him [Jesus] into an eternal deity, into a great, eternal world-miracle. He drew around the simple, timid, modest human child seven-layered, glittering, heavy gold brocade." Frenssen, *Hilligenlei*, p. 578.

[104] Dieterich, *Eine Mithrasliturgie*; Richard Pischel, *Leben und Lehre des Buddha* (Leipzig, 1906).

Wilhelm Bousset – who thought Gnosticism a synthesis of Babylonian and Iranian ideas – to describe it as the source of the Redeemer myth. In 1904, Richard Reitzenstein, reviving for the first time since the seventeenth century the study of the *Pimander*, found in it evidence of a pre-Christian Egyptian Gnosticism, in which a primal man acts as the redeemer of all humankind. At the time, Reitzenstein suggested *ur*-Persian and Babylonian origins for the redemption myth, but by the 1920s, he had settled on a point of origin that coincided both with recent orientalist speculation and racist speculation: Aryan Iran.[105]

The number of treatises on Paul and early Christian cults in the 1900s is astonishing, and virtually all of them have as their central problematic explaining (or denying) Paul's debts to the pagan Orient. There were studies arguing for the secondary impact of mystery religions on Paul, such as Gustav Anrich's *Das antike Mysterienwesen in seinem Einfluss auf das Christentum* (1894), and those arguing for heavy influence, such as Reitzenstein's *Die hellenistischen Mysterienreligionen* of 1910. There were studies like Wilhelm Wrede's *Paulus oder Jesus?* (1907) that contrasted the syncretic, oriental intellectual Paul and the plain-spoken, universal ethicist Jesus, and counter-studies like Paul Feine's *Paulus als Theolog* (1906), which claimed that Paul's Christology was untainted by Hellenistic conceptions. The debate remained so lively and so important that Albert Schweitzer returned to it in 1930, in *Mystik der Apostels Paulus*, a volume dedicated to refuting Reitzenstein, Bousset, and Deissmann and establishing Paul as heir to Jewish, not Hellenistic traditions.[106]

As in the case of *Hilligenlei*, and the Babel-Bibel Streit, this was a debate held before a rather large public; Wrede's 1904 *Paulus* (in the RGV series) was printed in 10,000 copies to start and Feine's work appeared in the widely circulated conservative series appropriately titled *Biblische Zeit- und Streitfragen*. Here, as in other debates we have discussed, the question of *ur*-origins was critical, for, as Schweitzer recognized, if Christianity was simply a "syncretic" religion, its purported prime-mover – Jesus – was no longer necessary.[107] For this, as well as simply for reasons of scholarly caution, many contributors warned against pushing Paul's "orientalism" too far – but as the reception of this material by Arthur Drews and its heavy usage by Jung, K. H. E. De Jong, Rudolf Steiner, and numerous other members of alternative avant-gardes indicates, the genie had escaped its scholarly bottle.[108]

Earlier in this chapter, we saw how Drews, the Monist, was able to spot the weaknesses in *Religionsgeschichte*'s apologetics and to use its findings in the service of his own quasi-religious ideas. At the heart of his *Christusmythe*, it should be added, was a critique of Pauline Christianity, which drew on and radicalized

---

[105] Baird, *History of New Testament Research*, pp. 240–7; Marchand, "From Liberalism to Neo-romanticism," pp. 155–8.

[106] On Feine, Baird, *History of New Testament Research*, p. 364; Schweitzer, *The Mysticism of Paul the Apostle*, trans. William Montgomery (Baltimore, 1998), pp. xxiii, 26–40.

[107] Schweitzer, *Paul and His Interpreters: A Critical History*, trans. W. Montgomery (New York, 1956), p. 234.

[108] On Jung, see Richard Noll, *The Aryan Christ: The Secret Life of Carl Jung* (New York, 1997); K. H. E. De Jong, *Das antike Mysterienwesen in religionsgeschichtliche, ethnographische und psychologische Beleuchtung* (Leiden, 1909).

both the liberal theological and orientalist literature of his day. Drews emphasized, first of all, Paul's lack of personal contact with Jesus and his vague knowledge of Jesus as a historical person. Paul did not care about Jesus' "real" being or
his actions and presented him as a purely divine being, not as a man. A man of
Tarsus, a Greek town where the Hittite god Sardanapaul was also worshiped and
where Mithraism and other mystery cults thrived, Paul simply reworked old myths
about self-sacrificing gods to fit his context. The pagans to whom Paul preached,
in any event, were much more likely to fall for the idea of a self-sacrificing god
rather than be impressed by tales of a wandering preacher who had cultivated
uneducated fishermen and day laborers. Paul was the key to Christianity's success;
Jesus was very likely his invention and, Drews concluded, one the modern "Christian" could do without.[109]

Drews, strikingly, was one of the very few German writers of the period to
draw Frazer's *Golden Bough* into his discussion of Paul. For a proponent of monist
spirituality, Frazer's usefulness should be obvious; *The Golden Bough* offered a
naturalistic explanation of the desire for a self-sacrificing god (to ensure nature's
rejuvenation and the gods' concern for the fate of humankind). Interestingly,
however, Drews did not simply deploy Frazer's universalistic reasoning and insist
on the functional necessity of the Christ-myth; his aim was an historical exposition
of the construction of this myth in Paul's orientalized world. To do this, Drews
followed his exposition of the English ethnologist cum classicist by drawing on the
work of virtually every "furious" orientalist discussed in the previous chapter:
Winckler, Lagarde, Jensen, Jeremias, Seydel, and Dieterich, as well as younger
theologians like Bousset, Albert Schweitzer, and Gunkel, and older iconoclasts like
Creuzer and Dupuis.[110] Funneling this work into an analysis of Paul's syncretism,
Drews clearly believed that he was updating D. F. Strauss's claim that the historical Jesus was a "myth" and one that needed to be exposed and overcome. Of
course, Drews' book also provoked enormous controversy, culminating in his
public defense of his theses at a lecture in the Berlin Zoological Gardens in the
deep winter of 1910. Drews' anti-Christian rant proved so offensive – and so long –
that a number of the 2,000 people who turned out to hear him fell into hysterics
and had to be carried out of the lecture hall.[111]

A less sensational but more substantial contribution to the controversy was
Wilhelm Bousset's *Kyrios Christos* (1913). Bousset's massive study of early Christian cults attempted to sum up the religious-historical school's work on Hellenistic
religions and to answer critics like Drews and Schweitzer. By tracing Paul's preferred designation for Christ, *Kyrios* (Lord) to pagan-oriental sources, Bousset
tried to show the deep Gnostic tendencies of the primitive Christian cults. In
Bousset's masterpiece, one sees again characteristic aspects of the furor orientalis
being put in play; the critique of Eurocentric (and Judeo-centric) perspectives, the
pushing back of developments before datable texts emerge; the hostility to "high"

[109] Drews, *Christusmythe*, pp. 125–37, 140, 225–30.
[110] Ibid., pp. 35–87.
[111] George S. Williamson, "Debating *The Christ Myth*: Radical Theology and German Public Life, ca.
       1910," paper delivered at the American Historical Association Conference, January 5, 2009;
       quoted by permission of the author.

philosophy and preference for what Adolf Deissmann called the "völkischness of primitive Christianity."[112] In the preface, Bousset refutes Franz Cumont's insistence on later dates for the influence of the mysteries on Christian practices, as well as the Harnackian liberals' misleading focus on Greek philosophy:

Rome and especially Greece, in spite of all the syncretistic currents, are not the Orient. What breaks forth into the open here in the second half of the second century has a long prehistory which has transpired especially in Syria (Asia Minor) and Egypt. But Christianity came out of the Orient. And further, in its beginnings, to which especially Paul, John, and Gnosticism belong, Christianity has nothing, nothing at all, to do with the truly philosophical literature of the educated circles in its historical development. What here first begins to climb up the ladder in the course of the second century can have been lively for a long time in a lower stratum.[113]

Christianity was much more than a synthesis of Greek philosophy and Jewish prophecy, as the liberals had claimed; it was heir to the older and perhaps finer mystical thinking and popular piety of the Orient as a whole.

As suggested in the earlier part of this chapter, Bousset's work was, from the beginning, controversial, and it took him nearly thirty years after finishing his doctorate to receive a full professorship. Perhaps politics played a role here; Bousset was an active supporter of the left liberal Friedrich Naumann, which put him to the left of virtually all of his colleagues; in response to an appeal to bring Bousset to Berlin, Prussian Cultural Minister August von Trott zu Solz is supposed to have said, "For people like Bousset there are no Ordinariates in Prussia!"[114] But more importantly, liberal theologians with considerable clout strongly disliked his work. Even those who not so "furious" as Bousset came in for considerable criticism; in 1913, Harnack lumped Eduard Norden's *Agnostos Theos* together with the work of Reitzenstein, Hermann Usener, and Johannes Geffcken, accusing them all of constructing illegitimate theories about the dependence of one text on another, creating combinations without a sound basis, in which "the most secure chronology is thrown on the dustheap."[115] It is certainly the case that Norden – who was also a philologist by training, and not a theologian – was challenging the liberal view by insisting on a more syncretic character for Pauline Christianity, and that he, like Reitzenstein, sometimes offered questionable inferences. But on the whole, the liberals did not respond by checking these claims but by renouncing the line of inquiry as a whole, or in the case of claims made by classicists (like Norden and Reitzenstein), by insisting that only theologians had the right to pass judgment on religious texts. Again, the "fathers" failed to listen to their sons, something that left the older generation behind the times and the younger embittered and increasingly less restrained enemies of established institutions and conventional beliefs.

---

[112] Deissmann, *Licht vom Osten*, p. 282.

[113] Bousset, *Kyrios Christos*, p. 15.

[114] Letter from Hugo Gressmann to his family of 1920, but referring to the prewar era, quoted in Klatt, "Die 'Religionsgeschichtliche Schule' in Giessen," p. 113.

[115] Quoted in Hans Dieter Betz, "Eduard Norden und die frühchristliche Literatur," in B. Kytzler et al., eds, *Eduard Norden*, p. 120.

In the eyes of later, especially Anglo-American, commentators, what most skewed the work of these Christian "orientalizers" was that they tended to retain a Wellhausian view of petrified Hellenistic Judaism even as they eagerly unveiled a more vital and richer pagan Orient.[116] Hermann Gunkel, in the introduction to his very important book on the sources of Genesis of 1895, claimed that he was not demoting the Jews, just adding new cultures to the mix[117] – but this was not entirely believable then or now. The same could be said for Bousset, whose first book was entitled *Jesu Predigt in ihrem Gegensatz zum Judentum* (1892). Indeed, the school of *Religionsgeschichte* as a whole suffered from its conflicting commitment to raise pagan religions to the level of monotheistic ones while still insisting on the superiority of Christianity, almost always without the prefix Judeo-attached.[118] The tendency was to emphasize commonalities between Christian and oriental pagan beliefs and practices, something that meant a subtle demotion of ethics and prophecy (where the ancient Jews excelled) in favor of theories of salvation and festivals of rebirth (where they did not). Naturally, with respect both to source materials and ethics, this was a flawed attempt at universalization, and as in the case of Panbabylonism, numerous scholars, Jewish and not, were able and willing to pinpoint *Religiongeschichte*'s shortcomings.

The younger generation's use of sources also had dangers. If the "liberal"-era work of Theodor Mommsen and Georg Wissowa had focused too exclusively on state rituals and official practices, as Arnaldo Momigliano pointed out, even by the late twentieth century, there was little evidence about what many of the mystery cults actually taught or how believers came to their faiths.[119] Dates for the texts Reitzenstein and his fellows used ranged widely, but even more importantly, given the often meager knowledge of eastern cultural contexts, it was difficult to decide whether the ideas these texts contained were archaic or contemporary, indigenous or borrowed. The *traditionsgeschichtliche* method offered new insights, but few chronological strictures: how far back could one reasonably go? Omission was as risky as addition; in an important sleight of hand, Bousset eliminated from his portrayal of Hellenistic Judaism all non-contemporaneous sources, which meant that he excluded the rabbinical sources Judaism itself regarded as authoritative.[120] That these two, like their contemporary Gunkel, drew on oriental sources without actually knowing all the relevant languages also made them vulnerable to the criticism of the older generation.[121] But for many who had seen the vast cultural territory between the two testaments open up over the course of the nineteenth century, who had experienced the discovery of

---

[116] There were some exceptions, including R. Kabisch, E. Bruckner, and Johannes Weiss. Schweitzer, in fact, found precisely in this literature the means to defend a rather old-fashioned view of Jewish-Christian uniqueness. See Baird, *History of New Testament Research*, p. 237.

[117] Gunkel, *Schöpfung und Chaos in Urzeit und Endzeit* (Göttingen, 1895), p. vi.

[118] See, e.g., Gunkel, *Zum religionsgeschichtlichen Verständnis*, p. 96; Rudolf Otto, *The Idea of the Holy*, trans. John W. Harvey (London, 2nd ed., 1950), p. 142.

[119] Arnaldo Momigliano, "Ancient Biography and the Study of Religion" (1985), in idem, *On Pagans, Jews, and Christians* (Middletown, CT, 1987), pp. 159–65.

[120] See George Foot Moore, "Christian Writers on Judaism," in *Harvard Theological Review* 14 (1921): 197–254, esp. pp. 241–8.

[121] See Marchand, "From Liberalism to Neoromanticism," pp. 142–6.

Assyrian, Persian, Coptic, Manichean, and Mandaen texts, and who had read the new studies of Buddhism and Vedic religions, the "history of religions" approach seemed the only way to make theology scientifically respectable. Here, as in the case of Assyriology, there were both dangers in departing from older humanistic practices and insights to be gained from expanding theology's horizons.

Unquestionably, liberal theology was shaken by the furor orientalis – indeed, it was much more profoundly transformed by the encounter than were classical philology or positivist oriental philosophy. But one cannot say that either *Religionsgeschichte* or hyper-diffusionism "won." Bousset died in 1920, weakened by wartime malnutrition. Max Weber, a close follower of religious-historical work, died in the same year, without having written the book on early Christianity he intended to write. There were certainly some, like Hans Lietzmann, who continued their studies of the early church and deep readers of the new theological literature, like Rudolf Bultmann, who carried forward some of Bousset's inquiries. Rudolf Otto's classic comparative study *Das Heilige* (1917) is unthinkable without religious-historical preparation. But after the death of Ernst Troeltsch in 1923, much of this work went overseas, where it ran into the more philo-Judaic work of W. F. Albright, G. F. Moore, and Elias Bickermann, whose ideas were confirmed, moreover, by new finds in Palestine.[122] At home, it was existentialist philosophy, not oriental philology or comparative religion, which younger (Protestant) theologians seized upon to renew and revitalize their faith after the Great War; and given what we have seen, it is hardly surprising that the first texts to which the leader of this profoundly anti-historicist movement, Karl Barth, turned were those of Saint Paul. As for the orientalists, debates about *ur*-Christian origins helped to generate interest – popular as well as scholarly – in another hyper-diffusionary line the radicals hoped to pursue, one that had always been there in some way, but which highly influential fin de siècle Indological popularizers were increasingly pushing to the fore, namely, the history of the Aryan race.

[122] By this time, Zionist archaeologists had begun to push forward the study of Jewish settlements in Palestine. Steven Fine, *Art and Judaism in the Greco-Roman World: Toward a New Jewish Archaeology* (Cambridge, 2005), pp. 22–34.

7

The Passions and the Races

A brilliant series of scholars of Indology and Germanic culture has, half unconsciously, completed their great deeds at the right moment; now we too possess our "holy books," and what they teach is more beautiful and nobler than what the Old Testament records. The belief in our strength, which we have drawn from the history of the nineteenth century, has been enriched to an incalculable degree by this discovery of our independent ability to develop the highest [cultural goods], whereas we once saw ourselves as mere borrowers. In particular the myth of the peculiar aptitude of the Jew for religion is finally exploded; and for this, later generations will thank our century.

    – Houston Stewart Chamberlain, *Die Grundlagen des Neunzehnten Jahrhunderts* (1900)[1]

Don't fall in love with the Aryans; every race has its portion of inhumanity.
    – Ignaz Goldziher to Martin Hartmann, February 11, 1903[2]

For the first time in this book, the subject of race appears prominently in the epigraph and will remain central throughout the chapter. But prominent in these passages is also the historiographically less familiar issue of passions – national passions, in the case of racist dilettante Houston Stewart Chamberlain's celebration of rising appreciation of the Aryan Orient; personal passions, in the case of Ignaz Goldziher's warning to his fellow Semitist, Martin Hartmann. Attention to the "passions" articulated in these passages tells us that by the fin de siècle, racial categories were becoming sources of deep individual and cultural self-understanding, as well as matters for public discussion. And understanding the direction both Chamberlain and Goldziher saw German affections flowing warns us against something else – and that is the presumption that all passions were equal, in the orientalist guild, in the eyes of the state-funded university and museum establishments, or in the hearts and minds of the wider culture-consuming public. While in the course of this chapter we will keep in mind the ever-diversifying landscape of oriental studies, we will focus not only on the ways in which racial thinking had a particularly powerful effect on some of its branches, but also on the ways in which the wider German culture embraced some passions, and not others. For it makes all the difference, in the history of scholarship as in life, if one's passions are reciprocated – or remain unrequited.

[1] Chamberlain, *Die Grundlagen des Neunzehnten Jahrhunderts*, vol. 1 (Munich, 1900), p. 29.
[2] Goldziher quoted Róbert Simon, *Ignác Goldziher*, p. 197.

From the romantic era forward, the study of Sanskrit and its related cultures and languages was consistently, if not primarily, linked to Germanic ancestry in a way that was easily racialized. Already in the works of Friedrich Schlegel and Friedrich Schelling, the antiquity and presumed cultural autonomy of the northern Indians laid the foundations for a long-lasting supposition that seeds of *ur*-wisdom might have been sown here, but transplanted with wandering family members to Persia perhaps and then to Central Europe. This idea of a primeval revelation lived on in figures like Friedrich Rückert, who, in an 1860 letter to his student Paul de Lagarde, suggested that the "highest goal" of oriental philology remained that of proving to Christians that a "pure (theistic) kernel of Christianity" was already contained in the Upanishads.[3] This was a religious vision, of course, along the lines of "the ancient theology"; and as Lagarde realized, it could also be made into a means to cleave the Old Testament from the New, and to destroy precisely what Chamberlain called "the myth of the peculiar aptitude of the Jew for religion." But it also formed the basis for racialized, diffusionist histories, for which the culture's passions increased at the fin de siècle, as the questions of German identity and the Reich's destiny became increasingly pressing.

Racial thinking was particularly salient in Indological circles, but of course the study of "Semitic" languages and cultures also featured older, quasi-racist elements; and here, too, changes at the century's end made for the clearer articulation of supposed racial identities. We have seen "Semitic" racial stereotypes evolve in the linkages made between the ancient Israelites and the Arab beduin, in the increasingly specialized study of language families, and in the contrasting of Jews with Greeks. In the mid-century, Ernest Renan repackaged these caricatures to create a widely popularized contrast between desert-dwelling, myth-less Semites and the myth-creating pagan Aryans, whose richer imaginations had been shaped by their less monotonous environments. While the Old Testament remained a book that could raise the passions of Christian orientalists – like Ewald, Nöldeke, and Wellhausen – and while there remained influential scholars like Heinrich Fleischer, committed to working with Jews, on Judeo-Arabic projects – there was still passion in these scholarly pursuits; and we should not forget that many theologians, and especially conservative ones, defended the uniqueness of Hebrew culture during the Babel-Bibel Streit. But just at the time interest in and knowledge about the ancient "Aryans" was growing, one can also observe the Semites, ancient and modern, becoming something of an arcane or marginal subject. Those who committed themselves to Semitic studies (other than Assyriology) after the 1880s tended to be either liberals with political rather than religious interests, or Jews and converts from Judaism. And even for those who committed themselves to historicist *Wissenschaft*, the passion for Greek antiquity, inculcated in the schools, made it hard to fully appreciate Semitic antiquity. As Ignaz Goldziher remarked in 1876: "For the well-educated, the Semitic is as it always was more distant than the Aryan, which, through studies of classical antiquity from elementary school on, ensnares us with its irresistible charms, and never stops

---

[3] Rückert to Lagarde, March 8, 1860, in Lagarde, *Erinnerungen an Rückert*, p. 28.

determining the direction of our thoughts and deeds.''[4] Though specialized studies mounted, this affective "distance" remained, or even increased over the next decades.

In the Jewish scholarly world, one could identify a fin de siècle movement parallel to the furor orientalis – one that stressed exoticness, easterness, mysticism, and deep cultural differences.[5] But this movement, even more than its gentile equivalent, was largely kept out of mainstream German cultural institutions. As had been the case at mid-century, men who taught at or studied in Jewish seminaries wrote for specifically Jewish publications and were usually ignored by university academics.[6] Christians tended to leave the study of post-biblical Hebrew and Jewish culture to Jewish scholars in Jewish institutions; while Indology flourished, the state continued to veto funding for a post-biblical Jewish seminar.[7] On the other hand, it was becoming increasingly possible for credentialed scholars to study Aryan pagan religions and even to champion the spiritual primacy of the ancient Indians and Persians. This imbalance – exemplified in this chapter's focus on the Aryans – too belongs to the history of the rise of racialized orientalism.

In what follows, I will first offer a few comments on the increasing racialization of oriental studies after about the 1880s and then turn to a consideration of the furor orientalis in Indology. Here, I have chosen to focus on Paul Deussen, a figure who is at present chiefly known as Nietzsche's school chum, but whose wider career deserves much more scrutiny. Deussen was instrumental in introducing a set of Schopenhauerian ideas which made possible both German Indology's full racialization and its linkage to an evolving form of Hindu nationalism. The second major chunk of the chapter is devoted to a scholar who was Deussen's exact contemporary, but in many ways his opposite, the Hungarian-Jewish *Islamforscher* Ignaz Goldziher. Like Deussen, Goldziher gained recognition right about 1890 – though Goldziher's fame was almost entirely among academics. Goldziher's passionate attachment to Semitism was surely as deep as Deussen's to Indo-Aryanism and his reputation has been much the more enduring and favorable one. But in their day, it was Deussen's legacy that left the deeper mark – something I will illustrate by describing two important popularizers who followed

---

[4] Goldziher, *Der Mythos bei den Hebräern und seine geschichtliche Entwicklung* (Leipzig, 1876), p. ix.

[5] One could certainly examine the work of Martin Buber and Gershom Scholem in this light.

[6] The *OLZ* (edited, remember by a Jewish scholar) did review some of their work, and when Senior D. Behrmann published a pamphlet honoring *Hamburgs Orientalisten* in 1902, he included, quite extraordinarily, rabbis and yeshiva teachers in his survey. Senior D. Behrmann, *Hamburgs Orientalisten* (Hamburg, 1902), pp. 3–7.

[7] In 1913, the Cultural Ministry seems to have approved Hermann Strack's plan to create one and to hire a Jewish assistant (who would understand the needs of the students better than a non-Jew), but the Finance Ministry said no. (Cultural Ministry to Finance Ministry August 25, 1913, and Finance Ministry to Cultural Ministry, November 15, 1913, in B-GSPK, I, 76Va, Sekt 2, Tit. X, Nr. 186.) In the middle of the war – and as debates about Zionism were rife – another proposal was declined. After Strack's retirement in 1921, his Berlin theology chair was not filled, and Talmud Judaism was taught first by an assistant (who was also a pastor) and then by our old friend Alfred Jeremias, who had cut down on his Panbabylonist publications and proclivities, but was still writing mass-circulated religious-historical pamphlets. Even he left, for Greifswald in 1928, leaving Strack's position unfilled.

in his traces, Leopold von Schroeder and his friend Houston Stewart Chamberlain. And in terms of global politics too, it was Deussen's anti-Semitism that won out over Goldziher's attempt to build Jewish-Arab bridges. Though both started out as latter-day lonely orientalists, by the time they died (Deussen in 1919 and Goldziher in 1921), one (Deussen) was clearly swimming with the tide and the other (Goldziher) struggling to keep clear of the rocks.

Racial family trees were more or less presumed by both to exist, though Deussen did far more work to elaborate his and to celebrate its superiority. But in both cases, race was thoroughly bound up with a set of older questions that still had great relevance for nineteenth- and early twentieth-century Europeans, questions which had chiefly to do with religion. All too often we treat these issues separately, or consecutively, as if religion and religious categories died and were replaced by racial ones.[8] Contemporary experience was, however, much more complicated, and as we have already seen in previous chapters, often the desire to reconcile science and faith or to purify Christianity paved the path backward into racialized prehistories. In the profiles of Deussen and Goldziher in this chapter, we will see how key questions derived from centuries of theological debate – such as the trustworthiness of the Old Testament and the dependence (or not) of Christianity or Islam on Judaism, the meaning of "law" and of Christian "freedom" – were still central to orientalism in the later nineteenth century. We will also see these figures rework the Greek tradition, and in the process, reduce its importance and normativeness for the modern world. The chapter then sounds some newer themes, but also recapitulates some of the old and introduces the reader to two idiosynchronic orientalists whose unequal shadows still fall, from time to time, across oriental studies today.[9]

ON ARYANS AND SEMITES

We start here with a brief discussion of the deployment of racial ideas in German orientalist thought since the days of Friedrich Schlegel. We must work carefully here and not be too obsessive about the use of the term "Rasse" – either supposing too much about its earlier usage or making too much of the infrequent use of the word in fin de siècle philology. After all, philologists and theologians – still the overwhelming majority of those considered professional orientalists – specialized in the interpretation of texts and considered relationships in "spirit" not in bodily form paramount. To speak too much of "Rasse" and of physical differences would be to admit that language and religious heritage were not the fundamental factors in human society, and our scholars were not about to give the physical anthropologists the keys to the kingdom of cultural history. On the other hand, what we would see as racial characterization (and often caricature) had always been part of the study of the East. It was generally assumed that lighter peoples

---

[8] But see now Colin Kidd's masterful *The Forging of Races: Race and Scripture in the Protestant Atlantic World, 1600–2000* (Cambridge, 2006).

[9] Our passions are clearly not those of the fin de siècle; while Deussen is now almost completely forgotten, Ignaz Goldziher's work is still widely studied and admired, and indeed has been the subject of several recent international conferences.

were more civilized and that darker peoples either languished in states of savagery or had degenerated into barbarism; Jews were presumed to be a "nation" or a "people" who looked, behaved, and even smelled differently from Christians. Race, on the one hand, was everywhere; on the other, it was not something to be dwelt on.

The same, in a way, might be said of the terms "Indo-German," "Indo-European," and "Aryan." Having been invented to describe a group of related languages, these terms always had the potential to describe ethnic differences as well, especially as behind these groupings lay, in one way or another, the attempt to map the dispersal of Noah's sons. It was easy, and no doubt appealing, to make linkages between the languages known to have been spoken by the highest castes and the cultural and physical attributes educated Europeans (and Brahmins) preferred, namely, creativity, intelligence, light skin, and tall stature. Philhellenes like Winckelmann had already equated moderate climates with beautiful bodies, and Friedrich Schlegel made it conventional to think that the more beautiful and culturally productive peoples, like the Greeks, spoke the most beautiful and flexible languages. Thus even when German scholars were not speculating about skin color or head shape, they did tend to associate cultural superiority – the product of caste, deep antiquity, linguistic flexibility, and cultural autonomy – with the ideals of physical beauty accepted by their European contemporaries. Still, as Thomas Trautmann has shown, "Aryan" was, for quite a time, a term used to forge a bond between Indians and Englishmen; it implied in it a kind of sub-colonial condescension (you, younger brother, ought to do as your wiser and more evolved older sibling tells you), but it was a term primarily used to throw a bridge, not to create a separate species.[10] In Germany too, it was sometimes used in this way, especially when the writer sought to appeal to members of the Indian or Persian elite.

It should also be noted that racial conclusions were often described as tentative or simply alleged and not emphasized. Many authors, speculating on the question of Aryan character or origins, insisted that their results were preliminary or their evidence uncertain; especially in the liberal positivist era, they often admitted, as did Wilhelm Geiger in 1882, that social and economic divisions could not necessarily be identified with racial differences or identified racial purity as a function of geographical isolation, not as the measure of a culture's worth.[11] And for some, the term "Aryan" was simply shorthand, its utility sanctioned by its appearance in ancient Indian texts. When Martin Haug set about trying to clarify meaning of the Gathas and to piece them together, he turned to songs of the *Rig Veda*, as they are (he decided) of more or less the same age and written in a closely related language. At the time of his inquiries (1850s) there was no dictionary or lexicon for either the Zend Avesta or for the *Rig Veda*, but there was enough work on the latter to be able to fix the significance of important Vedic words and passages and use them to interpret parallel passages in the Gathas. In attempting this philological high-wire act, Haug turned to the younger languages related to Bactrian (Middle-Persian, Modern Persian, and Armenian, as well as to the fragmentary remains of

---

[10] Trautmann, *Aryans and British India*, pp. 14–18.
[11] See, for example, Geiger, *Ostiranische Kultur im Altertum* (Erlangen, 1882), pp. 168–83.

earliest-known form of cuneiform, usually known as Old Persian). Haug suggested a change in nomenclature: "it would be more correct to use the name Aryan [*arisch*], as it is used in the Turanian translation of the Bisutun inscription" but he made nothing more of the term and in fact proceeded to differentiate these languages of the "iranischen Familie" from the Sanskrit "Sprachfamilie."[12] This is no recipe for genocide.

But by the fin de siècle, there was less religion and more biology behind the designation "Aryan" and the connotations of the term were changing. It was certainly being used more, and it was being used in a context in which Eastern European Jews and the colonial world were a much greater part of at least urban-dwellers' experience. Debates about degeneration, miscegenation, and assimilation, and about the "backwardness" of the Africans, Asians, and Slavs certainly gave racial identities new purchase. Intellectually, too, a new wind was blowing, and it was one that favored deep identities over recently acquired ones, and diffusion over independent evolution; it seemed to many increasingly important to discover origins and originators – and if possible to claim a kindred relationship to them. The lengthening of developmental chronologies and ebbing of faith in humankind's ability to make rapid improvements and adaptations meant that scholars could no longer believe, as had William Jones, that physiognomic differences between, for example, Africans, Indians, and Europeans might be explained by relatively swift effects of climate change. Humanistic specialization, too, made its contribution, demanding that scholars define their subjects according to the languages they read well. And once this choice was made, it became increasingly difficult for individuals to think across disciplinary lines; in Germany in particular, this was true not only for philologists, but for mythographers and historians of religion as well.[13]

As scholars focused on indigenous texts and new materials flooded libraries and museums, the gap across which scholars like Rückert and Ewald could still leap yawned ever wider. Writing about more than one linguistic family began to look distinctly *unwissenschaftlich*, and on each side of the divide, the families increasingly took on a sort of timeless cultural incommensurability that was tantamount to, if not explicitly described as, a racial identity. Though they continued to contribute papers to the *Zeitschrift der Deutschen Morgenländischen Gesellschaft* and to attend the orientalists' conferences, the fields lost touch. In terms of teaching obligations, too, oriental studies fragmented. As the number of theology students fell, and the number of secular orientalists grew, it was no longer necessary for Arabists to learn Sanskrit or for Indologists to teach Old Testament exegesis. The lapsing of Old Testament exegesis as a shared practice is, I think, a particularly important clue that passions were shifting, and that the long tradition of German-Christian Hebraism was under siege. As specialization and increasingly fixed racial borders drove apart studies of the Aryan and the Semitic East, the former

---

[12] Martin Haug, "Die fünf Gâthâ's," p. x.

[13] Thus, for example, in 1882, Rudolf Seydel cut short his discussion of similarities between Buddhist and Chinese birth-myths, noting: "But Buddhism is of Indian, that is, Aryan origin, and thus we are compelled to investigate the linkages with its birth-myths which are are offered from this side . . ." Seydel, *Das Evangelium*, p. 116.

took with it much of the affective and esoteric Orientophilia characteristic of the romantics like Rückert and Creuzer. East Asia, which – at least since the days of Frederick the Great – had attracted little German scholarly attention and even less passionate cultural association was also largely left out in the non-affective cold. Even most of the Buddhists and scholars of Buddhism identified more thoroughly with India than with China or Southeast Asia, though Japan did begin attracting some admirers after 1905. The affection nurtured for the ancient Indians and Persians, by contrast with the relative lack of passion kindled for the Egyptians, Arabs, and Chinese, is noteworthy – the study of the uninflected or agglutinative languages might stir a bit of interest on occasion, but these cultures were rarely the subject of paeans. Literature on the ancient Jews, of course, could raise passions, those of Jewish scholars and converts, and of some orthodox Christians. But it was Sanskrit, not Hebrew, whose pure linguistic forms were lovingly cultivated by many of the late romantics, and it was the ethical wisdom of the *Rig Veda*, Hermann Brunnhofer claimed, which represented the "ethno-psychological foundation" of the Germans, Celts, Slavs, Greeks, and Indians; "in reading the Vedas," he wrote in 1893, "tat tvam asi, 'that art thou' resounds in our racial subconsciousness and fills us with pride...."[14]

It is no coincidence that the places treated with reverence were, on the whole, places where Germans had no colonial presence (India, Japan), while the cultures its scholars were likely to treat critically or with indifference (China, the Islamic world) were those over which Germans were seeking to exert political, cultural, and/or economic overlordship. We will postpone a full discussion of imperialist entanglements until the next chapter; but it is important here to note that the evolution of the Aryan/Semitic divide within German oriental studies was propelled forward not only by an increasing racial association being made between Teutons and Aryans, but also by the different sorts of involvement each subfield developed with European colonial practices. While some Indologists were led by their affection for ancient Indian religions, their desire to revolutionize Christianity, and their associations with indigenous religious traditionalists to take up anti-colonial and anti-modernist stances (at least with respect to affairs in India), *Semitistik* was increasingly practiced by Jews who focused on Jewish traditions (and remained largely active outside the universities), or by liberal secularists, many of whom began to associate themselves rather more with the Reich's colonial projects. As Christian scholarly interest in the Old Testament waned, *Semitistik* became a field characterized less by passions than by *Realpolitik*.

It is dangerous to generalize about those who practiced Indo-German studies at the fin de siècle, for in addition to the neoromantic racists profiled below, there were also some who continued to work along Boppian lines, on comparative grammar, and others who devoted themselves to narrowly framed studies in Sanskrit philology. Of one of the latter, Heinrich Lüders, his student Heinrich Zimmer

---

[14] Hermann Brunnhofer, *Urgeschichte der Arier in Vorder- und Centralasien: Historisch-Geographische Untersuchungen über den ältesten Schauplatz des Rigveda und Avesta*, vol. 1 (Leipzig, 1893), p. xxvii. On the (mis)use of this phrase by Schopenhauer and others, see Paul Hacker, *Philology and Confrontation: Paul Hacker on Traditional and Modern Vedanta*, ed. Wilhelm Halbfass (Albany, NY, 1995), pp. 277–9.

wrote: he was "a plain liberal citizen from the republic of Lübeck, anti-philosophic, indifferent to mysticism, and with a meager sense for artistic qualities and implications." Zimmer complained bitterly about his prewar, hyper-positivistic education under Lüders and his kind (one of whom was Zimmer's own father, Heinrich Zimmer the elder, professor of Sanskrit and Celtic Philology at the University of Berlin); he and his fellow Gymnasium students were fed, in his words, on stones rather than spiritual bread – while outside the classroom they had feasted on avant-garde delicacies – Ibsen, Hofmannsthal, Kokoscka, and Stefan George.[15] His books and his teachers had spoken of India, but not in the way Zimmer, inflamed by his extramural readings, wanted it described. "The current representation of India," he recalled, "lacked color, depth, intensity, consistency, life. For years I was in search of the 'real' India, of 'my' India, of Schopenhauer's India."[16]

This anecdote reminds us that much, if not most, of the Indological establishment in the years before the war remained quite resolutely positivist, uninterested in or hostile to the Schopenhauerian India Zimmer longed for. But as in Assyriology, theology, and classics, here too a new generation was coming of age, one that found inspiration in reading Schopenhauer, Jakob Böhme, or, remarkably, the New Testament, not, as had been the case for Otto Boehtlingk, in reading Bopp's *Sanskrit Grammar*.[17] They were aware of the progress made in Indology since the 1850s, in works such as Martin Haug's *Dictionary of the Rig Veda* (1873) and Boehtlingk and Roth's *Sanskrit Dictionary* (1852–75).[18] But they were frustrated, predictably, with the liberal era's reticence in sketching "the big picture" – that is, the whole series of relations between cultures and religions in the ancient East.

Like the younger theologians too, some "furious" Indologists were eager to capture the attention of an expanding and increasingly distracted public before the Heinrich Zimmers among them gave up on science entirely. In an essay of 1900, the Viennese professor Leopold von Schroeder offered the following warning to colleagues who disdained the notion of "popularizing" their ideas, a warning that echoes Hermann Gunkel's call to his fellow theologians of the same year:

The younger generation in the German lands is emancipating itself more and more from the site of scholarship's intellectual dominance, the universities. A new drama by Sudermann or Hauptmann, a chapter of Nietzsche excites the nation's interest more powerfully than the most solid, or even the most significant specialized scholarly work. If the men of science, if the universities, want to meet the danger of isolation, the danger of being increasingly pushed into the background, if they want to escape losing a feeling for the great strains of cultural life of the nation, then they will have to learn not to "popularize" – but to speak

---

[15] Zimmer, "Some Biographical Remarks," in idem, *Artistic Form and Yoga in the Sacred Images of India*, ed. and trans. Gerald Chapple and James B. Lawson (Princeton, NJ, 1984), pp. 246–7.

[16] Ibid., pp. 258–9.

[17] Leopold von Schroeder claims that Boehtlingk found Bopp's *Grammar* a "revelation"; on reading it, he suddenly understood language's laws and thought himself the happiest man on earth. Schroeder, "Otto Boehtlingk" (1900), in idem, *Reden und Aufsätze*, p. 317.

[18] Schroeder, "Erste Vorlesung: Einleitung: Alter, Umfang und Originalität der indischen Literatur. Ursprung und Entwicklung der Indologie in Europa," in idem, *Indiens Literatur und Cultur im historischer Entwicklung* (Leipzig, 1887), pp. 13–16.

to the larger public in the highest and most noble sense of the word – in a language that this public understands, that grabs it, that forces it, willingly to listen to the voice of the speakers.[19]

Schroeder was only one among many to articulate this sense that it was no longer necessary, or possible, to work in the same way as his philological fathers. He was one of a smaller number of those who actually attempted to reach this greater public with his Indological writings, but his efforts, and the racialized perspective he adopted in them, would be amongst the most culturally influential and socially destructive of the endeavors spawned by the furor orientalis.

Schroeder was not, however, working alone and to understand his contributions to the racialization of popular Indology, we have to take a step backward to examine two critical predecessors. One is Schopenhauer himself and the other is Paul Deussen, whose remarkable project of knitting together Schopenhauer, Vedic philosophy, and Christian reform was one of the most disquieting aspects of fin de siècle German orientalism. We will find here plenty of passion, directed both at understanding the Indian past – and perfecting Germandom's future.

PAUL DEUSSEN, SCHOPENHAUERIAN CHRISTIAN

I will not attempt here a full account of Schopenhauer's relationship to Indology or describe in detail his comments on Buddhism; others have done that already.[20] But a few comments are necessary to show what parts of Schopenhauer's work could, and which could not, be adopted by fin de siècle Indologists and Buddhists. Roger-Pol Droit has convincingly shown that Schopenhauer's real affection for and self-identification with Buddhism came near the end of his life in the later 1840s and 1850s; but he did, as early as the 1810s, read Anquetil's *Oupnekhat* and live next door to K. C. F. Krause, a philosopher trying to blend his ideas with *ur*-Indian wisdom. He had met another romantic Indologist, Friedrich Majer, in his mother's salon. Moreover, as Rüdiger Safranski has noted, the few remarks Schopenhauer does make about Indian philosophy in the years before the first edition of *The World as Will and Representation* (1819) point to linkages the young pessimist was making between Indian thought and major aspects of his own philosophy.[21] Perhaps most importantly, Schopenhauer found in Indian thought a metaphysics without a God and the means by which he could transform Kant's world of appearances into a world of delusions. This in turn gave him real leverage on the modern European world he despised, without turning him into a materialist-revolutionary or a Christian ascetic (who would, presumably, have had to give up the art, literature, and music Schopenhauer so loved). And it made him, as many have since argued, the first western philosopher to delight in the tortures of individualization without thinking he could or should do anything to overcome them.

---

[19] Schroeder, "Vom Popularisieren," in idem, *Reden und Aufsätze*, p. 314.
[20] For example, Paul Hacker, *Philology and Confrontation*, pp. 273–318; Droit, *Cult of Nothingness*.
[21] Droit, *Cult of Nothingness*, pp. 93–6; Rüdiger Safranski, *Schopenhauer and the Wild Years of Philosophy*, trans. Ewald Osers (Cambridge, MA, 1990), pp. 201–2.

Schopenhauer was certainly no political liberal; but in religious matters, he was closer to Voltaire than to the conservatives of his day. In a dialogue on religion, he has his mouthpiece rage:

Think of the fanaticism, the endless persecutions, the religious wars, that sanguinary frenzy of which the ancients had no conception! Think of the crusades, a butchery lasting two hundred years and inexcusable, its war cry "It is the will of God," its object to gain possession of the grave of one who preached love and sufferance; think of the cruel expulsion and extermination of the Moors and Jews from Spain! Think of the orgies of blood, the inquisitions, the heretical tribunals, the bloody and terrible conquests of the Mohammedans in three continents, or those of Christianity in America, whose inhabitants were for the most part, and in Cuba entirely exterminated.[22]

The speaker then reverses himself: "Perhaps I go too far in saying all religions. For the sake of truth, I must add that the fanatical enormities perpetrated in the name of religion are only to be put down to the adherents of monotheistic creeds, that is, the Jewish faith and its two branches, Christianity and Islamism. We hear of nothing of the kind in the case of Hindoos and Buddhists."[23] It is monotheism that is intolerant, not religion as a whole; and elsewhere, Schopenhauer argues, the whole idea of a single God – creator and judge of humankind and the world – is absurd and sadistic; Buddhist metempsychosis or Zoroastrian dualism make more sense and are better guides to ethical behavior.

With a few modifications, this is the voice of the late Enlightenment: the critique of Judaism and its offspring in pursuit of a more rational, universal, and tolerant philosophy of ethics. Where Schopenhauer diverged from Voltaire, however, was in his conviction that such a system could not and would not in fact evolve in the world for us, and his recommendation that individuals seek to renounce the will or transcend it briefly through aesthetic contemplation. Here were the grounds on which he established the concordances between his Kantian idealism and Indian-Buddhist philosophy, especially in the concept of nirvana. This concordance helped Schopenhauer to move from a Kantian worldview to an all-encompassing renunciation of the world of appearances, something Kant did not contemplate. Ironically, this move would also enable a linkage between a highly ascetic form of Protestantism and Buddhist thought, one which Schopenhauer himself seems to have glimpsed, but never pursued.

Another stream of thought Schopenhauer tapped, at least briefly, from its esoteric underground springs was the one that posited an *ur*-oriental origin for Christian ideas. In an essay on "The Christian System," he argued that the visions of the Old and New Testament are so unalike that the latter "must be in some way traceable to an Indian source: its ethical system, its ascetic view of morality, its pessimism and its Avatar, are all thoroughly Indian."[24] Schopenhauer did not, however, have the tools, or even the desire, to push this genealogical argument further; nor did his ideas appeal much to mid-century men who might have had the

---

[22] Schopenhauer, "Religion: A Dialogue," in *The Essays of Arthur Schopenhauer*, trans. T. Bailey Saunders (New York, 1941), part 3, p. 42.

[23] Ibid., pp. 43–44.

[24] Schopenhauer, "The Christian System," in *Essays of Arthur Schopenhauer*, part 3, p. 92.

skills to attempt this. The return to this romantic program would await the fin de siècle. Regrettably, there is no good study of the mechanisms through which Schopenhauerianism infiltrated Indological circles – but the presumption that Schopenhauer was there at the discipline's birth cannot be maintained. As is well known, Schopenhauer's philosophy itself was only just becoming popular with a small set of disaffected and deeply anti-clerical younger men at the time of his death in 1860. Into the 1870s, however, Schopenhauerianism still belonged to what we might call the counter-culture and had made little if any impact on academic Indology or even on Buddhist sympathizers (if indeed there were any in Germany or Austria-Hungary at the time). Schopenhauer is not mentioned in Oldenberg's very popular *Buddha* of 1881 nor even by Oldenberg's younger contemporary, Ernst Windisch, in his much later, two-volume history of Sanskrit philology. He does not appear in either of Rudolf Seydel's treatises on Buddhism, written in 1882 and 1897, which is especially surprising, as Seydel had, already in 1857, written a long essay evaluating Schopenhauer's philosophy.[25] There is no sign of Schopenhauer in Leopold von Schroeder's 1887 collection, *Indiens Literatur und Cultur in historischer Entwickelung*, which included an essay on the history of Indological work in Germany.[26] This seems even more extraordinary in light of the fact that Schroeder later became an avid promoter of Wagnerian ideas, with which Schopenhauerianism was so closely linked, and that only six years later, in an essay written in 1893, Schroeder described Schopenhauer as one of the pro-genitors of the dawning Renaissance of Indian antiquity and his work as "nour-ished and suffused with Indian ideas."[27]

We have then to do mainly with a very late and rapid period of reception, stretching (if we follow Schroeder's indications) between about 1887 and 1893. These are the years in which Karl E. Neumann began to publish his Buddhist translations and the period in which elsewhere one sees strong signs of the furor orientalis emerging. But there is one great exception to this periodization, Paul Deussen, a man whose career trajectory, in fact, shows just how difficult it was to be a Schopenhauerian Indologist in the years before neoromanticism (and Buddhism) began to take hold.

Like most of the individuals profiled in this book, Deussen's passions and pursuits cannot be reduced to a single formula. Some of his behavior fits the conventional paradigm of the scholarly philologist; soon after settling in at Kiel he began composing his 900-page edition of the Upanishads, which was, as Chamberlain later averred, a testimony to the tradition of "German diligence."[28] Other aspects of his career, such as his enormous investment in popularization, and his close contacts with Indian scholars, do not. We will have to get to know him a bit to understand why he believed combining Schopenhauer and Indian philosophy made sense and to see how forging that particular bond both created and closed off intellectual possibilities for those working in his wake.

---

[25] Seydel, *Schopenhauers philosophisches System* (Leipzig, 1857), pp. 100, 115–16.
[26] Schopenhauer is quoted in an 1878 essay republished in Schroeder's *Reden und Aufsätze* (1913), but this is likely to have been a later intrusion.
[27] Schroeder, "Buddhismus und Christentum," p. 125.
[28] Chamberlain, *Arische Weltanschauung* (Munich, 3rd ed., 1916), p. 30.

Deussen's career trajectory is revealing. Though like Nietzsche a pastor's son, Deussen's father was Dutch and pastor to an "evangelisch-uniert" rather than a Lutheran community; Deussen in fact had to learn the Lutheran catechism on the train to attend school at Sculpforta.[29] He was already interested in things biblical, but had to learn most of his Greek at secondary school – where the students read the whole of the *Odyssey* and *Iliad* in the original language. His account of the effects on schoolboy faith of the school's exacting philological training are highly interesting: "Imperceptibly this [faith] was buried as a result of the exercise of the historical-critical method, with which the ancients were pummeled, and which then one wholly on one's own carried over to the biblical realm, as, for example, did [Karl] Steinhart in explaining the 45th Psalm entirely as a secular wedding-song in Hebrew class in Prima."[30] The challenge was surely intensified by Deussen's picking up, at Nietzsche's insistence, the new edition of D. F. Strauss's *Life of Jesus* a few years later; after reading it, Deussen found the theology lectures at the University of Bonn boring and even, for a time, lost his faith entirely. About the same time, in the mid-1860s, Deussen began to study Sanskrit – and although his autobiography does not record why he chose to study this difficult language, it seems related to the disillusionment he experienced with the classical seminars of Bonn's leading philologists, Friedrich Ritschl and Otto Jahn; their emphasis on conjugations and variants, he wrote, "worked powerfully on me, alienating my heart from classical philology, though not from classical antiquity." At first, Sanskrit was little better. His teacher, the now venerable Christian Lassen, had few students and Deussen had no books to practice with at home. Gradually he grew more interested – though he continued to feel guilty for devoting himself to the "Luxusstudium" of Sanskrit, ("a wholly impractical art") and in 1866, allowed his brother to convince him to return to the study of theology, this time at the infamous Tübingen Stift.[31]

But Tübingen had changed since Strauss's day, and its prevailing mysticism and anti-Prussian sentiment irritated Deussen. He returned briefly to Bonn, where he polished his Sanskrit and studied briefly with Jacob Bernays. By 1867 he had moved on to the study of philosophy at the University of Berlin. Here Sanskrit and his long-standing interest in the Bible were forgotten as Deussen was seized by what he called "a true Furor Platonicus." This was followed by an obsession with Kant, which then led, unavoidably, he claimed, to intense absorption in the work of Schopenhauer, coinciding with the upheaval of the Franco-Prussian War. Studying Kant and Schopenhauer turned him away from materialism and led him "to ground my Christianity in the Christ in us, in the fact of the moral consciousness, which is the only source from which also a Jesus and a Paul created their revelations."[32] As he later described his reconversion:

[T]he study of Schopenhauer, combined with the reading of the New Testament, shaped itself inside my mind into a harmonic whole, which united the most powerful claims of

---

[29] Deussen, *Mein Leben*, p. 60.

[30] Ibid., p. 70.

[31] Ibid., pp. 87, 88; on Lassen and Sanskrit, pp. 87–9.

[32] Deussen, *Mein Leben*, pp. 98; Deussen, *Allgemeine Geschichte der Philosophie mit besonderer Berücksichtigung der Religionen*, vol. 2, part 2, *Die Philosophie der Bibel* (Leipzig, 1915), p. x.

science with the equally imperative needs of the religious mentality in a completely satisfying way. Schopenhauer's name was always on my lips; I plagued people I hardly knew with
it; the whole day, in so far as it belonged to me, I devoted myself to his ideas and at night,
they followed me into my dreams. ... .[33]

Deussen had found, at last, a means of squaring science and belief, and a heroic
philosopher who needed a champion. But he had not yet found a job. Though he
now had good Hebrew and Sanskrit skills, it seems not to have occurred to him
until about 1873 that he might make a career as an orientalist. His doctorate had
been on Plato; his habilitation lecture was on Lucretius. When the notion came to
him, he reveled in the idea of finding his satisfaction "equally in the delight of
eternally increasing knowledge as in the fascination with which the public treats
the rare, the exotic [*Fernabliegende*] and the difficult to encompass."[34] But he
could not bear to leave aside the world of ideas for the usual orientalist's pursuit,
philology – and this is where Nietzsche's erstwhile friend took his most innovative
step. He chose to study Indian *philosophy* – a composite last taught at German
universities by Othmar Frank, whose dates (1770–1840) put him firmly in the
generation of the late romantics.

Deussen's innovative idea required innovation too in the job hunt. From 1869
to 1872, he taught at a Gymnasium in Minden, but left that post to serve as a
private tutor to a Russian family in Geneva and then in Aachen. Here he signed on
as a *Privatdozent* at the Technische Hochschule, and in 1876 offered a course on
Indian philosophy. That summer he attracted, remarkably, more than 100 people
to lectures in which he sang the praises of Schopenhauer and the Vedas so ardently
that he was accused of having claimed that compared to the Indians, Jesus Christ
was an idiot. The conservative Catholic press alleged him to be an emissary of the
liberal Prussian Cultural Minister Adalbert Falk, sent to carry forward the
Kulturkampf. Ultimately, these rumors were picked up by a Prussian Landtag
delegate, who complained in the chamber about the heretical "student of Schopenhauer," and Deussen was forced to give up lecturing on India and teach the
history of philosophy from Plato to Kant; he was even barred from discussing
post-Kantian philosophy because it was thought this would give him the opportunity to glorify Schopenhauer's unbourgeois and anti-Christian ideas. Deussen
obliged, selecting instead another subject at odds with liberal philhellenist proclivities: the pre-Socratics. Strikingly, this series of lectures, their appeal surely
enhanced by the controversy, attracted over 400 listeners.[35]

Deussen then moved with another Russian family to southern Russia. His
habilitation in Sanskrit occurred, finally, in 1881 – but the Schopenhauerian
scholar would have to wait until 1887 for the powerful Cultural Ministry bureaucrat Friedrich Althoff to create a professorship for him. He received his first
salaried academic position at the University of Kiel only in 1889. He was, through
the 1880s, still largely unknown as a scholar, despite having produced a study of
metaphysics, which contained much Indian material, an important translation of

[33] Deussen, *Mein Leben*, p. 121.
[34] Ibid., p. 165.
[35] Ibid., pp. 177–86.

Sankara's Brahmasutra commentary, and a pioneering study of Vedanta philosophy, all published by the Indophilic F. A. Brockhaus Verlag.[36] In 1889, the year his school friend went mad, Deussen finally made his name as a result of standing in for Max Müller as keynote speaker at the Congress of Orientalists in Stockholm.

Yet even after this time, Deussen remained very much a fringe member of the guild, something he reinforced by actually going to the Orient. He visited Egypt in 1890 and India in 1892. On returning home, instead of pursuing more specialized projects, he began work on a five-volume general history of philosophy (see below) and wrote remembrances of Nietzsche and of his travels in India. He published studies of Greek philosophy as well as a book on the fiery prophecies of Jakob Böhme. In 1911, he founded the Schopenhauer Gesellschaft – of which he would remain president until his death in 1919 – and began producing a luxurious edition of the great pessimist's work. In recognition of his wide-ranging efforts, the Kaiser made him a Geheimrat in 1907. He remained, however, a professor at the unexalted University of Kiel, as his philological colleagues seem to have found his popularizing efforts embarrassing and worried about his abilities to train future specialists.[37] To say that this career trajectory differed from that of the average nineteenth-century German orientalist is to assert the obvious – but that this new sort of orientalist did, after 1889, achieve a large measure of institutional and cultural influence should signal to us that the cultural politics of the Reich, and with them orientalism, were undergoing grand-scale change.

A closer look at Deussen's most popular and synthetic work, *Allgemeine Geschichte der Philosophie mit besonderer Berücksichtigung der Religionen* (five volumes, 1894–1917), reveals a great deal about the Indologist's view of world history.[38] When histories of oriental studies mention this text at all, it is usually to credit it with being the first western history of philosophy to make a serious attempt at treating Indian thought. This Deussen did do, devoting the whole of the first two volumes (technically, volume 1, parts 1 and 2) to Indian philosophy from the Vedas to the Upanishads. But the *Allgemeine Geschichte* is a much more interesting and complicated study than these passing compliments suggest. In the foreword to volume 1, Deussen collapses the categories of "religion" and "philosophy" in a way that would have horrified liberal-era practitioners of the history of philosophy, but which permitted him to give eastern thought equal footing with western (secular) philosophy. He argues that religions themselves, "seen internally and after stripping away their mythical garments, are themselves philosophy," and that, vice versa, philosophy, even modern European philosophy, was shaped at

---

[36] *Die Elemente der Metaphysik*, 1877; *Das System des Vedanta* (1883); *Die Sutra's des Vedanta* (1887).

[37] Betty Heimann, "Paul Deussen und die heutige Indologie," in *Achtzehntes Jahrbuch der Schopenhauer Gesellschaft* (1931): 246. They do not, however, seem to have questioned Deussen's own abilities as a linguist.

[38] This was meant to be a popular series and the set sold well; volume 1 had reached its 5th edition by 1922 (and volume 2, completed much later, its 4th edition by 1923). One wonders, however, if the "wider audience of friends of philosophy" Deussen coveted really read the whole thing; the chapters on Indian and Greek philosophy, in particular, were packed with largely unexplained and untranslated passages from original works.

least as much by religious beliefs as by philosophical ones.[39] This was certainly an innovation, but Deussen had others up his sleeve. Perhaps the most obvious was his decision to delay the telling of the European story until the survey's third volume. India, he explained, was just as big as Europe, and moreover, the inhabitants of the subcontinent had begun to think about "the puzzle of existence" earlier than the West. Moreover, the autonomy and differentness of Indian thought could have a very healthy impact on Europeans, "who have been born and bred on classical antiquity and the Bible"; the encounter, he believed would result not in "a superficial transformation, but one that stirs the [western tradition's] very depths." Those who had met Indian thinkers personally, he continued, could appreciate their profundity and breadth of knowledge, while also seeing the one-sidedness in them that they do not perceive. "Who knows," he continued, "if a similar sort of one-sidedness and narrowness also inheres in us, and in all of the traditional conceptions, in which we were raised, and if we might not learn just as much from the Indians as they can from us, if perhaps in a different way?"[40]

In the universal quest for knowledge, recent European "progress" in the natural sciences did not matter, for the ancients – Indians and Europeans – already understood nine-tenths of Being; indeed, natural forces and human nature "were grasped in a more pristine and clear way by the ancient philosophers 'who lived much nearer the gods' … than the later ones, that is, by [those] whose vision was not muddied by a jumble of traditions."[41] The volumes would focus, then, not on overcomings, but on moments of genesis in Indian, Greek, and Christian philosophy and the "high points" of each tradition: the Upanishads, Plato, and the New Testament – and the new foundations provided by Kantian philosophy. The other traditions and periods – in which "operating with inherited traditions outweighed the creation of original knowledge based on nature itself" – could be passed over quickly. For only in engaging with the latter was the history of philosophy fruitful for philosophy itself.[42]

There is something afoot here in Deussen's *General History* that needs closer specification, though his discernment of particular high points should already have given us some clues. As the "Provisional Overview" Deussen wrote for the series in 1894 clearly shows, this is not merely an inclusive history of philosophy: it is also a racial one. One of the reasons for ancient India's greatness in philosophy is not, as Hermann Oldenberg had suggested thirteen years earlier, that the whole lives of one special caste were devoted to thought, but that it had been isolated from others and thus had produced a pure, original culture, unlike that of western Asia. A largely Semitic West Asian *Kulturkreis* had produced Christianity. The third cultural area, that of the Greeks and Romans, had ultimately found its paganism and science insufficient, and sought help; it "stretched its hands out to the East, but encountered there not the wisdom of their primeval ancestors, the Indians, but Christianity which, among the Semitic tribes … was then preparing to

---

[39] Deussen, *Allgemeine Geschichte* 1, part 1, *Allgemeine Einleitung und Philosophie des Veda bis auf die Upanishad's* (Leipzig, 1894), pp. viii–ix, quotation p. viii.

[40] Ibid., 1, part 1: x.

[41] Ibid., 1, part 1: 31.

[42] Ibid., 1, part 1: 32.

make its conquering thrust into the world." This encounter laid the foundations for the medieval world, he wrote, one that represented a world-historical mixing of "rivers of two different kinds of water [the classical and the Semitic] ... but the union was an unnatural one and could not endure. The human spirit at the end of the medieval period awoke to consciousness of its own power and attempted to free itself from the fetters the Middle Ages had put on it. Modern philosophy [beginning with Kant] is this struggle for freedom."[43] In later pages, and extensively in what would be volume two, part two, Deussen further complicated this history of Aryan "struggles for freedom," arguing that ancient Iran had in fact participated heavily in the bringing about of Christianity; fitting their influence on the Jews into a Wellhausian trajectory for Jewish development, he tried to show that the ideas in Judaism that paved the way for the Christian conceptions of the New Testament were the product of the era of Jewish subjugation to the Persian Empire and thus probably borrowed from the Zoroastrians.[44]

In many ways, Deussen was simply enlarging the story of Christian synthesis by arguing, for example, that Jesus was a conscious student of Moses and an unconscious pupil of Zoroaster;[45] but his clear attempts to deny or diminish Semitic contributions to "true" philosophy and the thread that held the story together – the "Befreiungskampf" that modern German philosophy supposedly represented and in support of which Indian philosophy was to be enlisted – gives the *General History* an ominous quality. This is definitely not, as both Deussen's (Jewish) student Betty Heimann and the great historian of India-Europe exchanges Wilhelm Halbfass claimed, a return to the "perennial philosophy."[46]

What it was, more accurately, was an esoteric and implicitly racist form of Christian apologetics. Already in 1871, Deussen had found comforting commonalities between Schopenhauer's teachings and those of Paul – once the latter's "mystical shell" had been stripped away. But clearly too, as Deussen applied neoromantic philological techniques and idealist philosophy to his Sanskrit texts, he perfected a new means to provide his own reconciliation of science and faith.[47] This road led through the Vedas and the Upanishads, of which he completed a massive new edition in 1897. The epigraph to Deussen's *Sechzig Upanishads* comes from Schopenhauer, and announces to the reader that in this book, the iconoclast can luxuriate in the pure Indian air, where the pure spirit shrugs off its "early inoculations of Jewish superstitions and all such slavish philosophy." In the introductory section that follows, Deussen continues the theme of "stripping away," comparing his work to Luther's translation of the Bible and the editions of classical texts made by Renaissance humanists which, despite their errors, "had greater effects than the later critical editions and translations based on better documents..."[48] He is readying his world for conversion on the basis of a fully de-Judaized set of scriptures.

---

[43] Ibid., 1, part 1: 11.

[44] Ibid., 1, part 1: 16; and ibid., 2, part 2: 123–88. Thus, for example, he dated the Psalms, that suggested immortality of the soul to the post-Persian period and declared that older text (Deuteronomy, Ezekiel) showed no signs of this idea. Ibid., 2, part 2: 181.

[45] Ibid., 2, part 2: 229.

[46] Halbfass, *India and Europe*, pp. 130–3; Heimann, "Paul Deussen," p. 247.

[47] See his comments in *Mein Leben*, pp. 121, 344.

[48] Schopenhauer, quoted in Deussen, epigraph to *Sechzig Upanishads*, p. vi and "Vorrede," p. xiii.

But conversion to what? Here the preface to 1913 *Philosophy of the Bible* is perhaps most revealing:

The excellent textual critic [Kritiker] but philosophically less well-advised writer of the famous *Life of Jesus*, David Friedrich Strauss, in the publication of his old age *The Old Faith and the New*, throws out the question: "Are we still Christians?" and answers it with a clear and decisive No. But he who is able to remove the philosophical kernel from the historical and therefore accidental shell, he who no longer holds to mere words and is able to recognize a thing when it appears under a different name and in new clothing, he will, even in the wake of all the achievements in historical research, natural science and philosophy answer Strauss's question: Are we still Christians? With an equally clear and decisive Yes. For the essence of Christianity extends far wider than its name and consists in an idea, which is as eternal as the world and will never be extinguished: it is the Indian-Platonic-Christian idea, that our life on earth is not an end in itself . . . that indeed the highest task of life consists in . . . separating ourselves from all inborn egoism . . .[49]

For Deussen, the central feature of Christianity was the recognition that the ego was the only place in nature where the thing in itself is revealed to itself, where the consciousness of both freedom of action and the need to subject all actions to the categorical imperative can reside.[50] This was, for him, an eternally present and eternally valid idea – though only the Aryans seem to have been able to cognize it. Caught in their optimistic-realist worldview, with their distant God, the Semites were not likely to get this far. But the works of the Indians, Saint Paul, Kant, and Schopenhauer had proved by means of metaphysical, not natural, truths that there is an authentic, eternal world beyond the world of appearances. Thus "after all the undermining of belief in the Bible through historical and natural-scientific critiques we may yet dare to answer the original question, 'Are we still Christians? with a confident Yes!'"[51] Reversing the course charted by the Hegelians and rejecting, at the end of the day, liberal historicism, Deussen used the history of philosophy to prove the eternal truth of Aryan religion.

Deussen's linking of Indian ideas and Schopenhauerian ones was surely misleading, forcing a whole tradition into one highly pessimistic man's train of thought. This is, of course, a subject beyond the scope of this book and its author's competence, but I think it can be said that few scholars now would find Schopenhauer a suitable key to unlock the whole of Indian philosophy or, for that matter, Christian theology.[52] But we can assess here the impact of Deussen's innovations on the image of India in the German-speaking world, and this was undoubtedly quite profound. It was from Deussen that most Germans learned to associate the Orient with Schopenhauer; Nietzsche learned much of what he knew about Indian philosophy from Deussen and his works, and it was surely through Deussen that

---

[49] Deussen, *Allgemeine Geschichte* 2, part 2: v.
[50] See also ibid., 2, part 2: 114.
[51] Ibid., 2, part 2: ix.
[52] See Hacker's critique in his *Philology and Confrontation*. But a new book on the subject has just appeared, too late for my consideration: Douglas A. Berger, *The Veil of Māyā: Schopenhauer's System and Early Indian Thought* (Binghampton, NY, 2009).

the Basel philosopher learned to see India through a Schopenhauerian lens.[53] Deussen wrote for, and was read by, an educated elite for whom the reconciling of religion and science was still an aim, if also an often-frustrated passion. In his ceaseless advocacy of Schopenhauer, culminating in the founding of the *Schopenhauer Gesellschaft* in 1911, and his updating of the philosopher to make him speak to a neoromantic public, Deussen was instrumental in cementing elective affinities between the culturally pessimistic avant-garde and the early Aryan world.

Race was neither the beginning of Deussen's investment in the Indians (though vague notions of Aryan *ur*-wisdom may have shaped his decision to study Sanskrit) nor the object of his scholarship. In some respects, his promotion of "Aryan" ideas was a continuation of that anti-clerical, iconoclastic liberal tradition practiced by Voltaire or by Max Müller – which, as we have seen, also already contained elements of racist thinking as well. Deussen hoped, above all, to use Schopenhauer and Indian philosophy to clean up Christianity, rather than to denigrate the Jews. But his need to contrast a pristine, authochthonous, primeval India with the elements in Christianity he found problematic or distasteful culminated in the caricaturing of "Semitic Realism" and its complete opposition to Indo-Aryan idealism. In his model, the gulf between the Semites' vengeful God and supposed devotion to this-worldly materialism and the Aryans' faith in immortality and God's benevolence was so wide and deep that Deussen had to posit an intermediary role for the Persians in shaping the Old Testament ideas that had carried over into the New.[54] This was again no universalist project, à la Lessing, and even Friedrich Schlegel would have blanched at the tacking on of the Germanic *Befreiungskampf* at the story's end. Deussen was reducing both "Christianity" and "Indian philosophy" to purified and ultimately ahistorical forms, and defining them in such a way as to preclude the participation of Judaism and Islam, Egypt and China, the *Naturvölker* and the Slav, in the search for truth. Understanding Deussen in the context of earlier quests for the origins of revelation on the one hand, and iconoclastic attempts to modernize Christianity by divorcing the Old from the New Testament on the other, we can see how he got here; a few contemporaries were also able to see where he was heading. As one sympathetic observer wrote in 1917, Deussen, though he wrote very little himself about the ancient Germans, had contributed heavily to the cult of "Germanic Christianity" and, by drawing distinctions between Semitic and non-Semitic religious conceptions, to the creation of "a canon of Aryan piety."[55]

This does not mean, however, that Deussen should be described simply as a writer still beholden to Eurocentric forms; as we have seen, his debts to hyper-Protestantism, Plato, and Schopenhauer made him critical of many aspects of European Christian orthodoxy. Moreover, he had developed an anti-English set of prejudices that divided him from the previous generation of Indologists as well

---

[53] See Hans Rollmann, "Deussen, Nietzsche and Vedanta," in *Journal of the History of Ideas* 39, no. 1 (Jan.–March 1978): 125–32.

[54] Deussen, *System of Vedanta*, pp. 40–1; *Allgemeine Geschichte* 2, pt. 2: viii–ix, 28–37.

[55] Constantin Grossmann, "Schopenhauer und das Problem einer 'Germanisierung des Christentums,'" in *Sechstes Jahrbuch der Schopenhauer Gesellschaft* (1917): 273–4.

as from some of his colleagues in Islamic studies. These prejudices were confirmed and exacerbated by his travels in India and contacts with Indian anti-colonial elites. In fact, his travel diary, published in 1904, explicitly advertised itself as a non-English view of the subcontinent, written by one who "is not accustomed to kneeling before the golden calf of success or to believing that something is bad just because it has been subordinated."[56] It is also striking that, though his hero Max Müller apparently hoped that drawing out similarities between Indian and Christian thought might prepare the way for Christianization in India, Deussen recommended not Christianity, but a return to the Vedanta to his Indian audiences. Perhaps this is what endeared him so much to the Brahmins he visited during his travels in India in 1892–3; he was so well received by the Indian elite that he was given a Sanskrit name: Devasena.[57]

It should be noted that Deussen was one of the first German Indologists to actually visit the subcontinent – and by no means would all of his successors do the same. Even more unusually, Deussen took his wife along, and thanks to his ability to speak Sanskrit and some Hindustani, as well as English, spent his time chiefly with learned Brahmins and pandits, not with colonial officials or missionaries. He contrasts the many friendships he was able to form with the indigenous Indians to the arrogant and ignorant English, one of whom apparently told Deussen that it might be possible for a German Indologist to befriend the Indians, "'but we have to rule them, and that is something entirely different.'"[58] Deussen's visits to schools and ritual burning sites and his interviews with holy women and maharajas deepened his respect for the Indian past – and he conveyed clearly his contempt for the long line of colonizers of India, all of whom demonstrated "the brutal superiority of the Willing over the Knowing."[59] This conception, closer to that of Herder or Peter von Bohlen than to the views of Deussen's "liberal" contemporaries, is indicative of the ways in which a neoromantic orientalism could be coupled with a critique of Eurocentrism and of (somebody else's) empire.

At the World Parliament of Religions in Chicago in 1893, Deussen met Swami Vivekananda, a leading Hindu nationalist who had his own reasons for emphasizing the racial and spiritual superiority of the Aryans.[60] Deussen was apparently intrigued by Vivekananda (and enjoyed the chance to speak Sanskrit) and invited him to Kiel in 1896; after a three-day visit, Deussen traveled with Vivekanada to England, where they saw much of one another.[61] Their conversations during this time apparently had a greater effect on Vivekanada than on Deussen; Vivekanada adopted Deussen's interpretation of Vedantic ethics, making "Tat tvam asi" equivalent to Jesus' second great commandment, "Thou shalt love thy neighbor

---

[56] Deussen, *Erinnerungen an Indien* (Kiel, 1904), p. 1.
[57] Deussen, *On the Philosophy of the Vedanta in Its Relations to Occidental Metaphysics* (lecture given in Bombay, February 1893) (Bombay, 1893), p. 251; Friedrich Wilhelm, "The German Response to Indian Culture," in *Journal of the American Oriental Society* 81, no. 44 (Sept.–Dec. 1961): 399.
[58] Deussen, *Erinnerungen an Indien*, p. 45.
[59] Ibid., pp. 169–70.
[60] See Figueira, *Aryans, Jews, Brahmins*, pp. 134–41.
[61] Deussen, *Mein Leben*, pp. 305–6.

as thyself." On Paul Hacker's account, Deussen's philosophy also shaped the ethical thinking of the Ramakrishna Mission and the foremost Indian nationalist before Gandhi, Bāl Gangādhar Tilak, to whom certainly Deussen's hostility to the "defects" and "later corruptions" of Vedic systems of thought had significant appeal.[62] While Hacker focuses on the misunderstandings introduced into neo-Hinduism as a result of importing Schopenhauer and Deussen, Reza Pirbhai has recently demonstrated a deeper and longer-lasting set of political and cultural prejudices.[63] As this example demonstrates, the orientalists who facilitated British rule in India surely have much to answer for; but we should not forget that anti-imperialist friendships too have their consequences and costs.

POPULARIZING THE ARYAN INDIAN: LEOPOLD VON SCHROEDER AND HOUSTON STEWART CHAMBERLAIN

Deussen did write for non-expert audiences and seems to have enjoyed some success in having his voice heard. But more influential in this sphere were two slightly younger writers, whose common interest in things Indian and Aryan laid the foundations for a highly consequential friendship. The two men profiled below, Leopold von Schroeder and Houston Stewart Chamberlain, can, even more than Deussen, be said to belong to the group of "furious" orientalists described in Chapter 5. And much more clearly than the Schopenhauerian Indologist too, they can be said to have racialized the study of India.

This section will tack between the work of the two men, one of whom (Schroeder) was a credentialed orientalist, in order to sketch the racialized image of India being put forth in some circles by the 1900s. Chamberlain needs to be included here not only because he exerted formative influence on Schroeder at a critical moment in his career, but also because it was in the pages of his books and especially in his blockbuster *Foundations of the Nineteenth Century* (1900) that so many Wilhelmine readers got to know the ancient Orient. Though modern commentators on Chamberlain's *Foundations* do not dwell on the subject, that book focused very heavily on the ancient Orient; 512 of 531 pages of volume one treated events that predated the Resurrection; the book's footnotes are densely packed with references to the orientalist and theological scholarship described in the last few chapters. Even before the Babel-Bibel Affair, Chamberlain recognized the tendency of the new orientalism to attribute Judaism's "innovations" (like monotheism) to other oriental cultures, and sought to make his own, racialized attempt to purify Christianity. Schroeder's work gave him the Indological building blocks – and the patina of scientificness – with which to construct a highly influential history of Aryan-Semitic entanglements.

---

[62] Hacker, *Philology and Confrontation*, pp. 277–79, 293–302.
[63] Reza Pirbhai, "Demons in Hindutva: Writing a Theology for Hindu Nationalism," in *Modern Intellectual History* 5, no.1 (Apr. 2008): 27–53.

Leopold von Schroeder was born in 1851 to a German family in Dorpat (Tartu), Estonia. This area, home to numerous Prussian aristocrats, but subjected to intense Russification in the later nineteenth century, produced a large number of passionate German patriots, of whom Schroeder's father was one.[64] Schroeder's first passion was German antiquity, from which he moved, thanks to Friedrich Schlegel's lectures on ancient and modern literature, to comparative topics and, by 1869, to Sanskrit studies. By this time, specialization was beginning to drive wedges between orientalists, and it was becoming less and less common for younger scholars to be expected to cover both Indo-German and Semitic fields. Schroeder surely did know Hebrew, but he was not compelled, as were Peter von Bohlen and Justus Olshausen in the pre-1850 era, to teach Old Testament exegesis nor did he – unlike many of the early Indologists – publish anything in the field of *Semitistik*. He studied in Jena, Leipzig, and Tübingen, where he learned the Vedas and the Avesta from Rudolf Roth. He habilitated at the University of Dorpat and in 1879 was nominated for membership in the Russian Academy of Sciences by the great positivist linguist – and model anti-popularizer – Otto Boehtlingk. But his nomination was scuttled by nationalist infighting in the academy; in 1890, the Education Ministry overrode the Berlin University faculty's recommendation that Schroeder receive an Indological chair. He was offered a job in what he called American "Dollarlande" (at the University of Chicago) in 1892, but turned it down because – ironically – the pay was insufficient.[65] In 1894, chafing under renewed Russification at the University of Dorpat, he elected to go to the University of Innsbruck, where he took up a junior professorship for "Ancient Indian History and Antiquities, with Respect to General Ethnography"; in 1899, he was made Professor of Indology at the University of Vienna. Schroeder, an ardent Protestant and Baltic patriot, would never feel at home in the heavily Catholic – and Jewish – Habsburg capital.

Schroeder seems to have had an agnostic or even quasi-Buddhist period in the 1870s and 1880s; but shortly thereafter, inspired by a revelatory performance of *Tannhäuser* and Adolf Stoecker's campaigns against the evils of industrial society, he returned to the Christian fold.[66] Schroeder's piety was strengthened by the death of his beloved wife in 1901, the only consolation for which, he declared, could be found in prayer and in his friendship with Chamberlain, whom he had met after reading the *Foundations* in 1900.[67] His recovery, however, also entailed reviving his old interest in comparative mythology and especially in ancient Aryan religion. The way in which he pursued comparisons and his conclusions deserve some scrutiny, for they are not what one might expect to find in early

---

[64] Schroeder notes his father's intense sorrow at the Russification of the school he had directed and his resignation from his post, rather than agreeing to speak Russian on the job. Julius von Schroeder also kept a bag of German dirt in his home so that when he died, he could rest under German soil. Schroeder, *Lebenserinnerungen* (Leipzig, 1921), pp. 38, 69, 54.

[65] Ibid., pp. 139–40.

[66] Ibid., pp. 239–40; also idem, "Buddhismus und Christentum," in idem, *Reden und Aufsätze*, p. 87. Stoecker was a highly influential Protestant pastor, founder of the Christian Social Workers' Party and court chaplain to Wilhelm II; among the evils he denounced were socialism, rampant capitalism, and, viciously and persistently, Jews.

[67] Schroeder, "Aus meinem Leben," in *Aus baltischer Geistesarbeit* 9 (Riga, 1909), p. 129.

twentieth-century, supposedly secularized, Indology. In 1902, Schroeder delivered a lecture to the Vienna Anthropology Society which attacked the claims of English Darwinians that religion was not a fundamental part of human experience, but evolved along with civilization. The problem, Schroeder argued, was an overly restrictive definition of religion; so Schroeder came up with a new one: "Religion is belief in a spiritual Being or power, who reigns outside and over the sphere of men, the feeling of dependence on such a being, and the need to put oneself in harmony with him."[68] This could be observed in all peoples, he claimed; though some "special [bestimmt] people" had made progress beyond what he argued must have been a *ur-*, universal monotheism. There was evidence of belief in one high being in the "Aryan Urzeit," he argued, but the first real step was taken by the ancient Persians, in developing their Zarathustra religion. Schroeder then turned to Indian Buddhism, Greek mythology, and, in a dismissive half-sentence, Egyptian "monotheism." Only then did he turn to the Jews, whom he did credit with developing "true monotheism" (alongside persistent paganism), and even criticized those who would denigrate Jewish belief. But the essay concluded with claims that Judaism had been superceded and that Christ had brought the highest and purest revelation of God's truth to humankind. If Christianity had had its travails, he concluded "we still believe and trust in the conquering power that it carries in itself, we believe and trust in its further development, and it will always be new, and even raise up and purify the old, and shine on in luminous purity, for the good of mankind."[69]

This lecture apparently appealed so strongly to a young priest in the audience, Father Wilhelm Schmidt, that it inspired him to undertake the wide-ranging ethnographic studies of monotheism that culminated in Schmidt's important book, *Der Ursprung des Gottesidee* (1912) and in the studies of the Catholic-dominated Viennese School of Ethnology.[70] But Schroeder's interests after this time turned to a set of concerns less reconcilable with Schmidt's Catholic modernism: as he noted in a footnote to the 1909 printed version of this lecture, his studies of Christianity's "further development" led him to focus on "the great significance of the Aryan (that is, Indo-German) essence, Aryan culture and religious development ..."[71] Numerous essays written in the immediate prewar years, as well as his huge *Arische Religion* (note, not religion, not religions) of 1914 focused attention not on universal beliefs, but on those of one branch, the one "culture-carrying" branch, of Noah's family tree. This was a subject, Schroeder argued, in which his contemporaries took a keen interest; for his generation, "... the drive to track down the primeval roots of our spiritual existence is even stronger than that other drive to spiritual progress, which fills every living spirit."[72] But there was no room in this history for an Old Testament that was, in the view of Schroeder and many of his Protestant contemporaries, narrowly provincial,

---

[68] Schroeder, "Wesen und Ursprung der Religion, ihre Wurzeln und deren Entfaltung," in *Aus baltischer Geistesarbeit* 9 (1909): 135.

[69] Ibid., pp. 157, 167.

[70] Schroeder, *Lebenerinnerungen*, p. 165.

[71] "Wesen und Ursprung," p. 167, n. 1.

[72] Schroeder, *Arische Religion*, vol. 1 (Leipzig, 1914), p. 10.

materialist, legalistic, and riddled with historical errors and with ideas borrowed or stolen from other, older oriental cultures. Nor was there much room, really, for the *Naturvölker*, even for a person whose job title had once included "general ethnology"; the peoples whose spiritual history counted were only those related by language – and blood – to "us."

Blood was certainly important to Schroeder – but we should not underestimate either the seriousness of religious questions, both for him and for his readers. In the opening of *Arische Religion*, he writes:

> The great battle [Kampf] – the greatest the new century has to fight, is not a world war, which many anticipate.... But the question of all questions is another one, a more central one. It is the question of the whence, where, and why of the evolution of humankind and the world, the question of the meaning and purpose of our lives, which science is unable to answer. The battle of all battles is the great battle over *faith* [Glauben] – in which science must assist, precisely where it, by nature, breaks off and demurs – the battle over *Religion*, over *God*, over the question, if we want to have any religion, any faith, any god, and if so, what this religion should look like.[73]

Directly following this question, Schroeder describes the threat posed by the natural sciences and by historical-critical scholarship to belief and insists on the need for scholars to overcome "a tyranny of unbelief, a tyranny of negation," which he sees rampant among the educated elite. Sounding eerily like modern defenders of "intelligent design," he insists on the necessity of scholarly freedom for believers and of a purified form of religion in which they can put their trust.[74] Faith in the old forms of Christianity may be gone, but can and should be replaced by an Aryan worldview, which appeared "at the peaks of philosophical thought of the Indians, Greeks and *Germanen*, each in their turn, and which Kant has brought to scientific completion. This worldview, rightly understood, clears away all intellectual barriers and difficulties that stand between scientific thought and faith."[75] The way to put an end to skepticism and atheism, to win the battle of religion, is to believe in the truths propounded by your own race.

Schroeder's work on "Aryan" religion certainly represents a step further into racial segregation and intolerance; perhaps by virtue of being born on the Germanic periphery and then consigned to teaching there as well, Schroeder was also a more avid nationalist than was Deussen, who pled with subscribers to the *Schopenhauer Jahrbuch* during the Great War not to destroy international scholarly comity.[76] Schroeder was also even more passionately interested in popularization and closer to the arts than was Deussen; he wrote poetry and plays, one of which ("König Sundara") was staged at the Riga city theater in 1890, and he was an active Wagnerian. Schroeder too cultivated something of an outsider status with respect to other academics – the cantankerous Josef Strzygowski was a good friend – and he went much further than most of his colleagues in criticizing

[73] Ibid., 1: 1–2.
[74] Ibid., 1: 4–5.
[75] Schroeder, *Lebenserinnerungen*, p. 235.
[76] Deussen, "Vorrede des Herausgebers," in *Viertes Jahrbuch der Schopenhauer Gesellschaft* (1915): v–xi.

specialization and positivistic scholarship.[77] All of these qualities made him attractive to Chamberlain – and vice versa – and laid the foundations for an enduring friendship between the Indologist and the racist popularizer. As we turn now to describe the projects and passions these two shared, we should keep in mind that Schroeder remained throughout the less radical and outspoken of the two, but not necessarily the originator of all of their shared ideas; after 1900, we have to do not with the bastardization of (Schroeder's) scholarly ideas, but with the forming, between the two, of a shared conception of Aryan history and German-Christendom's future.[78]

To investigate the shared project, we must start with Chamberlain's *Foundations*, which clearly supplied Schroeder with a larger and semi-coherent trajectory in which to situate his studies of Aryan cultural history. Space forbids us from examining Chamberlain's biography or even his "orientalism" at length; suffice it to say that he was born in Britain, but considered himself a Germanic knight-cum-connoisseur; though his interest in matters Asian probably owed more to Gobineau than to Christian piety, he believed himself to be a Christian, frequently averred his faith, and convinced many that he was a Christian, albeit of an unorthodox sort.[79] Like Nietzsche, he remained a vehement critic of established churches and priestly intolerance. But in the preface of his *Foundations*, he insisted that a major cause of Teutonic culture's sickness unto death was not its ascetic will to nothingness, but its settling for an impure faith; "We have stopped up the spring that welled up in our own hearts and made ourselves dependent upon the scanty, brackish water which the beduins of the desert draw from their wells."[80] Like Deussen and Schroeder, Chamberlain criticized Nietzsche and Schopenhauer for their negativity and even distanced himself from Lagarde, who had blamed Saint Paul for destroying Jesus' true message.[81] His recovery of Paul involved racial arguments (he floated the possibility that Paul was not a pure Jew), but he wove his theses into evidence culled from specialized work by theologians and philologists, which suggested that Paul's ideas had been more heavily shaped by Hellenistic mystery religions than by Hellenistic Judaism.[82] Chamberlain's genius was that he was able to knit together biological and theological claims in a way that made him seem an earnest campaigner for the reform of Christianity and of

[77] See passages from Schroeder, "Vom Popularisierung," quoted above.

[78] Geoffrey Field has also called attention to the cross-fertilization and relations between academics and race popularizers. Field, *Evangelist of Race*, p. 212.

[79] He published a volume of the sayings of Jesus – *Worte Christi* – in 1901 and another study of Christian doctrine – *Mensch und Gott: Betrachtungen über Religion und Christentum* – in 1921. His work was frequently reviewed, and not always negatively, in liberal Christian publications. For another contemporary discussion of his piety, see, Franz Spemann, *Vom Heinrich W. Riehl bis Oswald Spengler: Ein Beitrag zum Verständnis der Bibel in unserer Zeit* (Berlin, 1926), pp. 82–85.

[80] Chamberlain, *Grundlangen* 1: 26.

[81] Chamberlain, *Mensch und Gott: Betrachtungen über Religion und Christentum* (Munich, 1921), pp. 179–217.

[82] Ibid., pp. 178–82. Chamberlain noted that he had already suggested that Paul might not be a full Jew in the *Foundations*, as early as 1900.

German culture against those who had debased and denigrated these "Aryan" achievements. And the linkage of this project to orientalist scholarship begins to explain how he and Schroeder could find common ground.

Importantly, Schroeder and Chamberlain held similar views not just on racial prehistory, but also on the culturally resonant question of Greek normivity; here too, they were eager to advertise their rejection of bourgeois norms. Early on, Schroeder showed signs of the tendency we have dubbed "furious" orientalism; his first major publication was a book entitled *Pythagoras und die Inder* (Leipzig, 1884), in which he made a passionate case for the dependence of Greek mathematics and science on Indian ideas – and he would continue throughout his life to underline the *ur*-originality of the Indo-Aryans. While for Deussen, the absolute autonomy and originality of Indian ideas was not so important as their correspondence with Kantian and Schopenhauerian truths, for Schroeder and Chamberlain, the self-sufficiency of the Indians, as compared to the mixed culture of the Greek world, gave the former greater depth. Not surprisingly, the emphasis on "cultural" mixing was a means of not so subtly suggesting that the Indians were racially more pure than their descendants to the West. As Schroeder wrote in 1887, responding to the conventional philhellenist insistence that the Greeks were able to form everything in their own image: "But the whole cultural evolution of the Indians can be said to be unique and autonomous to a higher degree than that of the Greeks, who were, already very early on, influenced by the Egypt, Phoenicia and other countries."[83] In addition to questioning their purity and originality, Schroeder claimed that the Greeks, while noteworthy for their aesthetic achievements, lacked the depth and interiority of the ancient Indians, whose characteristic preoccupations were not (superficial) forms, but religion and philosophy.[84]

Chamberlain too was eager to expand his contemporaries' critique of desiccated classicism and nowhere, before the *Foundations*, do we find the polemics put so vehemently: "That Indian thought has clearly exercised a determinative influence upon Greek philosophy is now a settled fact; of course, our Hellenists and philosophers have long disputed this with the violent obstinacy of prejudiced scholars; everything was supposed to have originated autonomously in Hellas; at most the Egyptians and Semites were supposed to have exercised a shaping influence ..."[85] The popularizer was even willing to carry this critique of scholarship into a critique of Gymnasium education:

That still today, for example, – when so many big and important things need our whole attention, when we have piled up endless treasures of thought, of poetry and above all of knowledge, of which the wisest Greeks had not the faintest idea and to a share of which every child should have a natural right – that today we are still compelled to waste valuable time learning every detail of the pitiful history of the Greeks, to stuff our poor brains with endless registers of names of boastful heroes ending in -ades, -atos, -enes, -eiton, &c., and, if possible, wax enthusiastic over the political fate of these cruel, short-sighted democracies,

---

[83] Schroeder, "Erste Vorlesung: Einleitung: Alter, Umfang und Originalität der indischen Literatur. Ursprung und Entwicklung der Indologie in Europa," in idem, *Indiens Literatur und Cultur in historischer Entwicklung: Ein Cyklus von fünfzig Vorlesungen* (Leipzig, 1887), p. 2.

[84] Ibid., p. 3.

[85] Chamberlain, *Grundlagen* 1: 80.

blinded with self-love, and based upon slavery and idleness – this is indeed a hard destiny. But if we think about it, the blame for this lies not with the Greeks but with our own narrow-mindedness.[86]

Chamberlain surely knew he was speaking to the disaffected youth, who were by now engaging in regular assaults on "dry as dust" classicism, while Schroeder, who knew too how "dry" oriental philology could be, referred to the more general "Moloch" of specialized science, "to whom great things, and even the best parts of [students'] being, must often be sacrificed."[87] But for both, the decentering of liberal classicism was central to the birth of a healthy new German culture.

A few years later came the fullest expression of this anti-Greek worldview, Chamberlain's *Arische Weltanschauung*, written in 1905 and dedicated to Schroeder. Here, Chamberlain argued explicitly for the need to replace the old (classical) humanism with one grounded instead in Indo-Aryan civilization in order to give *Kultur* religio-racist rather than secular-aesthetic roots. The advantages of India as a foundation for cultural revival for Chamberlain were, first of all, its great antiquity and thus its supposed autonomy from Semitic influences, something the Greeks (who adopted Judaized Christianity) could not boast. But more importantly, in his view, while the focus of Greek life was on art and on formal philosophy, India's "life" emphasized religious-philosophical thought, freedom from inner fragmentation and mechanization, and the experiential grasping of the unity of experience that German culture now needed.[88] While in the West, religion, philosophy, and science are in constant battle, in India – where, he argued there has always been complete freedom of thought – the three are harmonized; moreover, the true (Vedic) religion of the Indians "was never ... an attempt to explain external, temporal things but rather represents a symbolic shaping of internal, non-mechanistic, timeless experience – there was never an attempt to prove the existence of God ..." This God has nothing to do with the Jahwe of Genesis and Christian church doctrine; "Precisely that god of the Indo-Aryan 'whose existence cannot be proved,' (as it says in an Upanishad), since he is not given to experience externally, but only through inner experience, is in reality the god of all inwardly religious German Christians of all times, no matter which confession they had externally to adhere to; that can be proven in the mystics and philosophers, from Erigena and Eckhart to Böhme and Kant."[89] What India offers, ultimately, is the foundation not for a cultural revival, but for a spiritual one, one that – unlike the Renaissance – does its work from within and works only for Aryans, not for humankind as a whole.

Let me draw attention to one more striking aspect of this text. Early on, Chamberlain offers a short history of Indological work, in which Max Müller plays an interesting role. Chamberlain chastises the great German-British scholar for having as his ideal a sort of "Pan-eclecticism" (or, in Luther's phrase, a "Grundsuppe"), one in which all religions and philosophies claim essentially the same thing, "For difference is a natural law," Chamberlain writes, "and

---

[86] Ibid., 1: 91.
[87] Schroeder, "Vom Popularisierung," p. 312.
[88] Chamberlain, *Arische Weltanschauung*, quotation p. 33; p. 20, also pp. 77–84.
[89] Ibid., pp. 83–4.

Darwin has proved the tendency to strive toward differentiation (even where original similarity reigned).... Max Müller's claim, that there exists 'no specific difference' between a Chinese Taoist and an Indian Brahmin simply makes you want to tear your hair out." Müller's Indology then certainly could not provide the key to the inner truths of India – but Deussen's Vedic idealism could. Deussen's "deep religious instinct" had made possible the use of the Indo-Aryan worldview to effect humanistic and cultural ferment in the life of the present – or at least, the Aryan life of the present. Now it was necessary to separate out the foreign elements from those that belonged to our *Eigenart*. "We have sacrificed a whole century to the fad for unlimited tolerance.... It is high time that we raise our consciousness; not to reduce the spiritual freedom of others, but so that we are masters in our own house, which today we are not."[90] There is an oriental Renaissance in this text, and there is even a plan for Christian reform; but it goes far beyond that of Müller or of Friedrich Schlegel. Here the aim is racial not cultural renewal, and intolerant self-assertion, not the seeking of revelation's first sparks.

As their friendship grew, Schroeder moved increasingly in Chamberlain's direction. Before he met Chamberlain, he had already been interested in genealogical relations between Indians, Greeks, and early Germans, but he had not really fleshed out relations between the Aryan family members. Nor had he really integrated his Wagnerism into his scholarship. But this he had certainly done by 1906, when he identified the Indo-Aryan homeland not in the Hindu Kush or the Caucausus, but in Europe.[91] Though there were others, especially among the prehistorians, who had begun to push for a Scandinavian origin for the Aryans and/or Germanic tribes, this was, when Schroeder articulated as if it were common knowledge in 1906, still a rather marginal, recognizably right-wing view. After this time, racial conceptions suffused his work, offering him the opportunity to streamline and naturalize the Nordic-Aryan story. Thanks to the growth in the last century of "a previously unknown, even impossible, Aryan tribal consciousness [*Stammesbewusstsein*]" he wrote in 1908, it was now possible to reach deep into the Aryan past and to find help in tracking the origins of, for example, German mythology, with the help of the Indian "Aryan brothers."[92] Thus the Vedas could simply be assumed to be strongly related to medieval German legends (of which the Grail story was uppermost in his Wagnerian mind) and Aryan nature cults (Indian, Greek, and German) assumed to be similar and their impact on the Grail legend formative, without any comparative analysis of other cultures' practices.[93] Racial presumptions made possible the overcoming of all those tricky questions about diffusion so many members of his generation were still dealing with. And

---

[90] Ibid., pp. 25, 41.

[91] Schroeder, "Indien, ohne die Engländer," in idem, *Reden und Aufsätze*, p. 347.

[92] Schroeder, "Die Bedeutung der arischen Sagenquelle" [1908], in idem, *Reden und Aufsätze*, pp. 393, 398. Stefan Arvidsson also suggests that Schroeder's work of this period was instrumental in laying the foundations for the male fellowship ideal taken over by the Nazis. See Arvidsson, *Aryan Idols*, pp. 208–9.

[93] Schroeder, "Bedeutung der arischen Sagenquelle," and "Der arische Naturkult als Grundlage der Sage vom heiligen Gral" [1911], in idem, *Reden und Aufsätze*, pp. 393–406, 406–30.

too, they simplified the articulation of the sort of purified Christianity Schroeder wanted so passionately to sell.[94]

This is the Indian renaissance the three wanted, though Deussen and Schroeder did not articulate their vision with either the vehemence or the malice characteristic of Chamberlain. Deussen did not, to my knowledge, discuss the present-day Jewish Question in public, and in 1899, Schroeder explicitly denounced Nietzschean racism, "the brutal-egoistic master morality, the cult of the blond beast and of the criminal, which that so thoroughly un-Zarathustra-ish modern Zarathustra has conjured up."[95] Even after he befriended Chamberlain, Schroeder rarely discussed the Jews' contribution to civilization – his biography of Chamberlain is completely silent on his friend's anti-Semitism. Either the two agreed to disagree on this or perhaps Schroeder's professional position and more orthodox Christianity led him to keep his polemical fingers out of that particular pie. Though many of Chamberlain's comments on ancient Judaism were consistent with both liberal and religious-historical work on the subject, the theologians and orientalists of the day did not share his desire to meddle in what he called the present-day "struggle for life and death" of the Teutonic race against mongrelization.[96]

This is a big difference and one that makes it possible to make clear linkages between Chamberlain's work and Nazi Jewish policy, which are absent in the case of the others. But it is worth emphasizing again the way in which this Indological renaissance departed much more obviously from the perennial philosophy than earlier ones – with the possible exception of the one Giordano Bruno sought to stage. But, strikingly, Bruno was burnt by the Catholic church, while Chamberlain, Schroeder, and Deussen were able to sign onto the German Christian movement – by no means a mainstream community, but an active and influential cultural minority, which helped to lay the foundations for the debased Protestantism practiced by "German Christians" and "God-Believers" during the Third Reich.[97] They continued to be iconoclasts with respect both to academic institutions and to the larger Christian world; but in the cultural context of the twentieth century, they were able to spread their radical ideas for spiritual purification to an ever-widening set of racist readers.

There were, of course, specialists in things "Aryan" who resisted the tendency to seek sources for Christian ideas in the ancient East and even resisted comparing religions, as did Christian Bartholomae, in a 1918 lecture on "Zarathustra's Leben und Lehre."[98] We saw in the last chapter that numerous Indologists – including Schroeder – were also involved in debates over Buddhism; though defending a particular version of Christianity was also central there, this literature was not nearly so racialized as the discussions I have just profiled. Nor does the

---

[94] See, for example, the conclusion to "Der arische Naturkult," p. 430.

[95] Schroeder, "Indiens Geistige Bedeutung für Europa" (1899), in idem, *Reden und Aufsätze*, p. 170; on Nietzsche, pp. 183–4.

[96] *Foundations* 1: 578.

[97] See Uwe Puschner, *Die völkische Bewegung im wilhelminischen Kaiserreich: Sprache, Rasse, Religion* (Darmstadt, 2001), pp. 203–62; and now Susannah Heschel, *The Aryan Jesus: Christian Theologians and the Bible in Nazi Germany* (Princeton, NJ, 2008), pp. 41–7.

[98] Bartholomae explicitly refused to make comparisons with other religions, especially with Christianity, "as close together as they may lie." *Zarathustra's Leben und Lehre* (Heidelberg, 1924), p. 12.

work going on in comparative linguistics (which often involved Sanskrit) seem to have anything to do with the Schopenhauerian neoromantic racism of Schroeder and Chamberlain. In the new field of sociology, one noteworthy comparativist, Max Weber, seems to have drawn heavily on the liberal tradition – on Oldenberg, Garbe, and Koeppen in Indology, on Wellhausen and Meyer in Old Testament interpretation, for example – and deliberately avoided the neoromantic work of Deussen and Schroeder.[99] In his work on Indian religions, Weber depends upon Max Müller's *Sacred Texts* rather than the translations made by Deussen or by the Schopenhauerian Karl Eugen Neumann; in fact, Weber cites a great many more English and French authors than German ones. Perhaps most striking, in reading Weber against the abundant neoromantic orientalism of the period, is Weber's total disinterest in the question of who borrowed what from whom; what he wants to know is, how did religious systems function and interact or enable various political, social, and economic institutions. In this context, Weber appears not only more original, but I would argue, much more appealing, than many critics of his "orientalism" have claimed.

Indeed, neoromantic orientalism increasingly entangled itself in racist thinking. This was not necessarily a choice philologists made consciously, or with the desire to persecute others – though it should be noted that many who publicly disavowed racial thinking, like Renan and Müller, Rudolf Virchow and Franz Boas, were aware enough to understand that racialized science had dangerous implications, and the same powers of recognition were presumably available to their contemporaries as well. But for some, charting racial relations offered a "scientific" path back behind and in addition to scanty texts, and, for Indologists, making the case for racial relatedness gave them a powerful means of defending their own relevance to current national concerns. Moroever, racial ideology helped to streamline the project of purifying Christianity and determining its oriental origins, making it possible to identify the "essence" of the faith historically, without having to deal with the complications of the Old Testament. It should also be noted that in the case of Indian studies, the work of Deussen, Schroeder, and even Chamberlain had, from the perspective of post-colonial world history, the salutary effect of decentering perceptions of ancient history, of giving non-Mediterranean cultures credit for their innovations and of appreciating their religious and philosophical conceptions in something closer to their own terms. Ultimately, for the neoromantic or "furious" Indologists, identifying genealogical relationships between religions and racial groups in the ancient period was simply of more widespread and deeper importance than discussing internal Indian social relations or India's modern fate. The former were the questions that aroused their passions – though of course there were other resentments, prejudices, and anxieties also at stake. In the end, fin de siècle Indology had not really freed itself from the desire to serve as a theological surrogate; as Chamberlain himself complained with respect to the Assyriologists in the wake of the Babel-Bibel Streit, the tonsure had never quite grown back in.[100] This was, however, a

---

[99] Max Weber, *The Religion of India: The Sociology of Hinduism and Buddhism*, trans. Hans H. Gerth and Don Martindale (New York, 1958), p. 358, n. 6; p. 351, notes 1 and 2; p. 369, n. 63.
[100] H. S. Chamberlain, *Dilettantismus, Rasse, Monotheismus, Rom* (Munich, 1903), p. 64.

much more dangerous surrogate priesthood, one that did believe, as the Jesuits, Anquetil, Herder, and even Friedrich Schlegel did not, that biology was destiny.

SEMITISTIK IN THE POST-LIBERAL PERIOD

If Indo-European studies habored both the Aryanizing neoromantics described above, as well as positivist linguistis like Heinrich Lüders and comparative linguists like Ferdinand Saussure, *Semitistik* was a field with even less coherence; to begin with, the languages, experts agree, are more diverse and less amenable to comparative study. The field includes (among many others) Assyrian cuneiform, hieroglyphics, Aramaic, Arabic, Mandaen, Syriac, and Amharic. Many of these languages also evolved simultaneously and/or their linguistic changes have proved very difficult to date. Even more importantly, the foremost languages in this group, Arabic and Hebrew, were for Christians the languages of the peoples who should have known better – though of course Hebrew was also a sacred language, and Aramaic, by the mid-nineteenth century, acknowledged to be the language Jesus himself spoke. As we have seen, in the wake of the Reformation, Christian humanists had been extremely active in studying the Old Testament and in trying to determine which parts of it they could consider their own; orientalists involved in the study of New Testament texts written in Aramaic, Syriac, or other Semitic languages who might also be considered "Semitists" exhibited a similar desire to use their language skills to interpret and if possible to fix the text.

We should recall that the study of Arabic and Syriac, in particular, developed in strong proximity to Hebrew studies and were for most of the early modern period, not really secular fields at all. The eighteenth century saw the flowering of studies of Arabic and Persian poetry and tales, and many orientalists were certainly partisans of this literature – and in the world of Goethe's *Divan*, there was room for the enjoyment of Semitic as well as Sanskrit literature. But mid-nineteenth-century studies of the Islamic world, as we have seen, tended to focus more on warfare, high politics, and pure linguistic developments; one does not catch here the same sorts of underground strains of romantic longing as one catches from time to time in mid-century Indology. Philo-Islamism was much more common among Jewish scholars (or Jewish converts), for whom there were linguistic and, it was increasingly felt, racial linkages (remember Michaelis and the beduins!).[101] Nor were indigenous scholars, ancient or modern, much trusted for their textual practices, as compared to the sporadic return of Christian scholars to the work of indigenous Indian grammarians. One begins to feel a separation out of scholars, if not by political or religious allegiances, then by temperaments; the realists adopt the Semites; the dreamers the Aryans.

We have here not only to do with the collapsing of Christian universalism, but also, perhaps, with the end of an old dream, and that is, the conversion of the

---

[101] See Martin Kramer, ed., *The Jewish Discovery of Islam: Studies in Honor of Bernard Lewis* (Tel Aviv, 1999).

Jews. This dream, as we have seen, lay behind August Hermann Francke's Institutum Judaicum (Halle, founded in 1728), which encouraged commerce between learned rabbis and Christian Hebraists, in the interest of provoking the former to convert.[102] It was still alive in the work of Franz Delitzsch and H. L. Strack, in the third quarter of the nineteenth century, but thereafter fades from view. Perhaps we should see this as another sign of the fading fortunes of theology as a university subject or as an indication of the shift in oriental studies to more secular topics. In any event, it represents the end of another tradition, that of "informed evangelizing," at least as far as the Jews were concerned. And it had intellectual as well as institutional consequences: the lack of academic interest in the study of Judaism after the time of Christ meant that just as the study of other "Orients" was increasing, this subject continued to be left almost entirely to Germany's numerous yeshivas and Hebrew schools. Here, generations of Jewish scholars were produced who studied things Semitic not as outsiders, but as passionate protectors of a great cultural tradition. And these men, like Markus Horovitz (1844–1910), rabbi in Frankfurt and Rabbi Eduard Ezekiel Baneth (1855–1930), who taught Midrash and Talmud at the Jüdisches Hochschule in Berlin, would pass on to their students and sons (respectively, the Arabists J. J. Horovitz and David Baneth), their much more sympathetic style of *Semitistik*.[103]

During the eighteenth century, these scholars were little read – or at least little cited – by their Christian peers. But between the 1810s and 1860s, there was some traffic passing between the Christian and Jewish worlds. In the 1820s and 1830s, Peter von Bohlen and Wilhelm Gesenius attempted a large number of Persian/Hebrew etymologies, derivations that, to an observer eighty years on seemed wild.[104] We know that Wilhelm von Humboldt read the work of Julius Fürst (and begged Franz Bopp to read it too) and that Theodor Nöldeke read and was inspired by Abraham Geiger's book on Muhammed. Rabbinically-educated scholars like Gustav Weil brought their learning to bear on linguistic and cultural histories; even though sidelined and disappointed by their colleagues' still-powerful anti-Semitism, Jakob Bernays and Arminius Vambéry did hold university positions. At mid-century, it was still possible to believe in a common Semitic-Aryan *ur*-ancestor (as did Heinrich Ewald) or in strong similarities between Semitic and Indo-European mythology (as did Heymann Steinthal). Despite the pressures of specialization and the increasing consensus about the divergence of the Semitic and Aryan linguistic trees, for a time it remained possible to keep channels of conversation open, even across a widening historical and cultural gap.

After the 1860s, however, such conversations were becoming increasingly rare. The grammarian descendants of Bopp had become pure linguists, interested in the

---

[102] Dominique Bourel, "Die deutsche Orientalistik im 18. Jahrhundert. Von der Mission zur Wissenschaft," in *Historische Kritik und biblischer Kanon in der deutschen Aufklärung*, ed. Henning Graf Reventlow et al. (Wiesbaden, 1988), p. 116.

[103] On Baneth, Jr. and Sr., see Hava Lazarus-Yafeh, "The Transplantation of Islamic Studies from Europe to the Yishuv and Israel," in Martin Kramer, ed., *Jewish Discovery of Islam*, pp. 256–9; on Horovitz, pp. 250–3. There are, of course, some exceptions here, including the Christian scholar of Judaism Paul Kahle. For more on this tradition, see Henry Wasserstein, *False Start: Jewish Studies at German Universities During the Weimar Republic* (Amherst, NY, 2003).

[104] D. Behrmann, *Hamburgs Orientalisten*, p. 81.

structures of language in a more anthropological or social-scientific rather than philological way, while the school of A. W. Schlegel, devoted to the culture-historical development of the Indo-Europeans, was moving in the directions sketched in the section above. Persian specialists were caught in between, as students of an Indo-European language, whose modern culture was Islamic, but, as always, the pull toward ancient, in this case pre-Islamic, topics was powerful, and those who went this route tended to move in racist directions. As the great continent of oriental studies broke apart, the Indo-German floe took with it most of descendants of Creuzer and Schopenhauer, while the Semitic landmass was populated with the legacies of *Realpolitik* nationalists like Wellhausen and Jewish liberals like Heymann Steinthal.

As is the case in Indology, it is dangerous to generalize about German Semitists. In the chapter that follows we will profile in detail two men – not surprisingly, both Christians – who followed essentially in the Wellhausian tradition and contributed centrally to the shaping of pro-colonialist forms of Islamic studies. But there were also positivist Arabists, like Carl Brockelmann, who stayed out of modern politics (at least until 1914), and a few "furious" ones, like Georg Jacob (see Chapter 5). Although a few of these men developed some sympathy for Islam, most never felt the sort of affective affinity for their subject that Deussen or Schroeder felt for ancient Indian religions or even for Hindu revivalism. Neo-romantic passions simply did not run in this direction, a reality that deeply shaped the field's twentieth-century trajectory, just as the racialization of Indological romanticism shaped the evolution of Aryan studies.

But there was one great scholar of their era who did feel a deep affinity for both ancient and modern Semites, a man whose scholarship was so innovative and exemplary that it made him universally respected in the years before the Great War, despite his refusal to take one of the many orientalist chairs offered to him and despite his open adherence to the faith of his fathers, Judaism. The scholar I refer to is Ignaz Goldziher, who figures in this chapter not as the equivalent in the Semitic sphere to any of the Aryan sphere figures profiled above, though they are almost exact contemporaries; he was neither a popularizer nor a racist, and far from being reviled, his work continues to be greatly admired by scholars of many persuasions. He was, like Deussen and Schroeder, deeply interested in religion and its modern fate, and he did admire indigenous scholars – feelings most of his fellow *Islamforscher* did not share. He was, in truth, a one of a kind orientalist, and many of his ideals and hopes either died with him or left Central Europe after his passing in 1921. Although he was neither German nor a typical academic, his intellectual, if not his personal, life was intertwined with developments in German scholarship – to which, as we shall see, he reacted negatively as often as positively. We will be missing an important player in the field, as well as an insightful voice from the margins, if he is left out of this survey.

IGNAZ GOLDZIHER: MAN BETWEEN TWO LAWS

It has been argued in various places in this book that religious institutions and beliefs continued to shape oriental studies long into the twentieth century; that this was the case for Jews and Catholics, as well as for Protestants, should also be

noted. In the case of Ignaz Goldziher, there is little question but that his Judaism –
and by this I mean not just Judaism in his day, but *his* unique and passionate
system of beliefs – was central in framing his inquiries into the history and meanings of Islam. The men he admired most were, for the most part, secular Jews or
converts – Abraham Geiger, Heymann Steinthal, Mór Karman, Georg Ebers; and
many of those he hated most were also Jews. But he was also, in many respects, a
classic liberal; he believed in reason, meritocracy, assimilation (to a point), scientific specialization, and that religion should be a private matter. His proudest
moments were those of scholarly virtuosity performed on European stages, at
his bar mitzvah (during which he lectured the audience for an hour), and at the
1889 Congress of Orientalists, where he earned a Gold Medal for his achievements.[105] But his happiest months were those he spent in Cairo and Damascus in
1873–4, reading and conversing with reform-minded, religiously educated Arabs
(see below). He might, indeed, have converted to Islam at this time – but, as if a
character in the Torah, precisely at the most dangerous moment he was called
back to Budapest to attend his dying father. He would leave Budapest again, but
never for long, and die there in 1921, deeply saddened by the collapsing of both
the liberal Judaism, and the intellectual cosmopolitanism, which had made his
work possible in the years before the war.

Goldziher's career trajectory was a highly unusual one; that it involves early on
one brush with imperialist institutions is interesting, but as we will see, unimportant in the longer run. Even before his hour-long bar mitzvah lecture, Goldziher was recognized as a "Wunderkind" and encouraged by his parents to study
hard; in his diary, Goldziher connects this with his father's desire to save his son
from frustrating and painful experiences in the world of commerce, but this could
well be the trade-hating son's later invention. At the University of Budapest, he fell
under the spell of Arminius Vambéry. Vambéry, recently returned from his dervish
tour, was, in the mid-1860s, quite famous, especially one would guess among the
Jewish intelligentsia, who were well aware of Vambéry's origins – and probably
too of the Emperor's favor. Perhaps the non-Jews also knew about the controversies surrounding Vambéry's appointment – or perhaps it was simply another
manifestation of the "lonely" age of orientalism that Vambéry, on Goldziher's
arrival, had only two other students in his course, and these (said Goldziher) were
not really serious scholars. Vambéry took the young man under his wing and set
him to work translating and transcribing; in the process, Goldziher was also
admitted to Vambéry's personal library, where he was exposed to new work in
biblical criticism and Protestant theology.[106] By 1868, Goldziher was talented and
lucky enough to come to the attention of the liberal Hungarian cultural minister
Josef Eôtvös, who arranged a scholarship for Goldziher to study in Berlin and
Leipzig.

In Austria-Hungary, Goldziher certainly had to deal with Christian anti-
Semitism; in the northern German cities, he had also to endure jibes about
Austrian science, which was considered little better than dilettantry. For his part,
Goldziher was unimpressed at first by German academe, though he admitted later

[105] *Ignaz Goldziher: Tagebuch*, ed. Alexander Scheiber (Leiden, 1978), p. 23.
[106] Ibid., pp. 25–9.

that it was scholars such as Emil Rödiger and J. G. Wetzstein who introduced him to the Islamic material he would make his life's work. Again he profited heavily from time spent in a private library – that of a Talmud critic with whom Goldziher roomed in Berlin. And, by getting to know Gustav Jahn, one of the "martyrs" of Hegelian theology, he was inspired to read F. C. Baur and D. F. Strauss, an encounter which, he reported, made him at last really able to understand the work of the scholar he so resembled, Abraham Geiger.[107] In Leipzig, his studies with Heinrich Fleischer provoked him to study not languages, but Islamic Law, while through conversations with another Jew, Mór Karman, he got a thorough introduction to Higher Criticism as practiced by Wilhelm Vatke and Abraham Kuenen – at a moment, moreover, when this work was also beginning to spread more widely into other orientalist circles, turning up, for example, in the works of Nöldeke, Eberhard Schrader, and Julius Wellhausen. Goldziher also apparently spent some hours in these years discussing the Talmud and Jewish philosophy with Franz Delitzsch, the learned Hebraist famous for his attempts to convert well-educated Jews; but he never liked Delitzsch's "Asiatic mysticism." In 1870, Goldziher was appointed the first Jewish *Privatdozent* to the Leipzig faculty; Eôtvös made a reciprocal offer, despite the opposition of the Budapest faculty, and seemed poised to find Goldziher a paying job in Hungary. But in February 1871, Goldziher's liberal patron died, and the path upward, never easy, grew that much steeper.

What we should notice here was the process of Goldziher's formation by his encounters both with learned, but marginalized Jewish intellectuals and with Protestant orientalism and Higher Criticism; it is certainly possible, in fact, that his diary (written primarily for his children) overstated his dependence on Jews, but it is surely the case that this side of his development was instrumental in making him the sort of orientalist he became. It should also be noted that after leaving Leipzig, he spent some time in Leiden where he attended lectures on the history and philosophy of religion, and also imbibed large doses of English scholarship, especially travel literature and cultural history.[108] All of this material helped to form a mature Goldziher, a scholar who respected the German philological tradition, but also could see its limitations, and even, one might say, the forms of violence it imposed on the past.

But perhaps Goldziher's divergence from German norms is best explained by his "muhammedanisches Jahr" of 1873–4, which he spent in Egypt and Syria. Ironically, this trip was funded by the Hungarian Cultural Ministry, which sent Goldziher abroad to learn "the language of the streets" (*vulgäre Umgangsprache*) and the Arabic "bureaucratese" (*Amtsstile*) practiced in the consulates with a view to founding a Hungarian Oriental Academy, with clear colonial intent. Goldziher did prove remarkably adept at "street language" – perhaps because those with whom he tended to converse were thoroughly educated in classical Arabic. But he

[107] Ibid., pp. 34–9.
[108] Ibid., p. 92, quotation p. 50.

had no intention of simply, in his words, being made into a "Parlier Machine à la Vambéry" or even of performing the subcolonial task of acquiring oriental manuscripts. "I set myself the task of living in Islam and its scholarly world, of making myself a member of the Muslim republic of scholars, to learn the driving forces which, in the course of centuries formed the powerful world religion of Islam out of the judaicized cult of Mecca." For this, his timing was ideal, and he succeeded in finding a number of like-minded Arab reformers who appreciated his learning and shared with him their anti-European dreams (though perhaps he did not introduce the subject of the "Judaized Mecca cult" very directly).[109] By his account, the only inhabitants who mistrusted him were the Jews; though Goldziher conceded that, thanks to European pressure on the Sultan to tolerate the Christian "infâme," the Jews were justified in fearing that he might be a missionary.[110] Goldziher learned a great deal during his year that might have been of interest to colonizers; but one of the things he also learned was to see what colonialism looked like from the other side, and that knowledge, one suspects, was unlikely to suit the perquisites of any Oriental Academy.

One must appreciate the impact his warm reception in the East had on the young scholar, who had often enough experienced European intolerance himself. To hobnob with the military governor of Damascus, to be invited to the home of important scholars, engaged in serious and perhaps epoch-making discussions about Arab cultural reform, and even to be allowed to study at the Azhar – how much more thrilling and ego-gratifying than the Leipzig philological seminar! During a feast day declared to celebrate the marriage of the Viceroy's daughter, Goldziher was provoked to agitate in the bazaar against preferential treatment for Europeans. And here, he learned too to reverse in certain ways the presumption that Islam was simply a degenerate form of Judaism. On the contrary, after a few weeks in the East, Goldziher concluded that Islam was the only religion that even in its official, doctrinaire forms could be satisfying for philosophical minds. "It was my ideal to raise Judaism to a similarly rational level. Islam, my experience taught me, is the only religion, in which superstition and pagan rudiments were prohibited by orthodox teachings, not by rationalism."[111]

To understand Goldziher's form of *Kulturgeschichte*, and how it both entered into and diverged from German scholarly debates, let us examine two important areas of his work; first, his work on Hebrew "myths" and second his work on Hadith, that is, the large body of commentaries and interpretations of the words of Muhammed used to make political and legal decisions in the Islamic world after the death of the Prophet. The subject of myths was the one he treated in his first book of 1876, *Der Mythos bei den Hebräern*, which was, as we have seen, a response not only to Renan's insistence that the Jews had no myths, but also to Friedrich Delitzsch's indictment of Hebrew borrowing from the Babylonians.[112]

---

[109] Ibid., pp. 55–7, quotation p. 56. On Goldziher's travels, see Lawrence I. Conrad, "The Dervish's Disciple: On the Personality and Intellectual Milieu of the Young Ignaz Goldziher," in *Journal of the Royal Asiatic Society of Great Britain and Ireland* (1990): 240–3, and also below.

[110] *Goldziher: Tagebuch*, pp. 61–5; the Arabs did not fear this because it was still impermissible for Christians to attempt to convert Muslims in the Ottoman Empire.

[111] *Goldziher: Tagebuch*, p. 59.

[112] See the discussion of Goldizher and the diffusion problem in Chapter 5.

Goldziher's book was written after his near conversion in 1874 and after the appointment of an unqualified Catholic to the Budapest University chair Goldziher thought was his.[113] The book tried to show that the Jews too were myth-makers, forming, like the Aryan pagans, their stories and figures from aspects of their environs and daily lives, borrowing here and there, but transforming all according to their own needs and cultural traditions.

Regrettably, however, Goldziher's attempt in *Mythos* to weave the Hebrew experience into the religious life of the ancient world more generally pleased neither the orthodox Jews – some of whom apparently accused him of heresy – nor the German theologians. The latter dismissed the book as (Jewish) special pleading, while *Mythos* was much better received in England than Goldziher had hoped. The comments in his diary are worth quoting, both because they underline the variation in the book's reception and because they reveal something interesting about Goldziher's view of his own relationship to the study of Islamic culture, which we will take up later: "Institutionalized, confessional factors were never very influential for me; my confession was the universal religion of the prophets, whose chosen representative I felt myself, thanks to my Jewish birthright. I have to admit that the church-going English were able to perceive this side of my soul-life with sympathetic recognition, while the German Tübingen [scholars] could not free themselves from their Protestant prejudices in their estimation of my youthful writings. The English critics all understood me, friends and opponents; among the Germans, it was only Steinthal – one understands why – who could share the feelings of my soul."[114]

Now Goldziher was, at least inwardly, a sensitive plant, whose brilliance was already appreciated by Fleischer and Vambéry, both of whom actively promoted his career.[115] The reason why Goldziher believed Heymann Steinthal to be the only empathetic German was that the great comparative linguist was also a Jew and a liberal, reform-minded Jew as well. Fundamentally Goldizher felt – and probably rightly – that in Germany, liberal Jews alone could really understand his travails, and perhaps even his views on cultural history. Among German readers, he had more than the Protestant prejudices of the Tübingen School against him; Graecophilia was another barrier here to comparativism, one that Goldziher himself recognized.[116] And then too, as we have seen, mid-century Germans were not terribly keen on cultural evolution and preferred a Hegelian version, in which *Geist* moves from nation to nation, to a Tylorian picture of universal stages of development. It is striking that those who shared Goldziher's views would turn out to be Jewish left-liberals like S. D. Goitein or Anglophiles like Carl Becker.

It was, however, a Frenchman – Ernest Renan – whose ideas gave Goldziher most trouble. From the beginning of his career to its end, Goldziher was in the perpetual business of refuting Renan's stereotypes, which in turn had recognizable

---

[113] See Goldziher's account in *Goldziher: Tagebuch*, pp. 74–8; apparently Peter Hatala, an "old" Catholic, received the job after he had protested Papal Infallibility, and thus could no longer remain in the theological faculty.

[114] *Goldziher: Tagebuch*, p. 87.

[115] On Fleischer's support, Simon, *Ignác Goldziher*, pp. 37–8.

[116] Goldziher in introduction to *Mythos*, p. ix.

roots in Friedrich Schlegel's characterizations of uninflected (and therefore stationary) Semitic languages, as compared to lively, dynamic Indo-European ones. To this Renan added religio-geographical generalization – Semites were all monotheists because they came from the undifferentiated desert, while Aryans hailed from more complicated climates and therefore were *ur*-polytheists. And, though Renan recognized the importance of Semitic commitments to "righteousness," he, much more than Schlegel and the romantics, treated polytheism as a healthy, progressive thing.[117] In private letters, Goldziher often tried to refute Renan's caricatures of static, unchanging Semites and to dissuade his friends from a Manichean juxtaposition of Semitic intolerance and slavish obedience to their cruel, faceless God, and Aryan love of nature, humanness, and adaptability.[118] On the other hand, where he did agree with Renan – in his New Testament criticism – Goldizher could not publicly concur, without being seen (again) as a Jewish apologist. Asked to give a memorial tribute to Renan before the Hungarian Academy in 1893, Goldziher avoided the trap, as he saw it, of celebrating Renan's Jesus-demystification, and instead focused on Renan's contributions to the study of Islam.[119] Goldziher recognized that though they were both "Semitists," at the end of the day, he and Renan stood in opposite camps, Renan with the Aryans and he with the Semites.

When Goldziher failed to get the chair he thought had been promised to him, his friend (and rabbi) Samuel Kohn organized a job for the unemployed orientalist as administrative head of the Jewish community in Budapest. Although Kohn meant to do Goldziher a kindness, this appointment – which Goldziher kept from 1876 until his retirement in 1905 – turned out to be "slavery" for Goldziher, who developed during the course of his service a furious hatred for the hypocrisies of liberal Judaism. He resented the community's failure to appreciate his scholarly achievements and even developed a persecution complex, directed not at the social structures of the Austro-Hungarian Empire, which prevented full Jewish emancipation and equal treatment, but at the Jewish community itself. Other than in 1874, Goldziher never flirted with conversion; he was too loyal to his father's memory, too fearful of being accused of opportunism and too certain that his form of Judaism was the right form to contemplate such a move. But he was, after the mid-1870s, an embittered loner, who struggled mightily to keep his resentment and disappointment to himself.

It is undoubtedly the case that when, after *Mythos*, he took the decision to leave behind universal *Kulturgeschichte* and (professional) Old Testament studies, Goldziher did so in response to time pressures; he now had a full-time day job and was reduced to producing his scholarly articles at night and during vacations.[120] But he had also been bitterly disappointed by the Jews' response to his work and the rumors that continued to circulate about his iconoclastic beliefs. In focusing on Islam – where his hero Geiger had begun – he could, perhaps, continue

---

[117] Ignaz Goldziher, *Renan als Orientalist*, trans. Peter Zalan (Zürich, 2000), p. 56.

[118] E.g., Goldziher, *Renan*, pp. 37–9; idem, *Mythos*, p. xv.

[119] See Friedrich Niewöhner, "Kritik und Liebe," introduction to Ignaz Goldziher, *Renan als Orientalist*, trans. Peter Zalán (Zürich, 2000), p. 8.

[120] Simon, *Ignác Goldziher*, p. 46.

in a less polemical way his reading of Judaism and Christianity. Having experienced acceptance and tolerance in the Middle East unlike anywhere he had visited in Europe, he also clearly perceived his mission as conveying to Europeans the positive aspects of Islam. In any event, his decision proved to be an excellent professional choice and would have been a savvy career move – had he allowed himself to have an academic career. By the late 1880s, he was no longer seen as a Jewish polemicist, but rather as a great specialist in things Islamic. He began to produce scores upon scores of specialized articles, publishing them in German as well as in Hungarian and sometimes in French.[121] He also wrote for more popular audiences and on a diverse range of Islamic topics; he was interested in "provincial" as well as Arab versions of Islam, and in practices and customs as well as texts.[122] In 1892 he became the first Jewish member of the Hungarian Academy of Sciences. He was offered chairs, successively, in Prague, Heidelberg, and Cambridge; in 1894, the University of Budapest gave him the title of Ordinarius in 1894 (the first Jew to be so honored), but a full salary and teaching privileges only in 1905.

In the period of his mature production, Goldziher made many important contributions to the study of Islam and especially to the study of Islamic law. Jacques Waardenburg, one of the first scholars to attempt an overview of his career, divides his contributions into three groups: works concerning the general character of Islam; studies of its internal development; and considerations of external influences exerted on it – a list that represents Goldziher's enormous reach.[123] But his work in each of these categories concerned very specific subjects and texts rather than addressing itself to broad diffusionist, philosophical, or macro-historical concerns; like his friend Nöldeke, Goldziher was too careful a scholar to be given to broad surveys. Thus I will single out only one of Goldziher's major contributions, his reformulation of work on Hadith, without suggesting that this exhausts his contributions to the field as a whole.

Two of the fundamental questions Goldziher asked of the Qur'an were the following: what did it mean to Muhammed to be a prophet, and what did this mean to his followers? Or, to put it another way, how were the words of the prophet actually understood and used over time? This was essentially a set of questions created by combining Talmudic studies with *Religionsgeschichte*; it represented a quite different approach than that of simply deriving Muhammed's principles and life story from the Qur'an, and then presuming, as most Christian interpreters had, that the word of the Prophet had always been heard and interpreted in the same way, from the eighth century to the nineteenth – or that where divergences occurred, these were always misinterpretations. Goldziher recognized that Muhammed had seen himself in different ways at different times – as a prophet in Mecca, then as a rebuilder of the corrupted religion of Abraham in

---

[121] Some of these where collected in his *Muhammedanische Studien*, published first in Hungarian and then in German by Max Niemeyer (Halle, 1889–90).

[122] Two good examples, in which he treats the survival of customs in Islam, and also the interaction of Arab culture with the culture of other regions, are Goldziher, "On the Veneration of the Dead in Paganism and in Islam," and "'Arab' and 'Ajam'" both in idem, *Muslim Studies*, pp. 209–38, 98–136.

[123] Jean-Jacques Waardenburg, *L'Islam dans le miroir de l'occident* (Paris, 2nd ed., 1963), p. 266.

Medina; he had adapted to practical circumstances, now raging at the corruption of Arab pagan society, but then softening his rhetoric where necessary to recruit believers. Above all, Muhammed did not think of himself as a moral model; this was Goldziher's attempt to refute Christian apologists, who gleefully pointed to the Prophet's failings, as well as fundamentalist Muslims, who sought to impose their leader's most puritanical teachings on all his followers. For Goldizher, Muhammed was a *Wegweiser* (pathfinder; a softening of the "prophet" function), a flawed mortal whose work was greater than he was.[124] The corollary to this was that his teachings (viz. the Qur'an) could also be understood by his followers to be a flexible set of precepts, which, with equal textual legitimacy, had been used in different ways over time. This body of interpretation, the Hadith, then was central to whatever "the essence" of the religion was; one needed to do much more than read the Qur'an to understand Islam.[125]

Indebted as it was to Talmudic scholarship, this insight was revolutionary. Over and against the tradition of Christian Semitic philology – in which both Jewish and Islamic law were seen as "survivals" – the idea that Islam represented a living, breathing, malleable tradition opened the way, quite obviously, for a new set of studies of post-Qur'anic Islam. As C. H. Becker wrote just after Goldziher's death in 1921, "[Goldziher] gave us the tools, with which we work; he created the categories, in which we think."[126] But for his generation, Goldziher was, in a number of respects, still a loner; while men like Wellhausen and Meyer were concerned with state-building, and Becker and Martin Hartmann with Islam's relationship to the political economies of the West, Goldizher was centrally concerned with Islam as a system of belief.[127] He did not want to peel away layers of irrational custom and historical falsehood in order to find fragments of Truth; religion, he argued, for its believers had an absolute value, which should not and could not be dissected away.[128] A religious man himself, as well as a man who loved and respected tradition, Goldziher could understand Islamic history without wanting to overcome it. Indeed, in his letters he warned repeatedly against trying to eradicate Islam or using Islam's supposed backwardness as a pretext for further exploitation. "One does not make men better with foreign dogmas," he told Martin Hartmann in 1911. Saving his passionate outbursts for his diary, Goldziher refused to be either a popularizer or a propagandist. But then again, for his brand of iconoclasm there was not likely to be an audience, or many converts.

It is testimony to his wide-ranging genius, but also to his diplomacy, that Goldziher got on well with most of Europe's leading orientalists – though he had no time

---

[124] Goldziher, "Mohammed und der Islam," in idem, *Vorlesungen über den Islam*, ed. Franz Babinger (Heidelberg, 2nd ed., 1925), pp. 9–11, 22.

[125] Goldziher, "Mohammed und der Islam," p. 29; also idem, "Der Entwicklung des Gestzes," in idem, *Vorlesungen*, pp. 30–70.

[126] C. H. Becker, "Ignaz Goldziher zum Gedächtnis: Ein Geleitwort," in Goldziher, *Vorlesungen*, p. vi.

[127] In 1915, Goldziher complained to Nöldeke about the tendency (and not just among German scholars) to explain Islam's rise and continued appeal in purely functionalist terms: "It is getting so that Mohammed seems a totally insignificant figure for the rise of Islam and instead the price of grain in Mecca is the most important factor in its rise." Goldizher to Nöldeke, February 7, 1915, in Simon, *Ignác Goldziher*, p. 374.

[128] Goldziher, "Mohammed und der Islam," p. 15.

for "furious orientalists" like Hugo Winckler, or for those like Friedrich Delitzsch, engaged in Christian purification projects. He was very close to Nöldeke, the avowed atheist, and to Ebers, the Jewish convert. He exchanged numerous letters with Martin Hartmann, with whom he shared an interest in and concern for the *modern* Islamic world – something one cannot take for granted among German orientalists. These highly interesting documents show Hartmann, unhappy in his subordinate and marginalized position, trying to draw the unwilling Goldziher into a grand critique of the German establishment, as well as to convince him of the justness of the German imperial cause. On neither subject could Goldziher be cajoled into agreement. These were not Goldziher's fights; and he knew better than to be dragged into them. He believed his religion, and perhaps even his racial identity, obliged him to defend the "Semites" and to perfect their understanding and appreciation for their own traditions;[129] but he chose to do this quietly, through scholarship that reached across the Judeo-Islamic divide. Perhaps he realized that this was not a subject, like Indo-Aryan relations, that would have deep personal and cultural resonances for Christian Central Europeans. Or perhaps he was content to follow his own passions, and to measure his success in his own, very personal, terms.

Nor could Goldziher be swayed to express sympathy for any side in the Great War; by November 1914 he had developed his own (private) interpretation of the causes of the conflict. In his diary, he noted his growing anxiety "... about the general world-murder, which represents the true bankruptcy of the Christians. What did this system, with its nineteen-hundred years of world conquest create? Dogmas and piles of rubble."[130] When in 1916, a new Cultural Center for the Study of the Orient was formed in the midst of eager anticipation about relationships between the Central Powers and the Ottomans when the war concluded, Goldziher was put on the board of directors; but he resigned soon afterwards, disgusted, he claimed, by the dilettantism of its members. Though in that same year, 1916, he received his twentieth honorary degree, owing to his odd career trajectory, he had not produced a student to carry on his intellectual legacy. And when in December 1918, his beloved daughter-in-law succumbed to the Spanish flu without producing a grandson, Goldziher felt that the logic of his life had disappeared.[131] Deeply depressed by her loss and by the series of vicious pogroms that followed the demise of Béla Kun's short-lived Hungarian socialist republic, Goldziher died in November 1921.

Becker, by this time German Cultural Minister, penned an affectionate elegy for him for *Der Islam*, in which he called Goldziher (whose Judaism he openly acknowledged) the "Shaykh" of the younger generation of *Islamforscher* and a man who had earned "the love of his students."[132] Goldziher's achievements and friendships should remind us that it was still possible, in the late Wilhelmine era, for Jews to be revered for their scholarly credentials – at least when they were extraordinarily talented and did not openly criticize Christian society or

[129] As he wrote to Martin Hartmann, October 7, 1898: "I imagine in my fantasies an age, in which criticism of the Qur'an and the Hadith will be taught at the Azhar, as criticism of the gospels was begun in Europe from theological lecterns. Then the religious life of Islam will climb to a higher level." In Hanisch, ed. *Briefwechsel Goldizher/ Hartmann*, p. 115.

[130] *Goldziher: Tagebuch*, p. 283.

[131] Ibid., pp. 292, 312.

[132] Becker, "Goldziher," in *Der Islam* 12 (1922): 214.

"apologize" for Judaism. But the quiet industry of Goldziher contrasts very vividly with the loquacious Aryan advocacy of Deussen, Schroeder, and Chamberlain; while the Indo-Aryans were being sold as national heroes and racial ancestors, the defence of the Semites remained a scholarly, and narrowly Jewish one. And by the 1890s, even those who could call Goldziher their teacher had been seized by a new set of passions, and thrown themselves into evangelizing of a wholly different kind.

8

Orientalism in the Age of Imperialism

If I am not mistaken, we in Germany are faced with a partial transformation of our oriental scholarship. No longer do we sit by lonely little lamps, so far away from the real world in our little libraries; we too have stepped outside and feel the life pulsing through our people as a whole. There will always be men among us who revere serious linguistics, but who think nonetheless that a certain sort of grammatical pedantry has long enough been widespread here, and that those...who turn to [subjects] which are closer to us as acting and willing men, exhibit a more vital form of understanding, and contribute more to the common good. We want the doing of useful things no longer to be an embarrassment. In their pursuit, we can also demonstrate thoroughness [Gründlichkeit] and scientificness.

 – Georg Kampffmeyer, *Die Welt des Islam*, 1913[1]

There have always been, and will always be, people who want to be useful – to their families, their communities, their nations, or to humankind as a whole. Some institutions are dedicated to the production of such people – examples such as nursing colleges and foreign service schools come readily to mind. And there are eras and environments, in which utility is highly prized – as it was, for example, in the Scottish Enlightenment and in 1950s America. Certain political or economic events, such as wars or depressions, generate the need and desire for resources and personnel to be devoted more heavily than usual to utilitarian ends. As we have seen, German *Orientalistik* was formed by individuals who for the most part evinced little interest in being "useful" – unless, of course, one considers historical biblical criticism a utilitarian science (which most pastors, in any event, did not). Nor were its scholarly norms and practices shaped in a utilitarian age; rather, they developed in 1820s–1840s and in the context of the Humboldtian university, dedicated specifically to *Wissenschaft* not to *Nutzbarkeit*. Of course, there were mid-century men who went to university in this era simply to obtain a "trade" credential – to become teachers, lawyers, doctors, pastors, or bureaucrats. But those who passed through the philosophical faculty, in particular, were supposed to learn fundamentals, including ancient languages, to be formatted, as it were, for future self-enrichment and specialized research productivity and to believe too that knowledge was good for its own sake. To think of themselves as simply learning how to do things contemporary society needed done would have been to do violence to both the concept of *Bildung* and that of *Wissenschaft*.

[1] Georg Kampffmeyer, "Plane perspicere," in *Die Welt des Islams* 1 (1913): 4.

Like the other sub-departments of the philologic-industrial complex, nineteenth-century *Orientalistik* wanted above all to be considered "scientific"; and in this milieu, usefulness was often considered the direct opposite of *Wissenschaftlichkeit*. This was, in part, because the practitioners of "useful" orientalism – especially missionaries and diplomats – were seen as people who had only superficial knowledge (enough to do their work and no more) or who were constitutionally, as well as professionally, unable to perform "disinterested" science. Of course, this does not mean that academic scholars were themselves disinterested parties or that they were unwilling to draw on materials or ideas generated by more interested parties. Sometimes, missionaries, travelers, and diplomats too were admitted into academic circles, societies, and journals. Often there was little choice; the "practical" people were the data collectors on the ground and the ones who spoke the languages needed to do the research. Because such a high premium was put on new knowledge, they could sometimes parlay mere acts of collecting and translation into "scientific" achievements. But, stretching from the eighteenth to the twentieth century, there was also a discourse among academics of disapproval of missionaries in particular, either for not caring or knowing enough about local culture and history, or for trying to shove Christian doctrines down unprepared throats.[2] University scholars also frequently disdained members of the foreign service, feeling (usually rightly) that their linguistic abilities and historical knowledge were not up to snuff. This illustrates one of the most obvious problems in applying Edward Said's critique of "orientalism" to German *Orientalistik*, one that was already stated, in a theoretical way, by Said's contemporary Pierre Bourdieu: the academic world often operates as a market upside down, privileging precisely what the wider culture (including its political leaders) finds useless, trivial, or obscure.[3] It was not easy then, and it is not easy now, to be both relevant and profound; and we should recognize that those who preferred profundity tended to gravitate to the universities and those who preferred relevance to politics, journalism, or diplomacy.

One would have thought these attitudes might change as the German Empire joined the colonizing powers; and indeed, this did happen, at least to a certain extent. This chapter will focus on that period, between 1884 and 1914, when Germany did have an empire – most of it in Africa, but some of it (Samoa, Qingdao) in Asia. It was also in this era that Germans developed sub-imperial designs on the failing Ottoman Empire and that Austria-Hungary, in occupying and then annexing Bosnia-Herzegovina, added some 600,000 Muslim subjects to its empire.[4] In this brief but eventful period, numerous utilitarian and pro-colonial institutions and organizations were founded and orientalists, academic and nonacademic, were important players in them. Younger scholars in particular

---

[2] E.g., von Bohlen, *Das alte Indien*, pp. 77–80 (see Chapter 2); Garbe, *Indien und das Christentum*, pp. v–vi (see Chapter 6).

[3] Pierre Bourdieu, *The Field of Cultural Production: Essays on Art and Literature*, ed. Randal Johnson (New York, 1993).

[4] In the wake of this annexation, the Habsburgs passed an "Islamgesetz," Europe's first formal concession allowing Muslims to worship freely (see Fichtner, *Terror and Toleration*, p. 16). Perhaps they were borrowing from British India's colonial playbook, but applied to the European continent, this was a sign that tolerance had indeed made headway.

began emphasizing the collection of artifacts (not the study of words) and concerning themselves with the peoples, languages, economies, and social practices of the modern Orient. For them, one of the great benefits of colonial extension, especially in an increasingly competitive market, was that one could collect new data and objects virtually unhindered, data that not only added to the storehouse of (European) knowledge, but also gave interpreters new opportunities. Ironically, one of the by-products of this new orientation to *Realien* was the formulation of more embracive cultural histories of Islamic, and to a lesser extent, Chinese, and Indian civilizations. The imperial experience, along with the institutions and opportunities that arose with it, helped to destroy the hegemony, if not the lasting power, of the older Christian humanist and philological-historical traditions.

It should be noted that "imperialism" meant, and means, many things to many people, and in the period 1880–1914, there were almost as many views of Germany's proper "oriental" policy as there were individuals voicing them.[5] One recent commentator has described German debates about Middle Eastern policy in the Wilhelmine period as "a cacophony of voices representing different interests, badly coordinated and often ill-informed about political, social, and cultural conditions"; only when economic investments climbed – after the turn of the century – did powerful, well-organized networks begin to appear.[6] The same could be said about the Reich's Far East policy. Scholars certainly contributed to this "cacophony," but were by no means always able to make their voices heard. Indeed, military and business interests retained the upper hand when it came to making colonial policy – even after a new, purportedly more humanitarian, and scientific approach to colonization was introduced in the wake of the atrocities committed by German colonial troops in Southwest and East Africa in 1904–5. It must also be said that there were rather few professional orientalists who wanted to participate directly in the messy, all-too-practical process of conquest, conversion, and/or exploitation. And even among those who did want to use their expertise to perfect imperial rule, there were profound disagreements over such major questions as whether or not Islam was dangerous for Germany's colonies and whether Chinese modernization was a good thing. As we will see later in this chapter, everyone who wanted to be useful did not want to be useful in the same way.

THE CULTURE OF GERMAN IMPERIALISM

Though this chapter focuses on the ways in which knowledge was, intentionally or not, put to use in conquest, it also attempts to show the ways in which older forms persisted – all of these, of course, not purely objective, but shaped by the other aspects of cultural politics described in the preceding chapters. Most fundamentally,

---

[5] Independently arrived at, my conclusions here echo those of George Steinmetz, whose excellent study of German "native policy" in three different colonial theaters demonstrates the great importance of traditions of representation and scholarship, local conditions, and individual personalities in determining how colonial policy was actually derived and applied. See Steinmetz, *The Devil's Handwriting* (Chicago, IL, 2007).

[6] Gottfried Hagen, "German Heralds of Holy War," in *Comparative Studies of South Asia, Africa and the Middle East* 24, no. 2 (2004): 148.

I want to avoid the conclusion that we must choose between viewing German orientalism either as totally politicized and oriented entirely to the project of empire-building, or as totally objective and without any political or cultural commitments at all. As we have seen, orientalism was always intertwined with developments in the larger cultural and political world – it was shaped by factors such as church-state relations and Jewish emancipation, by philhellenism and by liberal nationalism. All of these "external" developments left their mark, affecting some sub-disciplines more than others. Even in the years 1884–1918, it was not exclusively "about" empire.

The same could be said about the culture of the Reich as a whole. It used to be a truism that Germany was little touched by the colonial project – but recent literature, taking its cue from work on British and French "cultures of colonialism" has tended to move toward the opposite, equally distorted, view that Wilhelmine culture was absolutely suffused with imperialist images and longings.[7] It is certainly true that by the 1890s, there was more involvement and interest in the East than before, and that the pace and intensity of involvement increased rapidly after this point – as the older literature stressed, the aggressiveness and novelty of German intervention here was fundamental to destabilizing the British-dominated balance of power across the globe. After 1884, a powerful procolonial lobby began to exert its influence on the Kaiser and the bureaucracy; there was broader support for the Reich's attempts to seek new cultural, economic, and political influence in areas where Germans could reap profits without ruling. We need only mention here the Ottoman Empire's employment of Germans to help modernize its military and its railroads and the Japanese importation of German specialists in pedagogy, medicine, botany, chemistry, law, and other subjects as part of its rush to modernize in the 1870s and 1880s. Trade and travel increased; new journals and associations devoted to cultural exchange were founded. Art, literature, and theater in both East and West began to show signs of contact, first at the elite level and then rather swiftly at the popular level as well. While the consumption of "exotic" goods – such as oranges or chocolate – may not signify much,[8] the lively trade in Persian carpets and Japanese lacquer tables does suggest that to the middle classes, at least, the Orient meant something – whether that was affordability, luxury, sensuousness, exoticism, or good taste – and they wanted to share in it.

But inter-cultural exchange should not be overemphasized; in terms of investment dollars and number of cultural establishments, the French and British far outdistanced the Germans, even after 1900 when the Germans picked up the pace considerably.[9] German "oriental" exhibits were small compared to those devoted to European arts, and the museums continued to be populated largely by classical

---

[7] For example, Kamakshi P. Murti, *India: The Seductive and Seduced "Other" of German Orientalism* (Westport, CT, 2001).

[8] See Porter, *Absent-Minded Imperialists*, pp. 34–5.

[9] Helmut Mejcher estimates that German exports to the Ottoman Empire rose 350 percent and Ottoman exports to Germany increased 700 percent in the period between 1888 and 1893. But by 1905, total German investment in the Empire was only 1 billion Marks, of an estimated 20–30 billion total invested abroad. Mejcher, "Die Bagdadbahn als Instrument deutschen wirtschaftlichen Einflusses im Osmanischen Reich," in *Geschichte und Gesellschaft* 1, no. 4 (1975): 453.

and Renaissance works. Leisure activities of all kinds – soccer, cabaret, magazine reading, and café-going – continued to focus on domestic, personal, national, and classical themes and images, even as the Orient increased its popular profile. For the Austrians, proximity to the Ottoman Empire and involvement in the Balkans made exposure to "oriental" arts and landscapes more common, but for many, it was the classical and Renaissance architecture of the Croatian coast that proved more interesting than the artifacts and structures of the Ottoman-ruled interior. Though the Austrians did annex Bosnia-Herzegovina in 1908, and invest considerable sums and much newsprint in attempts to solve the "southern Slav" problem, by no means were the artists, politicians, and scholars of fin de siècle Vienna exclusively concerned with eastern questions.[10]

Nor was every instance of "orientalism" an act of colonial domination; many were updated versions of much older European uses of eastern cultural elements. Just as Voltaire used Chinese, Persian, and Indian figures to show up the West's limitation, Buddhists and theosophists invoked eastern wisdom to critique western intolerance. Just as decorative artists for centuries had borrowed eastern styles, proponents of the arts and crafts movement at the fin de siècle employed Islamic designs to beautify western household goods. Finally, we should note that most cultural energy in this, as in every other modern nation, was spent on images and issues that hit closest to home: love and family life, faith, local news, food, work, sickness, and death. The East continued to be, as Margaret Anderson's wonderful essay underlines, "hinten, weit" (far, far away) and of central and lasting concern to only a handful of people, most of whom were bankers, investors, soldiers (or sailors), politicians, and colonial officials.[11] For everybody else, thinking about the Orient was, at best, infrequent and, for the most part, politically inconsequential, though it is doubtless the case that without some sort of support for the regime's increasingly expansionist, racist, and jingoist policies, Wilhelm II and the Navy League, the railroad magnates and the Hamburg shipping interests would have found it much more difficult, if not impossible, to dream their imperial dreams.

It may well be, as Susanne Zantop famously argued, that some Germans had "imperial fantasies" long before they had an Empire.[12] But unquestionably, before the 1880s, the Reich did not have a "culture of empire." Even after Bismarck officially threw Germany's hat in the colonial ring, the cultural world of the Kaiserreich responded slowly, as a brief examination of the patronage system suggests. The German state's investment in colonial science definitely increased over the course of our period, but state patronage was never very extensive or selective. Political aspirations did provoke the creation of utilitarian institutions such as the Seminar für Orientalische Sprachen, founded at the University of Berlin in 1887 and the Hamburgisches Kolonialinstitut (HKI) in 1910 – though

---

[10] The subject of Austrian cultural relations with the Ottoman Empire and with the Balkans after 1850 is a subject that needs and deserves further study.

[11] Margaret Lavinia Anderson, "'Down in Turkey, Far Away': Human Rights, the Armenian Massacres, and Orientalism in Wilhelmine Germany," in *Journal of Modern History* 79, no. 1 (March 2007): 80–111.

[12] Susanne Zantop, *Colonial Fantasies: Conquest, Family and Nation in Precolonial Germany, 1770–1870* (Durham, NC, 1997).

inspiration for the latter really came from the Hamburg business community rather than from the Reich itself. The Kaiser joined the Deutsch-Orient Gesellschaft, founded to promote the archaeological exploitation of the Ottoman Empire, and he financed the Turfan expeditions to Central Asia. But the Kaiser was, at the time, supporting a vast array of other projects, from excavations of Roman-German fortifications to deep-sea exploration; and his interest in African ethnography, to take one salient example, was very limited indeed. Despite a plea from the high-society Gesellschaft für Erdkunde, he could not be bothered to attend the funeral of Ferdinand von Richthofen in 1905, Germany's leading scholar-colonizer of the period.[13]

Railroad interests hoped to use scholars to their ends; the builders of the Berlin to Baghdad line, as Friedrich Althoff explained to the Kaiser in 1900, were quite interested in Oskar Mann's work on Kurdish dialects, as their lines extended some distance through Kurdish territory. But the railway was apparently not interested enough to fund Mann's work directly, for it was the Kaiser, as usual, who was touched for two years of travel expenses (15,000 Marks).[14] Nor were the railway magnates impressed by the *Orientalistische Literaturzeitung*'s enthusiastic endorsement, and refused to take up the editor's suggestion that the builders take along a team of orientalists.[15] The *Bagdadbahn* was primarily a money-making endeavor and the *OLZ*'s vision of a sort of railway version of the Cook voyages went nowhere.

Those who did want to make their scholarship relevant lamented the shortage of patrons and disinterest of large sections of the population. In 1911, Martin Hartmann deplored the Germans' ignorance and indifference with respect to colonial matters, and urged his fellow citizens to think of colonization as an affair of national importance:

How deeply the intensive development of overseas colonialization is bound up with all the circumstances of the Motherland is shown, above all, by Great Britain, where there is hardly one family that is not in some way involved with overseas settlement, and where economic life has, to the greatest extent, grown up with overseas trade, and is dependent on it. In Germany we have not, by a long stretch, come to this point. But conditions are paving the way. Whether one complains about it or not, it is a fact, and the organization of colonization by the state is to the highest degree everybody's affair.[16]

One can read this as a desperate appeal for help and involvement that did not seem to be forthcoming; on the other hand, it is certainly the case that some members of the procolonial lobby (including Hartmann) would not have been satisfied with anything else than society's total commitment to their project. We should also recognize that by 1911, even without the grand cultural investment Hartmann desired, German colonization was proceeding rapidly, as German Southwest

---

[13] Civil Cabinet to Gesellschaft für Erdkunde, October 24, 1905, B-GSPK, I, 89, 21371.

[14] Friedrich Althoff to Foreign Ministry, May 26, 1900, P-ZSA, AA/R 37675 (now B-BArch R 901/37675). Oskar Mann's detailed linguistic work, compiled between 1901 and 1903, was published under the title *Kurdisch-Persische Forschungen*, in four volumes between 1906 and 1910.

[15] F. E. Peiser, "Zum Jahresschluss," in *OLZ* 2 (1899): 395–6.

[16] Martin Hartmann, "Mission und Kolonialpolitik," in *Koloniale Rundschau* 3 (1911): 168.

Africa and East Africa, as well as Qingdao, Samoa, and the Bismarck Archipelago came under the Reich's control. The Germans had also by this time enormously increased their cultural, political, and economic presence in the Ottoman Empire – though they still lagged behind Britain and France. Many an African or "oriental" artifact had been shipped to the Royal Museums in Berlin (mostly to be stored in the basements). Exploitation could go on, apparently, with relatively little help from the culture-makers at home.

But some assistance was required – and some gladly lent to the cause. As we shift now to discussing the ways in which "orientalism" did respond to new imperial conquests and ambitions, we should keep in mind that we are talking here about a small minority of professional scholars – though these were, as we shall see, very active and sometimes influential people. Most of those considered here were specialists in the Islamic world or in China; the Indologists, Egyptologists, Assyriologists, and Old Testament scholars, as we have seen, were engaged in other sorts of projects, though in the course of my analysis, I will try to assess their contributions to imperialist worldviews and practices as well. I will also, particularly at this chapter's end, try to illustrate the forms of orientalism that the Reich rejected; the self-critical studies of Japanese culture by the expatriate doctor Erwin Baelz, for example, were not gratefully, or even graciously, accepted back home as proper guides to German behavior in the region. From the perspective of the state, there were limitations on the usability of orientalist knowledge that should just remind us again that "the discourse on the Orient" was anything but a univocal, unilateral, and unchanging debate.

German Orientalists and the Actuality of Empire

In this chapter, it will be harder than ever to define who should count as a "professional" orientalist, in part because in the imperial era, an increasing number of individuals began to claim expertise based not on their ability to read ancient texts and exotic languages, but on time spent "on the ground" or together with real-existing "orientals." Understandably, some thought diplomatic service, missionary endeavors, or business experience in the East gave them better credentials to speak about "the Orient" than armchair specialists in Old Testament Hebrew – and the advent of Wilhelmine *Weltpolitik* emboldened them to make their voices heard. After 1884, one finds, in particular, a host of journalists or travelers, only a few of whom had been trained in university programs, working outside the academy, and publishing articles or books as authoritative orientalists.[17] This was another natural consequence of the "open door" – and of the democratization of the cultural marketplace. But it does not make it easy to

---

[17] Friedrich Schrader is one example; after completing his dissertation in Indology with Pischel at the University of Halle (on a Vedic theme!), he took up a teaching post near Istanbul in 1891 and then moved to the Armenian-French lycée in Pera; after teaching for a Russian trade school in Baku for a year (1907–8), he helped to found the *Osmanischer Lloyd* and became one of the editors of this leading voice of German banking and industrial interests. His philo-Turkish and left-liberal stance (he also contributed anonymously to the socialist journal *Vorwärts*) made him an on-the-ground expert with quite different interests and ideas to air. Thanks to Jochen Schrader for guiding me to http://de.wikipedia.org/2/index.php?title=FriedrichSchrader, and confirming its accuracy.

determine who should count as a German orientalist in this era, a predicament that patrons and policy makers at the time never fully resolved – and thus I too will in the next three chapters survey a wide array of figures, focusing, however, on those who can meet our previous test, namely, men and women who did actually learn eastern languages or devote themselves to intense study of eastern cultures.

The confusion over oriental expertise was reflected in ministerial memos, as the bureaucrats tried to decide whom to hire to teach "oriental" subjects. In the more "exotic" fields, where Germany did not have a long tradition of scholarly achievement, men (but not, yet, women) were hired with unusual credentials; in 1908, the first chair for Sinology went to a man who had studied Sanskrit at university, spent thirteen years in China as a diplomat, and then written essays on contemporary politics for the newspapers. Even then, Otto Franke probably got his chair at the HKI (not at a traditional university) because he had also written on ancient subjects and because Carl Becker wanted him as a colleague. But when a chair at the University of Berlin was created in 1911, it went not to Franke but to the philologically-trained Dutch scholar of Chinese religions J. J. M. de Groot.[18]

It was even harder to decide whose projects deserved state funding. For instance, a prospective Central Asian traveler's credentials were suspect because he had been an actor for eight years and now seemed chiefly interested in photographing mountains; moreover, complained a member of the Calcutta consulate staff, his clothes were inappropriate for entry into India's high society.[19] Another traveler to Tibet, despite the hardships he had suffered, was not considered worthy to be called a "serious scholar-traveler" ". . . for, apart from his tendencies toward sensationalist reportage," wrote geography professor Albrecht Penck, "he makes unjustified and untenable claims to discoveries that others have made."[20]

These were the relatively easy decisions; in other cases, the applicants had the right clothes and did not lie about their exploits, but had questionable political aims – as in the case of Max Freiherr von Oppenheim, who volunteered in 1894 to trek across the Sahara to Chad, both for scientific reasons and to get better information on the revolutionary potential of the Wahabite beduin prince Ibn Raschid. In the end, the Foreign Ministry vetoed his trip, fearing that other nations would send "scientific" expeditions to the area as well, which might be dangerous for the Porte. Oppenheim was told to do his traveling in Mesopotamia instead.[21] Oppenheim was disliked by professional scholars and the usually cautious Foreign Ministry, but as a rich amateur he could operate outside the usual institutions and networks and did not need to perform the usual kinds of deference. To the vexation of the Deutsches Archäologisches Institut, he did carry out his own

---

[18] On Franke's career, see Fritz Jäger, "Otto Franke (1863–1946)," in *ZDMG* 100 (n.f. 25) (1950): 19–24. De Groot was actually a more vehement defender of imperialism than Franke. See Sinology section later in this chapter.

[19] Calcutta Embassay to Caprivi (Foreign Ministry), November 1, 1890, in P-ZSA, AA/R, 37672 (now B-BArch R 901/37672).

[20] Albrecht Penck to Kaiser, n.d., c. spring 1911, seconding the opinion of Sven Hedin and the Cultural Ministry, in B-GSPK, I, 89, 21369.

[21] Max Freiherr von Oppenheim to Caprivi, July 24, 1894, in P-ZSA AA/R 37672 (now B-BArch R 901/37672); Radolin (Therapia) to Caprivi October 13, 1894, and Oppenheim to Caprivi October 25, 1894, in P-ZSA AA/R 37673 (now B-BArch R 901/37673).

excavations, and pursued diplomatically problematical friendships with the young Egyptian viceroy, Abbas II Hilmi, and with other well-placed Arab nationalists in Egypt.[22] Seizing the opportunities presented to him, Oppenheim was one of many "men on the spot" who could not be fully controlled by the supposed decision-makers back home.

Opportunists like Oppenheim were always ready to follow the flag. But where did the flag lead? If, as noted above, German orientalists' choices were limited by the political and intellectual horizons of the period they inhabited, it should be said that those horizons were themselves hard to discern from the standpoint of 1885, or 1905, or even 1913. The Reich's leadership sent conflicting messages about its intentions toward the East. Having insisted, famously, that Germany had no interests to pursue in the Orient "which would be worth the sound bones of even a single Pomeranian musketeer," Bismarck after 1884 changed tack and began pushing investment in China and pursuing territory in the South Pacific. When, shortly after Bismarck's death in 1898, Wilhelm II set off on a six-week *Orientreise* (taking with him 230 tents, 60 waiters, and upwards of 1400 horses and mules), he seemed to be signaling another new departure. During this trip, however, Wilhelm made contradictory statements – or at least statements that had contradictory policy implications.[23] He declared his sympathetic support for the Christians of the Ottoman Empire, but he also visited the tomb of Saladin. At a dinner in Damascus after his visit, Wilhelm called the great defender of the House of Islam a hero and expressed his hopes that Abdul Hamid and the 300 million Muslims of his caliphate be assured of the German Emperor's sincere friendship. Muslim newspapers in the region covered these statements extensively, one of them concluding that history would eventually appreciate Wilhelm's anti-European stance: "At the end of the 19th and the beginning of the 20th century, Germany was ruled by a young monarch whose greatness and justice detested to join the greedy vultures flying eagerly over the lands of the Ottoman Empire."[24]

But did Wilhelm really detest, or more importantly, disdain the idea of joining the scavengers? The putative main event of his pilgrimage was not the visit to Saladin's tomb but the consecration of the Evangelical Church of the Redeemer in Jerusalem, one calculated to underline Germany's role in protecting Protestants in the Muslim world. Was Wilhelm, perhaps, encouraging Pan-Islamism to unsettle the colonies of his rivals and simultaneously readying himself to claim spoils of his own at the end of the day? Was he, in the end, for or against advancing the rights of Christians in the Ottoman Empire? It was also possible to read the whole trip simply as a product of Wilhelm's well-attested vanity and his view of ideal Germanic rulership. As Thomas Scheffler has shown, Wilhelm fancied himself as something of a reincarnated late Roman Emperor, tolerant and yet all-powerful, uniting in his person classical culture (without democracy), oriental kingship

---

[22] On Oppenheim, see Chapter 10.

[23] Thomas Scheffler, "The Kaiser in Baalbek: Tourism, Archaeology, and the Politics of Imagination," in *Baalbek: Image and Monument, 1898–1998*, ed. Hélène Sader, Thomas Scheffler, and Angelika Neuwirth (Beirut, 1998), pp. 13–27.

[24] Quoted from an Arabic language journal (*al-Jami'ah al-'Utmaniyyah*) of April 1, 1899, in Abdel-Raouf Sinno, "The Emperor's Visit to the East as Reflected in Contemporary Arabic Journalism," in Sader et al., eds., *Baalbek*, p. 133.

(without being an "oriental"), and Christian sacrality (without any actual Christian content), and accordingly, his journey was largely devoted to visiting the sites of non-Christian sacred rulership.[25] Perhaps this was chiefly a performance for domestic consumption? With respect to East Asia, Wilhelm was equally hard to read, and hard to follow; on the one hand, he coined the phrase, "the Yellow Peril"; on the other hand, he sent his son, Prince Heinrich, to visit the Empress of China. In this context, it is not surprising that German eastern policy would be confusing and unpredictable, even if one did know the players and kept a reasonably accurate scorecard.

Moreover, during a period of rapidly changing diplomatic relations, in the wake of events such as England's formal colonization of Egypt, the Sino-Japanese War, the Armenian massacres of the 1890s, the Russo-Japanese War, and the Balkan Wars, even coherent policies necessarily changed. Sometimes these were the result of repositioning in order to thwart other powers' ambitions; that was the case in the Reich's relations with Japan between 1896 and 1905. German claims on Moroccan territory had to be given up after the summer of 1911 not because Wilhelmstrasse thought better of taking on new colonial territory, but because the British came to the immediate and unequivocal aid of the French. Germany's indispensable alliance with the Austrians also made maneuvering in the Balkans treacherous and made the pursuit of an independent line with respect to the Ottomans virtually impossible. Finally, in an era in which some liberals, in particular, sought to use the more subtle methods of *Kulturpolitik* to extend Germany's overseas influence, it was rather hard to know which agency or private organization might have the sanction of state officials – and even when one could discern official involvement, there were institutional conflicts between organizations (between for example, the Foreign Office, the Colonial Society, and Navy League) and internal divisions within institutions (within the German Archaeological Institute, for example). In such circumstances, planning a successful utilitarian career as an orientalist was almost laughable. The life of a *Privatdozent* trained in Sanskrit linguistics, by contrast, looked secure.

This does not mean, naturally, that the two decades of closely-packed imperialist ventures that followed Bismarck's change of course did not fire the imaginations of some and have the tacit backing of many professional orientalists. In his memoirs, the Sinologist Otto Franke recalled the powerful impression made on his generation when Bismarck, addressing the Reichstag, proclaimed: "We Germans fear God, and nothing else in the world."[26] In the course of my research, I have encountered very few academics who actively and consistently opposed German conquest – though as we shall see, there were many who criticized particular projects or more frequently the ways in which operations were being undertaken. The reason for this may lie less in their choice of fields than in the narrow socio-cultural stratum from which most scholars came. The individuals treated in this book, as we have seen, came preponderantly from the middle classes; the universities in which they were trained excluded socialists and discriminated

---

[25] See Scheffler, "The Kaiser in Baalbek," pp. 34–41.
[26] Otto Franke, *Erinnerungen aus zwei Welten: Randglossen zur eigenen Lebensgeschichte* (Berlin, 1954), pp. 37–8.

against left-liberals, and the proximity of oriental studies to the Higher Criticism meant that most of these scholars too came from liberal Protestant or Jewish households. This was the demographic group that was most likely of any to support some sort of imperialism in the first place – but also, perhaps, most likely to feel entitled to criticize when their expectations were not met.

Given this narrow spectrum, it is actually quite surprising how much divergence of opinion one finds on the question of the proper kind of empire Germany should have. One of the most liberal, Theodor Nöldeke, preferred Bismarckian *Realpolitik* to messy annexations and was happy to leave the "wasp's nest" of Morocco to the French. Freiherr Ferdinand von Richthofen believed it suicidal for Europeans to assist in the process of Chinese economic modernization; they should instead work together to *prevent* Chinese development.[27] Otto Franke, on the other hand, thought Germany should befriend China and help it to avoid race wars instigated either by the Japanese or by other Europeans.[28] Both Franke and the Arabist Martin Hartmann thought the Germans should act aggressively, setting up secular cultural institutions in China and the Ottoman Empire to win over pro-modernizing factions. But others wanted their countrymen (and women) to back off. Before the Great War, the Near Eastern archaeologist Ernst Herzfeld thought Germany should stop meddling in Persia and let the English run it properly.[29] Some – like Nöldeke – liked the Ottoman "old" Turks; others like the Arabist Karl Süssheim and the journalist Ernst Jaeckh made friends with Turkish modernizers. There were Zionists (like Gershom Scholem), ardent anti-Zionists (like Leopold von Weiss), and those who wanted to make peace, like Ignaz Goldziher. As Malte Fuhrmann has suggested, some of the archaeologists in particular believed themselves duty-bound to rescue Asia Minor's classical heritage.[30] But others, probably the majority, did not think much about the modern East at all and continued to think of themselves as scholars pursuing knowledge for its own sake – or for the sake of increasing German prestige in the eyes of the "cultured people" of the West.

One of the biggest divergences, indeed, revolved around religious issues or to be more specific, around the question of exporting Christianity to the East. In an address to the Reichstag of April 30, 1912, Wilhelm Solf, the colonial minister (and trained orientalist), claimed that it was Germany's duty "to make propaganda for Christianity, without taking other coexisting religions into consideration. The history of [the Islamic world] has shown that the impact of Islam on the indigenous peoples has proved not to be favorable. Islam has accomplished nothing in the larger world; it is no culture-carrier."[31] The missionary groups surely

---

[27] Theodore Nöldeke to Becker, December 31, 1914 and October 12, 1914, in B-GSPK, Nachlass Becker, M. 3138; on Ricthofen, see Chapter 3.

[28] Otto Franke, "Was lehrt uns die ostasiatische Geschichte der letzten fünfzig Jahre?" in *Abteilung Berlin-Charlottenburg der Deutschen Kolonial-Gesellschaft, Verhandlungen 1903–05*, vol. 8, no. 4 (Berlin, 1905): 110–14.

[29] Ernst Herzfeld to Carl Becker, March 26, 1911 in B-GSPK, Nachlass Becker, M. 4023.

[30] Malte Fuhrmann, "Den Orient Deutsch Machen: Imperiale Diskurse des Kaiserreichs über das Osmanische Reich," available at www.kakanien.ac.at/beitr/fallstudie/MFuhrmann1.pdf.

[31] Quoted in Traugott Mann, review of Martin Hartmann, *Islam, Mission, Politik* (1912), in *OLZ* 15 (1913): 467.

concurred with this, but most *Islamforscher* did not. Goldziher wholeheartedly disagreed with this assessment of Islam and disapproved of attempts to uproot local religious traditions. Carl Becker thought Islam could and should be modernized and opposed heavy-handed Christian missionization, offering in one pamphlet an exceedingly crude argument for preferring conversions to Islam in the African colonies: "If, ...the black becomes a Christian, he misunderstands from the beginning the idea of the brotherhood of Christians, and his outrage is not to be doubted if he is also long under the tutelage of the prostelyzers.... Considered from the vantage point of religion, the internal distance [between men] Islam creates is perhaps regrettable, but it facilitates the maintaining of European authority."[32] In a period in which missionaries both provoked anti-colonial violence and were victimized by it, the exportability of Christianity was a hugely contentious topic, and one on which German orientalists did not agree.

The necessity, for those who chose to study the modern Orient, of taking a public stand on such controversial questions made this speciality seem a particularly risky career choice; even if one's positions were carefully considered, one had constantly to defend one's inquiries against accusations that they amounted to "a descent into the political fights of the day."[33] That is to say, while some, and especially younger scholars, were tempted by the siren song of "relevance," there remained professional advantages in resisting these temptations. To drive this point home, it is worth noting the difficulty "modernist" orientalists had in obtaining both prestige and academic jobs right through the Wilhelmine era. Martin Hartmann, the most prolific of Germany's modern Arabists, raged perpetually against the field's orientation toward antiquity and "pure" languages – to little avail. One would think, he wrote in 1899, that the fact that 130 million of the world's 260 million Muslims lived under European (including German) rule would mean that there would be careful studies of the history of Islam, but there were very few. "The cause of this phenomenon? That the 'science of Islam' has, up to now, not yet come into its own. It was the stepchild partly of Arabic linguistics and partly of comparative religious studies. In the former, the linguistic side and perhaps even some superficial details were given consideration; in the latter one was content to synthesize what was to be found in well-known works about the ideas of the Islamic world."[34] Even when authors did touch on the modern history of the Islamic states, he raged, they did not take the subject very seriously.

Nor was the Islamic world the only arena in which antiquities were preferred to things modern. The same could be said of Indology, which continued to focus on the ancient Aryans and had little time for study of modern Indian languages or cultures. Sinologists were expected to know the whole of the Chinese tradition, all 4,000-plus years of it, though this usually meant that one combined expertise in its early period (or in classical Chinese literature) with willingness to discuss, in more popular fora, the events of the last year. Though Berlin and Hamburg were home to powerful colonial lobbies and businesses increasingly interested in exploiting

---

[32] Carl Becker, *L'Islam et la colonization de l'Afrique* (lecture at the Union Coloniale Francaise, January 22, 1910) (Paris, 1910), p. 14.

[33] Martin Hartmann, *Die arabische Frage* (Leipzig, 1909), p. 5.

[34] Martin Hartmann, "Islamologie," in *OLZ* 2 (1899): 1–2, quotation p. 2.

the East, orientalism's most prestigious and prolific leaders continued to lodge themselves in Leipzig, Bonn, Strasbourg, Göttingen, and Tübingen and to produce works focused chiefly on language and on the ancient world. Outside agitation did not swiftly, if ever, change their views on what university orientalism should be. Though in 1905 influential members of the colonial lobby declared it a "pressing necessity" to create professorships for Sinology in Germany, by 1911, there were still only two, the most prestigious of which was held by de Groot (a Dutchman) at a time the state could boast eighteen chairs and eight assistant professorships for Indology and seventeen chairs and twelve assistant positions in Semitic languages.[35]

Indeed, despite the fact that Germany did have a colony or, in official parlance, a leased territory (Qingdao) in China after 1898, the state of Sinological studies did not improve much at all and may only have been prevented from declining by the interest generated by the Turfan expeditions and the Japanese victory in the Russo-Japanese War of 1904–5.[36] When, in 1911, Germany's only full professor of East Asian languages, Otto Franke, surveyed the state of Sinology in Germany, his essay was anything but a celebration of the country's achievements. Sinology in Germany, he argued, had been and was impaired in its development by the nation's lack of cultural middle ground, its polarization in the "medieval scholasticism" of the universities on the one hand and the exclusively practical orientation of the commercial and industrial world on the other. Franke's pamphlet reflected, once again, the frustrations of the fin de siècle orientalists: on the one hand, they were convinced that classicism had become narrow and desiccated – "... we need a new humanism, a more expansive form," he argued.[37] On the other, he wrote, Sinologists did not want to be simply the tools of state officials or businessmen, who, after all, had little time or interest in appreciating the complexities of the cultures to which scholars devoted intense study. Franke was sure that Germany needed a new, and more "relevant" humanism; but he wanted the scholars, not the politicians, to create and implement these new forms of thought.

It is worth quoting Franke here at some length, as his claims underscore the persistence of the rivalry between *Orientalistik* and classics that has been emphasized throughout this book. Germany's philosophical faculties, Franke bitterly complained, were still suffused with:

the anachronistic conception that Greece and Rome alone should be considered sources of culture for us, and that therefore they must remain for all time the focal point of historical-philological research. [Classicists] still practice that orthodox philology, which claims and possesses an influence, which it has not for a long time deserved, [and] that intolerant onesidedness which only accords the oriental sciences a hearing in so far as they are related to the history and culture of Greece, but otherwise are blind and want to be blind to the enormous field of Asian knowledge, which has brought us into contact with the modern

---

[35] Otto Franke, "Die sinologischen Studien in Deutschland," in idem, *Ostasiatische Neubildungen: Beiträge zur Verständnis der politischen und kulturellen Enwicklungs-Vorgänge im Fernen Osten* (Hamburg, 1911), pp. 373, 375.

[36] The Berlin chair, according to Erich Haenisch, was founded in response to the Turfan finds. Christina Leibfried, *Sinologie an der Universität Leipzig* (Leipzig, 2003), p. 15, n. 39.

[37] Otto Franke, "Die sinologischen Studien," pp. 376–77.

world. [They are still beholden to] that real "unworldliness" in the scholarly sense, which takes no part in the widened historical conceptions of our day. Those are the forces with which *Orientalistik* has always had to struggle, and which today too block Sinology's path. ... And added to this is another fact, that one ought to think, should offer [Sinology] a leg up, but actually because of the weirdness of our academic [canons of] scientificness hinders it; and that is its vital connection with the present. If Sinology only had to do exclusively with a long finished, ruined and then re-excavated culture, then perhaps there would be a possibility of finding grace in the eyes of the philological right-thinkers...

But instead, Franke lamented, Sinology was seen by his colleagues as "a branch of today's politics; as a means to [address] the economic questions of the day, it might serve 'practical' goals, but in the city of 'pure science' there is no room for it."[38] Like many other members of his generation, Franke resented classicism's enduring power to define knowledge worth knowing and realized that the very usefulness of Sinology would make it even more difficult for the new science to gain the cultural respectability it deserved.

Of course, orientalism can and has contributed to imperialist projects without meaning to do so directly, and that was certainly the case for the Germans. The fact that German intellectual culture did not for the most part sanction the direct engagement of scholars in practical matters does not mean that anyone disapproved of applying scientific ideas to colonial problems – when, that is, they could be useful. As the above discussion suggests, it is not so much that academics were against colonization that limited their involvement in the process; it is rather that their work was largely irrelevant to the tasks at hand. German orientalist scholarship, as we have seen, evolved largely from biblical interpretation and focused on the ancient world and its languages. It was hard to turn this ship around quickly and to root out older values and traditional scholarly pursuits for the sake of being "useful" – even if everyone had been on the same political page.

Scholars were most useful in the implementation of "indirect" colonialism, the practice of working with and through local customs, institutions, and officials rather than seeking wholesale and immediate Europeanization. But this was an evolving set of practices, support for which in the relevant state bodies really only began to evolve after German colonizers had demonstrated their corruption, incompetence, and even genocidal tendencies in the series of scandals stretching from Carl Peters' 1897 conviction for extreme cruelty in East Africa to the massacre of the Herero in 1904–5. Following the latter debacle, the Reichstag's vociferous denunciations of colonial policy led to the promotion of the banker Bernhard Dernburg from Director of the Colonial Section in the Foreign Ministry to the new cabinet post of colonial secretary (1907–10). Dernburg's job was to maintain Reichstag – and public – support for colonialism by substituting what he called "scientific" colonialism for the corrupt and violent methods which had culminated in the near genocide and the loss of German troops, and which made doing business in the colonies so difficult.[39] He was followed in office by his

---

[38] Ibid., p. 362.

[39] We might see, in this moment, a German equivalent of the Hastings trial, as described by Nicholas Dirks, in *Scandal of Empire*; blame for the evils of colonization is not placed on colonization itself, but on corrupt individuals and practices.

protégé Wilhelm Solf, who was by training a Sanskritist, and one of the foremost proponents of what Fritz Fischer called "world policy without war," that is, satisfying Germany's desire for colonies while also preserving good relations with England.[40] This period did see considerable collaboration between orientalists and imperial policy-makers; but we should also keep in mind that the period of German "scientific" colonialism was quite short, ending in 1914 – for the war brought with it other sorts of colonial rule. Though we can certainly find arguments for cultural colonization before this time, it is really only after the "Dernburg Turn" that the state, the scholars, and, to some extent, the business elite were on the same page.

And even then there were conflicts, as the case of Solf shows. Solf was an industrious and outspoken advocate of German colonial annexations, from the time he was a junior official in Calcutta in 1889–90, up to and including his postings to German East Africa (1898) and Samoa (1900–11). But he persisted in believing that colonial governance should be in the hands of civilian rather than military officials. He was never a Pan-German and spoke out consistently in favor of humanitarian treatment of indigenous peoples. Of course, like the other indirect colonizers of that ilk, he thought indigenous workers the key to colonial profitability and thus believed non-exploitative forms of governance practical as well as ethical[41]; he did not hesitate to use colonial subjects to help win Germany's war, and he sought to preserve the empire even at the expense of losing territory in Europe. Solf's views echoed those of Friedrich Rosen, the Persian scholar posted to the Portuguese Embassy in 1912; Otto Franke's were similar – though Franke's China experience led him to develop quite a different view of England. All of them would criticize, at one time or another, the more aggressive and ham-fisted policies of the Kaiser, the greedier bankers, the linguistically and culturally tone-deaf members of the Foreign Ministry, the most intolerant and high-handed missionaries. Perhaps they learned some of their ethnographic sensitivity from their orientalist educations? Let us listen to Wilhelm Solf, paying tribute to his recently deceased Indologist mentor in a letter of 1910: "Insofar as I have had success in handling the indigenous races, [in finding] understanding for their ways of thinking and feeling, in [employing] the conception of the colonizer as the conveyor of culture and not as the one who paves the way for those lusting for booty, that is the intellectual tincture which I bore with me, from [Richard] Pischel's colloquium into life."[42] Of course, Pischel did not teach him to see the pernicious aspects of cultural colonization (even had that honestly been all that Solf sought to further); but we must recognize that there were different kinds of colonizers and that they often disagreed about how best to rule.

All of these men were imperialists and contributed in important ways to the extension of German power and the colonization (or pseudo-colonization) and exploitation of hundreds of thousands of people. I do not wish to quarrel with this

---

[40] See Fritz Fischer, *War of Illusions: German Policies from 1911 to 1914*, trans. Marian Jackson (London, 1975), pp. 258–7, 310–19.

[41] See Eberhard von Vietsch, *Wilhelm Solf: Botschafter zwischen den Zeiten* (Tübingen, 1961), pp. 40–54, 89.

[42] Quoted in ibid., p. 23.

reality or to blunt critiques of scholarly complicity. But it is important that we understand the service orientalists provided in the context of the exploitative actions and cultural representations going on around them – the Reich surely would have colonized without them, and perhaps they complicated colonial policy as often as they facilitated it. We move on now to a closer study of the institutions erected to serve Germany's needs for colonial knowledge, seeking to understand their patrons, employees, and students against the larger backdrop of Wilhelmine cultural and imperial politics.

Colonialism and Its Orientalist Institutions

We have seen, earlier in this chapter, the ways in which older forms of orientalism persisted and surveyed the institutional disincentives to scholarly engagement in the practical pursuit of empire. And yet we must also acknowledge the attraction of many academics to power – cultural power as well as political power – and their willingness to capitalize on opportunities to advance their careers and cultural visions. As self-appointed captains, determined to "steer" German culture toward greater achievements, many German professors also felt it was their duty to provide aid and sometimes even comfort to the colonizers. "Who should study the conditions in our colonies, if not us?" asked Georg Kampffmeyer in 1913.[43] And some of his colleagues heartily agreed.

Enthusiasm for jumping on this bandwagon was especially keen among those who felt their talents and fields had been under-appreciated and under-utilized by the Reich. This was, of course, the case for many of our "furious" orientalists. Felix Peiser's celebration of the coming of the Baghdad Railway was just one of the *OLZ*'s effusions in this line: "Now the doorway to a goldmine of scientific discoveries will be opened to the orientalists, who have long yearned for [this opportunity]...Germany long stood by the side and let other nations complete the initial work. With hasty steps, in the last decades [we] have attempted to make up for lost time."[44] Museum officials and field archaeologists, as we have seen, used the rhetoric of "catching up" to the British, French, and sometimes Russians or Dutch repeatedly, and many a student of the Islamic world would echo Carl Becker's pronouncement: "The times, during which Germans could be indifferent when 'far away, deep in Turkey, the peoples battle one another,' are finally over."[45] For those who had long felt undervalued or ignored, it was some comfort to think that in the era of *Weltpolitik*, they could, at last, find favor and help their belated empire pull even with the others.

But the numbers of trained men were few, and the support systems for training more experts weak. Where would a new, much larger generation of "real" orientalists come from? The institutions that promoted the study of the *modern* Orient were few: Maria Theresa's Oriental Academy had been in business, training translators and diplomats since 1754, and in the mid-nineteenth century, a

---

[43] Kampffmeyer, *Plane perspicere*, p. 4.

[44] F. E. Peiser, "Zum Jahresschluss," in *OLZ* 1 (1899): 395–6.

[45] Carl Becker, "Die orientalistischen Wissenschaften: Der vordere Orient und Afrika," in *Deutschland unter Wilhlem II* (Berlin, 1914), p. 1183.

second Austrian oriental academy was founded in Vienna; little is known about this institution at present, but a contemporary noted it had 216 students (including ladies) in 1914.[46] Although a Königlich-ungarische orientalische Handelsakademie was founded in Budapest in 1883 to teach Hungarians the languages needed for the Balkan trade, farther to the north and west, there was no Germanophone equivalent of the Viennese schools or France's École spéciale des langues orientales vivant (founded 1795). Moreover, in the Germanies, modern oriental languages were rarely taught in universities, in contrast to Russia and England, where university faculty at King's College and Vilnius University (not to speak of their colleagues in Poona and Almaty) regularly taught living languages. German diplomats received their training in local affairs when they arrived at their stations, and their language skills were often so poor that German offices had to borrow interpreters from other consulates.[47] Though archaeological "schools" were founded in Rome (1829), Greece (1871), and Egypt (1907), there were none in the newer areas (Mesopotamia, Persia, India, and China), and thus oriental archaeologists too were trained (if at all) in European museums or on the fly.

Nor were there, in 1884, many scholarly outlets for work devoted to the modern Orient. Early in the century, a few German-language journals had been attempted and finally one took – the *Fundgrube des Orients* – but it lasted only nine years, from 1809 to 1818, folding when its aristocratic patron retired to his estates (see Chapter 2). The next major secular journal (the *ZDMG*) began publication only in 1847. Though the *Fundgrube* (thanks to the fact that Hammer-Purgstall wrote most of its articles) had published some essays on modern developments, the ZDMG published almost none. The semi-popular geographic or later ethnographic journals carried the most information – or one could turn to travelogs, to British and French journals like the *Journal of the Asiatic Society*, or speciality newspapers like the *Osmanisches Lloyd*. The OLZ, founded in 1898, carried a few editorials and reviews, but focused mostly on the ancient Near East and Mesopotamia – as did the specialized philological journals. Of course there were plenty of smaller-scale journals, such as *Der Orient* (published by the Austrian Orient-Klub, between 1898 and 1906), and materials produced by missionary or colonization societies. There was no dearth of information about the East – and there were plenty of organizations, by 1900, willing to publish one's findings. But associating oneself with some of these organizations was sometimes risky, or at the least, did little for one's respectability amongst one's peers. Not until Becker established *Der Islam*, in 1910, and Hartmann the rival journal *Welt des Islam* (in 1913) were there any German periodicals devoted to publishing scholarly work on the "modern" Orient. And even then, one could not be sure one's colleagues would be impressed.

---

[46] William H. Worrell, "An Account of Schools for Living Oriental Languages Established in Europe," in *Journal of the American Oriental Society* 39 (1919): 193. Worrell lists attendance at Hammer's alma mater for 1914 as 53. Ibid., pp. 191, 193.

[47] Lothar Burchardt, "The School of Oriental Languages at the University of Berlin – Forging the Cadres of German Imperialism?" in *Science across the European Empires, 1800–1950*, ed. Benedikt Stuchtey (Oxford, 2005), p. 64.

In fact, for quite some time, there was no real sense that a study of "living" oriental languages was necessary, at least not in academic establishments; missionaries and diplomatic or military officers could learn a few phrases in special schools designed exclusively for members of those guilds. In any event, learning the "classical" forms of the languages and the fundamental (read ancient) characteristics of Arab, Indian, or Chinese culture was thought to provide the scholar the tools to understand the modern (read degenerate) forms of these worlds. Many of the big oriental "cultural histories" of the 1840s and 1850s, such as Lassen's *Indische Altertumskunde* and Koeppen's work on Buddhism, began in the deep past, but took the story up to the present day (or nearly). But for many decades thereafter, German orientalists preferred to work on ancient and long dead cultures – recall Franke's complaints about Sinology's handicap, namely, that it had to deal with a culture that had *not* expired. All of this meant that the infrastructure and incentives for investing the necessary years in learning, say, modern Turkish or Chinese were very weak, and the academic world was, in the 1880s, showing very little likelihood of responding to the demands of modern empire without external pressure, or more accurately, without some combination of outside pressure and the investment necessary to make change practicable and attractive.

That pressure, it seems, came from Bismarck, though his intervention began in a rather haphazard fashion. Seeking in vain a qualified translator for a Chinese envoy in 1883, the Chancellor wondered aloud if it might be useful, in the interests of the foreign service, to have a means to produce young officials "who are in a position to engage in linguistic exchanges with the great peoples of Asia and Africa, and to do so in a reliable manner."[48] The Prussian Cultural Ministry, eager to promote cutting-edge cultural projects, took note, and by August 1885, the Ministry had a memo in hand from Professor Paul Haupt, suggesting the founding of an Oriental Seminar at the University of Berlin on the model of Austria's Lehranstalt.[49] Intense discussions between the Foreign, Finance, and Cultural Ministries took place in 1886, and in 1887, after lively debate in the Prussian Landtag and Reichstag, modest funding was allocated and the Seminar für Orientalische Sprachen (SOS) opened its doors. In its first semester, it enrolled 108 students, 44 of them with law degrees (probably recruits for the diplomatic service), 26 businessmen, and 38 scholars and teachers.[50] Two of its first students were Wilhelm Solf and Otto Franke, both of whom had recently switched to Sinological studies from Indology precisely because the Foreign Ministry had let it be known they needed diplomats for the Far East and right away. The swift posting of these two trained Sanskrit philologists (Solf to India and Franke to China) strongly suggests that the state was seeking to move vigorously in an easterly direction and creating as quickly as possible a cadre of at least superficially knowledgeable administrators to carry out its aims.

[48] Bismarck quoted in Mangold, *Eine 'weltbürgerliche Wissenschaft,'* p. 226.
[49] Gossler to Althoff, April 8, 1885; Haupt to Althoff, August 20, 1885, in B-GSPK, Rep. 92, Althoff, AI, Nr. 109. See the detailed accounts in Burchardt, *School of Oriental Languages*, pp. 64–70; Mangold, *Eine 'weltbürgliche Wissenschaft,'* pp. 227–29.
[50] Gossler to Kaiser, May 9, 1888, B-GSPK, I, 89, M. 21531.

The SOS was, from the outset, an unusual institution; unlike the provincially supported universities, its funding was divided between the Reich and the Prussian state. The aim of instruction was not wide-ranging *Bildung* but unabashedly practical training; it cultivated students who aimed chiefly at business careers, careers as colonial officials, postal workers, and overseas military personnel, not at all the same sorts who frequented the philosophical faculty. If anything, the SOS's courses were even more heavily linguistic than those in the wider university – but the languages taught were not dead languages students were to learn to read, but living languages students needed to learn to speak. In its original design, the SOS was to devote itself exclusively to Asian languages, teaching Chinese, Japanese, Hindustani, Arabic, Persian, and Turkish; but in 1887, Carl Peters, chairman of the Gesellschaft für deutsche Kolonisation, successfully petitioned for African languages to be added. A decade later, European languages (Russian, English, and French) were introduced.[51] Gradually, more and more courses in "Colonial *Realien*" were taught – tropical medicine, and the ethnography and geography of Germany's colonial territories, for example – and some of the Arabists in particular moved in the direction of the kind of cultural history we now regularly include in college courses.[52]

There can be no doubt that the SOS contributed to German colonial rule; in 1912 the director estimated that the Seminar had produced some 101 colonial officials, 64 postal officers for the colonies, and 228 colonial military officers.[53] Though Solf, as we have seen, credited his work in ancient Indian philology at the University of Halle with preparing him for his colonial ministrations, in fact it was his time at the SOS (and his law degree) that prepared him for day-to-day foreign service. Governors of East Africa (Gustav Adolf Graf von Götzen and Heinrich Schnee) as well as Togo (Julius Graf von Zech auf Neuhofen) also passed through. The raw number of students was relatively large; 98 in winter 1887–8, rising to 171 in 1900–1, and 274 in 1909–10, though many, by this time, were there to study European languages, and especially Russian.[54] By 1912, the students' presence in the colonies was, according to Cultural Minister Trott zu Solz, pervasive. As he informed the Kaiser: "Almost all the officers in your majesty's colonial forces and in the colonial administration, insofar as they enjoyed any sort of specialized training at home, have come out of the Seminar."[55]

In the same year as the founding of the SOS, the Deutsche Kolonialgesellschaft (DKG) was created, pulling together several older and smaller pro-colonial pressure groups. The DKG boasted some 15,000 members already in the year of its founding, 1887, and by 1914 had 43,000 members, divided into 442 branch associations. Most of these members were businessmen, bureaucrats, and military officers and their wives; but scholars were also active participants. Carl Becker, together with Gymnasium professor Heinrich Zimmerer, president of the Regensburg DKG,

---

[51] Jürgen Kloosterhuis, '*Friedliche Imperialisten': Deutsche Auslandsvereine und auswärtige Kulturpolitik, 1906–1918*, part 1 (Frankfurt, 1994), pp. 396–7; Burchardt, "School of Oriental Languages," pp. 68–9.

[52] See discussion later in the chapter.

[53] Mangold, *Eine 'weltbürgliche Wissenschaft*,' p. 234.

[54] Burchardt, "School of Oriental Languages," p. 72.

[55] Trott zu Solz (Cultural Ministry) to Kaiser, October 11, 1912, in B-GSPK, I, Rep. 89, M. 21531.

pushed hard for German "civilizing" work in the Ottoman Empire. The host of other *Vereine* founded after 1900 to promote various forms of "friendship" or economic cooperation with Turkey, Japan, or China testify to the swift rise in interest in the East in German middle- and upper-middle-class society, including the educated elite and academics – as well as to the increasing presence in Germany's bigger cities of individuals of Chinese, Japanese, or Turkish descent. But there was little time to get organizations like the Ostasiatischer Verein (Hamburg, 1900; Bremen, 1901) or the Deutsch-Türkische Vereinigung (founded in Berlin in 1914) up and running before the Great War came; and though these associations did have educative functions, we should also recognize their primary purpose as interest or pressure groups, or as social clubs. Perhaps the most explicitly imperialistic was the Deutsches Vorderasien-Komitee, founded by geographer Hugo Grothe in 1908, and dedicated to the promotion of German "cultural work" in the Orient.[56] Grothe himself was so vigorous a promoter that in 1911, the Interior Minister advised against allowing him an audience with the Kaiser to present his recent book; Grothe, though a real scholar, would simply use this opportunity to push his plans for German cultural and trade expansion in Asia Minor.[57]

Another of Wilhelmine Germany's great imperialist cultural institutions was the Deutsch-Orient Gesellschaft (DOG), whose founding in 1898 was briefly described in Chapter 4. We should underline here its origins in German frustration with limitations on the belated nation's ability to acquire archaeological treasures from the Orient. To understand the context, it should be noted that a mere two years earlier, the French had established monopoly rights over all excavation sites in Persia, while the rich Egyptian sites were largely in the hands of the British (with Frenchmen running the Egyptian Antiquities Service). The Greeks were enforcing antiquities laws and prices for artifacts on the open market were skyrocketing. The Germans had extracted the Pergamon Altar on its entirety from Ottoman soil, but by the later 1890s, despite a secret agreement between the Germans and the Porte, it was getting harder to acquire from this source the Hellenistic artifacts the Royal Museums coveted.[58]

This competition and Germany's increasing resentment at its failure to acquire major monuments provoked Rudolf Virchow, in a speech to the Prussian Landtag in March 1898, to regret that since Richard Lepsius's visit to Egypt in the 1840s, Germany had been largely shut out of oriental acquisitions. The French and British had been accommodating, he claimed, but of course took the lion's share of finds for themselves; it was rather embarrassing that Germans had to go abroad to study Egyptian and Assyrian artifacts or be satisfied with casts. Even the Austrians had better Asia Minor collections![59] The upshot of the elderly professor's lament was the appointment of Ludwig Borchardt as scientific attaché to the Imperial *Generalkonsulat* in Cairo in 1898; in the same year, the young Egyptologist joined a non-German dig in Abusir, and when those (private) funds ran

---

[56] Kloosterhuis, '*Friedliche Imperialisten*,' pp. 401–3, 574.
[57] Interior Ministry to Civil Cabinet, May 12, 1911, B-GSPK, I, 89, M. 21369.
[58] For more on the DOG, see Marchand, *Down from Olympus*, pp. 188–227.
[59] Virchow's speech reprinted in "Die orientalische Altertumsforschung im preussischen Landtag," in *OLZ* 1 (1898): 120–24, esp. p. 121.

out in 1901, the Germans obtained the right to excavate the site. Thanks to continued pressure on the British and French, in 1911, German excavators were even given part of the plum site of Tell el Amarna. In early 1913 Borchardt would bring home the celebrated head of Nefertete, displaying it to the Kaiser and the DOG's executives alone for fear that the Cairo museum would be vexed at his having appropriated this treasure.[60] When Borchardt published his find in 1923, the Egyptian government demonstrated its vexation by refusing to grant any more archaeological concessions to Germany until the bust was returned; but by then it had become a cult object – both for its beauty and, one suspects, for its demonstration that Germany had played a role in the Egyptological Great Game.[61] It remains the Berlin Egyptian Museum's most iconic object.

Finally, plans were made to create something like a colonial university. The HKI was Dernburg's pet project, part of the liberal colonial minister's attempt to create a cadre of well-educated colonial officials to assist him in putting Germany's empire in order. It was enthusiastically backed by Hamburg merchants interested in overseas trade; but as Jens Ruppenthal has shown, other Hamburg notables also saw the project as a means to lay the foundations for a "real" university in their hometown.[62] Like the SOS, the HKI was a hybrid, meant to offer useful courses to neophyte colonizers as well as to further specialized knowledge. Again, its structure was unusual; it was subordinated to the Colonial Ministry in Berlin (rather than the provincial ministry of culture) and subject to pressure from a "businessmen's advisory board" composed of members of the Hamburg Chamber of Commerce. The ideal and only candidate for its position in Islamic History and Civilization was Carl Heinrich Becker, assistant professor at the University of Heidelberg, who had taught Germany's first lecture course on modern Islam in 1906–7. In negotiations over the position, Becker insisted that his purview be the cultural, not the linguistic, world of Islam and that languages at the HKI would be taught without the technical apparatus demanded in comparative Semitic studies. The time saved could be spent on *Realien*: institutions, customs, art, and geography.[63] Becker was also a political animal and ambitious – at least on Germany's behalf; the idea of having political influence was for him – unlike many other orientalists, who restricted their aims to cultural influence – enticing.

Sabine Mangold rightly sees Becker – and Martin Hartmann, who began offering courses in "Islamkunde" at the SOS in 1910 – as proponents of a new kind of cultural history, one that played down philology in favor of history, sociology, and political ideas. But she also correctly underlines the uniqueness of the Kolonialinstitut and the SOS, intellectually, as well as in institutional structure. Hartmann could (and did) complain all he wanted about "armchair Arabists" and "philological pedants"; but they continued to inhabit most of the Reich's academic jobs,

[60] Olaf Matthes, *James Simon: Mäzen im wilhelminischen Zeitalter* (Berlin, 2000), pp. 261–3.

[61] John A. Wilson, *Signs and Wonders upon Pharaoh: A History of American Egyptology* (Chicago, 1964), pp. 156–7.

[62] See Jens Ruppenthal, *"Kolonialismus als Wissenschaft und Technik": Das Hamburgische Kolonialinstitut, 1908 bis 1918* (Stuttgart, 2007).

[63] Josef van Ess, "From Wellhausen to Becker: The Emergence of *Kulturgeschichte* in Islamic Studies," in Malcolm Kerr, ed., *Islamic Studies: A Tradition and its Problems* (Malibu, CA, 1980), p. 30.

publish the largest number of books and articles, and dictate the profession's standards.[64] Nor did attendance at the HKI ever meet expectations; there were only 109 regular students and 254 auditors as late as 1913–14 – low enough that Becker was confident that by moving to the University of Bonn, he could interest more students in Germany's world mission.[65] The Berliners were jealous and the Reich did not contribute as much to the project as expected. The HKI did offer cutting-edge forms of pedagogy – it had a phonetic laboratory and employed as often as possible native-speaking language instructors; students were even taught practical survival skills such as swimming and cooking. But, as one outside observer commented, its strongest field was African languages;[66] in oriental studies its contribution was significant, but not culture-altering.

Indeed, there were pervasive problems in the introduction of colonial institutions into a German cultural world built around the Humboldtian ideals of *Bildung* and *Wissenschaft*. The mere idea of practical science clashed with the deep-seated conviction that the state should encourage learning for its own sake – or for the sake of developing citizens with patriotic rather than confessional loyalties; learning "vulgar" Arabic in order to do business in Syria or to command troops in Dar-es-Salaam was not *Bildung* in anyone's book. The conservative Berlin *Staatsbürger-Zeitung* thought breaking with the tradition of academic freedom in order to found a "drill academy" was "a fateful step."[67] Even worse, the University of Berlin faculties remained largely contemptuous of its supposed appendage institution; in the words of Otto Franke, the university's reaction to the founding of the SOS was that of "an honest woman, who had had a bastard put in her crib."[68]

Personnel issues, internal conflicts, and funding problems continued to dog both the SOS and HKI throughout the colonial era. Staffing the schools with the right sort of teachers was problematic. Even after the first years, it continued to be difficult to find individuals skilled in speaking modern languages who also could be respected as scholars, and the SOS and HKI frequently tried to steal each other's faculty. Eduard Sachau, whose specialty was Arabic translations of Greek prose and who had occupied a Berlin university chair since 1875, did not deal well with his underlings, and by 1889, the SOS was already characterized by rivalries among the faculty members and struggles over rank, some of these openly aired in front of students.[69] The bureaucratic entities who supported the SOS – including the postal service, the War Ministry, and the Foreign Office – all wanted different things from it, but no one wanted to pay for its expansion, least of all the Prussian

[64] Mangold, *Eine 'weltbürgerliche Wissenschaft,'* pp. 256–73, Hartmann quoted, pp. 252, 254.

[65] Kloosterhuis, '*Friedliche Imperialisten,*' pp. 421–2; Becker to Enno Littmann, July 9, 1913, Nachlass Becker, M. 4579. Becker had also tired of the provisional and unstable nature of the HKI.

[66] Worrell, "Schools for Living Oriental Languages," p. 194.

[67] Mangold, *Eine 'weltbürgerliche Wissenschaft,'* p. 235.

[68] Franke, *Erinnerungen,* p. 37.

[69] A. Arendt to Althoff, July 4, 1889, B-GSPK, Rep. 92, Althoff, AI, Nr. 109. Martin Hartmann, in particular, hated Sachau, whom he called "… that criminal (I can't call him anything else) who forces every ambitious [man] with talent to the wall, for fear of being overshadowed. My sin is only that I let Sachau force me to the wall!" Hartmann to Goldziher, June 30, 1906, in *Briefwechsel Goldziher/Hartmann,* p. 255.

Cultural Ministry, which feared expanded SOS programs would compete with those already offered by its universities. Private businessmen failed to develop enthusiasm for the school's offerings.[70] In Hamburg, there were conflicts between the professors, who wanted the respect and independence accorded to faculty members at other universities, and the Hamburg merchants, who had something more like a technical *Fachschule* in mind.[71] There were constant clashes between the two interest groups, especially as, after 1912, the faculty pressed for the transformation of the Kolonialinstitut into a proper university – something that would actually happen in 1919, when colonial training, of necessity, disappeared.

Nor did other colonial institutions quite live up to their grand plans for the thoroughgoing exploitation of the East and the orientalization of the German cultural market. Large sums of money were spent on the excavations of the DOG: Olaf Matthes estimates the contributions of its major patrons at 1.8 million Marks from Prussia, 415,000 Marks from the Kaiser, and 562,000 Marks from businessman James Simon.[72] But a goodly bit of this was spent on excavations in Asia Minor which brought home mostly Greek, rather than "oriental" artifacts. As for excavations elsewhere, the Tell el Amarna digs had to be stopped in 1913 when money ran out; Jericho and Hattusa were excavated chiefly with private funds supplied by Simon. Of course, excavations in Mesopotamia, not only at Babylon, but also at Assur, cost a great deal and turned up much-touted material. But as we will see in Chapter 9, Germany's museums were not very good at making room for "oriental" acquisitions; the Mschatta Gate, acquired in 1903, was housed in a dark basement, and the Ishtar Gate did not go on display until 1934. A few of Albert von Le Coq's Turfan murals were on view by 1913 (in the Ethnography Museum), but most of the Turfan finds remained in boxes long after their arrival in Berlin. There was no room in the Egyptian Museum for the major pieces of architecture acquired by Borchardt from Abusir (1907–8); in fact, they could not be displayed until the opening of Charlottenburg Egyptian museum in 1989.[73]

By 1914, then, a number of institutions and organizations had been founded to further German cultural and colonial penetration into the East; significant numbers of trainees had been produced and a large number of scholarly and artistic treasure brought home. Publishers had greatly expanded their "oriental" offerings, and museum exhibits had exposed viewers to more authentic Asian art than ever before (see Chapter 9). Some "modern" directions had been charted in the study of the East, and the state had begun to fund some "relevant" cultural projects. But, as we have seen, the success of these projects was mixed, and their rivals and critics remained powerful and outspoken.

In what follows, I turn to two of the major players in the study of *Islamforschung* and in the linking of orientalist scholarship to Germany's wider political ambitions. Though the two men profiled here, Martin Hartmann and Carl Becker, are relatively well known to those who study the history of *Orientalistik*, they are

---

[70] Burchardt, "School of Oriental Languages," pp. 84–93.
[71] Becker to Carl Bezold, July 8, 1909, in B-GSPK, Nachlass Becker, M. 6431.
[72] Matthes, *James Simon*, pp. 263, 344.
[73] Ibid., pp. 248, 251–2.

not much known outside this field and offer us the opportunity to come to grips with individual orientalists who did seek to put their knowledge to political use. We have come to know quite well the world their more theologically and philologically inclined colleagues inhabited; this is our opportunity, at last, to meet the colonizers.

MARTIN HARTMANN, ENLIGHTENED ARABIST

Martin Hartmann (1851–1919) considered himself a good friend of Ignaz Goldziher – and although he was not Jewish, Hartmann was, in his own way, just as marginal as was Goldziher or even more so, with respect to academia's pecking order. Carl Becker called him "a wild weed in the so well-ordered and properly-trimmed French garden of the Fleischer school;" no establishment man himself, Hugo Winckler described Hartmann as "a white raven," unique amongst the philologists in preferring the real-existing Orient to grammatical treatises.[74] What Hartmann and Goldziher had especially in common was the recognition that Islam was alive and well and indeed had a modern history worth studying. They differed, however, on whether or not Islamic modernity was a good thing; nor was Hartmann, to borrow a phrase from Max Weber, "religiously musical," as Goldziher most assuredly was. In a letter, Hartmann summed up, succinctly, what separated him from the much more Islamophilic Goldizher: ". . . it is that you try to save the most from tradition, while I am the sworn enemy of tradition . . ."[75] This would be true for his politics and for his scholarship, and would make Hartmann both a spokesman for progressive change, and a harsh critic of both orthodox Islam and of the German academic establishment.

What made Hartmann a "wild weed" was both his willingness to address in print the major political issues of the day and his resistance to the Turcophilic line taken by most contemporary *Islamforscher*. Perhaps Hartmann's divergence can be explained in part by his "real life" experience in the East; after intense philological training in Fleischer's seminar, he had been a tutor in Adrianople and then served as dragoman at the General Consulate in Beirut from 1875 until his appointment at the SOS in 1887. Beginning in 1879, he had taken a number of trips around greater Syria with the military mapmaker Heinrich Kiepert.[76] These expeditions laid the foundations for his interests not only in *Realien*, but also in Ottoman domestic politics. By 1899, he had sufficient knowledge of Arab cultural history to publish (in English) *The Arabic Press of Egypt*; the subject, Carl Becker noted, gave Hartmann keen insight into the reaction of the Orient to the intrusion of the "frankish" thought-world – an elliptical way of saying that Hartmann had learned much from Arab nationalists. Before Hartmann, Becker claimed, no one

---

[74] Becker, "Martin Hartmann," in idem, *Islamstudien* 2: 481; Hugo Winckler, review of Hartmann, *Der islamische Orient*, vol. 3 (1910), in *OLZ* 13 (1910): 363. For the best treatment of Hartmann, see Martin Kramer, "Arabistik and Arabism: The Passions of Martin Hartmann," in *Middle Eastern Studies* 25, no. 3 (1989): 283–300.

[75] Hartmann to Goldziher, May 17, 1900, in *Briefwechsel Goldziher/Hartmann*, p. 155.

[76] Ludmila Hanisch, ed., *Islamkunde und Islamwissenschaft im Deutschen Kaiserreich: Der Briefwechsel zwischen Carl Heinrich Becker und Martin Hartmann (1900–1918)* (Leiden, 1992), pp. 15–18.

had dared take up this vastly important subject, for fear of lacking sufficient historical distance to judge it – and perhaps because their political sympathies lay elsewhere. "But Martin Hartmann had the courage to swim against this current . . . thank God, others have followed in his wake, but he deserves the credit." Not that Hartmann's contemporaries had given him any, as Becker added wryly: "Under prevailing conditions, naturally, he never made it onto a German faculty's short list."[77]

Hartmann was to remain, from 1887 forward, a professor of Arabic at the SOS, a job far below his ambitions and even, at least in the view of many of the "modernists," below the position his talents merited. He had very few students – and discouraged those who did try to study with him by treating them badly and making extraordinary demands on them.[78] During his years at the SOS, he proved remarkably prolific, writing – like any good "furious" orientalist – chiefly for well-educated but not specialist audiences. He traveled frequently – much more than did the others in this chapter – making his way even to Turkestan in 1902–3. He learned Chinese and Russian in order to better understand Islamic culture's evolution in these non-Arabic speaking domains, and he took a keen interest in Islamic archaeology. He sometimes described his method as "sociology," but admitted he did not read the specialized sociological literature. His colleagues, Becker wrote, raged about him or laughed at him according to their own temperaments; but if they wanted to know something about the modern Islamic world, they had to read his work: "In Germany, Martin Hartmann was the first, and for a long time the only one, who directed his studies to the forms of the state, the political battles, [and] the cultural condition of the modern Orient, and [who] attempted to raise the study [of these subjects] in the field of contemporary history out of the domain of pure journalism into the higher realm of scholarly investigations."[79]

Though Hartmann's father was a Mennonite preacher, he seems to have had no background in Old Testament exegesis or any apparent affection for Christianity; Becker remarked on his "hatred of the church and of Popery."[80] Among his other passions was an antipathy to Islam and a desire to free the peoples of the Ottoman Empire and Africa from its culture-killing yoke. Unquestionably, Hartmann hated Islam and hoped Europeans would eradicate it (at least in Africa) by the year 2000.[81] Though Islam might once have been a noble religion, he argued, in the present it simply produced a culture of barbarism and intolerance, one that cut its followers off from the highest goods of humankind; he could not believe, he told Goldziher in 1911, that "ethical progress and advancement on the basis of

---

[77] Becker, "Martin Hartmann," pp. 485–6.
[78] Hartmann's student Schabinger von Schowingen described how he dragged on his apprenticeship, scheduled lectures (in which he was the only student) in the early morning hours, and threw tantrums over small misreadings. Schabinger, *Weltgeschichtliche Mosaiksplitter: Erlebnisse und Erinnerungen e. kaiserlich. Dragomans* (Baden-Baden, 1967), pp. 7–8.
[79] Becker, "Martin Hartmann," pp. 484–9, quotation p. 484.
[80] Ibid., p. 490.
[81] Martin Hartmann, "Der Islam in Westafrika," in *OLZ* 3 (1900): 164.

indigenous tradition" was anything but a "beautiful dream."[82] Islam needed to be
rooted out and replaced not by Christianity (though that would be in his view an
improvement) but by European secular culture and capitalism.

Indeed, Hartmann is almost a caricature of the sort of Eurocentrism practiced by
the Enlightenment's heirs. He did not approve of Ottoman "absolutism," especially
as the Sultan's corruption and inability to rule made the imposition of work
discipline impossible. He did not like clerical interference in cultural matters,
whether the issue was European missionization or the tyranny of Islamic law. He
criticized both westerners and Islamic writers who defended the closeting of women,
though he admitted that women's liberation created social disruptions and could
well introduce western immorality into the East.[83] "The worst thing is that he
[Muhammed] has been falsely taken to be a 'prophet' instead of seeing him simply
as a poet!" he exclaimed, making the same move toward desacralization de
Wette had made for Old Testament figures and Renan had made for Jesus.[84] But
we should also attend to the remark that follows this exclamation: "What suffering
has this error brought the world, and still threatens it!" Though Hartmann's view of
world history was suffused with condescension and prejudice, he did harbor a real
desire to liberate the East from what he saw as the tyranny of the theocratic old
regime.[85]

Central to this liberation, for Hartmann, was secularization [*Entkirchlichung*]
and work discipline. The former directive, spelled out first by C. H. Becker,
amounted to what one might call *Kulturprotestantismus* for Muslims – that is,
the making over of Islam into mere cultural glue, its detachment from centralized
institutions and hierarchies, and, crucially, the secularization of the educational
system. Islam did not have to disappear as a system of belief, but it did need to
subordinate itself to European ideas and practices. Hartmann refuted the arguments of cultural pessimists, who tried to terrify their fellow Europeans by ranting
about the evils of over-civilization; ". . . we know very well," he insisted, "that the
culture-less people suffer physically and morally from far worse maladies than do
the cultured peoples."[86] Similarly, Hartmann advocated work discipline as the
means toward economic development and individuation, certain that this was the
key to happiness in both East and West. He was a champion of the "Dernburg
Turn" in colonial policy, not only because milder regimes seemed less likely to foster
violent opposition from the colonized, but also because he abhorred "the perception, that the white [race] has the right to exploit and mishandle the black [race]."[87]
Europe would benefit from colonization, he hoped, but it would cost not millions,
but billions, to accomplish the grand goal: "The filling of hearts and minds with

---

[82] Martin Hartmann to Goldziher, July 25, 1911, in *Briefwechsel Goldziher/Hartmann*, pp. 385–6.

[83] Martin Hartmann, *Die Frau im Islam* (lecture, March 3, 1909) (Halle, 1909), pp. 15–31.

[84] Martin Hartmann to Goldziher, August 29, 1906, in *Briefwechsel Goldziher/Hartmann*, p. 261.

[85] Colonizers had to ask themselves a critical moral question: "Should the indigenous people always
remain the subservient ones (*Höriger*), or not?" Martin Hartmann, "Mission und Kolonialpolitik,"
in *Kolonial Rundschau* 3 (1911): 194.

[86] Ibid., p. 188, n. 1.

[87] Ibid., p. 173.

Frankish [viz., European] ideas such as the saving power of work, the liberation from tradition and the struggle against the ever-renewed attempts to force the people as a whole into political and spiritual subservience to a small group (the court, the church, the bureaucracy), or to a combination of such groups."[88]

Why Europe would and should pay this price was, in his view, a matter of self-interest – but he cast self-interest in quite a different way than did the Hamburg and Berlin business elite who frequented his lectures. As he explained to Goldziher: "The Orient, as it now is, is the most dangerous reserve army for all backward elements in Europe, for all those who, here at home, want to beat a return to the Middle Ages with its 'nobles' and its 'serfs' and its linking of the throne and altar to enslave the people. The Orient, as it is now, is an inexhaustible storehouse of valet-souls and hangmen's apprentices..."[89] Hartmann seems really to have believed, as he told Munich's Oriental Society in 1909, that Europe was leaving the era of pure nationalism behind and straining toward a new age in which the nations "opt to forge themselves together into one higher [entity]."[90] He did not want reaction in the East to reverse progress toward this colonial version of Kantian perpetual peace.

Unlike most of the other professional orientalists of his day – generally a conservative, tradition-loving bunch – Hartmann detested the Ottoman Turks, young and old; they were liars, he said, exceeded only by the Russians. Like Goldziher, he had learned to sympathize with Arab modernizers during his visits to Syria and Egypt.[91] Before 1914, Hartmann regularly referred to the "terror-regiments of Abdul Hamid," whose regime, in Hartmann's view, was characterized by a corrupt and irresponsible central bureaucracy and a tendency to think force was the only way to create development. He was one of the first Europeans to argue (in 1905) that the Ottomans had lost the support of their Arab subjects; though he also realized that the Arabs were not organized enough to achieve liberation without the help of a foreign power.[92] By 1913, he had despaired of the reforms undertaken by the Committee of Union and Progress (CUP); the Young Turks, like the old, used force instead of reason, had no interest in or intention of improving the standard of living for their people, and worst of all were pursuing a bloody and counter-productive policy of Turkification. Perhaps worst for Hartmann was that despite its European-liberal leanings, the CUP too had failed to destroy the Caliphate or to break the power of Islam, a religion that preached destruction of non-believers and offered no incentives for hard work on earth. All of this fits together in a certain way; what Hartmann thought he was advocating for the eastern Mediterranean was "raising of the standard of living (in the broadest sense, spiritually as well) of the oriental population."[93] He was not

---

[88] Martin Hartmann, "Deutschland und der Islam," in *Der Islam* 1 (1910): 91–2.

[89] Martin Hartmann to Goldziher, *Briefwechsel Goldziher/Hartmann*, August 11, 1899, p. 126.

[90] Martin Hartmann, *Die Frau im Islam* (lecture, March 3, 1909, for the Munich Orientalische Gesellschaft) (Halle, 1909), p. 32.

[91] Becker, "Martin Hartmann," p. 488. Becker claimed that Hartmann's wartime conversion to Turkish friendship was also the product of a real change in his emotions.

[92] Kramer, "Arabistik and Arabism," pp. 290–1.

[93] All of these ideas can be found diffused through Hartmann's publications, and condensed in the introduction to his *Reisebriefe aus Syrien* (Berlin, 1913). Quotation in ibid., p. xxiv.

interested in promoting Islamic culture, but in giving the Ottoman Empire's minority groups – and especially the Arabs – a jumpstart along the road to a secular, liberal-capitalist future.

Hartmann was not really typical of the younger generation of scholars, among whom there were many whose views of Islam were rather less harsh. Some, like the young Arabist Traugott Mann (b. 1881) in Berlin, regularly reminded their still ill-informed and prejudiced readers that Christians – perpetrator of the Inquisition and long-time persecutor of the Jews – had no business scapegoating Muslims for having declared holy wars. The "Aryans," he continued, had no right to denounce the "Semites" (Mann was one of the few in his day to use these terms in scare quotes) for sensuousness; most Arab pornography was of "Aryan" origin and in any event was much more chaste than the efforts of the "master race" in this area. Mann believed in "Islam's capacity for development" – as long as modernization did not mean the wholesale replacement of Muslim mores and practices by "our essentially foreign culture" but rather a "an indigenously-based, self-designed culture... but for that," he wrote, "we can only supply the inspiration, and not in any way the forms in which it is implemented."[94] Hartmann found this tepid support for modernization frustrating and raged against both younger scholars who did not want to get their hands dirty and the old philological "big wigs," who were contributing nothing to educating their contemporaries about the real-existing Arabic world.

A means to rectify the situation, Hartmann proposed in 1898, was to found a scholarly institute in the Orient. Here, a new generation of Arabic teachers could learn the Orient from their own *Anschauung*, and link their teaching more closely to "life" and to practical politics. Moreover, not all Arabs were ignorant, and one might learn something from a few of the educated ones. Local labor was cheap and might be used in "highly successful collecting operations."[95] Such an institute was never founded, and in 1913, Hartmann was still lamenting the poor training possessed by most German officials in the Ottoman Empire and demanding that those stationed in minority areas, such as the Arab lands, learn to speak the indigenous language as well as Turkish. Even German capitalists, he complained, did not really understand the Ottoman economy and the promise it held for riches, if only a sensible agrarian policy could be pursued.[96] Germany's exploitation of its opportunities was still in future – though we know, as Hartmann could not have done, that in 1913, there was very little time left on that particular clock.

Hartmann neither had powerful friends in academia nor advocates in the state bureaucracies, and his plans – regardless of their "relevance" – fell on deaf ears. His arguments for the importance of understanding the contemporary world did not seem to have had much impact; though his work did help to entice our next subject, Carl Heinrich Becker, into the fray. Becker, who made his career at almost

---

[94] Traugott Mann, review of Carra de Vaux, *La Doctrine de l'Islam* (1909), in *OLZ* 12 (1909): 504. Mann expressed similar concerns in a review of Hartmann's *Islam, Mission, Politik* (1912), in *OLZ* 16 (1913): 467–9.

[95] Hartmann, "Die Arabistik – Reformvorschläge," in *OLZ* 1 (1898): 333–42, quotation p. 341.

[96] Hartmann, *Reisebriefe*, pp. xiv–v, xxiii.

precisely the same time as Hartmann,[97] would prove much more influential – politically, indeed, he was probably modern Germany's most influential academic orientalist – perhaps because he advocated ideas and policies that did not aim to eradicate Islam, but to put it to European use.

CARL BECKER: COLONIALISM AND *KULTURGESCHICHTE*

Surely much of Becker's originality owes to his rather unusual (for a German orientalist) background; he was born not in Saxony or the Baltic region but in Amsterdam and was the son not of a clergyman but of a liberal, Protestant, and wealthy Frankfurt banker. He began his studies not in Tübingen or Leipzig, but in Lausanne, proceeding in 1896 to Heidelberg, Friedrich Creuzer's old stomping grounds. Here he studied Old Testament criticism (he had already read Wellhausen) and was introduced to the new *Religionsgeschichte* by Hermann Usener and his son-in-law Albrecht Dieterich.[98] Having transferred to the philosophical faculty, he studied Assyriology with the non-"furious" Carl Bezold, then Arabic with the Fleischer-Nöldeke student Jacob Barth in Berlin, where he also met Martin Hartmann. Up to this point, he later claimed, he had heard nothing about the post-Qur'anic Orient: "In the opinion of the schoolmasters, modern Islam was 'petrified' and scientifically uninteresting. Added to that was philology's disapproval of all sociological and modern-historical studies. Politically, the scholars were entirely uninterested in domestic problems, and the germinating new life even of their own nation remained, to the philologists, and even the historians, foreign." But Hartmann, who was beginning to publish the first installations of his *Islamische Orient* (1899) just at this time, offered Becker "a new world," which Becker, at least in part, embraced. It was only later that the younger man recognized the "dark side" of Hartmann's work, its deep prejudices and also the disapprobation for it among the great scholars Becker admired and wanted to please.[99]

Eager to explore Hartmann's new world, Becker wrote a doctorate, for Bezold, on a manuscript of Ibn Jawzi about Caliph Omar II and then spent some time learning spoken Arabic and Persian at the SOS; he left Europe for Egypt in August 1900, returning via Istanbul in April 1901; that December, he made another trip to Egypt, Syria, and Palestine, returning in 1902 to habilitate in oriental philology at the University of Heidelberg. It is noteworthy that Becker, owing to his family's wealth, could travel in the Orient without working as a tutor, diplomat, or journalist, as so many other German orientalists had done to finance their travels. And it is also worth noting that Becker's studies to this point were "modern" only by virtue of being focused on the post-Hellenistic world. Though he wrote a 1904 essay on the subject of "Pan-Islamism" (for, notably, Dieterich's *Archiv*

---

[97] Born in 1876, Becker was a quarter-century younger than Hartmann, but Hartmann's late start, and Becker's early death, at 56, in February 1933, made their careers almost exactly contemporaraneous.

[98] These two men played an important part in the disciplinary re-convergence described in Chapter 5, and in this chapter, and in making acceptable a broader range of cultural history topics. See also Marchand, "From Liberalism to Neoromanticism," pp. 129–60.

[99] Carl Becker, "Martin Hartmann," p. 484.

für Religionswissenschaft), his publications up to about 1907 focused on Egypt in the early period of Islamic history. Becker had strayed a bit from the well-worn paths of Semitic philology, but not very far.

But during his years at Heidelberg, especially after his appointment as assistant professor in 1906, Becker interested himself in broader themes and more "relevant" questions. This was undoubtedly the result of his relationships with a circle that included Max Weber, Ernst Troeltsch, Wilhelm Windelband, and Eberhard Gothein. This intense world, where neo-Kantian philosophy met sociology of religion and where evolutionary and materialist development was being rigorously tested against the findings of historicist-philological scholarship, surely shaped Becker's understanding of Islamic history. Perhaps, too, its intense interest in social theory and the commitment of many of its personalities (including Weber) to engaging in the social and political issues of the day gave Becker the confidence to work in different ways than most of his predecessors and contemporaries. Of course, some inspiration came to him from his own generation of "furious" orientalists, from Winckler, Strzygowski, and Georg Jacob, though both in temperament and in his generally positive view of the Reich's institutions he was closer to the older "liberals," Wellhausen, Meyer, and Nöldeke.[100] In any event, by about 1908, Becker was becoming, as Alexander Haridi has pointed out, not really an old style "orientalist," but already as quite a young man something more of a philosopher of history.[101] Rejecting philological positivism, Becker, both for political and intellectual reasons, now wanted to work on a larger canvas and have a broader impact than his teachers – a set of ambitions that also made him much more suited to colonial propagandizing than his philological brethren.

Becker's greatest mission as an orientalist – one he thought more important than his contribution to the imperial cause – was to make Islam part of world history. It was, he said repeatedly, the "central link," the "mediator," linking East and West, and should not be excluded from the history of the Christian *Abendland*. And it was a living tradition that could claim millions upon millions of adherents; one could not simply consider it a false faith or a medieval survival on its way to sure extinction. European Christians needed to come to grips with it and to recognize the ways in which Islamic history was entangled with their own. These ideas run through his work and lay behind the journal he founded, *Der Islam*, which was not primarily envisioned as a political or policy-oriented journal, but as one designed to promote the historical study of the Islamic world and to make that history accessible to educated, but non-orientalist readers.

---

[100] While he endorsed the articulation of new and daring ideas, he distanced himself from the more outlandish theses of his contemporaries; he publicly called Panbabylonism "eine Kinderkrankenheit," and refuted Leo Frobenius's theory that the descendants of the island of Atlantis had settled in Yorubaland. Becker, "Der vordere Orient und Afrika," in B-GSPK, Nachlass Becker, M. 6813, p. 1186; idem, "Leo Frobenius und die Brille des Islam," in idem, *Islamstudien* 2: 45–62. His moderate views might have been, in part, the result of his academic success; unlike Winckler and Hartmann, he did not have to wait long for academic appointments, or suffer condescending critiques from his "betters."

[101] Alexander Haridi, *Das Paradigma der 'islamischen Zivilisation', oder die Begründung der deutschen Islamwissenschaft durch Carl Heinrich Becker (1876–1933)* (Würzburg, 2005), pp. 16–17.

Becker thought of himself as an *Islamforscher* rather than a Semitic philologist, theologian, or even cultural historian, and indeed Islam – as religion, as political idea, and as cultural formation – lies at the heart of his work. To understand its complexities, he believed, one had to abandon *Orientalistik*'s traditional philological approach, in part because it presumed that "Asia" could be reduced to a set of participle forms, but also because it was essentializing and primitivizing (though he did not use those terms) rather than historical. Moreover, the philologists' way of writing history led to the misapprehension that because Islam's oldest literary texts were in Arabic, the civilization itself was Arabic. It was not, he argued; it was *vorderasiatisch* (early on) and in the present, also African.[102] Nor, however, could Becker countenance a pure "religious-historical" interpretation of Islam. To think that reading the Qur'an was the key to understanding modern Islam, he argued, was equivalent to believing one could understand today's Catholic peasants by reading the Vulgate.[103] Nor, finally, were narrow national or ethnic histories what his generation needed or desired. Though he greatly respected Wellhausen's *Das arabische Reich*, he distanced himself from the positivist generation of those who silently rejected "intellectually-productive speculations about connections between neighboring cultures," because they, like Wellhausen, "did not feel at home in the areas brought into the comparison."[104] The method of *Islamforschung* had to escape the limitations imposed by the sciences of the previous generation; it had to produce synthetic and useful, not philologically fragmented and culture-isolating, histories.

Becker began rethinking Islamic cultural history by making the now-typical, liberal, move to "normalize" Islam, making it a civilization with a history rather than simply a religion based on one, false, book. Where Becker made a more innovative, and in our terms, a rather "furious" move, however, was in his analysis of the foundations of Islam. For him, these lay in the syncretic culture of the Hellenistic world, not in the language and ideas of the Qur'an. Islam represented the "orientalizing of Christian Hellenism" or in the words of his oft-quoted motto: "Without Alexander the Great, no Islamic civilization!"[105] This was to take Droysen farther forward and eastward than the great historian of Hellenism would have gone, but Becker's emphasis on the formative power of late Greek culture was recognizably Droysenesque. We could, perhaps, easily dismiss such a view as still too Hellenocentric – as indeed Strzygowski delighted in doing. But it should be noted that at the same time Becker was integrating Islam into European as well as world history, he was, in effect, also "orientalizing" western cultural history. Both cultures, he insisted, were rooted in the Hellenistic world and were made up of essentially the same components: "1) the ancient Orient, especially with respect to Semitic prophesizing, Jewish religious law, Persian dualism and eschatology, Babylonian-Magian conceptions of the world and bureaucratic-absolutist forms of the states; 2) classical antiquity in the form of Hellenism,

---

[102] Becker quoted in Mangold, *Eine 'weltbürgerliche Wissenschaft,'* p. 254; Becker, "Der Islam als Problem," in *Der Islam* 1 (1910): 13–14.
[103] Becker, "Ist Islam eine Gefahr für unsere Kolonien?" in idem, *Islamstudien* 2: 158.
[104] Becker, "Julius Wellhausen," in *Der Islam* 9 (1919): 98.
[105] Formulated already in Becker, "Der Islam als Problem" [1910], p. 15.

especially in daily life, in science, and in art, 3) Christianity, in its dogmatic, cultic and mystical form."[106] In fact, according to Becker, throughout the Middle Ages, Islam and Christianity had been joint (and equally deserving) heirs and had continued to exchange ideas on the basis of a "relationship based on cultural foundations." This historical-cultural relationship, he explained in a famous 1922 response to a characterization of the western tradition (without Islam) by his friend Ernst Troeltsch, is stronger than any supposed "Indo-Aryan-European relationship" and the key to understanding both the Near East and West – down at least to the time of Dante.[107]

If one accepted Becker's view of Islamic cultural history as "Asiaticized Hellenism," the next question to ask was, why then did the Islamic world of, say, 1910, look so different than that of contemporary Europe? Becker's answer was simple: the divergence of the two spheres was the product not of the West's sole ownership of the classical tradition nor of the East's conversion to Islam, but of the Renaissance, the self-conscious revival of the classics that took place in the West alone. "*The great divergence in the experience of the West is the phenomenon of humanism,*" he wrote, in italics, in 1922: "In the West antiquity did not only live on as it did in Islam; no, [in the West] it was reborn."[108] One can certainly see this as re-importing western hubris, but we should also recall that the payoff, for Becker, in conceiving Islam this way was that it demolished the conventional view that Muslim and European cultures were completely dissimilar and unable to communicate. Representing the two sides of a single cultural circle, the break between them was, in his view, relatively recent and susceptible to being healed.[109] Becker's theory also meant to give hope to Ottoman modernizers that Islam could adapt to modern times and not become wholly European. He had numerous occasions to apply and extend his ideas in essays endorsing the Kaiser's policy of increasing German-Turkish "friendship," both before and during the Great War. Indeed, after September 1914, he found he could do no other. In the chapter to follow, we will see how hazardous Becker's Turkophilia proved, in the end, to be.

Becker's historical work offered hope for a conversation between Germans and well-educated Turkish modernizers. But he was also an ambitious man, eager to play a role in extending German cultural and economic, if not political, power abroad. Particularly after his Hamburg appointment, he took an aggressively nationalist line, becoming increasingly impatient with what he saw as Foreign Office foot-dragging in the competition for global economic and cultural influence. In a 1910 letter to Ernst Herzfeld, he objected vociferously to the faint-heartedness of German politicians and diplomats who regarded any sort of friction as tantamount to "the terrors of Hell. I am certainly no Pan-German," he continued, "but I believe German expansion, not only in matters of trade, but also in the form of cultural stations like missions and schools, is a simple necessity of

---

[106] Becker, "Der Islam im Rahmen einer allgemeine Kulturgeschichte," in *Zeitschrift der Deutschen Morgenländischen Gesellschaft* 76, no. 1 (1922): 23.

[107] Ibid., p. 22.

[108] Ibid., pp. 29, 30.

[109] Mark Batunsky, "Carl Heinrich Becker: From Old to Modern Islamology," in *International Journal of Middle East Studies* 13 (1981): 297.

Germany's position in the world. How did England, France, and Russia achieve their predominance in Asia? Do we want, for all eternity, to deprive those who come after us, and remain, with our 75 millions, quietly inside our narrow Fatherland, just because here and there diplomatic difficulties could arise?"[110] He knew, however, that to have influence in Asia, Germans needed to better understand the current state of the Islamic world where, *pace* Hartmann, economic progress and technological modernization was happening, As early as 1904, in fact, he had argued that the movement coming to be known as Pan-Islamism was the product of the expansion of European power and of European technologies like the telegraph, press, and the post, as well as a reaction, fostered by the Sultan to the crumbling of the Ottoman Empire.[111] The Reich needed to understand how to tame these processes if it was to succeed in its quest for world power.

Since at least the time of his habilitation, Becker had high hopes that his work might be "relevant" to contemporary political concerns; but it was the events of 1905–9 that really made Islam – and Becker's expertise – interesting to a wide array of readers. Becker was not alone among Europeans in beginning to fear that the power of Islam was waxing, not waning, in response to European inroads. Though neither the Herero revolt nor the Maji Maji uprising (1905–7) was thought to owe much to Islamic convictions or instigation, it was widely feared that malcontents might turn in this direction for assistance against the Europeans. The Balkans, of course, and especially Serbia, seemed in the thrall of Russian-backed Pan-Slavism; but there were also Bosnian Muslims to worry about, and the Sultan, despite having his power severely curtailed by the 1908 Young Turk Revolution, was trying to turn his own Pan-Islamic trick. Not only did Abdul Hamid vigorously assert his claim to the title of Caliph (a claim Wilhelm II himself approved and encouraged), he also insisted on getting a rail-link to Mecca and Medina out of the *Bagdadbahn* project. Western complaints about the persecution of Christians in the Ottoman Empire had been on the rise since the 1890s. The increasingly bruited "danger of Islam" was a subject Becker felt supremely suited to comment on – and one that brought his essays to the attention of a wide, and politically influential, public.

Becker's colonial essays lay out clear racial and religious hierarchies; just as black Africans were inferior to "orientals," and "orientals" to white men, paganism was ranked below Islam, and Islam below Christianity. Interestingly, however, this ranking made Islam potentially quite useful to European colonizers in Africa – as long as it could be tamed and if it could be prevented from taking over the whole continent. In a 1910 address to the Union Coloniale Française (also published in German), Becker addressed himself once more to the "facts," rather than to the ideals, with which colonialism had to contend. In his view, Europeans simply had to come to grips with the reality that Islam had become a cultural, political, and economic force in Africa, and was not likely either to melt away with increased modernization and colonial penetration, or to be forced out by Christian missionization or state-backed persecution. The reason African pagans were

---

[110] Becker to Ernst Herzfeld, December 9, 1910, B-GSPK, Nachlass Becker, M. 4023.
[111] Becker, "Panislamismus," in *Archiv für Religionswissenschaft* 7 (1904): 169–92, quotation p. 192.

converting to Islam and not Christianity, Becker argued, was not only that it gave them tools to counter the further spread of European power, but that Islam was closer to "the natural forms of black thought"; "Islam brings a new and more elevated sensibility to the traditional practices of the blacks; Christianity wants to change the laws of their thought."[112] It had spread rapidly through Africa, more quickly in fact where Europeanization had laid foundations for it by increasing trade and travel and by spreading literacy and the press. "Islam is also a great threat to the spread of Christianity, but the state can do nothing to change that"; and indeed, Becker was very much in favor of a religiously-neutral policy administered by the state, fearing that missionary activity was turning Africans against the colonial states.[113] The point was not to eradicate Islam, but to defang it, something best done indirectly, by Europeanizing it; practically speaking, methods for this defanging might include the creation of "islands of Christianity" to foster internal disunity, the suppression of "fanatics," and the co-opting of educated and wealthy Islamic interests.[114] In the long term, one could use Islam to complete the "evolution" (*Entwicklung*) of inner Africa.

There is much more to Becker's work and career that might be discussed; in Chapter 10, we will treat his involvement in the cultural politics of the Ottoman alliance and the Great War. We can, however, offer a few conclusions. First of all, Becker, in insisting on a secular, historical approach, and in moving past the strictures of Semitic philology, was instrumental in laying the foundations for a new sort of Islamic *Kulturgeschichte*. By removing both positivistic objectivity and romantic origin-seeking from the study of Islamic history and by insisting on the need for comparative perspectives, he made possible a rich means of understanding East-West cultural interactions in the ancient and medieval worlds. Second, although trained to focus on the ancient Orient, he willingly embraced both the opportunities and the challenges of writing about the modern world. He was one of the few to truly appreciate the efforts of men like Hartmann, who risked being labeled "dilettantes" by those who preferred to avoid "actual" problems and keep their heads stuck safely in the sand.[115] But his essays, his letters, and the hectic pace of his life, before, during, and after the war, suggest the strain his commitments to "relevance" put on him. He was constantly called upon by politicians, bureaucrats, businessmen, and even some of his colleagues to present scholarship's "popular" and "actual" face – for the very good reason that he was one of the few men who was both respected in the scholarly world and able to comport himself outside of it (though of course he had many enemies there as well as critics within academia). When, during and after the Great War, he agreed to involve himself directly in politics, this for all intents and purposes put an end to his orientalist scholarship. He might have settled for a quiet life in the ivory towers of the

---

[112] Becker, "L'Islam et la colonization de l'Afrique," pp. 10, 11.

[113] Quotation in Becker, "Ist der Islam eine Gefahr," p. 182. On missionaries, Becker, "Staat und Mission in der Islamfrage" [1910], in idem, *Islamstudien* 2, pp. 215–18.

[114] Becker, "Ist der Islam eine Gefahr," p. 184; practical advice in idem, "L'Islam et la colonization de l'Afrique," p. 14.

[115] Becker, "Martin Hartmann," p. 485.

University of Bonn; but he wanted to be "useful" and he was, in ways that proved both progressive and reprehensible.

Finally, Becker embroiled himself, deeply and willingly, in the colonial politics of the Reich and endorsed the conquest and exploitation of Africa; but he never seems to have thought himself a partisan politician. He openly championed German colonization and Germany's pursuit of her own interests, "which happily are identical with the true advantage of the colonies, in the long run..."[116] This was, of course, self-serving propaganda. But he, like most of his orientalist colleagues, did not believe himself compromising science in serving the state; the way they saw things, as Ludmila Hanisch has argued, "one distilled 'pure knowledge' in the study and then put it at the state's disposal."[117] Indeed, Becker was terribly upset when in 1914 his Dutch friend Christian Snouck Hurgronje refused to side with the Germans and accused them of practicing politicized science. This was, indeed, rather rich, coming from a man who had been an official in the Dutch colonial service in Aceh for seventeen years; but Becker's heartfelt anger and dismay at being told that German science (and his own scholarship) was not interest-free suggests just how difficult it was for him to reconcile his own ambitions.[118] Making oneself both useful and "scientific" remained difficult for those trained in the philological-historical tradition, no matter how much they departed from it. And it would be just as complicated for those who specialized in the study of an area even more distant from the humanist academy's predilections: East Asia.

EAST ASIA'S PLACE IN THE SUN

The study of East Asian languages, history, art, and literature was one of the few fields of *Orientalistik* in which the Germans, it was universally agreed, lagged behind the other Europeans. There are, I think, a number of reasons for this: the predominance early on of Jesuits in the collection of Chinese materials (among whom there were Germans, but not many); the strong association of China with Baroque culture and enlightened ideas, rather than romantic ones; and the fact that the Chinese had a living tradition of historiography, one that could not easily be replaced by philological-historical criticism. There was no fully dead culture or body of undeciphered texts from which to conjure a great past. Most crucial, however, was the irrelevance of Japanese and Chinese to the interpretation of the Old Testament and to the history of classical antiquity, which placed the study of the Far East outside the perimeter defined by the humanist tradition. All of this meant that what nineteenth-century German scholars did best, the Lachmannian recreation of early texts, was not, in East Asian studies, a very meaningful or consequential enterprise; and though there were quite a number of autodidacts or French-trained orientalists who knew some Chinese and several German

---

[116] Becker, "Staat und Mission," p. 215.
[117] Ludmila Hanisch, "Gelehrtenselbstverständnis, wissenschaftliche Rationalität und politische 'Emotionen'," in *Die Welt des Islams* 32 (1992): 113.
[118] Ibid., pp. 115–22; Becker's letters of 1914–15 return quite obsessively to Snouck's position (and essay on the question); see Chapter 10.

doctors who returned from Japan with artifacts and ethnographic materials, there was not much incentive for making East Asia a speciality; and as a handful of risk-takers found out, few rewards for those who did.

There had, of course, been a period of eighteenth-century Sinophilia, typified by Frederick the Great's Sanssouci teahouse. But more than any other nonwestern culture, China fell out of fashion sometime after the 1760s – losing out, above all, to Greece on the one hand and India on the other. Hegel and his contemporaries thought the Qing Empire hopelessly immobile and despotic; in 1848, the high liberal *Staatslexikon* repeated the refrain: "China has no history, at least none in the commonly understood sense," a sentiment Ranke would reiterate again in 1881 in volume 1 of his *Weltgeschichte*.[119] Marx, of course, thought it the epitome of "oriental despotism." As in Indology, there was a counter-tradition available, one that drew on both the enlightened, rationalist praise of China's non-religious ethics and meritocratic bureaucracy and the Jesuit tradition of "ancient theology," revived in volume one of Karl Joseph Windischmann's *Die Grundlagen der Philosophie im Morgenland* in 1827.[120] But the tradition's rationalism and the barriers dividing both Semitic and Indo-European *ur*-languages from East Asian ones offered few footholds for romantic, esoteric theorizing and made thinking *à la chine* more difficult for German Christians who simply wanted to stretch traditional conceptions of religion or ancestry. Then too, China had not been formally colonized and thus could not be pitied as a means of criticizing other European nations. When Japan was "opened," its small size and sudden eagerness to adopt western ideas made it, at most, an object of condescension – until the Russo-Japanese War necessitated according it more respect. Seen as more foreign than the Near East and South Asia, China and Japan would only appeal to Germans for whom classical aesthetics, Christian orthodoxy, and traditional humanistic institutions had been fully discredited.

Is it accidental that three of Germandom's early Sinological specialists did jail time for political liberalism? Perhaps this was the inevitable outcome of a tradition rooted in Leibniz's universalism and Athanasius Kircher's iconoclasm. The first, early victim was Andreas Müller, the provost at Berlin's *Nikolaikirche* and inventor in 1667 of a key to the secrets of Chinese pictographs. Trained in Near Eastern languages, Müller never published his key; the Great Elector did not, in his view, offer him enough recompense. But he did, to his cost, publish a disquisition claiming that the solar eclipse of the original Good Friday could be reconciled with one recorded in Chinese annals. For this and for other attempts to reconcile Christian and Chinese traditions (as against claims of the more orthodox that Chinese picture-writing was the work of the devil), Müller was accused of heresy and imprisoned at Spandau.[121] The other two scholars in question were not heretics, but liberal partisans of the 1830 revolutions. Heinrich Kurz (1805–1873) learned

---

[119] Quoted in Thomas Fuchs, "Das Chinabild im frühneuzeitlichen Europa," in *Berliner China-Hefte* 17 (1999): 52.

[120] Mechthild Leutner, "Weltanschauung – Wissenschaft – Gesellschaft: Überlegungen zu einer kritischen Sinologie," in *Berliner China-Hefte* 14 (1998): 5.

[121] Donald Lach, "The Chinese Studies of Andreas Müller," in *Journal of the American Oriental Society* 60, no. 4 (1940): 564–75.

his Chinese in Paris and then taught briefly at the University of Munich before being locked up in 1832 as a result of his editorship of a liberal weekly; when he got out two years later, he moved to Switzerland, where he focused almost exclusively on the history of German literature.[122] Kurz's contemporary, Johann Heinrich Plath (1802–1874), who had habilitated in classical philology at the University of Göttingen in 1829, was sentenced to a twelve-year term for his participation in political unrest in 1831. Though he actually served only seven years, this experience ruined him financially and damaged his health, not to mention dooming his short-term career prospects. The 1848 revolutions changed the picture somewhat, and Plath – who continued, despite his hardships, his autodidactic pursuit of Chinese studies – was made state librarian in Frankfurt. When the revolutionary moment passed, he moved to Munich and must have become an upstanding citizen, as in 1860 he was elected a member of the Bavarian Academy of Sciences.[123] But he was still something of an iconoclast; against conventional bourgeois presumptions, Plath continue to insist that China possessed a self-sufficient religion which, though unrelated to Christianity, could compare with it in the loftiness of its ethical precepts.[124]

Philipp Freiherr von Siebold had his political troubles on the other end, namely with the Japanese government. This Würzburg doctor ventured to Japan in the employ of the Dutch colonial army in 1824 and was stationed in Nagasaki for six years. During that time, his remarkable healing skills won him access to Japanese officialdom and he befriended a number of Japanese intellectuals. Unfortunately, especially for the latter, in 1830 one of Siebold's interlocutors was accused of sharing cartographic information about Japan with Europeans. An investigation began and much of the material Siebold and his friends had collected was confiscated and a number of his friends were executed. Only the exertions of the Dutch representative commuted Siebold's sentence into permanent banishment. Interestingly, when he was allowed to return home to Japan in 1859 – still in Dutch military service – he found former students and curious intellectuals eager for contact with Europeans and information about European science. His Dutch superiors, however, were anxious about rising anti-foreigner sentiment and forced him to return to Europe in 1861.[125] This vignette should remind us that Europeans could not travel, collect, and inter-relate freely with East Asians for much of the nineteenth century; those who tried often undertook considerable personal risks – though their risks would be considerably less than those of their indigenous friends.

Siebold never held a professorial post. Though he published a great deal, Plath never taught formally at the University of Munich; but then again, neither did most of Germany's East Asian specialists actually hold regular academic posts. Julius Klaproth, though professor at the University of Berlin, spent his time in

---

[122] Christina Leibfried, *Sinologie an der Universität Leipzig*, p. 12; Hermann Franke, *Entwicklung*, pp. 9–10.

[123] Hermann Franke, *Entwicklung*, p. 10

[124] Mechthild Leutner, "Weltanschauung – Wissenschaft – Gesellschaft," p. 6.

[125] Felix Schottlaender, *Erwin von Baelz (1849–1914): Leben und Wirken eines deutschen Arztes in Japan* (Stuttgart, 1928), pp. 29–30.

Paris; Wilhelm Schott, who published an occasional Chinese piece, held an unpaid professorship for Altaic, Tatar, and Finnish at the University of Berlin, beginning in 1833; that Chinese did not even rate a mention in his title suggests just how little his colleagues valued his expertise in this field. Georg von der Gabelentz learned his East Asian languages by dabbling in his father's polyglot library; he was hired to teach *allgemeine Sprachwissenschaft*, not Chinese, at the University of Leipzig and owed his Berlin chair in "ostasiatische Sprachen" to Friedrich Althoff.[126] His appointment in 1889 coincides exactly with the appointment of Paul Deussen, also thanks to Althoff's intervention, at the University of Kiel (see Chapter 7). When Gabelentz died in 1893, the obvious candidate, assistant professor Wilhelm Grube, did not get the call (no one did); Grube died underpaid and bitter in 1908.[127] Remarkably, in an era in which Germany was setting up a colony in China and expanding its trade with East Asia, there was still no professorship in Sinology or Japanology until 1908 and 1914, respectively – and those were sited at the little-respected HKI.

Even the fin de siècle generation of German Sinologists usually learned Chinese later in life, and often abroad, or by self-guided study. Those who did learn the language often went abroad in search of secure positions. Friedrich Hirth (1845–1927) learned his Chinese as a tariff collector and in 1902 took a job at Columbia University in New York; unable to find a German post, Berthold Laufer (1874–1934) signed on at the Field Museum in Chicago. Karl Florenz went to Japan in 1888 and stayed as a professor at the University of Tokyo for twenty-six years until he was called to Germany's first chair in Japanology.

It was, after all, rather hard to get there and get home, though travel to East Asia was facilitated by the opening of the Suez Canal in 1867. Information from the Far East traveled slowly; at the time of the Taiping Revolution (1850–64), it still took six weeks for a letter to get to Europe from the Chinese coast – in summer; in winter, it took eight weeks. The first transcontinental telegraph was laid in the early 1870s, and Reuters news service opened a Shanghai office in 1871 – making it easier, for example, for Chinese businessmen to estimate currency and commodity prices in the West.[128] But monopolization of the telegraph service made using it prohibitively expensive even in 1890 (7.50 Marks a word), and Otto Franke and his colleagues at the Beijing Embassy preferred to send messages by camel to Kiachta, on the Russian-Mongolian border, and then over Russian lines, a process that took 18–20 days.[129] News from China's interior arrived much more slowly, if at all, and mail service was more or less non-existent, a reality that offered Elisabeth von Heyking a convenient conceit for her sensationally popular one-sided epistolary novel, *Briefe, die ihm nicht erreichten* (*Letters that Never Reached Him*, 1903). The Chinese "wild West" was still fair game for mapmaking pioneers and antiquities' rushes down to the time of the Great War. It

---

[126] Christina Leibfried, *Sinologie an der Universität Leipzig*, pp. 40–2.

[127] Otto Franke, "Die sinologischen Studien in Deutschland," p. 368. Wilhelm Schott (1807–1889) also held an assistant professorship at the University of Berlin beginning in 1838.

[128] Jürgen Osterhammel and Niels P. Petersson, "Ostasiens Jahrhundertwende: Unterwerfung und Erneuerung in west-östlichen Sichtweisen," in *Das neue Jahrhundert: Europäische Zeitdiagnosen und Zukunftsentwürfe um 1900*, ed. Ute Frevert (Göttingen, 2000), p. 280.

[129] Otto Franke, *Erinnerungen*, p. 47.

is surely the case that Europeans, following the travails of Stanley and Livingstone in their newspapers, knew much more about inner Africa in 1900 than they did about East Asia. It cannot be said that what they did "know" was especially flattering. The European public's general view of the Far East remained, as one specialist caricatured it: "In general, the territories in the Chinese cultural realm are seen as a place where one can sell goods at a profit, and from which, if one wants, one can at any time obtain work-slaves. No one knows about the cultural life of the people there – nor do they want to learn about it."[130]

The stronger presence in this field of *Orientalistik* than in any other (unless one counts *Byzantinistik*) of the Universities of Munich and Vienna may have to do with the Jesuit legacy in Sinology. At Munich, Karl Friedrich Neumann (1793–1870) first specialized in Armenian studies and then learned Chinese from the famous French Sinologist Abel Rémusat in Paris. Neumann did teach at the University of Munich, beginning in 1833, designated professor for Geography and Ethnography and also for Chinese and Armenian. Such a post was typical, Hermann Franke later wrote, of the period of Sinological dilettantism, and indeed, Neumann did not leave much of scholarly import behind. Thanks to having actually sailed to China on an English ship, Neumann accumulated a collection of some 6,000 Chinese books; in 1830, his collection was divided between the state libraries in Munich and Berlin. It is unclear, however, how widely used Neumann's books were in either of their two depositories. According to Otto Franke, the Munich portion still had not been cataloged in 1911 and until just before that date, the Berlin portion of the collection had been unusable, both because a catalog had not been made and because there were no employees available who could read the book titles.[131]

Neumann's designation, in the first instance, as a professor for geography and ethnography, points to another unusual feature of German Sinological studies: here, alone among the orientalist subfields, studies of geography were far in advance of those in philology or literature. Surely this was the result of the combination of the source differences described above as well as of moderate interest in Asian geography, reaching back into the eighteenth century, but promoted in particular by Carl Ritter and Alexander von Humboldt. This was the tradition that generated Ferdinand von Richthofen, who was certainly the most widely recognized "China-Kenner" of the mid-century, and Johann Justus Rein (1835–1918), the Bonn Professor of Geography who was Germany's only Japan specialist between Siebold's death (1866) and the Sino-Japanese War.[132] Richthofen's atlas of China (three volumes, 1877–1912) was indeed a monumental achievement – but even he had trouble funding its publication and interesting other students in the "Silk Road" questions he wanted solved. His most successful protégé in this field was a Swede, Sven Hedin, who never became a professional geographer, much less a Sinologist. It is instructive too that Richthofen looked

---

[130] Otto Franke, "Was lehrt uns?" p. 101.
[131] Hermann Franke, "Entwicklung," p. 9; Otto Franke, "Die sinologischen Studien in Deutschland," pp. 374–5.
[132] Rein visited Japan in 1874–5, thanks to funding from the Prussian Trade Ministry, and published a two-volume work on his trip 1881–86.

upon the study of Chinese as a necessary inconvenience – not an aesthetic or scholarly experience in itself – and that amongst the specialists it was an open secret that his language skills were at best dilettantish.[133]

Perhaps the Ritter-Richthofen school's emphasis on territory, rather than on language, history, or culture, explains why the field never really underwent specialization, and Sinologists were long expected to practice both ancient and modern Chinese studies and to cover literature, law, religion, archaeology, and political history, at a time when other fields were undergoing specialization. The Sinologists had, moreover, to deal with an enormous and hard to access secondary-source literature, for Chinese and Japanese scholars had continued to produce interpretations of classical texts for centuries, something Egyptologists and Assyriologists, for example, did not have to worry about. Before 1900, interested parties simply read the English, Dutch, and French studies; they were, in any event, more sophisticated and better informed. As late as 1953, Herbert Franke, professor at the University of Munich and son of Otto, argued that Sinology remained "a young science." "A long time must yet pass before anything comparable to the status of classical antiquity is achieved, until one can, in good conscience, link up minute details. We still lack a *Thesarum Linguae Sinicae*, a corpus of inscriptions, and a *Realenzyklopedia* based on modern points of view....."[134] In other words, Sinology had not yet had its 'second renaissance': how could it compete with its sister sciences?

The fact was, it could not, certainly not until the early 1920s, and even then its prospects were bleak. It was simply too difficult to apply humanistic methods here and too hard to link the Far East to the classical or Christian self. There were some who tried to make a case for linkage; Friedrich Hirth's 1885 *China and the Roman Orient: Researches into their Ancient and Medieval Relations as Represented in Old Chinese Records* (published in English) claimed that Chinese records could throw light on classical history.[135] The strongest case for relevance, however, could be made by way of art and archaeological finds, once scholars began to study Buddhist art – for the Bodhisattva form was found to be a synthesis of Central Asian, East Asian, and Greek forms, with its roots in Alexander's empire. This was a legacy upon which, as we will see, the Turfan expeditions played – but without much success. It was also hard to make a case for an alternative canon of East Asian literary and philosophical classics. There was no East Asian equivalent to *The 1,001 Nights*, the Vedas, or *Sakuntala*, and though there was some understanding of the teachings of Confucius (thanks chiefly to French scholars) there were few translations of the writings themselves. Indeed, even after the turn of the century, Richard Wilhelm had terrible trouble selling his translations of

---

[133] Otto Franke, "Die sinologischen Studien in Deutschland," pp. 364–5. To his detriment, Friedrich Hirth had pointed out Richthofen's weaknesses in the popular press, and sent copies of his attack to scholars and Reichstag members; embarrassment at this assault on the powerful professor was one reason that Hirth's search for a position in Prussia failed. Studt (Cultural Ministry) to Kaiser, 1903, in B-GSPK, I, 89, M. 21531.

[134] Hermann Franke, "Sinology," part 1 of "Orientalistik" in *Wissenschaftliche Forschungberichte: Geisteswissenschaftliche Reihe*, vol. 19, ed. Karl Hoenn (Bern, 1953), p. 13.

[135] See, for example, Friedrich Hirth, "Die Chinesischen Annalen als Quelle zur Geschichte Asiatischer Völker," in idem, *Chinesische Studien*, vol. 1 (Munich and Leipzig, 1890), pp. 68–75.

Confucius; publishers doubted there was an audience. As Wilhelm noted bitterly: "... [T]he publishers devote themselves to singing the refrain: 'We can't do that, who here cares about China?,'"[136] In 1900, the integration of Chinese texts into the canon of world "classics" was still a far-off dream.

But hopes for an East Asian renaissance were made a bit more plausible by, first of all, the political events of 1895–1905 and, secondly, the emergence of an avant-garde cultural pessimism that called into question the West's cultural superiority. The two were already linked in the first best-selling work of fiction written by a German woman: Elisabeth von Heyking's anonymously published *Briefe, die ihn nicht erreichten*. Appearing serially in 1902 in the *Tägliche Rundschau* and then passing through fifty-six editions in the next two years, Heyking's work was comprised of a set of letters supposedly written by a world-weary German woman to her diplomat lover, who dies heroically in the course of the Boxers' assault on the European community in Beijing. Heyking's novel – like the contemporary writings of Lafcadio Hearn and Pierre Loti – was suffused with primitivist condescension toward East Asians, but also cast a jaundiced eye on western fortuneseeking and even on the imperialist "civilizing mission" itself. Heyking's heroine sends many of her letters from America, where she finds the gulf between the cultureless rich and the forsaken poor much less sympathetic than picturesque, traditional China. This is not to say that Heyking's work – or Hearn's, which enjoyed enormous popularity in Germany after 1905 – gave German readers any deep insight into Chinese or Japanese affairs; their central subject was, after all, European world-weariness. But staging these self-pitying dramas on East Asian territory did draw new attention and add emotion to events unfolding in the East. One might say they offered opportunities for engagements with new kinds of "otherness" for those weary of other forms of alterity, and sick of bourgeois culture at home.[137]

Indeed, part of the genius of Elisabeth von Heyking's letters was the staging of the drama of the worldweary European self against the backdrop of the well-publicized events of the Boxer Rebellion, in which German Ambassador Baron von Ketteler was murdered. The Boxer Rebellion, and especially its dramatic conclusion, marked the opening of an era in which China suddenly began to seem "relevant" – now Germans and other Europeans were involved, which made events in China seem quite suddenly "world-historical." Ironically, part of their becoming "world-historical" also entailed the East Asian nations' equally sudden recognition that the Germans were, just like the other Europeans, angling for concessions and playing self-interested games. Violent contact and the news media's newfound ability to transmit sensational stories quickly gave rise to wider public interest in Pacific Rim affairs. Jürgen Osterhammel and Niels Petersson call the siege of the Beijing embassies and the eight-party invasion that followed "one of the earliest global

---

[136] Richard Wilhelm quoted in Salome Wilhelm, *Richard Wilhelm* (Düsseldorf, 1956), p. 154.

[137] For Hearn's popularity, see Katherine M. Webb, *Lafcadio Hearn and his German Critics: An Examination of his Appeal* (New York, 1984); for more on Heyking, see Chapter 10. On American avant-garde pessimists who, similarly, sought solace in the Far East, see T. J. Lears' *No Place of Grace: Antimodernism and the Transformation of Modern American Culture, 1880–1920* (New York, 1981).

media events."[138] In fact, these events, on the heels of the Sino-Japanese War and Germany's seizure of Qingdao, did bring East Asia into sudden focus. After his return from China in 1900, a Berlin correspondent wrote: "Up to now, when we used the term 'world history,' we Europeans really only meant the history of the peoples of the western cultural sphere ... in the general understanding of world history, the powerful East-Asian cultural sphere, with its autonomous, millennia-old, in its way extremely significant history, was pretty much completely ignored."[139] But, sudden peaks in interest were mostly that, and China would almost certainly have faded from view, had not a near neighbor really shown signs of becoming "world-historical" – and that neighbor was, of course, Japan.

After Japanese grudges against the Prussians for forcing them into an unequal trade treaty in 1861 had faded, the Japanese had largely viewed the Germans as leaders in science, medicine, pedagogy, and especially military affairs; Japan's modernizing elite quite liked the Kaiserreich's conservative political system too, and the Meiji Constitution was heavily informed by German ideas. Moreover, Bismarck's disinterest in taking Pacific colonies made Germany seem, alone among the Western nations, a potential friend rather than foe, a notion encouraged by Germany's support of Japan's efforts to end extraterritorial concessions (the treaty went into effect, finally, in 1899). This meant that, especially after the Franco-Prussian War, the Japanese often sought German advisors and a series of German experts in law, chemistry, engineering, philosophy, pedagogy, medicine, and military affairs made their way to Japan in the 1870s–1890s. But in 1895, rapid disillusionment with the Germans set in, as the Kaiserreich, desperate to get some part of the Chinese spoils, abandoned its non-intervention policy and joined with Russia and France to prevent the Japanese from seizing Port Arthur.[140] Such services won Germany Chinese gratitude in the form of a greater role in financing the Chinese debt, but also inclined Japan in the direction of the English, something exacerbated by Germany's seizure of Qingdao and designs on Shandong Province as a whole and by the Reich's provisioning of the Russian fleet during the Russo-Japanese War.[141] By 1905, as Erwin von Baelz experienced, the Japanese press had become thoroughly, bitterly, anti-German.[142]

This did not mean, however, that Germans were equally interested in Japan, and one can sum up the German attitude to Japan for most of this period as "off the radar screen." The Sino-Japanese War had been something of a wake-up call, attended as it was with the Kaiser's infamous articulation of the "Yellow Peril," in the form of a cartoon, sent as an overture to the Czar in 1895. In addition to being a calculated effort to engage the sympathies of the pious and autocratic Nicholas II, the cartoon nicely sums up what Wilhelm, and probably many Germans, thought of Japan in the 1890s. As Wilhelm's caption describes, the image "... shows the powers of Europe represented by their respective genii called together

---

[138] Jürgen Osterhammel and Niels P. Petersson, "Ostasiens Jahrhundertwende," p. 281.

[139] Quoted in Otto Franke, "Was lehrt uns?" p. 102.

[140] Frank W. Iklé, "Japan's Policies Toward Germany," in *Japan's Foreign Policy, 1868–1941: A Research Guide*, ed. James William Moorley (New York, 1974), pp. 265–71.

[141] Kurt Bloch, *German Interests and Policies in the Far East* (New York, 1978), pp. 1–3.

[142] Schottlaender, *Erwin von Baelz*, pp. 79–80.

by the Archangel Michael – sent from Heaven – to unite in resisting the inroads of Buddhism, heathenism, and barbarism for the Defense of the Cross. Stress is especially laid on the united resistance of all European Powers, which is just as necessary also against our common internal foes, anarchism, republicanism, and nihilism."[143] Note that religion, once again, is the central category to which race has been added. There is no recognition of Japanese modernization, and the use of the Cross to suggest a unified Euro-Christendom which both Kaiser and Czar knew did not exist was entirely cynical. In fact, the Kaiser's whole Far Eastern policy was driven by the desire to divert Russian expansionism away from Central and Southeastern Europe and to use the Russians to counter-balance the British. No wonder the Kaiser and the vast majority of his subjects were not prepared for Japan's victory in 1905 – they had been too self-absorbed and too convinced by their own rhetoric of "oriental stasis" to notice Japan's dramatic modernization.

Japan's shocking victory in 1905 – again an event widely reported and commented on in the press – did, at last, provoke a reevaluation in some circles of China's much smaller neighbor. Having beaten a European power in a major conflict, Japan now seemed to have a history, and perhaps even lessons for Europeans. In 1905, Leopold von Schroeder praised Japan's transformation of Buddhist nihilism into heroic self-sacrifice for the state. Schroeder was relieved to find in Japan no trace of the "overly-exuberant enthusiasm for life" so prevalent in the West.[144] More culturally conservative Germans were inclined to disapprove of this technology-savvy and bureaucratically efficient "new" Japan, some fearing a "Yellow Peril" and others lamenting the loss of traditional, more picturesque and "authentic," ways of life, memorialized in the romanticizing works of Lafcadio Hearn – who also had the good fortune to die in 1904.[145] The young military geographer Klaus Haushofer was posted to Japan as a Bavarian military observer between 1908 and 1910; Haushofer's observations of Japanese expansionism would be instrumental in developing his view of geopolitics, a subject he would elaborate and teach to German students in the 1920s. The title of Haushofer's first book, *Dai Nihon: Betrachtungen über Gross-Japans Wehrkraft, Weltstellung und Zukunft* (*Dai Nihon: Observations on Greater Japan's Armaments, World Status, and Future*, Berlin, 1913), sums up the aggressive opportunity-grabbing posture the young geographer thought noteworthy about Japan.

East Asia, wrote Erwin Baelz in August 1905, had entered the world stage: "What happens in the Far East will not henceforward have an exclusively local interest, but will necessarily concern us in Europe as well. People here hardly realize the significance of this as yet, but they will learn it as time goes on. My earnest wish is that Germany will, now that the time is ripe, see the right path and follow it."[146] But how should Germany act in East Asia? Opinions, even among the small circle of specialists, differed. For Ferdinand von Richthofen, the events of

---

[143] Quoted in Iklé," Japan's Policies," p. 281.

[144] Leopold von Schroeder, "Die kriegerische Bedeutung des Buddhismus in Japan" (1905), in idem, *Reden und Aufsätze*, pp. 226–35, quotation p. 234.

[145] Katherine M. Webb, *Lafcadio Hearn*, p. 74.

[146] Erwin Baelz, *Awakening Japan: The Diary of a German Doctor*, ed. Toku Baelz, trans. Eden and Cedar Paul (Bloomington, IN, 1974), p. 385.

the fin de siècle were more ominous than exciting. A veteran of the first Prussian trade mission, Richthofen had been instrumental in mapping coal deposits, laying out Chinese railways and in interesting German investors in China.[147] But after the events of 1895–1900, Richthofen turned against modernizing policies, fearing that China would use western technology to threaten Europe's world hegemony. In 1902, he submitted a memorandum to the Foreign Ministry, in which he urged the German Empire to join with other European nations to avoid "suicide" by keeping modern technology out of Chinese hands.[148] Otto Franke disagreed, arguing that Germany should cultivate a friendship with China and pointing out that the "yellow peril" rhetoric simply played into the hands of the Japanese.[149] Baelz, an expatriate who had been teaching medicine and dabbling in ethnography in Tokyo since 1876, agonized at the Kaiserreich's ham-fisted diplomacy and ill-informed policies, all of which conduced to push Japan into British arms. All of these men did have influence in decision-making circles; but in fact Wilhelmine Far East policy continued to be driven neither by knowledge of, or interest in, modernization in China or Japan, but by the desire to entangle Russia in the East, thus relieving pressure on the Balkans and assuring Germany and its troubled partner Austria-Hungary a free hand in Central and Eastern Europe. Once again, the Orient mattered – and mattered now more than ever; but intra-European relations still drove policy choices and, to a large extent, cultural institution-building as well.

The circle of those involved in East Asian policy and scholarship was very small and in some ways more closely knit than Islamic studies circles; given the paucity of Germans with proper linguistic credentials and/or interest in East Asia, this is not too surprising. Here too, it is rather hard to divide the "on-the-ground" experts and/or career Foreign Ministry men from the scholars, as many of these individuals were trained in unconventional ways and played numerous roles. A good example of this is Otto Franke, whose career we trace in the section to follow. A number of other "on-the-ground" experts had no prior academic training in the fields to which they would ultimately contribute a great deal. Erwin Baelz's interests in Japanese art and ethnography were the result of curiosity and enhanced by his marriage into Japanese society; similarly, the missionary Richard Wilhelm knew almost nothing of the Chinese language or of China's history, literature, and culture, until he arrived on the mainland in 1899. Wilhelm Solf and Karl Florenz, like Franke, started their careers as Sanskritists; Germany's other diplomats had even less linguistic or cultural training than did they – but then again, these posts were not ones the Reich thought particularly crucial or sensitive, nor ones that ambitious candidates were particularly eager to fill.

Perhaps the small size and non-specialization of the field made those in it more inclined to address themselves to "relevant" subjects. Even the more retiring and

---

[147] "Denkschrift betreffend Ferdinand von Richthofens Chinawerk und seine Vollendung," p. 5, attached to letter of Vorstand, Gesell f. Erdkunde to Kaiser, April 2, 1906, in B-GSPK, I, 76V, Sekt I, Tit XI, Teil VB, Nr. 20.

[148] See Osterhammel and Petersson, "Ostasiens Jahrhundertwende," pp. 282–3.

[149] Otto Franke, "Geistige Strömungen im heutigen China" (lecture for the Deutsche Kolonialgesellschaft, February 18, 1904), published in *Deutsche Kolonialgesellschaft: Verhandlungen der Abteilung Berlin-Charlottenburg* 7 (1902–3): 26.

"irrelevant" East Asian specialists occasionally wrote about or tried to intervene in present-day politics – though not only on the imperialists' side. In 1904, the Dutch scholar J. J. M. de Groot penned an essay justifying European missionization and even military action on the basis of the Chinese state's history of suppressing of religious freedom – though that was before he left Holland for Germany. Leipzig professor August Conrady, on the other hand, as early as 1897 rejected European expansionism and pled for better understanding between West and East. His student, Eduard Erkes, became even more critical of European expropriation and missionization, arguing in 1918 that the importation of Christian elements into China had caused a "retreat [from liberal progress] of the worst kind."[150]

Yet teaching or preaching modern history and foreign cultural policy was not what these scholars did most of the time. De Groot's interest in China's religious affairs was undoubtedly the result of his long series of studies of ancient Chinese religions, which culminated in the publication of his six-volume *The Religious System of China* (1892–1910). Georg von der Gabelentz, Conrady's predecessor, spent his time on comparative philology and on composing the first Chinese grammar not based on analogies drawn from Latin (though its idiosyncrasies and complexities made it useless, Otto Franke argued, as a way to learn the language). Conrady and Erkes were essentially linguists, as was F. W. K Müller. Like several others who gravitated into Chinese territory or occasionally poached on it – Hermann Oldenburg, de Groot, and later Ferdinand Lessing – Müller's main interest, beyond the pure love of exotic languages, was the history of Buddhism. But he was best known for his service in deciphering the Estrangelo script; his decipherment allowed scholars, and especially theologians, to read the important Manichean texts brought home by the first Turfan expedition (see Chapter 9).[151] Müller did not get a chair, but he did get the directorship of the Berlin Ethnography Museum and was probably more respected in academic circles than was Franke. Even in this field, small and late developing, non-theological and with little or no connection to the classical world, linguistic, religious, and ancient historical studies tended to outweigh, in prestige terms, the modern, "relevant" work being done by men like Franke – which is probably why de Groot, and not he, received the call to Germany's first fully academic chair in Sinology at the University of Berlin in 1910. But it was Franke who played the more important role in East Asian cultural politics before the war; and it is to his career that we now turn.

Otto Franke: Orientalism in the Age of "Indirect" Colonialism

Otto Franke (1863–1946) had no burning childhood desire to study the Orient; indeed, it was only in his second year of college that he discovered – having heard Droysen's last lectures on the philosophy of history (1882–3) – that he liked

---

[150] Leutner, "Weltanschauung – Wissenschaft – Gesellschaft," pp. 8–9.
[151] Ferdinand Lessing, "F. W. K. Müller zum Gedächtnis," in *Ostasiatische Zeitschrift* 16, no. 6 (1930): 142.

history and then – having tried various philological courses at the University of Göttingen – that he liked Sanskrit. But orientalism was not an equally viable alternative to the legal career his father was pushing, especially at the time he obtained his promotion (which concerned a phonetic work useful in interpreting the Vedas) in 1886. Academic Indology jobs were scarce, and in the years just after the "war in sight" crisis, getting on with the English colonial service in India did not look likely. Thus, when a friend informed Franke that the Foreign Office was eager to hire young talent for the diplomatic service in East Asia, both Franke and his seminar-mate Wilhelm Solf signed on. Franke would later argue that a move from Indology to Sinology was prepared by his readings in the history of Buddhism.[152] He did continue to interest himself in Buddhism and Lamaism, making several visits to the important Manchu temple at Jehol and writing essays about Tibet as it was (forcibly) drawn into the Great Game. Like the other Sanskritists of the day, he found Buddhism worrying, and in 1905 charged the Japanese with using monks to spy on the Chinese and, more danger-ously, with advertising religious commonalities as a means to link together Asian peoples against the West – the East Asian form, as it were, of the Pan-Islamic threat.[153]

An understanding of Buddhism could then be made "relevant" – but of more immediate usefulness were Franke's studies at the newly opened SOS. He enrolled in October 1887 and was able to learn at least something of northern Chinese dialect from Karl Arendt, a translator with long experience at the Beijing Embassy. Franke's studies could not have been especially deep and broad, as he was called to a post in Beijing already in June 1888; but, unlike most of the diplomats and missionaries sent to the Far East in the prewar era, he could at least speak and read some Chinese. Moreover, Franke soon convinced himself that understanding the China in which he was stationed, rather than the ancient Orient, was the proper course to pursue. He was, then, in a different way than envisioned in the title of his autobiography, a man between two worlds, oscillating between the old oriental-ism and the new.

Franke proved an adaptable diplomat, able to understand legal and commercial matters despite little formal training. But he could never quite accustom himself to the culture of the diplomatic corps, in which, as he wrote, learning too much about their nonwestern environs was a disadvantage: "Our local bureaucrats, whose knowledge of foreign lands does not extend past Switzerland, wanted to send out officials like themselves: lawyers, no 'philologists.' The former were the ones in charge, the latter, the interpreters, subaltern minds, who had already proven their [subalternity] by their preoccupation with such irrelevant things as oriental languages."[154] Having made his way home from Beijing in 1896–7 by the uncon-ventional northern land route (over Manchuria, Mongolia, and Russia), Franke was disappointed to find that no one at the Foreign Office in Berlin was interested

---

[152] Otto Franke, *Erinnerungen*, p. 35.
[153] Otto Franke, "Die Propaganda des japanischen Buddhismus in China" (1905), in idem, *Ostasia-tische Neubildungen*, pp. 158–9.
[154] Otto Franke, *Erinnerungen*, p. 68.

in his economic observations about the areas soon to be traversed by the Siberian Railroad.[155] During his stay in China, Franke was instrumental in negotiating the treaty that which gave Germany a ninety-nine-year leasehold over Jiaozhou Bay and its surrounding territory on the Shandong peninsula; in his usual high-handed fashion, Ambassador Edmund von Heyking had refused to speak directly with the Chinese officials. But rather than being rewarded for his services, Franke was demoted afterward to a post in Amoy. Disillusioned, he resigned from the Foreign Service in 1902 and took up writing articles on East Asian politics for the *Kölnische Zeitung*. In 1903, having encountered his old friend Yin Chang (now Chinese consul) on the streets in Berlin, he actually went to work for the Chinese Embassy as *Legationssekretär*.[156]

But Franke was making a number of other important friends in Berlin as well. He continued his association with Admiral Alfred von Tirpitz, who would play a role in a later stage of his career. But he also moved into academic circles, interesting Ferdinand von Richthofen with his studies of the spread of Chinese imperial power into inner Asia. Also interested in Franke's work was Sanskritist Richard Pischel, who set the young scholar to work deciphering a fifth-century Buddhist inscription in Chinese. Pischel urged Franke to habilitate, but for some time the Sinologist resisted; there were no full professorships anyway. Franke commented: "The sciences in Germany at that time held their gates closed to Sinology."[157] He relented in 1907 and easily passed his exams, as no one on the faculty knew enough about his field to ask probing questions. But in that same year, Tirpitz called; the "Dernburg Turn" was being taken in Far Eastern matters, too, and the Admiralty, in whose hands administration of Jiaozhou had been placed, was suddenly interested in a *kulturpolitisch* approach to China. The French, it was known, had hatched a plan for a higher school in China that would promote cultural relations and trade with France. The Germans wanted to follow suit, planning their own state takeover of the territory's missionary schools. Missionaries like Richard Wilhelm had mixed feelings about the takeover idea; as he wrote in a letter, "For we were and are always ready to support the German state in all its endeavors that are appropriate, and yet it must be said that our actual desires cannot be limited to representing the political goals of a European great power; we are children of Jesus and want to serve the Chinese people as such...." But Wilhelm was also disappointed that he was not offered the job himself.[158] The Reichstag also balked, but ultimately Franke (and Tirpitz) got his way and by 1908 was on his way to Qingdao, the fishing village that had become the capital of the German territory.[159]

What is interesting about this project is, first of all, the resistance Franke continued to meet from his own countrymen; when he arrived in Beijing, Ambassador Graf Rex (to whom, Franke wrote, "everything Chinese was a book with

---

[155] Ibid., p. 94.

[156] Fritz Jäger, "Otto Franke," pp. 22–3; Otto Franke, *Erinnerungen*, pp. 112–14.

[157] Otto Franke, *Erinnerungen*, p. 117.

[158] Wilhelm quoted in Salome Wilhelm, *Richard Wilhelm*, p. 144. Ursula Ballin, "Richard Wilhelm (1873–1930): Eine biographische Einführung," in *Richard Wilhelm: Botschafter zweier Welten*, ed. Klaus Hirsch (Frankfurt, 2002), p. 16. For more on Wilhelm, see Chapter 10.

[159] Otto Franke, *Erinnerungen*, pp. 121–2.

seven seals") denied any responsibility for the school plan and declared it over-ambitious; but Franke, who had followed the progress of reform movements in the Chinese newspapers from Berlin, insisted, and this time, managed to get backing for this culture-political foray. The agreement he hammered out for the elusively named *Hochschule für Spezialwissenschaften mit besonderem Charakter* ("Higher School for Specialized Sciences with Extraordinary Status") entailed support for the school from both the German Admiralty and by the Chinese government. The school was to serve the ends of both parties; for the Chinese students, it offered practical courses in agriculture and law, for example, which could pave the way to a civil service job; for the Germans, it was a useful prop-aganda instrument, designed to convince the Chinese that German economic and political intervention did not have to come at the price of sacrificing traditional Chinese culture. At the opening ceremonies, Franke went so far as to instruct students to be diligent especially in studying Chinese language, Confucian books, and Chinese history – even though he personally hated Confucianism, and thought Chinese scholarship was a waste of time.[160] Such were the compromises one made in pursuit of cultural "friendship." But even then, Franke's plans were repeatedly criticized by the military governor, Oskar von Truppel, who thought the Germans should have a "free hand" in its organization rather than "be chained to Chinese perceptions and methods..." As a concession to Truppel, in addition to Confu-cian lessons, the students were compelled to exercise – and, after final exams, to hold military parades.[161]

When Franke returned from China, a new opportunity presented itself; the newly founded HKI was now seeking a Professor for the Languages and History of East Asia, and thanks to Becker's recommendation, Franke was the preferred candidate. He accepted and began a new series of bureaucratic battles, this time with the Hamburg business community, which resisted the faculty's attempts to transform the HKI into a "normal," that is, not particularly relevant university. The drawn-out negotiations left Franke bitter – though his attitude toward his utilitarian antagonists was not nearly so vituperous as were his feelings about England's greed and deceitfulness, which he aired in a passionate lecture in October 1914.[162] The loss of his eldest son at the Somme and the crushing of Germany's colonial ambitions in 1918 were blows from which he never recov-ered, though he did finally get de Groot's Berlin chair in 1923 and would spend

---

[160] Roswitha Reinbothe, "Deutsche Kulturpolitik in China und der Beitrag deutschsprachiger China-wissenschaftler," in *Berliner China-Hefte* 14 (1998): 61–4; Jäger, "Otto Franke," p. 35. On Franke's view of Confucius, see Mechthild Leutner, "Kontroversen in der Sinologie: Richard Wilhelms kulturkritische und wissenschaftliche Positionen in der Weimarer Republik," in Hirsch, ed., *Richard Wilhelm: Botschafter zweier Welten*, pp. 71–7.

[161] Truppel quoted in Klaus Mühlhahn, *Herrschaft und Widerstand in der 'Musterkolonie' Kiaut-schou: Interaktionen zwischen China und Deutschland, 1897–1914* (Munich, 2000), p. 249. Mühlhahn suggests the impact of the Hochschule was ultimately minimal; many Chinese students could not follow the German language lessons, translators were always in short supply, and in the end, only about 30 students made it through to graduation before the outbreak of the war. Mühlhahn, *Herrschaft und Widerstand*, pp. 247–50.

[162] Otto Franke, "Deutschland und England in Ostasien," in *Deutsche Vorträge Hamburgischer Professoren*, no. 3 (Hamburg, 1914).

the next eight years there, training a group of Sinologists who would spread over the world.[163] Like a number of products of the "liberal" generation, Franke was also very active in the Prussian Academy of Sciences and in distributing patronage and ultimately, despite his unconventional training, at least as influential in the internal politics of East Asian studies as Eduard Meyer, Adolf Erman, and Theodor Nöldeke were in their specialized fields. And being younger (born in 1863, compared to Nöldeke [1836], Erman [1854], and Meyer [1855]), Franke also lived longer than these three, long enough indeed to offer his services to the Nazi state.[164]

Franke took to writing history in the 1920s, beginning, of course, with the ancient world; volume five of his *Geschichte des chinesischen Reiches* was published after the author's death in 1952. In some respects, the impress of Droysen was still evident; Franke's focus on the state and its exigencies recapitulated the Prussian historicist tendency to justify the sovereign's actions to secure stability against all challengers, internal and external. Like Becker, Franke criticized the narrow world histories of Hegel and Ranke – but in some ways, his insistence on the inclusion of "historyless" China was an even more radical move than was Becker's call to take cognizance of the third form of Mediterranean monotheism.[165] Franke's work also entailed some new endeavors in source criticism, including the demonstration that the great text of Zhu Xi (1130–1200), the *Tongjian Gangmu*, on which most European knowledge of Chinese history rested, could not be read as a straightforward historical work. It is a testimony to Franke's daring – perhaps he was something of a "furious orientalist" after all – that he attempted to write a synthetic history of China before German Sinology had passed through a full-on "Second Oriental Renaissance."[166] And of course, that daring has had the predictable result that his work was heavily criticized and quickly superseded.

What Franke's career shows us is that specialists who offered their services to the German Empire could indeed be useful; though the services they wished to provide were sometimes also superfluous or undesirable in the eyes of political decision-makers. It also shows that even the most dedicated agents of empire sometimes contributed to the diversification of European culture, even though their intentions were openly to spread and strengthen it. Culturally and affectively, Franke was not,

---

[163] Jäger, "Otto Franke," pp. 28–9. His influence on the profession was undoubtedly greater than that of Conrady, who was promoted to Ordinarius at Leipzig in 1922, and Richard Wilhelm, who received a chair at the University of Frankfurt in 1925. See Chapter 10.

[164] A 1934 essay rather bravely criticizes the "primeval error," from which China had not yet entirely freed itself, "that idea of chosenness, the belief, that a certain people or a certain race, naturally always one's own, created all of the world's culture." Otto Franke, "China," in *Der Orient und Wir: Sechs Vorträge des Deutschen Orient-Verein Berlin* (Berlin, 1935), p. 112. But Franke seems to have been willing to cooperate with the action Ritterbusch during the Nazi era. See Frank-Rutger Haussmann, '*Deutsche Geisteswissenschaft*' *im Zweiten Weltkrieg: Die 'Aktion Ritterbusch' (1940–1945)* (Dresden, 1998), p. 214, n. 300.

[165] Mechthild Leutner, "Otto Frankes Konzeption zur Chinesischen Geschichte: Die 'Geschichte des Chinesischen Reiches' neu gelesen," in idem and Kuo Heng-yü eds., *Deutsch-chinesische Beziehungen vom 19. Jahrhundert bis zur Gegenwart: Beiträge des Internationalen Symposiums in Berlin* (Munich, 1991), pp. 185–92.

[166] Jäger, "Otto Franke," pp. 30–1, 35–6.

in any meaningful way, "a man between two worlds" despite the title of his auto-biography; his passions were thoroughly German. But he did care about China, and try at least in part to understand it in its own terms. And that, at the very least, was more than could be said for most of his contemporaries.

I would like to make one further point. It is certainly true that "indirect" colonialism encouraged the participation of scholars and that a good number happily contributed to the cause; others surely would have helped out had they been willing and/or able to reorient their studies to make them relevant. There were very few critics of colonization among the German orientalists. But we should perhaps consider the perception, if not the reality, that "scientific" colonialism, in addition to being more efficient, was also less brutal and intolerant. We are likely, today, to be cynical about this, but it is possible that Otto Franke, in advocating German understanding of Chinese culture and politics, as against the fatalist pre-sumption that the "yellow" and "white" races were doomed to Darwinian racial war, was considering the fate of the Chinese people as well as the interests of the German Empire. Unquestionably he was more sympathetic to their aspirations and able to recognize them as human beings than his diplomatic superior, Edmund von Heyking, who thought the Chinese barbarians and social development in China hopeless.[167] In a 1905 lecture to the Berlin branch of the Colonial Society, Franke instructed his audience to work to achieve the higher goals of world peace that were common both to German philosophy and to Confucian universalism; "For the people who stand on the highest [plane of civilization] have the biggest obligation to further the moral ordering of the world, to work for cultural exchange between the races and not to lose sight of the ethical unity of the human race as their final goal."[168] And, thanks to an afterward appended to the lecture, we know that Franke's message was understood by at least one influential figure, the Society's president Prinz von Arenberg, who concluded the meeting with the following words: "We have all learned from history that the chief causes of conflicts are misunderstandings, and even if we only have contractual obligations, it is the most elementary duty of justice and wisdom that we understand and take care to respect the culture of these people, and for this reason...this lecture is for us of immeas-urable practical utility and practical applicability."[169]

Though we can be sure many of Arenberg's contemporaries did not take these words to heart or that they did so purely for self-interested purposes, it should not be denied that this sort of orientalist "usefulness" had nobler ends also. The purpose of setting up European-style girls' schools in China, in the words of Richard Wilhelm's father-in-law and spiritual advisor Christoph Blumhardt, was the same as the aim of schools for peasant girls in the German provinces: "...that they become sufficiently conscious of their value that they do not let themselves be treated like slaves."[170] There is a good case to be made that the rhetoric and institutions of indirect colonialism did exactly that, offering nonwestern people

---

[167] Osterhammel and Petersson, "Ostasiens Jahrhundertwende," pp. 287–8.
[168] Otto Franke, "Was lehrt uns?" p. 110. Also, idem, "Geistige Strömungen," p. 28.
[169] Arenberg's closing statements reported at end of Otto Franke, "Was lehrt uns?" p. 114.
[170] Christoph Blumhardt to Wilhelm, March 21, 1905, in Christoph Blumhardt, *Christus in der Welt: Briefe an Richard Wilhelm*, ed. Arthur Rich (Zürich, 1958), p. 152.

some new sympathy as well as new tools – which could be, and often were, used against the West or against their internal oppressors and enemies. Though it was not intended as such, "scientific" colonialism often had as its consequence the undermining of older forms of oppression and even of colonialism itself.

Erwin Baelz: The Orientalism the Kaiserreich Could Not Use

In the final section of this chapter, we treat, all too briefly, the beginnings of serious scholarship on Japan, the last field of oriental studies to gain standing in German academia before the Great War. The individual profiled below, however, is not the man who got that first chair – that honor went to Solf's Seminar-mate Karl Florenz. Rather, the focus in this section is on the doctor, ethnographer, and collector Erwin Baelz (1849–1913), who might have played roles in Japan and Germany similar to that played by Franke in his stomping grounds – except that Baelz was a man cut from quite a different cloth. The point here is to highlight again the differences displayed by individual orientalists in their works and in their daily lives and to demonstrate that there were limits to the kind of men the Reich found "useful." Indeed, Baelz was one of those beyond the "useful" pale.

After a tour as a field doctor in the Franco-Prussian War, Erwin Baelz returned to the University of Leipzig to complete his medical studies, aiming, apparently, at a normal clinical career. Though he had already developed an interest in anthropology – not at all uncommon for doctors in the high liberal era of Virchow and Bastian – Baelz's initial encounter with things East Asian was through contact with Japanese medical students, sent to Leipzig to learn western practices. Unlike most of his German contemporaries, Baelz took these students seriously and befriended them; yet he was so surprised by an offer of a teaching post in internal medicine from the University of Tokyo that he first believed it to be a joke.[171] He happily accepted a three-year posting, not suspecting that he would not return to Germany for eight years and not resettle there until 1905. In the 1870s–80s, Baelz saw xenophobic violence wane, and he saw anti-German sentiment rise again after 1895, as Japan moved closer to England and Kaiser Wilhelm made awkward overtures to the Russians. Over the years, he also experienced Japanese modernization at first hand. While his predecessors, just a few years earlier, had worked in a badly-heated operating room and depended on poorly-trained translators, Baelz worked in increasing comfort, linking himself not only to the German community and wider university circles, but also to Japan's state bureaucracy and then to the court.[172]

Baelz himself improved the quality of contacts he enjoyed with local residents by learning to speak fluent Japanese and by marrying a Japanese woman, though he insisted on sending his son Erwin Toku to Germany when he reached Gymnasium age. He also made careful studies of indigenous Japanese dietary and hygienic practices, and learned, from Japanese connoisseurs, to appreciate Japanese art. To understand current politics, he read the Japanese newspapers as well as the

[171] Schottlaender, *Erwin von Baelz*, p. 14.
[172] Ibid., pp. 34–49. There were about 300 Germans in Japan in the later 1870s.

European ones. He was, on his account, almost single-handedly, responsible for reviving jiujitsu, which had been spurned by the younger generation in the early Meiji years, and insisted, even against the arguments of his friend Marquis Ito, that European dress was unbecoming to Japanese women. Baelz was no great fan of modernization; but neither was he, like Lafcadio Hearn, nostalgic about Japan's pre-industrial folkways. European culture in his view should not be transplanted, but its useful elements grafted onto organic Japanese customs: "We must surely begin by discovering all that is good in the Japanese cultural heritage," he wrote shortly after arriving in Japan in 1876, "and then attempt to adapt it, slowly and purposively and carefully, to the changing conditions of the present and the future."[173] And as time passed, he would become even more skeptical about and critical of the role of Europeans in "reforming" the culture of East Asia.

By the 1890s, Baelz was writing essays on medicine, hygiene, and ethnography for both Japanese and German consumption. Though no one would have accused him of having "gone native," his positions were frequently critical of European ethnographic practices and often defended Japanese traditions against European criticisms. In a paper presented to the *Berliner Medizinischen Gesellschaft* in 1901, he refuted claims that a vegetarian diet was insufficient for top physical performance, a question that was of central importance in assessing the Japanese army's fitness.[174] The latter was something Baelz did not doubt, and the failure of his countrymen to recognize the growing strength and sophistication of the Japanese was a source of deep frustration for the German doctor. Politically he was even more radical, noting in his diary that since the Boxers had done no more than murder the envoy of a power "which, in peacetime, stole territory from their country," Kaiser Wilhelm's "take no prisoners" speech was wholly unjustified.[175] He despaired at the replacement of the tactful Theodor von Holleben with Freiherr von Gutschmidt at the German Embassy in Tokyo in 1893 (the same year that Max von Brandt was replaced with a more aggressive and intolerant ambassador in Beijing) and thought Germany's seizure of Jiaozhou was a political as well as an economic blunder.[176] He thought the Kaiser tyrannical, reckless, and unbalanced, and believed most of his fellow Germans ignorant as well as arrogant.[177] He rooted for the Japanese in 1904–5 and when the Kaiser sent condolences to the Czar over the death of Admiral Makaroff, commodore of the Russian fleet at Port Arthur, Baelz wrote: "Wasn't the Krueger Telegram enough? The lack of political tact in Germany makes one want to cry."[178]

At the ceremony celebrating his twenty-fifth anniversary at the University of Tokyo, Baelz told his audience that the era of foreign tutelage was over; the seeds

---

[173] Baelz, *Awakening Japan*, pp. 239, 17.

[174] Schottlaender, *Erwin von Baelz*, p. 71.

[175] "Apart from the brutality and inhumanity of the thing," he added, "politically considered it is sheer lunacy." Erwin Baelz, *Awakening Japan*, p. 136.

[176] Schottaender, *Erwin von Baelz*, pp. 74–6; Gutschmidt's successor Graf Leyden was even more obviously contemptuous of the Japanese.

[177] See, for example, Erwin Baelz, *Awakening Japan*, pp. 139, 188, 252–3, 273.

[178] Quoted in Schottlaender, *Erwin von Baelz*, p. 80. Baelz is referring to the highly publicized telegram in which Kaiser Wilhelm congratulated the Boer president of the Transvaal Paul Krueger on defeating a British "invasion" of his territory.

had been sown and now the "tree of science" could develop by itself in Japan. Though he lauded the results of European *Geist* – even the finest Japanese statues and paintings, he argued, bore the traces of (Alexandrian) Greek influence – he also portrayed the development of European knowledge as a painful and difficult road: "... and it is characterized by sweat, much noble sweat, and also by spilt blood and by burning heaps of ruins."[179] This is not the language of liberal optimism – or at very least, one can say that a dark cloud has passed over the progressives' sun. Back in Germany, Baelz continued to be critical of western views of the East; in 1904 he wrote a scathing reply to an article in the journal *Globus* written by one Dr. ten Kate which portrayed the Japanese as lacking in individuality, stupid, unstable, and jingoistic. Baelz replied that, first of all, ten Kate's knowledge of the culture was superficial and based on a few (and outdated) impressions. The Japanese were not at all stupid – in fact, Baelz was able to quote some observers who thought the average Japanese worker was smarter and more diligent than his average German counterpart. They might have appeared "hypnotized" by European science and technology in the 1870s, but now (1904), "the hypnosis is over, the people are waking and have now adopted a critical, in many ways a hyper-critical, stance with respect to their own culture. National and individual consciousness have awakened, the people are consciously going their own way." Nor was this a superficial form of imitation; the Japanese now had a parliament and a citizen army, mandatory schooling, and vaccinations. They were modern, and moreover, they did not need Christianity. Their kindness to strangers almost certainly exceeded that practiced in Europe.[180]

Interestingly, upon his return to Germany, Baelz was not offered a position at the SOS, HKI, or any other university. It is true that he was, by training, a doctor, not a philologist – but he might well have been invited to teach tropical medicine or Far Eastern ethnography, fields in which practicing doctors were still accepted. It is also the case that he was rather old (fifty-six years) to take on a new career – although Karl Florenz was not much younger (fifty-one years) when his call came in 1914. But more importantly, some of Baelz's views were not particularly conducive to acceptance in orientalist circles. His personal comportment was unconventional; he practiced jiujitsu, embraced Japanese customs, and had abandoned Christianity (he had his wife baptized and the couple were officially married only in 1905, just before their boat sailed for Germany and simply for the sake of appearances). But even more importantly, his politics diverged from that of most university mandarins; in a 1906 newspaper article he argued that Jiaozhou was an embarrassment, the naval base there pointless, and the port unprofitable; rather than improving the situation by altering the Reich's approach to the *Pachtgebiet* (the classic Dernburgian answer), he insisted that Germany should simply give the territory back to China. A subsequent article, explaining why the Japanese had become so deeply anti-German (there were, in Baelz's mind, entirely rational reasons and he named names), was so likely to be controversial that the papers

---

[179] Erwin Baelz, "Ansprache: Gehalten bei seinem 25-jährigen Universitäts-Jubiläum am 22. November 1901," reprinted in Schottlaender, *Erwin von Baelz*, p. 128.

[180] Erwin Baelz, "Zur Psychologie der Japaner" (1904), in Schottlaender, *Erwin von Baelz*, pp. 139–42, quotation p. 140.

rejected it on political grounds. Baelz, evidently, was not the sort of "relevant" orientalist with whom the Kaiserreich felt comfortable.[181]

Baelz himself offered an analysis of the unpopularity of his sort of "orientalism" in relating in his diary a conversation with a like-minded official from Qingdao. Baelz's friend warned the doctor, who was about to return home, that he might find Germany vexingly close-minded. There is much talk there, he said, of the Great Wall of China;

Well, the Germans, too, are surrounded by a "great wall." This wall is not built of masonry, but is spiritual. Anything outside the wall is regarded with contempt. But when such a superior person goes abroad, and finds how much he has been misinformed, he is apt, unless he is a person of very stable temperament, to rush to the opposite extreme, and thence to look down upon all that he has previously venerated. That is why so many Germans who go abroad are lost to Germany. But one who, having gone abroad, remains a good German and wants to enlighten his fellow-countrymen is not understood at home and is despitefully used.

The official, Baelz added, "was voicing my own sentiments."[182] While he could reflect on his successes in learning from and sharing ideas with the Japanese, Baelz found this German "wall" impossible to scale.

Naturally, Baelz and his friend were generalizing from their own experiences and indulging in a bit of self-pity. But perhaps there is something to this analysis after all. "Going there" was, for German orientalists and for Germans in general, still rather new at the fin de siècle and processing that new experience, and that new knowledge about the modern Orient, remained difficult at both the personal and the institutional level. Moreover, the naval, entrepreneurial, and missionary supporters of colonialism often had conflicting interests and plans, some of which were served by "knowing more" about the East and some of which were not. There were some orientalists who could, and did, make themselves "relevant" in one way or another and many who, intentionally or not, supplied knowledge that could be used to further colonial plans. We have seen several examples of this in this chapter, from Becker and Hartmann to Otto Franke. But there is also the case of Baelz, whose expertise was chiefly put to use by his Japanese hosts and who did try to use his "orientalist" knowledge to critique colonial policies. That he was "despitefully" used, or simply not "used" at all, by German policy makers and cultural institution builders is a more telling indictment of German imperialist hubris than a Saidian critique of his participation in some purportedly European-wide "discourse on the Orient."

---

[181] Erwin Baelz, *Awakening Japan*, pp. 215–17, 221–9, 374. Small wonder that he bestowed his benefice on Japanese and not German universities and students. He gave 10,000 Marks to the Tokyo medical faculty in 1908, and in his will set aside 20,000 Marks for needy Japanese students to study at German universities. Baelz, "Upshot," in idem, *Awakening Japan*, p. 390.

[182] Erwin Baelz, *Awakening Japan*, p. 273.

9

Interpreting Oriental Art

What explains our astonished admiration as we stand before this oriental art? Does it not show us, mockingly, the one-sided narrowness of our European concepts of painting [?]. Its thousand-fold deeper art of coloration and composition puts our conventional theories to shame.

— Franz Marc, on viewing the Munich Mohammedan Exhibition, 1910[1]

The eyes of the visitor glide curiously over these forms and examples, the colors and materials, and here and there are caught by a glimpse of a gemstone, occasionally excited by a familiar animal design or a tendril ornament; but it seems as if the monotony of this ever-repeating surface ornamentation ... calls forth an irrepressible exhaustion, as a result of which European attention is soon enfeebled and lost ... the uniform rhythm of Egyptian columned halls, the unaccented repetitiveness of oriental story-telling, art and music, the formless eternity of the Asian steppe landscape find in this ornament, with its simple and similar parts a counterpart, one which offers the achievement-desiring agility of the westerner no delight.

— Review of the same exhibition for the *Neue Zürcher Zeitung*[2]

If imperialist ventures and aspirations were making the Orient increasingly "relevant" for German *Islamforscher* and East Asia experts, there were other ways too in which increasing contact with the world's people and products mattered to German cultural producers. In this chapter, we delve seriously into a subject treated only in passing in earlier chapters, and that is the study of "oriental" art. While largely separate from the pursuit of oriental philology, the study of Asian arts and artifacts followed roughly the same trajectory, from something like a passionless positivism at mid-century, through fin de siècle renaissance and "furor." Here I focus on these later developments, which played an important part in decentering classicizing aesthetic presumptions, and thereby opened the way for new forms of *Kulturgeschichte* – for better and for worse. The chapter not only insists on the cultural importance of the wider accessibility of oriental artifacts – through reproductions, colonial exhibitions, museum collections, and archaeological excavations – but also notes the diversity of ways in which eastern forms were understood and used; again, the widening cultural marketplace and

---

[1] Quoted in Annette Hagedorn, "The Development of Islamic Art History in Germany in the Late Nineteenth and Early Twentieth Centuries," in *Discovering Islamic Art: Scholars, Collectors, and Collections, 1850–1950*, ed. Stephen Vernoit (London, 2000), p. 124.

[2] Arthur Weese, "Die Teppiche in der Münchner Muhammedanischen Ausstellung," in *Neue Zürcher Zeitung*, October 6, 1910, and October 7, 1910, p. 276; in M-BHSA, II, MH 9286.

the expanding diversity of cultural offerings play a role. We note ways in which the consumption of oriental imagery in the public sphere was continuous with older traditions, but enhanced by imperialist hubris and the increased accessibility of nonwestern goods, and we suggest that, paradoxically, the same political and economic context shaped the avant-garde artists' and elite scholars' desire to appreciate oriental art in its own terms. The book's focus remains on the history of oriental scholars and scholarship, but here we get to know some usually over-looked contributors to study of art history, namely, museum assistants, private collectors, and bureaucrats, all of whom were especially important in promoting a field of inquiry little regarded by most members of the academy. The study of German "orientalism" in art and in art-historical scholarship is just beginning.[3] But we can begin to map this landscape and to show how it fits into our larger sketch of the cultural politics of German orientalism.

By no means can I offer here a full history of the reception of oriental imagery in German-speaking Europe – one would have to begin in the Middle Ages, if not even earlier. From the seventeenth century forward, artists and readers could consult a wide range of pattern books or illustrated works, in which eastern art-works and architecture were depicted, including Athanasius's Kircher's *China Illustrata* (1667), Carsten Niebuhr's *Travels*, and Thomas and William Daniell's multi-volume *Oriental Scenery* (1795–1808). Many elite Central Europeans – perhaps especially Austrians and Russians, thanks to their proximity to the Otto-man Empire – saw and admired finely-crafted weaponry, carpets, textiles, and porcelains; the great age of Chinoiserie also came to Prussia, as Queen Sophie's porcelain collection demonstrates. The repertoire of forms was, however, limited and much of it based on indirect sources such as coins, china designs, travelers' sketches, or pattern books used by masons, clock makers, or furniture designers; for the most part, Germans, like other westerners, knew and cared about oriental art primarily as ornamentation, as what we now call "decorative" art, rather than "art" in the high romantic sense. Of course, long into the nineteenth century, many if not most western artists and connoisseurs worked in and greatly valued the "decorative" arts sector as well. But it is important for what follows that this was the context in which oriental art was chiefly valued.

In the nineteenth century, certain aspects of the arts of the East did appeal to artists, and especially to decorative artists; interlaced designs, brilliant colors, and formalized organic patterns drawn from "Turkey" carpets and mosque exteriors were used in modern spaces like glass and iron conservatories or in railway station designs. The exoticizing effect helped to create contrasts between new spaces and conventional Renaissance or classical building types, making the Orient seem less

---

[3] We lack, for example, a full-scale treatment of the reception of oriental art in Central Europe on the model of John Sweetman's *The Oriental Obsession: Islamic Inspiration in British and American Art and Architecture, 1500–1920* (Cambridge, 1991). But on popular orientalism, see Wolf-Dieter Lemke, *Staging the Orient: Fin de Siècle Popular Visions* (Beirut, 2004); on orientalism in art, Erika Günther, *Die Faszination des Fremden: Der malerische Orientalismus in Deutschland* (Münster, 1990); M. Haja and G. Wimmer, *Les Orientalistes des Écoles allemande et austrichienne* (Paris, 2000); on art history, the essays in *Islamic Art in Germany*, ed. Joachim Gierlichs and Annette Hagedorn (Mainz, 2004), and Vernoit, ed. *Discovering Islamic Art* (London, 2000).

an unknowable "other" than a consumable, "alternative" style – one which also evoked, through old linkages to the spice and silk trades, lives of luxury and pleasure that respectable bourgeois Germans were not supposed to covet, but often did.[4] The "otherness" of the Orient was also sometimes employed in religious architecture – as a contrast to the all-too-secular and dehistoricized context of modern western experience. For some who were already internal others, or who sought to distance themselves from conventional norms, the Orient could be an identity one might invoke or even adopt. As Ivan David Kalmar has argued, the "Moorish" style was used for synagogues throughout Central and Eastern Europe after the 1830s by Jews who did not find the appellation "Orient" objectionable; rather, the style seemed to ratify the great history of the Semites and to evoke, in particular, the glory days of medieval Spain.[5]

There was "orientalist" painting in the German-speaking world, though until the 1870s and 1880s, the Orient invoked in oils seems to have been chiefly that of the Bible. The very popular genre painter Carl Spitzweg did do a series of opium-smoking men and veiled women – but these do not seem to have been very popular or widely reprinted. In 1875–6, the Austrian painter Carl Leopold Müller had organized a trip to Egypt for several friends, including Hans Makart and Franz von Lenbach, to revel in "oriental" light and color; this was something few German painters had done before and little art of this kind was on display in German galleries. In creating his high-end travelogue *Ägypten in Bild und Wort* (two volumes, 1879–80), the Egyptologist Georg Ebers would commission work from a number of these painters and make it accessible at least to upper-class audiences. A friend of the British painter of classical reveries Lawrence Alma Tadema, Ebers wanted to bring Egypt, ancient and modern, to life – but he did not really want to exoticize it. The illustrations in his book depicted Egyptians as normal citizens of a modernizing country (though he did not hesitate to render women in headscarves and burkas). Contemporary Egyptians were interesting to Ebers and he made sure they were portrayed in their diversity, as mothers and workers, teachers, and beggars. But his work also made clear that the most interesting thing about Egypt for Europeans remained its Old Testament sites and scenery – and these too Ebers' artists rendered in elaborate detail.[6]

What inspired Ebers' project and the proliferation of oriental imagery after the 1870s was certainly the hubris and excitement provided by the "open door" and by international competition to take advantage of the new accessibility and exploitability of the East. But we should note that this expansion was also the result of the creation of more democratized cultural forms, many of which simply allowed more Europeans to consume the same sort of oriental imagery as had courtly connoisseurs of jeweled snuff boxes or readers of *The 1,001 Nights* in the eighteenth century. The exhibits at the Paris World Exhibition of 1867, for

---

[4] The tastes of Ludwig II, King of Bavaria, in particular ran in this direction. See Eva-Maria Troelenberg, "Orientalismen im Königreich Bayern: Islamisierende Architektur bei König Ludwig II," in *Eothen*, 4 (2007): 392–406.

[5] I. D. Kalmar, "Moorish Style: Orientalism, the Jews and Synagogue Architecture," in *Jewish Social Studies* 7, no. 3 (2001): 68–100.

[6] See Marchand, "Popularizing the Orient," in *Intellectual History Review* 17, no. 2 (2007): 181–8.

example, seem to have been particularly influential for arts and crafts designers, who sought to bring highbrow taste to middle-class consumers. The panoramas depicting the crucifixion or the great cities of the East – such as Jerusalem, Cairo, and Istanbul – offered to ordinary citizens the kind of imagery their betters already knew from religious paintings. Cabarets and circuses often featured "oriental" acts, complete with matching costumes, props, and scenery – recognizable descendants of eighteenth-century orientalizing operas.[7] By the century's end, there were more images of the Orient available than ever before, available in these forms as well as in popular journals, travelogues, coffee-table books, and inexpensive knick-knacks and home furnishings; it is especially important that printing illustrations and photos was rapidly getting easier, faster, and cheaper, meaning that access to images became almost universal.[8] But these were images drawn from a contemporary or perhaps timeless East; their audiences were attracted to oriental alterity as a consumer good, but were not particularly interested in what we would call "art."

If we shift to a discussion of the study of oriental art proper, it is obvious that here too imperialist hubris and the "open door" shaped the fin de siècle story – but not in the same way, in part because artistic objects were drawn into a different context and used in different ways. Still, of course, imperialist politics underwrote the process by which they came, in increasingly large quantities, to the West. We still have more to learn about the private trade in eastern artifacts, but judging by scattered references, it seems that imperial officials, telegraph operators, Europeans employed by the Ottoman, Japanese, or Chinese governments, and businessmen often began collecting Persian carpets or Chinese porcelain for themselves, taking advantage where possible of the willingness of hard-pressed elites to sell their treasures. Many of these collectors then published catalogs of their possessions and/or scholarly studies of the field more generally, and many went on to work in and around museums, using their "on-the-ground" contacts and linguistic experience to assist them in trafficking or pilfering more objects, often in ways that would have made Lord Elgin blush. We know rather more about the extractive methods of state-supported museum officials – though here too we have more to learn.[9] Much more than in the case of philological studies, the study of oriental arts depended on "being there" – and on having leverage, political, financial, or both, over indigenous owners of artifacts or of excavation rights.

---

[7] At the Sarrasani circus, German spectators could see Indians, a Singhalese temple dancer, and Chinese acrobats; variety shows featured "Negro," "Indian," and "Chinese" or "Egyptian" dancers – although, as Jill Lloyd contends, most of these performers were in fact Europeans. Jill Lloyd, *German Expressionism: Primitivism and Modernity* (New Haven, CT, 1991), pp. 89–95.

[8] Until 1869, Bruckmann Verlag employed silver-plated photography, which was expensive and suited only for editions of fifty copies or less. But after that time a series of technological innovations made it possible to publish, by 1882, up to 1,000 an hour, and then to perfect the printing of half-tone photographs. This made possible the publishing of broadly circulated reproductions and "improving" illustrated journals such as *Die Kunst für Alle* (founded 1885). Erhardt D. Stiebner, "Einleitung," in *125 Jahre Bücher: 1858–1983 Verlag und Graphische Kunstanstalten F. Bruckmann KG* (Munich, 1983), pp. 7–12. For an excellent treatment of the democratization of Wilhelmine taste, see Beth Irwin Lewis, *Art for All? The Collision of Art and the Public in Late Nineteenth-Century Germany* (Princeton, NJ, 2003).

[9] On private collectors' deals, see, e.g., Julia Hankey, *A Passion for Egypt*, pp. 171–206; on museum-funded extractions, see Marchand, *Down from Olympus*, Chapters 3 and 6.

The Germans, with no imperial toeholds until the 1880s and a powerful tradition of classicizing aesthetics, were especially late to enter this field; but when they did, as we shall see, they too adopted imperious methods of extraction in the formation of their collections and directed much of their prewar energy to acquisition, rather than interpretation, of eastern art.

In the period between 1865 and 1890, as Annette Hagedorn has shown, academic scholars largely ignored oriental art, while theorists of the reform movement in the decorative arts published more than sixty books and articles on Islamic applied arts (especially on ceramics and carpets).[10] Most of the early collectors and patrons of oriental arts were individuals connected with commerce and industry (*Besitzbürgertum*), rather than products of the Gymnasium, and most of them were neither interested in nor credentialed enough to attempt to write synthetic or historical studies. Generalizations about oriental art outside the circle of travelers, architects, and designers continued to be based not on actual encounters with artworks or even reproductions of authentic works, but instead on texts. This was especially apparent in Islamic art, for non-Muslims were forbidden from entering all but a few mosque interiors.[11] It continued to be normal practice for German Indologists writing about Indian aesthetics to subsume plastic arts under "Kunst und Poesie" and then to devote sections almost exclusively to poetry (*Dichtkunst*).[12] Very often, generalizations drawn from assessments of the foreign culture's religious or mythological texts were transferred to the arts, as in Carl Schnaase's claim that Islamic art's combination of riotous ornament and despotic form reflected the Qur'an's juxtaposition of severe monotheism with excessive sensuousness.[13] Even more clearly than in the world of texts, in art history, the Second Oriental Renaissance was a product not of the romantic era, but of the fin de siècle.

The archaeological excavations and the expanding trade in oriental artifacts after the 1870s did result in the exhibiting, explaining, and imitating of a wider range of styles and genres. Of course, not all "oriental" goods were equally valued by European society as a whole or by the German elite in particular; Egyptian and Assyrian and later Chinese and Japanese art appealed most, probably because these traditions of figural representation were most like those of the West. Indian art was representational – but as Partha Mitter showed many years ago, its representations were considered monstrous.[14] Islamic art's rich decorative tradition made it respected by those who appreciated or practiced ornamentation; but there was little interest in its history. Though excavations at classical and Near Eastern sites had been turning up Islamic artifacts for decades (often destroying them in the process), the first organized dig at a purely Muslim site did not begin until 1898 when the French began to excavate ancient Qal'at Bani Hammad, capital of the Hammadids in eleventh/twelfth century in Algeria; the first German dig at an

---

[10] Annette Hagedorn, "The Development of Islamic Art History," pp. 117–23.

[11] Ettinghausen, "Islamic Art and Archeology," in Young, ed., *Near Eastern Culture and Society*, p. 28.

[12] For e.g., Heinrich Zimmer (the elder), *Altindisches Leben* (Berlin, 1879).

[13] Schnaase, *Geschichte der bildenden Künste im Mittelalter*, vol. I, *Altchristliche, byzantinische, muhammedanische, karolingische Kunst* (Düsseldorf, 2nd ed., 1869), pp. 480–1.

[14] Mitter, *Much Maligned Monsters*.

Islamic site, Samarra, began in 1911. The exception here was Persian art, which, like Persian poetry before it, enjoyed much higher status, in part because of its lyricism and in part because it was assumed to exhibit at least some intermixture of "Aryan" elements. By the 1880s, Persian ceramics were reputed to be the most refined and Persian carpets were widely seen to be the Orient's greatest aesthetic achievement.[15]

But could these be compared to, say, Donatello's bronzes or Dürer's paintings? Were Persian carpets "art" in the same sense as were these masterworks from the western, representational tradition? Texts and religious ideas were one thing – and Europeans had long been accustomed to the notion that luxury goods and belief systems might come from the East. But it took rather longer to get used to the idea that "art" – in the way Vasari and the romantics saw it, as a perfectly balanced synthesis of the ideal and the natural – might be found in Asia. If one looks at major art-historical surveys of the 1860s – Gottfried Semper's *Der Stil in den technischen und tektonischen Künsten* or Carl Schnaase's *Geschichte der bildenen Künste*, for example – the characterizations or rather caricatures they offer of "oriental" art are quite striking, as are their very open insistence that Greek styles are unquestionably the most natural and the most beautiful. Though Schnaase claimed in the opening to the second edition of his work (1869) that Islamic, Byzantine, Carolingian, and early Christian art were interesting not only historically but also "because elements of the beautiful are also present in these epochs," the real reason for such a study was to better understand the "epochs of more mature artistic accomplishment."[16] The man who thought all of oriental art reflected the touching of the extremes of despotic abstraction and crass sensuality can hardly be said to have been an unbiased historian of the arts. It took the changes in museum practices and personnel as well as the entrance of more technologically progressive voices into the discussion to push scholars to undertake deeper studies of eastern art.

By the 1890s, western artists were themselves debating which forms of craftsmanship really counted as "art" and which were merely decorative; as the "minor arts" such as weaving, glass-blowing, porcelain-making, and furniture design received new attention, questions about the status of Asian art were also raised. Could oriental art be beautiful or even sublime in the sense that Schiller and Kant defined these words, or was it merely ornamental? If the latter was the case, was it to be classed with the products of the *Naturvölker*, or displayed only in the contextless collections of arts and crafts? Was it interesting simply for ethnographic reasons, or for mercantilist ones (so that European decorative artists could copy its patterns) – or was it appealing in its own terms? There were some scholars and connoisseurs, in Germany and elsewhere, beginning to believe that some works at least, such as the Ajanta cave paintings or Chinese landscapes, should

---

[15] On carpets, see David Sylvester, "On Western Attitudes to Eastern Carpets," in *Islamic Carpets from the Joseph V. McMullan Collection* (London, 1972), pp. 4–19. In 1882, William Morris pronounced: "To us pattern-designers, Persia has become a holy land, for there in the process of time our art was perfected." Quoted in Sweetman, *Oriental Obsession*, p. 178.

[16] Schnaase, *Geschichte* 1: vi.

be classified as real "art."[17] But by no means had this battle been won. As we will see, where such battles were fully joined was in the museums, where tempers ran hot enough for one chronicler to declare the conflict a "museums war."[18]

ORIENTAL ART AND THE ETHNOGRAPHIC MUSEUM

Throughout the nineteenth century, oriental art fit uneasily into the emerging system of museums. It was not considered imaginative and original enough to deserve a place in museums of fine arts (though Egyptian sculptures sometimes snuck in), but it was also seen as different from and higher than the arts of "primitive" peoples. Collections were generally divided between arts and crafts exhibits, whose purpose was to expose European artists to exotic designs, and ethnographic museums, where artifacts were generally used to typify nonwestern religious practices. Neither or these were particularly suitable for the pieces displayed, and museum officials were by no means in agreement about which objects belonged where. In 1835, in the course of founding the Munich Ethnography Museum, the traveler Philipp von Siebold suggested a distribution of artifacts according to which the Ethnography Museum would hold materials belonging to living cultures, while the antiquities museums took things belonging to "untergeganener Völker," whether these were Indian, Egyptian, Greek, or Roman, and including both "monuments and surviving folkloric items."[19] But the curators of the classicizing *Glyptothek* were not about to mix classical and oriental artifacts, and the same was generally true for other museums. After all, aside from being something like laboratories for university professors, museums were supposed to present exemplary forms and styles of art and no one told German artists that they should imitate the ancient Indians or even the Egyptians and Persians; even those involved in the production of "minor" arts like carpets, porcelain, funerary monuments, and clocks were supposed to lift designs, but to adapt them to European needs and tastes. This meant that there were few public venues for the display of authentic oriental art and little money or effort was spent trying to acquire more of it.

Things began to change in the 1880s, as the Wilhelmine world joined the race for colonies and a number of new ethnographic museums were founded, most importantly the Berlin Ethnography Museum in 1886. Strikingly, this museum was built not on the Museums Island, near the Royal Palace, where the great collections of classical and modern German art were exhibited, but quite a distance away, in Prinz Albrecht Strasse. As H. Glenn Penny describes, this collection was from the beginning a hodgepodge of objects of all sorts; it contained Siebold's Japan collection as well as Amazonian shrunken heads, Papuan idol images

---

[17] Non-Germans, such as the English scholar of Indian art Ernest Binfield Havell, were also working in this direction. Sweetman, *Oriental Obsession*, p. 206.

[18] Karl Scheffler, *Berliner Museumskrieg* (Berlin, 1921).

[19] Siebold quoted in Sigrid Gareis, *Exotik in München: Museumsethnologische Konzeptionen im historischen Wandel am Beispiel des Staatlichen Museums für Völkerkunde München* (Munich, 1990), pp. 158–60, quote p. 158.

displayed next to Benin bronzes.[20] By the 1890s, it also contained Schliemann's Troy treasure, which was insufficiently classical to merit exhibition in Schinkel's Altes Museum – the latter was, in any event, packed to the rafters with plaster casts. Large quantities of orientalia found their way to the Ethnography Museum, some of the artifacts clearly of higher and some of lower aesthetic value; some could claim great historical value (like the Trojan treasure), some – like those collected by Leo Frobenius in Africa – were interesting chiefly for their folkloric significance. The jumbled nature of these collections offended several groups – the connoisseurs of oriental arts, who wanted to accord them aesthetic status equal to that of European forms; the historicizing scholars, who wanted things grouped in clear lines of development; the ethnographers, who were beginning to think of ethnographic museums as places exclusively for the artifacts of *Naturvölker*; and members of the general public, who simply found the tangle of stuff – crowded together and often unlabeled – impenetrable.

What is interesting here is the inclusion of the Orient in a jumbled category that can only be defined by what it was not: classical or modern European art. In fact, for those trained in the classical tradition, only the latter counted as art; the rest was just exotic junk, some too explicitly sexual to be aesthetically improving. In response to the eclectic collecting practices of Max Buchner (a ship's doctor who served as director of the Munich Museum between 1887 and 1907), one philology professor exclaimed: "What are we to do with these jagged sticks and this dreary idol-rubbish? That stuff deserves to be packed off to Hamburg, for the red light district." Small wonder Buchner thought the ethnographic collection, overshadowed by the impressive classical and Renaissance collections at the Glythothek and Pinakothek, counted as the "stepchild" of the Munich Museums.[21]

One of the problems in sorting out where oriental art belonged was that the public collections were largely miscellanies formed of the sometimes quite eclectic collections of private persons; putting them together did not necessarily make for an integrated or even coherent collection. The collection of the Munich Ethnographic Museum, for example, was chiefly formed of objects that had belonged to the house of Wittelsbach and like many royal or ducal collections contained "oriental" "booty" that had been seized by western armies from Ottoman commanders or presented as gifts to western dignitaries.[22] This included, for example, the audience tent of Grand Vizier Suleiman Pasha, captured by Bavarian soldiers in 1687, an interesting object, but one that could only be awkwardly juxtaposed to Siebold's collection of Japanese arts and crafts. Travelers, diplomats, and traders, of course, frequently purchased art objects as well as manuscripts abroad and in the nineteenth century, began selling or donating them to public museums or libraries instead of passing them on to their heirs; as we saw in Chapter 3, some travelers, like Ida Pfeiffer, even used this practice to fund further travel. Many museum curators – like Wilhelm von Bode or the first director of the

---

[20] H. Glenn Penny, *Objects of Culture: Ethnology and Ethnographic Museums in Imperial Germany* (Chapel Hill, NC, 2002), pp. 193–6.

[21] Gareis, *Exotik in München*, pp. 72–3, quotation, p. 78.

[22] Ernst Aichner, "Bavarian Army Museum in Ingolstadt," in Gierlichs and Hagedorn, eds., *Islamic Art in Germany*, p. 126. See the other essays in this volume for more examples.

Berlin Islamic Department, Friedrich Sarre – were also collectors and eventually gave their artifacts to their museums. These donations and/or fire sales were crucial to Central European museums at the mid-century; with very little in the way of funds to buy artifacts or to send expeditions to the East, this was practically the only means of acquiring authentic objects. But the number of objects acquired, as well as their diversity, began to increase rapidly once such practices became conventional, and once excavations were begun, they skyrocketed. In fact, the Berlin museums long resisted accepting Max Freiherr von Oppenheim's important Tell Halaf collection: there simply was not enough room in their overstuffed basements to house the sculptures.[23]

Some "oriental" objects, of course, were accorded higher status; ancient oriental art and especially Egyptian and then Assyrian monuments were rather more acceptable to those responsible for the nation's major exhibition spaces. But we should not overestimate the quantity and accessibility of these collections even at the peak of the Second Oriental Renaissance. Egyptian obelisks and sphinxes, captured by Roman armies, had long been familiar to those who had visited Mediterranean cities; eighteenth- and early nineteenth-century engravings and paintings, culminating with the Napoleonic *Description de l'Egypte*, made it even more familiar to artists, architects, and craftsmen. A few aristocratic Central Europeans owned authentic Egyptian artifacts, but large quantities of real Egyptian art only became accessible to the German public after Richard Lepsius's expedition of 1842–5. Well stocked in the wake of Lepsius's return, the Berlin Egyptian Museum opened on the Museum Island in 1850 and impressed the public with its combination of authentic objects, plaster casts, and historicizing murals. But most other Egyptian collections were much less elaborate and accessible. Although founded in 1840, until after 1893, the Egyptian collection at the University Museum in Leipzig – where some of Germany's most important Egyptologists worked – consisted of one good mummy, a few authentic but minor pieces, and a number of plaster casts. Like Germany's other museums, it was conceived chiefly as an extension of the university's library – though it was open to the public on Sundays.[24] Similarly, though German readers saw depictions of the Mesopotamian monuments excavated by A. H. Layard and his successors in the late 1840s, the Berlin museums actually began their own forays into Mesopotamia fifty years later and the fully restored Ishtar Gate was only installed for public viewing in 1934. As late as 1922, Wilhelm von Bode complained that the Islamic section of the Kaiser Friedrich Museum remained "almost unknown; thanks to the very off-putting entryways, by our reckoning, hardly even one of 15–20 museum visitors accidentally stray into the Islamic department."[25] Some of the new departments created in the wake of Richard Schöne's appointment as General Director of the Royal Museums (in 1880) were staffed only by unpaid

---

[23] This material, some of it excavated as early as 1911, was still housed in Oppenheim's private Tell Halaf Museum in 1934. See *Führer durch das Tell Halaf-Museum: Berlin, Franklinstr. 6* (Gräfenhainichen, 1934).

[24] Anon., "Zur Geschichte der Sammlung," in Renate Krauspe, ed., *Das Ägyptisches Museum der Universität Leipzig* (Mainz, 1997), pp. 1–4.

[25] Quoted in Klaus Brisch, "Wilhelm von Bode und sein Verhältnis zur islamischen und ostasiatischen Kunst," in *Jahrbuch der Berliner Museen* 28, Beiheft "Kennershaft" (1996): 46.

volunteers and given virtually no exhibition space. To put it rather crudely, they were expected to buy stuff for the basement and to publish specialized books about it, not to put it on view or explain it to the general public.

But this does not mean that the system lacked dynamism, for it was from those very basements and those underpaid museum assistants that new engagements with oriental art were made possible.[26] Let us start with those museum basements and storehouses; how and when did they get so stuffed? Again, I would suggest that a quiet period of collecting lies behind the increase in public attention given to the material at the fin de siècle. The process was a cumulative one, beginning as early as the 1840s, with Lepsius's Egyptian campaign, and escalating over time. By the time we reach the 1870s – when Berlin's museum budgets, in particular, expanded enormously – there were already a considerable number of artifacts in storage. But the greatest period of increase comes after that time, as an imperialist urge to conquer and display coincided with a historicist desire to possess one of every possible type and to document every step in a developmental process. At the same time, curators were seized by the fear that all unspoiled cultures were about to be spoiled by modernization (and all prices increased by the intrusion of the market). In the "open door" era, competition between nations and museums increased dramatically the pressure on both scholars and buyers to "get there" more quickly; heads of individual museum departments were also eager to outcompete their rivals, both at home and abroad, and to create collections that would attract scholarly, if not popular, attention. Their methods were sometimes confrontational – as in Adolf Erman's attempts to force the Anglo-French antiquities service in Egypt to allow German scholars to help decide which sites to excavate, and to whom digging rights should be given.[27] But more often officials preferred secretive tactics. As one collector described the approach he had used successfully on his recent trip to China, Japan, and Korea: "The adage, that the best women are those about whom one speaks least, can with justice be applied to the serious, goal-oriented collector, for if he lets his intentions show, if he trumpets his coming and the reason for it to the whole world, he creates for himself unnecessary competition, [rivals] who seek to upset his plans, to complicate his work, and to cause the prices to skyrocket."[28]

As the basements filled up, new discoveries were made and the museums sought to extend their collecting activities to new fields, it became common practice for university professors – many of them trained as philologists, not as archaeologists or art historians – to head up individual departments and for credentialed scholars in certain fields, especially young ones awaiting a call, to work for a time in the museum. Naturally, orientalists in such positions – such as Erman or Friedrich Delitzsch – hired their own students or other university-trained orientalists to take these jobs. This made for a highly competent workforce, linguistically-gifted, well read, and eager to impress higher-ups with their cataloging skills, and it gave

---

[26] The dynamics of cultural change described here are remarkably similar to those Lynn Nyhart has profiled in her innovative new book on the study of natural history in Wilhelmine Germany, *Modern Nature: The Rise of the Biological Perspective in Germany* (Chicago, IL, 2009).

[27] On the prologue to Erman's efforts, see Reid, *Whose Pharoahs?* pp. 113–15.

[28] Adolf Fischer to Museums, July 3, 1905, P-ZSA, AA/R, 37679 (now in B-BArch R 901/37679).

younger scholars a chance to immerse themselves in "the stuff," which was becoming daily more and more exotic.

For a time, these collections served primarily as laboratories where scholars who depended on objects – art historians, natural historians, archaeologists, folk-lorists, and ethnographers – spent most of their time simply sorting, authenticat-ing, and trying to date and catalog the mass of new objects. But out of this experience came a generation with new skills, men like the classical archaeologist Adolf Furtwängler, who transformed the study of Greek *Kleinkunst*.[29] Among the orientalists, Adolf Erman was one of the first to benefit; he was employed in the late 1870s to integrate the 15,000-item coin collection of British officer Seton Guthrie into the Royal Coin Cabinet in Berlin, a task that surely helped him expand his understanding of everyday life in Egypt.[30] But there would be many more, from Josef Strzygowski to Albert Grünwedel, from Otto Kümmel to Richard Ettinghausen, who would earn their scholarly spurs as catalogers and curators. Some of these apprenticeships were long-lasting; Kümmel, who would become Germany's foremost scholar of East Asian art, served as an apprentice at the Hamburg Museum für Kunst und Gewerbe, at the City Museum in Freiburg, at the Berlin Zeughaus, and finally at the Berlin Ethnographic Museum before being recognized as an expert in the field. The inventories and catalogs produced by these scholars served as the art-historical equivalent of positivist translations, editions, and dictionaries in the realm of textual scholarship and laid the founda-tions for the non–aestheticizing art history and oriental cultural history practiced in the twentieth and twenty-first centuries.

This process helps to explain the remarkable specialization and diversification in late nineteenth-century archaeological and art-historical studies and also the amazingly detailed knowledge many members of this generation possessed with respect to a diverse and non-canonical set of artifacts. The fact that this work was extremely time-consuming, poorly compensated, and usually thankless, also helps to explain the advent of "furious" orientalists like Josef Strzygowski and his antagonist, Ernst Herzfeld, precisely from the world of museum curatorship. These were men who made their careers by knowing the non-European stuff better than anyone else and figuring out how to turn this advantage – which would have made them, before the 1880s, merely obscure antiquarians – into cultural clout.

It is perhaps telling that the man who had the most cultural clout and who contributed most to the rising appreciation of oriental art in late Wilhelmine Germany was not an art historian or an archaeologist, but a private collector and a bureaucrat, Wilhelm von Bode; here again, as in Chapter 2, we see how important a single, well-placed patron can be in furthering cultural change.[31] Bode had purchased his first oriental carpet in Italy in 1871, the year before he began work for the Berlin museums, and in the next decades acquired many more for

---

[29] See Marchand, "From Antiquarian to Archaeologist? Adolf Furtwängler and the Problem of 'Mod-ern' Classical Archaeology," in Peter N. Miller, ed., *Momigliano and Antiquarianism: Foundations of the Modern Cultural Sciences* (Toronto, 2007), pp. 248–85.

[30] Stefan Heidemann, "Collections of Oriental Coins in Germany," in Gierlichs and Hagedorn, eds., *Islamic Art in Germany*, p. 26.

[31] Information in this paragraph is drawn from Klaus Brisch, "Wilhelm von Bode," pp. 33–48.

himself and for Berlin's Museum of Decorative Arts. Although he became department head for European painting and sculpture, Bode continued to collect carpets and even to write specialized studies about them; in the course of this "hobby," he learned to know travelers and collectors like Friedrich Sarre and to respect the arts of the Islamic world. By 1900, he was pushing for the creation of an Islamic museum, to be stocked with materials removed from the arts and crafts and ethnography museums. His superior, however, the classicist Richard von Schöne, opposed this move as did the director of Berlin's *Kunstgewerbe* Museum, Julius Lessing, as well as many other museum officials, and the press. Bode managed to realize his plans by the roundabout method of acquiring something so big and impressive (the Mschatta Gate) that it could not be put in the storehouse and by getting Friedrich Sarre to agree to be the unpaid director of the new department, and to put his own collections on display. In 1905, Schöne resigned over the affair. Bode became General Director, and by 1907, the Islamic Department was up and running – though it had to be housed in the dark basement of the Kaiser Friedrich Museum, and as we have seen, visitors often had trouble locating the two-room exhibit. Bode had less success with his plans for an East Asian art museum and for a museum for Near Eastern and Islamic art – though he fought for these for many years, he never got the bureaucracy to agree to display these works together, and as art, rather than as ethnographic or decorative objects. Instead, state money went for the building of the chiefly classical Pergamon Museum.[32]

We can see Bode's story as a glass half empty or one half full; it is clear that the visibility of oriental art increased significantly between 1890 and 1914 – but also that appreciation for the aesthetic and even historical importance of eastern forms remained limited. But looking carefully at this story, we can also see how one category of objects, oriental carpets, did undergo significant reevaluation and in the process change the minds of a few influential culture-makers and institution builders. Bode was deeply involved in a set of cultural changes here whose origins lay much more in the marketplace than in the university, but did finally have a transformative impact on art-historical studies. We need now to abandon, if briefly, the library and the lecture hall, and immerse ourselves in the complexities of the carpet trade.

ORIENTAL CARPETS AND AUSTRIAN ART HISTORIANS

As Renaissance paintings amply attest, Europeans have long admired the luxurious color and ornamental intricacy of eastern carpets and used them both in domestic settings and in sanctuaries to brighten dark rooms and warm up cold floors. Relatively expensive in the early modern era, their affordability increased as transportation systems evolved and European wealth and influence spread; by the mid-nineteenth century, "oriental" carpets adorned many a bourgeois floor, wall, or tabletop. But it was not until the 1870s, as David Sylvester has argued, that "collecting governed by a sense of history" began. Interestingly, this was in part a reaction to increasing European interference in indigenous carpet production, as merchants tried to dictate designs and colors to local craftsmen, exporting

---

[32] Marchand, *Down from Olympus*, pp. 288–94.

too one of the European chemical industry's proud new achievements: synthetic dyes.[33] European workshops began turning out imitations at even more affordable prices, forcing traditional carpet–makers to the wall. By 1891, one connoisseur admitted regretfully that the last best hope for saving authentic carpet weaving was its adoption by western firms and arts and crafts schools. "The lovers of the splendors of oriental carpets might hope that these imitative endeavors will have reached a satisfying stage of development at the moment when the last inner-Asian nomads have buried the last operating handwoven carpet-workshop in its grave."[34]

In Berlin, the two museum curators we mentioned above, Julius Lessing and Wilhelm von Bode, began quietly researching and buying older carpets, realizing that their scarcity would sooner or later make prices skyrocket. They took advantage of a wave of carpet sales occasioned by a devastating famine in Iran in 1871–2;[35] as usual, savvy collectors seized their opportunity to buy when sellers were desperate. But gradually the market caught up with the speculators as critics of mass production like William Morris began to sing the praises of handmade, premodern carpets. By the 1890s, the search for "authentic" carpet-makers began, precisely on the model of contemporary anthropologists' quests for unspoiled indigenous peoples. In 1893, outbidding numerous other would-be buyers, the South Kensington Museum paid an eye-popping 2,500 pounds for the universally admired Ardabil carpet (1539–40). Thereafter, early Persian carpets, in particular, became enormously desirable[36] and Europeans moved to take over both the study and the making of "real" oriental textiles.

As suggested in the earlier part of this chapter, the project of saving authentic carpet-weaving went hand in hand with deeper studies of carpet history. Not surprisingly, one of the first of the latter came from Lessing, whose job as curator at the arts and crafts museum in Berlin put him in touch both with the early arts and crafts movement and with actual carpets. His 1877 *Altorientalischen Teppichmustern nach Bildern und Originalen des XV–XVI. Jahrhunderts* moved a bit beyond the use of carpets simply to improve domestic manufactures, but retained, as its title made clear, the utilitarian functions of the traditional pattern book. Though Lessing had begun to collect Islamic artifacts after the 1867 World Exhibition, his book relied heavily on the depictions of carpets in western paintings. In 1882, the Austrian orientalist Josef Karabacek pioneered the use of Ottoman sources and textile inscriptions in his work on Persian "needle-painting" (*Die persische Nadelmalerei Susandschird*); regrettably, the few other specialists in the field quickly realized that Karabacek's work was riddled with errors and flights of fancy.[37] Over the course of the next decade, one of these specialists wrote, two things continued to bar the way to further progress in writing the history of carpet design: lack of comparative material older than the late Middle Ages and lack of

[33] Sylvester, "Western Attitudes to Eastern Carpets," pp. 4–5.

[34] Alois Riegl, *Altorientalische Teppiche* (Leipzig, 1891), p. 214.

[35] Vernoit, "Islamic Art and Architecture," p. 12.

[36] See here Sylvester, "Western Attitudes to Eastern Carpets," pp. 12–18.

[37] See Becker, "Joseph von Karabacek," in idem, *Islamstudien* 2: 491–8, and Richard Ettinghausen, "Islamic Art and Archeology," pp. 26–7.

scholarly interest in the art of Byzantium and the Near East.[38] He might have added that, Karabacek aside, the carpet enthusiasts of the age continued to be chiefly travelers and museum men and not readers of oriental languages. When Wilhelm von Bode in 1892 published the long essay that would form the basis for his later important study *Vorderasiatische Knüpfteppiche* (1902), he, like Lessing before him, depended upon depictions of carpets in European paintings, not "oriental" sources, to establish upper dates for certain types of carpets. His carpets, mostly acquired in Italy, were largely housed in the museums' basements, though before the founding of the Islamic Department, he did hang some to set off Renaissance sculptures.[39] Though what we called the Second Oriental Renaissance was certainly underway in the collection of and increased interest in oriental textiles, the frame remained very much a European one.

The man who helped to change this perhaps more than any other was not himself an orientalist, and he was, in any event, most keenly devoted not to the Orient, but to the cultural world of the late Roman Empire. Alois Riegl, curator of textiles at the Museum für Kunst und Industrie in Vienna from 1885 to 1897, began his service to Asian art by staging in 1891 the largest exhibition of carpets ever seen in Europe. In the same year, he published an important little book entitled *Altorientalische Teppiche*, which integrated the study of early carpets into contemporary debates about the origins of medieval European art. Here, Riegl quietly dismissed the relevance of classical art for understanding the modern world and rejected the Hegelian presumption that oriental art had stopped developing after the battle of Marathon. Instead, he set himself the task of answering, in non-aestheticizing terms, an extensive set of art-historical questions that earlier scholars, and especially classicists, had sidelined. "Unfortunately, classical archaeology has up to now pretty much exclusively concerned itself with pure masterworks of Attic art," he wrote.

Even the threads that bind pre-Hellenic and archaic art to that of the people of the Levant have been much more energetically and lucidly studied than the many-sided inter-mixture of ancient oriental and Greek art in the age of the Diadochi; [and the] outcome [of this inter-mixture] has been seen in a much too one-sided way, as decline and fall. It was believed one could ignore [this art]; actually, however, the contact between the old and immobile and the young, fluid and adaptable [cultures] ought to be understood as the beginning of a new period of art and culture, one which is much more closely connected with the coming middle ages than with the era of the Persian Wars.[40]

Riegl made it his business to emphasize the importance of these ignored Hellenistic forms, a mission that inevitably involved rethinking not only the question of Roman "decline" but also the Orient's creative impact on western culture.

A few words about Riegl's background may be helpful before we delve more deeply into his contributions to the history of oriental art. As a young man, Riegl had studied technical historical research methods (chronology and

---

[38] Riegl, *Altorientalische Teppiche*, pp. vii, viii.
[39] See Volkmar Enderlein, *Wilhelm von Bode und die Berliner Teppichsammlung* (Berlin, 1995), pp. 6, 13–15.
[40] Riegl, *Altorientalische Teppiche*, pp. 111–12.

paleography), empirical psychology, and Indo-Germanic linguistics, among other subjects, in Vienna; his initiation into the world of art history came by way of another empiricist, Moriz Thausing, the curator of the Albertina collection of sketches and one of the early advocates of monument preservation. Riegl wrote his dissertation on a medieval monument, and his *Habilitationsschrift*, inspired by viewing sections of the Pergamon Altar in Berlin, traced the origins of medieval calendar iconography to the Hellenistic era. As Margaret Olin has shown, the *Habilitationsschrift* demonstrated already Riegl's interest in Hellenistic art as the fount of Byzantine, Sassanid, and ultimately European medieval art, and his determination to play down the destructiveness of Rome's "barbarian" invaders.[41] And yet, Riegl, born in 1858 and a loyal defender of the multicultural Austrian Empire, continued throughout his life to trace modern styles to the Roman Empire and to resist the temptation to lay out racial trajectories. Though Riegl did open the way for a highly consequential debate on artistic relations between East and West, his own diffusionist tendencies were tempered by an understanding of the ways in which different cultures adapted designs to their own materials and ends. His critique of high classicism was one that did not become a shrill defense of *völkisch* purity or a paean to primeval eastern origins.

Already in *Altorientalische Teppiche*, Riegl found himself arguing with several hypotheses, all of which had been sketched but not fully worked out by scholars of the positivist generation before him: first, that Persian art was autochthonous, having evolved from a combination of ancient Assyrian and ancient Persian designs; second, that eastern decorative art was the pure product of Arab culture, which is why Europeans had never made good carpets; and third that the art of the *Germanen* had come to them from an indigenous Nordic *Urkultur*. It was not necessary, Riegl thought, to have recourse to these quasi-racial explanations when a perfectly good historical one would do: the similarities between Islamic and medieval art, between European folk art and the arts of Persia, were to be explained by a historical phenomenon: their shared roots in what he called "international Hellenistic-Roman Art" or sometimes "late Roman-Byzantine Art."[42] Differences could be explained by the persistence of local traditions or adaptations to the environment, and Riegl was perfectly willing to give the (ancient) Orient credit for new ideas and fine craft traditions which had helped to shape what one might call the Roman "international" style. But Riegl was quite sure, like most of his contemporaries, that the modern Orient was a place of decadence and indolence, and quite explicit about the new opportunities offered by the Austro-Hungarian occupation of Bosnia-Herzegovina to gather information about traditional carpet-weaving techniques.[43] Once again, his was a politics driven by domestic, European concerns and debates, and his interests ran typically to the ancient, not the modern world. He did not, to my knowledge, travel in the Orient nor pretend to speak to its present-day concerns. At the heart of his inquiries, as

---

[41] Margaret R. Olin, *Forms of Representation in Alois Riegl's Theory of Art* (University Park, PA, 1992), pp. 5–10.

[42] Riegl, *Altorientalische Teppiche*, pp. 112–47, quotations pp. 146, 147. See also Olin, *Forms of Representation*, pp. 18–23.

[43] Riegl, *Altorientalische Teppiche*, pp. 173–6.

Jaś Elsner has noted, lay "axiomatic assumptions about evolutionary progress and change in a multicultural empire."[44] This is an important point; once again, our scholar was a man shaped by his context, but it was not global colonial affairs but the political and cultural world of the Austro-Hungarian Empire about which Riegl, an exemplary Austro-German liberal monarchist, cared most.

In his first major theoretical work, *Stilfragen* (1893), Riegl described the history of art as a teleological process, in which design – he focused especially on the acanthus leaf motif – evolved as a means of solving problems of representation posed by previous makers of artworks. Born of an age of new archaeological discoveries, accelerating artistic experimentation, and enhanced appreciation of carpets, Riegl's approach effectively undercut both the tendency to treat non-naturalistic representation as inept and the presumption that all cultures at all times aimed at the same aesthetic goals. In his even more important (and lucid!) *Spätrömische Kunstindustrie* (1901), Riegl made perfectly clear one of his major aims: his determination not to see late antique and medieval art as "decline," compared to the Olympian beauties of Greek sculpture. Late antique art, he complained, remains a "dark continent on the map of art historical research," not because materials and information are lacking but because of persisting neo-classical prejudices.[45] It is high time, he insisted, that modern scholars recognize that "the aim of the fine arts is not completely exhausted with what we call beauty nor with what we call animation" and that "modern art, with all its advantages, would never have been possible if late Roman art with its unclassical tendency had not prepared the way."[46] What held scholarship back, he intimated, was not lack of materials but lack of desire; again, we find passion, or its lack, important in structuring what is studied and how studies proceed. Riegl was not really a "furious" orientalist; he died in 1905, before many of the artifacts from Minoan Crete, Assur, Babylon, Ugarit, Susa, Samarra, Persepolis, or "Turfan" had come to light. Riegl's specialty was the art of Byzantium and of the late Roman Empire, not oriental art as such. But as we shall see, the study of early Christian and Byzantine art proved to be a useful jumping off point for many of the eastward-looking art historians after him.

Something that does appear extensively in *Stilfragen*, but which will largely drop out in the twentieth century is prehistorical art, including carved bones and cave paintings. This was highly relevant to Riegl's central argument: that vegetal designs do not arise, independently of one another, from the observation of nature, but are the product of the human imagination and similarities in style are likely to be the result of diffusion (borrowing and trade), rather than from independent evolution. This was, for Riegl, an argument against an ancient source, namely Vitruvius, who claimed that the acanthus leaf design originated in the observation of the plant, but it was also an argument against what he called a Darwinist "theory of the technical-materialist origin of

---

[44] Jaś Elsner, "The Birth of Late Antiquity: Riegl and Strzygowski in 1901," in *Art History* 25, no. 3 (2002): 375. Also, Suzanne Marchand, "Professionalizing the Senses: Art and Music History in Vienna, 1890–1920," in *Austrian History Yearbook* 21 (1985): 23–57.

[45] Alois Riegl, *Late Roman Art Industry*, trans. Rolf Winkes (Rome, 1985), p. 6.

[46] Ibid., p. 11.

all primitive art forms."[47] Though Riegl's art-historical successors may have differed on other aspects of the *Stilfragen*, they seem to have been convinced to jettison both Vitruvius and Darwin, leaving prehistorical art to the prehistorians and ethnographers. In the next generation, oriental and ethnographic art really began to part ways – though it would take some time for museum exhibits to catch up. Here we see, in another realm, the same sort of backing away from ethnographic universalism we saw in the study of religion; and as we will see in the section to follow, what tended to take the place of this form of cultural Darwinism was again a hyper-diffusionist search for origins.

JOSEF STRZYGOWSKI: THE ART-HISTORICAL FUROR ORIENTALIS

Riegl was then innovative, but understanding oriental art in its own terms was never really his goal. The scholar much more willing to press for the Orient's agency and autochthony – and one who fully deserves the title "furious orientalist" – was Riegl's malevolent student Josef Strzygowski (1862–1941).[48] In examining Strzygowski's career, we have the opportunity to observe the transformation of what was, in the work of Friedrich Schlegel and Jacob Grimm, a dimly envisioned anti-classical cultural history and its replacement with a fully racialized history of art. But if we blame Strzygowski for racializing art history, we also must give him credit for a deep and abiding interest in oriental art, one which generated many new inquiries and inspired many a more moderate student of Asian forms. His deplorable politics have made it difficult, since 1945, to cite his publications, though they are undeniably the product of remarkable familiarity with the major and minor arts of a large number of little-known cultures and broke much new scholarly ground. Like the others studied in this chapter, his work was made possible by the positivist collecting and documenting work that had gone before him, especially work undertaken by the museums. But Strzygowski had the passion, the daring, the resentment, and the opportunity – offered by changes in academic culture and in publishers' wares – to mold the proceeds of the museological version of the Second Oriental Renaissance into an all-out attack on liberal neohumanism.

Of his biography, it is important to note that Strzygowski grew up in a German family (his mother hailed from an aristocratic line) in Austrian Silesia, an area in which the generally well-heeled Germans were far outnumbered by the generally lower-class Poles and Czechs. Rejecting a career like his father's in textile manufacturing, but non-plussed by his early studies at the Institut für österreichische Geschichtsforschung, in 1883, Strzygowski moved to Berlin and then to Munich, where he studied with the classical archaeologist Hermann Brunn. Brunn almost certainly set Strzygowski's dissertation topic (on the iconography of the baptism of Christ) and arranged for him to spend a year in Rome. But Brunn probably did

---

[47] Riegl, *Problems of Style: Foundations for a History of Ornament*, trans. Evelyn Kain (Princeton, NJ, 1992), pp. 7–11, quotation p. 23.

[48] Since drafting this section, I discovered Jaś Elsner's essay, which makes very much the same point. Elsner, "Birth of Late Antiquity," pp. 358–79. For my more detailed view, see Marchand, "Rhetoric of Artifacts," pp. 106–30.

not anticipate the direction Strzygowski's arguments would take; for Strzygowski's focus was not on the survival of classical forms, but rather on the contributions of Byzantine styles to the evolution of medieval Italian art.[49] Already Strzygowski was bucking trends, emphasizing the contributions of Constantinople rather than those of either classical or Christian Rome, and in his next major piece, *Cimabue* (1887), he again insisted on the powerful influence of Byzantium on the West. It was as a Byzantinist that Strzygowski was hired by Wilhelm von Bode to go to Istanbul and to compile a list of artifacts that the Sultan could (and did) give the Kaiser for the early Christian collection to be housed in the Kaiser Friedrich Museum. As Bode's ally, Strzygowski would later be instrumental in the acquisition of the Mschatta Gate as well.[50]

It is a sign that neoclassicism's power was waning that Strzygowski's unconventional tastes netted him a professorship at the University of Graz in 1892. But the young scholar's iconoclastic tendencies were not yet fully developed, and the next steps, in the peak years of our furor and the axial period in the formation of Austro-German hyper-nationalism, were surely decisive ones. In 1894–5, Strzygowski went to Egypt to inventory the collections of Coptic art at the Cairo Museum. He later said that he recognized there that many regions where Christian and Islamic art flourished had been untouched by Mediterranean influence – and shaped instead by artistic traditions rooted in Egypt and Mesopotamia.[51] Strzygowski here still had a role for the Jews. In fact, he noted happily that their mediation between Hellenistic and Byzantine art made it possible to dispense with another set of mediators, namely, the Romans.[52]

But Strzygowski was beginning to connect oriental origins with an anti-Catholic, anti-classical view of European cultural history. The title of his polemical masterpiece of 1901, *Orient oder Rom?* – a specialized study of the eastern origins of European medieval art – gives us even more proof of Strzygowski's increasingly pan-German, anti-Catholic politics; in it, he attacked the Viennese art historian Franz Wickhoff's highly esteemed interpretation of an illuminated medieval text, *Wiener Genesis*, arguing against the notion that late Roman forms had quite logically become Christian ones (just as the Roman Empire had quite logically evolved in the Holy Roman Empire). *Orient oder Rom?* veiled its political, if not its personal, animosities, but Strzygowski's contemporaries would all have understood his reference to the contemporary "Los von Rom" campaign pursued by radical German nationalists, which sought to detach Austrian and Bavarian

---

[49] Josef Strzygowski, "Ikonographie der Taufe Christi" (dissertation, University of Munich, 1885), pp. 11, 28ff.

[50] Strzygowski, *Aufgang des Nordens: Lebenskampf eines Kunstforschers um ein deutsches Weltbild* (Leipzig, 1936), p. 13; on Mschatta, Brisch, "Wilhelm von Bode," pp. 37–41; Marchand, "Rhetoric of Artifacts," pp. 123–6.

[51] Strzygowski, *Aufgang des Nordens*, pp. 13–14. It is striking that in his catalog, which appeared in 1904, the year after the death of the great liberal Theodor Mommsen, the first paragraph attacked the idea that Egypt had been Hellenized, or Romanized; the first footnote asked readers to compare Strzygowski's insistence that Egyptian gods had triumphed with Mommsen's much more syncretic view. Strzygowski, *Koptische Kunst. Service des antiquités de l'Égypte: catalogue général des antiquités égyptiennes du Musée du Caire* (Osnabrück, 1973; reprint of 1904 edition), p. xv.

[52] Strzygowski, *Orient oder Rom? Beiträge zur Geschichte der spätantiken und frühchristlichen Kunst* (Leipzig, 1901), p. 9.

Catholics from Rome and to link them, over and against the Habsburg Empire's other ethnic groups, to Bismarck's increasingly powerful Reich.[53] Less and less convinced of the enduring impact of classical forms and willing to credit early dates for oriental innovations, sick of Franz Josef's concessions to minority groups and eager to see a new generation of artifact-oriented scholars prevail, Strzygowski, like the Panbabylonists and the religious-historical school, began to push the envelope further eastward.

Strzygowski was clearly also emboldened by his on-the-ground experience, which he believed gave him the right to criticize his senior Austrian colleagues; the fundamental flaw from which both Riegl and Wickhoff suffered, he charged in 1902, was that they did not know the Orient. It is interesting, and indicative of changes in his generation, that for Strzygowski, knowing the Orient did *not* mean knowing oriental languages, but rather having seen art and architecture in situ. Experience of the East and close contact with its monuments legitimized his attack on the Hegelian "Phantasiebild" of the "fathers" and his assertion that Greek culture had expired in the Orient's embrace.[54] Having learned the value of direct encounters with *Realien* from his museum experience, Strzygowski would take an evolving art-historical critique of philology to its logical end, arguing in 1928 that the study of art should replace Latin as the basis of education and of the humanities as a whole.[55] Like Winckler's bid to make Assyriology the *ur*-science, Strzygowski's plan aimed at undermining Germandom's classicizing institutions by opening up a wider, deeper world than the one available to the classical philologist.

In his prewar work, Strzygowski was determined to challenge his fellows, jealous of their successes, and eager to trade on his "oriental" experience. He was an iconoclast, one whose iconoclasm took the form of pushing harder and further the Austrian school's arguments about the importance of late Roman and Hellenistic art for the forming of medieval and Islamic (viz., non-classical) tastes. He was roundly disliked by other members of the academy and considered too opinionated and mean-spirited in treating the work of others. But his work was sufficiently pathbreaking, compelling, and plentiful that he was a favored candidate for the job he coveted: Franz Wickhoff's chair at the University of Vienna (Wickhoff died young, at age 52). Typically, for the late Habsburg world, the contest between liberal and non-liberal factions was fierce, and there was very little ground upon which to broker a compromise between divergent conceptions of Austria's lineage – Strzygowski seeking a pure *Urheimat*, the liberal loyalists emphasizing ethnic diversity under Roman Catholic auspices. Typically, too, a decision was made which produced less, rather than more harmony: Wickhoff's position was split between Strzygowski and the western-oriented Max Dvořák. In 1909 Strzygowski was made chair for non-European (*ausser-europäisch*) art

---

[53] This movement, which sought to destroy Catholic influence in southern Germany and Austria, was at its peak in the late 1890s. Much agitation went on at the University of Graz, where Strzygowski taught from 1892 until 1909. Strzygowski later denied that he had meant the book to be interpreted in a confessional sense. Strzygowski, *Aufgang des Nordens*, p. 57.

[54] Strzygowski, *Hellas in des Orients Umarmung* (Sonderabdruck aus der Beilage zur *Allgemeinen Zeitung* Nr. 40 und 41 vom 18 und 19 February 1902; Munich, 1902), pp. 4–5, 9.

[55] Strzygowski, *Forschung und Erziehung* (Stuttgart, 1928), p. 31.

history, the first such chair in Europe.[56] But it did not make him happy or reconcile him to the academic establishment. On the contrary, it gave him a soapbox and the opportunity to train students to share his point of view.

This is perhaps a good moment to outline the steps by which Strzygowski became a "non-Europeanist" – and to indicate the extent to which he deserved this title. Throughout his life, Strzygowski's major objective was to explain the origins of Christian art and to increase appreciation for medieval German forms. These were recognizable aims shared with Riegl, but as we have seen, Strzygowski took them further, moving first to explicate the origins of Christian art in Byzantium and then the origins of Coptic forms. Predisposed to iconoclasm, he moved, as his autobiography notes, gradually further East, writing on Islamic art, on the art of the Seleucids and Sassanids, on an Albanian treasure, on the art of the nomadic Germans, and on Balkan and Scandinavian art. In 1918, he published a very important and richly documented study of early Armenian art and architecture, arguing (without shedding a tear for the Armenians' recent fate) that they must be seen as the mediators between the Northern cultures and the "hothouse" world of the ethnically-mixed eastern Mediterranean.[57] In the 1920s, he even championed ancient Croatian art, arguing for the autonomy of this art from *both* the Roman and the Byzantine Empires.[58] What drew him to these very different cultures was their supposed independence from the classical tradition, and often from representational forms. That was enough for him to make them part of his repertoire, even had he not developed a grand-scale theory about their common descent and westward diffusion.

It should be said that Strzygowski opened up many new areas for scrutiny and inspired many a young student to enter the fields of Byzantine, Islamic, Indian, or Iranian art history; and it is also the case that Strzygowski was a vehement critic of humanistic prejudice and narrow-mindedness. What is also remarkable about Strzygowski – and what has contributed to his long-lasting influence and appeal beyond the realm of the racist crazies – is that he was a remarkable collector of data and able to marshal vast quantities of it; his publications offered curious readers new topics for contemplation, and a remarkable number of photographs of obscure and not easily accessible monuments and artifacts. His books appeared during a period in which there were very few specialists in the area and very few researchers in the field. Ernst Herzfeld, one of the few who had visited a number of the places Strzygowski wrote about in his important study of Islamic art, *Amida* (1910), had to engage in what the archaeologist called "a labor of Hercules" to

---

[56] "Protokoll aufgenommen in der Dekanatskanzlei der philosophischen Fakultät der k. k. Universität in Wien," June 16, 1909, and Redlich (Dekan) to Austrian Cultural Ministry, July 12, 1909, in V-UA, Philos. Fac. Mappe Strzygowski. Later in life, Strzygowski would also be offered a number of other jobs, at Santiniketan University in India (1920), at the Universities of Warsaw and Dorpat (1922, 1923) and at Bryn Mawr (1926). Anon., "Nachruf Josef Strzygowski," in V-UA, Mappe Strzygowski.

[57] Strzygowski, *Die Baukunst der Armenier und Europa*, 2 vol. (Vienna, 1918).

[58] See Strzygowski, *Die altslavische Kunst: Ein Versuch ihres Nachweises* (Augsburg, 1929). It is a testament to the power of Strzygowski's urge to emancipate European art history from neoclassicism that this Germanophile product of the Austro-Polish borderland was willing to find beauty and Aryan ancestry in Slavic art.

identify the problems in Strzygowski's interpretation – his tendency, for example, to throw irrelevant material at a problem, to offer superficial readings of monuments, and to persist in giving Persia credit for all innovation.[59] In response, Strzygowski admitted: "It could well be that in the attempt to answer the questions, I often make false steps or go too far – that is only natural when one is throwing light on wholly unknown terrain."[60] He then went on to argue, quite rightly, that Herzfeld had not visited all the sites he described either and that because Strzygowski did not have funds for an excavation himself, Europeans actually knew very little still about ancient Persian art. Relatively new to the profession compared to the Viennese professor's twenty-year track record, Herzfeld should shut up and work quietly with the monuments for a few years before he passed judgment on Strzygowski's theories.[61] One might draw instructive parallels here with the philological work of Paul de Lagarde, whose mean-spirited Orientophilia similarly tried to destroy conventional Christian and classical prejudices in the name of correcting European history and purifying German *Geist*. As in the case of Lagarde's Septuagint project, it would take intense, specialized work on little-studied topics to demonstrate clearly how much of Strzygowski's critique of Eurocentrism was justified, and how much was simply the product of ideological fervor.

The combination of sweeping ethno-historical narratives and positivist embrace of detail remained characteristic of Strzygowski, but it was only in the course of the Great War that he finally found a way to make his oriental pursuits and passions relevant. Having already decided upon the importance of Persia before the war, he now put even more emphasis on the originality and deep antiquity of Iran, where he found a pure enough *ur*-culture to satisfy his longings. Here too he could find confirmation for his claims for the Orient's influence on the German medieval world, claims he argued were simply reiterations of romantic-era philology.[62] Indeed, he writes in his autobiography: "The discovery of Iran was only the first step toward a much greater surprise: I recognized that something stood behind Iran and its significance, something that linguistics has been occupied with for the last one hundred years without really getting anywhere: the Indo-German question."[63]

In answer to that question, a North-South contrast came into play and in fact began to obscure, though not wipe out his earlier anti-Roman polemics (Strzygowski was not one to forget a slight, or concede an error). In his *Baukunst der Armenier und Europa*, he writes:

The war has taught us what the designation "barbarian" in certain conditions means. The Armenians of the fourth century like the Iranians in general, were [called Barbarians] in the

---

[59] Ernst Herzfeld, review of Max van Berchem and Josef Strzygowski, *Amida*, in *OLZ* 14 (1911): 397–435, quotation p. 434.

[60] Strzygowski, "Das Problem der persischen Kunst," in *OLZ* 14 (1911): 505.

[61] Ibid., pp. 507–10.

[62] Strzygowski, "Mschatta II: Kunstwissenschaftliche Untersuchung," in *Jahrbuch der königlichen preussischen Kunstsammlung* 25 (1904): 373; idem, *Altai Iran und Völkerwanderung* (Leipzig, 1917), pp. 296–7.

[63] Strzygowski, *Aufgang des Nordens*, p. 25.

same sense as today the Germans and German Austrians are [so designated] by the battle cries of [our] enemies. In the period in which Christianity came to [the Armenians] and then, c. 300 became the state religion, they still had primeval völkisch strength and defended this against the hothouse culture of the Greeks, Syrians and southern Persians. It is in the plastic arts, if in any area, that we in Europe can be shown what we have to thank this Aryan folk-power for.[64]

The Armenians had saved Aryan art from Semitic debasement, just as the modern Germans (and German Austrians!) were trying to save Aryan-European culture from western-Semitic civilization. Finally, Strzygowski had found a script – and this one he would stick to for the rest of his long life.

Relevance did not, however, tame Strzygowski's passions, in part because he still felt his field was vastly understudied and hemmed in by persistent humanist prejudices. Thirty years of work, he wrote in 1918, had been ignored by the Viennese museums; "Even the phil-historical section of the academy [of sciences] has only ignorance and contempt for [my work]. Court-air and ossified humanism has partly enervated the human sciences and made them incapable of operating with healthy energy."[65] He blamed not only the scholars of classical and Renaissance art but perhaps especially the moderate orientalists, as enemies of real science and servants of aristocratic-papist "power art," *Bildungschauvinisten*, who valued humanism above truth and Germandom's need to cultivate a "völkisch mentality."[66] His work had never been appreciated and the state of the field was no better in 1936 than it had been when he wrote his Mschatta study in 1904. After his retirement, the humanists had even had the temerity to destroy the world-famous institute he had built.[67] Clearly, despite Aryanism's new currency, Strzygowski did not feel he had won.

In the course of his anti-humanist rantings, Strzygowski occasionally offered interesting insights into the difficulties of studying oriental *Realien* in a culture steeped in specialized philology. The orientalists, he claimed in 1917, were in fact even less disposed to give up their textual studies than the classicists. This made it extremely difficult for someone who wished to take stock of "the Orient" as a whole to garner academic legitimacy:

... for an oriental philologist who undertook the study of art history was not seen as fully respectable, and an art historian, on the other hand, who worked without knowledge of the different languages was seen ever afterwards as a dilettante by the powers that be. Thus the difficult research on the transitional areas between antiquity and medieval art, one characterized by numerous national and linguistic opposing forces, has been left to colleagues who are ready either, as specialists, to die of hunger, or as pariahs, to knock about between the well-established research areas. Under such conditions it was not at all possible to establish the necessary foundations, and to do so [based on] philological fundamentals.[68]

---

[64] Strzygowski, *Baukunst der Armenier* 2: 604.
[65] Ibid., 2: 877.
[66] Strzygowski, *Forschung und Erziehung*, pp. 17–18, 45–6.
[67] Strzygowski, *Spuren indogermanischen Glaubens in der Bildenden Kunst* (Heidelberg, 1936), p. 452.
[68] Strzygowski, *Altai Iran*, p. 225.

Ernst Herzfeld, though he disagreed with Strzygowski on many subjects, might well have seconded these sentiments, as his letters to Carl Becker in the years before the war suggest. Herzfeld was then excavating in Samarra under the direction of Friedrich Sarre and trying to figure out in which field to habilitate, as "oriental archaeology" did not yet exist in German universities – though it manifestly did exist on the ground. But that was rather cold comfort; as Herzfeld fully recognized, the professors tended to like the archaeology student when he was out in the field doing the dirty work, but then treated him as an annoyance, and as an inferior job applicant, when he returned home.[69] In 1912, one young archaeologist wrote of Assyriology: ". . . it has been so preoccupied with its linguistic-historical tasks that for the portion of its realm that goes beyond writing, it has neither sense nor schooling."[70] Even the orientalists did not care very much about oriental art.

One reason for this, as Strzygowski also realized, was that dating oriental art was even more difficult than dating oriental texts. Moreover, much of it – made of wood, paper, or textiles – had disappeared. How could its history be reconstructed? Here Strzygowski was again highly innovative, if also ideologically tendentious. The oriental art historian, he argued, needed to go outside the museum (stocked entirely of Mediterranean wares anyway) and perform the equivalent of Grimmian *Mythenforschung*.[71] Always one to value the "minor" arts, he also advised his readers to examine and collect folk art, in which older traditions were better preserved than in the art commissioned and consumed by the upper classes. The right-thinking cultural historian could not accept silence, he argued; the subject of Mazdaen art, for example, could not be avoided simply because no monuments had been found. Instead, one should opt for "the path of backward deductions, from the early Christian, Central Asian and Islamic." In the absence of contemporary documentation too, it was allowable to use later, indigenous sources; indeed, for Strzygowski, tracing the (Aryan) origins of Armenian art, for example, this was actually preferable to using the misleading classical sources.[72] Here there are parallels to be drawn to the work of Gunkel and Bousset; it was time to break the stranglehold of historicism and to reconstruct traditions and "cultural circles" using fragments of evidence, and faith in the homogeneity of ethnic groups and the persistence of styles over the *longue durée*.

One of the striking things about Strzygowski, in retrospect, are his passions, passions that sprang undoubtedly from contemporary political and personal relations, but which were worked out meticulously and relentlessly on the terrain of the ancient Near East. Though Strzygowski did write occasionally on modern (German) art, his engagement with it remained rather superficial and lacked the

---

[69] Herzfeld to Becker, April 17, 1911, September 10, 1911, in B-GSPK, Nachlass Becker, M. 4023. In April 1911 a depressed, and perhaps even suicidal Herzfeld told Becker he was about to give up his scholarly career – by May, fortunately, some of the problems he was facing (including, apparently, one of transporting excavated artifacts) were solved, and the crisis passed. Herzfeld to Becker, April 20, 1911, in ibid.

[70] Ludwig Curtius, "Studien zur Geschichte der altorientalischen Kunst. I. 'Gilgamesh' und 'Heabani,'" *Sitzungsberichte der Königlichen Bayerischen Akademie der Wissenschaften*, Philos-philhist. Klasse 1912, no. 7, p. 3.

[71] For example, Strzygowski, *L'Ancien art chrétien de Syrie* (Paris, 1936), p. 188.

[72] Strzygowski, *Baukunst der Armenier* 2: 625, quotation p. 630.

passion he lavished on the ancient Iranians and Armenians, Germanic tribes, and early Islamic craftsmen. He cared more deeply about the Orient than did virtually all of his contemporaries; but it would be difficult to understand Strzygowski's worldview, not to mention his lifelong, painstaking, and vast study of the artifacts of the East by imposing a colonial frame. Strzygowski did not become a scholar of the "oriental" world in order to intervene in it; he did so rather in order to explore under-studied realms and to undermine a "liberal" classicism he – for both political and personal reasons – had come to detest.

Strzygowski did have a large following, especially outside the charmed circle of credentialed humanists.[73] Ironically, however, his fame and influence seems to have been greater in Armenia, Sweden, Turkey, and Croatia than in Germany or Austria.[74] He did, however, have at least one "furious" follower in the Germanies, Ernst Diez, who also moved from Byzantine art to deep-Orient advocacy. Already before the war, Diez was trying to prove the Syrian, rather than Sicilian, origin of painted ivory work and would generate in the course of the 1920s–1940s, a large number of popular books on Islamic, Indian, Iranian, and East Asian art history.[75] Diez, like his mentor, would advocate Iranian-Aryan purity and ingenuity. But Strzygowski would also train and promote a large number of female students, who would make careers outside Central Europe and remain relatively free from racist ideologies. What they, like many other readers of Strzygowski's work, took away from it was his insistence on seeing eastern art in nonwestern frames. The man Ernst Gombrich would call "the Attila of art history" attacked western humanism for his own destructive and ideological reasons; but he also taught his students to throw away their classicizing spectacles and their Renaissance norms.[76]

Seeing eastern art in its own terms was something also being attempted by those with more direct influence over the public's exposure to real-existing artifacts. In what follows, we move from Austria back to Germany and from art-historical narratives to exhibitions of art, hoping to show how scholars tried to introduce the wider public to a new view of oriental art – and to assess the successes and failures of those endeavors.

EXHIBITING THE ORIENT IN MUNICH AND BERLIN

As we have seen, museum officials and a few academic experts, by the time of the Great War, had learned a good deal about the art of the Near, Middle, and Far

---

[73] Cf. Herzfeld, review of Berchem and Strzygowski, *Amida*, p. 398.

[74] See Christina Maranci, "Medieval Armenian Architecture in Historiography: Josef Strzygowski and his Legacy" (Ph.D. dissertation, Department of Art and Archaeology, Princeton University, 1998); Talinn Grigor, "Orient oder Rom? Qajar 'Aryan' Architecture and Strzygowski's Art History," in *The Art Bulletin* (Sept. 2007): 562–90; Scott Redfield, "'What Have You Done for Anatolia Today?' Islamic Archaeology in the Early Years of the Turkish Republic," in *Muqarnas* 24 (2007): 243–7.

[75] Diez' Strzygowski-esque tendencies are already evident in his Byzantine work; see Diez' "Die Miniaturen des Wiener Dioskurides," in Diez and Josef Quitt, *Ursprung und Sieg der altbyzantinischen Kunst: Beiträge* (Vienna, 1903), pp. 62–9.

[76] E. H. Gombrich, "An Autobiographical Sketch," in idem, *Topics of Our Times* (Berkeley, CA, 1991), p. 14. Gombrich attended Strzygowski's lectures in the 1920s, but found his approach and his conceit repellant.

East and were increasingly able to make sense of it outside Eurocentric frames. But what did the public know about "oriental" art? This is a question to which we can only give fragmentary answers, in part because the question has been little studied and in part because of the inherent difficulties of studying "reception." It can certainly be said that, thanks to circuses and traveling exhibitions, to cheap imported wares and department-store displays, to cabaret performances and the first movies, urban populations at least would have seen or even owned some bits of what upscale critics called "bazaar ware" or "shop-window" Japanoiserie. Tea sets, carpets, fans, embroidered divan covers, and lacquer boxes would have given even lower-end consumers the sense that they knew something about oriental design. Of course, this same consumerist familiarity bred in experts the conviction that the real art of the East must not be so easily accessible. Thus, throughout this section, we will have to keep in mind the divergence between the two publics, a popular, market-oriented public and an elite, anti-commercial one, something that would be clearly and even painfully obvious in the wake of the Kaiserreich's two great exhibitions of eastern art: the Munich Muhammedan Exhibition of 1910 and the Berlin East Asian Art Exhibition of 1912.

The Munich show was apparently inspired by Crown Prince Rupprecht, who had traveled in the Near East, and purchased carpets for himself. In 1909, Rupprecht found some seventeenth-century Persian carpets in the royal residence in Munich and decided they should be exhibited. That the Prince's attention would have been drawn specifically to seventeenth-century Persian carpets surely owed to a series of earlier carpet exhibitions, beginning with Riegl's 1891 exhibition in Vienna and culminating in the Louvre's big Exposition des Arts Musulmans in 1903. As we have seen, early modern Persian carpets, in particular, had been raised to the status of art objects as a result of these exhibitions and the effusions of taste-makers like William Morris, and it is not surprising that the Prince would have found his "masterpieces" exhibition-worthy.[77]

Somehow, however, in the course of consulting with Islamic art experts F. R. Martin and Friedrich Sarre, the exhibition concept was greatly expanded, and the idea of an all-embracing Islamic art exhibit was born. Some 250 lenders – European and non-European – agreed to send their treasures to Munich so that the exhibition could offer a comprehensive overview of all the genres and diverse developments subsumed under the rubric "Islamic art." When the exhibit finally opened, it comprised some 3,600 objects. Carpets there were, in abundance, but by no means were all of them Persian. Grouped by region and genre, there were works from Persian, Turkish, Spanish-Moorish, Syro-Egyptian, and other cultural areas, as well as exhibits demonstrating the impact of oriental art on Russia, Poland, Scandinavia, and Italy, amounting finally to more than eighty rooms of Islamic art.[78]

The exhibition was a mammoth undertaking and one that could only have been brought together by individuals who possessed detailed knowledge of the private

---

[77] I am indebted to Eva Troelenberg for sharing with me her unpublished paper, "History Within? The Munich Exhibition and its Attitude towards the Object."

[78] Friedrich Sarre, "Vorwort," in idem and F. R. Martin, eds., *Die Ausstellung von Meisterwerken Muhammedanischer Kunst in München 1910*, vol. I (Munich, 1912), pp. 1–5.

as well as public collections of Europe — and, incidentally, collections of their own. The organizers clearly believed that their efforts would show off the great scholarly progress and the lucrative collecting ventures that had transpired in the previous 10–15 years and would also, as one of them wrote, appeal powerfully to the "world's finance-aristocracy," which had been especially active in carpet connoisseurship of late. The huge exhibition, wrote co-organizer Ludwig von Bürkel, "will undoubtedly bring a high-aristocratic and rich elite in unusually-high numbers to Munich and the surrounding area. . . ."[79] In creating the exhibit, the young art historian Ernst Kühnel wrote, the organizers had opted not to exhibit "commonplace bazaar trash" or to recreate "harem interior with soft divans, jolly fountains and a thousand geegaws, clouded and scented with intoxicating perfumes. . . ."[80] In organizing the exhibit, Sarre said, ". . . we were seeking, intentionally, to form a front against the popular conception of oriental art, against fairy-tale splendor and bazaar-goods."[81] Oriental objects were instead exhibited in isolation, as worthy of contemplation in and for themselves, "the only right way," Kühnel argued, despite complaints about the "dull and joyless feel of these rooms."[82] Nor did the catalog's text or even Kühnel's review, for that matter, make many concessions to the wider public. Both demanded familiarity with Near and Middle Eastern chronologies and geography and made only rare and incidental mention of the classical and western forms and events that Gymnasium-educated readers would have known well. Knowledge had progressed enough here that the old frames could be dispensed with and oriental art understood in its own terms and contexts – this, scholars knew, was the "only right way" to proceed.

Regrettably, for Kühnel and the organizers, this approach did not particularly please the "finance-aristocracy" and even the Gymnasium-educated visitors did not care much for the exhibition. Kühnel was crushed: "Seldom has an undertaking with the scholarly and artistic range to reach beyond specialist circles found so prejudiced and unreceptive a public as the Exhibition of Muhammedan Art. . . . For what the educated or uneducated Central European . . . thinks of when he thinks of the artistry of the Islamic world is, as a rule, nothing but an imaginary extract from the realm of oriental legends and fables, [a realm] which has, since the time of the Crusades, driven out all concrete perceptions. . . ."[83] Attendance fell far below expectations – though perhaps those expectations had been rather grand. When the exhibit closed in October 1910 after about a five-month run, more than 620,000 tickets had been sold, but costs, including rent, exceeded 1.6 million Marks. Thus, the Bavarians ended the project with a profit of 10,000 Marks; slight compensation, to be sure, for the many months of preparation the exhibit had cost, but black ink nonetheless.[84]

---

[79] Bürkel, "Ausstellung München 1910," in M-BHSA, II, MH 9286 (printed proposal for the exhibition).

[80] Ernst Kühnel, "Die Austellung Mohammedanischer Kunst München 1910," in *Münchner Jahrbuch der bildenden Kunst* 5 (1910): 210, 209.

[81] Sarre, "Vorwort," p. 3.

[82] Kühnel, "Austellung," p. 210.

[83] Ibid., p. 209.

[84] "Finanzbericht" [c. December 1910], in M-BHSA, II, MH 9286.

The money was one thing – but clearly more dispiriting for oriental art experts was the reaction in both the elite and the popular press. "Rarely has an endeavor of scholarly and artistic power, one that had the potential for effect far beyond specialized circles, found such a tasteless and unreceptive public as the exhibition of Muhammedan art," wrote Kühnel, in the opening sentence of his review, and Friedrich Sarre, in his forward to the massive exhibition catalog, acknowledged too that there had been widespread criticism of the exhibit.[85] An anonymous reviewer in one of Bavaria's major newspapers, the *Münchner Neueste Nachrichten*, identified the source of the problem: Bavarians, whose knowledge of the Orient had been formed by circuses and operas, were bound to be disappointed by the exhibition's modesty.[86]

Here, of course, was the avant-garde's problem in a nutshell; they knew what the "right" kind of art was and the "right" way to exhibit it, but the public found the Munich Exhibition tedious and incomprehensible – not surprisingly, since the very definition of what was "right" for the avant-garde was based on opposing sophisticated appreciation to popular taste. Centuries of western appropriation of Islamic decorative forms and the mass marketing of imitations, combined with nineteenth-century stereotypes about the unchanging Orient, made it very difficult for experts to historicize and differentiate styles, and poor exhibition techniques made the displays seem monotonous. Confronted with so much unfamiliar material, most Europeans were left cold. As the reviewer in the *Neue Zürcher Zeitung* – quoted in this chapter's epigraph – noted, many viewers found the exhibition boring and exhausting.[87] Some, like the expressionist painter Franz Marc, were impressed; it was the context of viewing this exhibition that he remarked on the "one-sided narrowness of our European concepts of painting"; but then again, Marc was already seeking to escape European conventions. Contemporary aesthetic theorists were pioneering new understandings of nonwestern forms, as the work of Wilhelm Worringer and Karl Einstein suggests.[88] But both modern theory and avant-garde practice were moving further away from public taste – and the public increasingly was demanding its right to have museums suited to its proclivities. Such demands were ever more difficult to negotiate, as we shall see in the attempt, just two years after the Munich Exhibition, to stage an East Asian Exhibit in the Reich's other cultural capital, Berlin.

The 1912 East Asian Art Exhibit, put on by the Berlin Academy of Arts in 1912, offers a similar story of public/expert divergence, though the press, in this case, seems to have been more widely appreciative of the organizers' achievements. The exhibition was not a blockbuster; only eleven rooms were open to the public, as against more than eighty in the case of the Munich Exhibition. But, as Hartmut Walravens's collection of ninety-one press clippings indicates, many thought the occasion marked a turning point, and these reviews offer, for our

---

[85] Kühnel, "Austellung," p. 209; Sarre, "Vorwort," p. 3.
[86] "M," "Eine englische Stimme über die Ausstellung München," in *Münchner Neueste Nachrichten*, August 31, 1910, in M-BHSA, II, MH 9286.
[87] See n. 2, above.
[88] Worringer's *Abstraktion und Einfühlung* (Neuwied, 1907); Karl Einstein, *Negerplastik* (Leipzig, 1915).

purposes, highly interesting insights into the German reception of East Asian art in the years before the war.

The reviews range from very brief notices to quite extensive essays and the reviewers from anonymous reporters to well-known connoisseurs. Universally, the quality of the pieces – none made after 1850 and most datable before 1700 – was praised. Many notices too contrasted the discernment of the curators to the poor taste shown by previous East Asian art enthusiasts like the Goncourt brothers, who preferred, as one commentator put it, "the later, especially decoratively refined, shop-window Japan."[89] What was different about this exhibit was its treatment of East Asian art not as purely decorative, nor simply as exotic and ethnographic, but as the product, one admirer wrote, of "a soul strong enough for [this] life ... the pure expression of the drive to enoblement."[90] Again, as in the case of the Munich exhibit, admirers portrayed the new perspective as a triumph over classical aesthetics and orientalizing trash, and one summed up the history of oriental art appreciation in a way that would have greatly pleased Sarre and Kühnel:

It is self-evident that with [the onset of] classicism all interest for oriental art, so different from that of [classical] antiquity disappeared; and if in the Romantic era it surged up here and there, this was only sporadic and always occurred as a tribute to difference. Only since the middle of the nineteenth century, since the world exhibitions brought the peoples into closer contact, has the interest in the Orient become more lively and above all deeper. The attempt has now begun to get aesthetically and scientifically closer to East Asian art, to get beyond the faddish taste which has flooded the market with inferior crafts and bad imitations.[91]

Some reviewers emphasized the difficulty westerners had had, both in appreciating and in collecting East Asian art, gesturing in passing to the nineteenth-century changes in power relations which had made it possible for westerners to improve their knowledge and taste. Each Asian connoisseurs, one writer claimed, had long exploited western naïveté, hiding the good stuff from European collectors and thus making it hard for them to understand the arts of China and Japan. Another reviewer actually criticized the destructive impact of western civilization on the "ideal spirituality" of other cultures; "Most collectors, too, rise from the ranks of the destroyers and opportunists, who love and want to take care of the earlier expressions of the culture they have destroyed."[92] Another had trouble squaring recently published photos of the execution of Boxer rebels with the ahistoric spirituality of Chinese art: "To [the record of] the Mongoloid race's

---

[89] Robert Breuer, "Die ostasiatische Ausstellung der Berliner Akademie," *Weimarische Landeszeitung*, September 29, 1912, reprinted in Hartmut Walravens, ed., *Bibliographien zur ostasiatischen Kunstgeschichte in Deutschland*, vol. 4, *Die Ostasienausstellung Berlin 1912 und die Presse* (Hamburg, 1984), p. 40.

[90] Max Krell, "Ostasiatische Kunst," in *Weser-Zeitung*, October 3, 1912, in Walravens, ed., *Ostasienausstellung Berlin*, p. 47.

[91] W. Baer, "Ausstellung alter ostasiatischer Kunst in Berlin," in *Leipziger Volkszeitung*, November 27, 1912, in ibid., p. 114.

[92] Hans Kaiser, "China-Japan," in *Berliner Neueste Nachrichten*, October 17, 1912, and *Deutsche Zeitung*, October 18, 1912, in ibid., p. 76.

barbarization of humankind one must now contrast its art. One stands before a conundrum."[93] It is perhaps instructive that the exhibit actually emphasized Japanese art, the specialty of the youngest curator, and the one most steeped in authentic oriental art, Otto Kümmel. As we have seen (Chapter 8), in the wake of their westernizing reforms and their victory in the Russo-Japanese War, the Japanese had earned new respect from the West. Kümmel himself had recent experience in negotiating with Japanese collectors and dealers, whose taste he respected and evidently tried to emulate.[94] Imperial politics clearly had much to do with both the new opportunities for exploitation and the new forms of admiration that characterized Germany's prewar reception of East Asian art.

Of course, there were some who felt that East Asian art was too difficult and foreign for western scholars to grasp – and its forms too lifeless and abstract for European artists to emulate.[95] The critics cited above, writing for the *Kreuz-Zeitung* and the *Deutsche-Tageszeitung*, both thought the exhibition costs could have been spent more wisely, as did the exhibition's most vehement critic, Willy Pastor. Pastor's reviews for the popular *Tägliche Rundschau* protested the Prussian Academy's investment in East Asian art over and against, he claimed, the art of the ancient Germans. Pastor could not understand this perverse attraction to a weak artistic tradition, which had rejected both Greek and Hindu forms as too worldly; their limp-limbed and sightless Buddhas were even worse than "the granite monstrosities of ancient Egypt," which "have, even in their severity, some sort of manly beauty, compared to the slow-working poison of vampire-Buddha, the hideous freak [born] of oriental fantasizing." Pastor deplored the academy's intention to use the exhibition as the launching pad for a new East Asian art museum, warning that the adoption of such foreign forms and ideas posed the aesthetic equivalent of the "yellow peril."[96]

Pastor's review was passionate, but it was surely easier for specialists to dismiss his criticism than that of Marie von Bunsen, whose long, appreciative review of the exhibit appeared in the avant-garde journal *Die Zukunft* in 1913. Bunsen, the daughter of our old friend Christian, and a well-traveled writer and artist in her own right, concluded her review with some remarks about the organizers' aims and their failure to reach out to the public. "Could this learned exhibition, prepared with delicate taste, an exhibition which according to foreign authorities is one of its kind, cover its heating bills? If one wanted to prove the excellence of our purchases, then the goal has been met; [but] if the point was to awaken interest in the founding of an East Asian Museum, then the [exhibitors'] wishes have not been fulfilled. The boundaries have been so painstakingly drawn, and there is so little explanation and clarification [of the materials displayed] that all too many

[93] "W-r.," "Die Ausstellung ostasiatischer Kunst," in *Welt am Montag*, October 14, 1912, in ibid., p. 72.

[94] Yukio Yashiro, "Dr. Otto Kümmel," in *Bulletin, Society of Friends of Eastern Art* 17 (1941), reprinted in Walravens, ed., *Bibliographien zur ostasiatischen Kunstgeschichte in Deutschland*, vol. 3, *Otto Kümmel* (Hamburg, 1984), pp. 8–9.

[95] For example, Fr. V. Khaynach, "Ostasiatische Kunst: Die Ausstellung in der Königliche Akademie der Künste," in *Kreuz-Zeitung*, October 5, 1912, in Walravens, ed., *Ostasienausstellung Berlin*, p. 50.

[96] Willy Pastor, "Der Gott des fernen Ostens," in *Tägliche Rundschau*, October 1, 1912, in ibid., p. 41, 43.

people, shivering, have perceived [the exhibit's] high-minded inaccessibility. 'That is all too foreign to me,' one hears constantly. And yet it would have been easy, to pave the way for many [to enter] this delightful world."[97] Whether or not "many" might really have changed their minds is disputable; it is indisputable that, had a grand-scale popular education program in the oriental arts been attempted, it would not have been as "easy" to win over the German public as Bunsen suggested.

But popular or not, oriental art was becoming a hot field both for scholars and especially for museum officials, if for no other reason than that the opportunities to study and to acquire it were better, by 1900, than ever before. This is particularly true of East Asian art, the supply of which in Europe had been, until this time, rather limited. In the wake of China's defeat by the Japanese in 1896 and the internal unrest caused by the Boxer Rebellion of 1899–1900, just as businessmen leapt at new opportunities to expand their trade, scholars too saw a "wild East" opening and rushed to take advantage of the situation before too many other claims were staked, and while the foreigner-friendly Qing dynasty still had nominal dominion. Far from Beijing, Central Asia in particular experienced what can only be called an "antiquities rush" between 1900 and 1914, one that must be seen not only in the context of European imperial rivalries, but also in the context of museological scrambles for nonwestern treasure. Ironically, however, despite the collectors' poor preparation and hasty methods of extraction, this "antiquities rush" would also succeed in changing chronologies, inspiring new comparisons, and challenging Eurocentric aesthetic categories.

In Egypt and Assyria, the Germans had been largely locked out of the competition for major treasures; India belonged to the British, and the Southeast Asian sites to the French. In western China, however, the German Empire was deeply engaged in the antiquities rush, one scholars recognized as parallel to and inextricable from the simultaneous race for colonial possessions. The four Turfan expeditions of 1902–14 were Germany's first series of state-funded "excavations" which concerned themselves exclusively with a world beyond the reach of biblical or classical sources and chronologies; they also represent one of Europe's blindest quests for archaeological booty – and a turning point in the appreciation and understanding of oriental art.

THE TURFAN EXPEDITIONS AND THE INTELLECTUAL CONSEQUENCES OF THE CENTRAL ASIAN ANTIQUITIES RACE

The series of rapidly organized "scientific" trips known as the Turfan Expeditions are little known outside the specialized worlds of Sinology and Turkology, but there they are recognized to be of fundamental importance to the history of art in East and Central Asia. In the course of four short trips undertaken by German museum officials, the first in 1902–3, the second 1904–5, the third 1906–8, and the fourth 1913–14, the ancient Uighur settlement near the Chinese town of Turfan was just one of many sites visited, but its riches and renown earned it

---

[97] Marie von Bunsen, "Ostasiatische Kunst," in *Die Zukunft* 21 (1913), in ibid., p. 149.

the right to represent all the rest. Before the fin de siècle, only a few western travelers had ventured into this climatically inhospitable and politically-fraught part of Chinese Turkestan, but afterward, a large number of travelers would cross these deserts and mountains, seeking manuscripts and sculptures, wall paintings, and ethnographic artifacts. Non-German scholar-adventurers would also raid deserted Silk Road settlements, some of them, like Aurel Stein and Sven Hedin, making names for themselves and bringing home large amounts of important material in the process. But the German expeditions were both the most thorough and perhaps the most intellectually profitable. In the course of their four trips, the Prussian Academy of Sciences and Berlin's Ethnographic Museum reaped enormous scholarly benefits from the approximately 16,115 kilos of manuscripts, murals, statues, and other artifacts shipped back with fantastic difficulty over deserts and treacherous mountain passes.[98] The manuscript cache was particularly rich; the Turfan expeditions brought home manuscripts in 17 languages, written in 24 scripts, a tremendous boon for the "armchair" orientalists at home.

Remarkably, neither a political and critical nor a positivist and celebratory history of the Turfan expeditions has yet been written (though there is a German TV documentary). The major accounts of these expeditions remain the romantic memoirs of Albert von Le Coq, who describes, for example, crossing a 17,840-foot peak thrice, one in a blizzard, and subsisting on a diet limited to flour balls made with yak lard. An occasional museum catalog describes the expeditions in order to explain how the works of art were brought to the West, and they are treated, in passing, by Peter Hopkirk in his engaging *Foreign Devils on the Silk Road* (London, 1980). But no one has yet given the Turfan expeditions their due, which requires, on the one hand, appreciating the extent to which they were shaped by colonial politics and, on the other, recognizing the role the collected texts and objects played in opening up new perspectives on the Orient in an age of growing dissatisfaction with western culture.

The context and consequences of the expeditions had much to do not only with the personalities involved but also with the precise cultural and political moment at which they commenced. Russian travelers had been the first to comb Central Asia, seeking to map and if possible subdue territory both inside and outside Russia's official borders. In 1873, the military officer Nikolai Przhevalsky returned from his travels so heavily laden that he was able to supply the Russian Imperial Academy of Sciences with a huge collection of Central Asian flora and fauna, including 5,000 plant specimens and 3,000 insects.[99] In Przhevalsky's day, only a few scholars in Europe were interested in the region – but one of them was Berlin geography professor Ferdinand von Richthofen, whose youthful travels we described in Chapter 3 and whose politics we surveyed in Chapter 8. By this time, Richthofen's traveling days were over, but he was still working on his atlas of China and interested in the multi-national trade routes that had connected China to the West, routes for which he coined the term "Silk Road." For some years Richthofen had little success in inciting his students to visit the area; in the later

[98] See Le Coq, *Auf Hellas Spuren in Ostturkistan* (Leipzig, 1926), pp. 8–9.
[99] Frances Wood, *The Silk Road: Two Thousand Years in the Heart of Asia* (Berkeley, CA, 2002), p. 167.

1870s and 1880s, Xinjiang Province was in the midst of a war between the Chinese and the Muslim overlord Jacob Bey; moreover, it was assumed that traversing the Silk Road was in any case no longer possible because climatic changes had dried up the oases that once relieved the rigors of the Taklamakan Desert. After the political situation stabilized, and as the Great Game intensified Russian and British rivalry along the Indian and Tibetan borders, a series of individual travelers skirted the Taklamakan and the Turfan areas. But it was only after China's defeat by the Japanese in 1896, and after the Qing emperor called in European support to suppress the Boxer Rebellion in 1899–1900, that the great Central Asian antiquities rush began.

In the course of this rush, both emerging eastern powers (Russia and Japan) and western powers (England, France, and Germany) moved aggressively to claim new legal, economic, political, and archaeological privileges from the failing Qing Empire. Germany's new importance in the region, thanks to its establishment of a colony at Qingdao, made it possible for a handful of men to contemplate the actual accomplishment of a scholarly endeavor that would have been, before 1899, a pipe dream. The man chiefly responsible for setting in motion the exploration of a part of the world wholly unknown to most Central Europeans was Albert Grünwedel, an artist's son who had chosen to study *Orientalistik* in 1876, during the era, that is, of lonely orientalism. The story of Grünwedel's rise from lowly museum assistant and narrowly-focused linguist to director of a major archaeological endeavor is indicative of the new opportunities beginning to open for scholars and especially for excavators of oriental artifacts; but its denouement also suggests the limited welcome that even those who brought home great treasures could receive from the Reich's academic and cultural elite.

At the University of Munich, Grünwedel had studied Sanskrit, Pali, Avestan, and Indian religions – though he also pursued his studies of classical art and literature, which he had learned to love at Gymnasium.[100] After two years of poorly-paid work in Berlin's Ethnographic Museum, in 1883, Grünwedel was appointed director's assistant, with the mandate of caring for the collections of ethnological and especially "Nordic" antiquities. It is likely that he spent much of his time in these early years reading books rather than working with artifacts – for the Indological collections were extremely small. By 1893, however, Grünwedel had seen sufficient pieces in illustrations or in private collections to write a book, *Buddhistische Kunst in Indien*, which claimed that the Indians themselves had little talent for plastic art. "Insofar as it is a cultured nation," he added, "the character of the [Indian] people oscillates between sensuousness and pessimism."[101] Indian art really interested Grünwedel only insofar as Persian and Greek forms were mixed with it – making it not only more aesthetically appealing but also offering the means for tracking the history of separate styles. A pioneer in the field, Grünwedel remained in many ways a lonely positivist, eager to fill in historical gaps, especially where "Aryans" were concerned, but without real passion for his specialized material.

---

[100] Waldschmidt, "Albert Grünwedel," in *Ostasiatische Zeitschrift* 21, no. 11 (1935): 215.
[101] Grünwedel, *Buddhistische Kunst in Indien* (Berlin, 1893), pp. 1–4, 29–72, quotation p. 162.

Not surprisingly for a museum assistant in a quite obscure field, Grünwedel sought out foreign literature and contacts – though he did not seek to go to India, prevented either by his prejudices or his poverty – or some combination of both. In 1900, he published a heavily illustrated study of Buddhist mythology, which was at the same time a guide to the collection of Russian Prince Esper Uchtomsky.[102] By this time, he was also in touch with the Russian collector Dimitri Klementz, who showed the German scholar examples of materials he had found on his recent visit to the Turfan region in 1899; in the course of discussions, Klementz proposed a collaboration between German and Russian scholars, probably hoping to secure German financial assistance.[103] Grünwedel was even more excited by this prospect after Klementz's finds were publicly bruited at the Congress of Orientalists in Rome; there is nothing like validation by fellow experts to convince a scholar to follow his or her instincts. This excitement inspired the founding of a scholarly group, the Association Internationale pour l'Exploration Historique, Archéologique, Linguistique, et Ethnographique de l'Asie Centrale et de l'Extrême Orient, with its headquarters in St. Petersburg.

An association, however, was of no use to Grünwedel or the Russians unless it had the financial wherewithal to send scholars to the field. Like Bode, Grünwedel ran into resistance from Richard Schöne, still the General Director of the Museums, who was already funding a large number of excavations all over Asia Minor and could not be interested in supporting work in so remote and non-classical a region as Central Asia.[104] The Prussian Academy of Sciences also said no.[105] The Prussian *Kultusministerium* saw real value in Grünwedel's proposal and sent a copy to the Kaiser Wilhelm II, who not only seemed a soft touch but also showed new interest in "oriental" projects after his travels to the Levant.[106] But in the end, most of the costs of the first expedition were paid by private patrons, Friedrich Krupp and James Simon, and the Berlin Committee for the Advancement of Ethnography. The Ethnography Museum put up only about 8,000 Marks; thus public funds paid for only about 25 percent of the first expedition's costs.[107]

This balance would change significantly in the wake of the first expedition's successes. Though Grünwedel and his fellow travelers, Georg Huth, a *Privatdozent*

---

[102] Albert Grünwedel, *Mythologie des Buddhismus in Tibet und der Mongolei: Führer durch die lamaistische Sammlung des Fürsten E. Uchtomskij* (Leipzig, 1900).

[103] Herbert Härtel, "Introduction," in *Along the Ancient Silk Routes: Central Asian Art from the West Berlin State Museums* (New York, 1982), pp. 24–5.

[104] Schöne to Grünwedel, February 8, 1902, in B-MfIK, Acta betreffend die Expedition des Prof. Grünwedel nach Turfan, vol. 1.

[105] [Grünwedel] to Akademie der Wissenschaften (draft), July 22, 1901, and Akademie to Grünwedel, January 3, 1902, both in ibid.

[106] In addition to helping to fund DOG excavations at many sites in Asia Minor, in the decade before the war, the Kaiser was also funding Oskar Mann's ethnographic travels in Kurdistan, Dr. Leutnant Filcher's cartographic work in Tibet, the Deutsche Verein zur Erforschung Palästinas's topographic work in Palestine, and Hugo Grothe's geographic and geological studies in Southern Persia. See the correspondence in B-GSPK, 89, 21369.

[107] Both Krupp and Simon contributed 10,000 Marks, for a total of 20,000 Marks; if Haertel's estimate of 25 percent public funding for the full costs of the expedition (36,000 Marks) is correct, this means the museums contributed about 8,000 Marks. See Haertel, "Introduction," p. 29. On Krupp's contribution: Grünwedel to [Museums Administration], January 3, 1902, in ibid.

specializing in Tibetan philology, and Theodor Bartus, a museums assistant, had little notion of where they were going or what they might find, they managed not only to bring back several lovely murals but also to purchase a number of very ancient manuscripts. Grünwedel's report compared the progress of their work in bringing home Central Asian original art to the gradual progress classicists had made in excavating Greece; Central Asian work too "must first begin with sad fragments; it is not so lucky as was Egyptology, which, thanks to the thunder of Bonaparte's cannon and Champollion's genius, was forged, fully-formed, with one stroke."[108] Cannon perhaps, they lacked, but in 1904, the philologist F. M. K. Müller (who was also employed by the Ethnography Museum) presented a paper to the Prussian Academy showing that one of the Turfan manuscripts was in fact a Manichean text, enflaming hopes among theologians and orientalists as well as museum officials and the Cultural Ministry for a second expedition.

In pressing for a second venture, the German chapter of the Association Internationale could count among its members the most exalted and influential of orientalist scholars: the Berlin Ordinarius for Sanskrit, Richard Pischel; Germany's most prominent orientalist, Eduard Meyer; the director of Berlin's Orientalisches Seminar, Eduard Sachau; and the most important theologian of the late Kaiserreich, Adolf von Harnack. In February 1904, this eminent group composed a spirited memo to the Prussian Cultural Ministry, calling for the abandonment of Germany's "purely theoretical standpoint" toward oriental studies; instead, the Reich should opt for a hands-on approach, which would secure Germany's great reputation in the field. Times had changed, they argued, in language that showed how international competition in scholarship as in politics had taken on new urgency and bitterness; the Germans should muscle into the competition and fight threatened export restrictions or risk exclusion from large-scale endeavors, and be forced "to resign ourselves to dealing with minor bits of trash."[109] The *Kultusministerium* was so convinced that it suggested a "pre-expedition" go out to secure Germany's "sphere of influence," not only against foreign competitors but also against Jewish dealers, who, it was claimed, were trying to hire Bartus to help them carry off mounds of treasure.[110] The Kaiser signed on and the expeditions gained an enthusiastic new backer when Wilhelm von Bode replaced Schöne as General Director of the Royal Museums in 1905. Private funding now dwindled in importance, and in the course of the next ten years, the state dedicated a total of more than 200,000 Marks, collected from the Kaiser's private disposition fund and the Prussian budget to the Turfan expeditions, a sufficiently lavish sum to attract comment from the foreign press.[111]

---

[108] Albert Grünwedel, "Einige praktische Bemerkungen über archäologische Arbeiten in chinesische Turkistan," in *Bulletin de l'Association Internationale pour l'Exploration historique, linguistique et ethnographique de l'Asie Centrale et de l'Extreme Orient* 2 (Oct. 1903): 7, in B-GSPK, Rep. 76Vc, Sekt. 1, Tit. XI, Teil Va, Nr. 8, vol. 1.

[109] Memo, Committee in support of Turfan Expedition to Cultural Ministry, February 12, 1904, in ibid.

[110] Studt [Kmin] to Kaiser, August 14, 1904, B-GSPK, 89, 21368.

[111] For example, "Gilded Sculpture: Discoveries in Central Asia," in *The Standard*, December 26, 1906, in B-MfIK, Turfan Komitee, Acta betreffend Allgemeines; Gaston Migeon, "Les Fouilles du Turkestan," in *Journal des Débats*, November 2, 1908, in ibid.

Realistically, Germany had no hope of claiming territory in Central Asia, but the scholars deliberately used the language of imperialism to cajole the state into financing a great "scientific" act. In a letter written in support of the second expedition, Harnack insisted: "... we Germans must use all our powers to secure for ourselves our rightful place in this sun."[112] The backers of the Turfan digs continually emphasized the importance of speed and tried to scare the *Kultusministerium* by threatening, in 1903, that the locals would pillage the sites; in July 1904, that the French would get there first; in August 1904 that a team of Jewish traders was on its way; in 1912 that rich Americans were planning excavations; and in 1913–14 that Chinese turmoil and Russian expansionism would end all chance of new expeditions to the region. Germany had to get its foot in the door, as it were, before Turfan's goodies were all shared out.[113] But if they talked the talk, the expedition members also acted the part of imperious conquerors. While in Greece and Italy, and to some extent in the Ottoman Empire, the home country supervised the excavations and kept many, if not all, of the finds, in Chinese Turkestan supervision was non-existent and no diplomatic niceties were required, even after the 1911 Revolution. Le Coq simply ignored Chinese attempts to close down his operations. "The Chinese," he told the Cultural Ministry in 1913, "must be presented with a fait accompli – they won't dare to obstruct my excavations by using force."[114] The snatching up of manuscripts and choice artifacts was much more frenzied and crude in Turfan than in Babylon and would have been intolerable in the Peloponnesus; the sawing off of murals from the walls of the caves of the cloisters at Qyzil, much more hasty and destructive than contemporary excavations at Olympia and Ephesus, is just one example of what was meant by "excavation" in the age of the great Central Asian antiquities rush.

Born of the era of high colonialism, the Turfan expeditions nonetheless opened the way for an intensive study of non-European cultures that insisted precisely on the understanding of other cultures in their own terms. Wholly embedded in colonial cultural politics, the expeditions also represented a highly positivistic enterprise. Having little idea of what they would find and little ability to judge the significance of materials on site, the excavators simply hoped to bring home some important "stuff" before others carried it all off to the Louvre and the British Museum – though Le Coq reports interestingly that the first three expeditions were occupied with finding temples whose paintings bore on Hellenistic–East Asian

---

[112] Harnack to Cultural Ministry, July 22, 1904, in B-GSPK, Rep. 76Vc, Sekt. 1, Tit. XI, Teil Va, Nr. 8, vol. 1.

[113] Grünwedel, "Einige praktische Bemerkungen," pp. 8–11, in ibid.; R. Pischel to Althoff, July 8, 1904, and R. Pischel to Althoff, August 1, 1904, in ibid.; H. Lüders to Cultural Ministry, October 21, 1912, in ibid., Nr. 8, vol. 2. On the conditions in 1913–14, see the documents in ibid., Nr. 8, vol. 3. I found no evidence in the documents that the Turfan expeditions had any political function; though the excavators occasionally report on political matters, such as the degree of Chinese hostility toward the Russians, these issues seem to be raised only in connection with the conduct of the expedition and the secure shipping home of its finds.

[114] Le Coq to Cultural Ministry, October 16, 1913, in ibid., Nr. 8, vol. 3.

relations or on Iranian influences on Buddhist art, as Grünwedel had little interest in styles that inclined in the direction of Chinese art.[115] What they did bring home was startling; "For the history of oriental art, the finds have been nothing short of a revelation," the Indologist Heinrich Lüders wrote in 1914. "We can now recognize the threads that run from Greece and Rome through Persia and India, running out as far as China, Tibet, and Japan; West and East are no longer cleft by the gaps that we previously had to postulate."[116] Gaps had been filled – and for German *Wissenschaftler*, that meant real progress.

But if one takes note of the ad hoc and often quite unprofessional way in which the collecting was actually done and the internal battles over the publication and exhibition of the Turfan materials in the Wilhelmine and Weimar periods, one sees much more clearly the complicated, combative, and halting process through which oriental archaeology and artifacts made their modest mark on German cultural history. To begin with, many of the travelers themselves were quite unlike the armchair philologists at home and none of them ever found full acceptance in academic circles. Grünwedel and Huth were the only expedition members with a university degree; Huth made only one trip (and then died), and Grünwedel was mostly a museum-man. Grünwedel was certainly not the model "scientific traveler" Ferdinand von Richthofen had sought to cultivate; though he ventured on a second expedition, he was an ineffectual excavator and traveler even when not (as he often was) deathly ill. Although he did try to record details about the situation of the finds, Grünwedel was neither able nor willing to do careful excavations of the type now routinely practiced in Greece and Asia Minor. And he had something of the "furious" orientalist about him too. Though he was made Director of the Indian Department of the Ethnographic Museum in 1904, Grünwedel fell out with other scholars after he claimed that he, not the philologist Müller, deserved credit for recognizing the Manichean character of the first Turfan finds.

In the postwar period, a new generation of connoisseurs of Indian art attacked Grünwedel in the public press for failing to appreciate the unique beauties of Indian art and using precious exhibition space simply for ethnographic displays. He replied that he opposed "renaming Asian manufacturers 'art' and, after all, found Indian artifacts boring and enervating. When he finally published what should have been a major overview of the finds (*Alt-Kutscha*, 1920), it still offered, one reviewer wrote, only "crumbs" – most of the finds were not treated – in fact, they had not even been unpacked! Moreover, the book did not hesitate to fill in the holes with unproven hypotheses, especially as to the *ur*-Iranian origins of East Asian art.[117] Having little energy or perhaps desire to give his Turfan finds proper public exposure, Grünwedel left the battle for their display to his deputy Albert von Le Coq and retired in 1921, isolated and bitter, glad, he said, to turn

---

[115] Le Coq, *Von Land und Leuten in Ostturkistan: Berichte und Abendteuer der 4. deutschen Turfan-expedition* (Leipzig, 1928), p. 136. Le Coq says that this changed in the fourth expedition, as a result of a more general change in European appreciation for Chinese art. Ibid., pp. 136–9.

[116] Lüders to Cultural Ministry, May 28, 1914, B-GSPK, Rep 76Vc, Sekt 1, Tit. 11, Nr. 8, vol. 3.

[117] H. Haas, "Grünwedels 'Alt-Kutscha'" (part 1), in *OLZ* 24 (1921): 101–9.

everything having to do with Buddhism and Turfan over to his successor (who was incidentally none other than F. M. K. Müller).[118]

Other expedition members have equally interesting stories. Albert von Le Coq, who led the second, third, and fourth expeditions, was a businessman-turned-medical doctor-turned orientalist. Before leaving for Turkestan, he had studied a smattering of Persian, Kurdish, and Arabic, assisted briefly at the DOG excavations at Sendschirli, and organized the oriental weapons in the Royal Armory.[119] He participated in the excavations as a poorly paid "wissenschaftlicher Hilfsarbeiter" and only received a full salary at the Museum in April 1914. For all his years of service to the Indian Department, he was official director only for the two years preceding his retirement, 1923–5. The scholars thought him a dilettante and he never received a university appointment. If the traveling and collecting was exhausting and perilous, it was only after the expeditions were over that Le Coq's domestic travails commenced. On his return, wrote a friendly elegist, "A perpetual battle began for the proper display and for public recognition of the results of the expedition"; and indeed, the struggle for recognition and funding, so easily won in the prewar period, would occupy most of the rest of Le Coq's life.[120] Shortly before his death, he wrote to thank the orientalist and Weimar-era cultural minister Carl Becker for support that had eased the burden of the last few years. "If you had not, with, I happily testify, your generally-recognized broad-mindedness, supplied the space and the means for the Turfan project (Excellenz Bode never wished to recognize their importance), all of our acquisition-work would have been wasted."[121] But, Turfan promoter that he was, Le Coq could not embrace the sort of "furious" orientalism that Strzygowski was selling; perhaps – as in the case of Grünwedel – his Gymnasium years (in the 1870s) had made too indelible a mark. He found Buddhist art ultimately "horrid" or "boring" and cherished the notion that the few attractive qualities of Buddhist painting and sculpture might be ultimately rooted in Hellenistic forms; his very popular account of the third Turfan expedition was titled *Auf Hellas Spuren in Ostturkistan*, despite the fact that there were very few of these "tracks" to find. In the 1920s, younger (and even more "furious") critics accused him of seeing everything Asian through Greek spectacles.[122] Though a treasure trove of fragmentary details, his seven-volume masterwork, *Die Buddhistische Spätantike in Mittelasien* (1922–33) testified that the Turfan "revelation" still needed plenty of scribes as well as interpreters before it achieved universal acclaim.

It remains only to mention the most elusive member of the Turfan team, Theodor Bartus. The only man to accompany all four expeditions, Bartus had been a ship pilot and a squatter in Australia; tired of life at sea, he had then signed on as an assistant at the Ethnography Museum and in the course of a few years, become an expert on Buddhist art. It was a testimony both to Bartus's ingenuity

[118] Ernst Waldschmidt, "Albert Grünwedel," in *Ostasiatische Zeitschrift* 21, no. 11 (1935): 218–19.

[119] Albert von Le Coq, biographical statement, August 3, 1904, in B-GSPK, 76Vc, Sekt. 1, Tit. XI, Teil Va, Nr. 8, vol. 1.

[120] Waldschmidt, "Albert von Le Coq," in *Ostasiatische Zeitschrift* 16, no. 6 (1930): 146.

[121] Le Coq to Becker, February 9, 1930, in B-GSPK, Nachlass Becker, M. 4476.

[122] Waldschmidt, "Albert von Le Coq," pp. 147–8.

and to the obscurity of the field that in 1903 Grünwedel could claim that he "knew [Buddhist art forms] better than many scholars. . . ." But Bartus had other skills that were critical to the Turfan expeditions' success. He was able to climb cliffs jutting out over raging rivers, "a pleasure," Grünwedel wrote, "that I unfortunately had to deny myself."[123] He also learned to converse with the Turkic, Tibetan, and Chinese natives, which is more than could be said for Grünwedel. Bartus's high spirits and robust constitution made him widely loved – he was a diplomat of quite a different stripe than the genteel philologists who gathered at the yearly *Orientalistentag*. Finally, and most importantly, Bartus, as Le Coq later testified, was the only European to really understand how to rip a Buddhist mural off a cave wall.[124] He was, luckily for the museums' administration, the direct opposite of the typical Berlin philologist and simply one indicator of the enormous shift in art-historical work that had occurred over the course of the nineteenth century, as scholars exchanged a science built chiefly on casts and sketches for one so obsessed with possession, novelty, and authentic artifacts that it could adopt Grünwedel, Le Coq, and even Bartus into its ranks.

It must be emphasized that Le Coq and Bartus were no more exploitative or less "scientific," than their Russian, French, English, and Japanese competitors in the East; the depredations of Aurel Stein and Paul Pelliot are well known, and the Russian and French collections were certainly no better treated than the German ones: Le Coq may have been right to insist, in the 1920s, that it was better to study the Buddhist art of Central Asia in Berlin than anywhere else in the West.[125] All of these teams were well aware that they were working in a subcolonial setting, where there were no antiquities laws or governmental oversight. Moreover, they were dealing not with Greek sculptures or biblical texts, but with little-understood manuscripts and aesthetically unappreciated art. It is no wonder that the tales of their feats read like adventure novels, in sharp contrast to descriptions of the contemporary excavations at Olympia or even Pergamon, where there is no humor, no danger, and no luck. Digging up Greek temples was seen as serious business, and individual personalities were not supposed to interfere in the work of science; trawling Asia for treasures, however, allowed or even required the personality of the excavator, whether prankster or hero, to be emphasized.

But narratives featuring the excavator or the adventure do not necessarily make the quarry more appealing – or, as Schliemann found out, convince scholars of one's seriousness of purpose. Although Asian art was gaining a new following and new respect, at a time when it was unthinkable to send a non-scholar on a classical dig, men like Bartus and Le Coq were sent to bring home the riches of East Asia. Nor is this an isolated case; Hugo Winckler's work at Hattusa (Boghazkoi) was not taken seriously despite its novelty and importance, perhaps because the excavator had already been dubbed a "Panbabylonist." Walter Andrae, whose only qualification for going to dig in Mesopotamia was his ability to draw, went to Babylon as Robert Koldewey's assistant in 1899, and by 1902, was in charge of

---

[123] Grünwedel, "Bericht über die Expedition nach Turfan in den Jahren 1902 und 1903," August 1903, B-GSPK, 89, 21368.
[124] Le Coq, *Auf Hellas Spuren*, p. 10.
[125] Ibid.

his own excavation at Assur. Otto Kümmel received an honorary professorship – nothing more – from his academic brethren in 1927 though he was made General Director of the Berlin Museums by the Nazis. And, as a final indignity, in the 1930s, Gestapo headquarters was located next to the Berlin Ethnography Museum, where so many of the Turfan finds and Kümmel's treasures were displayed. Because curators were unable to remove them all to safety (some of the Turfan murals were cemented to the walls), many precious East and Central Asian pieces were destroyed in the last year of the Second World War or sent back to Russia after the war's end.[126] Those murals and sculptures, carried by camels, yaks, and ponies over deserts and glaciers, were destroyed neither by nomads nor by greedy archaeologists but by Allied bombs. In a letter written just after the most serious devastation took place, a despairing Otto Kümmel wrote to a friend: "Beneath my life, in any event, 'Finis' has been written in big letters."[127]

This is, of course, to paint too black a picture of the expeditions' legacy, and of the reception of Asian art as a whole. The documents and images brought back from "Turfan" offered a wealth of new information for linguists, art historians, philologists, classicists, historians, and scholars of comparative religion. The importance of the Turfan texts to orientalist philologists is hard to overestimate; in addition to forming the basis for the modern study of Turkic languages,[128] the Turfan texts also offered great riches to Sanskritists and Sinologists. The deciphering of Tocharian – which should logically have been an Indo-European language, but did not fit the usual criteria – was a major blow to conventional Indo-European genealogies. For historians and theologians, the materials were equally rich and disruptive. Richard Reitzenstein used the Turfan finds to expand the frame of Hellenistic history and theology beyond Egypt and thus initiated a great debate on the "oriental" origins of Gnosticism and of Christianity itself.[129] Turfan's wall paintings and sculptures inspired unprecedented interest in Central Asian art, allowing for the elaboration of stylistic and historical trajectories never before suspected or attempted. It is certainly too much to say, with Carsten Colpe, "that now [after the Turfan finds] a new form of humanism arose, this one arrayed under the sign of the inner-Asiatic-European [spiritual community (*Geistesgemeinschaft*)]."[130] Perspectives had been altered at least in some quarters. But the old humanism was still there, as Strzygowski knew all too well, and it would not give up its ideals, institutional prerogatives, or cultural respectability without a fight.

---

[126] Even after the return of many objects in 1956, more than 2,000 Indian, Southeast Asian, and Central Asian objects (and 8,000 books) were still missing; some were returned as the Soviet Union collapsed, but, as of 2002, there were still many Turfan materials in the basements of the Hermitage, and probably other Russian museums as well. Marianne Yaldiz, "A Journey of Exploration: Objects d'Arts of the Museum of Indian Art, Berlin, in the State Hermitage, St. Peterburg," in *IDP News* (Newsletter of the International Dunhuang Project) 25 (Spring 2005): 2–3.

[127] Kümmel to Frl. Dr. R.-M. Hempel, February 8, 1945, in Walravens, *Otto Kümmel*, p. 73.

[128] George Hazai, "Annemarie von Gabain und die türkische Sprachwissenschaft," in *Turfan, Khotan und Dunhuang*, ed. Ronald E. Emmerick et al. (Berlin, 1996), p. 167.

[129] See Marchand, "From Liberalism to Neoromanticism."

[130] Carsten Colpe, *Die religionsgeschichtliche Schule: Darstellung und Kritik ihres Bildes vom gnostischen Erlösungsmythus* (Göttingen, 1961), p. 31

The Turfan expeditions also had a culture-political legacy, which the West is still trying to live down. The despoilation of Central Asian art in the years before the war gave Chinese nationalists an issue to use against the Qing Empire, the Chinese Republic, and the Europeans themselves in subsequent years. Sven Hedin and Aurel Stein, among others, would reap this whirlwind, when in the 1920s and 1930s they found the "open doors" closed.[131] Europeans had learned a lot about oriental art, and Germans and Austrians, in particular, had generated sweeping new theories about contacts and conquests. The ancient Orient had been integrated into discussions about the origins of western styles. But all this new work, and the infrastructure that supported it, depended on virtually unlimited European access to the treasures of the East, and that, not only in China but also increasingly in Egypt, Persia, and Turkey, was no longer possible. Late into the colonial field and forced early from it, German art historians in the 1920s were some of the first to realize that they would now have to abide by the rules made by others – or return, as did others, to those rich, but still rather lonely, museum basements.

[131] Suzanne Marchand, "Traversing the Silk Road in a Post-Colonial Age: Sven Hedin and the Sino-Swedish Expeditions of 1927–35," paper delivered at Transnationalism Conference, University of North Carolina, Chapel Hill, April 2006.

Orientalists and "Others"

What will this Europe be for the Orient in the future? A band of swindlers and oppressors, without honor, without shame!
— Otto Franke to C. H. Becker, May 26, 1915[1]

As travel to the East became less difficult and more advantageous for scholars, as Germany's imperialist appetite grew, German orientalists increasingly came into contact with indigenous peoples, and this contact took on new qualities. We can date these new relations quite precisely, and tie them to a series of political events that were changing relations between Europeans and nonwestern peoples globally; these events, including the Sino-Japanese War, the Boxer Rebellion, the Boer Wars, the Russo-Japanese War, the Herero Uprising, the Maji Maji Rebellion, the Young Turk Revolution, and the Balkan Wars, would all impact, in one way or another, Europe's view of "others" — and the "others'" view of Europeans. This was also the period in which policies of "scientific" colonization or "peaceful penetration" were increasingly being implemented; these policies, more tolerant of local practices on the one hand and more invasive attempts at population control on the other, did further Europeanization, but in the long run also intensified and broadened hatred of colonial masters — and of Eurocentric orientalism. This era produced a much larger cadre than ever before of indigenous anti-colonial intellectuals, some of them trained in Europe, and Asian leaders willing and sometimes able to play the great powers off against one another. At their command were new tools — railroads, schools, newspapers, and excavation permits; many of these had been created by the imperial powers for furthering their own ends, (but might, like the Berlin-Baghdad Railway, be could be put to local ends as well.) And, ironically, the period also produced orientalists increasingly dependent on the coercion or cooptation of indigenous elites, a reality that came home powerfully when, during the Great War, the Kaiserreich allied itself with the Ottoman Empire.

As we enter the twentieth century, it no longer becomes possible to tell the story of German (or any European) orientalism without describing its entanglement with the lives, political aspirations, and cultural preoccupations of real-existing "orientals." There is simply too much intercontinental traveling, visiting, teaching, arguing, and exchanging going on and too much reciprocity for us to tell an essentially one-sided story. This is not, of course, to say that roles were equalized

[1] Otto Franke to C. H. Becker, May 26, 1915, in B-GSPK, Nachlass Becker, M. 703.

or that Europeans gave up their prejudices, chronologies, and/or classifications for local ones. Nor did they give up their personal ambitions or change their political convictions to suit others, though they did try, more and more often, to enroll individuals on the ground in their projects. What is different is that indigenous intellectuals increasingly were forming political and cultural projects of their own and working assiduously to enroll Europeans in *their* endeavors. Competing on the world stage for the hearts and minds (not to mention the resources) of peoples from Samoa to Samos and from the Cape to the Polish Pale, Europeans began thinking of nonwesterners, and especially the relatively independent and increasingly literate peoples of the Orient, as consumers of their books and newspapers. And their readers began to demonstrate that they were discerning and not necessarily docile consumers. Some professional orientalists, of course, did not realize that relations were changing; they continued to practice their trade in European libraries and to write exclusively for domestic consumption. Some – especially Kaiser Wilhelm's friends and advisor – remained as high-handed as ever before and presumed the West had the right and power simply to tell everyone else what to do and what to believe. But it was becoming increasingly clear to others, even before 1914, that direct imposition did not work, either to run an empire or to engineer an indigenous renaissance or reformation. And that meant one had to play differently, though not necessarily more "nicely," with others.

It would be wrong to take too seriously German claims to be the natural "friends" of colonized others; many of these "friendships" were of short duration and purely self-serving (sometimes on both sides). On the other hand, we cannot say that they related to indigenous intellectuals in Egypt, Algeria, or Indonesia in the same way as did the British, French, or Dutch; relationships between individuals and ideologies also varied greatly. We will not be able to find a single "Indian" or "Chinese" view of Germany, any more than we could find a unitary "German" view of India or China. Some Chinese intellectuals admired Germany for its combination of authoritarian politics and modern military machinery; others wished to emulate its social democratic traditions and efficient bureaucracies; and some others were sympathetic simply because Germany was the least threatening of the modernized imperial powers.[2] Some others still disapproved of German militarism, thought the language ugly, and/or thought the Reich a less advantageous trading partner than, say, the United States. Nor did the positions of groups or even of individuals necessarily remain constant over time; views changed as interests changed; Chinese Republican leaders, for example, grew less enthusiastic about things German as the great military power began to lose the World War, but then conceived a new appreciation for the defeated state after the western powers failed to return Shandong Province to China at the end of the war. As this example suggests, images can change quickly and are bound up too with relations with third or fourth parties: Germany inevitably looked friendlier and more attractive as a model the more England and Russia appeared imperialistic or dangerous. Economic and cultural factors also played a role; Germany's attraction to "the Orient" was perhaps never so strong as in the years 1918–23, years of such

---

[2] See, e.g., Roland Felber, "Das chinesische Deutschlandbild in der Zeit des Vierten Mai," in *Berliner China-Hefte* 17 (1999): 27–40.

great economic and political turmoil that many Germans, like Oswald Spengler, gave up on the West.[3]

Though of course a process of reciprocal learning and sharing of materials had been going on since at least the Jesuit missions of the seventeenth century, now this set of exchanges became more and more frequent; and as specialization and the shift to indigenous sources and authentic artifacts moved orientalism away from classical studies and familiar (European) texts, the knowledge and material culture of "the other" took on a new value. While in 1890, the excavating and collecting of manuscripts and artifacts overseas was only gradually becoming a pursuit for scholars, by 1910 orientalists who had actually "been there" were earning new respect and new visibility in academic and cultural institutions. And, increasingly, these were orientalists whose view of the East had been shaped in some rather deep way by their encounters with Asian cultures and indigenous individuals, especially the sort of individuals who had been exposed to European ideas but were also deeply steeped in, and often defensive of, local traditions and artifacts.

This chapter then focuses on these changing relations over a period that ranges from about 1900 to 1918, with a few excursions into the 1920s. The first section attempts to show briefly a range of interactions between orientalists and their purportive "subjects" and/or their colleagues abroad and to tease out some of the intellectual, cultural, and political consequences of their interaction. The next section examines a much better-known series of relations, that is, relations between Germans and Turks and describes the orientalists' many attempts to lend their services to the state during the Great War. The final section focuses on one exemplary individual, Richard Wilhelm, a missionary-turned orientalist, whose career was determined much more by events in China than by German developments and whose Sinological stance was, in more or less equal parts, shaped by Chinese neo-Confucianism and by German hyper-Protestantism. Regrettably, space and the author's linguistic limitations do not allow us to do full justice here to the nonwestern side, or to investigate a wider range of German-speaking scholars; there is much more work to be done here and I hope others will help to explore this terrain.

ORIENTALISTS AND OTHERS, 1900–1918

We open with the usual reminder that there are continuities here that reach back centuries or even millennia; Europeans, some Europeans have always learned things from others (and not just others' texts) and by "going there." Most readers seem to have treated the travelogues of Herodotus, Marco Polo, John Mandeville, and Matteo Ricci as truthful reportage despite the fantastical nature of some of their information. Beginning in medieval Spain and increasing after the fall of Constantinople, contacts between eastern intellectuals (Jews, Greeks, and Arabs) and western scholars laid the foundations for Renaissance science and Reformation-era biblical criticism – though eastern nations for some time seem not to have found western ideas particularly useful or interesting. In the seventeenth century,

---

[3] See Marchand, "Eastern Wisdom in a Time of Western Despair: Orientalism in 1920s Central Europe," forthcoming in Peter Gordon, ed. *Weimar Thought: A Critical History* (Princeton, N.J., forthcoming).

the Safavid rulers of Persia encouraged cultural contacts with the West and adopted European artillery techniques to fight the Turks more effectively; but, like the Chinese court's dalliance with the Jesuits, this did not really lead to creative or sustained intellectual interaction.[4] Quite suddenly, in the early decades of the nineteenth century, things changed; early modern cross-continental cultural exchange – never harmonious, but based on a less lopsided balance of power – gave way to a western game plan that dictated that the East should evolve, at least in material and external ways, toward a European model. The British abandoned attempts to understand India's subcultures and languages in favor of forcing their Indian subjects to learn English and to adopt English institutions and mores; the French made new efforts to impose French culture on their dominions. Those who had not yet come under European control adopted some forms of Europeanization as a defense. Threatened by Russian expansionism, the Qajar shahs, for example, sought to import western military technology, and in 1852 founded an Academy of Arts and Sciences, staffed by Europeans who taught (western) natural science, history, and literature. The Japanese similarly began to import all manner of western experts in the decades after the nation's ports were forcibly "opened" by the Americans. In this context, the old model of "informed evangelizing" (Chapter 1) broke down, and Europeans abroad did not seek to adapt to local conditions, but simply to replace indigenous cultures with their own.

Of course, there were already signs, for those perceptive enough to see them, that straightforward impositions or imitations were not going to effect sudden and thorough going western-style modernization. The British or French models could not succeed over the long run: firstly, because the Europeans were not satisfied with allowing locals to manage the process in their own ways, and secondly, because interests, customs, and belief systems were under threat, and indigenous traders, believers, and political leaders not willing to go down without a fight. Finally, the model itself was rife with injustices and inconsistencies and usually applied with extreme prejudice for European interests. The Indian Rebellion (1857) and the Boxer Uprising (1899–1900) might have been wake-up calls – but they were not. Then European rivalries began to make themselves felt, abroad as well as at home, and even non-colonized nations like Japan and Persia began to be suspicious of their advisors, of European overtures made to them, and of travelers and archaeologists who insisted their motives were purely scientific. Of course, some nations had too little power (or too much debt) to resist such overtures, but in other cases, they were able to pick and choose their "friends" and often get something for themselves out of the deal. As Nasir-al-Din Shah (of Iran) commented: it would have been preferable "that never a European had set foot on my country's soil: for then we would have been spared all these tribulations. But since the foreigners have unfortunately penetrated into our country, we shall at least make the best possible use of them."[5]

Hamdi Bey, the Ottoman Empire's Minister of Cultural Affairs and founder of the Imperial Museum in Istanbul, did precisely this. By making friends with

---

[4] T. Cuyler Young, "Islamic and Western Thought: Iran," in idem, *Near Eastern Culture and Society: A Symposium on the Meeting of East and West* (Princeton, NJ, 1951), pp. 131–2.

[5] Nasir-al-Din quoted in ibid., p. 138.

German archaeologists and using secret as well as formal agreements to control the flow of artifacts, Hamdi not only contributed greatly to the Reich's supply of treasures, but procured a collection for his own museum quite cheaply. Gradually, Hamdi began to train an indigenous cohort of archaeologists and archaeological overseers and to move toward more and more Ottoman control of excavations.[6] The same dynamic worked even more quickly in Japan; Germans were engaged to reform medical education in the 1870s, but by 1905, when Erwin Baelz retired and left for home, the system had been put entirely in Japanese hands. The period in which the Japanese were "hypnotized" by everything European, Baelz recognized, was already over by 1900, as disillusioned inhabitants mused about the actions of all the Great Powers in response to the Sino-Japanese War.[7] In this case, self-confidence, not to mention an effective navy, bred respect, and it was not long before Europeans began to feel they might have something to learn from the Japanese.

Learning processes were formalized, of course, in the planting of European schools in colonized areas and in the sending of foreign students to Europe for instruction. Some of these students would end up working for the colonial regimes and some would end up fighting them too. To take one striking example: the Chinese nationalist Cai Yuanpei learned to respect German philosophy during his studies in Japan, but his actual plans to study in Germany evolved after he had committed himself to overthrowing the Qing and recognized the revolution's need for outside expertise. In 1907, he left China for Leipzig, where the Sinologist August Conrady treated him kindly – but Cai had no intention of becoming a conventional German orientalist. In 1909, he translated Friedrich Paulsen's *System der Ethik* into Chinese and in the following year published his own *Geschichte der chinesischen Ethik*, which tried to give traditional ethical thought an order and history. After the revolution he became China's education minister, and in 1916, was appointed Beijing University's first chancellor; he was later instrumental in founding the National College of Music, Academia Sinica, and the Beijing Institute for Esperanto. His goals throughout, argues Cai Jianguo, lay in the defeudalization and reform of Chinese science and education, and not in mimetic westernization; it is not an adequate characterization of him to call him either simply a Chinese nationalist or a Europeanized intellectual.[8]

Indeed, we need to pay particular attention not only to the *European* generation of the 1890s to understand changes underway in early twentieth-century orientalism; we need also to understand the *non-Europeans* of this generation, men and women like Cai Yuanpei and the Indian nationalist (and then communist) M. N. Roy, who used their European contacts and exposure to western ideas for the sake of their own domestic cultural ends. Though they often drew on traditional learning, these intellectuals also benefited from the increased circulation of books and newspapers, from telegraphic connections and faster travel to spread their messages, both in the East and in the West. They worked between worlds, often becoming celebrities in both, though they were often caught in the

---

[6] On Hamdi, see Wendy M. K. Shaw, *Possessors and Possessed: Museums, Archeology and the Visualization of History in the Late Ottoman Empire* (Berkeley, CA, 2003).

[7] See Chapter 8.

[8] Cai Jianguo, "Cai Yuanpei und die deutsche Kultur," in *Berliner China-Hefte* 14 (1998): 78–87, 99.

political crossfire. We cannot generalize too much about them; not only did their cultural and political positions depend on the particularities of their location – Cairo versus Hong Kong, Ceylon versus Isfahan – but they too were individuals with disparate life experiences, interests, education, and aims. If it is wrong to stereotype orientalists, it is also wrong to make sweeping generalizations about their counterparts in the nonwestern world.

However, to many of these individuals and especially to those who saw themselves as enemies of thorough-going westernization, things and persons "German" often had a special set of connotations.[9] This was due to a number of factors: the late leap of the Kaiserreich into colonization; the monarchy's generally defensive position with respect to traditional authority; the long legacy of Herderian *völkisch* nationalism; and Germany's association with the latest developments in the humanities, natural sciences, and especially military training and armaments. The latter, that is, military might, was not something prewar German scholars advertised openly – though they were fully aware of its importance and welcomed Germany's rise to world prominence. They preferred, of course, to emphasize their nation's cultural power. But, to those watching Germany's meteoric rise to world power status, military prowess was perhaps the most attractive feature of the Kaiserreich. To those who still had control of their own countries, such as the Ottomans, Japanese, and Chinese, it suggested that authoritarian regimes could modernize rapidly without too much democratization or erosion of elite culture and influence (Germany's internal dissensions were less often recognized). To those who had been colonized, like the Indians, Egyptians, or Moroccans, Germany appeared a possible ally in the struggle against British or French domination. This seemed especially likely after the Kaiser openly gloated over Britain's floundering in the Boer Wars. Of course, Polish and Arab nationalists were likely to seek military assistance elsewhere and throughout the period, nonwestern radicals coursed through all of Europe's major cities, looking for inspiration and assistance from local and expatriate support groups. But Germany, the new power on the block, with its now well-established scientific credentials and its crack troops, its reputation for profundity and efficiency, its powerful social democratic party and growing communist intelligentsia, and its grand ambitions and open desire to challenge established balances of power and spheres of influence, had a special appeal. It was already a "third way" between traditional political and cultural practices and totally westernized modernity, and though there were enormous disparities in images of what that "third way" might look like on the ground, for nations (or would-be nations) trying to survive the era of high colonialism, the German model had deep resonance.

This appeal of the Germans, I hasten to add, was neither Germany's fault nor to Germany's credit; it was, in large part, simply the result of its growing power and the geopolitical lay of the land circa 1900. Probably most Germans, and even most German orientalists, did not recognize this and attributed foreign overtures and the increasing tide of nonwestern students coming to Germany, to their own magnanimity and scholarly repute. Of course, the more cynical and

---

[9] See Andrew Sartori, "Beyond Culture-Contact and Colonial Discourse: 'Germanism' in Colonial Bengal," in *Modern Intellectual History* 4, no. 1 (2007): 77–93.

those tied to the business community recognized that there were convenient "communities of interest" that underwrote the launching of projects like the Baghdad Railway and the numerous "friendship" societies that sprang up in the years before the war. There were some who, like Otto Franke, also recognized that nonwesterners might take European culture on board, and still hate Europeans; ". . . fear, combined with the hatred, toward ever-thrusting Europeandom forms the key to understanding the cultural trends and internal-political processes in China since 1898," Franke wrote in 1902, soon after returning home from China.[10] But many seemed to have believed that these friendships would hold, despite the Reich's usually superficial and self-interested reasons for advertising them, and would try to inflame subaltern sentiment against European colonial regimes. No wonder their efforts failed so miserably; the only internal revolutions they were able to foment were not "oriental" rebellions, but Irish (briefly) and, infamously, Russian ones.

It might be noted that one aspect of the German orientalist tradition played directly into the failure of these wartime plans and that is the tradition's emphasis on pure and ancient language learning, and its disdain for modern oriental cultures, events, and individuals. As we saw in Chapters 8 and 9, in the era of high imperialism, Germans did begin to engage more avidly in the study of the modern East, to travel more, and to interact more with local intellectuals and political figures. Yet their presence in the East and their practical knowledge of contemporary affairs was still, in 1905, or even 1914, quite limited. The German community in Hong Kong in 1914 numbered only about 300 souls, of 320,000 total inhabitants, substantially fewer than the 4,000 Britons and 2,500 Portuguese.[11] By Erwin Baelz' count, in 1905, there were 1866 foreigners in Tokyo, of whom 954 were Chinese, 296 Americans, 186 English, 104 Koreans, 91 French, and 77 Germans.[12] The German communities in Syria, Egypt, Persia, and even Istanbul were similarly small – though there were upward of 100,000 Jews in Palestine by 1914, most of them Yiddish speakers and many of them Germanophilic.[13] One did not necessarily have to "be there," or even to study things modern to feel solidarity with friends abroad; Paul Deussen had demonstrated this already in the 1890s. In June 1914 he underlined, in the first article in the first volume of a Zürich-based Indian nationalist journal, the linguistic kinship that linked the Germans to "our brothers in the East," adding: "But supremely surprising, more surprising than the relationship of our languages, is the fact that Indian and German genius, the first [expressed] already in the Vedas and Vedanta, the latter only in Kant and Schopenhauer, have arrived by different paths at a single worldview. . . ."[14] In fact, this would have been surprising only to Indian nationalists, as Deussen had been telling his German readership the same thing for a

---

[10] Franke, "Geistige Strömungen im heutigen China," in *Deutsche Kolonialgesellschaft: Verhandlungen Abteilung Berlin-Charlottenburg* 7 (1902–3): 5.

[11] Winfried Speitkamp, "Die Deutschen in Hongkong, 1860–1914: Wirtschaftliche Interessen und nationale Identität," in *Berliner China-Hefte* 17 (1999): 17.

[12] Baelz, *Awakening Japan*, p. 337.

[13] Isaiah Friedman estimates at most 2,500 Germans in Palestine in 1914. Friedman, *Germany, Turkey and Zionism, 1897–1918* (Oxford, 1977), pp. 155, 192.

[14] Deussen, "Unsere Brüder im Osten," quoted in Walter Leifer, *Indien und die Deutschen: 500 Jahre Begegnung und Partnerschaft* (Tübingen, 1969), p. 377.

long time. But Deussen was now a rather elderly man and no political organizer; in promoting the next stage of inter-cultural relations, it helped to know something about contemporary politics, economic matters, and religious groups – and that was characteristic neither of the German academy nor even of the Reich's diplomatic service.

Nor did many Germans who did spend time abroad model inter-cultural understanding; many kept as much as possible to themselves and/or to the German and European encampments and did not mix much at all with the natives. Some of the members of the foreign service were themselves quite reluctant to mix or condescend to learning the local languages. One visitor to Istanbul, in 1914, was amazed to learn how little the German ambassador and his staff knew about contemporary "cultural trends," and especially about Pan-Turkism.[15] Both the German ambassador to China, Edmund von Heyking, and his novelist wife Elisabeth, Otto Franke claimed, were convinced that the Chinese were universally dirty, weak, and ignorant: in their view, "To concern oneself with Chinese cultural questions was the sign of a subaltern mind...."[16] Franke, as we have seen, eventually resigned from the diplomatic service himself, frustrated at the whole organization's contempt for *Kulturpolitik*. Among businessmen, missionaries, scientific emissaries, and journalists, there were some, like Erwin Baelz, who learned languages, became avid collectors of Asian artifacts, and even married local women. But there were others who simply wanted to do their jobs and return home, hopefully with domestically useful profits, souls, or stories in their pockets.

By the time of the Great War, there were many new converts to the esoteric sciences and more Buddhists than ever before. Corinna Treitel has shown not only how popular occult sciences became in the late Wilhelmine and Weimar eras but also how often they attracted scientists, artists, and other intellectuals dedicated to "spiritual" reform; occult practices seemed to them, she argues, less a form of anti-rational behavior than a means to further expand the sphere of human consciousness.[17] This would hold too for many of those who had begun to look eastward for inspiration; usually their aims were to reform or perfect western ideals rather than to adopt wholly different lifestyles or to oppose European expansionism. Rudolf Steiner was a particularly influential exemplar of this movement – and it is interesting to note that his break with the Theosophical Society was precipitated by the American members' insistence on giving messianic status to an Indian boy, Jiddu Krishnamurti. On the whole, Steiner and the Anthroposophical Society seem to have been less enamored with "eastern wisdom" and less interested in Indian politics than many of their erstwhile Anglo-American colleagues. But Steiner did introduce many a member of the educated elite to nonwestern ideas and even managed to convince Field Marshall Helmuth von Moltke, after his dismissal as Chief of the General Staff in November of 1914,

---

[15] Karl Emil Schabinger von Schowingen, *Weltgeschichtliche Mosaiksplitter: Erlebnisse und Erinnerungen eines kaiserliches Dragomans* (Baden-Baden, 1967), pp. 106–8.

[16] Otto Franke, *Erinnerungen*, p. 98.

[17] Corinna Treitel, *A Science for the Soul: Occultism and the Birth of the German Modern* (Baltimore, 2004).

that he was the reincarnation of Pope Nicholas (died 867), whose role was to build new bridges to the East.[18]

Of course, there were some genuine friendships and real mutual respect that linked orientalists (as well as consular officials, businessmen, and missionaries) and their nonwestern interlocutors, teachers, or students, and it is certainly a tribute to the rising status of "orientals" that one begins to see, after 1900, more and more acknowledgments of their help in the prefaces of European works and more frequent mention of particular individuals in the orientalists' autobiographies.[19] One could be cynical about such things, but there were feelings of gratitude, loyalty, and affection behind such gestures as Richard Wilhelm's dedication of a major work to his friend Cai Yuanpei or Paul Deussen's friendship with Swami Vivekananda. There were a few noteworthy marriages: of Ida Stieler to the Bengali intellectual Benoy Kumar Sarkar and of the last king of the Sikhs, Dulip Singh, to the daughter of a German merchant living in Alexandria.[20] Books do make real friends; Richard Pischel had longed for many years to see India for himself, a personal passion that made his death on arriving in Madras, before he had a chance to see the subcontinent, particularly tragic.[21] There is probably even truth in H. L. Strack's story about a German captain, who happened to be a professor of oriental languages, riding through a Polish town after a vicious Great War battle. Spotting a rabbi calmly reading his books in his destroyed house, the unnamed captain approached, announced his familiarity with biblical Hebrew, and the two sat down to an animated discussion of an obscure passage in the Talmud.[22] Strack does not report what happened next; did the captain take the rabbi home to Leipzig or Hamburg to practice his scholarship in peace? That is possible, but we may have grounds for being more cynical and assuming that this one moment of intellectual friendship, like many others, was heartbreakingly brief.

Books of course also make enemies, and gradually, some Europeans did begin to realize that "other" people were reading their work, and rejecting their ideas. The signs of this are certainly faint to begin with and certainly not evident in every orientalist's work – the vast majority of European scholars continued to think that they were producing for the domestic market alone, just as political leaders consistently underestimated the sophistication of their "oriental" interlocutors. Most Germans surely did not know or care that the Arabic press gave

---

[18] See T. H. Meyer, ed., *Light for the New Millennium: Rudolf Steiner's Association with Helmuth and Eliza von Moltke: Letters, Documents, and After-Death Communications* (London, 1997), p. 264.

[19] Enno Littmann acknowledged his assistant in the published version of his translation and commentary on 715 Tigre-language songs; and in a private letter admitted: "If I had not discussed this material line for line and word for word with my Abyssinian, I would never have been able to make heads or tails of it." Littmann to Becker, March 30, 1909 in B-GSPK, Nachlass Becker, M. 4579.

[20] Walter Leifer, *Indien und die Deutschen*, pp. 381–2.

[21] Otto Franke, *Erinnerungen aus Zwei Welten*, p. 127.

[22] Felix Perles, review of H. L. Strack's *Jüdisches Wörterbuch mit besonderer Berücksichtigung der gegenwärtig in Polen üblichen Ausdrücke* (Leipzig, 1916), and idem, *Jüdische Texte: Lesebuch zur Einführung in Denken, Leben und Sprache der osteuropäische Juden* (Leipzig, 1917), in OLZ 21 (1918): 200.

extensive coverage to Wilhelm II's visit to the Near East and that Egyptian newspapers, in particular, were very critical of German political and cultural ambitions in the Ottoman Empire.[23] But there are some indications even before the war that sensitivities or even target audiences were changing, together with the rise of more systematic forms of cultural colonialism. Though the editors of the first edition of the *Encyclopedia of Islam* were not anxious enough to have indigenous elites read their work to include any Muslim contributors or to issue their work in Arabic or Persian editions (it appeared in German, French, and English), some of them, at least, were interested in indigenous response. One *OLZ* reviewer hoped educated Muslims might read it. Their first reaction might be an apologetic defense of the faith, but then "a second stage will then perhaps awaken scientific consciousness and lead, without misgivings, to the testing of the evidence."[24] Of course, men like Hartmann, Franke, and Baelz, who had spent time abroad, knew well that local elites had access to a wealth of information and that they could easily discover – simply by reading European newspapers – what plans were afoot or what derogatory terms were being bandied about. But it would take the Great War for the mentalities and ambitions of the "others" to really count – and even then, who counted continued to depend on who was needed (or not needed) at the moment.

THE ORIENTALISTS AND THE GREAT WAR

For most of Germany's professional orientalists, the Great War came rather too soon, before a large cadre of "modernist" scholars could be trained – before they had exhausted their treasure-trawling in Central Asia, and before they had gained full backing for the policies of peaceful penetration and cultural colonization most of them endorsed. Long before the war's outbreak, virtually any observer could have predicted that the next European conflict would have at its core two central issues of concern to orientalists: Germany's role as a colonizing power and the future of the "sick man of the Balkans," namely the Ottoman Empire. But intellectually, no one, perhaps least of all the Germans, was ready for such a conflict. When war came to the colonies as well as to mainland Europe and the question of the Ottomans' direct engagement in the conflict arose, the relatively small pool of specialists in modern Asia were confronted with an unexpected but important opportunity to demonstrate their "relevance" and value to the Reich. Though a few were horrified at the prospect of world war – Nöldeke initially wished himself already dead – most adapted to the reality of it quite swiftly. By mid-September, in the wake of German victories, even the aging Strasbourg professor was enthusing over the prospect of adding a Great War victory to those he had seen in 1866 and 1870–1.[25]

One of the professional orientalists' first reactions to the war's outbreak was to decry England's "perfidy." After all, many (including Wilhelm Solf and Friedrich Rosen, the highest placed orientalists at the time) had hoped, right

---

[23] Sinno, "The Emperor's Visit," in Sader et al., eds., *Baalbek*, pp. 115–33.

[24] J. Horovitz, review of *Enzyklopädie des Islam* (1908), in *OLZ* 13 (1910): 32–3.

[25] Nöldeke to Becker, September 20, 1914, in B-GSPK, Nachlass Becker, M. 3138.

down to Franz Ferdinand's assassination, that some sort of deal could be brokered between the two powers, allowing Germany its rightful place in the colonial sun without causing a general war.[26] But on August 3, when England entered the conflict, that hope was dashed. Franke immediately produced an essay denouncing England's East Asian policies and Carl Becker followed suit, underlining Britain's double game with respect to Islam. On the one hand, Becker argued, the English treated Muslims favorably, especially in India, where Islam was being used as a means to forestall Hindu nationalists' attempts to liberate the country. On the other hand, the English had sold out the Young Turks and Turkey itself.[27] By early 1915 Eduard Meyer had already written a 200-page book blaming England for the war; though, of course, France did not escape severe criticism nor did Russia, whose world-historical mission was, according to Meyer, to destroy European culture.[28]

But this sort of outrage was not particularly effectual, and there were other causes in which orientalist involvement was far more important and extensive. As we will see in this chapter, there were numerous ways in which scholars and para-academic orientalists tried to make themselves useful in Germany's war effort and numerous debates in which they engaged. But perhaps the most consequential and telling of these engagements was the one that began with the Ottoman Empire's entry into the war on October 31, 1914, which was followed quickly by the Sultan's declaration of "holy war" or *jihad* on November 11 to a small circle of officials, and its public announcement three days later by the Shaykh-al-Islam (Shiite clerics in Najaf and Karbala also issued *fatwa*s calling their people to arms).[29] Fear of "the East set aflame" had already been simmering before the war, and thus the *jihad* declaration fell on prepared soil; Entente newspapers were quick to blame German "barbarians" for conceiving the idea of raising the Muslim East against Christian Europeans.[30] Whether or not the idea was "made in Germany" is debatable, and the role of one orientalist, Max Freiherr von Oppenheim, in devising the whole policy remains controversial (discussed later in this chapter). But the declaration and its ideological consequences certainly did shape the roles German orientalists would play during the war and the ways in which their relations with non-European "others" evolved, and so we begin our analysis by delving into the prehistory and fallout of the Ottoman-German *jihad*.

---

[26] See Fritz Fischer, *War of Illusions: German Policies from 1911 to 1914*, trans. Marian Jackson (London, 1975), pp. 318–19.

[27] Otto Franke, "Deutschland und England in Ostasien," in *Deutsche Vorträge Hamburgischer Professoren*, 3 (Hamburg, 1914). Becker, "England und der Islam" [1914], in idem, *Islamstudien* 2: 385–92.

[28] Meyer, *England: Seine staatliche und politische Entwicklung und der Krieg gegen Deutschland* (Stuttgart, 6th and 7th eds., 1915); on Russia, p. 212.

[29] Thanks to Mustafa Aksakal for clarifying the announcement of the declaration. Personal correspondence, January 2, 2009.

[30] Well before the war's outbreak, Herbert Landolin Müller has shown, "the themes of Pan-Islamism and jihad as well had been everywhere instrumentalized." Müller, *Islam, gihad ("Heiliger Krieg") und Deutsches Reich: Ein Nachspiel zur wilhelmischen Weltpolitik im Maghreb 1914–1918* (Frankfurt, 1991), p. 182.

DECLARING *JIHAD*

For many years, historians essentially accepted the Entente's interpretation of events, blaming Germany for tricking the Ottomans into joining the war and for provoking the declaration. This tendency was compounded by attempts by post-1945 historians like Fritz Fischer to emphasize Germany's guilt in inciting the Great War – and there are still many who follow this line of interpretation.[31] There is some good evidence for it; on July 30, 1914, three days before the Germans and Turks signed a secret accord, Wilhelm instructed diplomats and intelligence agents to do their best to inflame the Muslim world. On August 5, Moltke wrote a memo to the Foreign Office to the same effect.[32] Others in Foreign Office circles, especially of the anti-English school, pushed the idea too: Arthur Zimmermann and Ernst "Türken" Jaeckh, for example, and Sven Hedin, Germanophile traveler, apparently endorsed the feasibility of the plan.[33] On August 2, Max Freiherr von Oppenheim, a retired diplomat and amateur archaeologist, was recalled from his excavation site in Syria to Berlin.[34] Drawing on his own, long exposure to Islamic anti-colonial circles as well as these plans, by mid-October, Oppenheim drafted a highly detailed 136-page memorandum on how, in practical terms, the Reich could use Islam as "one of our most important weapons" especially in the fight against England. Islam's use was to be organized by the Germans, though for the most part secretly, convincing or bribing local religious and political leaders to spread their message as necessary. The Turks in particular were vital; the Caliph's participation was, he wrote, "the best propaganda tool" one could imagine. "Turkish Propaganda," he continued, "should be centralized in Constantinople; it should perpetually be directed and supported by the German side, but [it should be directed] in such a way that the Turks believe that we are simply standing next to them as friendly advisors, so that they can, ever after as before, see and proclaim themselves the actual authors."[35] The memo carefully laid out plans for how to "revolutionize" Egypt, India, Persia, Morocco, Afghanistan, and the Islamic areas of Russia, how to deal with the various nationality groups in each area and what sort of supplies would be needed (not only *Orientkenner* but also camels, land mines, airplanes, armaments, and food).

---

[31] For example, Hagen, "German Heralds of Holy War"; Peter Hopkirk claims it was Wilhelm's own idea. Hopkirk, *Like Hidden Fire: The Plot to Bring down the British Empire* (New York, 1994), p. 62. Seçil Deren goes even further, arguing that it is probable that "... Turkish nationalism as an original and systematic ideological formulation was moulded and propagated by German politicians, academicians and policy-makers, rather than the Turks themselves." Deren, "From Pan-Islamism to Turkish Nationalism: Modernisation and German Influence in the Late Ottoman Period," in *Disrupting and Reshaping: Early Stages of Nation-Building in the Balkans*, ed. Marco Dogo and Guido Franzinetti (Ravenna, 2002), p. 139.

[32] Vahakn N. Dadrian, *German Responsibility in the Armenian Genocide* (Watertown, MA, 1996), pp. 50–81.

[33] Hopkirk, *Like Hidden Fire*, p. 54.

[34] See R. L. Melka, "Max Freiherr von Oppenheim: Sixty Years of Scholarship and Political Intrigue in the Middle East," in *Middle Eastern Studies* 9 (173): 81.

[35] Oppenheim, "Die Revolutionierung der islamischen Gebiete unserer Feinde," in Tim Epkenhaus, "Geld Darf keine Rolle Spielen (part II)," in *Archivum Ottomanicum* 19 (2001): 123.

Oppenheim estimated the costs of his policies (including propaganda and materiel) to be at least 100 and probably more like 300 million Marks.[36]

On the basis of this memo, Fritz Fischer made Oppenheim the brains behind the Reich's decision to think of Pan-Islamism as a weapon, arguing that Oppenheim had inspired the Kaiser's visit to Saladin's tomb as well as his speech in Damascus, in which Wilhelm assured the Sultan and the Empire's 300 million Muslims of his true friendship.[37] But many years ago, Wilhelm Treue noted that there is no evidence that Oppenheim's ideas reached the Kaiser at this point and that the memos Oppenheim wrote in 1896 were less concerned with "revolutionizing the East" than with promoting his own career.[38] It is quite possible that Oppenheim reiterated his ideas to his friend on later occasions, though their correspondence just before the war focused on archaeological matters (Oppenheim was excavating at the Hittite site of Tell Halaf, while the Kaiser was working at his own prehistorical site on Corfu).[39] There were other orientalist operatives in on the plan; Oppenheim's friend, Karl Schabinger von Schowingen, as we shall see, was in Istanbul for the declaration and it is possible that Arthur Zimmermann's agent Fritz Klein bribed the Shiite clerics to issue their *fatwas*.[40] In any event, Oppenheim was allowed to organize his agency, the Nachrichtenstelle für den Orient (NfO), within the Foreign Ministry and to employ numerous orientalists in the task of "setting the East aflame."

This account is cogent, but a more nuanced view of Ottoman entry into the war and responsibility for the *jihad* declaration is supported by recent studies that take seriously Turkish agency in the matter.[41] If we look at eastern affairs between about 1908 and 1914 from the Turkish point of view, neither the German alliance nor the "holy war" declaration seem irrational acts. The Young Turk Revolution of 1908 briefly interrupted the "friendship" Wilhelm II had cultivated with the Ottomans; but in subsequent years, the Committee of Union and Progress (CUP) had found the Germans not only useful investors but also counterweights to the French, British, and Russians. In early 1914, the Turks were still reeling from the Balkan Wars; not only had the army experienced a large number of defections by Christian soldiers during these battles (which made the Turks suspicious, thereafter, of calling up Greeks and Armenians for service) but also many Muslims from lost Ottoman territories had now resettled in Turkey and were,

---

[36] Ibid.

[37] Fritz Fischer, *Griff nach der Weltmacht: Die Kriegszielpolitik des kaiserlichen Deutschland 1914/18* (Düsseldorf, 2nd ed., 1962), pp. 136–48.

[38] Wilhelm Treue, "Max Freiherr von Oppenheim: Der Archäolog und die Politik," in *Historische Zeitschrift* 209 (1969): 52–3, 57–9.

[39] Apparently the two talked chiefly archaeology at a dinner in November 1912. Oppenheim to Wangenheim, November 20, 1912, in B-PAAA, Kultur Abtelung, Kunst und Wiss. IIId, 27–468d, vol. 2 (now in B-BArch). A letter from Oppenheim – who was then still at Tell Halaf – to Wilhelm in April 1914 concerned exclusively the fate of his archaeological finds, Oppenheim to Kaiser, April 3, 1914, in ibid.

[40] Martin Kröger, "Revolution also Programm: Ziele und Realität deutscher Orientpolitik im Ersten Weltkrieg," in *Der Ersten Weltkrieg: Wirkung, Wahrnehmung, Analyse*, ed. Wolfgang Michalka (Munich, 1994), p. 379.

[41] See now Mustafa Aksakal, *The Ottoman Road to War in 1914: The Ottoman Empire and the First World War* (Cambridge, 2008).

understandably, suspicious of or hostile to groups they saw as persecutors. Moreover, in February 1914, the Russians, backed by the Germans, had signed a Reform Agreement, guaranteeing Armenian autonomy in parts of Anatolia and threatening Russian intervention if this autonomy was disturbed.[42] Hundreds of thousands of Greeks were already being forced out of Mediterranean coastal towns, thought to be too close for comfort to Greece's recently conquered islands of Lemnos, Imros, and Mytilene. The Turks were also well aware that Arab nationalism was stirring, though during the Italo-Turkish War in 1911, the CUP had managed to convince some Arabs to fight by means of declaring *jihad*. The Turkish Minister of War, Enver Pasha, had been instrumental in organizing the resistance to the Italians and had come out of the conflict with the reputation of being a hero of Islam; Enver was certainly pro-German and would be, according to Halidé Edib, instrumental in pushing for the *jihad* declaration in 1914.[43] On August 2, when it was clear that Europe – or at least the arch-enemy, Russia – was heading for war, the Turks signed an alliance with the Germans, extracting for themselves promises on a wide range of issues, from assistance in abolishing capitulations to protection of Ottoman territorial integrity or even annexations in case of a victory.[44] Even after the war started, the Ottomans still had to be bribed with a considerable amount of materiel as well as promises of debt relief to join the conflict, which they finally did, only on October 31, 1914. The Turks had calculated their self-interest in making their alliance with the Kaiserreich – though their options were limited and their calculations proved disastrously ill-considered, they had their own reasons for choosing this fate. And the Turks would guard their own interests as closely as possible throughout the war.

The Ottoman alliance, then, was not simply the result of German dirty tricks; and the same might be said for the *jihad* declaration. We might first of all ask where Oppenheim got his ideas about Pan-Islamism – it is doubtful that it was from German sources, for as we have seen, the study of the modern Middle East in Germany was very weak indeed in the 1890s, when Oppenheim was said to have been forming his ideas. As a young man, Oppenheim had longed to be a scholar-traveler on the model of Gerhard Rohlfs or Georg Schweinfurth, an activity that called for deep interactions with local populations. In his memoirs, he makes much of his "double life" during the years he was at the Cairo Embassy (1896–1909) and his close contacts with Arab notables and intellectuals. One of these was the Khedive, Abbas II Hilmi, who, Oppenheim reports, was passionately opposed to English occupation and who stood "absolutely for the ideas of Pan-Islamism"; another was Muhammed Abduh, an Egyptian intellectual whose passionate endorsement of Islamic modernization and revival resulted in his exile in 1882.

---

[42] Isabel V. Hull, *Absolute Destruction: Military Culture and the Practices of War in Imperial Germany* (Ithaca, NY, 2005), p. 266.

[43] Stephen Casewit, "Background to the Holy War of 1914: Towards an Understanding," in *Islamic Quarterly* 29, no. 4 (1985): 225, 229.

[44] For a list of these concessions, see Ulrich Trumpener, *Germany and the Ottoman Empire, 1914–1918* (Princeton, NJ, 1968), p. 28. Isabel Hull, who gives more agency than most to the Turks in the forming of the alliance, even suggests Talat and Enver, in particular, were anxious to go to war in order to "solve" the Armenian question – and thought declaring *jihad* would be useful in accomplishing the solution (genocide) they had in mind. Hull, *Absolute Destruction*, pp. 266–8.

Oppenheim also had contacts with representatives of the Senussi, whom he knew to be "a thorn in the side" of the English.[45] Moreover, some of the ideas in Oppenheim's memorandum seem to have come from Enver Pasha's own anti-colonial agents, who had been reporting secretly to the Turkish war minister for several years, and as we have seen, the CUP already recognized that *jihad* might be useful in rallying Arab and perhaps Persian subjects to its cause.[46] By late October, Enver's friend Shaykh Salih ash-Sharif at-Tunisi, who had been active in the *jihad* against the Italians, had prepared an Islamic defense of the *jihad* declaration; Enver made sure this passionate and well-born figure returned to Berlin just after the announcement, to carry forward the propaganda campaign.[47] If we give up our Eurocentric presumptions, we might well give Oppenheim's Egyptian, Sudanese, and Moroccan friends, rather than the man himself, credit (or blame) for his conversion to this point of view. This would not at all be inconsistent with the other learning processes we have seen orientalists undergo when they came into contact with anti-imperialist intellectuals elsewhere (Deussen and Goldizher are just two examples). Oppenheim's real significance for Germany's wartime *Orientpolitik*, Herbert Müller judiciously concludes, lay in his gathering together of "all the confusing, uncoordinated, and partially fanciful plans" produced by prewar German and Turkish provocateurs, anti-colonial radicals, and Islam-fearing journalists, missionaries, and scholars, and forging from them an overall program and a supposedly coordinating institution.[48]

We will discuss later in this chapter the operations of the institution Oppenheim created, the Nachrichtenstelle für den Orient (NfO) and its use of orientalist expertise. What is interesting, for our purposes here, is firstly that the idea was mutually useful to both the Germans and the Ottomans, and secondly, that it appears that no orientalists, other than Oppenheim, Klein, and Schabinger (a dragoman) – all of whom the *Fach* held at arm's length – were consulted on the *jihad* policy, though Becker apparently had heard about it by September 23, well before it was officially declared by the Shaykh-al-Islam and even before Oppenheim's memorandum was circulated.[49] But from that time forward, the *jihad* declaration would be a major focus of their public as well as private discussions. Most defended it publicly, even though they knew that justifying it was tricky and knew too that the religious diversity of the Ottoman Empire would make its implementation difficult.

German orientalists recognized this question not only as one on which their historical and linguistic talents could be brought to bear but also as one central

---

[45] Oppenheim quoted in Treue, "Max Freiherr von Oppenheim," p. 50; on his early longings, ibid., pp. 40–9. Cf. Hagen, "German Heralds of Holy War," pp. 149. On Oppenheim's friends, see Müller, *Islam, gihad*, pp. 61, 194–5. Abduh was also a student of Goldziher's old anti-colonial contact, Jamal al-Din al-Afghani. Oppenheim quoted in ibid., p. 195.

[46] Ibid., pp. 202–3, 238–43; also Hull, *Absolute Destruction*, pp. 263–79; Daniel Bloxham, *The Great Game of Genocide: Imperialism, Nationalism, and the Destruction of the Ottoman Armenians* (Oxford, 2005), pp. 115–33.

[47] Wolfgang Schwanitz, "Djihad 'Made in Germany'; Der Streit um den Heiligen Krieg, 1914–1915," in *Sozial Geschichte* 18, no. 2 (2003): 12–17.

[48] Müller, *Islam, gihad*, p. 203.

[49] Carl Becker to Enno Littmann, September 23, 1914, B-GSPK, Nachlass Becker, M. 4579.

to the effective participation of their ally in the conflict. Moreover, they had for a long time been practicing various sorts of what one might call "*Schadenfreude* orientalism," that is, exulting in their own tending of indigenous oriental cultures as a way of underlining the western powers' imperialist hubris. Inciting holy war, if seen in a pragmatic light, as Becker wished to do, was nothing more than increasing the self-consciousness of oppressed peoples and working for their liberation. Perhaps it was even most useful simply as a scare tactic that would frighten the Entente[50] – which it definitely did, as exemplified by British intelligence director John Buchan's popular novel, *Greenmantle* (1916), which features precisely a plot to cause religious upheaval in the East. Once they had rationalized the policy, the orientalists naturally bridled at the suggestion that they were inciting murderous fanaticism – though of course that is exactly what they wanted to do, provided the objects of it were English, French, and Russian soldiers, and perhaps civilians as well. Their complicity in attempting to implement this policy and in trying selling it to the public is something German orientalists must answer for, especially since, as Vahakn Dadrian has argued, the policy may have contributed to the unleashing of violence against the Empire's internal "others," especially the Armenians.[51]

There were three major issues here that the orientalists felt they had to address in the European press, doing so, however, without offending the Turks, whose ability to seek a separate peace was a perpetual worry; maintaining "German-Turkish friendship" – not to mention the military alliance – now depended upon taking the opinions of an "oriental" population into consideration. First, they had to refute the accusation that *jihad* was "made in Germany" – for this made the Germans, seeking to use religious fanaticism to raise the infidels against European Christian rule, appear more "backward" than the Turks themselves, and the Entente propagandists liked nothing better than to underscore the barbarism of "the Hun." The "made in Germany" claim was also dangerous because it played into the hands of those who wanted to suggest that Germany was simply establishing a subcolonial protectorate over the Ottoman Empire, which it would exploit when the war ended. Some Germans also (and rightly) thought that the accusation failed to take seriously the power of anti-imperialist sentiment welling up within nonwestern countries without German provocation. On the other hand, to suit their own racial and religious prejudices, German orientalists wished to stress that their relationship with the Muslim world was not eternal or ideological. It worried many Germans – not just the Kaiserin! – that rumors were said to be rampant in the bazaars that Wilhelm II had secretly performed the hajj and converted to Islam.[52] Liberals and socialists, of course, objected to an alliance with an authoritarian power, one that also had an abysmal record of human rights abuses. The line most commentators took was to emphasize the purely economic and political communion of interests that linked the two states. Luckily for them, this was also acceptable to the Turks, who wanted to emphasize their own political and military independence and their real, as opposed to merely expedient, belief in Islam.

[50] Nöldeke to Becker, September 20, 1914, in ibid., M. 3138.
[51] Dadrian, *German Responsibility*, p. 52.
[52] Thomas L. Hughes, "The German Mission to Afghanistan, 1915–1916," in *German Studies Review* 25, no. 3 (2002): 449–50.

But there were other issues that had to be addressed, especially for those who thought of themselves as professional students of Islamic history. The first was whether or not this *jihad*, officially proclaimed as a *jihad Akbar*, was an authentic *jihad*. There were complicated questions here: was it possible to declare holy war against just *some* Christians? The normal understanding of a *jihad Akbar* (the greatest holy war) was the battle for faith within oneself . . . surely that was not the same as a Pan-Islamic revolution? Was this *jihad* to be interpreted as obliging all Muslims as individuals or just the Muslim community as a whole to fight? Since the Sultan also claimed to be the Caliph, was not every war the Ottoman Empire declared already a *jihad*? If so, did a *fatwa* from him apply to Muslims in, say, West Africa or Dutch Indonesia? Of course Entente propagandists tried to make all these negative points, arguing that it was not a proper *jihad*, or if it was, that meant nothing more than a war launched by a Muslim state. Entente-friendly commentators also claimed that the concept was a medieval one and could not be modernized; that the declaration was going to reap religious zealotry against Christians everywhere; and that real, believing Muslims would never take it seriously. Naturally, all of these claims took a considerable amount of ink to address – especially when they were made, as in one very prominent set of exchanges, not by French journalists, but by respected orientalists in neutral countries.

The case I am alluding to is that of the exchange of vehement words on the *jihad* declaration between the Dutch orientalist Christian Snouck Hurgronje and Carl Becker, who during the war became something like the spokesperson of the academic orientalists. Before 1915, Snouck had been much beloved by the Germans; he and Nöldeke were especially close friends, but the Dutch scholar also knew most of the other prominent scholars well and had even written his best-known work, an account of his (incognito) trip to Mecca, in German. But Snouck was also a colonial official; he had served for seventeen years in Dutch Indonesia and had been the spiritual and actual overseer of the implementation of his own version of cultural friendship in Aceh. Clearly, the *jihad* declaration struck both at his heart and his head; he was distressed at the idea that his life's work of promoting Indonesian modernization and evolution (toward the Dutch model, of course) could be undone by enflaming the colonial population and also distressed at the prospect of his long-time trusted friends selling their scholarly credentials for the sake of an opportunist and disastrous policy. In early 1915, he published in the liberal journal *De Gids* a long essay entitled "Heilig Oorlog 'Made in Germany'". Written by their erstwhile friend, this vituperative piece pushed all the German orientalists' buttons and occasioned numerous public and private responses.

The Becker *Nachlass* is full of letters dated 1915–16, which deal with the Snouck question; this is in part because Becker was the one to reply and to do so most forcefully, but many of Becker's colleagues also found it hard to come to grips with the breakdown of international collegiality, especially between the Dutch and Germans. "For me," wrote Enno Littmann, "Snouck's pamphlet was a dagger to the heart."[53] Nöldeke, of course, was especially hurt, though he did

---

[53] Examples include, Franke to Becker, May 26, 1915, B-GSPK, Nachlass Becker, M. 703; Nöldeke to Becker, January 12, and January 28, 1915, in ibid., M. 3138; Littmann to Becker, January 13, 1915, in Ibid., M. 4579.

not reply in public, hoping perhaps to salvage the friendship for later. Wellhausen apparently agreed with Becker, but like Nöldeke, did not respond publicly.[54] Predictably, Goldizher refused attempts to be drawn in on either side of this debate; he rejected Becker's request that he break with Snouck (whom he had known for thirty years) and opposed the issuing of a collective response to Snouck, hoping the matter would blow over and intellectual friendships across borders rebuilt.[55]

Becker's lengthy responses are extremely interesting, both in what they suggest about orientalist accommodation to state policies and in what they say about Becker's own political and scholarly development. Becker had spilled a good deal of ink before the war on Pan-Islamism; though he generally did not think Islam dangerous to European civilization, he described how the Sultan had attempted, with some success, to use the movement to his advantage and acknowledged that as an "eschatological" (as opposed to a political) force, Islam might well pose dangers to colonial overlordship.[56] In his first wartime salvo, he argued that even if this were an old-fashioned *jihad* (which it was not), medieval religious conflict was not necessarily worse than "organized murder . . . [and] the starvation policies of economic warfare." Moreover, it is "an obvious means of fighting a war" to exploit internal social tensions in enemy nations "and it is laughable to treat religious differences as sacrosanct, but to [see] the national and social [ones] as unimportant." Several times, in fact, in the course of the essay Becker reiterates his *Realpolitik* view that "war is war, and not a sport. When defense is vital, the rules which govern business as usual do not apply."[57] But even more interesting is his insistence that this *jihad* is a modern one, really a political and tactical call to arms by a state that just happens to be Islamic, just as the Russians are Orthodox and the Austrians Catholic. If some aspects of it do not fit the model created by "study-bound scholars," that is not because the Germans tailored the concept to their needs, but because the Muslim world has actually escaped from the "petrifaction" Europeans perpetually accused it of exhibiting. One has to understand this new form of *jihad* not by studying "obsolete volumes of the Shari'a" or religious history at all, but by understanding it as the product of "awakened national-ities."[58] In short, the Entente is engaging again in a kind of orientalizing (in Said's sense) or primitivism, assuming the East is incapable of modern forms of behavior, including the cunning pursuit of its own interests and the tactical use of religion for other ends.

It may be recalled that this very issue, the question of religious or political motivations in Islamic history, already divided Wellhausen's approach from Gold-ziher's; as we have seen, most of the German *Islamforscher* in the prewar period tended to take a Wellhausian line. They felt uncomfortable with Islam as a religion (most of them did not like any form of organized religion) and would, on these grounds, have sided more with the Young Turks than the Old,

---

[54] Littmann to Becker, January 23, 1915, in ibid., M. 4579.
[55] Goldziher to Becker, January 18, 1915, and January 25, 1915, in ibid., M. 449.
[56] Becker, "Ist Islam eine Gefahr," pp. 165–8.
[57] Becker, "Die Kriegsdiskussion," pp. 288, 299.
[58] Ibid., p. 298.

had the Young been less threatening to Ottoman stability. But many (like Becker) had already bought Friedrich Naumann's arguments about the necessity of splitting domestic from foreign politics and not pushing liberalism or secularism too hard, lest it undermine the Ottomans. Their writings are clearly indebted to the Prussian historicist tradition which emphasized *Staatsraison*; and their war propaganda often applies the "encirclement" theory to the Ottoman Empire, making it all the more certain that the war was a battle for both states' survival. This was the meaning of the new *jihad*, Eugen Mittwoch explained; it was declared "to designate the war, for the Muslims, as one for Islam, while the Turks, beset by a world of enemies ... muster all the forces they have at their command to fight a war for their very existence."[59] All of this would make it ultimately rather difficult to argue, later in the war, that the Turks should stop massacring Armenians or that either side should seek a negotiated peace. The German scholars had already convinced themselves that, as Nöldeke said in a letter to Becker: "in war, one uses every means."[60]

But not all the orientalists, even those who worked happily for the German state during the war, were enthusiastic about the *jihad* declaration, and those who were grew less and less sanguine about it as the war went on. Friedrich Rosen refused to take the ambassadorial post in Teheran offered to him in 1917, seeing his posting as another sign of the Foreign Ministry's fantasies of raising Central Asia in order to undermine British rule in India. He warned Undersecretary Bussche-Haddenhausen that Persian nationalists were simply trying to use Germany to push out the English, which was, with Percy Sykes' gendarme army on the ground, unthinkable. "Dazed by German oriental romanticism, you dream and hope that perhaps a German deus ex machina will succeed in saving an unsalvageable situation." But Rosen did not apprise the Kaiser of his doubts, thinking Wilhelm too weak for serious concerns.[61] Did anyone else tell the Kaiser? Becker was depressed enough about the failure of the declaration to admit to Herzfeld in June 1915 that the policy might have been a mistake. It is unlikely that he voiced his criticisms in his interview with Wilhelm II in January 1916, for it was not long afterward that he took up his post in the Cultural Ministry.[62] Martin Hartmann, who had been quite brave in criticizing Turkish authoritarianism and countering the "interest-community" rhetoric before the war, did not criticize the eastern policy or comment on the Ottoman execution of some of his Arab nationalist friends in 1915.[63] Here again German orientalists have sins to answer for – it may have made no difference to the course of events for those who knew the Reich's eastern policy was a failure to speak truth to power; but at the very least, they had the responsibility to try.

Some orientalists were responsible not just for selling the *jihad*, but for propagating it too. One little-known example here should nicely illustrate both the

---

[59] Eugen Mittwoch, *Deutschland, die Türkei und der Heilige Krieg* (Berlin, nd [1914]), p. 4.

[60] Nöldeke to Becker, March 29, 1915, in B-GSPK, Nachlass Becker, M. 3138.

[61] Rosen, quoting his own letter of December 5, 1917, in Rosen, *Aus einem diplomatischen Wanderleben*, quotation pp. 127, 136.

[62] Becker to Herzfeld, June 4, 1915, in B-GSPK, Nachlass Becker, M. 4023; Becker mentions the upcoming interview in a letter to Carl Bezold, December 30, 1915, in ibid., M. 6431.

[63] Martin Kramer, "Arabistik and Arabism," pp. 297.

amateurishness of these efforts and their typically desultory endings. In late October 1914, Oppenheim's friend Schabinger von Schowingen was instructed to go to one of Berlin's special camps for Muslim prisoners of war and to cajole seven POWs to venture with him on an anti-Entente mission. Posing as a diplomatic courier who had accidentally fallen in with a traveling circus, Schabinger then put his team on the Orient Express to Istanbul (though they rode in third class and he in first). Arriving in time for the *jihad* declaration, Schabinger stood his "acrobats" on the German Embassy's balcony, whispering lines into their ears such as "Long live the Sultan, the Caliph!" Interestingly, Schabinger found the chaos that followed scary and retreated to his lodgings (a hotel owned by an Armenian). "I had seen enough of this 'holy war.'" he wrote later, "... as to what happened afterwards – the measures against the Armenian population [during the hours and days after the decree] – I did not know about them from my own experience, for I was tired and didn't bother myself about them. In any event, I didn't then or afterwards expect much from the 'holy war.'"[64] And yet, he too played the game to the bitter, indeed very bitter, end.

UTILITY, AT LAST

It is apparent that many of the most consequential "orientalists" – those who influenced the Kaiser and Foreign Office, guided economic policy, and directed efforts in propaganda and spying – were not the most-respected academics, but rather those who had already joined the Foreign Service, like Oppenheim, or who were already heavily engaged in politics like the pro-Ottoman propagandist, Ernst Jaeckh. Many of the more "careful" types had been backers of the "pacify the English" strain of thought before the war and it is not really surprising that Oppenheim's NfO would turn elsewhere in 1914. Those the NfO did cultivate were known hotheads (Oskar Mann and Martin Hartmann), younger scholars (Rudolf Tschudi, Helmut von Glasenapp, and Georg Kampffmeyer), or dragomans without scholarly ambitions (Schabinger). For more direct operations, military officials were even more inclined to embrace adventurers, like Leo Frobenius, Wilhelm Wassmuth, or Otto Werner von Hentig; their attempts to organize anticolonial resistance were usually laughable boondoggles. Wilhelm Wassmuth, who, disguised as a Muslim, was supposed to raise Persia and then Afghanistan against the English, made the most spectacular and perhaps consequential blunder; having been captured by tribesmen he was attempting to "revolutionize," he also abandoned his codebook, which fell into British hands and thenceforth made it possible for the Entente to read secret German cables to Washington, including the Zimmermann telegram.[65]

These intrigues gave some grounds for arguing after the war, as did Friedrich Rosen, that the Reich's oriental policy was guided by romantic zealots, who looked to Karl May for intellectual guidance and were seduced by alliterations like "Berlin-Bagdad, oder Hamburg-Herat" into believing the Pan-Islamic rhetoric. "This whole oriental policy was executed by fantasy-prone opportunists with

---

[64] Schabinger, *Weltgeschichtliche Mosaiksplitter*, pp. 106–8.
[65] On Wassmuss's capture, see Hopkirk, *Like Hidden Fire*, p. 225.

the exclusion of all of those who were actually familiar with the conditions in these countries," Rosen commented.[66] Rosen's comments notwithstanding, "real," scholarly orientalists did show themselves energetic proponents of the war and many eagerly volunteered to help Germany win it. Enno Littmann and Eduard Sachau, among others, bombarded the Foreign Ministry with offers to help beat the English.[67] Naturally, most wanted to use their own special talents, namely, their knowledge of oriental languages, to help the cause. They did so primarily for patriotic reasons; though some hoped for better career chances as a result of Germany's enhanced position in the Orient after a presumptive victory. It was also logical, however, given the academy's anti-utilitarian proclivities, for others to worry that too much propagandizing might actually *hurt* their reputations.[68] Most of them seem to have been willing to collaborate with the government, in one way or another, ranging from producing anodyne essays about Germany's Turkish "friends" to spying, from censoring POW mail to writing incendiary pamphlets in Persian. Sometimes their work remained philological (like Gotthold Weil's 1917 *Grammatik der Osmanisch-Türkischen Sprache*), but sometimes it took them far beyond the library or embassy offices, as in the case of Arabist Curt Prüfer, who served as liaison to the fourth Ottoman army. It was a war – perhaps the first – in which *Orientalistik* really did matter: but as usual, it did not matter exactly as the orientalists wished or as anyone planned.

We will probably never really be able to count how many orientalists worked in the war effort; but we can be pretty sure that there was something like full employment available for all speakers of oriental languages who wished to be employed.[69] We can get a glimpse of the sub-academic economy by a notice in the official Seminar für Orientalische Sprachen (SOS) report that between 1914 and mid-1916, the war ministry sent some 352 private persons seeking employment as prison camp translators to the SOS for testing.[70] We shall say something more about the SOS and the need for translators and language teachers later in this chapter; but here it is necessary to specify a bit more carefully what sorts of roles orientalists would play in Germany's war effort and what the leading figures were actually trying to accomplish. Here we enter rather tricky terrain, for we have to do with secret missions and grandiose plans, internal and personal conflicts, and propaganda of all kinds. There are also highly important, but complicated pieces to the puzzle that cannot be treated in detail here, namely the orientalists' involvements in and reactions to the Armenian massacres, Egyptian and Indian anti-colonial agitation, and the Zionist movements. Our task must be to assess the

---

[66] Friedrich Rosen, *Aus einem diplomatischen Wanderleben*, pp. 54, 140. Remarkably, a number of these same individuals – Oppenheim and von Hentig most prominently – would try the same sorts of tactics again in the next world war. See Melka, "Max Freiherr von Oppenheim," pp. 81–93.

[67] Treue, "Max Freiherr von Oppenheim," p. 73.

[68] Becker to Herzfeld, November 7, 1914, in B-GSPK, Nachlass Becker, M. 4023; *The Diary of Karl Süssheim (1878–1947)*, ed. Barbara Flemming and Jan Schmidt (Stuttgart, 2002), p. 104.

[69] Margaret Lavinia Anderson, "'Down in Turkey, Far Away': Human Rights, the Armenian Massacres, and Orientalism in Wilhelmine Germany," in *Journal of Modern History* 79, no. 1 (2007): 80–111.

[70] "Seminarchronik für die Zeit vom Oktober 1915 bis August 1916," in *Mitteilungen des Seminars für Orientalische Sprachen an der KFWU zu Berlin* 19 (1915): ii.

complicity of many of Germany's scholars in wartime intrigues and propaganda campaigns, something the *Fachliteratur* has been loathe to do,[71] while not over-sensationalizing their roles. These roles were, in any event, far less important than those played by professional diplomats, military officers, and political leaders (German and Turkish). We should also note that scholars from other fields – and especially from classics – also were very active and committed prowar propagandists, and some of them also heavily engaged in "secret" intrigues abroad.[72] Above all, what limited the participation of both classicists and academic orientalists in war work was their age and the irrelevance of most of their expertise to the Reich's practical needs, not their greater humanitarianism or more skeptical stance toward German war aims.

Perhaps the least taxing way academics could contribute to the cause was by writing encouraging brochures and articles for the domestic market. A large number of these had appeared already in 1914, insisting on Germany's friendship with the Turks and the harmony, or at least compatibility, of Islam and German *Kultur*. A particularly weird and egregious example of this sort of propaganda came from the pen of the now elderly Assyriologist Friedrich Delitzsch, who had never before shown any interest in the modern Middle East. In 1915, Delitzsch published *Die Welt des Islam*, in which he praised the "peace-loving" but victimized Turks, the genius of Muhammed, and the integrity of Muslim theology, which in his rendition looked remarkably like Protestant doctrine.[73] Enno Littmann, the embodiment of the tradition of apolitical philological orientalism, also contributed to this discussion. His "Der Krieg und der islamische Orient" reiterated the familiar rhetoric of German-Turkish friendship, but went further than usual in defending the Turkish *Herrschervolk* and in blaming non-Turks for the Ottoman Empire's corruption. "The so-called 'Turkish economic chaos' is above all the result of the fact that dubious individuals from oppressed ethnic groups have converted to Islam and forced their way into the bureaucracy; hidden behind many an Ibrahim Bey or Ahmed Effendi is a name ending with – pulos, -wic, or – ian."[74]

We shall get to the Armenian and minority population questions presently; for the moment let us stick to the question of who said what, for opinions and tactics differed even within this rather small community. Eduard Meyer, the most influential (insofar as cultural institutions are concerned) of Germany's orientalists, bitterly attacked the Entente, but wrote little about "oriental" questions, sticking rather to mainline issues like England's guilt, American neutrality, and unrestricted submarine warfare (he was for it). In his polemics, Meyer drew extensively on his knowledge of classical antiquity, but not on work in the history of the

---

[71] The Vorderasiatische Museum's recent book on Max Freiherr von Oppenheim, *Kopf Hoch! Mut hoch! Und Humor hoch: Der Tell Halaf und sein Ausgräber Max Freiherr von Oppenheim* (Berlin, 2002), for example, says nothing whatsoever about his deep engagement in the anticolonial propaganda campaigns in both the First and the Second World War.

[72] See Marchand, *Down from Olympus*, Chapter 7.

[73] Delitzsch, *Die Welt des Islam* (Berlin, 1915); on theology, see pp. 10–32.

[74] Littmann, "Der Krieg und der islamische Orient," in *Internationale Monatsschrift für Wissenschaft, Kunst und Technik* 9, no. 5 (1914): 281–92, quotation pp. 290–1.

ancient Near East.[75] But then again, Meyer knew little about the modern Orient or about Islam and unlike Delitzsch, he recognized the limits of his "orientalism." The others were, for various reasons, less outspoken: Wellhausen was too ill to contribute, Deussen too absorbed in his Schopenhauer studies – though he did write essays seeking to foment Indian nationalism in the interest of toppling the Raj. Unlike Meyer, Nöldeke did not think Germany would or should annex new territory, and even more unusually, did not think Germany should necessarily be dominant in Europe: "In general, I find all the ideas for Germany's world domination unpalatable, even the idea that in Europe Germany should be the completely controlling power. The Holy Roman Empire showed us where that leads."[76] (His reasoning, it should be noted, was not entirely noble: he thought states with large minority populations problematic and he also hated Catholicism.) And, although he was susceptible to the arguments from military necessity, both with respect to Belgian atrocities and in launching the holy war, Nöldeke was unhappy that the army was making all the decisions and very doubtful that *jihad* would work.[77] But Nöldeke expressed his ideas only to his close friends; his temperament, as we have seen, was not suited to expressing grand, non-philological ideas in print.

Among the members of the slightly younger generation (touched, i.e., by the furor orientalis, and by colonization), many were active. Hartmann, earlier a deep critic of the Ottomans, became an ardent Turkophile, taught at the SOS, and worked for the NfO. The young Indologist Helmut von Glasenapp worked for the NfO throughout the war; Friedrich Sarre spent the war, by his own admission, in western Persia, not doing archaeological excavations, but seeking to deepen the population's love for its nation and its great past; his evidently anti-Entente operations were successful enough that after the war he was blacklisted and prevented from returning to Persia for ten years.[78]

Becker, though not working for the NfO, was heavily involved in propaganda efforts. In the war's first months he produced quite a lot of pro-Turkish propaganda, arguing in a June 1915 lecture that the German-Turkish brotherhood was "worth not only the sweat, but even the blood of noble men."[79] He reiterated these themes at the end of another long essay, "Islampolitik," insisting on Germany's consistently friendly relationship to the Ottoman Empire – and indeed to all of autonomy-seeking *Asiatentum* – though he stopped well short of renouncing colonialism as a whole. Evidently, he, like most of his other colleagues, had no intention of allowing his commitment to the self-determination of peoples to apply

[75] On his wartime polemics, see Jürgen von Ungern-Sternberg, "Politik und Geschichte: Der Althistoriker Eduard Meyer im Ersten Weltkrieg," and Bernd Sösemann, "Der künste Entschluss führt zm sichersten zum Ziel: Eduard Meyer und die Politik," both in [William M. Calder III and Alexander Demandt, eds., *Eduard Meyer: Leben und Leistung eines Universalhistorikers*] (Leiden, 1990), pp. 484–504, 446–83.

[76] Nöldeke to Becker, November 8, 1914, B-GSPK, Nachlass Becker, M. 3138.

[77] Nöldeke to Becker, November 8, 1914, January 12, 1915, March 29, 1915, in ibid., M. 3138.

[78] Sarre, *Die Kunst des Alten Persien* (Berlin, 1923), p. viii. Sarre was also married to the daughter of Karl Humann, the excavator of Pergamon; Humann's son Hans (Sarre's brother-in-law) was very close to Enver Pasha and other high-ranking members of the Turkish government.

[79] Becker, "Unsere türkischer Bundesgenossen" (June 9, 1915), published by the Volksheilstätten-Vereins vom Roten Kreuz, Hohenlychen, in B-GSPK, Nachlass Becker, M. 6872, p. 18.

to the German colonies in Africa, a position that he defended by racial argumentation: "We wish, everywhere, for the preservation of the independence of the oriental states, since these Asiatic peoples, as opposed to the Negroes of Africa, are intended for self-determination."[80] Producing such essays, however, did not satisfy Becker's longing to be useful, and in mid-1916 he joined the Cultural Ministry as liaison for oriental matters. As he explained to his friend Nöldeke, "... particularly in this time of negotiating and action, entirely silent work in my study and the sybaritic comforts of my existence in Bonn were simply unbearable."[81] Though more moderate than Eduard Meyer, Becker believed that the war had been forced on Germany because of its geographic position and that compensations were needed in the future, including sovereignty over Belgium and parts of Poland. His studies of Ottoman minority problems, however, had taught him something. In creating new state boundaries, he informed his student Helmut Ritter, one needed to follow a simple principle: "In the East as in the West [annexations] must be completed without allowing a foreign population political significance in domestic affairs of the Reich."[82]

Another important player was Eugen Mittwoch, who was born in Posen (Poznán) in 1876. By 1914 Mittwoch was a professor at the SOS and a widely respected specialist in Ethiopic and Amharic; he was considered for Becker's Hamburg job, but was not selected; "For the Hamburgians, Mittwoch seemed too Jewish," Becker explained to Theodor Nöldeke in May 1914.[83] But he as evidently not "too Jewish" to be taken on by the NfO (Oppenheim himself hailed from a Jewish family), and even to take charge of it in March 1916 after Oppenheim had left for Turkey and Schabinger for Jerusalem. After the war, Mittwoch was selected for a Berlin University chair – though the Nazi regime would, in 1935, revert to Hamburg's judgment, forcing him to retire, and in 1938 to emigrate.[84] The Foreign Ministry had more trouble convincing another orientalist of Jewish extraction, Karl Süssheim, to do its bidding; when approached in 1917 with a request to collect information on the Reich's allies in Istanbul, Süssheim, who had already endured six years of *Privatdozent* existence, refused to go until promised a professorship on his return. No promises could be made and Süssheim never left Munich, where, in any case, he was needed to help censor mountains of Arabic, Turkish, and Persian POW mail.[85]

These are but a few illustrative cases, indicating some of the ways in which orientalists contributed to the war effort. There were, of course, other ways in which Germans related to their "oriental" allies and friends. (The number of "friendship" *Vereine* had,) as we have seen, skyrocketed in the run-up to the war; according to Jürgen Kloosterhuis, some fifty of these organizations were founded in the years 1912–14. And these continued to be founded during the war; umbrella organizations such as the Auslandsbund Deutscher Frauen

[80] Becker, "Islampolitik" [1915], in idem, *Islamstudien* 2: 329–30.
[81] Becker to Nöldeke, May 20, 1916, in B-GSPK, Nachlass Becker, M. 3138.
[82] Becker to Ritter, August 30, 1915, in ibid., M. 3521.
[83] Becker to Nöldeke, May 25, 1914, in ibid., M. 3138.
[84] Enno Littmann, *Ein Jahrhundert Orientalistik*, pp. 128–33. Mittwoch moved to England in 1939, and died in exile in 1942.
[85] *Diary of Karl Süssheim*, pp. 111–13.

(founded 1915) were supplemented by more specific ones (Deutsch-Bulgarischer Verein, founded 1914) and by organizations transparently devoted to producing propaganda (such as the Balkan-Orient-Film GmbH, founded 1916).[86] Scholars – academically respectable as well as marginal ones – as well as businessmen and Foreign Ministry officials played prominent roles in many of these organizations. Academics gave public lectures on war topics; how many we shall never know exactly, but some like Eduard Meyer, Carl Becker, and Otto Franke were very active. Others took up their pens. A quick glance at the *OLZ* for this era reveals a large number of new publications, intended especially for more popular audiences, put out by various presses, including Diederichs, Teubner Verlag, Dietrich Riemer, and Max Niemeyer. Here are just a few the *OLZ* reviewed: Paul R. Kraus *Die Türkei* (Leipzig, 1916); Joesph Heil, *Die Religion des Islam* (Jena, 1915); Ewald Banse, *Die Türkei: Eine moderne Geographie* (Braunschweig, 1916). More thorough research would surely show a huge jump in the number of these publications after 1914 – though this popularizing tendency, as we have seen, was also partly the product of the furor orientalis and already underway before the war's outbreak.

Turning now to more formal institutions, it is evident that they too were eager to be of use, none more so than the SOS. This was, of course, the obvious place for the Reich to turn when it needed to train both military officers and civilians in the languages of the war theaters. There were overall huge increases in enrollment despite perpetual staffing problems, as some teachers were called up to regular service or seconded to one or the other special operation. Tracking the numbers taught in each category gives one an interesting insight into the Reich's personnel requirements – except that, because of some odd turns of fate, training in Turkish lagged far below need until the winter of 1915–16. In winter of 1914–15, there were 263 students enrolled in a course devoted to Russian for army personnel (though this was down to 101 in the summer semester of 1915, perhaps because everybody had been deployed to the Russian front to make up for the Austrian army's frailties). There were only eleven students in courses on "Cultural Conditions in Mesopotamia Today" in these semesters – precisely the ones in which the Armenian atrocities were occurring. The faculty officially included thirty-four teachers and twelve readers, but seven of these were drafted and one interned. The Turkish teacher (Friedrich Giese) was serving in the field and had to be replaced by Martin Hartmann, an ironic move given Hartmann's well-publicized prewar disdain for the Turks.[87] It is unclear how many students he taught; the SOS chronicle does not list Turkish as an offering until summer of 1915.[88] In the winter of 1915–16, the numbers jumped and 684 students were enrolled in "Turkish for Members of the Armed Forces" (305 were studying Russian and 112 Polish). The balance changed again in summer of 1916: 410 in Turkish, 71 in Russian, and a

---

[86] Jürgen Kloosterhuis, *'Friedliche Imperialisten': Deutsche Auslandsvereine und auswärtige Kulturpolitik, 1906–1918*, vol. I (Frankfurt, 1994), p. 273; on these *Vereine*, ibid., pp. 349–51, 447–8.

[87] He recommended, in fact, that the Turks willingly cede the Caliphate to Arab control, in order to reduce Arab antipathy toward the Empire. Hartmann, "Abdulhamid," in *Das freie Wort* 9, no. 4 (1909): 130.

[88] "Seminarchronik für die Zeit vom Oktober 1914 bis August 1915," in *Mitteilungen des Seminars für Oriental Sprachen an der KFWU zu Berlin* 18, no. 3 (1915): i–iii.

whopping 198 in Polish and Bulgarian.[89] Other languages were still being taught of course – sixteen of them in 1914–15 and nineteen in 1915–16, the new ones being Serbian, Haussa, and Bulgarian. By mid-1915, thirty-three graduates had already fallen, the large majority of them, for some reason, Swahili speakers.[90]

The SOS and the various *Vereine* would continue their work throughout the conflict, but from the outset it was apparent – to the Foreign Ministry in any event – that these bodies could not carry out all the tasks required in time of war, and in any event, a coordinating propaganda office was necessary. That office was to be Oppenheim's NfO, an organization founded in October 1914 with a small handful of his friends and housed in the Colonial Office. By November it was under the control of the Foreign Ministry and the political section of the General Staff.[91] It grew quickly enough so that by March 1915 it had to move its office to a larger building; by then Oppenheim had gone to Turkey and the leadership was taken over by Schabinger. In February 1916, Eugen Mittwoch replaced Schabinger and continued as director throughout the rest of the war. By August 1918, an organization that had occupied five rooms now required thirty-two. It was at first, an internal report admitted, "no easy task" to find proper personnel, "since in Germany there are only a few people who can be considered knowledgeable about the Orient, or at least [only a few] who also can be considered knowledgeable about the Orient's political affairs."[92] Some had been interned abroad, some had been drafted and were hard to retrieve; by early 1915, there were about ten to twelve people on the job. At its peak in early 1918, the NfO employed as many as fifty-nine people, including secretaries. Many of these were German nationals, but there were "others" too. In 1918, two Turks, three Arabs, three Indians, and two Tatars were sufficiently established as part of the "smaller circle of colleagues" to have their own offices.[93] Their budget was quite small, especially compared to the grand deeds Oppenheim had envisioned in his memorandum; the organization's official budget, in 1914–16, was a meager 5,000 Marks, and most of the rest of the expenditures were covered by Oppenheim's private contributions. But even then, by April 1916, there was considerable sentiment among the Foreign Office higher-ups that the NfO was not worth its costs.[94]

---

[89] "Seminarchronik für die Zeit vom Oktober 1915 bis August 1916," in *Mitteilungen des Seminars für Oriental Sprachen an der KFWU zu Berlin* 19 (1915): i.

[90] "Seminarchronik 1914/15," pp. iv–v.

[91] Gerhard Höpp, *Arabische und islamische Periodika in Berlin und Brandenburg, 1915–1945: Geschichtlicher Abriß und Bibliographie* (Berlin, 1994), p. 9.

[92] "Die Nachrichtenstelle für den Orient, 1914–1918: Ein Bericht" [c. August 1918], in B-GSPK, 76Vc, Sekt 1, Tit XI, Teil 1, Band 58, p. 4.

[93] "Die Nachrichtenstelle," p. 4; (1917 figures see) "Denkschrift der Nachrichtenstelle für den Orient betreffend die Gründung eines Deutschen Orient-Instituts" (Streng vertraulich. Als Manuskript gedruckt) (July 30, 1917), also in B-GSPK, 76Vc, Sekt 1, Tit XI, Teil 1, Band 58, p. 13.

[94] Schabinger, *Weltgeschichtliche Mosaiksplitter*, pp. 142, 150. The amounts devoted to the NfO were surely not as high as estimated by Fritz Fischer (382 million Marks); but Oppenheim clearly contributed a great deal of his own money. The budget in 1916 has been estimated at about one million Marks. Wolfgang Schwanitz, "Djihad 'Made in Germany': Der Streit um den Heiligen Krieg, 1914–1915," in *Sozial. Geschichte* 18, no. 2 (2003): 19, n. 48.

They were evidently quite busy, given the duties they were supposed to carry out, which included organizing Germany's "oriental" inhabitants into "national committees," receiving and guiding foreign visitors, and reading and writing for the "oriental" press in an era when indigenous, not to mention underground, newspapers were expanding rapidly. Members were also engaged in translating official documents; publishing newspapers in nonwestern languages for the benefit of allied POWs; and censoring official correspondence as well as private letters written in nonwestern languages.[95] Their organizing efforts seem to have consisted, in part, in working through existing "friendship" or student-support associations or in founding new groups with less ambiguous purposes, such as the Vereinigung zur Befreiung Ägyptens. Short-handed from the outset, the outfit sometimes called upon non-orientalists; a journalist who admitted he could not understand a single word of Arabic was at first made editor of the journal *Al Gihad; Zeitung für die muhammedanischen Kriegsgefangenen.*[96] There were journals in other languages, targeted at Indian prisoners and Russian Tatars. Though nominally overseen by German specialists, most of the articles were written by the NfO's non-European *Mitarbeiter*, who, as Gerhard Höpp has shown, had their own anti-Entente axes to grind. Some of the Muslims who worked for the NfO were apparently recruited for service by the Turkish authorities and were quite close to Enver Pasha.[97] But they were thought useful enough that men like Abd al-Aziz Sawis, who was close to the president of the Egyptian nationalist party, Muhammad Farid, was allowed to produce a journal for Germans too: *Die Islamische Welt: Illustrierte Monatsschrift für Politik, Wirtschaft und Kultur* (founded November 1916). The Germans were aware enough of the possibility that colleagues like Sawis might well strain at the ideological leash that the Reich censored their mail too; but German editorial control was weak enough to allow the publication of, for example, articles by Farid invoking Pan-Islamism against the Central Powers as well as the Entente.[98]

Oppenheim and the NfO evidently counted quite heavily on help from allied POWs, whom they hoped to convert into anti-colonial warriors. One of their chief tasks – if not, Schabinger said, the most important one over time – was producing newspapers and other propaganda for prisoners in special German camps. The NfO took these publications very seriously (even if the prisoners did not) and when there were complaints about their style, the writing of the articles was given over to "oriental" colleagues in the hopes that a more authentic style of reportage would prove more convincing.[99] Camp officials were to be solicitous of Muslim customs and even to encourage Muslim piety; instructors were appointed to teach the Qur'an to prisoners, on the theory that the *suras* would bear out justness of the *jihad* decree.[100] Somehow by mid-1918 the NfO had managed to produce some

[95] "Denkschrift der Nachrichtenstelle" (1917), pp. 12–14; "Die Nachrichtenstelle," pp. 2–3. In 1917 alone the organization censored some 4,117 letters and 400 "gramophone records" just in Turkish "Die Nachrichtenstelle," p. 6.
[96] Gerhard Höpp, *Arabische und islamische Periodika*, p. 9.
[97] Gottfried Hagen, "German Heralds of Holy War," pp. 150.
[98] Höpp, *Arabische und islamische Periodika*, pp. 10–14.
[99] Schabinger, *Weltgeschichtliche Mosaiksplitter*, pp. 130–1.
[100] Hagen, "German Heralds of Holy War," p. 152.

1,012 publications in fifteen oriental and nine European languages (for the "neutral" markets). They also had a hand in spreading some "Writings by Orientals for Orientals" especially those that treated the Caliphate question (suited for defending the Sultan's authority) and that encouraged "the self-consciousness of the oriental peoples."[101]

Nonetheless, the NfO was quite discouraged by its lack of tangible achievements over the course of the war. In mid-1917, one memorandum emphasized the absolute necessity of expanding Germany's study abroad programs, which might well be needed after the war. Especially emphasized here was the need for more practical knowledge – indeed, the memorandum proposed founding an Institut für den Orient (with branches in China, Turkey, North Africa, and possibly Turkestan) precisely not to deal with objects of knowledge (*Wissen*) but with means to further cooperation and exchange (*Einwirkung und Handlung*). Thus employees would be missionaries, diplomatic service employees, officers, businessmen, journalists, and farmers, and *not* professors of oriental languages. The training students were to receive at this proposed Institut für den Orient was more like that of the traditional dragoman than that of the professor of oriental studies.[102] The fact that the NfO was desperate enough for practical assistance to call upon such orientalist "dilettantes" as missionaries and businessmen and to invoke the despised model of the dragoman suggests just how ineffectual they knew themselves to be, despite their insistence otherwise. As we shall see, by the war's end, it was depressingly clear that Germany had no future in the East. The NfO itself was disbanded, its "modernist" knowledge now of little utility for the post-imperialist Weimar Republic.

LOSING THE EASTERN PROPAGANDA WAR: TURKS, ARMENIANS, AND JEWS

In the section to follow we have briefly to consider the consequences, domestic and foreign, of the orientalists' wartime efforts. As suggested in the earlier section, none of the Foreign Office's more spectacular plans panned out; Wassmuth failed to invade India with Afghan help; Hentig failed to bring the Persians into the war on the German side; Frobenius's mission to raise the Libyan Senussis to invade Egypt from the West resulted only in a series of skirmishes and minor battles.[103] Those in the field quickly realized the *jihad* declaration was a non-starter; as Ernst Herzfeld – who had been digging for some time at Samarra – asked in January 1915, why would the Empire's subjects fight for a hated, corrupt, and deceitful regime?[104] Later that spring, Curt Prüfer, sent to Egypt with the Ottoman Fourth Army early in the war, called the effort a fiasco; Helmut Ritter in Jerusalem agreed, reporting to Carl Becker that the level of anti-Turkish sentiment was now "unbelievable" – it was getting worse and worse, he reported, as a war none

[101] "Die Nachrichtenstelle," pp. 9–10.
[102] "Denkschrift der Nachrichtenstelle," pp. 2–10, quotation p. 2.
[103] These did, however, as Trumpener argues, keep tens of thousands of Italian and British troops in the area for more than two years. Trumpener, *Germany and the Ottoman Empire*, pp. 119–21.
[104] Ernst Herzfeld to Becker, January 23, 1915, B-GSPK, Nachlass Becker, M. 4023.

of the locals cared about imposed many new discomforts and as new "Turkifying" measures, such as the teaching of only Turkish in schools, were announced.[105] The policy had backfired, inspiring no one except a Shaykh who issued a call in a local newspaper for the driving out of all unbelievers. "It appears," he wrote, "as if here [everyone] is already too enlightened to still think about combining theocratic religion and politics."[106]

German (and CUP) "primitivism" was bad enough – but far worse was the semi-sanctifying effect the alliance and the *jihad* declaration had on Turkish domestic policies. As suggested above, both in Schabinger's account of events in Istanbul on the day of the declaration and in recent assessments of Turkish war aims, declaring holy war meant, in effect, that the Armenians, Jews, and Greeks could now be treated as enemy aliens and compelled to leave (at best) the "house of Islam." In practice, Greek men in coastal towns were already being conscripted into labor battalions before the war began, and in the days just after the *jihad* declaration, there were attacks on Armenians and wild rumors that "an end had come to the Jews."[107] By no means were the Turks the only ones to clear war zones of possibly disloyal ethnic groups; blaming their initial setbacks on the Jews, the Russians executed more than 100 Jewish "spies" and expelled several hundred thousand from the border regions.[108] But when Enver Pasha's winter campaign in the Caucasus collapsed, the decimated Third Army was forced to retreat through heavily Armenian territory and fears of Armenian treachery escalated. Thereafter, Turkish Special Operations thugs provoked the feared Armenian unrest in Van and elsewhere, resulting, by late April, in the rounding up, intentional deprivation, and outright murder of Armenian civilians.[109] As Ulrich Trumpener, Isabel Hull, and Margaret Anderson have shown, the German and Austrian ambassadors in Istanbul, as well as numerous consuls on the ground, knew what was happening and protested Turkish atrocities, but to no avail. Not only did Berlin and Vienna show little interest and less backbone in pressing the Turks to relent; the Turks persistently objected to interference in their domestic affairs and carried on their murderous policies without heeding warnings about the effects of the atrocities on attitudes in neutral countries.[110] As Trumpener nicely puts it, "The statesmen of both Central Powers and some of their representatives in Constantinople were guilty of extremely poor judgment, a considerable degree of moral callousness, and an altogether excessive concern with what was or seemed to be politically expedient."[111] But they did not condone, much less incite, the massacres.

Many professional orientalists signed the call for members issued by the *Deutsch-Armenische Gesellschaft* just after its founding – for the promotion of

---

[105] Ritter to Becker, March 31, 1915, on Prüfer; April 19, 1915, on the new measures, in ibid., M. 3521.

[106] Ritter to Becker, March 6, 1915, in ibid., M. 3521.

[107] Hull, *Absolute Destruction*, p. 273; Friedman, *Germany, Turkey, and Zionism*, pp. 199–200.

[108] Steven E. Aschheim, *Brothers and Strangers: The East European Jew in German and German Jewish Consciousness, 1800–1923* (Madison, WI, 1982), p. 143; also Peter Gattrell, *A Whole Empire Walking: Refugees in Russia during World War I* (Bloomington, IN, 1999), Chapter 1.

[109] Hull, *Absolute Destruction*, pp. 274–5.

[110] See Trumpener, *Germany and the Ottoman Empire*, pp. 200–70.

[111] Ibid., p. 204.

cultural and economic relations as well as for humanitarian reasons – in April 1914. But for some time after the war's outset, the Armenian Question was not uppermost in their minds – there were other nationality questions, of course, involving Arabs, Persians, and Jews that occupied them more – and indeed this would continue to be the case throughout the war. This was not the result of ignorance on their part. Hans Freiherr von Wangenheim, at the Istanbul Embassy, first informed Berlin of the "clashes" at Van on April 24; already by May 1915 Becker was hearing reports of the massacres from his student Helmut Ritter.[112] By this time the Entente had protested the massacres, and reports of them had begun to appear in the British, Swiss, and French media, to which Germans had ready access. Enno Littmann discounted the reports of Armenia's suffering because the stories fit too perfectly the atrocity propaganda model: "Rape of women and girls, forcible drafting of men into war service (as if the Turks would put any stock in these soldiers!), forced conversion to Islam ... etc." The deportation of the Polish and Lithuanian population, he argued, had been no milder than that of the Armenians and the pogroms in Russia were even worse.[113]

Had Littmann wanted facts, he might have turned to Johannes Lepsius, pastor and president of the German-Armenian society. Lepsius had access to Foreign Office dispatches and by early June was concerned enough to volunteer to go to Istanbul to negotiate some sort of deal with the Turks; but the Turks refused and Wangenheim insisted this would be counter-productive. Lepsius would stay with the issue; in August 1915, he was permitted to meet with Enver Pasha, but the latter refused to stop the persecutions or even to allow any foreigners to organize aid for the Armenians. Lepsius returned to Germany where he tirelessly spread the facts about the massacres and Germany's weak effort to stop them, cultivating support almost exclusively in evangelical Christian communities.[114] In general, the *Islamforscher* seem to have thought Lepsius something of a fanatic and a nest-dirtier; none of them signed his October 1915 petition to Bethmann Hollweg. In the wake of this petition, on October 7, the censorship guidelines dictated silence on the Armenian question unless the international community directly accused the Germans of *Mitschuld*, in which case writers should proceed with the greatest caution and reserve. This decree remained in place through 1917, though it is likely that it was scholarly self-censorship – the fear that good, *wissenschaftlich* citizens would be associated with a cause championed by evangelical Christians – that chiefly impeded wider debate on the subject.[115]

---

[112] On May 24, Ritter wrote to Becker about the expulsion of a 1,000-family village (Hasan Begli) because two policemen had been shot; Ritter's letter explained Turkish hatred of Armenians as a result of long-smoldering resentment of the local Turk against those who did not have to send their sons to the [Balkan] wars, and thus were able to prosper. Ritter to Becker, May 24, 1915, in B-GSPK, Nachlass Becker, M. 3521.

[113] Littmann to Becker, October 29, 1915, in ibid., M. 4579. When he was convinced of the Armenian massacres, he commented: "[England and Russia] surely are the most guilty parties in the tragic history of this unfortunate people." Littmann to Becker, May 2, 1916, in ibid.

[114] See Trumpener, *Germany and the Ottoman Empire*, pp. 211–12, 217–18; also see Anderson, "'Down in Turkey, Far Away'," pp. 91–108.

[115] Kröger, "Revolution als Programm," pp. 384–5. On self-censorship, see Anderson, "'Down in Turkey, Far Away'," pp. 104–7.

After this point, the orientalists could not, of course, address the question publicly, but they did discuss it in private. Ritter, who had seen the atrocities at first hand, told Becker in September that although he appreciated the necessity of not making "sentiment and horror" the basis of political action, he could now hardly stomach the panegyrics of the pro-Turkish propagandists.[116] This was also Becker's position; by October 1915, he was convinced that atrocities had happened and was eager to write something explaining the whole situation.[117] He wrote an essay, "Armenians, Turks, and Us," which was rejected by a publisher under Ernst Jäckh's influence – even though Becker's analysis was hardly conscience-searching. Here, as in an essay written just slightly later, Becker attacked the Russians for provoking the Turks and blamed the Armenians themselves: "Already before the war certain Armenian circles attempted to use violent means to force Europe to intervene; during the war itself [the Armenians] ought to demonstrate their complete loyalty and at the same time revenge themselves fearfully on those [members of their community] who were led astray by the voices of seduction."[118]

In the months to follow, Becker's articles were censored, and Mittwoch, now head of the NfO, informed him that he was not to criticize the Old or the New Turks and to be cheerful about the alliance.[119] "Our censors are now more Turkish than the Turks," Becker told Littmann; "As long as subaltern officers incapable of serving in the field command the scientists, it is best to remain silent."[120] He complained bitterly about the government's solicitousness of Turkish sensibilities, which meant that the German people were misinformed and German economic interests were being slighted in favor of strengthening Turkish ones.[121] This was a big mistake, he told Reinhard Junge, president of the Deutsch-Türkisch Vereinigung: "The Turks are much too clever to see in this anything other than German weakness and German fear of Turkey's pursuit of an independent policy, and the necessary consequence is then that the Turks will become ever more shameless...."[122] Indeed, an "Information Department for German-Turkish Economic Issues" was created in 1915 and expanded in 1917, chiefly in order to fight the false hopes of German businessmen and to prevent them being swindled by Near Eastern entrepreneurs – that is, to undo the damage done to market realities by the puffing of the German-Turkish "community of interests."[123]

---

[116] Ritter to Becker, September 19, 1915, in B-GSPK, Nachlass Becker, M. 3521.

[117] Becker to Littmann, November 9, 1915, in ibid., M. 4579.

[118] Becker, "Die Türkei," in *Deutschland und der Weltkrieg*, ed. idem et al. (Leipzig, 2nd ed., 1916), pp. 287–8; "Armenier, Türken und wir," in B-GSPK, Nachlass Becker, M. 7836. Information about the rejection of Becker's article from Margaret Anderson, personal communication, June 9, 2006.

[119] Becker to Littmann, March 27, 1916, in B-GSPK, Nachlass Becker, M. 4579; Becker to Carl Bezold, October 16, 1915, in ibid., M. 6431.

[120] Becker to Littmann, February 18, 1916, in ibid., M. 4579.

[121] Becker to Littmann, March 27, 1916, in ibid., M. 4579; Becker to Ritter, May 12, 1915, in ibid., M. 3521. Becker may be referring in the latter case to debates over the canceling of capitulations that the Ottomans were pushing for in 1915.

[122] Becker to Junge, November 23, 1915, in ibid., M. 176.

[123] See the secret memo titled, "Die künftige Entwicklung der Zentralgeschäftsstelle für Deutsch-Türkische Wirtschaftsfragen," by Dr. Mayer [nd] (Auskunftsstelle für Deutsche-Türkisch Wirtschaftsfragen).

By 1916, Becker, for one, saw that "friendship" propaganda had in some ways worked too well; the Turks now expected to be treated as cultural as well as economic and military equals. This meant that German *Kulturpolitik* would have to become even more solicitous of "the other" if it were to succeed in its aims. In a fascinating 1916 essay entitled "The Problem of Turkish *Bildung*," Becker reflected on the inadvertent effects of European orientalists' critique of Eurocentrism: "The ancient oriental and medieval world of the East first became known as a result of [Asian] contact with European scholarship. People were carried away with the idea that Europe was sunk in barbarism during the time Baghdad and Cordoba were flourishing.... In French and in German writings, there is no lack of unflattering parallels: 'Here auto da fé and Inquisition, there, oriental spiritual freedom.' Such ideas naturally greatly pleased the orientals." Recent military victories, he wrote, first against the Greeks, then against the Entente, would only increase Turkish self-confidence and renew faith in the Islamic state's ability to achieve great things without western help. This meant, he argued, that after the war, policy makers were going to have to contend with a quite different set of realities. "There is nothing more false than to represent the future relationships between Germany and Turkey as if the Orient will throw open its brotherly arms and joyfully press German businessmen and German culture-bearers to its breast."[124] There were two ways one could operate in these new circumstances, he continued: one could let European culture filter, unsystematically, into the East, as occurred in the Hellenistic age; or Germans could throw themselves behind Turkish-directed educational reforms and demonstrate that Germany really did desire an internally strong Turkey. This was an option only for Germans, whose "fateful objectivity" had so often inclined them to devote themselves to furthering foreign interests. The reality was, Becker concluded, that the will to retain autonomy was stronger in the Orient than the will to reform and that to be effective, Germans had to develop the tact and talent to execute "the correct handling of the indigenous psyche...." "We should also never forget," he added, "that we are only guests in the Orient and that one wins over the oriental most easily, when one treats him as if he were our guest."[125]

Ironically, Becker's clever attempt to save *Kulturpolitik* by deepening Germany's solicitude toward the Turks was exactly what military leaders ordered; in mid-1916, the Turks were trying to force Germany to give up the special privileges enjoyed by German religious institutions and schools in the Ottoman Empire and the General Staff, anxious to keep the Turks in the war, pressed the unwilling Foreign Ministry to accede to their demands.[126] By "acting the guest," Becker also hoped that Germany could salvage its special advantages, perhaps especially its economic interests, in postwar Turkey; the problem was that this now meant not only deceiving one's citizenry and allies but also stifling one's own voice and peacetime values. Of course, the Turks were not deceived and insisted on extracting more autonomy and more financial concessions. After considerable bartering, a "gentleman's agreement" was worked out with the intent of ending

[124] Becker, "Das türkische Bildungsproblem" [1916], in idem, *Islamstudien* 2: 375, 376–7.
[125] Ibid., pp. 378, 384.
[126] Trumpener, *Germany and the Ottoman Empire*, pp. 129–30.

the Reich's high-handed policies in order to salvage its cultural influence. But when the war ended, this "gentlemen's agreement," too, was nullified; already in the Bulgarian-Turkish truce agreement of October 31, 1918, promises were made that all German "cultural pioneers" would be expelled from their territories.[127] Thus, did one of the most Machiavellian uses of the rhetoric of "friendship" come to its well-deserved dead end.

After 1916, events conspired to give the orientalists an increasingly (and correctly) pessimistic view of the Ottoman Empire's future: efforts in Persia, Afghanistan, and India were going nowhere and the recruitment of POWs to fight the Entente had become something of a joke. In 1917, the Americans joined the war and the Arab revolt against the Turks gained momentum. After the Balfour Declaration (November 9, 1917), the Zionist card was being played against, rather than for, German influence in the region. The collapse of the Russian war effort and the signing of the Treaty of Brest-Litovsk gave the Central Powers hope for a mutually profitable end to the war, but in the peace negotiations, severe disagreements broke out between the Turks and Germans over Transcaucasian annexations.[128] Frustrated with the Turks' refusal to allow for any sort of devolution or retreat from Turkification policies, some orientalists began to criticize their allies more publicly. Outlining the various threats to the CUP's ability to hold the Empire intact in mid-1918, Carl Brockelmann criticized the Turkish annexationists' desires to reincorporate the Turkic people of the Crimea. These people, he argued, might well infect the whole state with their revolutionary ideas. But the Arab problem, he concluded – in what was, remarkably, his inaugural lecture as Rector at the University of Halle – was the most grave and could not be solved simply by invoking Islamic brotherhood. "Only when [the Turks] once again decide to operate on the basis of European culture, renounce all racial idiocy and make an attempt to respect the national feeling of their fellow citizens can they reach their goal – for which we too have suffered considerably – to be the supreme Islamic power and a forceful member of the coalition for preserving, in defiance of Anglo-Saxondom, national and economic freedom on the earth."[129] But by this time it was too late for the Turks to win back Arab allegiance, even had they been able to "respect the national feelings of their fellow citizens," for T. E. Lawrence and Anglo-Saxondom had given them gold and arms and promised them their own state – something the Turks and their treaty-bound allies could not do.

The orientalists might well have been frustrated; for by 1917, another of their great plots had gone awry. This was the plan, conceived before the war, to expand German influence in the Near East by working through Jewish settlers in Palestine, most of whom spoke Yiddish and were quite naturally inclined to anti-Russian sentiments. Between 1908 and 1917, in an attempt to counter the cultural influence of the Franco-Jewish Alliance Israélite Universelle, the *Hilfsverein der deutschen Juden* with Foreign Ministry backing had organized a series of German and Hebrew language schools in Palestine. From the outset, this project had to be

[127] Kloosterhuis, '*Friedliche Imperialisten*,' pp. 262–3, 266.
[128] See Trumpener, *Germany and the Ottoman Empire*, pp. 167–99.
[129] Brockelmann, *Das Nationalgefühl der Türken im Licht der Geschichte* (Halle, 1918), p. 22.

carefully managed so that Germany could, on the one hand, seem to be acting as protector of the Jews, and on the other, not seem to threaten Turkish territorial integrity.[130] When war broke out, the Germans realized that they might cultivate Jewish friends in Poland, Russia, and America by looking after the 50,000-plus Russian Jews already in Palestine as well as new emigrants fleeing Russian evacuation policies. (Harping on these refugee crises,) for one thing, gave the Central Powers material to counter the all-too-successful advertisement of German atrocities in Belgium. Thus, at the war's outset, the Central Powers issued a call in Yiddish "To the Jews of Poland" and outfits like the Komitee für den Osten produced many newspaper articles that treated political and religious questions relevant to eastern Jews and the fate of Jewish refugees forced to flee to the Russian interior.[131] Backing the Zionist movement also played well among anti-Semites at home, who were eager to reduce the population of impoverished Jews in territories the Reich was quickly conquering and to close the borders to potential immigrants. Even western Jews, as Steven Aschheim has argued, were sometimes tempted to take this line, hoping to distance themselves from the uncivilized, poor and it was often bruited, disease-carrying *Ostjuden*.[132]

One of those who did was Gotthold Weil, a student of Eduard Sachau and Josef Horovitz, and *Privatdozent* in post-biblical Jewish history and literature at the University of Berlin. In 1916, Weil contributed an essay entitled "Zionism" to Hartmann's *Die Welt des Islam*, in which he described Zionism as beneficial both to Jewish and to German interests. It would forestall total assimilation – which neither Jews nor non-Jews wanted – and it would not endanger Ottoman territorial sovereignty. The Jews in Palestine were loyal to the Empire and economically useful to it; the Zionists wanted no more than "a homeland for the homeless." Moreover, the German-speaking Jews were of "the very greatest significance for the furthering of German *Kultur* and German trade in the Near East." "The possibility of emigrating to Asiatic Turkey," he continued, "offers a way out that seems to serve both parties: the Jews, who are thereby put in the position to lead a quiet and healthy life on their own soil in the land of their fathers, and the Germans, who can hope for the progressive development of the Polish lands through a reorganization of population relations and a revitalization of the economic situation."[133] Weil would incidentally continue to support Zionism during the Weimar period and move to Jerusalem in 1934 when forced out of his recently attained chair for Semitic Philology (1932) at the University of Frankfurt.[134]

[130] Friedman, *Germany, Turkey, and Zionism*, pp. 154–60; for further complications in these plans, pp. 161–88; also Thomas Scheffler, "The Burden of Geography: Germany and the Middle East, 1871–1945," in *Journal of Arab Affairs*, 12, no. 2 (1993): 130–1.
[131] See Perles' review of Strack's *Jüdisches Wörterbuch*, in OLZ 21 (1918): 200 (as cited in n. 23, above).
[132] Aschheim, *Brothers and Strangers*, pp. 139–82; Aschheim also argues that by the war's end, some German Jews had come to realize that their fates were inseparable from those of the *Ostjuden*. ibid, pp. 183–4.
[133] "Der Zionismus," in *Die Welt des Islam* 4 (1916): 5, 11, 12.
[134] Jacob Landau, "Gotthold Eljakim Weil (Berlin, 1882–Jerusalem, 1960)," in *Die Welt des Islams* 38, no. 3 (1998): 280–5.

But, as much as the support for Jewish settlers and moderate Zionists might suit the Germans, the Porte, from early on, was suspicious and in any event, none too happy about the expansion of another minority population in its territories. Indeed, in late 1914, even before the anti-Armenian policies began, Jamal Pasha made an attempt at forcing the Jews out of Palestine into Egypt, a policy that was stopped only by the energetic intervention of the Germans and the Americans and by the Turks' responsiveness (in this case) to pressure.[135] Still, the Turks insisted on Ottomanization measures and kept an eye on Zionist activities, and especially after the Armenian atrocities became known, the Germans tread carefully too, fearful of another propaganda disaster. Posted to Jerusalem in 1916, Schabinger was entrusted with the task of "harmonizing of the Jewish nationalist movement with the ambitions of the Turkish nationalists. That was in any event a tricky problem, and precisely for a German envoy a very difficult one. One the one hand, he had to make sure that in his political-propaganda work he kept his sights on the condition and the unity of the Turkish Empire, while on the other hand, he had to understand and respect the legitimate longings of the Jews. That was a problem very much like that of squaring the circle!"[136]

The long-feared anti-Jewish violence and ensuing propaganda debacle arrived in 1917, as the Entente began to advance on Jerusalem. On March 27, 1917, Izzet Bey, the Mutasarrif of Jerusalem, summoned the leaders of all the religious communities of Jaffa and told them that all civilians were to be evacuated – but then quickly backed down and allowed the Muslim, as well as non-Jewish European nationals to stay. Jewish leaders and the German Consul, Schabinger, immediately recognized that this was in fact an effort to rid Jaffa of its Jews – and that Jerusalem, with a much larger Jewish population, would be next.[137] Schabinger tried to intervene, telling Izzet on March 31 that this was a big mistake: "'Think about public opinion in Germany [and] abroad,'" but the reply was "'That doesn't concern me.'" Schabinger then countered: "'Consider that these measures will let loose a pogrom [*Judenverfolgung*], which makes people in Germany upset; in neutral countries, Turkey will be compared with Russia. One of our most powerful propaganda tools against that country was [that it commits] pogroms against the Jews!'"[138] But the Turks, once again, were not particularly concerned with the blackening of their allies', or for that matter, their own, human rights record, especially when they had the chance to rid themselves of a troublesome minority population. They began deportations in April 1917, expelling about 9,000 Jews by foot, some of whom died of exposure or hunger, though many were saved by the quick response of the Jewish communities in surrounding areas. The Entente press had the story by May 8, and there was worldwide outcry in defense of the Palestinian Jews. Though it would be, according to Isaiah Friedman, chiefly German efforts that prevented more expulsions and protected Jerusalem from Jamal Pasha's depredations, the Germans predictably got no propaganda "bounce" out of the affair. In November 1917, the provisions of the Balfour Declaration made

[135] For the full and gripping account, see Friedman, *Germany, Turkey, and Zionism*, pp. 200–25.
[136] Schabinger, *Weltgeschichtliche Mosaiksplitter*, p. 182.
[137] Friedman, *Germany, Turkey, and Zionism*, pp. 347–8.
[138] Schabinger, *Weltgeschichtliche Mosaiksplitter*, pp. 194–5.

life even harder for German propagandists, for inevitably Zionists were won over by promises of an autonomous state, something the Germans could not match. The Jews of Palestine might have been grateful for German protection after the war and the Zionists, like the Arabs, disillusioned by the failure of the British to make good on their promises, but they were unlikely to devote themselves to "the furthering of German culture and German trade in the Near East." They too had their own interests to look after and had learned not to trust European promises of "friendship."

All over the map, from Persia to Morocco, from China to Egypt, the Great War raised "oriental" self-consciousness, not by inciting *jihad* or even anti-colonial violence, but simply by demonstrating to the supposedly "less civilized" peoples just how barbaric Europeans could be. Already in May 1915, Otto Franke was deeply depressed about the propaganda war, for its cynicism, together with the brutality of the war itself, threatened to wholly discredit not just Germany but all of Europe in eastern eyes; he was terribly concerned, he told Becker, about "the terrible fact that the last remains of the prestige and the honor that Europe once possessed has been destroyed. What will this Europe be for the Orient in the future? A band of swindlers and oppressors, without honor, without shame!"[139] At this point, Franke thought Germany might be exempted from this ignominy, but Ernst Herzfeld thought otherwise. In August 1915 he called the *jihad* a farce and the war itself a crime. "There are clear signs that with this war, Europe has surpassed the peak of its power. Asia will pull itself ever more away from [European] domination and we have yet perhaps to experience some of the destructive consequences [this will have] for Africa. When in 1000 years Europe is only an outpost of Asia, the cause of all that will lie in European civilization."[140]

These were privately expressed anxieties, but even in public, the same sentiments were coming to the fore. In his long polemic against English perfidy, Eduard Meyer offered an historical analogy to the present day that he would repeat numerous times thereafter. What was happening in his day (1915), Meyer argued, ran parallel to the situation Rome faced in the wake of its wars with the Macedonian empires of the eastern Mediterranean, one that amounted to "the emancipation of the Orient. Until that point, the universal Hellenistic culture spawned by the Greeks reigned unchallenged from the Indus and the Aralo-Caspian steppe . . . the consequence of the sacking of Rome was that Asia beyond the Euphrates wrenched itself away from the West; and political reaction followed as swiftly as did the cultural one: [the result was] the reawakening of the oriental peoples and cultures." Japan's rise, he argued, was the first sign of the waning of Europe's influence over the East; but that was a limited phenomenon until the outbreak of war. Now Japan threatened to exert domination over China and perhaps over the whole of the Pacific rim; an Indian independence movement had been unleashed (and would sooner or later would prevail;) but most important was the use of Islam to rally mass opposition not just to Christian threats, but to European modernization as well, the final results of which were at present unforeseeable, but after which "a whole new epoch of world history begins." European culture

---

[139] Otto Franke to C. H. Becker, May 26, 1915, in B-GSPK, Nachlass Becker, M. 703.
[140] Herzfeld to Becker, August 7, 1915, in ibid., M. 4023.

was discredited, even in Africa, so much so that it was likely "that in a century's time, the European colonies and European domination in Africa (will belong just as much to the past,) as, since the second century before Christ, do the Greek colonies and Greek domination in Bactria and Persia."[141] Here, in a nutshell, was Spengler's "decline of the West" (though Meyer put the blame squarely on English perfidy, not on fate).[142] A new "oriental renaissance" was in the offing, though not at all the one German orientalists had desired.

Meyer's polemic was widely circulated (it reached a seventh edition already in 1915), and as the war ground on, his pessimism about Europe's future influence seemed more and more to be justified. Given their particular disappointments, the Germans seem to have realized before most of the rest of their European brethren that no matter who won the war, the Orient was lost. Its peoples increasingly kept their own counsels and sought their own ends, and when their interests diverged from those of the Reich, they did not feel bound by any propagandists' claims to "friendship." The Turks are the best example of this counter-European *Realpolitik*, but there are other groups too – the Persians, for example, or the Indian nationalists – who practiced it. After 1917, Indian and Egyptian nationalists began to look to the new Soviet state, which promised support for their independence movements. This was also true of many Chinese nationalists – though some liberal Republicans, especially after the Entente failed to restore the Shandong peninsula to China in the postwar treaties, apparently decided the Germans might be useful allies after all. Some of these schemers were still trying to enroll the Germans in their plans; in early 1918, Mahendra Pratap, who had gone on the German mission to Afghanistan as Muhammed Pir, tried to organize a joint German-Russian army to invade India by way of Turkestan. Naturally, his plan met with little enthusiasm from either party.[143] There would be more intrigues to follow – German military advisors serving Chiang Kai-shek, Indian communists congregating in Weimar Berlin – but these "friendships" would never seem so promising, or so threatening, as had the German relationship with the East in 1914. In yet another way, the world would never see such innocence again.

RICHARD WILHELM, GERMAN MANDARIN

But German orientalists had other ways of making friends, and there were many other paths into and out of the Great War for those who made the Orient a career. We cannot track them all, and perhaps do better to trace one important career, that of Richard Wilhelm, whose passions and proclivities bring us back to some of our earlier concerns, including Protestant iconoclasm and the "furious" orientalists' longing to enlighten the public. For Wilhelm too, the war and its aftermath were sobering experiences; but perhaps because his prewar "friendships"

---

[141] Eduard Meyer, *England*, pp. 209, 211, 212.

[142] Not surprisingly, Meyer quite liked Spengler's work, and the two became personal friends. See Meyer's "Spenglers Untergang des Abendlandes," in *Deutsche Literaturzeitung* 25 (1924): 1759–80; also Alexander Demandt, "Eduard Meyer und Oswald Spengler," in Calder and Demandt, eds., *Eduard Meyer*, pp. 159–81.

[143] Leifer, *Indien und die Deutschen*, p. 385.

were more than pure expediency, he committed himself afterward to keeping them. In the Weimar era, he sought to make himself "useful" to Germany, but did so in an unconventional way: by pointing out the narrowness of Europe's understanding of culture, history, and spirituality and by insisting on the need for the West to take seriously the nonwestern soul.

Even before he reached the Tübingen Stift, Richard Wilhelm was a man touched by fin de siècle religious crises: he had, after all, already had one of his own. He had studied Goethe, chemistry, music, and astronomy; experiencing his family's downward mobility after the death of his artisan father in 1882, he had despaired of the collapse of the well-ordered bourgeois world of his childhood. His mother's attention to outward forms of piety without much apparent inward conviction irked him; he thought deeply about death and developed a longing to do something great; he experienced a sort of revelation while examining the night sky.[144] As a young man, he did not, apparently think much at all about East Asia, though at the Stift he fell in love with radical writers – Spinoza, Wellhausen, and Lagarde – whose work would have familiarized him with the latest debates in biblical criticism. His first job (1896) was as a *Volksschullehrer* in the village of Göppingen near Stuttgart; here he met the local pastor, who was apparently obsessed both with Assyrian and Babylonian studies and with the new German colonies.[145] But all of this was simply prologue – a neoromantic, iconoclastic preparation for what came next.

In early 1897, Wilhelm was called to serve as vicar in the nearby village of Bad Boll. Here he came under the influence of Christoph Friedrich Blumhardt, who quickly became his spiritual advisor, and soon his father-in-law as well. Blumhardt too was a product of the Tübingen Stift, and had followed in the wake of *his* father, Johann Christoph Blumhardt, an iconoclastic pastor who had been forced to give up his official clerical post in 1844 because of the charismatic "healings" he had championed in his parish.[146] At the time of Wilhelm's arrival, Christoph Blumhardt had been running his father's healing center for seventeen years, ministering to spiritually-needy locals like the young Hermann Hesse, who came to Bad Boll after his suicide attempt in 1892. He had grown increasingly outspoken about the plight of the working class, and in 1899, on rumors that he had joined the socialist party, the Lutheran consistory requested that he give up his pastor position. Blumhardt resigned, depressed by the church's narrow view of how Christ might be served in the world.[147] Under Blumhardt's influence, Wilhelm developed a Pietist-inflected doctrinal radicalism and concern for the victims of modern capitalism that would underlie and structure his encounter with nonwesterners as well.

---

[144] Ursula Ballin, "Richard Wilhelm (1873–1930): Eine biographische Einführung," in *Richard Wilhelm: Botschafter zweier Welten*, ed. Klaus Hirsch (Frankfurt, 2003), p. 7; Salome Wilhelm, *Richard Wilhelm* (Düsseldorf, 1956), pp. 37–56.

[145] Wilhelm, *Richard Wilhelm*, pp. 65–6.

[146] "Blumhardt, Johann Christoph," in Biographisch-Bibliographisches Kirchenlexikon, www.bautz.de/bbk/b/blumhardt_j.shtml.

[147] "Blumhardt, Christoph," in Biographisch-Bibliographisches Kirchenlexikon, www.bautz.de/bbk/b/blumhardt_c.shtml.

A word or two about this radical form of Protestantism must precede our discussion of Wilhelm's move to China. It is important to recognize the signs in Wilhelm's earlier biography that he was prepared for such radicalism: he had experienced spiritual crisis; he had read Spinoza and Wellhausen; he had thought hard (together with his Göppingen friend) about relationships between Assyrian and Babylonian texts and the Old Testament. And he had liked Lagarde, that most radical of Protestant thinkers, for whom a contentless, dehistoricized *Evangelium* was the only credible bit left of Christian dogma. Blumhardt was working from a different direction, namely, from the radical Pietism of Nikolaus Zinzendorf and the Moravian brotherhood, supplemented by the anti-doctrinal charismatic and social Christian movements that shaped his father's commitments; but much of his thinking resonated powerfully for Wilhelm. Blumhardt was heir to a tradition in which, as Arthur Rich puts it, "Christianity is not reducible to the Gospel, and the Gospel is not merely Christianity." All religions, including Christianity, were seen as the work of men; at the second coming, all of these religions would pass away, and humankind would be united in a higher form of Truth. For Blumhardt, Christian missionizing was a form of religious propaganda and one that turned non-Christians away rather than bringing them to the table. One had to show the reality of Jesus Christ's humanness by one's actions in the world, not merely (or even usually) to proclaim it in words. It was part of Blumhardt's practice among the proletarians not to worry about converting them, but simply to minister to their needs; and it was the same strategy that he would recommend to Wilhelm, in person, and in letters they exchanged regularly throughout Wilhelm's stay in China.[148]

Blumhardt's engagement with the workers was peaking (and his confrontation with the consistory brewing) when Wilhelm read in the newspapers that missionaries were needed in the new German territory on the Shandong peninsula, Jiaozhou. Blumhardt, who like Leibniz apparently thought China an ideal place to begin a sort of world salvation that championed Jesus over and against Christian dogma,[149] approved the idea and recommended Wilhelm to the Allgemeine Evangelisch-Protestantische Missionsverein [AEPMV], a non-sectarian mission society devoted to charitable and cultural work, which would later rue its involvement with these radical pastors. Wilhelm arrived in London in January 1899 to learn a little English (he still knew no Chinese) and prepare to sail; while waiting, he received a letter from Blumhardt with the following advice: "The first thing to do is to find the path of the Savior, who also appeared to the Chinese as a man to men, not criticizing them, only shining with holy life, teaching only in and through his loving life. Only in this way can a change of heart be effected .... Create empathy with the Chinese on the basis not of religion, but of daily life and commerce. You must not at first be a Christian, perhaps never [be one]."[150]

[148] Rich, "Einführendes Vorwort," in Christoph Blumhardt, *Christus in der Welt: Briefe an Richard Wilhelm*, ed. Arthur Rich (Zürich, 1958), pp. 5–21, quotation p. 8.
[149] Lydia Gerber, "Richard Wilhelms Missionsarbeit im deutschen Pachtgebiet Kiautschou, 1899–1914," in Hirsch, ed., *Richard Wilhelm*, p. 168.
[150] Blumhardt quoted in Wilhelm, *Richard Wilhelm*, p. 75.

True to Blumhardt's advice, Wilhelm never converted a single Chinese. On reaching Qingdao, Jiaozhou's major port city, in April 1899, he did not seem especially eager to work among the simple "needy" people, as did many of the more zealous missionaries, whom Wilhelm, like the German business and military elites, often disdained. It was more comfortable to take a page from the Jesuits' book and to cultivate the educated elite. This Wilhelm was better able to do after the arrival in Qingdao of another German missionary, who was able to take over much of the pastoral work, freeing up Wilhelm to learn Chinese.[151] His negotiating skills got a first important test in the fall of 1900, as the Boxer Rebellion sent ripples of fear and violence into the northern areas where German railway surveyors had begun work. When locals, fearing the builders would disturb their ancestors' gravesites, sabotaged railway work, the German officials sent out "punitive expeditions," and whole villages in the province of Gaomi were destroyed; estimates of those killed range between 200 and 400 Chinese (no Germans died). Wilhelm bravely ventured into the area, with only his "helper" – his Chinese teacher Li Benjing, who was medically trained – at his side. What he saw shocked him; "Our troops in Gaomi, who were there to restore order, are guilty of allowing themselves such transgressions that I am embarrassed to speak about them. I had there a very, very deep look into a yawning abyss," he wrote in one letter. In another, several months later, he summed up his experiences. "One [conclusion] at least I have reached, and that is that we have no longer any right to place ourselves above China. All the inhumane and brutal acts [of the Boxers] were repaid with interest in the name of *Kultur*."[152] Less admirable than these insights was the credit Wilhelm took for negotiating with the village elders and setting up a field hospital for the wounded – it appears that Li Benjing did most if not all of the negotiating, raised the money for the endeavor, and took care of most of the patients.[153] The agreement he brokered entailed the elders' formal apology to the German overlords for the "stupidity" of the Chinese peasantry who did not understand the value of the railway and their promise that from now on the local elites would punish severely those who created unrest.[154] This was perhaps a pragmatic solution; but it was not exactly a model of reciprocally respectful cultural exchange.

The Boxer experience surely shook Wilhelm's faith in Europe's civilizing mission. Yet it was his success in Gaomi that gave him credibility with both Chinese and German officials, and allowed his institution building to go forward. Grateful Chinese citizens donated money to the AEPMV cause, which gave Wilhelm resources with which to begin his Deutsch-Chinesische Seminar (1901); in the wake of Chinese reforms, Wilhelm also founded a three-year girls' school in 1905 and

---

[151] Ballin, *Richard Wilhelm*, pp. 14–15. It offers some insight into conditions in Qingdao that the chief occupation of the pastors here was, according to Lydia Gerber, burying of the many soldiers and civilians who succumbed to typhus and dysentery. Gerber, "Richard Wilhelms Missionsarbeit," p. 169.

[152] Wilhelm's letters, of November 26, 1900, and January 29, 1901 quoted in [Gerber, "Richard Wilhelms Missionsarbeit,"] pp. 171–2.

[153] Ballin, "Richard Wilhelm," pp. 11–12.

[154] Roswitha Reinbothe, "Deutsche Kulturpolitik in China und der Beitrag deutschsprachiger Chinawissenschaftler," in *Berliner China-Hefte* 14 (1998): 65.

an upper school for girls in 1911. In all of these institutions, Christian and Confucian texts were read interchangeably and as equally valid sources of moral wisdom.[155] These practices – welcomed by Chinese officialdom – were probably what made it necessary for Otto Franke to include Confucianism in the program of his schools, much as Franke disliked the philosophy.[156] After Franke (and the Navy) took over the schools, Wilhelm moved on to more diffuse efforts to influence the elites of both China and Germany. He increased his reputation as a China expert by publishing scores of essays in local (German) newspapers and by translating Chinese "classics," finally finding, in 1910, a publisher in Eugen Diederichs Verlag in Jena. And yet, his most successful and consequential cultural association would be one founded less on his initiative than on that of his conservative Chinese friends.

When revolution came to China in 1911, there were numerous mandarins seeking shelter for themselves, for their books, and for the traditional Chinese culture the reformers insisted should be supplanted by modern, European-style philosophy and science. A number of these men, most Qing loyalists and Confucians, made their way to Jiaozhou, where they believed (as it turned out, correctly) German authorities would protect them from persecution. Wilhelm did more than that; he befriended many of the exiles, including the highly accomplished scholar Lao Naixuan, who would help Wilhelm above all with his work on the *I Ching*, which he began in 1913. After a long and intense evening of discussing European militarism and China's future, parallels between ancient Jewish and Buddhist conceptions of the divine, cosmic prophesies and secret universal truths, a group of these intellectuals resolved to found a Confucian Society. The society devoted itself to saving Chinese cultural treasures, as well as to furthering exchanges between East and West.[157] The mandarins donated money to replace Wilhelm's private tennis court with a library, where their books could be protected and shared.[158] It was in interacting with these scholars – whose accomplishments and high offices under the Qing surely made the glass-painter's son feel he was in elite company – that Wilhelm developed his abiding love for China's ancient culture and stable, uninterrupted "life wisdom." His increasing regard for Confucius too surely increased pressure on his already doctrinally-thin Christian persona and also on his commitments to European and German culture, whose materialism and "externality" he criticized more and more openly and whose frail presence abroad he – like Blumhardt – increasingly appreciated.[159]

In an earlier century – even in an earlier generation – Wilhelm would have been dubbed a heretic and forced out of the Church. [Despite the fact that after the "Dernburg Turn," the missionary societies too seemed to moving toward more

---

[155] Gerber, "Richard Wilhelms Missionsarbeit," pp. 170–5; Ballin, "Richard Wilhelm," pp. 13–15.

[156] See Chapter 8.

[157] See Wilhelm's account, in "Die Alten von Tsingtau. Aus den Chinaerinnerungen Richard Wilhelms," in Wolfgang Bauer, ed., *Richard Wilhelm: Botschafter zweier Welten*, pp. 46–52.

[158] Wilhelm, *Richard Wilhelm*, pp. 220–1; Ballin, "Richard Wilhelm," pp. 16–17. The building was hardly completed when the war began; during the conflict, it served as a theater for the Germans interned in Qingdao. Wilhelm, "Die Alten von Tsingtau," p. 53.

[159] See Wilhelm, *Richard Wilhelm*, pp. 186–7. For Blumhardt's views – including his disgust at the suppressing of missionary critiques of the Herero massacres – see Blumhardt, *Christus*, esp. pp. 148, 156–7, 164–5, 257.

culturally sensitive forms of interaction,[160] and Wilhelm still felt uneasy in the company of other missionaries. It is testimony indeed, either to the AEPMV's desperate need for boots on the ground or its ideological flexibility (or both), that Wilhelm not only continued in their employ but also the organization even touted his Diederichs' translations of Confucius, Laozi, Liezi, and Zhuangzi as contributions to "their" literary work.[161] During the Great War, he was even made pastor in Qingdao – rather against his will – though as he was one of the few Germans not interned by the Japanese, this is hardly surprising. But his real break with orthodox Protestantism came in the 1920s – after Blumhardt's death in 1919 and after he had become even more disillusioned with missionization and with the West's "anthropomorphic" religion.[162] He had never been a fan of "churchly" Christianity, but it is clear by the 1920s that he no longer saw "being with others" as a means to change their hearts – in a more or less one-directional way. He saw himself now as a mediator between two equally needy cultures, both of which lacked proper understanding of "humankind as a unified whole." What he now hoped, in founding a China Institut in Frankfurt in 1924, was "that China and Europe now actually for the first time see each other eye to eye." He had come a long way since Tübingen – which is perhaps why he resisted being taken to the university town in 1929, despite the fact that the tropical medical specialist with the best chance of curing his Coeliac disease lived there. Tübingen, he said, just before he died there, was too "pious" for him now[163] – and he was right.

In the war's wake, Chinese liberal nationalists developed a rather more sympathetic attitude toward Germany – but one based on Germany's usefulness for their own purposes. Some, like Zhang Junmai, a leader in the May 4 movement, hoped Germany might represent a third way between the capitalist West and Soviet Russia; others, like Sun Yat-sen, looked for economic and military support.[164] In 1923, Zhang Junmai, who had studied philosophy in Germany before the war, delivered a highly important lecture on "life intuition" (*Lebensanschauung*) at Beijing University; as the lecture showed, Zhang found German neoromantic thought perfectly suited to a defense of autochthonous Chinese culture.[165] Already accustomed to, in Becker's words, "acting the guest," Wilhelm was able to accommodate himself to this line of thought with little difficulty. He returned to China as a scientific advisor to the Beijing Embassy in 1921 and increased his friendship with men like Zhang and Cai Yuanpei, the German-educated chancellor of Beijing University from 1916 to 1926; thanks

---

[160] See Wilhelm, *Richard Wilhelm*, p. 138, on discussions of new methods at a conference at Weihsien, 1907.

[161] Ballin, "Richard Wilhelm," p. 17.

[162] Wilhelm, *Richard Wilhelm*, p. 271. In the postwar era, in fact, he became even more outspoken in his criticism of other missionary efforts. The bitter criticisms of missionary ignorance and intolerance he made in his *Die Seele Chinas* (pp. 223–34) caused the AEPVM to ask him to give up his honorary membership, which he did in 1926. Wilhelm, *Richard Wilhelm*, p. 331.

[163] Wilhelm quoted in Wilhelm, *Richard Wilhelm*, pp. 340, 341; on Tübingen, p. 390.

[164] Felber, "Das chinesische Deutschlandbild in der Zeit des Vierten Mai," in *Berliner China-Hefte* 17 (1999): 40.

[165] Wolfgang Bauer describes the debate that followed the lecture the most important intellectual exchange in modern China before 1949. Bauer, "Einleitung," in idem, ed., *Richard Wilhelm*, p. 22.

to his diplomatic skills, Wilhelm was able to organize support and money (especially from Chinese donors) for the founding of an "Oriental Institute" at Cai's university and invite speakers from both the new Germany and the new China to visit. In 1929, he spelled out his accommodationist policy to a friend: "We must embrace this era, not out of blind optimism – believe me, I am well-informed, in all respects, about 'young China' – but because this is our duty. The ancient world is gone, unsalvageable. It was a beautiful world. . . . But then it was decided to go forward, into chaos. Let us devote ourselves to making the chaos creative. Only please don't stand still. . . ."[166]

That was, in essence, his attitude toward Germany too – which makes him, insofar as he said anything about German politics in the 1920s, something of a *Vernunftsrepublikaner*, of a rather *sauve qui peut* type. Unlike many of his colleagues, he did not pine for the old days of colonial control or even of monarchical reign and he refused to pay court to the deposed Kaiser in exile, though many of his friends did so. He was critical of Allied behavior in the East during the war and after; but he also knew that German businessmen, officials, and missionaries were similarly prone to greed, arrogance, and unnecessary violence. When, during a discussion at the preparatory meeting of the Konferenz des Weltbundes für Freundschaftsarbeit der Kirchen in the 1920s, the organization's (German) president remarked that the Germans would have had no part in the scandalous "coolie trade" during the Great War, Wilhelm quietly noted that it was (only) by God's grace that they had not had the opportunity to be tested on this point.[167] In general, he endorsed Chinese nationalist desires to determine China's destiny without European intervention; China had the right, he insisted in the mid-1920s, to save itself from the "white peril," without being accused of being xenophobic or backward. "People sometimes speak of the animosity of the Chinese to aliens. The Chinese are not at all hostile to foreigners. They merely defend themselves against being dragged into the mire which, emanating from the West, threatens to choke the world." In fact, he thought the Chinese had been saved from soul-death by the Great War, which had shown them just how morally bankrupt technological Europe really was; Europe itself needed considerable enlightenment from the East if it were to avoid technological self-destruction and the twin dehumanizing evils of fascism and bolshevism.[168]

As a result of the hyper-inflation of 1923, Wilhelm's Embassy post was struck; he was offered additional teaching at Beijing University, but now clearly hoped instead for an academic position in Germany. De Groot died in 1923, but his post went to Otto Franke. Wilhelm relied heavily on the patronage of Hermann Graf Keyserling, who invited the Sinologist to give many lectures at his esoteric Schule der Weisheit (see Epilogue). Finally the theologian Rudolf Otto arranged for a private donation from an aristocratic devoté of Keyserling's "School"; this funded a position for Wilhelm at the University of Frankfurt, where he became a full professor in 1927. By this time, however, Wilhelm had already founded a German

---

[166] Wilhelm quoted in Wilhelm, *Richard Wilhelm*, pp. 383–4.
[167] Ibid., pp. 317, 331.
[168] Wilhelm, *The Soul of China*, trans. John Holroyd Reece (New York, 1928),pp. 368–73. quotation pp. 256.

sister to his Beijing Oriental Institute, the China Institut (CI), funded by both the Chinese government and German public and private money.[169] The list of German supporters of the CI was a distinguished one, featuring especially liberal philosophers, among whom were Max Scheler, Ernst Cassirer, Edmund Husserl, Paul Natorp, and Hans Vaihinger. In the next four years, Wilhelm would devote an enormous amount of time and energy into building up, acquiring funding for, and popularizing the CI. Schlepping notes and slides all over Germany, he delivered lectures on such diverse subjects as Buddhist psychology, meditation practices in China, Chinese lyrical poetry and landscape painting, and one of his favorites, Goethe and Chinese philosophy. This, in addition to editing the journals *Sinica* and *Chinesisch-Deutscher Almanach* and his regular university lectures, surely did not enhance his health; but China was, quite suddenly (and notably after Germany's colonial experiment there failed), in fashion and Wilhelm's services were in high demand.[170]

Strikingly, the sort of Sinological service the Weimar elite wanted was not the same as what was desired, either before or to a large extent after the war, by the university faculties. Carl Becker, education minister for a large part of the 1920s, gave Wilhelm strong backing, but his appointment was rather a hard sell, and it is noteworthy that the job Wilhelm got was not in a traditional philosophical faculty, but at the new and unusually progressive University of Frankfurt. It is certainly true that Wilhelm's credentials were unorthodox; and there were apparently some specialists who thought his translations were unpardonably loose and his language skills weak.[171] As Mechthild Leutner points out, Wilhelm was much more a cultural philosopher than a philologist, and though he did want to produce scholarly works, "objectivity" was never one of his highest aspirations. His notion of "civilization" too was quite different than that of the nineteenth-century historians and showed the deep impress of western *Religionsgeschichte* and ethnography as well as deep and almost exclusive dependence on Chinese source materials.[172] In translating the *I Ching*, in particular, Wilhelm had relied to an unusual degree on the assistance of native scholars, something he defended in 1926 as a scientific necessity.[173] But old prejudices die hard, and many professionals thought Wilhelm too much a product of China. Precisely because of his long stays in Jioazhou, his immersion in the original sources, and his affectionate embrace of traditional Chinese culture, Wilhelm always remained on the scholarly margins. The other Sinologists of his day kept their distance from him, often criticizing his translations and editions for failing to include critical annotations

---

[169] Ballin, "Richard Wilhelm," pp. 19–20.

[170] Wilhelm's Weimar writings are highly interesting, and touched many an important intellectual; this subject definitely warrants further study.

[171] Ferdinand Lessing, "Richard Wilhelm zum Gedächtnis," in *Ostasiatische Zeitschrift* 16, no. 6 (1930): 64.

[172] His 1928 *Geschichte der chinesischen Kultur* begins with a long description of available sources, including a great deal of material evidence such as bronzes, coins, and architecture, then passes into a discussion of religious and folkloric customs, some of which are said to be characteristic of "solar" cultures, and have present-day equivalents in Africa. Wilhelm, *A Short History of Chinese Civilization*, trans. Joan Joshua (Port Washington, NY, 1929), p. 69.

[173] Wilhelm quoted in Wilhelm, *Richard Wilhelm*, p. 342.

or even for their tendency to render Chinese ideas in the languages closest to Wilhelm's heart: those of Luther's Bible and of Goethe's *Faust*, and, of course, the *West-östliche Divan*.[174]

Central to his disputes with other specialists was Wilhelm's love for Confucius, which had been forged in his Qingdao days. While liberal imperialists like de Groot and Franke saw Confucianism as the philosophical underpinning of Chinese absolutism and intolerance, Wilhelm saw in the sage a combination of Goethe and Christ, the founder of Chinese ethics and the fount of Chinese "universalist" wisdom. If the fundamental error Christians had made was founding a church on the basis of Jesus' teachings, the power of the Chinese tradition was precisely that it had avoided turning "the way" into a full-fledged religion.[175] Here Wilhelm was interestingly reverting to something like the Jesuit "ancient theology" that had so inspired Christian Wolff, Leibniz, and Voltaire[176] – and continuing too that radical strain of Protestant thought we have seen manifest itself in Lagarde and Wellhausen, Friedrich Delitzsch and Karl Lachmann.

There were, in Wilhelm's thought, odd echoes of Friedrich Creuzer's *Symbolik* – and also of that hyper-Protestant commitment to purification we have seen arise so often among German orientalists. He believed his main purpose and that of his CI was to explore the "the relationship of the human being to the ultimate sources of life," which, at some fundamental level, would be the same in the East as in the West. "The deduction of these truths, which were, in the religious sense, hidden in the ancient traditions and ancient myths, does not represent, historically, the final answer." Like Albert Schweitzer – whom he greatly admired – Wilhelm believed it was vital for Europeans to give up the demythologizing game – if, that is, the West were to save whatever might be left of its soul.

I do not invoke the word "soul" unadvisedly, for Richard Wilhelm was deeply concerned that the West's materialism might have completely destroyed its spiritual life. Nor could the western soul be reclaimed by a simple return to Christianity. A fascinating 1928 essay entitled "Der Priester in Europa" lays out the credentials Wilhelm thought necessary for the proper "priest" of the future – credentials (such as total loyalty only to one's God and freedom from all institutional and ritualistic commitments, complete courage of one's convictions, complete lack of dogmatic principles or judgments) which in fact could not have been held by any real-world Christian clergyman. But it was to this "order of monks" that Europeans should look to save their lives and redeem their souls.[177] It was an age that called for deep introspection and contemplation of the secrets of Being; it resembled, he wrote elsewhere, nothing so much as the late Hellenistic, eastern reaction to the Roman Empire or the "mystical" Gothic reaction to the failed Crusades – eras in which, predictably, light came from the East.[178]

[174] Leutner, "Kontroversen," p. 70.
[175] See his remarks in *Kung-Tse: Leben und Werk* (Stuttgart, 2nd ed., 1950), p. 187.
[176] Leutner, "Kontroversen," pp. 71–7.
[177] Wilhelm, "Der Priester in Europa," in idem, *Der Mensch und das Sein* (Jena, 1931), esp. pp. 96–7.
[178] Wilhelm, "Licht aus Osten" [1921], reprinted in Bauer, ed., *Richard Wilhelm*, p. 166.

There was, of course, more than a whiff of primitivism in Wilhelm's Weimar work on China; the picture he painted of "the soul of China" in his very popular book of 1926 was not much more than the nineteenth century's portrait of immobile China, now with the moral values reversed (change, mass participation in politics, imitation of the West, and mechanization are now bad rather than good things). China represented depth, peace, stability (remarkable he should stress this during the post–May 4 period), rest, and connection to nature, while the West represented externality and technology, but also individuality. And although he thought there were underlying universals, he consistently stressed the deep differences between East and West and the need for each sphere to find its own spiritual solutions. Much of Wilhelm's popular work belonged to the genre T. J. Lears has described as "therapeutic orientalism," which he finds rampant in the Boston Brahmin elite already at the turn of the century.[179] Its function was to help Germans fulfill themselves – to achieve full, global *Bildung* or non-demoninational salvation – not to explain Chinese history and culture in its own terms.

With the gift of hindsight, we can easily identify lingering Eurocentrisms in Wilhelm's work and ridicule his neoromantic affections for China's traditions, customs, and landscapes. His popular essays often portrayed the East and West as entirely different realms of being – but in practice he knew that not to be true. There was, also, a very human side to Wilhelm's interaction with the Chinese. He made good and lasting friends in China and respected their wisdom and scholarship; he tried to get Cai Yuanpei an honorary degree from the University of Frankfurt, and when that failed, he dedicated one of his major works – *Die Seele Chinas* – to him. He did not marry a Chinese woman, but Salome Wilhelm eagerly shared in his life and work and the couple even adopted a Chinese baby for a time when one of its parents died; the adoption would have been permanent had not the Chinese family decided it wanted the child back. When Wilhelm returned to Germany, he frequently invited his Chinese colleagues and students into his home; they also came for family holidays, such as Christmas and New Year's Eve. In 1929, in straitened circumstances and poor health himself, Wilhelm collected money for Chinese famine relief and publicly denounced the Red Cross for taking a Malthusian attitude toward the crisis.[180] Despite the pervasiveness of antiwestern nationalism in China by the end of the 1920s, Wilhelm continued to be admired there; at his death, Beijing National University held a memorial ceremony (and created a fund to support establishing of a chair) in his name at Frankfurt.[181]

During the few years of his adult life he spent in Germany, Wilhelm surely softened many a heart in China's favor; he produced large quantities of popular articles, as well as at least 125 book reviews and 28 books, including the hugely popular *I Ching* (1924) and *Die Seele Chinas* (1926).[182] This was unquestionably

---

[179] T. J. Lears, *No Place of Grace: Antimodernism and the Transformation of American Culture, 1880–1920* (New York, 1981), pp. 188ff.

[180] Wilhelm, *Richard Wilhelm*, pp. 354, 381, 388. Despite Wilhelm's age and illness, in the late 1920s he and his wife moved to a third floor walk-up, with no telephone, no central heat, and no telephone. ibid., pp. 367–8.

[181] Wilhelm, *Richard Wilhelm*, p. 392.

[182] Mechthild Leutner, "Kontroversen in der Sinologie: Richard Wilhelms kulturkritische und wissenschaftliche Positionen in der Weimarer Republik," in Hirsch, ed., *Richard Wilhelm*, p. 43.

his most effective "missionary" work. One of his most outspoken "converts" was C. G. Jung, who took it upon himself to deliver an elegy for Wilhelm, though he was neither a Sinologist nor a longtime friend, precisely because, as he said at the conclusion of his address, "I feel myself so very much enriched by him that it seems to me as if I had received more from him than from any other man...."[183] Of course, Jung here was taking a subtle swipe at his *ur*-intellectual father, Freud, and conversion was hardly involved; Jung found in Wilhelm confirmation of theories he had derived quite independently. But there was something in Wilhelm still of the Blumhardtian missionary, of his old faith in "being with" individuals as a means to conversion. He clearly looked at his work in Weimar Germany in that way and devoted himself much more to popular lectures and informal get-togethers than to intense specialized scholarship in his study. And his personal charisma was vital to China's appeal to non-specialist audiences. Under his leadership, the CI developed an impressive public face, but after his death, it retreated very quickly into specialized scholarly studies.[184] Though they too tended to the neoromantic and conservative, Wilhelm's successors were in no way able to carry on his counter-western "missionization," and were, in any event, either forced out or completely ignored by the Nazis.

Richard Wilhelm cannot be said to have been typical of virtually any group: certainly not of prewar missionaries (most of whom did not take on so much of the cultures they lived in), nor of wartime orientalists, nor of Weimar intellectuals, though he did share some interesting elective affinities with a number of other maverick neoromantics such as Keyserling, Jung, and Hermann Hesse. But did any of them steep themselves so willingly and so continuously in another world as did Richard Wilhelm?[185] We close this chapter accordingly with an image of the sort of East-West interaction he promoted, one that not only has its stereotypical qualities, but also conveys a hopeful universalism still not entirely destroyed by the horrors, intrigues, and deceptions of the Great War. Imagine, in conclusion, the party Wilhelm held for his colleagues at the CI to celebrate the Chinese festival of the harvest on September 29, 1928. Present were not only his coworkers (Chinese and western) but also the director of the Goethe Museum – for Wilhelm's one lasting western hero, aside from Christ, was Goethe. The guests were served curry for dinner; then Chinese poems and stories were read, presumably in translation. Finally, a (Chinese) friend of the family played the Chinese flute.[186] If this chapter's first section offered a damning description of German orientalism's participation in imperialist and military affairs, this section should end with the perhaps overly *gemütlich*, but well-intentioned, face-to-face multiculturalism of Richard Wilhelm's harvest festival.

[183] Jung, *Richard Wilhelm*, in *The Secret of the Golden Flower: A Chinese Book of Life*, German trans. (from Chinese) by Richard Wilhelm, English trans. from the German by Cary Baynes (London, 1931), p. 151.

[184] Bauer, "Einleitung," in idem, ed., *Richard Wilhelm*, p. 29

[185] Jung, "Richard Wilhelm," p. 140.

[186] Wilhelm, *Richard Wilhem*, p. 367.

Epilogue

The European invasion of the East was a deed of violence on a great scale, and it has left us the duty – noblesse oblige – of understanding the mind of the East. This is perhaps more necessary than we realize at present.
> – Carl Jung, *Secret of the Golden Flower*[1]

If these new worldwide perspectives [drawn from India, China, Egypt, etc.] must really have a relativizing effect on our European cultural consciousness, as it appeared in the first imposing moments [of their articulation], if they will, in particular, seriously disrupt the inborn "humanistic" value-relationship to ancient culture in which we are so deeply rooted, that is indeed another question, on which the last word has not yet been spoken.
> – Werner Jaeger, "Plato's Role in the Shaping of Greek *Bildung*" (1927)[2]

We begin this epilogue where we ended the last chapter: in ambivalence. On the one hand, by the 1920s, we find widespread recognition among German scholars that, as Jung claimed, understanding the mind, or minds, of the East was a western necessity. Understanding had become imperative both because new texts and artifacts now demonstrated clearly Asia's many contributions to western cultural development, but also because the modern histories of East and West had been so inextricably, and, at least for the latter, disastrously, entangled. (We will deal with Jung's condescending "noblesse oblige" presently.) On the other hand, we must register classicist Werner Jaeger's skepticism about the extent to which orientalism had actually convinced Europeans of the relevance of Asian cultures to their own development, or shaken their faith in their classical roots. Just as the last chapter offered examples of the cynical manipulation of others, and real attempts at understanding, just as earlier sections of the book suggested both gains in displacing Eurocentric narratives and the limited forms of universalism that emerged, so too this epilogue will leave this story not at a conclusion, but at a crossroads, with paths leading away from it in different directions. For the history of German orientalism certainly did not end in 1918, or in 1933; it is still ongoing, and there are many chapters left to be written.

1918, however, did represent a critical juncture, for reasons that will be described below, and that is why this book concludes most of its analysis here.

---

[1] Jung, "Richard Wilhelm," in *The Secret of the Golden Flower: A Chinese Book of Life*, German trans. (from Chinese) Richard Wilhelm, English trans. from the German, Cary Baynes (London, 1931), p. 137.
[2] Jaeger, "Platos Stellung im Aufbau der griechischen Bildung," in idem, *Humanistische Reden und Vorträge* (Berlin, 1960), pp. 118–19.

As will be argued below, the war and its end dealt the traditions we have been following several powerful blows. It resulted in the loss of all of Germany's colonies (though not all colonial dreams) and the collapse of its great "oriental" ally, the Ottoman Empire; it also did serious damage to both institutional structures and academic traditions. Intellectually and emotionally, as well as financially, the experience of the war made it difficult for humanists to return to positivist practices – and the enormous tide of grief, suffering, and resentment made theologians who continued to focus on deep historical or exegetical matters seem profoundly out of touch, if not a bit ridiculous. The Higher Criticism, heir to the tradition of Reformation Christian Hebraism, had already been under siege by 1914, and few, by 1918, believed any longer that it was up to "science" to uphold faith (though this idea has returned, from time to time, ever since). The quest for the historical Jesus, as Albert Schweitzer had predicted in 1905, had ended only in despair. The esoteric traditions, Hermetic or Jesuit, might still be faintly perceived in modern theosophy, or in the neoromantic *Mythenforschung* of Heinrich Zimmer.[3] But in the scholarly world, this tradition was essentially dead. Creuzerian-Schlegelian romanticism had mostly been turned in the direction of Aryanist fantasies and Panbabylonism had been tempered and toned down a notch. In 1921, the founder and guiding spirit of the *OLZ* Felix Peiser retired from his editorship; his farewell statement put a positive spin on the petering out of the furor orientalis: ". . . many ideas," he wrote, "which in earlier times created controversy because they destroyed established prejudices, have now prevailed and have achieved acceptance, against all resistance."[4] As we shall see in this chapter, Peiser was not entirely mistaken here; nor was he correct, however, to presume "resistance" – from positivists and classicists, Germanists and theologians – snuffed out. Intellectually, as well as physically, the old world was in ruins, but a new one had not yet risen to replace it.

What follows is a brief attempt to survey developments in German *Orientalistik* between 1919 and 1945; there is much more to be done here, both to explore more deeply the institutional and intellectual developments "at home" and to scrutinize more carefully German linkages with scholars, statesmen, and nationalist intellectuals abroad. No attempt is made here to detail either the institutional changes of the Weimar era or the orientalists' engagement with the Nazi regime. There has been some work on these subjects already,[5] but much more legwork

---

[3] On Keyserling and Zimmer, see later in the chapter.
[4] F. E. Peiser, "An meine Leser!" in *OLZ* 24 (1921): 49–50.
[5] See Ludmila Hanisch, *Die Nachfolger der Exegeten: Deutschsprachige Erforschung des vorderen Orients in der ersten Hälfte des 20. Jahrhunderts* (Wiesbaden, 2003); idem, "Akzentverschiebung – Zur Geschichte der Semitistik und Islamwissenschaft wahrend des 'Dritten Reichs,'" in *Berichte zur Wissenschaftsgeschichte* 18 (1995): 217–26; Martin Kern, "The Emigration of German Sinologists, 1933–1945: Notes on the History and Historiography of Chinese Studies," in *Journal of the American Oriental Society* 118, no. 4 (1998): 507–29; Sheldon Pollock, "Deep Orientalism? Notes on Sanskrit and Power Beyond the Raj," in Carol A. Breckenridge and Peter van der Veer, *Orientalism and the Postcolonial Predicament: Perspectives on South Asia* (Philadelphia, 1993), pp. 76–133; Robert P. Ericksen, *Theologians Under Hitler: Gerhard Kittel, Paul Althaus and Emmanuel Hirsch* (New Haven, CT, 1985); Susannah Heschel, "For 'Volk, Blood and God': The Theological Faculty at the University of Jena during the Third Reich," Alan E. Steinweis, "Nazi Historical Scholarship on the 'Jewish Question,'" and Suzanne Marchand, "Nazism, 'Orientalism and Humanism,'" all in Wolfgang Bialas and Anson Rabinbach, eds., *Nazi Germany and the Humanities* (Oxford, 2007), pp. 365–198; 399–412; 267–305. One of the difficulties here is, once again, the diverse and diffuse nature of orientalism that makes it very hard to generalize across all the subdisciplines.

remains to be done before we can really get a full picture of this rich, strange, and painful story.

ORIENTALISM'S INDIAN SUMMER: WEIMAR SCHOLARSHIP AND ITS DISCONTENTS

Let us start our survey by saying something about the cultural context in which oriental studies was practiced after the war, and about the individuals who practiced it. Here we see continuities with trends outlined in previous chapters, but also some novel developments. The war was particularly devastating to the second generation of "furious" orientalists and orientalists shaped by the "Dernburg Turn," the young men born between 1880 and 1895, who were just coming of age when it broke out. A large number of Carl Becker's students perished, as did many sons of both liberal and "furious" fathers. The impact of those fatalities on the profession and on the surviving members should not be underestimated. The war and its immediate aftermath also brought on an inordinately large number of deaths among the "furious" orientalists themselves: Hugo Winckler had already passed away in 1913; Paul Deussen died in 1919, and Wilhelm Bousset and Leopold von Schroeder the year after. Felix Peiser and Friedrich Delitzsch followed, in 1921 and 1922, respectively. The liberals seem to have survived longer, though Wellhausen perished (after a long illness) in 1918, Eduard Meyer and Theodor Nöldeke held on, and continued to be productive, until 1930, Erman until 1937. But even for those who survived, the war took a profound toll; it was impossible emotionally, as well as practically, to pick up one's studies where one left off. As Becker remarked in a 1920 letter to Littmann, another non-combatant, reviving oriental studies was not simply a matter of finding ex-soldiers jobs or funding for their research: "We must reckon with the nerves of those who fought the war."[6] Indeed, the Weimar era abounded in nervous tensions, tensions which would result both in innovative departures and in disastrous quests for security.

The experience of Heinrich Zimmer is evocative. Although already a Schopenhauerian before the war's outbreak, it was not Zimmer's vitalist reading list, but his war experience that made returning to his studies of Sanskrit grammar afterward seem intolerable. "The only benefit which I derived from my participation in the war," he recalled, "was a complete liberation from the authority of the older generation who had managed the war and managed it into catastrophe. I said to myself: 'I do not criticize anybody or anything. But henceforth I shall decide what I take seriously, if anything at all.'" In fact, it took Zimmer several years after he returned from the trenches to escape from the mind-numbing work of pasting together fragments of texts brought back by the Turfan expeditions. He read J. J. Bachofen, whose work on primitive, especially maternalist, myths and symbols would provide him a "master-key" in the unlocking of Indian symbolism; he studied Arthur Avalon's work on the Tantras, material that had long been ignored by scholars because of its relatively late date and its erotic components. And he began to study Indian art – and to take it seriously and to understand its aesthetic appeal, something, as we have seen, even Albert Grünwedel, who had devoted his

[6] Becker to Littmann, April 20, 1920, in B-GSPK, Nachlass Becker, M. 4579.

life to the subject, was not really able to do. But Zimmer did not make his choices without cost, for his positivist advisor Heinrich Lüders tried, and succeeded, in hindering the young iconoclast's career; "But," wrote Zimmer, "I had been reborn, and the price paid for it was negligible..."[7]

Zimmer might have believed that the costs of his choices were insignificant, but others knew that both cultural and institutional changes in the Weimar era signified real losses, the leaving behind, most obviously, of the founding fathers of both "liberal" and "furious" orientalism. Both the "liberals" and their critics had been shaped by the rigorous, text-centered educations they received in the nineteenth-century humanistic Gymnasium and by the specialized philology taught at the universities. Though some of them remained active through the 1920s, these men would lose much of their influence as reforms forced their retirements and patronage dwindled. When they died, their deep erudition and the traditions they had both tampered with and sustained were, at least in part, also put to rest. Already in 1919, Franz Babinger would notice the inability of his teachers to combine both a strong sense of history and philological expertise, as had Julius Wellhausen and even Carl Becker.[8] Much younger than Wellhausen and Eduard Meyer, Becker might have gone back to teaching, but committed himself instead to the much larger task of reforming German *Bildung* as a whole; he threw in his lot with the Weimar Republic, serving periodically as German cultural minister and working closely with allies on the left on school reform projects he thought crucial to national cultural survival. Indeed, Becker's dedication to a moderate plan of reform scandalized his old friend Nöldeke, who feared Becker's efforts would complete the degrading of German education that had begun with Kaiser Wilhelm's breaking of the Gymnasium's monopoly on university entrance in 1892. Students had to have good Greek by their final year of Gymnasium, the elderly orientalist argued, so that they could read Homer and the tragedies in the original; "Please excuse the meddling of an old man, who always gladly leaves aside the orientals to restore himself with Homer, the tragedians, and so forth....,"[9] Nöldeke wrote; and Becker did forgive him, knowing that there were costs as well as benefits to his reforms.

It is hard to know if the number of students entering or returning to oriental studies increased after the war; the field had been expanding rapidly before the conflict, more quickly than the universities could accommodate. The war's loss had delivered a big blow to the field's political relevance, but, on the other hand, its global nature had interested some younger people in non-European cultures (and the discrediting of the old establishment had certainly not done orientalism's old rivals, classics and theology, any good). If some orientalists had perished, there were plenty of archaeologists and librarians, former diplomats and "scientific" travelers, who returned to the Reich seeking jobs, students, and publishers; there were so many that some well-qualified candidates, like Strzygowski's student Stella Kramrisch, chose to abandon a world of collapsing and cash-strapped institutions

---

[7] Zimmer, "Some Biographical Remarks," in idem, *Artistic Form and Yoga in the Sacred Images of India*, trans. Gerald Chapple and James B. Lawson (Princeton, NJ, 1984), pp. 249–59, 249, quotation pp. 250, 249.

[8] Babinger to Becker, Sept. 2, 1919, in B-GSPK, Nachlass Becker, M. 6181.

[9] Nöldeke to Becker, May 2, 1921, and December 4, 1920 in ibid., M. 3138.

to seek opportunities in India. Had institutional support and private patronage been stronger, it is probable that the field would actually have grown over the course of the 1920s, for as we shall see later in this chapter, *Orientalistik* in the Weimar era was for once closer to the cultural pulse of the nation than its classicist rival.

Among those who did get jobs in the 1920s and early 1930s were, finally, a few women. If Kramrisch left Austria for India, other women stayed and fought for a foothold in academia. The travails and partial successes of Betty Heimann and Annemarie von Gabain are instructive. Heimann, Germany's first professionally trained female Indologist, received her doctorate for a study of Hegel's aesthetics in 1916;[10] though her thesis showed no signs yet of her interest in India, she was already beginning her studies of Sanskrit philology and Indian philosophy, inspired chiefly by Paul Deussen. She habilitated at the University of Halle in 1923 and began teaching – as a *Privatdozentin*, naturally; her lectures were popular, in large part because she focused not on close textual readings but on Indian culture more generally. Like Kramrisch, she emphasized the importance of intuition and of interpreting artifacts and texts in their local, indigenous contexts. An inter-academic battle ensued when Heimann applied, in 1929, for an assistant professorship in Halle; some of her male colleagues defended her new methods, while others denounced her for her descent from Deussen and her lack of philological skills. One detractor resentfully noted that she had gone to university while her male contemporaries were suffering in the trenches. Heimann eventually received a temporary assistant professorship in 1931 (fifteen years after her doctorate), as well as a fellowship to travel to India; during her eight-month sojourn, she apparently impressed many of her Indian colleagues with her dedication to fighting free from European modes of thought. Knowing the April 1933 Civil Service law would apply to her (both of her parents were Jewish), she accepted an invitation from the British Federation of University Women and departed for England in September 1933. She would spend the next thirteen years teaching at the School of Oriental and Asian Studies and complete her career with a three-year lectureship at the University of Colombo in Ceylon.[11]

Another woman, Annemarie von Gabain, was able to use her specialized skills to take advantage of the semi-meritocracy existing in newer fields of study (and especially in the study of *Realien*). By virtue of having a useful combination of two little-studied languages – Chinese and old Turkish – Gabain was hired in 1927 to work with the Turfan materials, then was promoted to *Privatdozentin* at the University of Berlin in 1930.[12] Like Heimann and Kramrisch, she had a supportive *Doktorvater*, in her case the Sinologist Willi Bang-Kaup. She was also wise enough to avoid being sucked into dead-end cataloging jobs. Throughout her

[10] Betty Heimann, "Hegels Ästhetische Anschauung: 1. Teil: Die Psychologie des ästhetischen Erlebens" (dissertation, University of Strasbourg, 1916).

[11] See [no author], "Betty Heimann (1888–1961): Die erste deutsche Indologin," in Johannes H. Voigt and Gerd Kreisel, *An Indiens Tempelstätten: Fotoimpressionen der Indologin Betty Heimann* (Stuttgart, 2003), pp. 15–34.

[12] Annette Vogt," Eine seltene Karriere," in *Berlinische Monatsschrift* 6 (1999): 24–31, www.luise-berlin.de. Called to a professorship at the University of Ankara in 1935, she returned to Nazi Germany to complete the *Habilitation* process and teach (again only as a *Dozentin*) in 1940, lost this job in 1945, but finally found a position at the University of Hamburg in 1950.

life, Gabain was repeatedly asked to create catalogs; "I said, 'Yes, sure,' but didn't do it, for [that stuff] takes a frightful amount of time...'"; instead she focused on "manly" tasks: finding new manuscripts, deciphering unknown scripts, and publishing texts and interpretations – and not surprisingly, thanks to her philological talents, her non-Jewish ancestry, and also perhaps her refusal to marry, she would become Germany's first fully respected female orientalist.[13]

In the war's wake, Jews too were getting more jobs. Eugen Mittwoch and Marc Lidzbarski got full professorships, and many younger Jewish scholars also found employment, like the Czech-born Islamicist Paul Kraus, who received a lectureship at the University of Berlin in March 1932. By 1933, Ludmila Hanisch estimates that one-third of the professorial posts at German universities were held by Jews; had professorships been permitted for the study of Jewish history and theology, the numbers would, of course, have been greater; and of course there were many Jewish "orientalists" too who were writing and teaching outside this system in Jewish schools or seminaries. As Michael Brenner has shown, the Weimar era witnessed a "Renaissance of Jewish Culture"; a wealth of new periodicals, community libraries, youth organizations, and cultural support groups were created including Franz Rosenzweig's influential adult education program, the *Frankfurter Lehrhaus*.[14] The emigration, dismissal, or annihilation of these scholars and the lay cultures and communities that inspired and supported them after 1933 would do irreparable damage to German *Orientalistik*.

In any event, we can say that the war did not kill oriental studies, though the postwar economic situation made its rebuilding, not to mention forward development, very difficult. The wreckage of the German economy, as Jürgen Kloosterhuis rightly argues, made it no longer possible to use money and organizations from the private sector to organize overseas *Kulturpolitik*, including archaeological excavations and research trips; nor was there an open-handed Kaiser to be touched for special subsidies. Now the Foreign Ministry or the Notgemeinschaft der Deutschen Wissenschaft had to pay for everything – and neither of these organizations was particularly well fixed.[15] Strapped universities seeking to cut unnecessary faculty were especially likely to dismiss extraneous humanists – and as Werner Jaeger correctly suggested, university faculties still believed orientalists were less vital to German *Kultur* than were their classicist cousins. Throughout academia, times were hard; Bousset's death was brought on partly by malnutrition, and Enno Littmann had his well-appointed Wilhelmine home bought from him by a haberdasher.[16] "We older [men] still recollect very happily earlier conditions,"[17] wrote Sinologist Ernst Haenisch in 1930, and there were surely many others who shared his sentiments.

---

[13] See Jonker, "Gelehrte Damen," pp. 144–6.

[14] Michael Brenner, *The Renaissance of Jewish Culture in Weimar Germany* (New Haven, CT, 1996).

[15] Jürgen Kloosterhuis, *"Friedliche Imperialisten,"* 1: 269. The Notgemeinschaft was a foundation established in 1920 to sustain German research and libraries through the lean postwar years; in an era in which university budgets were being slashed, it proved a highly important distributor of patronage.

[16] Littmann to Becker, April 2, 1919, in B-GSPK, Nachlass Becker, M. 4579.

[17] Erich Haenisch, "Sinologie," in *Aus fünfzig Jahren deutscher Wissenschaft*, ed. Gustav Abb (Berlin, 1930), p. 273.

The situation was even worse, of course, for those outside the ivory towers and perhaps especially for Germandom's nonwestern "friends," some of whom now found themselves marooned in depressed Central Europe. In 1920, Eugen Mittwoch, former director of the Nachrichtenstelle für den Orient (NfO), was still trying to find jobs for "orientals" who worked for Germany during the war and now could not go home. He petitioned both the Interior Ministry and the Cultural Ministry for money to start up a tobacco or sweet shop (for those without education), and for student stipends for those who could make the academic grade; perhaps a library job could be found for an Indian Muslim who had produced anti-English propaganda in Istanbul?[18] Neither agency, of course, was particularly happy to respond to this claim on their resources, and it is unlikely that Mittwoch's efforts produced many state-funded Persian tobacconists or Indian graduates.

In particular, travel, which had become increasingly crucial to oriental studies, became more difficult after the war for several reasons. First of all, it was expensive: terribly so, now that the Mark had lost so much of its value. Afflicted by bouts of hyper-inflation between 1918 and 1923, the German currency was so weak indeed that numerous expatriate radicals, as well as Russian emigrés, settled in Berlin because it was comparatively so cheap.[19] Second, Germany had not only lost its colonies – and its right to treat the Ottoman Empire as a sort of sub-colonial territory – but it had also lost most of the goodwill other Europeans had shown toward its citizens in the era of the "open door." And third, many colonized territories, dispensing with European ideals and promises, after the catastrophes and disillusionments of the war and postwar treaties, began limiting Europeans' unfettered access to their cultural goods. One sees this most obviously in the spate of new antiquities protection legislation and rise of indigenous antiquities services in Persia, Egypt, and China, for example; but one can also see a more general rise in nationalist scholarship and unwillingness to allow Europeans to dominate local cultural institutions. A few Germans did manage to travel and to engage in archaeological excavations after the war – at Medinet Habu in Egypt, and at Persepolis in Persia; but they had to give up, either for monetary or for political reasons, digs at Babylon, Assur, and Tell el Amarna, and on the plains of Turfan and Troy, and even where they did continue to work, they had to involve local officials and scholars more intimately than ever before. No longer could they simply cart away other people's stuff; the antiquities race, even in remote Central Asia, was now at its end.

For some, this did not much matter. Enno Littmann was not bothered; he had collected enough material before the war, he told Becker, to last the rest of his life.[20] Josef Strzygowski's protégé, Ernst Diez, had also amassed a collection of photographs, many of which ended up in his *Die Kunst der Islamischen Völker* (Berlin, 1915); Strzygowski's own lavishly illustrated *Baukunst der Armenier* was finished in 1918, before further devastation occurred, and western access to the

---

[18] Reichministerium des Innern to Kultusminsterium, March 9, 1920, in B-GSPK, Rep. 76Vc, Sekt. 1, Tit. XI, Teil 1, vol. 58.

[19] See here the remarkable story of Lev Nussimbaum told by Tom Reiss in *The Orientalist: Solving the Mystery of a Strange and Dangerous Life* (New York, 2006).

[20] Littmann to Becker, April 22, 1919, in B-GSPK, Nachlass Becker, M. 4579.

region became even more difficult. Littmann and Strzygowski already had chairs, in any event, and Diez too was well enough established to produce in succeeding years numerous highbrow, heavily pictorial coffee-table books about the arts of the East – though his scholarship, an *OLZ* reviewer claimed, would have benefited from close work with a philologist, who might have saved him from presenting in many places what were "more clever fantasies than certain facts."[21] A few scholars still could make professional hay from getting to the stuff, as for example was the case for Ferdinand Lessing, whose studies of Lamaism profited greatly from his signing on with Sven Hedin's "Sino-Swedish Expeditions."[22] But more budding archaeologists and art historians now had to be trained exclusively in museum basements – which meant less opportunity to make big breakthroughs – and even fewer philologists were exposed to indigenous cultures and obscure texts. It is hard to say definitively how much difference these political, institutional, and practical changes made to the pursuit of *Orientalistik* in Germany; but it is fair to say that poverty and isolation contributed to the survival, and perhaps even intensification, of the positivistic linguistic tradition in academic circles – and perhaps to the reaction against this tradition as well.

If the close philological studies of Heinrich Lüders typified the intensified positivism of some Weimar orientalism, two of the young scholars Lüders disapproved of – Betty Heimann and Heinrich Zimmer – represented a new romantic reaction. Both had trouble pleasing their mentors and making their way in German academia.[23] But their interests were much more in tune with discussions about the Orient outside the universities, discussions that tended to emphasize exoticism and mystery, sexuality and soulfulness. The early Weimar period was indeed the highwater mark of neoromantic orientalism, born in fin de siècle *Religionsgeschichte* and Schopenhauerian cultural pessimism. Before the Great War, as we have seen, scholars and amateur iconoclasts had written many detailed studies on the history of the early Aryan Indians, on early Buddhism, on Babylonian myths, on Persian proto-Christian ideas: now a much wider series of lay intellectuals and elite readers began to take this material seriously as the material from which new forms of *Bildung* might be fashioned. For many Weimar-era Jews, the orientalizing work of Martin Buber now seemed to show how faith in one's community and culture could be renewed and the evils of too much assimilation avoided. But Christians too were looking eastward. Comparing the idea of holiness as it was expressed in several eastern religions (including Christianity), Rudolf Otto's *Das Heilige* (1917) would prove the most widely read work of theology of the Weimar period[24] – perhaps because it defended the uniqueness of Christianity in a way that did not rely either on history or on philosophical rationalism. For the less pious, and more pessimistic, there were a host of other choices. Published in 1919,

---

[21] Hartmann, review of Diez, *Die Kunst der Islamischen Völker*, in *OLZ* 20 (1917): 244–9, 279–82, quotation p. 281.

[22] See Lessing's tribute to Hedin: "My Friend Sven Hedin: An Unfinished Portrait," in Walravens, ed., *Ferdinand Lessing*, pp. 419–23.

[23] Though he did receive an appointment at the University of Heidelberg late in the Weimar era, Zimmer lost it again in 1938, moving first to Britain and then emigrating to America in 1942; like Franz Boas more than a half-century earlier, he made his name, and his career, at Columbia University, not in his Central European home.

[24] Brenner, *Renaissance of Jewish Culture*, p. 42.

Hermann Graf Keyserling's *Reisetagebuch eines Philosophen*, a set of philosophical ruminations drawn from the Baltic dilettante's prewar travels in India and China, sold nearly as well as Spengler's *Der Untergang des Abendlandes* – a tome, incidentally, which drew heavily (if without acknowledgment) on the orientalist scholarship of the Wilhelmine world. In 1919, Keyserling also founded the so-called "Schule der Weisheit" in Darmstadt, an organization that was self-consciously half Platonic academy and half Buddhist outreach program; its remarkable series of speakers (ranging from C. G. Jung to Walter Benjamin) very frequently took the Orient as the starting point for critiques of European utilitarianism and spiritual shallowness. We could also mention here Hermann Hesse's *Siddhartha* of 1923 or the greatly increased sales of Richard Wilhelm's translations of Chinese texts, the extraordinary popularity of Rabindranath Tagore, Lafcadio Hearn, Gandhi, and the Buddha.

Works in this vein typically emphasized the power and endurance of the Orient and its spiritual depths; this totalized entity was seen not as part of the self, but as an indispensable aspect of individual or cultural wholeness, which the West had ignored at its own peril. The popularity of these self-critical manifestos surged during the hyper-inflation, flagging again with the onset of Neue Sachlichkeit realism.[25] But neoromantic orientalism continued to shape the careers of many of the writers Keyserling cultivated, including Karl Kerenyi, Jung, and Mircea Eliade, thinkers who would be fixtures of the Eranos conferences, beginning in Ascona, Switzerland, in 1933. And it informed other lives in other ways; the Austrian Jewish journalist Leopold von Wiese/Muhammed Asad was so drawn to the desert and to Islamic mysticism that he became a Muslim in 1927 and would go on to become a radical anti-Zionist and Islamic militant, becoming a friend of the Saud family and finally Pakistan's first delegate to the United Nations.[26]

Some academic linguists tried to discourage this neoromantic furor in their students, as did Lüders; but some were at least mildly attracted to it, and around the academy's fringes, at least, one begins to see it seeping into scholarly circles. Both Eduard Meyer and Carl Becker – arch enemies over university reform during the Weimar period – found much to chew on in Spengler's *Decline of the West*. The innovative, if peripheral, art historians Aby Warburg and Fritz Saxl were drawn together by their mutual interest in the impact of oriental astrology on western art – a subject near and dear to the hearts of the "furious" orientalists. Academic work in the circles that surrounded Rudolf Otto, Rudolf Bultmann, Martin Heidegger, Jung, Martin Buber, Richard Wilhelm, and Josef Strzygowski increasingly took eastern forms of mysticism seriously, and faced few – like Johannes Voss or August Lobeck in the 1820s – willing and able to drag students and scholarship back into neoclassical rationalism. Some of this ferment also touched literary writers like Hesse, Thomas Mann, Alfred Döblin, Hugo von Hofmannsthal, and Berthold Brecht, all of whom wrote orientalizing masterpieces – though of sorts that could not have been written in the mid-nineteenth century.

[25] Katherine M. Webb, *Lafcadio Hearn and his German Critics: An Examination of his Appeal* (New York, 1984), pp. 154–6.
[26] See, for e.g., Asad's *The Road to Mecca* (London, 1954).

In addition to the two lines of thought described above, recognizable heirs to older traditions of positivist and furious orientalism, we have to do in the Weimar era with two more strains of interpretation. Neither was particularly strong in academic circles at least until 1933, when one side definitively lost and the other presumably won. To take the losers first: we can see in the Weimar era some further elaboration of liberal-era sociology of religion and the study of living cultures, especially among *Islamforscher*, like Richard Hartmann, who continued Goldizher's work on Islamic law. There were also many new studies of modern Indian politics and social relations, such as Fritz Diettrich's *Die Gandhi-Revolution* (1930) and of current religious practice, such as Helmut von Glasenapp's *Der Hinduismus: Religion und Gesellschaft im heutigen Indien* (1922). Some of these studies had clear *völkisch* and anti-western proclivities, but some studies, like those of Karl Wittfogel, were more sociological and even showed strong signs of Marxist influence. A cursory survey of the *OLZ* in this period suggests this modernist orientalism was finally gaining traction against studies of the ancient world; East Asia too was receiving much greater coverage than had been the case in the years before the war. But changes were still tentative – Max Weber was no prophet in his own country – and many of the lines of liberal inquiry extended here would be snuffed out by the advent of the Nazi regime.

The fourth strain of orientalist thought, heir to the Aryanist and hyper-diffusionary traditions of Leopold von Schroeder, and more distantly, Friedrich Schlegel, was not at all new. It was bolder now, but as Strzygowski endlessly complained, still not entirely respectable. Racial language was becoming more attractive to many; unquestionably, "Aryans" were in vogue. Scholars such as Richard Reitzenstein or the German-influenced Franz Cumont and Mikhail Rostovtzeff expressed intense new interest in Iran – a function of the new work being done in the slower-to-develop field of Persian philology and archaeology, but also a deliberate departure from the Panbabylonism that had vaunted the achievements of the Semitic Assyrians.[27] Racism was more common in theological circles as well; as Susannah Heschel has shown, a "redemptive anti-Semitism" drove numerous theologians to deny Christianity's Jewish roots, hoping thereby to redeem German Christianity from "Jewish" soulless materialism.[28] In these circles, orientalist scholarship was being used not to build bridges, but destroy them, to beat the nineteenth century's linguistic lineages into prescriptions for ethnic partition.

Linguistically-constructed, ancient "orientals" could be dealt with. But real, existing "orientals" posed new problems for the field. Those orientalists who cared about their reputations abroad wanted simultaneously to convince Asian inhabitants of Germany's unique objectivity and its sympathy for their plight. The more conservative wanted their Asian interlocutors to put their efforts into preserving traditional customs and arts; the more "liberal" wanted to help push forward modernizing, that is, westernizing, reforms abroad. Many more non-western students came to study at German universities, where their reception

---

[27] See Marchand, "From Liberalism to Neoromanticism." For extensive coverage of fascist "Aryan" studies, see Arvidsson, *Aryan Idols*, 178–282.

[28] Susannah Heschel, "When Jesus Was an Aryan: The Protestant Church and Antisemitic Propaganda," in *In God's Name*, pp. 79–105. The term "redemptive antisemitism" was coined by Saul Friedländer.

was mixed. Some were welcomed; others were not. In 1923, Arab and other "colored" (*farbige*) students in Berlin and other cities were attacked by racists who confused them with the North Africans used by the French to occupy the Rhineland. As Frank Gesemann and Gerhard Höpp note, this was particularly absurd, as Arab nationalists had already voiced strong opposition to this new form of French imperialism – but of course, race did matter, and many Germans did not ask about political opinions, but simply vented their anger on those who seemed to exemplify "the black affront" [*der schwarze Schmach*].[29] Clearly, the Orient was more alluring the less one saw its face.

Some "Orients," then, if they remained safely dead and/or unseen, had new appeal, especially to the educated elite. Even the most vitalist East did not, however, have the same sort of gut appeal as the North, and here we meet again that other antagonist to nineteenth-century classicism, namely Germanic studies. Similarly disdained by upper-crust Gymnasium graduates before 1914, the study of early Germanic folklore and literature also took its revenge in the Weimar era. Naturally, as in oriental studies, there was a range of participants here, from university philologists like Konrad Burdach to amateur crazies like Lanz von Liebensfels. And in the initial years of Nazi rule, these Germanic specialists did manage to grab the majority of new positions. But the Nordicists never managed to defeat the orientalists entirely – nor did both wipe out the appeal of the Greeks. For the classicists, too, sought to respond to the challenges of the day by developing a neoromantic form of classicism that Berlin professor Werner Jaeger would call "the third humanism."[30]

As the preceding chapters have shown, the loss of humanistic autonomy to the state was in many ways the fault of the humanists themselves, many of whom reacted to school reform movements, German unification, the onset of colonialism, the deepening of international rivalries, and the coming of the Great War by volunteering their services and advertising their utility in achieving national goals.[31] Interestingly, the professoriate was eager, and (crucially) able, to criticize the state in the Weimar era; many, even most, found modernizing and democratizing tendencies unappetizing and bitterly regretted the loss of their Kaiser, their global prestige, and their domestic cultural clout. The Weimar state both could not, and would not, oblige them; restoring the halcyon days of the Second Empire was out of the question. Not only was money tight, but priorities were changing, and *Orientalistik*, especially now that it could not deliver impressive monuments or "useful" information, were not high on potential patrons' lists.

Fundamentally, "culture" was changing, and philological-historical humanism was of little use to state bureaucrats or to the marketplace more generally. Part of this has to do, again, with the diminishing cultural importance of Christian theology and biblical interpretation; part, too, has to do with the expanded range of culture-makers and cultural choices. Younger men, and a few women, some of them educated in *Realgymnasien* or worse, now felt they had the right to steer German culture, or at least to choose what culture they consumed. And of course there were now many more choices. Movies and soccer, phonographs and radio, lending

---

[29] Gesemann and Höpp, "Araber in Berlin (bis 1945)," p. 20.
[30] See Marchand, *Down from Olympus*, Chapter 10.
[31] This is true for classical scholarship as well. See Marchand, *Down from Olympus*, pp. 263–340.

libraries and adult education programs had now spread widely, and the palette of choices for those with even just a little leisure time and disposable income was far more diverse than had been the case a half-century earlier. With the further democ-ratization of visual and print media, fewer people had to depend on their pastors for their religious instruction – or on their university professors for their historical knowledge. The university itself, so central a force in the creation of German culture since the Reformation, was lagging behind the times and no longer able to hold back the non- or even anti-humanist tide. Carl Becker did use his clout to support his erstwhile profession; but he lacked the cash, and clout, of a Christian Bunsen, or an Alexander von Humboldt. It is certainly possible that professional orientalists in the Weimar era felt even more "lonely" than had their forefathers, a century before.

Ironically, *Orientalistik*'s return to political irrelevance, its struggles to find patronage, its excision from the antiquities' races, its inner schisms, and its new willingness, in places, to accept ideas from the wider culture gave some members of the discipline the liberty and courage to make a remarkable series of innovations. Even as the older generation passed, there were exciting other options opening, from the non-racist neoromanticism of Heinrich Zimmer to the Marxian sociology of Karl Wittfogel and the ecumenical history of Elias Bickermann. This was the era in which the theologian Hans Lietzmann put the finishing touches on a new field, known today as "late antiquity," and Heinrich Schäfer pioneered the study of Egyptian art in its own terms, without judging it by Greek standards. Weimar Germany – and/or Wittgenstein's Vienna – were the training grounds for Richard Ettinghausen and Karl Wittfogel, Fritz Saxl and Otto Neugebauer, Kurt Weitzmann and Heinrich Zimmer – but they all had to leave. The 1920s represented something of a *Nachsommer*, an Indian summer, in German oriental studies; it probably did not seem rich and restful to the participants at the time, but in retrospect it did seem idyllic, compared, of course, to the Hitler winter that followed.

Still, we can harvest from that Indian summer some fruits that would have to be stored up for a much later time. One of these was the sense that orientalist battles with classical and Christian chronology had not been in vain; the academy, and even the educated elite, had adopted a view of the ancient world that departed radically from the Graecophile accounts of the mid-nineteenth century. When in 1930 Enno Littmann published a popular lecture entitled "Abendland und Morgenland," he opened by listing a series of catch phrases: "Ex Oriente Lux" and "Babylon and the Bible," "Hellas in the Orient's Embrace" and "On the Tracks of Hellas in the Orient," knowing his readers would pick up his references to the orientalists' bruis-ing, but largely victorious, assaults on classicism and Christian orthodoxy in recent decades. He could offer twenty-eight pages of closely printed proof, much of it produced by the last two generations of German orientalists. If the West's roots lay in *Griechentum*, he wrote, "... [our western culture] has also been influenced and made fruitful by the Orient, in many and lasting ways, and that ought not to be forgotten or left unsaid. It was, precisely, German scholars whose hard work established these facts and contributed the foundations for a truly historical, and comprehensive, understanding of European cultural development."[32] German

---

[32] Littmann, "Abendland und Morgenland," in *Reden bei der Rektoratsübergabe am 30. April 1930 im Festsaal der Universität* (Tübingen, 1930), catch phrases p. 13, longer quotation p. 27.

orientalism had made a fundamental shift in western perspectives possible, and had made the more limited, Graecophile form of humanism obsolete. If this would have been neither exalted nor mystical enough for Friedrich Schlegel, it represented an oriental Renaissance, just the same.

Even more poignant were the later public lectures of Carl Becker. Delegated to a committee to report on possibilities for reforming education in China, Becker extended his travels to circle the globe in 1931–2. On his return, he produced a remarkable set of radio addresses in which he described the "complete change in perspective on the world" even an orientalist underwent as a result of spending three months in the Far East. He had discovered, for one thing, how very small Europe was, compared to Asia, and how little Germany's fate mattered to the rest of the globe. He was made to feel just how much Europe was still suffused with the traditions and symbols of the Bible and the humanistic tradition and how little even the orientalists understood of "the confusing riot of Asian symbolism." "We console ourselves, for the most part, with the superiority of our cultivation, which we consider to be qualitatively 'higher,'" he wrote. "One reveres the uniqueness of Greek *Geist*, but with closer contact with this Asian world one cannot help raising the suspicion that our feelings of superiority are built on the quicksand of igno-rance."[33] Here at last was the modest voice of the West, one that had been largely missing since Voltaire's musings on the deep antiquity of China, its history so incomprehensible to European scholars.

Becker then made some sobering predictions that read like a modernized ver-sion of Strzygowski's "Orient in Hellas' Embrace." The Asian masses were not inert or inflexible, he insisted, and fully capable of resisting European attempts at technological, economic, and political conquest. They could certainly react powerfully, he charged, "to save their cultural [*geistige*] autonomy, just as," he added, "the Near East [threw off] Hellenism and Roman rule."[34] In a contempo-rary lecture delivered in English, Becker reminded his audience again that the East had deep cultural roots and resources and that the Islamic world, like the West, owed significant debts to the Hellenistic world. European hegemony might well be fleeting and the East might yet get its revenge.

It is also important to bear in mind that this present struggle, tremendous and unique as it may seem, is not the first of its kind, but is really nothing other than the present phase of a contest which has been going on between East and West for thousands of years. Action on the part of one side has always immediately called forth a reaction on the part of the other, and one may rightly doubt whether the Occident has always supplied the action, and the Orient the response, as is now the case, or whether the initiative has not rather changed from one side to the other in the course of history.[35]

Becker predicted that it might not be long, in fact, before the pendulum swung again, with devastating consequences for the all-too-human Europeans.

Though they were still a minority, even within the humanities, the orientalists had historicized and relativized the "rise of the West." Some had recognized that

[33] Becker, "Von Peking bis Damaskus: Eindrücke von einer Studienrise durch Asien," in B-GSPK, Nachlass Becker, M. 6788, pp. 2, 4, 5.
[34] Ibid., p. 5.
[35] Becker, "Hellenism and Islam," in B-GSPK, Nachlass Becker, M. 8102, p. 5.

western imperialism was not only destroying venerable non-European cultures and traditions, but also that it was the duty of Europeans, as Becker wrote, "to replace the mentality of Asian exploitation with the recognition of the equality of the Asians, with all the consequences of this for Europe and America."[36] There was, to be sure, a major part of this that was self-interested and/or condescending (remember Jung's "noblesse oblige"). Still, Weimar orientalists were laying foundations for a non-Eurocentric history of the ancient world. Regrettably, they and their "fathers" had also provided the groundwork for a thoroughgoing racial reading of the past and present.

ORIENTALISM AND NAZISM

It would be the latter form of orientalism, of course, that would most appeal to the Nazi regime – insofar, that is, as any form of orientalism particularly interested the Nazi elite. Hitler's rise to power did not do *Orientalistik* much good in either the short, medium, or long term. Nazi purges of the universities were felt powerfully in this field, in which by 1933, according to Ludmila Hanisch's estimate, some 33 percent of academic positions (including 25% of the chairs).[37] In addition, there were a number of liberal-leaning Islamicists and Sinologists who were either purged or who departed Germany early in the Nazi period. The number of émigrés overall was large and included some of the younger and most innovative: the sociologically inclined student of Islamic law, Joseph Schacht; the scholar of Islamic philosophy, Richard Walzer; the Islamic art historian, Richard Ettinghausen; the Byzantinist Kurt Weitzmann; the historian of Hellenistic Judaism, Elias Bickermann; and the communist student of Chinese economics, Karl August Wittfogel. Some went directly to Turkey, England, Switzerland, or the United States, others like Bickermann, Walzer, and Otto Neugebauer made intermediate stops (in Paris, Rome, and Copenhagen, respectively). A handful of scholars who stayed (e.g., Heinrich Lüders) were forced into early retirement. Some Jews, like Isaak Heinemann and Yohanen Lewy, transferred first to Jewish theological seminaries or taught at the *Lehranstalt für die Wissenschaft des Judentums* before making their way to Jerusalem. Many would play major roles in establishing programs and centers for oriental studies in their new countries, as did Ferdinand Lessing, who built Berkeley's East Asian Studies department, or J. J. Horovitz and Gotthold Weil, who established the School of Oriental Studies in Jerusalem, directing it first in absentia, while careers in Germany still seemed attractive and possible, and then in situ, in permanent exile.[38] The heavy purging of this generation may help to explain why, as Frank-Rutger Hausmann notes in his study of the *Aktion Ritterbusch*, the orientalists tended to be rather older than others involved in this collaborative endeavor.[39]

---

[36] Becker, "Von Peking bis Damaskus," p. 5.

[37] Hanisch, "Akzentverschiebung," p. 218.

[38] On Horovitz and Weil, see Hava Lazarus-Yafeh, "The Transplantation of Islamic Studies from Europe to the Yishuv and Israel," in Martin Kramer, ed., *The Jewish Discovery of Islam*, pp. 252–3.

[39] Hausmann, *'Deutsche Geisteswissenschaften' im Zweiten Weltkrieg: Die 'Aktion Ritterbusch' (1940–1945)* (Dresden, 1998), p. 217.

There were also some scholars who did not make it into exile and who paid the ultimate price. We do not know for sure how many there were – of course, the counting is complicated by decisions taken as to who might or might not count as a "scholarly" orientalist. Ludmila Hanisch has published a limited-edition catalog containing biographical sketches of some of the émigrés – but she would be the first to argue that much more work needs to be done to document and commemorate the victims. Among the victims we know of were the Islamicists Fritz Wolff and Hedwig Klein and the Indologist Otto Stein.[40] If we count theologians and learned rabbis, we would arrive at a much larger figure. Then there were those persecuted but not killed, like the geographer Alfred Philippson, who returned from Theresienstadt to die in Bonn in 1953, or Paul Kraus, who made it to Cairo, but died by his own hand in 1944.[41] In addition to the successful transplants, there were undoubtedly other scholars who went abroad but could not find work, or solace, and whose careers and lives were ruined by the change of regime. Many lines of transmission were interrupted, making for fewer practitioners in the generations to follow. Indeed, the field as a whole suffered a precipitous decline over the course of the 1930s–1950s; using *Kürschners Deutscher Gelehrten-Kalender*, Hanisch notes that while in 1931, 360 individuals were listed as specialists in oriental languages, this number had fallen to 180 in 1940–1, and fell even further after the end of the Third Reich (to 130 in 1950).[42]

The number of émigrés might have been large, but it was easily matched by the number of gleeful collaborators. Interestingly, if we widen the *Kürschners* data above, we find that the number of self-identified orientalists actually rose immediately after Hitler's ascent (to 372 in 1935). In *Orientalistik* as in theology and other humanistic disciplines, there was much self-mobilization for little or no gain, motivated not only by ideological affirmation, but also by inter-field competition and the sense that there was nowhere else to go. Aside from some of the most outspoken racists – like Strzygowski, who remained in Vienna – in some cases, it would have been hard to predict who the collaborators might be. There were some prominent collaborators among the theologians involved in the study of Judaism; quite surprisingly, Gerhard Kittel, who had before 1933 argued vehemently against attempts to amputate Christianity's Jewish roots, joined the Nazi Party and pronounced the assimilated Jews to be the source of Germany's misfortunes; he now advocated offering ghettoized, "guest status" for the Jews to prevent them from corrupting the population as a whole.[43] In 1933, Kittel began editing and publishing a series of second-century Jewish texts – something he and his gentile colleagues had long ignored. His progress was halted after 1937, less, Robert Ericksen argues, because of Nazi opposition to the project than because he was increasing his activities for Walter Frank's anti-Semitic Institute for the History of

---

[40] See Hanisch, *Ausgegrenzte Kompetenz*, pp. 43, 97, 119.
[41] Paul Kahle, "Die Universität Bonn von und während die Nazi Zeit," in Marie Kahle, *Was hätten Sie getan? Die Flucht der Familie Kahle aus Nazi Deutschland*, ed. John H. Kahle (Bonn, 1998), pp. 106–7; on Kraus, see Joel L. Kraemer, "The Death of an Orientalist: Paul Kraus from Prague to Cairo," in Martin Kramer, ed., *The Jewish Discovery of Islam*, pp. 181–224.
[42] *Kürschners Deutscher Gelehrten-Kalender* 5 (1935) and 7 (1950). Hanisch, "Akzentverschiebung," p. 221.
[43] See Robert P. Ericksen, *Theologians Under Hitler: Gerhard Kittel, Paul Althaus and Emmanuel Hirsch* (New Haven, CT, 1985), pp. 50–70.

the New Germany.[44] In some fields, on the other hand, collaboration was no surprise; as we have seen, Indology, almost wholly devoted to the study of ancient Indian languages and literatures, had been inclined to romantic racism already in the late nineteenth century. In the 1930s, numerous Indologists sought to anchor Nazi racial theory in ancient "Aryan" history and literature, including Erich Frauwallner, Hermann Güntert, Hermann Lommel, Paul Thieme, and Ludwig Alsdorf; Sheldon Pollock estimates that one-third of the approximately twenty-five professors of Indology were active in the party or SS.[45] Some, like SS-*Hauptsturmführer* Ernst Schäfer, were extremely active. Returning from an official SS mission to Tibet in August 1939, Schäfer was able to present higher-ups detailed ethnographic (and sexual) details on the peoples of the Himalayas and very likely geopolitical information useful in planning a north Indian strike against Britain's most profitable colony. But, still exhibiting traces of the positivist collectors of yesteryear, the Sanskritist also sent home ancient manuscripts and, as the newspapers boasted, "a hitherto unknown wild goat."[46] Worst of all among the Indologist collaborators was Walter Wüst, the Vedic specialist at the University of Munich who became the director of the SS Ahnenerbe.[47]

The Indologists frequently advertised their usefulness in establishing *ur*-ancient Aryan linkages and/or in laying the foundations for an Indogerman religion, one that could do without Judaism as well as without clerical Christianity itself. We have seen the nineteenth-century roots of this quest and noted the ways in which it was given new force by the discovery of Mandaen, Gnostic, Manichean, Mazdaen, and Nestorian texts in the period 1880–1930. Often initially dated to the pre-Christian era, these texts permitted all too easily convinced scholars to fall back into the trap laid for Renaissance scholars by the Hermetic texts, that is to say, to presume that proto-Christian ideas were already pervasive in the pagan East *before* the time of Jesus' birth. After 1933, the refutation of the Jewish origins of monotheism could be accomplished even more openly and viciously than ever, as in Ernst Diez' 1940 paean to the Iranian "religion of light," Mazdaism. The ancient legend of Ahura Mazda's triumph over the powers of evil and light, proclaimed by the prophet Zarathustra, Diez claimed, was the real source of western religion; even Jesus, whose Jewishness had so long been problematical for Germanic Christians, was no longer necessary. "With the ethical teachings of this Aryan-Iranian reformer [Zarathustra]," Diez writes, "we find ourselves in one leap on Christian-European soil; this is the teaching of our blood and Christianity took it over from Iran. The significant step in the history of mankind, from the Sumerian and Semitic to the Aryan world view was taken by Zarathustra."[48] It should be noted, however, that by this time, those Christians inclined to throw in

---

[44] Robert P. Ericksen, "Genocide, Religion and Gerhard Kittel: Protestant Theologians Face the Third Reich," in *In God's Name*, ed. Bartov and Mack (New York, 2001), pp. 71–21.

[45] See Pollock, "Deep Orientalism?" esp. pp. 86–96, 94.

[46] Peter Levenda, *Unholy Alliance: A History of Nazi Involvement with the Occult* (New York, 2002), pp. 192–6.

[47] On Hauer, see Margarete Dierks, *Jakob Wilhelm Hauer, 1881–1962: Leben, Werk, Wirkung* (Heidelberg, 1986); on Wüst, see Reinhard Bollmus, *Das Amt Rosenberg und seine Gegner* (Stuttgart, 1970).

[48] Ernst Diez, *Entschleiertes Asien: Alte Kulturen vom Zweistromland bis zum Gelben Fluss* (Berlin, 1943) (originally Vienna, 1940), p. 130.

their lot with the regime had already done so, without reference to Iran, Zarathustra, or the Zend Avesta. Despite the efforts of radical orientalists and
Germanists, Zarathustra, like Wotan, might help to justify the extrusion of Jews
from Germandom's history, but would never really become an effectual god.

Among the Islamicists, there were also numerous collaborators – though of
rather a different type. The grounds for collaboration for the specialists in modern
Islamic languages were often, first, their usefulness as diplomats in the Middle East
or as *agents provocateurs* in India and Egypt; they had long experience in using self-
congratulatory anti-British rhetoric and in pandering to backward-looking conservative indigenous elites (e.g., the Chinese mandarins, the "old" Turks). Some,
like Curt Prüfer and Fritz Grobba, had long experience in the business of foment-
ing *jihad* and continued to do so through the Nazi era.[49] Many were ardent Nazis,
like Prüfer, who acknowledged in his diary the authenticity of his conversion to
"some of the beautiful ideas of National Socialism."[50] Others seem likely to have
been opportunists, like Hans Alexander Winckler, who had been a communist in
the mid-1920s, then joined the Nazi Party in 1939; having spent much time in the
mid-1930s studying Egyptian ethnology, he was sent by the Foreign Ministry to
Teheran, then served as a *Sonderführer* with the Afrikakorps.[51] Things looked
rather promising for this bunch in the period 1936–9, during which time there was
an outpouring of publications on Arab and Muslim affairs; Baldur von Schirach
toured Damascus, Baghdad, and Teheran, and Goebbels went to Egypt.[52] Intriguing with the Mufti of Jerusalem and Rashid Ali al-Gailani, the nationalist former
prime minister of Iran, these Foreign Ministry orientalists successfully dissemi-
nated Nazi principles throughout the Middle East, despite the fact that, for various
reasons, a real alliance was, from the outset, deeply problematic both before and
during the war.[53] Dreaming their own dreams of world conquest, many of these
policy experts – backed evidently by Alfred Rosenberg – were to be terribly disappointed by the lackluster efforts of their leaders in this theater and by the
backbiting of their fellow "experts" in the diplomatic corps. In November 1942
(that is, just after the battle of El-Alamein), Prüfer, now ambassador for special

---

[49] Prüfer, who entered the Foreign Service in 1907 at age 26, was, for example, minister to Ethiopia
1928–30; deputy director of the Foreign Ministry's Anglo-American and Middle Eastern Division,
1930–6; head of the Ministry's Personnel and Budget Division, 1936–9; ambassador to Brazil,
1939–42; ambassador for special duties in the Ministry's Middle Eastern section, 1942–3. Grobba
was German minister (Gesandter) in Iraq up to 1939, then attached to the Foreign Ministry,
heading up the Arab committee in the Political division. Donald M. McKale, ed., *Rewriting History: The Original and Revised World War II Diaries of Curt Prüfer, Nazi Diplomat*, trans. Judith
M. Melton (Kent, Ohio, 1988), pp. x, 5, n. 8.
[50] Ibid., diary entry for July 19, 1943, p. 115.
[51] Hanisch, *Ausgegrenzte Kompetenz*, p. 113.
[52] Lukasz Hirszowicz, *The Third Reich and the Arab East* (London, 1966), p. 18.
[53] Both the Nazi party elite and the Arab nationalists treated one another with circumspection; the
Arabs' loyalties were divided, plus they hesitated at siding with the Italians, who, in 1936, showed
themselves to be greedy colonizers. German economic investment in the Arab countries was quite
small, compared with investments in Turkey and Iran (Hirszowicz, *The Third Reich*, pp. 16–17).
Hitler's focus remained so concentrated on Europe and the Soviet Union that he seems to have given
little thought to Middle Eastern nations other than those which bordered the Soviet Union (e.g.
Turkey, Iran, and Afghanistan); moreover, Hitler did not want to offend either the Italians or
Vichy, or, early on, the English, by declaring his support for Arab independence. See Andreas
Hillgruber, "The Third Reich and the Near and Middle East, 1933–1939," in *The Great Powers
in the Middle East, 1919–1939* ed., Uriel Dann, (New York, 1988), p. 275.

duties in the Foreign Ministry's "oriental" section, complained bitterly in his diary: "Again, as in the first war, the Orient and the Mediterranean are being neglected."[54] A year later, a disgusted Prüfer summed up the futility of petitioning a Europe-centered Nazi regime: "I, a second-class ambassador, am comparable to a fly that is not shooed away from the cake it is crawling on because no one cares."[55]

Other forms of collaboration and fellow-traveling were also possible. Sven Hedin, the Swedish adventurer who became an ardent German patriot during the Great War, befriended Hindenburg and Hitler and was willing to lend his name to a Central Asian Institute created under Himmler's auspices at the University of Munich. The Japanese commercial and political contacts of Karl Haushofer, the geopolitician, undoubtedly smoothed the way for the German–Japanese alliance. Strzygowski, in the 1930s, let loose a new torrent of racist art-historical nonsense; the Indologist Ludwig Alsdorf penned a popular book on India, which clearly aimed at sabotaging British rule.[56] Carl Becker's conservative Catholic student Franz Babinger surely would have accepted a chaired professorship at the University of Munich in 1933, but he was ruled out after the Persian specialist H. H. Schaeder expressed doubts about Babinger's scholarship, personality, and Aryan origins; in 1934, Babinger's career prospects were crushed when *Der Stürmer* denounced him for being a *Mischlinge*.[57] The linguist Carl Brockelmann was powerful enough to retain the name *Semitistik* for his purely philological institute in Leipzig, but published an essay in 1944, which reproduced hackneyed disparagements of Semitic culture (its supposed lack of "flexible" aesthetic and philosophical qualities), speculated on the origins of the Jewish nose, and denounced the work of Jewish scholars as wholly unscientific.[58]

In some cases, insufficient political correctness was punished. The Assyriologist Albert Schott joined the party, but made the mistake of believing Rudolf Hess's claim that diverse opinions within the ranks were welcomed; to avoid persecution for his criticism of the Nazis' anti-Christian rhetoric, Schott had to be sent to dig in Mesopotamia. Schott's mentor, Paul Kahle, had a sufficiently impressive international reputation that he was allowed to continue in his post at the University of Berlin and to assume the editorship of the *ZDMG* in 1934, even though his close work with Jewish scholars and on "late" Jewish subjects was well known. Indeed, Kahle was tapped in 1935 to reorganize Berlin's now venerable SOS, folding into it all other Berlin bodies that specialized in oriental studies, ancient and modern. But Kahle would not dispense with a personal assistant who was a Polish rabbi, and he had a brave and humane wife, who helped Jews clean up their shops after *Kristallnacht*, tried to comfort her Jewish friends, and hid valuables for them. When she was condemned by a Nazi court,

---

[54] *Rewriting History* (Prüfer diary, entry for November 14, 1942), p. 7; also December 31, 1942, p. 27.

[55] Ibid., January 23, 1943, p. 41.

[56] Alsdorf, *Indien* (Berlin, 1940).

[57] German Grimm, "Franz Babinger (1891–1967): Ein Lebensgeschichtlicher Essay," pp. 317–20.

[58] Hanisch, "Akzentverschiebung," pp. 13, 14, 32; Carl Brockelmann, "Stand und Aufgaben der Semitistik," in *Beiträge zur Arabistik, Semitistik und Islamwissenschaft*, ed. Richard Hartmann and Helmuth Schell (Leipzig, 1944), pp. 4–12, 41.

Kahle lost his job and the couple, with their five children, left for England in March 1939.[59]

As this suggests, there were many dangers, as well as some new opportunities, for the Nazi-era orientalist. The old question of relevance or utility was still around, made even more urgent by the regime's conflicting tendencies to respect *Wissenschaft* on the one hand and to discourage over-investment in non-utilitarian and/or *unvölkisch* endeavors on the other. Even the collaborators faced the other party members' inevitable tendency to make a damning category mistake, as Paul Kahle explained. "They were often very surprised when they were told that there were many non-Jewish orientals, and, moreover, there was a difference between orientals and orientalists."[60] To counter this prejudice – one that incidentally harkens back to orientalism's long focus on the Old Testament and its appeal to Jewish converts – one could insist on one's Aryan ancestry and subject matter, or one could insist upon the usefulness to the regime of knowledge about Semites – though the tradition of "informed evangelizing" had to be redefined, as what might be called "informed expulsion," as racially defined Jews could no longer be converted. What was more difficult was to defend the study of cultures neither clearly Jewish nor Aryan, such as Islamic studies, Egyptology, Sinology, or Assyriology, where racial ideology did not offer much cultural purchase.

The problem of relevance was something the Nazi classicist Helmut Berve insightfully linked to another difficulty orientalists faced in the definitely anti-positivist climate of the mid-1930s: how to defend the continuing pursuit of "pure" linguistic studies or the non-utilitarian collection of ancient facts? In many fields of oriental studies, Berve argued in 1934, though painstaking linguistic and archaeological work remained to be done, there were fewer and fewer individuals willing to devote themselves to "naked fact collecting" – especially when the culture under study was a racially foreign one. In other fields, such as Egyptology, the "fact work" was largely complete and since, as specialists like Heinrich Schäfer and Helmut Junker had argued, the thought-worlds of these people were entirely un-Greek and unmodern, there was little point in studying them further. Given our racial distance from the Semitic world, Berve asked, was it even possible to write a post-positivist Egyptian cultural history?[61]

Berve's question amounted to a turning of the furor orientalis against itself: if the Orient needed to be studied exclusively in its own terms, could western orientalists ever fully understand it? Why should they even try to do so? These were clearly questions only thinkable in a fully post-Christian context; even though Berve conceded that "parts of the Old Testament today form a permanent part of our Christian thought-world," he did not even bother explaining how Jesus as Messiah could be understood without acknowledging Christianity's roots in Judaism. It was also a question posed by a man who had completely abandoned the ideals of universal history even on the Hegelian model and for whom Rankean objectivity was not a noble goal, but a seditious farce. "Treitschke, not Ranke, is the answer in our age, and not only for German history! The study of antiquity

---

[59] Kahle, *Die Universität Bonn*, pp. 105, 150–1; Marie Kahle, *Was hätten Sie getan?*
[60] Kahle, *Die Universität Bonn*, p. 148.
[61] Helmut Berve, "Zur Kulturgeschichte des alten Orient," in *Archiv für Kulturgeschichte* 25, no. 2 (1934): 230, quotation p. 227.

too will not be able to operate in the future without a decisive valuing of the material – and not a subjective [valuing] but a racially-grounded and a racially-uniting one. That poses a serious question for ancient oriental scholarship...," a question Berve posed most pointedly a few pages later: "Is knowledge, here, in the deeper sense, possible?"[62] In answering no, Berve was essentially reconstructing, in a new place, those walls of untranslatability – between orientalism and classicism, between the Christian Bible and pagan religions, between Europeans and "others" – so many orientalists had worked for centuries to tear down.

Berve was a major cultural player (he was a chaired professor, then after 1933, dean, and finally rector at the University of Leipzig, as well as a party member) and his essay a major challenge. W. F. Albright thought it a significant enough threat to devote his 1936 presidential address to the American Oriental Society to refuting it.[63] One of Berve's criticisms of *Orientalistik* was quite novel: the ancient Orient, he claimed, was incomprehensible simply because it was so very ancient. This is something new; in the nineteenth century, language, culture, religion, geography, and race were seen as barriers to understanding, but very few scholars thought their modernness posed an insuperable barrier to hermeneutical understanding. But here, perhaps, Berve was partly right. We have seen how the *OLZ* essays in the 1920s moved forward in time to modern subjects; this is even more observable in the *OLZ* in the 1930s. The ancient world was gradually fading even from the scholarly horizon, becoming less surely graspable, in part because the philological traditions of the theological seminaries and of the Gymnasium were beginning to wane.

But the real reason Berve questioned the possibility of deep knowledge in oriental studies was racial; for him, the non-Greek, non-Germanic aspects of the eastern worldview were, at the end of the day, so essential as to make these cultures totally incomprehensible to westerners. This was a challenge the orientalists who specialized in Aryan topics could answer – at the cost of reducing knowledge essentially to racial intuition. The Semitists could try to defend hermeneutical understanding – but that was already premised on the notion that Semites were "others," not in any way belonging to the German "self." Though we have seen the gradual division of oriental studies along racial lines, with relevance defended in different ways, and with different degrees of passion, Berve here was finally demanding that the orientalist say whether he or she studied "us" or "not us." With orthodox Christians, Jews, and even historicizing Protestants taken out of patronage system, and replaced by Nazi functionaries and ideologues, no one with money or power had any interest in defending knowledge of the Semites as part of "our" history or civilization.[64] In denying the possibility of a scientific orientalism, Berve was not only promoting a biological division of labor, but also destroying German orientalism's Christian humanist underpinnings – and asking for the final breakup of the great and diverse continent inhabited by *Orientalistik*.

---

[62] Berve, "Zur Kulturgeschichte des alten Orient," pp. 228, 220, 227.
[63] William Foxwell Albright, "How Well Can We Know the Ancient Near East?" [1936], in idem, *History, Archaeology and Christian Humanism* (New York, 1964), pp. 103–29.
[64] It is interesting that conservative Catholic prehistorians in Austria still attempted to do this. See Arvidsson, *Aryan Idols*, pp. 257–75.

Racial orientalism did prevail in Nazi Germany and left scars that perhaps will never heal. Both the purges that forced out so many talented and innovative scholars, and the ideological and institutional damage committed by the regime destroyed a long-standing philological-humanist tradition to which we owe so much of our knowledge of the ancient Orient. But racial orientalism could not triumph for long, both because Nazi officials seemed to have lost interest in supporting it and because scholarship abroad, energized by exiles, would not allow walls of untranslatability to be rebuilt or the world to forget what had been learned about cultural exchanges and indebtedness, religious parallels, and intertwined texts. Especially where evangelical Protestantism was weak (e.g., outside the United States, and to a lesser extent, Great Britain), there would continue to be questions about "relevance" – why should young Frenchmen (and women) know about ancient Egypt? And the "western civ" style of thought, indebted in many ways to Jaeger (but not to Berve), made this relevance in the 1950s–1970s hard to argue for. But some orientalists have always been content to be irrelevant, upholding thereby a humanistic principle some modern Europeanists could profit from. And now that they have become relevant once more, thanks to economic globalization and recent conflicts in Palestine, Iraq, and Afghanistan, it is hardly surprising that they find critiques of their own "Eurocentrism" and/or complicity in imperialist endeavors vexing; their forefathers, even the racists among them, fought long and hard to demonstrate Asia's contributions to world history, arguing against a host of others – many of them racists too – reluctant to give the Orient its due.

In exile, at any rate, some Germans retained their commitments to translatability. Carl Jung's orientalism, condescending and self-interested as it was (the East is important because it represents another side of ourselves), at least offered some promise of intercultural learning and exchange. Jung's perspective was shared, in essence, by two other important conservative pessimists, Keyserling and Spengler; in all three cases, after some initial soundings, the men backed away from collaboration with the Nazi regime and the Nazis disdained their sort of orientalism, for it threatened to relativize the virtues of Germandom along with those of western liberalism and technology. But another form was discernible in Thomas Mann's attempt, in his Joseph novels, to put the Old Testament back into the European imagination, and in Sigmund Freud's effort to universalize Moses, making him, in *Moses and Monotheism*, mankind's primeval father. It is striking that Mann opens his Joseph tetralogy, the first volume of which was published in 1933, with the line, "Very deep is the well of the past. Shall we not call it bottomless?" a phrase I read as a direct challenge to the hyper-diffusionism of his racist contemporaries, seeking pre- or non-Semitic roots in the mists of the Aryan past. Freud's text is harder to interpret – and many more interpretations have been lavished on it – but I am convinced that Jan Assmann is right in seeing it as reprise of Deist critiques of Christian intolerance and Jewish provincialism.[65] And it was also, as Carl Schorske showed in a brilliant essay, Freud's vindication of the Jews as a masculine *Kulturvolk*, a project that required abandoning Freud's earlier inquiries into the bisexual and mixed classical-oriental foundations of

---

[65] Jan Assmann, *Moses the Egyptian: The Memory of Egypt in Western Monotheism* (Cambridge, MA, 1997), p. 157.

European civilization.[66] In their different ways, both Mann and Freud were reviving the Old Testament as, in Herder's phrase, "the oldest document of mankind," now outside the Christian-humanist context. But by mid-1938, both authors were also outside Central Europe. That the "orientalists" who stayed in Germany and Austria were neither able nor apparently willing to pursue these lines of thought meant that the hope for a post-positivist, fully universal *Kulturgeschichte* would have to be put off for a later – perhaps a much later – time.

WHY GERMAN ORIENTALISTS LAID THE FOUNDATION FOR MULTICULTURAL THINKING, BUT COULD NOT DEVELOP IT

If the literature on Weimar- and Nazi-era orientalism remains thin, the work on *Orientalistik* after 1945 is even more so. It seems that very few of the Nazi-era collaborators were purged – and critical scrutiny of the field's history, with the exception of some Old Testament scholars like H. J. Kraus, has been lacking.[67] Perhaps the enormous outflux of émigrés so damaged the field's critical facilities and racism so distorted the romantic tradition as to make a return to positivist linguistics the only sensible response in the postwar world. And perhaps as West Germany sought to join NATO and the emerging EU, it made sense to return to lines of thought that stressed German links to European civilization, to fall in line, that is, with the "western civ" view of the world, in which Greek democracy, Renaissance individualism, and western capitalism are all too often seen as the defining moments in a self-enclosed history of the West. It is striking, however, that, again according to Kürschner's lexicon, while both orientalism and classics lost self-identified members sharply between 1935 and 1941, oriental studies, in the postwar period, had fallen to 38 percent of its Weimar strength, while classics retained 68 percent of its prewar strength (and chemistry 87 percent).[68] Though this is, of course, a crude measure, it is nonetheless part of a highly important and largely untold story of the retrenchment of German classicism in the post-1945 period.

There is an even less charted set of developments that also need to be studied here: those involving the triumph (or not) of "secularization" in oriental studies. In 1922, the editor of the *ZDMG* Carl Brockelmann declared that *Semitistik* had ceased at last to be the "ancilla theologiae," which had as its task the delivery of material for the upholstering of biblical commentaries or the opening up of new sources on the ancient church for clerical historians."[69] More than ever before, as we have seen, orientalists in the 1920s focused on modern languages, folklore (rather than religion), and economic and political history. The missionary tradition waned, as racists gave up on conversion, and as more secular sorts of emissaries – military advisors, communist agitators, environmentalists, and

---

[66] Carl E. Schorske, "To the Egyptian Dig: Freud's Psycho-Archeology of Cultures," in idem, *Thinking with History: Explorations in the Passage to Modernism* (Princeton, NJ, 1998), pp. 209–13.

[67] Kraus, *Geschichte der historisch-kritischen Erforschung*.

[68] *Kürschners Deutscher Gelehrten-Kalender* 5 (1935), 6 (1940–1), 7 (1950). Friedrich Wilhelm's "The German Response to Indian Culture," in *Journal of the American Oriental Society* 81, no. 4 (1961): 395–405, describes the history of Indology in Germany through 1961 without mentioning the Nazi era.

[69] Carl Brockelmann, "Die morgenländischen Studien in Deutschland," in *ZDMG* 76 (1922): 9.

novelists – traveled between West and East. Institutionally, the gaps between theology, philosophy, classics, and *Orientalistik* widened again. But *Religionsgeschichte* did not die, as witnessed by the great success of Rudolf Otto's *Das Heilige* and the prestige of Rudolf Bultmann; biblical studies were not wholly irrelevant, as the dedication of Martin Buber and Franz Rosenzweig to the creation of a deeply non-Christian Old Testament suggests. Though German scholars seem not to have paid much attention to the new excavations of the 1920s and 1930s in Palestine, for those who did there were surely implications for faith. Anyone who works in and around Near Eastern archaeology and philology today can testify that many of our contemporaries continue to be drawn to the subject by religious concerns, and the same is probably true, to a lesser extent, in other branches of ancient oriental studies. If we are to better understand the reconstruction of German oriental studies after 1945, we cannot assume once more that religious beliefs, longings, or prejudices are irrelevant parts of the story.

No one would, I think, dispute that Germany has lost its cutting-edge status in oriental studies, perhaps forever. This was not only the fault of the Nazis – though that regime must be held responsible for destroying lives and for the full-scale institutional wreckage it caused. In part, Germany was already beginning to lose its status at the time the Great War broke out – due to its sluggish adoption of comparative perspectives, its prejudices for the ancient as opposed to the modern world, its comparatively small toeholds in Asia, and its very late discovery of East Asian cultures. It lost more ground during WWI, as propaganda replaced scholarly inquiries, and in the war's immediate aftermath, as German colonies were taken away, the friendly Ottoman Empire collapsed, the patronage system was ruined, and indigenous elites learned to be suspicious of all their erstwhile European "friends."

Had the Weimar era gone on, it is possible that German orientalism would have evolved more fully in the direction of what we now call multiculturalism. It had many of the makings of such a worldview; as we saw in some of Littmann and Becker's effusions above, as well as in the whole line of thought we called "furious" orientalism, there was already a powerful understanding of the Eurocentric nature of conventional history-writing and the unsuitability of western models and norms for understanding the cultures of the East. There was an appreciation of the ways in which Europe was, for most of recorded history, the weaker continent, and of how many myths, ideas, inventions, and practices (including major ones like Christianity, paper, and astronomy) Europeans owed to the Orient. Critics of the humanist tradition like Josef Strzygowski and Hugo Winckler had repeatedly called for the demolition of the walls between the East and West which prevented Europeans from understanding the wider sweep of cultural development and allowed for the presumption that the West alone had agency. Iconoclastic Christians and Jews had exposed their religions' debts to and similarities with other world religions. And some European orientalists, like Martin Haug and Richard Wilhelm, had even acknowledged that the East knew more about its own traditions than westerners could ever really learn; Europeans should try to understand the great achievements of the East, but not attempt conversions of any sort. In Helmut Berve, we even saw a national-socialist version of the most radical forms of post-colonial argumentation: Europeans can never understand "orientals" (Berve would have said Semites) because the former are simply unable to comprehend the minds of the "other." For Berve, scientific orientalism, in the West at any rate, was simply not possible.

All of this sounds very familiar today and it is worth emphasizing again that such ideas were pretty much conventional in orientalist circles by the 1920s and that they were born of the study of the ancient, not the modern world. It is the conceit of too many modern historians that they are the first ones to have discovered the evils of Eurocentrism. But herein too lies the beginning of the other part of the story: why German orientalists could not completely effect the multicultural turn. In part, this was the result of their very deep immersion in the Christian and classical traditions and the attendant prejudices and institutional barriers that made thinking outside these boxes difficult and fraught with peril – as well as exhilaratingly iconoclastic. This meant further that the ways in which this "thinking outside" was done were often marked by inordinate passions for or resentment toward the normative peoples – Greeks and Jews – against whom other peoples of Asia and Africa were juxtaposed. Similarly, the continual return to the Hellenistic era, for sources and for intellectual weaponry, and the imbrication here of Neoplatonic forms of thought left deep and abiding tendencies to play the chronology cards against the better-documented, self-promoting Hellenes and Israelites. The new forms of "universal" history the orientalists sought to construct were then all too often antinarratives, constructed chiefly to subvert or sideline the Greeks, or more commonly, the Jews. As I argued in Chapter 6, this tendency increased at the fin de siècle with renewed longings to "purify" Christianity, intellectual and racially, and left its disastrous stamp on Indology and Persian studies. This impeded German scholars from moving in the direction of their French, American, and British colleagues, who were better able to assimilate material from sites like the Jewish–Hellenistic complex at Dura Europos and to recognize the need to embrace what James Henry Breasted called the "coherent and unified story of mankind."[70] The German orientalist quest, on the contrary, continued to be one characterized by origin-seeking and increasingly by West-bashing, by the desire to find a pure new religion, and the longing to debunk (or reattribute) the ideals of the old.

Another way in which German orientalism was not multicultural was in the continuing confidence of many scholars that the West had made a leap forward, morally and intellectually, in having a Renaissance as well as a Reformation. Perhaps this was simply too deeply ingrained in European culture to resist or perhaps it went along with Germans' abiding confidence in text criticism, so central an achievement of the early modern period. But it meant that once their analyses leapt beyond the Middle Ages, the orientalists' cultural relativism went out the window. This is something one sees quite clearly in Becker, who credited the rise of the West to the Renaissance rediscovery of the classical tradition, which gave Europeans the idea of the free citizen and the individualist ego.[71] Here,

---

[70] James Henry Breasted, *Oriental Forerunners of Byzantine Painting: First Century Wall Paintings from the Fortress of Dura on the Middle Euphrates* (Chicago, IL, 1924), p. 8.

[71] Becker, "Hellenism and Islam," pp. 12–15. The Islamicist recognized, however, that many parts of the West had not advanced to enlightened reading: "... wide swathes of America," he mused, "still maintain this sort of medieval standpoint with respect to the Bible." Becker, "Vom Peking bis Damaskus," p. 13.

Becker was no iconoclast, but was simply reiterating liberal, Hegelian claims no different from the storylines pursued by most other educated Europeans of his class.

Finally, the German orientalist world was deeply touched by imperialist hubris, both before and after the Kaiserreich's leap into colonization. One of the many compromising aspects of this arrogance was the presumption that non-European culture was something to master and own, not an ongoing living set of traditions into which one entered as a guest. Most orientalists did not really want to hear the voices or see the faces of real-existing "oriental" peoples; though there were moments in which they idolized individuals such as Swami Vivekananda or Rabindranath Tagore, their fascination usually carried with it a strong whiff of anti-British *Schadenfreude* or primitivist longing. There were some friendships across international borders, many more surely than have been detailed above. But prejudice and condescension were far more prevalent; although Germans regularly depended, as we have seen, on the knowledge, language skills, and collecting energies of "others," it was rare for a nonwesterner to be treated as an intellectual equal. Judging by the international character of twenty-first century *Orientalistentagungen*, that day is ending; but it was not an achievement this book's protagonists can claim.

In conclusion, we should not forget the strengths of the tradition analyzed above, its enormous appetite for hard work, its devotion to careful language study, its willingness to defy conventions and norms, and its deep immersion in original texts. It was a tradition that was dispersed far and wide, but has for the most part been lost; as Hava Lazarus-Yafeh noted of the generations who first taught at School of Oriental Studies in Jerusalem, from 1920s–1950s, largely German-trained: "They were schooled in Greek and Latin in the German Gymnasium, and later mastered an array of European and Semitic languages. They all had a solid grounding in Jewish studies, having studied not just in the university but in the rabbinic seminary or its equivalent. And they were widely read in history, literature and philosophy..." Lazarus-Yafeh continued, modestly, but probably correctly: "We lack their vast erudition and rich sources for comparison, and so do our students."[72] We do, however, have other strengths, new and respected non-Western interlocutors, wider access than ever before to materials, facilitated interdisciplinary exchange and thanks to our university systems (so far) no requirement to be relevant. It is the author's hope that this book has also given us the historical perspective to understand the ways in which our humanistic traditions have both failed to embrace a truly universalist perspective and given us the tools to develop one.

---

[72] Lazarus-Yafeh, "The Transplantation of Islamic Studies," p. 256.

Select Bibliography

Archival Sources

Bonn, Politisches Archiv des Auswärtigen Amt (B-PAAA); these files are now in the
Bundesarchiv, Berlin (and their new file numbers are cited with the prefix B-BArch)
Vienna, Universitäts Archiv (V-UA)
Berlin, Akademie der Wissenschaften Archiv (B-AWA)
Berlin, Deutsches Archäologisches Institut Archiv (B-DAIA)
Berlin, Museum für Indische Kunst Archiv (B-MIKA)
Berlin, Geheimes Staatsarchiv, Preussischer Kulturbesitz (B-GSPK)
    I, Rep. 76 Files of the Central Bureaucracy of Brandenburg-Prussia
    I, Rep. 89 Files of the Civil Cabinet
    Nachlass Carl Heinrich Becker (VI, HA Rep. 92) (M=Mappe)
Berlin, Staatsbibliothek; Handschriftsabteilung (B-SB) (K=Kasten)
Munich, Bayerisches Hauptstaatsarchiv (M-BHSA), Abteilung II
    Files of the Trade Ministry (MH)
Potsdam, Zentrales Staatsarchiv, files of the Auswärtiges Amt, Rechtsabteilung (P-ZSA,
AA/R). These files have now been transferred to the Bundesarchiv, and their new file
numbers are cited with the prefix B-BArch).
Vienna, Universitäts-Archiv (V-UA)
    Philosophical faculty file on Josef Strzygowski

Printed Sources

Aarsleff, Hans. *From Locke to Saussure: Essays on the Study of Language and Intellectual
History* (Minneapolis, MN, 1982).

Acton, Lord (John Emerich Edward Dahlberg-Acton). "German Schools of History," in
The English Historical Review 1, no. 1 (1886): 7–42.

Alder, Lory and Richard Dalby. *The Dervish of Windsor Castle: The Life of Arminius
Vambery* (London, 1979).

Anderson, Margaret Lavinia. "'Down in Turkey, Far Away'": Human Rights, the Armenian
Massacres, and Orientalism in Wilhelmine Germany," in *Journal of Modern History* 79,
no. 1 (2007): 80–111.

Arvidsson, Stefan. *Aryan Idols: Indo-European Mythology as Ideology and Science*, trans.
Sonia Wichmann (Chicago, 2006).

Aschheim, Steven E. *Brothers and Strangers: The East European Jew in German and
German Jewish Consciousness, 1800–1923* (Madison, WI, 1982).

Assmann, Jan. *Moses the Egyptian: The Memory of Egypt in Western Monotheism*
(Cambridge, MA, 1997).

Baelz, Erwin. *Awakening Japan: The Diary of a German Doctor*, ed. Toku Baelz, trans. Eden and Cedar Paul (Bloomington, IN, 1974).

Bammel, Ernst. "Judentum, Christentum und Heidentum: Julius Wellhausens Briefe an Theodor Mommsen, 1881–1902," in *Zeitschrift für Kirchengeschichte* 80 (1969): 221–54.

Barthold, Wassily. *Die geographische und historische Erforschung des Orients mit besonderer Berücksichtigung der russischen Arbeiten* (Leipzig, 1913).

Bauer, Wolfgang, ed. *Richard Wilhelm: Botschafter zweier Welten* (Cologne, 1973).

Baur, F.C. *Symbolik und Mythologie oder die Naturreligion des Alterthums*, pt. 1 (Stuttgart, 1824).

Bayly, C.A. *Empire and Information: Intelligence Gathering and Social Communication in India, 1780–1870* (Cambridge, 1996).

Becker, Carl. "Der Islam im Rahmen einer allgemeinen Kulturgeschichte," in *Zeitschrift der Deutschen Morgenländischen Gesellschaft* 76, no. 1 (1922): 18–35.

Becker, Carl Heinrich. *Islamstudien* (Leipzig, 2 vols., 1924, 1932).

Becker, Carl Heinrich. *L'Islam et la colonization de l'Afrique* (Paris, 1910).

Becker, Carl Heinrich. "Panislamismus," in *Archiv für Religionswissenschaft* 7 (1904): 169–92.

Benfey, Theodor. *Geschichte der Sprachwissenschaft und orientalischen Philologie in Deutschland* (Munich, 1869).

Benes, Tuska. "Comparative Linguistics as Ethnology: In Search of Indo-Germans in Central Asia," in *Comparative Studies of South Asia, Africa and the Middle East* 24, no.2 (2004): 117–32.

Benes, Tuska, *In Babel's Shadow: Philology and the Nation in Nineteenth-Century Germany* (Detroit, MI, 2008).

Berman, Nina. *Orientalismus, Kolonismus und Moderne: Zum Bild des Orients in der deutschsprachigen Kultur um 1900* (Stuttgart, 1997).

Berman, Nina. "Thoughts on Zionism in the Context of German Middle Eastern Relations," in *Comparative Studies of South Asia, Africa and the Middle East* 24, no. 2 (2004): 133–44.

Blumhardt, Christoph. *Christus in der Welt: Briefe an Richard Wilhelm*, ed. Arthur Rich (Zürich, 1958).

Bohlen, Peter von. *Das alte Indien, mit besonderer Rücksicht auf Ägyptens* (Königsberg, 2 vols., 1830).

Bollack, Jean. *Jacob Bernays: Un homme entre deux mondes* (Villeneuve d'Ascq, 1998).

Bopp, Franz. *Vergleichende Grammatik des Sanskrit, Send, Armenischen, Griechischen, Lateinischen, Litauischen, Altslavischen, Gothischen und Deutschen* (Berlin, 3rd ed., 1868).

Bousset, Wilhelm. *Kyrios Christos: A History of the Belief in Christ from the Beginnings of Christianity to Irenaeus*, trans. John E. Steely (Nashville, TN, 1970).

Bousset, Wilhelm. *Die Religion des Judentums im neutestamentlichen Zeitalter* (Berlin, 2nd ed., 1906).

Breckman, Warren. *Marx, the Young Hegelians, and the Origins of Radical Social Theory* (Cambridge, 1999).

Brenner, Michael. *The Renaissance of Jewish Culture in Weimar Germany* (New Haven, CT, 1996).

Brisch, Klaus. "Wilhelm von Bode und sein Verhältnis zur islamischen und ostasiatischen Kunst," in *Jahrbuch der Berliner Museen* 28 Beiheft *Kennershaft* (1996): 33–48.

Bryant, Edwin. *The Quest for the Origins of Vedic Culture: The Indo-Aryan Migration Debate* (Oxford, 2001).

Budde, Karl. *Das Alte Testament und die Ausgrabungen: Ein Beitrag zum Streit um Babel und Bibel* (Giessen, 2nd ed., 1903).

Bunsen, Christian Karl Josias von. *Ägyptens Stelle in der Weltgeschichte* (Hamburg/Gotha, 5 vols., 1845–57).

Calder, William M., III and Alexander Demandt, eds. *Eduard Meyer: Leben und Leistung eines Universalhistoriker* (Leiden, 1990).

Carhart, Michael C. *The Science of Culture in Enlightenment Germany* (Cambridge, MA, 2007).

Chadwick, Owen. *The Secularization of the European Mind in the Nineteenth Century* (Cambridge, 1976).

Chamberlain, Houston Stewart. *Arische Weltanschauung* (Munich, 1905).

Chamberlain, Houston Stewart. *Foundations of the Nineteenth Century*, trans. John Lees (London, 2 vols., 1912).

Clarke, J.J. *Oriental Enlightenment: The Encounter between Asian and Western Thought* (London, 1997).

Clemen, Carl. *Religionsgeschichtliche Erklärung des Neuen Testaments: Die Abhängigkeit des ältesten Christentums von nichtjüdischen Religionen und philosophischen Systemen* (Giessen, 1909).

Colpe, Carsten. *Die religionsgeschichtliche Schule: Darstellung und Kritik ihres Bildes vom gnostischen Erlösungsmythus* (Göttingen, 1961).

Conrad, Lawrence I. "The Dervish's Disciple: On the Personality and Intellectual Milieu of the Young Ignaz Goldziher," in *Journal of the Royal Asiatic Society of Great Britain and Ireland* (1990): 225–66.

Cooper, Jerrold S. "Posing the Sumerian Question: Race and Scholarship in the Early History of Assyriology," in *Aula Orientalis* 9, nos. 1, 2 (1991): 47–66.

Creuzer, Friedrich. *Symbolik und Mythologie der alten Völker, besonders der Griechen* (Leipzig, 2nd ed., 6 vols., 1819–28).

Dahlmann, Joseph. *Budda: Ein Culturbild des Ostens* (Berlin, 1898).

Darmesteter, James. *Essais Orientaux* (Paris, 1883).

Deissmann, Adolf. *Licht vom Osten: Das Neue Testament und die neuentdeckten Texte aus dem hellenistisch-römischen Welt* (Tübingen, 1908).

Delitzsch, Friedrich. *Babel and Bible: Two Lectures*, ed. C.H.W. Johns (New York, 1903).

Delitzsch, Friedrich. *Die grosse Täuschung: Kritische Betrachtungen zu den alttestamentlichen Berichten über Israels Eindringen in Kanaan, die Gottesoffenbarung vom Sinai und die Wirksamkeit der Propheten* (Stuttgart, 2 vols., 1921).

Deussen, Paul. *Allgemeine Geschichte der Philosophie mit besonderer Berücksichtigung der Religionen* (Leipzig, 5 vols., 1894–1917).

Deussen, Paul. *Erinnerungen an Indien* (Kiel, 1904).

Deussen, Paul. *Mein Leben*, ed. Erika Rosenthal-Deussen (Leipzig, 1922).

Deussen, Paul. *Sechzig Upanishad's des Veda* (Leipzig, 2nd ed., 1905).

Dirks, Nicholas B. *The Scandal of Empire: India and the Creation of Imperial Britain* (Cambridge, MA, 2006).

Donner, Eka. *Und Nirgends eine Karawane: Die Weltreisen der Ida Pfeiffer (1797–1858)* (Düsseldorf, 1997).

Drews, Arthur. *Die Christusmythe* (Jena, 2nd ed., 1910).

Droit, Roger-Pol. *The Cult of Nothingness: The Philosophers and the Buddha*, trans. David Streight and Pamela Vohnsen (Chapel Hill, NC, 2003).

Droysen, Gustav. *Johann Gustav Droysen*, vol. *1, Bis zum Beginn der Frankfurter Tätigkeit* (Leipzig, 1910).

Droysen, Johann Gustav. *Geschichte des Hellenismus*, vol. 1 (Hamburg, 1836).

Duchesne-Guillemin, Jacques. *The Western Response to Zoroaster* (Oxford, 1958).

Ebers, Georg. *Aegypten in Bild und Wort* (Leipzig, 2 vols., 1879–80).

Eichhorn, Johann. "Johann David Michaelis: Einige Bemerkungen über seinen litterarischen Character," in *Allgemeine Bibliothek* 3, no. 5 (Leipzig, 1791): 827–906.

Elsner, Jaś. "The Birth of Late Antiquity: Riegl and Strzygowski in 1901," in *Art History* 25, no. 3 (2002): 358–79.

Erman, Adolf. *Ägypten und ägyptisches Leben im Altertum* (Tübingen, 2nd ed., 1923).

Erman, Adolf. *Mein Werden und meine Wirken* (Leipzig, 1929).

Essner, Cornelia. *Deutsche Afrikareisende im neunzehnten Jahrhundert* (Stuttgart, 1985).

Ewald, Heinrich. *Geschichte des Volkes Israels bis Christus* (Göttingen, 3 vols., 1843–59).

Field, Geoffrey G. *Evangelist of Race: The Germanic Vision of Houston Stewart Chamberlain* (New York, 1981).

Fichtner, Paula Sutter. *Terror and Toleration: The Habsburg Empire Confronts Islam, 1526–1850* (London, 2008).

Figl, Johann. *Nietzsche und die Religionen: Transkulturelle Perspektiven seines Bildungs- und Denkweges* (Berlin, 2007).

Figueira, Dorothy M. *Aryans, Jews, Brahmins: Theorizing Authority through Myths of Identity* (Albany, NY, 2002).

Figueira, Dorothy M. "The Authority of an Absent Text: The Veda, Upangas, Upavedas und Upnekhata in European Thought," in Laurie L. Patton, ed., *Authority, Anxiety and Canon: Essays in Vedic Interpretation* (Albany, NY, 1994), pp. 201–30.

Fischer, Fritz. *Griff nach der Weltmacht: Die Kriegszielpolitik des kaiserlichen Deutschland 1914/18* (Düsseldorf, 2nd ed., 1962).

Fischer, Fritz. *War of Illusions: German Policies from 1911 to 1914*, trans. Marian Jackson (London, 1975).

Fischer, Hans. *Der Ägyptolog Georg Ebers: Eine Fallstudie zum Problem Wissenschaft und Öffentlichkeit im 19. Jahrhundert* (Wiesbaden, 1994).

Franke, Herbert. *Sinologie*, part 1 of *Orientalistik*, in *Wissenschaftliche Forschungberichte: Geisteswissenschaftliche Reihe*, vol. 19, ed. Karl Hoenn (Bern, 1953).

Franke, Otto. *Erinnerungen aus Zwei Welten: Randglossen zur eigenen Lebensgeschichte* (Berlin, 1954).

Franke, Otto. *Ostasiatische Neubildungen: Beiträge zur Verständnis der politischen und kulturellen Enwicklungs-Vorgänge im Fernen Osten* (Hamburg, 1911).

Frei, Hans W. *The Eclipse of Biblical Narrative: A Study in Eighteenth and Nineteenth-Century Hermeneutics* (New Haven, CT, 1974).

Frenssen, Gustav. *Hilligenlei* (Berlin, 1905).

Friedman, Isaiah. *Germany, Turkey and Zionism, 1897–1918* (Oxford, 1977).

Garbe, Richard. *Indien und das Christentum: Eine Untersuchung der religionsgeschichtlichen Zusammenhänge* (Tübingen, 1914).

Garbe, Richard. *Indische Reiseskizzen* (Berlin, 1889).

Geiger, Abraham. *Was hat Mohammed aus dem Judenthume aufgenommen?* (Bonn, 1833).

Geiger, Wilhelm. *Ostiranische Kultur im Altertum* (Erlangen, 1882).

Gierlichs, Joachim and Annette Hagedorn, eds. *Islamic Art in Germany* (Mainz, 2004).

Gérard, René. *L'Orient et la pensée romantique allemande* (Nancy, 1963).

Glasenapp, Helmut von. *Das Indienbild deutscher Denker* (Stuttgart, 1960).

Goldziher, Ignaz. *Ignaz Goldziher: Tagebuch*, ed. Alexander Scheiber (Leiden, 1978).

Goldziher, Ignaz. *Der Mythos bei den Hebräern und seine geschlichtliche Entwicklung: Untersuchungen zur Religionswissenschaft* (Leipzig, 1876).

Goldziher, Ignaz. *Renan als Orientalist*, trans. Peter Zalán (Zürich, 2000).

Graetz, Heinrich. *The Structure of Jewish History and Other Essays*, ed. and trans. Ismar Schorsch (New York, 1975).

Graf, Friedrich Wilhelm. "Rettung der Persönlichkeit," in *Kultur und Kulturwissenschaften um 1900*, ed. Rüdiger von Bruch, Friedrich Wilhelm Graf and Gangolf Hübinger (Stuttgart, 1989), pp. 103–31.

Grafton, Anthony. *Defenders of the Text: The Traditions of Scholarship in an Age of Science, 1450–1800* (Cambridge, MA, 1991).

Grafton, Anthony. *Joseph Scaliger: A Study in the History of Classical Scholarship* (Oxford, 2 vols., 1983, 1993).

Grigor, Talinn. "Orient oder Rom? Qajar 'Aryan' Architecture and Strzygowski's Art History," in *The Art Bulletin* 89 (Sept. 2007): 562–90.

Grünwedel, Albert. *Buddhistische Kunst in Indien* (Berlin, 1893).

Gruppe, Otto. *Die griechischen Culte und Mythen in ihren Beziehungen zu den orientalischen Religionen*, vol. 1 (Leipzig, 1887).

Gunter, Ann C. and Stefan R. Hauser, eds. *Ernst Herzfeld and the Development of Near Eastern Studies, 1900–50* (Leiden, 2005).

Hacker, Paul. *Philology and Confrontation: Paul Hacker on Traditional and Modern Vedanta*, ed. Wilhelm Halbfass (Albany, NY, 1995).

Hagedorn, Annette. "The Development of Islamic Art History in Germany in the Late Nineteenth and Early Twentieth Centuries," in *Discovering Islamic Art: Scholars, Collectors and Collections, 1850–1950*, ed. Stephen Vernoit (London, 2000), pp. 117–27.

Hagen, Gottfried. "German Heralds of Holy War," in *Comparative Studies of South Asia, Africa and the Middle East* 24, no. 2 (2004): 145–62.

Halbfass, Wilhelm. *India and Europe: An Essay in Understanding* (Albany, NY, 1988).

Hammer-Purgstall, Joseph Freiherr von. *Erinnerungen aus meinem Leben, 1774–1852*, ed. Reinhart Bachofen von Echt (Vienna, 1940).

Hammer-Purgstall, Joseph von. *Geschichte des Osmanischen Reiches* (Pest, 10 vols., 1827–35).

Hanisch, Ludmila. "Akzentverschiebung – Zur Geschichte der Semitistik und Islamwissenschaft während des 'Dritten Reichs,'" in *Berichte zur Wissenschaftsgeschichte* 18 (1995): 217–26.

Hanisch, Ludmila. *Die Nachfolger der Exegeten: Deutschsprachige Erforschung der Vorderen Orient in der ersten Hälfte des 20. Jahrhunderts* (Wiesbaden, 2003).

Hanisch, Ludmila, ed. *Islamkunde und Islamwissenschaft im deutschen Kaiserreich: Der Briefwechsel zwischen Carl Heinrich Becker und Martin Hartmann (1900–1918)* (Leiden, 1992).

Hanisch, Ludmila, ed. *"Machen Sie doch unseren Islam nicht gar zu schlecht": Der Briefwechsel der Islamwissenschaftler Ignaz Goldziher und Martin Hartmann, 1894–1914* (Wiesbaden, 2000).

Hankey, Julie. *A Passion for Egypt: Arthur Weigall, Tutankhamun and the "Curse of the Pharoahs"* (London, 2001).

Haridi, Alexander. *Das Paradigma der 'islamischen Zivilisation' – oder die Begründung der deutschen Islamwissenschaft durch Carl Heinrich Becker (1876–1933)* (Würzburg, 2005).

Harnack, Adolf. *Die Aufgabe der theologischen Facultäten und die allgemeine Religionsgeschichte.* (Giessen, 1901).

Harris, Horton. *The Tübingen School* (Oxford, 1975).

Hartmann, Martin. *Die arabische Frage* (Leipzig, 1909).

Hartmann, Martin. *Reisebriefe aus Syrien* (Berlin, 1913).

Haug, Martin. *Essays on the Sacred Language, Writings and Religion of the Parsis* (London, 1878).

Havemann, Daniel. *Der "Apostel der Rache": Nietzsches Paulusdeutung* (Berlin, 2002).

Hecker, Helmut, ed. *Lebensbilder deutscher Buddhisten*, vol. 1, *Die Gründer* (Konstanz, 1990).

Herder, Johann Gottfried. *Herders Sämtliche Werke*, ed. Bernhard Suphan (Berlin, 33 vols., 1879–1913).

Hertz, Martin. *Karl Lachmann: Eine Biographie* (Berlin, 1851).

Heschel, Susannah. *Abraham Geiger and the Jewish Jesus* (Chicago, 1998).

Hess, Jonathan M. *Germans, Jews, and the Claims of Modernity* (New Haven, CT, 2002).

Heyking, Elisabeth. *Briefe, die ihm nicht erreichten* (Berlin, 1902).

Hirsch, Klaus, ed. *Richard Wilhelm: Botschafter zweier Welten* (Frankfurt, 2002).

Höpp, Gerhard. *Arabische und islamische Periodika in Berlin und Brandenburg, 1915–1945: Geschichtlicher Abriß und Bibliographie* (Berlin, 1994).

Hoffmann, Christhard. *Juden und Judentum im Werk deutscher Althistoriker des 19. und 20. Jahurhunderts* (Leiden, 1988).

Hopkirk, Peter. *Foreign Devils on the Silk Road: The Search for Lost Cities and Treasures of Chinese Central Asia* (Amherst, MA, 1980).

Howard, Thomas Albert. *Protestant Theology and the Making of the Modern German University* (Oxford, 2006).

Howard, Thomas Albert. *Religion and the Rise of Historicism: W.M.L. de Wette, Jacob Burckhardt and the Theological Origins of Nineteenth-Century Historical Consciousness* (Cambridge, MA, 2000).

Hübinger, Gangolf. *Kulturprotestantismus und Politik: Zum Verhältnis von Liberalismus und Protestantismus im wilhelmischen Deutschland* (Tübingen, 1994).

Hull, Isabel V. *Absolute Destruction: Military Culture and the Practices of War in Imperial Germany* (Ithaca, NY, 2005).

Irwin, Robert. *For Lust of Knowing: The Orientalists and their Enemies* (London, 2006).

Israel, Jonathan I. *Radical Enlightenment: Philosophy and the Making of Modernity, 1650–1750* (Oxford, 2002).

Iversen, Erik. *The Myth of Egypt and its Hieroglyphs in European Tradition* (Princeton, NJ, 1993, reprint of 1961 edition).

Janssen, Nittert. *Theologie fürs Volk: Eine Untersuchung über den Einfluß der Religionsgeschichtlichen Schule auf die Popularisierung der theologischen Forschung vor dem Ersten Weltkrieg unter besonderer Berücksichtigung des kirchlichen Liberalismus in der lutherischen Landeskirche Hannovers* (Göttingen, 1993).

Jensen, Peter. *Das Gilgamesh-Epos in der Weltliteratur*, vol. 1 (Strasbourg, 1906).

Jeremias, Alfred. *Das Alte Testament im Lichte des alte Orients* (Leipzig, 1904).

Johanning Klaus, *Die Bibel-Babel Streit: Eine forschungsgeschichtliche Studie* (Frankfurt, 1988).

Kalmar, Ivan Davidson. "Moorish Style: Orientalism, the Jews, and Synagogue Architecture," in *Jewish Social Studies* 7, no. 3 (2001): 68–100.

Kern, Martin. "The Emigration of German Sinologists, 1933–1945: Notes on the History and Historiography of Chinese Studies," in *Journal of the American Oriental Society* 118, no. 4 (1998): 507–29.

Kippenberg, Hans G. *Die Entdeckung der Religionsgeschichte: Religionswissenschaft und Moderne* (Munich, 1997).

Klaproth, Julius. *Mémoires relatifs à l'Asie, contenant des rescherches historiques, géographiques, et philologiques sur les peoples de l'Orient*, vol. 1 (Paris, 1826).

Klatt, Werner. "Die 'Religionsgeschichtliche Schule' in Giessen" in *Theologie im Kontext der Geschichte der Alma Mater Ludoviciana*, eds. Bernhard Jendorff et al. (Giessen, 1983), pp. 111–37.

Kloosterhuis, Jürgen. *'Friedliche Imperialisten': Deutsche Auslandsvereine und auswärtige Kulturpolitik, 1906–1918* (Frankfurt, 2 vols., 1994).

Koeppen, Carl Friedrich. *Die Religion des Buddha*; vol. 1, *Die Religion des Buddha und ihre Entstehung* (Berlin, 1857); vol. 2: *Die lamaische Hierarchie und Kirche* (Berlin, 1859).

Kramer, Martin. "Arabistik and Arabism: The Passions of Martin Hartmann," in *Middle Eastern Studies* 25, no. 3 (July 1989): 283–300.

Kramer, Martin, ed. *The Jewish Discovery of Islam: Studies in Honor of Bernard Lewis* (Tel Aviv, 1999).

Kraus, Hans-Joachim. *Geschichte der historisch-kritischen Erforschung des Alten Testaments von der Reformation bis zur Gegenwart* (Neukirchen, 1956).

Kremer, Alfred von. *Kulturgeschichte des Orients unter den Chalifen* (Vienna, 2 vols., 1875, 1877).

Kreyenborg, Hermann. "Friedrich Rückert als Interpret orientalische Dichtungen," in *Friedrich Rückert im Speigel seiner Zeitgenossen und der Nachwelt*, ed. Wolfdieterich Fischer (Wiesbaden, 1988), pp. 261–86.

Kühnel, Ernst. "Die Ausstellung mohammedanischer Kunst München 1910," in *Münchner Jahrbuch der bildenden Kunst* 5 (1910): 209–51.

Lach, Donald. *Asia in the Making of Europe* (Chicago, 9 vols., 1965–93).

Lachmann, Karl. "Rechenschaft über seine Ausgabe der Neuen Testaments," in *Theologische Studien und Kritiken* (1830): 817–45.

Lagarde, Paul de. *Deutsche Schriften* (Munich, 4th ed., 1940).

Lagarde, Paul de. *Mitteilungen*, vol. 1 (Göttingen, 1884).

Lagarde, Paul de. *Purim: Ein Beitrag zur Geschichte der Religion* (Göttingen, 1887).

Lassen, C.A. *Indische Alterthumskunde* (Bonn, 5 vols., 1847–62).

La Vopa, Anthony J. *Grace, Talent and Merit: Poor Students, Clerical Careers and Professional Ideology in Eighteenth-Century Germany* (Cambridge, MA, 1988).

Le Coq, Albert von. *Von Land und Leuten in Ostturkistan: Berichte und Abendteuer der 4. deutschen Turfan-Expedition* (Leipzig, 1928).

Lefmann, Solomon. *Franz Bopp: Sein Leben und seine Wissenschaft*, vol. 1 (Berlin, 1891).

Legaspi, Michael Chris. "Reviving the Dead Letter: Johann David Michaelis and the Quest for Hebrew Antiquity." Ph.D. dissertation, Harvard University, 2006.

Lehmann, Reinhard G. *Friedrich Delitzsch und der Babel-Bibel-Streit* (Göttingen, 1994).

Leifer, Walter. *Indien und die Deutschen: 500 Jahre Begegnung und Partnerschaft* (Tübingen, 1969).

Lemke, Wolf-Dieter. *Staging the Orient: Fin de Siècle Popular Visions* (Beirut, 2004).

Lepsius, *Letters from Egypt, Ethiopia, and the Peninsula of Sinai*, trans. Leonora and Joanna B. Horner (London, 1853).

Leutner, Mechthild. "Kontroversen in der Sinologie: Richard Wilhelms kulturkritische und wissenschaftliche Positionen in der Weimarer Republik," in *Richard Wilhelm: Botschafter zweier Welten*, ed. Klaus Hirsch (Frankfurt, 2003), pp. 43–84.

Leutner, Mechthild. "Weltanschauung – Wissenschaft – Gesellschaft: Überlegungen zu einer kritischen Sinologie," in *Berliner China-Hefte* 14 (1998): 3–14.

Liebeschütz, Hans. *Das Judentum im deutschen Geschichtsbild von Hegel bis Max Weber* (Tübingen, 1967).

Littmann, Enno. *Ein Jahrhundert Orientalistik: Lebenbilder aus der Feder von Enno Littmann und Verzeichnis seiner Schriften* (Wiesbaden, 1955).

Lüdemann, Gerd, and Martin Schröder. *Die Religionsgeschichtliche Schule in Göttingen: Eine Dokumentation* (Göttingen, 1987).

Majeed, Javed. *Ungoverned Imaginings: James Mill's The History of British India and Orientalism* (Oxford, 1992).

Makdisi, Ussama. "The 'Rediscovery' of Baalbek: A Metaphor for Empire in the Nineteenth Century," in *Baalbek: Image and Monument, 1898–1998*, eds. Hélène Sader, Thomas Scheffler, and Angelika Neuwirth (Beirut, 1998), pp. 137–56.

Manjapra, Kris. "The Mirrored World: Cosmopolitan Encounter between Indian Anti-Colonial Intellectuals and German Radicals, 1905–1939." Ph.D. dissertation, Harvard University, May 2007.

Mangold, Sabine. *Eine 'weltbürgerliche Wissenschaft': Die deutsche Orientalistik im 19. Jahrhundert* (Stuttgart, 2004).

Manuel, Frank. *The Broken Staff: Judaism through Christian Eyes* (Cambridge, MA, 1992).

Marchand, Suzanne. *Down from Olympus: Archaeology and Philhellenism in Germany, 1750–1970* (Princeton, NJ, 1996).

Marchand, Suzanne. "From Liberalism to Neoromanticism: Albrecht Dieterich, Richard Reitzenstein and the Religious Turn in Fin de Siècle German Classical Studies," in *Out of Arcadia* (British Institute of Classical Studies Supplement, 79, 2003), ed. Martin Ruehl and Ingo Gildenhard (London, 2003), pp. 129–60.

Marchand, Suzanne. "Philhellenism and the Furor Orientalis," in *Modern Intellectual History* 1 (2004): 331–58.

Marchand, Suzanne. "Popularizing the Orient," in *Intellectual History Review* 17, no. 2 (2007): 175–202.

Marchand, Suzanne. "The Rhetoric of Artifacts and the Decline of Classical Humanism: The Case of Josef Strzygowski," in *History and Theory*, Beiheft 33 (1994): 106–30.

Masuzawa, Tomoko. *The Invention of World Religions: Or, How European Universalism Was Preserved in the Language of Pluralism* (Chicago, 2005).

Matthes, Olaf. *James Simon: Mäzen im wilhelmischen Zeitalter* (Berlin, 2000).

McGetchin, Douglas T. "Wilting Florists: The Turbulent Early Decades of the Société Asiatique, 1822–1860," in *Journal of the History of Ideas* 64, no. 4 (2003): 565–80.

McGetchin, Douglas T., Peter K.J. Park, and Damodar SarDesai, eds. *Sanskrit and "Orientalism": Indology and Comparative Linguistics in Germany, 1750–1958* (New Delhi, 2004).

Melka, R.L. "Max Freiherr von Oppenheim: Sixty Years of Scholarship and Political Intrigue in the Middle East," in *Middle Eastern Studies* 9 (1973): 81–93.

Mendes-Flohr, Paul. *Divided Passions: Jewish Intellectuals and the Experience of Modernity* (Detroit, MI, 1991).

Meyer, Eduard. "Die Bedeutung der Erschliessung der alten Orients für die geschichtliche Methode und für die Anfänge der menschlichen Geschichte überhaupt," in *Sitzungsberichte der Königlich Preussischen Akademie der Wissenschaften* 32 (1908): 648–63.

Meyer, Eduard. *Geschichte des Altertums* (Stuttgart, 5 vols., 1884–1902).

Miller, Peter N., ed. *Momigliano and Antiquarianism: Foundations of the Modern Cultural Sciences* (Toronto, 2007).

Mitter, Partha. *Much Maligned Monsters: A History of European Reactions to Indian Art* (Oxford, 1977).

Mohl, Jules. *Vingt-sept ans d'histoire des études orientales: Rapports faits à la Société Asiatique de Paris de 1840 à 1867*, vol. 1 (1840–54), vol. 2 (1854–67) (London, 2003; reprint of Paris 1879, 1880).

Moltke, Helmut von. *Briefe über Zustände und Begebenheiten in der Türkei aus den Jahren 1835 bis 1839*, ed. Gustav Hirschfeld (Berlin, 6th ed., 1893).

Momigliano, Arnaldo. *Essays in Ancient and Modern Historiography* (Oxford, 1977).

Momigliano, Arnaldo. *Essays on Ancient and Modern Judaism*, ed. Silvia Berti, trans. Maura Masella-Gayley (Chicago, 1994).

Momigliano, Arnaldo. *New Paths of Classicism in the Nineteenth Century* (Middletown, PA, 1982).

Moore, George Foot. "Christian Writers on Judaism," in *Harvard Theological Review* 14 (1921): 197–254.

Mühlhahn, Klaus. *Herrschaft und Widerstand in der "Musterkolonie" Kiautschou: Interaktionen zwischen China und Deutschland, 1897–1914* (Munich, 2000).

Müller, Herbert Landolin. *Islam, ǧihād ("Heiliger Krieg") und Deutsches Reich: Ein Nachspiel zur wilhelmischen Weltpolitik im Maghreb 1914–1918* (Frankfurt, 1991).

Mulsow, Martin. *Moderne aus dem Untergrund: Radikale Frühaufklärung in Deutschland, 1680–1720.* (Hamburg, 2002).

Mungello, David E. *Curious Land: Jesuit Accommodation and the Origins of Sinology* (Wiesbaden, 1985).

Nöldeke, Theodor. *Geschichte des Qorâns* (Göttingen, 1860).

Nöldeke, Theodor. *Orientalische Skizzen* (Berlin, 1893).

Noll, Richard. *The Aryan Christ: The Secret Life of Carl Jung* (New York, 1997).

Oldenberg, Hermann. *Buddha: Sein Leben, sein Lehre, sein Gemeinde* (Berlin, 1881).

Olender, Maurice. *The Languages of Paradise: Race, Religion and Philology in the Nineteenth Century*, trans. Arthur Goldhammer (Cambridge, MA, 1992).

Olin, Margaret R. *Forms of Representation in Alois Riegl's Theory of Art* (University Park, PA, 1992).

Oppenheim, Max Freiherr von. "Die Revolutionierung der islamischen Gebiete unserer Feinde," in Tim Epkenhaus, "Geld Darf keine Rolle Spielen" (part II), in *Archivum Ottomanicum* 19 (2001): 121–63.

Osterhammel, Jürgen. *Die Entzauberung Asiens: Europa und die asiatischen Reiche im 18. Jahrhundert* (Munich, 1998).

Osterhammel, Jürgen. "Forschungsreise und Kolonialprogramm: Ferdinand von Richthofen und die Erschließung Chinas im 19. Jahrhundert," in *Achiv für Kulturgeschichte* 69, no. 1 (1987): 150–95.

Osterhammel, Jurgen. "Neue Welten in der europäische Geschichtsschreibung (ca. 1500–1800)," in *Geschichtsdiskurs*, vol. 2., ed. Wolfgang Küttler et al. (Frankfurt, 1994), pp. 202–15.

Osterhammel, Jürgen, and Niels P. Petersson. "Ostasiens Jahrhundertwende: Unterwerfung und Erneuerung in west-östlichen Sichtweisen," in *Das Neue Jahrhundert: Europäische Zeitdiagnosen und Zukunftsentwürfe um 1900*, ed. Ute Frevert (Göttingen, 2000).

Paret, Rudi. *Arabistik und Islamkunde an deutschen Universitäten: Deutsche Orientalisten seit Theodor Nöldeke* (Wiesbaden, 1966).

Penny, H. Glenn. *Objects of Culture: Ethnology and Ethnographic Museums in Imperial Germany* (Chapel Hill, NC, 2002).

Pfeiffer, Ida. *Eine Frauenfahrt um die Welt: Reise von Wien nach Brasilien, Chili, Ostahaiti, China, Ost-Indien, Persien und Kleinasien*, vol. 3 (Vienna, 1850).

Polaschegg, Andrea. *Der andere Orientalismus. Regeln deutsch-morgenländischer Imagination im 19. Jahrhundert* (Berlin, 2005).

Pollock, Sheldon. "Deep Orientalism? Notes on Sanskrit and Power Beyond the Raj," in Carol A. Breckenridge and Peter van der Veer, *Orientalism and the Postcolonial Predicament: Perspectives on South Asia* (Philadelphia, PA, 1993), pp. 76–133.

Porter, Bernard. *The Absent-Minded Imperialists: Empire, Society and Culture in Britain* (Oxford, 2004).

Porterfield, Todd. *The Allure of Empire: Art in the Service of French Imperialism, 1798–1836* (Princeton, NJ, 1998).

Püschner, Uwe. *Die völkische Bewegung im wilhelminischen Kaiserreich: Sprache, Rasse, Religion* (Darmstadt, 2001).

Rabault-Feuerhahn, Pascale. *L'archive des origins: Sanskrit, philologie, anthropologie dans l'Allemagne du XIXe siècle* (Paris, 2008).

Reid, Donald Malcolm. *Whose Pharoahs? Archaeology, Museums, and Egyptian National Identity from Napoleon to World War I* (Berkeley, CA, 2002).

Reitzenstein, Richard. *Poimandres: Studien zur griechisch-ägyptischen und frühchristlichen Literatur* (Leipzig, 1904).

Renan, Ernest. "Des religions de l'antiquité et de leurs deniers historiens," in *Revue des deux Mondes* 23, no. 2 (1853): 821–48.

Richthofen, Ferdinand Freiherr von. *Entdeckungsreisen in China, 1868–1872: Die Erforschung des Reiches der Mitte*, ed. Klaus-Dieterich Petersen (Tübingen, 1982).

Richthofen, Ferdinand Freiherr von. *Ferdinand von Richthofen's Tagebücher aus China*, vol. 1, ed. E. Tiessen (Berlin, 1907).

Riegl, Alois. *Altorientalische Teppiche* (Leipzig, 1891).

Riegl, Alois. *Late Roman Art Industry*, trans. Rolf Winkes (Rome, 1985).

Riegl, Alois. *Problems of Style: Foundations for a History of Ornament*, trans. Evelyn Kain (Princeton, NJ, 1992).

Roider, Karl A. *Austria's Eastern Question, 1700–1790* (Princeton, NJ, 1982).

Rosen, Friedrich. *Aus einem diplomatischen Wanderleben: Aus dem Nachlass herausgegeben*, ed. Herbert Müller-Werth (Wiesbaden, 1959).

Rothermund, Dietmar. *The German Intellectual Quest for India* (New Delhi, 1986).

Rudolph, Kurt. *Die Religionsgeschichte an der Leipziger Universität und die Entwicklung der Religionswissenschaft: Ein Beitrag zur Wissenschaftsgeschichte und zum Problem der Religionswissenschaft, Sitzungsberichte der Sächsischen Akademie der Wissenschaften zu Leipzig*, Phil.-hist. Klasse, Band 107, Heft 1. (Berlin, 1962).

Rückert, Friedrich. *Rückerts Werke*, ed. Georg Ellinger, vol. 2 (Leipzig, 1897).

Rückert, Heinrich. "Friedrich Rückert als Gelehrter" [1866], in *Friedrich Rückert im Spiegel seiner Zeitgenossen und der Nachwelt*, ed. Wolfdieterich Fischer (Wiesbaden, 1988).

Said, Edward. *Culture and Imperialism* (New York, 1993).

Said, Edward. *Orientalism* (New York, 1978).

Sarre, Friedrich and F.R. Martin, eds. *Die Ausstellung von Meisterwerken Muhammedanischer Kunst in München 1910*, 3 vols. (Munich, 1912).

Schimmel, Annemarie. *Morgenland und Abendland: Mein west-östliches Leben* (Munich, 2003).

Schipper, Bernd U., ed. *Ägyptologie als Wissenschaft: Adolf Erman (1854–1937) in seiner Zeit* (Berlin, 2006).

Schlegel, Friedrich. *Kritische Friedrich-Schlegel-Ausgabe*, ed. Ernst Behler et al. (Munich, 35 vols. 1958–75).

Schmidt-Biggemann, Wilhelm. *Philosophia perennis: Historical Outlines of Western Spirituality in Ancient, Medieval and Early Modern Thought* (Dordrecht, 2004).

Schnaase, Karl. *Geschichte der bildenden Künste im Mittelalter*, vol. 1, *Altchristliche, byzantinische, muhammedanische, karolingische Kunst* (Düsseldorf, 2nd ed., 1869).

Schottlaender, Felix. *Erwin von Baelz (1849–1913) Leben und Wirken eines deutschen Arztes in Japan* (Stuttgart, 1928).

Schrader, Eberhard. "Gedächtnisrede auf Justus Olshausen," in *Abhandlungen der Königlichen Akademie der Wissenschaften zu Berlin 1883* (Berlin, 1884).

Schrader, Eberhard. *Die Keilinschriften und das Alte Testament* (Giessen, 1872).

Schroeder, Leopold von. *Indiens Literatur und Cultur in historischer Entwicklung: Ein Cyklus von fünfzig Vorlesungen* (Leipzig, 1887).

Schroeder, Leopold von. *Lebenserinnerungen* (Leipzig, 1921).

Schroeder, Leopold von. *Reden und Aufsätze, vornehmlich über Indiens Literatur und Kultur* (Leipzig, 1913).

Schulin, Ernst. *Die weltgeschichtliche Erfassung des Orients bei Hegel und Ranke* (Göttingen, 1958).

Schwab, Raymond. *The Oriental Renaissance: Europe's Rediscovery of India and the East, 1680–1880*, trans. Gene Patterson-Black and Victor Reinking (New York, 1984).

Schweitzer, Albert. *Paul and his Interpreters: A Critical History*, trans. W. Montgomery (New York, 1956).

Schweitzer, Albert. *The Quest of the Historical Jesus*, trans. W. Montgomery (New York, 1962).

Semler, D. Joh. Salomo. *Lebensbeschreibung von ihm selbst abgefasst*, 2 vols., (Halle, 1781, 1782).

Sengupta, Indra. *From Salon to Discipline: State, University and Indology in Germany, 1821–1914* (Heidelberg, 2005).

Seydel, Rudolf. *Die Buddha-Legende und das Leben Jesu nach den Evangelien. Erneute Prüfung ihres gegenseitigen Verhältnisses* (Weimar, 2nd ed., 1897).

Seydel, Rudolf. *Das Evangelium von Jesu in seinen Verhältnissen zu Buddhasage und Buddha-Lehre mit fortlaufender Rücksicht auf andere Religionskreise* (Leipzig, 1882).

Sharpe, Eric J. *Comparative Religion: A History* (London, 1975).

Simon, Róbert. *Ignác Goldziher: His Life and Scholarship as Reflected in his Works and Correspondence* (Leiden, 1986).

Shavit, Yaacov. "Babel und Bibel – The Controversy as a Jewish Event," in *Leipziger Beiträge zur jüdischen Geschichte und Kultur* 1 (2003): 263–79.

Sheehan, Jonathan. *The Enlightenment Bible: Translation, Scholarship, Culture* (Princeton, NJ, 2005).

Shuger, Debora K. *The Renaissance Bible: Scholarship, Sacrifice and Subjectivity* (Berkeley, CA, 1994).

Simon, Róbert. *Ignác Goldziher: His Life and Scholarship as Reflected in his Works and Correspondence* (Leiden, 1986).

Smend, Rudolf. "Julius Wellhausen and his Prolegomena to the History of Israel," in *Julius Wellhausen and His Prolegomena to the History of Israel*, special issue of *Semeia* 25 (1983): 1–20.

Smith, Woodruff D. *Politics and the Sciences of Culture in Germany, 1840–1920* (Oxford, 1991).

Sommer, Andreas Urs. *Friedrich Nietzsches 'Der Antichrist': Ein philosophisch-historischer Kommentar* (Basel, 2000).

Sorkin, David. *The Berlin Haskalah and German Religious Thought: Orphans of Knowledge* (London, 2000).

Stark, Gary D. *Entrepreneurs of Ideology: Neoconservative Publishers in Germany, 1890–1933* (Chapel Hill, NC, 1981).

Steinmetz, George. *The Devil's Handwriting: Precoloniality and the German Colonial State in Qingdao, Samoa, and Southwest Africa* (Chicago, 2007).

Stern, Fritz. *The Politics of Cultural Despair* (Berkeley, CA, 1961).

Stocking, George W., Jr. *After Tylor: British Social Anthropology, 1888–1951* (Madison, WI, 1995).

Stroumsa, Guy G. "Richard Simon: From Philology to Comparativism," in *Archiv für Religionsgeschichte* 3 (2001): 89–107.

Strzygowski, Josef. *Aufgang des Nordens: Lebenskampf eines Kunstforschers um ein deutsches Weltbild* (Leipzig, 1936).

Strzygowski, Josef. *Die Baukunst der Armenier und Europa*, 2 vols. (Vienna, 1918).

Strzygowski, Josef. *Orient oder Rom? Beiträge zur Geschichte der spätantiken und frühchristlichen Kunst* (Leipzig, 1901).

Stucken, Eduard. *Astralmythen (der Hebräer, Babylonier und Aegypten)*, 5 vols. (Leipzig, 1896–1907).

Süssheim, Karl. *The Diary of Karl Süssheim (1878–1947)*, ed. Barbara Flemming and Jan Schmidt (Stuttgart, 2002).

Sullivan, Michael. *The Meeting of Eastern and Western Art* (Berkeley, CA, 2nd ed., 1997).

Sweetman, John. *The Oriental Obsession: Islamic Inspiration in British and American Art and Architecture, 1500–1920* (Cambridge, 1991).

Sylvester, David. "On Western Attitudes to Eastern Carpets," in *Islamic Carpets from the Joseph V. McMullan Collection* (London, 1972), pp. 4–19.

Tal, Uriel. *Christians and Jews in Germany: Religion, Politics and Ideology in the Second Reich, 1870–1914* (Ithaca, NY, 1975).

Timpanaro, Sebastian. *The Geneis of Lachmann's Method*, ed. and trans. Glenn W. Most (Chicago, 2005).

Toews, John Edward. *Becoming Historical: Cultural Reformation and Public Memory in Early Nineteenth-Century Berlin* (Cambridge, 2004).

Trautmann, Thomas R. *Aryans and British India* (Berkeley, CA, 1997).

Treue, Wilhelm. "Max Freiherr von Oppenheim: Der Archäolog und die Politik," in *Historische Zeitschrift* 209 (1969): 37–74.

Trumpener, Ulrich. *Germany and the Ottoman Empire, 1914–1918* (Princeton, NJ, 1968).

Vambery, Hermann. *The Coming Struggle for India* (London, 1885).

Vambery, Arminius. *Travels in Central Asia, being the Account of a Journey from Teheran across the Turkoman Desert on the Eastern Shore of the Caspian to Khiva, Bokhara and Samarcand, Performed in the Year 1863* (New York, 1865).

Vambery, Hermann. *Der Islam im neunzehnten Jahrhundert: Eine culturgeschichtliche Studie* (Leipzig, 1875).

van Ess, Josef. "From Wellhausen to Becker: The Emergence of *Kulturgeschichte* in Islamic Studies," in Malcolm Kerr, ed., *Islamic Studies: A Tradition and its Problems* (Malibu, CA, 1980), pp. 27–51.

Vernoit, Stephen. "Islamic Art and Architecture: An Overview of Scholarship and Collection, c. 1850–c. 1950," in idem, ed., *Discovering Islamic Art: Scholars, Collectors and Collections, 1850–1950* (London, 2000), pp. 1–61.

Vietsch, Eberhard von. *Wilhelm Solf: Botschafter zwischen den Zeiten* (Tübingen, 1961).

Waardenburg, Jacques. *L'Islam dans le miroir de l'occident* (Paris, 1961).

Walker, D.P. *The Ancient Theology: Studies in Christian Platonism from the Fifteenth to the Eighteenth Century* (Ithaca, NY, 1972).

Walravens, Hartmut. *Bibliographien zur ostasiatischen Kunstgeschichte in Deutschland*, vol. 3, *Otto Kümmel* (Hamburg, 1984).

Walravens, Hartmut, ed. *Bibliographien zur ostasiatischen Kunstgeschichte in Deutschland*, vol. 4, *Die Ostasienausstellung Berlin 1912 und die Presse* (Hamburg, 1984).

Weber, Max. *Ancient Judaism*, trans. Hans H. Gerth and Don Martindale (New York, 1952).

Weber, Max. *The Religion of India: The Sociology of Hinduism and Buddhism*, trans. Hans H. Gerth and Don Martindale (New York, 1958).

Wellhausen, Julius. *The Arab Kingdom and its Fall*, trans. Margaret Graham Weir (Calcutta, 1927).

Wellhausen, Julius. *Evangelienkommentare* (Berlin, 1987).

Wellhausen, Julius. *Prolegomena to the History of Ancient Israel* (New York, 1957).

Wende, Erich. *C.H. Becker: Mensch und Politiker* (Stuttgart, 1959).

Wiese, Christian.*Wissenschaft des Judentums und protestantische Theologie im wilhelmi-nischen Deutschland: Ein Schrei ins Leere?* (Tübingen, 1999).

Wilhelm, Richard. *Chinesische Lebensweisheit* (Darmstadt, 1922).

Wilhelm, Richard. *Der Mensch und das Sein* (Jena, 1939).

Wilhelm, Richard, trans. *The Secret of the Golden Flower: A Chinese Book of Life*, English trans. from the German, Cary Baynes (London, 1931).

Wilhelm, Richard, *The Soul of China* (London, 1928).

Wilhelm, Salome. *Richard Wilhelm* (Düsseldorf, 1956).

Williamson, George S. *The Longing for Myth in Germany* (Chicago, IL, 2004).

Williamson, George S. "A Religious Sonderweg? Reflections on the Sacred and the Secular in the Historiography of Modern Germany," in *Church History* 75, no. 1 (2006): 1–18.

Wilson, John A. *Sign and Wonders upon Pharaoh: A History of American Egyptology* (Chicago, 1964).

Winckler, Hugo. *Die alte Orient und die Geschichtsforschung* (Berlin, 1906).

Winckler, Hugo. *Die babylonische Geisteskultur in ihre Beziehungen zur Kulturenwicklung der Menschheit* (Leipzig, 1907).

Winckler, Hugo. *Untersuchungen zur altorientalischen Geschichte* (Leipzig, 1889).

Windisch, Ernst. *Geschichte der Sanskrit-Philologie und indischen Altertumskunde*, part 1 (Strasbourg, 1917); part 2 (Berlin and Leipzig, 1920).

Yates, Frances. *Giordano Bruno and the Hermetic Tradition* (Chicago, IL, 1979).

Zimmer, Heinrich. *Artistic Form and Yoga in the Sacred Images of India*, ed. and trans. Gerald Chapple and James B. Lawson (Princeton, NJ, 1984).

Zimmermann, Andrew. *Anthropology and Antihumanism in Imperial Germany* (Chicago, 2001).

Index

18028748R00333

Made in the USA
Middletown, DE
28 November 2018